INTEGRATION AND INNOVATION ORIENT TO E-SOCIETY VOLUME 1

IFIP – The International Federation for Information Processing

IFIP was founded in 1960 under the auspices of UNESCO, following the First World Computer Congress held in Paris the previous year. An umbrella organization for societies working in information processing, IFIP's aim is two-fold: to support information processing within its member countries and to encourage technology transfer to developing nations. As its mission statement clearly states,

> *IFIP's mission is to be the leading, truly international, apolitical organization which encourages and assists in the development, exploitation and application of information technology for the benefit of all people.*

IFIP is a non-profitmaking organization, run almost solely by 2500 volunteers. It operates through a number of technical committees, which organize events and publications. IFIP's events range from an international congress to local seminars, but the most important are:

• The IFIP World Computer Congress, held every second year;
• Open conferences;
• Working conferences.

The flagship event is the IFIP World Computer Congress, at which both invited and contributed papers are presented. Contributed papers are rigorously refereed and the rejection rate is high.

As with the Congress, participation in the open conferences is open to all and papers may be invited or submitted. Again, submitted papers are stringently refereed.

The working conferences are structured differently. They are usually run by a working group and attendance is small and by invitation only. Their purpose is to create an atmosphere conducive to innovation and development. Refereeing is less rigorous and papers are subjected to extensive group discussion.

Publications arising from IFIP events vary. The papers presented at the IFIP World Computer Congress and at open conferences are published as conference proceedings, while the results of the working conferences are often published as collections of selected and edited papers.

Any national society whose primary activity is in information may apply to become a full member of IFIP, although full membership is restricted to one society per country. Full members are entitled to vote at the annual General Assembly, National societies preferring a less committed involvement may apply for associate or corresponding membership. Associate members enjoy the same benefits as full members, but without voting rights. Corresponding members are not represented in IFIP bodies. Affiliated membership is open to non-national societies, and individual and honorary membership schemes are also offered.

INTEGRATION AND INNOVATION ORIENT TO E-SOCIETY VOLUME 1

Seventh IFIP International Conference on e-Business, e-Services, and e-Society (I3E2007), October 10-12, Wuhan, China

Edited by

Weijun Wang
HuaZhong Normal University, China

Yanhui Li
HuaZhong Normal University, China

Zhao Duan
HuaZhong Normal University, China

Li Yan
HuaZhong Normal University, China

Hongxiu Li
Turku School of Economics, Finland

Xiaoxi Yang
HuaZhong Normal University, China

 Springer

Integration and Innovation Orient to E-Society, Volume 1

Edited by W. Wang, Y. Li, Z. Duan, L. Yan, H. Li, and X. Yang

   p.   cm. (IFIP International Federation for Information Processing, a Springer Series in Computer Science)

ISBN 978-1-4419-4533-4   eISBN: 978-0-387-75466-6
Printed on acid-free paper

Table of Contents
Volume 1

Conference Chair's Message

Organizing Committee

Program Committee

External Reviewers

e-Commerce Track

CONFERENCE CHAIR'S MESSAGE

This volume contains the papers presented at I3E2007, the seventh IFIP International Conference on e-Business/Commerce, e-Services and e-Society, which was held in Wuhan from 10-12 October 2007. The conference was sponsored by IFIP TC6/WG6.11 in co-operation with TC8, TC9, TC11, and TC6/WG 6.4.

The scope of six past I3E conferences was on e-Commerce, e-Business, and e-Government. It is changed to "e-Business, e-Services and e-Society" this time, which is not only a diction modification, but also represents the upcoming trends of integration and innovation in the growing areas of e-Business/Commerce, e-Services and e-Society. Modern Service Science based on e-Services is developing as a discipline in all over the world, which would undoubtedly improve the research and application of e-Commerce and e-Society. It really shows the integration and innovation of multidisciplinary research and application in e-Business/Commerce, e-Learning, e-Tourism, e-Government, e-Health, e-Payment, etc. All of these construct the base and bricks of the e-Society.

A total of 460 papers were submitted and 149 papers were accepted through double-blind reviewing, the submissions came from 20 different countries, and it is the first time for I3E to attract big attentions of so many Chinese scholars. We believe more and more Chinese authors will participate in the future activities of I3E.

I would like to express my sincere thanks to the many people that made this volume and the I3E2007 conference in Wuhan possible. The first thank you goes to Reima Suomi, co-chair of the IFIP WG6.11 and Executive Liason, who visited my university in 2005, encouraged me to attend the I3E2006 conference and trusts us to hold the I3E2007 in Wuhan. He has spent much time to discuss issues with us and answer our detailed questions on how to organize the conference. The next goes to Winfried Lamersdorf and Wojciech Cellary, co-chairs of the IFIP WG6.11. They have put forward many good suggestions to our team in preparing for the conference and this book. The third goes to Lefkada Papacharalambous and Narciso Cerpa, program co-chairs. The detailed help was always available from them. And total reviewers have paid great contribution for improving the quality of the already high-quality submitted papers. This conference would not have been possible without your huge support. Thank you very much, all of you.

I also would like to thank my leaders and several colleagues in HuaZhong Normal University. Our president, Ming Ma, vice-president, Zhongkai Yang and Dean, Xuedong Wang pay hight attention to this conference as a core academic activity in the university's and our department's portfolio. Dr.Yanhui Li, Zhao Duan and Li Yan have spent much time and paid much contribution works to edit book and perpare the conference. Our staff Yangai Cai, Tian Jie, Xiaoli Chi and postgraduated students Xiaoxi Yang and Jing Sun took care of the administration of the conference.

Special thanks go to our support institutes: Ministry of Education of People's Republic of China, Ministry of Commerce of People's Republic of China, Ministry of Information Industry of People's Republic of China, National Natural Science Foundation of China, Wang-Kuangchen

Education Foundation and HuaZhong Normal University.

Finally, I want to thank all the contributors to this book and the conference, as well as the I3E2007 conference participants. Because the quality and success of the IFIP I3E2007 was based on the sound work of all the committee members, reviewers and participants.

Weijun Wang
I3E2007 Wuhan Conference Chair

Organizing Committee

Honorary General Chair

Ming Ma, *Huazhong Normal University, Wuhan, China*

General Chair

Zongkai Yang, *Huazhong Normal University, Wuhan, China*
Xuedong Wang, *Huazhong Normal University, Wuhan, China*

Conference Chair

Weijun Wang, *Huazhong Normal University, Wuhan, China*

Program Co-Chairs

Narciso Cerpa, *University of Talca, Chile*
Lefkada Papacharalambous, *TEL of Halkida, Greece*

Liaison Chairs:

Executive Liason: *Reima Suomi, Turku School of Economics, Finland*
Europe: Volker Tschammer, *FhG FOKUS, Germany*
North America: Ranjan Kini, *Indiana University Northwest, USA*
South America: Manuel J.Mendes, *Unisantos, Brazil*
Asia-Pacific: Katina Michael, *University of Wollongong, Australia*

Members of Organizing Committee

Zhihao Chen, *Zhongnan University of Economics and Law, China*
Weiguo Deng, *South China Normal University, China*
Xiaozhao Deng, *Southwest University, China*
Tingting He, *Huazhong Normal University, China*
Jinyi Hong, *Ministry of Information Industry, China*
Yisheng Lan, *Shanghai University of Finance & Economics, China*
Hongxin Li, *Dongbei University of Finance & Economics, China*
Jun Liu, *Beijing Jiaotong University, China*
Qingtang Liu, *Huazhong Normal University, China*
Tenghong Liu, *Zhongnan University of Economics and Law, China*
Yezheng Liu, *HeFei University of Technology, China*
Yong Liu, *ZhengZhou Institute of Aeronautical Industry Managent, China*
Zhenyu Liu, *Xiamen University, China*
Haiqun Ma, *Heilongjiang University, China*

Shihua Ma, *Huazhong University of Science & Technology, China*
Weidong Meng, *Chongqing University, China*
Guihua Nie, *Wuhan University of Technology, China*
Zheng Qin, *Tsinghua University, China*
Yongzhong Sha, *Lanzhou University, China*
Xiaobai Sheng, *Nanjing Audit University, China*
Jinping Shi, *Hubei University, China*
Ling Song, *China Electronic Commerce Association, China*
Yuanfang Song, *Central University of Finance and Economics, China*
Baowen Sun, *Renmin University of China,, China*
Binyong Tang,*Donghua University, China*
Xinpei Wang, *Ministry of Commerce of the People's Republic of China, China*
Yuefen Wang, *Nanjing University of Science & Technology, China*
Yan Wu, *Ministry of Education, China*
Kang Xie, *Sun Yat-Sen University, China*
Yangqun Xie, *Anhui University, China*
Kuanhai Zhan, *South West Univesity of Finance & Economics, China*
Ning Zhang, *Beijing University, China*
Liyi Zhang, *Wuhan University, China*
Bangwei Zhao, *Xidian University, China*
Chengling Zhao, *Huazhong Normal University, China*
Shuangyi Zheng *South-Central University For Nationalities, China*

Local Arrangement Committee

Yanhui Li, *Huazhong Normal University, China, Chair*
Zhao Duan, *Huazhong Normal University, China*
Li Yan, *Huazhong Normal University, China*
Xiaoxi Yang, *Huazhong Normal University, China*
Jing Sun, *Huazhong Normal University, China*

Program Committee

Shanlin Yang, *HeFei University of Technology, China*
Jinglong Zhang, *Huazhong University of Technology and Sciences, China*
Jing Zhao, *China University of Geosciences, China*
Daoli Zhu, *Fu Dan University, China*
Hans-Dieter Zimmermann, *Swiss Institute for Information Research, Switzerland*

External Reviewers

Virtual Organization Theory: Current Status and Demands

Americo Nobre G.G. Amorim
Rua do Espinheiro, 854-Recife-PE
52020-020,Brazil
americoamorim@gmail.com

Abstract. The intense use of Information technologies in various functions caused many changes on organizations. The utmost in terms of technology usage are the virtual organizations: operating with virtual processes globally, by means of networks. This paper has the objective to present organizational theories and try to identify aspects which can be applied to virtual organizations and the ones which need more profound research. The main contribution of this work is to start the creation a strong theoretical approach for modeling these organizations. Managers working in this kind of companies might also benefit from a better understanding when designing and managing virtual organizations.

1 Introduction

During the last three decades, information technologies (IT) and telecommunications have been improved and spread worldwide. From small firms to multinational corporations, it became present in almost all management areas such as marketing, sales, human resources and controlling.

New technologies emerged during the nineties such as multimedia and virtual reality, and companies started to use them in activities such as product development, advertising and communication. In the same period, Internet connections became available to general public. This is the context where virtual organizations emerge and began to take place.

Several kinds of organizations labeled as been "virtual" or "digital" started to call attention in the media and academic circles during the so-called "dot.com bubble" period. Researches in fields such as management, economics and computer science argue that virtual organizations have different characteristics than "traditional" ones. That comes from their virtuality in terms of competing globally without geographical restrictions. Several studies focused on conceptualizing and defining the main business activities of virtual organizations, but some significant dimensions remain

Please use the following format when citing this chapter:

Amorim, A. N. G. G., 2007, in IFIP International Federation for Information Processing, Volume 251, Integration and Innovation Orient to E-Society Volume1, Wang, W. (Eds), (Boston: Springer), pp. 1-8.

unclear. Knowledge about the influences of virtuality in organizational dimensions is one of the most important issues to workers and researchers.

The objective of this paper is to discuss and bring to attention the theoretical issues that remain uncovered by literature and that need deeper research. This is done by confronting virtual companies with organizational theories, trying to identify points of convergence and issues that remain unclear. It's expected that this approach will reveal when classic management literature is still useful and issues for future research. The paper first presents a short review on organizational theories, discusses the main issues of virtual organizations and finally confronts them.

2   Organizational Theories

One of the main foundations to organization theories was the **Bureaucracy** [23]. It states that firms should be conducted by a rational-legal authority system. It stated that managers should create clear rules stating the tasks, responsibilities and requirements for each job position. Merton [17] argued that excessive bureaucratic rules and control can lead to serious dysfunctions.

The first scientific approaches to management were the studies of "**Classic Management**" [8, 20]. In their view, the organizations should be structured with work division, grouping common activities in departments and workers should be controlled closely by their superiors. Fayol [8] defined the four most important managerial activities: planning, organizing, leading and controlling. Workers are perceived as *Homo Economicus* taking rational decision to maximize their gains. In this context, the most evident motivational tool was the financial payment (wages).

This view is followed by the **Human Relations Movement**, with its psychological background applied to *Homo Social* [15]. They thought that workers were affected by complex needs such as affiliation in informal groups, affectivity and sociability. Motivation could be achieved by fulfilling personal needs such as the wish to be recognized. Organizations should be designed in a way to assure that workers interests are reflected in managerial objectives, providing psychosocial incentives.

The **motivation and leadership theories** considered workers with complex needs such as self-actualization and esteem [14, 16]. Complex man would have autonomous thinking, making predictions about behavior almost impossible. Maslow's [14] work about the hierarchy of human needs oriented managers about how to act in relation to their various types of workers. McGregor [16] named the classic management as "Theory X", considering that it didn't inspire satisfaction among workers. In his "Theory Y", workers were naturally dedicated and engaged. Managers should organize resources for production, stimulating the participation of workers in decision processes and inspiring responsibility behaviors.

One of the outcomes from McGregor theories is Argyris [2] work. He argued that there are two types of organizations: Organization "A" with centralized and hierarchized decision processes and organization "B" in which workers perform relevant role in decision making. "A" workers are specialized and have low knowledge about the organizational activities unrelated to their work. Organization

"B" offers a more clear vision about its information and objectives, making workers aware about medium and long-term plans. That makes them better informed and active in decision processes.

Structuralist approaches [10] tend to defend that the objectives and preferences of dominant groups are expressed in the bureaucratic rules of the organizations. Change resistance and conflicts take place by unprivileged groups. They could be co-opted by the dominant ones to gather support for their objectives. Structuralists see man as "organizational", flexible and resistant to frustrations. That leads to a strong need for self accomplishment in several social roles taken, which is achieved by formulating goals that will become reality by politically actions and work.

All those theories are related to internal issues of the organizations. The relationship of firms with the environment emerged with the **systems theory**. Katz and Kahn [12] used the open-system perspective to define the main characteristics of organizational change of energy, mapping inputs, transformation, output and renewed input.

Emery and Trist [7] stated that organization structure should be adapted to the environment needs and roles performed. In turbulent and complex markets organizations should give more attention to benefits offered to highly qualified workers. In stable markets, organizations can have simpler structure, employing less effort on gathering and processing information.

Reeves and Woodward [24] related production types with organizational characteristics. Process production requires horizontal structures and there are a lot of qualified professionals that control parts of the process. In mass-production the complexity is lower and there is a more apparent hierarchy. In unitary or project-based production, horizontal structure is present together with direct control.

Burns and Stalker [4] created two models for describing organizations: mechanistic and organic. Mechanistic organizations are traditional and suitable to competitively and technologically stable environments. Workers are specialized and have well defined roles, the hierarchy is vertical, decision making is centralized and bureaucratic controls are dense. Organic organizations are well suited for turbulent environments with intense competition and technological innovations. They are characterized by multi-functional teams where worker roles are dynamic and there aren't specific tasks. Control is decentralized and autonomy in decision making is strengthened. Workers competences are the main competitive characteristic of organic organizations.

After this brief review on the evolution of organizational thinking, the focus will change to the analysis of virtual organizations, looking for intersections between concepts and characteristics between this kind and the organizational theory.

3 Virtual Organizations

Virtual organizations (VO) emerged at the end of 1990s with the dotcom companies and the consolidation of internet usage among traditional companies. In organizational theory, one of the first published works about VO was Davidow and

Malone's [6]. Virtual organization was then used by several researchers with different meanings such as outsourcing, telework and others.

Goldman, Nagel e Preiss [9] argued that a virtual organization is an opportunistic alliance of core competences to fulfill a specific demand. Davidow and Malone [6] agree that VO conduct common activities trough series of relationships.

Other authors seek to define VO in terms of processes that characterize their activities. VO strategic approach would concentrate in creating and developing intellectual resources through several relationships [21]. Virtuality could be seen as an organizational dimension. Traditional companies could apply virtual configurations in strategic approaches. Mowshowitz [19] sees VO as means to manage organizations by key-activities such as the identification of demands that can be virtually fulfilled, search entities that can supply those demands and dynamic associate entities to the demands according to certain criteria.

Authors like Hale and Whitlaw [11] understand VO as companies that are in constant need of changing. The ability to change processes to achieve goals would be the essence of those organizations. VO can still be described as those that massively adopt technologies such as networks that reduces their geographic, time and information restrictions. For this paper, we will adopt the definition that a VO is a systemic arrange of entities (mans, autonomous agents, organizations, systems) trying to dynamically integrate, by IT means, demands and resources for their fulfillment with strategically defined operational rules [5].

4   Virtual Organizations and Organization Theories

Having emerged almost 100 years after the "classic management" period, VO exists in a completely different set in terms of economical, technological and social issues. VO seem to differ in many aspects: task-based work division was replaced by multi-roles approaches; centralized decision making changed to certain levels of autonomy for groups of workers and highly vertical hierarchy seem to have been cut down. Therefore, *Homo Economicus* is outdated and incompatible with VO workers.

The human relations approach represents one step further toward virtual organizations. However it's ingenuous to think that VO, highly based on knowledge and qualified professionals, don't recognize the importance of informal organization. On the contrary, there are evidences that VO deliberately promote its workers to interact and create informal relations. Additional types of ties to the organization are especially important in environments that present high turnover rates because of the competition among companies to hire qualified workers. The control and exercise of power among workers doesn't seem to be the main concern. Informal relations tend to be perceived as means for creating cohesive groups that can act independently. That said, *Homo social* conception is inadequate.

Virtual organizations also seem to act different than what is stated by bureaucracy theory. Explicit and stable formalization of job positions seems to be incompatibly with the flexibility requirements for VOs and their workers. Hierarchy also seems to be mutable, mainly when the VO is structured in autonomous teams assigned to perform certain tasks that change constantly.

The rational-legal system seems to be noted in VOs at a different level. It seems that transparency and governance mechanisms drive VOs rational-legal system. Horizontal hierarchy put managers and workers closer, making it easy to develop personal relations. Unfavorable managerial decisions to workers can't be blamed on higher and far away hierarchical levels, which echo some of Blau's [3] ideas.

Satisfaction and motivation of workers are vital to VOs. Highly qualified workers are valued and demanded by firms, which makes unemployment smaller than non-qualified positions. In some fields there is even a deficit of professionals [1]. The possibility of changing to other company tends to make workers to look forward higher levels of Maslow's [14] motivation such as esteem and self-actualization. Lower levels such psychological and safety seems to be fundamentals that should be presented. That said, it's clear that McGregor's X Theory [16] is completely out of question. VOs are closer to Y Theory, where workers are perceived as creative, responsible and hard workers.

These characteristics of VOs workers can place them as Argyris [2] type B. Information technology can be crucial to guarantee effective participation in decision processes, integrated organizational view and the flow of relevant information for workers. Regarding to power and authority, VOs can be perceived as adhocracies [18]. Even when teams of workers can take decisions related to their work, it's unclear if they can influence strategic decisions. The idea that dominant groups interests are expressed in organization rules [10] doesn't appear to fit straight. Dominant interests may be propagated more by influence in behavior, strategy and organizational policies.

To understand and work with VOs, systems perspective seems to be one of the best fits. In VOs, many links [13] between groups and systems, in operational and managerial levels, are provided by non-human entities, like information technologies (expert systems, artificial intelligence). It is reasonable to say that can lead to higher human interactions in strategic levels. That can indicate that one of the main executive tasks is to establish and maintain relationships with leaders of other companies in order to have connections for creating partnerships and explore business opportunities when necessary.

The contact between managers can be fulfilled by being present in events such as conferences, commerce chambers meetings and other. Social interaction in sports practice, parties and voluntary work is also another viable approach to keep relations active. When partners are geographically distant, what is normal to VOs, virtual contact might take considerable importance by using chats, VoIP, email and others.

Katz and Kahn's [12] perspective that organizational structure is defined by cycles of events seems to be useful for VOs. Probably these firms have shorter cycles, with faster changes than in traditional ones. Long term structures would not be viable. Regarding to the authors systemic model, several characteristics such as import/export energy, processing and feedback might occur virtually, by means of IT. As the technology is prevalent, it seems to be a strong need for service level assurance in adequate levels to perform such tasks.

Emery and Trist [7] turbulent environment seem to be adequate to VOs. Fast changes in technology and economic conditions affect these companies dramatically. The lack of geographic constraints can lead to hypercompetitive markers [22]. In this context, the search for qualified professionals and the maintenance of some levels of organizational redundancy seems to be adequate. Technology clearly works in both Zuboff's [25] mechanisms: replacing human efforts and improving operational and informational and levels.

Regarding to contingency perspective, VO seem to have project like production. That is accomplished by teams that work to create a product or service. These products are sometime also digital goods, which mean that after the first item is produced, replication takes place with reduced costs. One important issue in contingency approach [24] is that it defines unitary production as been of low complexity. VO frequently face highly complex projects like research and development activities, which require qualified professionals to fulfill complex activities.

Regarding to Burns and Stalker [4] approach, it's possible to say that VOs are closer to the organic model which is adequate for turbulent environments. Virtual organizations are clearly different from mechanicist ones: decentralized authority, mutant worker responsibilities, lighter bureaucratic controls and horizontal structure. These characteristics are highly supported by means of Information Technology.

The table 1 below presents a synthesis of the organizational theories analyzed in the context of virtual organizations. It mainly indicates aspects where theories are convergent with VO and issues that aren't compatible.

Table 1. Virtual Organizations and Organizational Theories

Virtual Org.	Theory	Convergent	Inadequate
Highly qualified professionals	Classic Management	-	Work specialization; Centralized decisions; Vertical hierarchy.
Structural flexibility	Power and Authority	Operational decisions taken by workers.	Dominant group interests in organizational rules.
Work flexibility	Human relations	Informal relations among members are encouraged.	Informal interactions are not perceived as means for assuring power and control.
Transparency and governance			
Proximity	Motivation	Higher motivational levels; Theory Y; Type B.	Lower motivational levels; Theory X; Type A.
among managers and workers	Bureaucracy	Rational-legal system	Explicit hierarchy; Well defined work activities; Hierarchy protecting managers.
Intense use of information technologies			
Roles performed by non-human entities	Systems	Virtual and non-human interactions; Cyclic structure; Virtuality in energy flows, processing and feedback; Turbulent environment; Levels of redundancy.	-
Service level requirements			
Global operation Virtual controls	Contingency	Decentralization; Horizontal structure; Organic organizations.	Unitary production with low complexity; Mechanic organizations.

5   Conclusions

Virtual organizations are different from the ones studied by several organizational theory researchers. Classic management and human relations are almost completely inadequate to study VO but bureaucratic theory has still some useful characteristics if it's known that its implementation takes place with virtual characteristics.

Contemporary approaches are better for understanding virtual organizations. Motivational and leadership theories use perceive the human in a suitable way to virtual organization workers. However, two components are not present in these approaches: high turnover rates and the constant interaction between organization and worker by means of technology.

Decision making in virtual organizations is more decentralized, especially regarding to operational issues. One issue that could be focus of future research is to check if and how strategic decisions are taken in VOs.

Systems theory offers good mechanisms for understanding VOs. The characteristics and impacts on organization and workers of the interactions between human and non-human entities are important research issues that should be addressed.

Still an extremely affected point in VO's approach is enterprise strategy. All traditional theories explain the strategy concept like a combination of two factors: the competition and the customers, both characterized to an external view. They are stipulated as the essential base for the development of a competitive strategy. But in VOs occurs that both support ideas, the slight knowledge of market and space, are completely diffuse for the virtual organizations.

In this context, tracking information regarding to current and potential competitors is a very difficult task. Mapping external changes is also critical to understand customer behaviour. This is extremely complicated due to the lack of knowledge on the customer space neither customer control. However, the VO is always exposed, in special in its critical resources and capacities for the organizational performance.

Therefore, while in the traditional organizational theory processes are stipulated to assure the competitive advantage with environmental guide tactics for VOs this is an integrated process and part of the chain of communication of the ordinary activity, an essentially technological procedure anchored in highly qualified professionals and intense use of IT means.

The information technology influence on business processes seems to be increasing. Several processes are migrating to be completely fulfilled without human interaction. What are the organizational consequences of this tendency? The requirement of higher service levels might be one possible outcome.

The existence of unitary production, almost like projects with highly complex tasks is an important issue where contingency-based approaches are frontally defied. This characteristic can generate important impacts in virtual organizations, such as stronger decentralization of decision making, new structure designs and the increment in productivity.

As it was made clear in this paper, virtual organizations aren't compatible with classic management theories. Contemporary approaches might be useful but there are important gaps that deserve further investigation. One interesting next step could be the development of a broad characterization framework to virtual organizations, and then start exploring the unclear issues.

References

1.   1.Alexander, Rodney, New York's Engineering and Technically Skilled Labor, 1999.
2.   2.C. Argyris, Personality and organization (Harper & Row, New Your, 1957).
3.   3.P. Blau, The dynamics of bureaucracy (University of Chicago Press, Chicago, 1955).
4.   4.T. Burns, G. M. Stalker, The management of innovation (Tavistock, 1961).
5.   5.C. B. Cano, J. L. Becker, H. M. R. Freitas, Organizações no Espaço Cibernético, Revista de Administração de Empresas Eletrônica, v. 1, n. 1 (2002).
6.   6.W. H. Davidow, M. S. Malone, The Virtual Corporation : Structuring and Revitalizing the Corporation for the 21st Century (Collins, 1993).
7.   7.F. Emery, E. Trist, The causal texture of organizational environments, Human Relations, v. XVIII (1965).
8.   8.H. Fayol, Administration industrielle et générale (Dunod, Paris, 1916).
9.   9.S.L. Goldman, R. N. Nagel, K. Preiss, Agile competitors and virtual organizations: Strategies for enriching the customer (Thomson Publishing, New York, 1995).
10. 10.A. Gouldner, Patterns of industrial bureaucracy (Free Press, Glencoe, 1954).
11. 11.R. Hale, P. Whitlaw, Towards the virtual organization (McGraw-Hill, London, 1997).
12. 12.D. Katz, R. L. Kahn, Psicologia social das organizações (Atlas, São Paulo, 1970).
13. 13.R. Likert, New patterns of management (McGraw-Hill, New York, 1961).
14. 14.A. Maslow, A theory of human motivation, Psychological Review, v.50, 370-96 (1943).
15. 15.E. Mayo, The human problems of an industrial civilization (Macmillan, New York, 1933).
16. 16.D. Mcgregor, The human side of enterprise, in: Leadership and motivation: essays of Douglas McGregor, edited by W. Bennis, E. Schein (MIT Press, Cambridge, 1966).
17. 17.R. Merton, The role-set: problems in sociological theory, British Journal of Sociology, v.VIII, p. 106-120 (1950).
18. 18.H. Mintzberg, A. Mchugh, Strategy Formation in an Adhocracy, Administrative Science Quarterly, v. 30(2), 160-197 (1985).
19. 19.A. Mowshowitz, Virtual organization, Communications of the ACM, v. 40(9), 30-37 (1997).
20. 20.F. Taylor, The Principles of scientific management (WW. Norton & Co, New York, 1911). Available at: <http://www.gutenberg.org/etext/6435>.
21. 21.N. Venkatraman, J. C. Henderson, Real strategies for virtual organizing, Sloan Management Review, v. 29(2), 33-47 (1998).
22. 22.H. W. Volberda, Toward the Flexible Form: How to Remain Vital in Hypercompetitive Environments, Organization Science, v. 7(4), 359-374 (1996).
23. 23.M. Weber. Bureaucracy, in: Max Weber: Essays in Sociology edited by H. Gerth and C. W. Mills (Oxford, New York, 1946).
24. 24.T. Reeves, J. Woodward, Industrial organization, behavior and control (Oxford University Press, Oxford, 1970).
25. 25.S. Zuboff, In the age of the smart machine: the future of work and power (BasicBooks, New York, 1988).

Application of Portfolio Theory in Controlling Supply Chain Crisis

Benxin Lao [1], Ningjie Liu [2]

1.ERP Laboratory, Guangxi University of Finance and Economics, Nanning, China, 530003, lbxwz@163.com

2.Industrial and Commercial Management, Guangxi University of Finance and Economics, Nanning, China, 530003, lnj1213@126.com

Abstract. Supplying chain cooperation has already become an important strategy that enterprises use to tackle market competition; however, the supply chain crisis caused by supply chain risk makes the supply chain operation of enterprises very fragile. This paper applies Portfolio Theory to explain the suppliers' combination plays an important role in dispersing the supplying chain risk and controlling its crisis, and point out, on the basis of analyzing the suppliers' expected return and risk, through choosing certain amount of suppliers and distributing the proportion of volume of purchase rationally, enterprises can find the efficiency front of suppliers combination.

1. Introduction

Home and abroad scholars have many research results on supply chain risk, including the qualitative and the quantitative. However, as supply chain system is a complicated system and its risk is very difficult to define, totally qualitative or totally quantitative method is all very difficult to be applicable in practical application. Portfolio Theory is a better risk controlling method combined nature and ration together, being widely applied to the investment field, but people have not realized its application value in controlling supply chain risk. This paper plans to probe into the application of Portfolio Theory in controlling supplying chain crisis.

2. Portfolio Theory

Portfolio theory is a systems approach that studies how to assign the fund available on more assets in various uncertain situation, in order to seek the most appropriate & satisfactory assets combination, under which different kinds of investor can accept

Please use the following format when citing this chapter:

Lao, B., Liu, N., 2007, in IFIP International Federation for Information Processing, Volume 251, Integration and Innovation Orient to E-Society Volume1, Wang, W. (Eds), (Boston: Springer), pp. 9-16.

return that match the risk. The start of Portfolio Theory can be traced back to Harry Markowitz's article entitled "Portfolio Selection" published in 1952, and the later (1959) monograph of the same name published.

Portfolio Theory introduces the concept of expect and variance in statistics into the research on assets combination. It assumes the probability of return ratio is definite and measures the mean deviation that variable of random return ratio deviates the average return ratio. It proposes the thought of measuring the prospective returns with expectation of the return ratio of the assets, of measuring the risk with the standard deviation of the assets return, of making the risk quantitative.

Illustrate Portfolio Theory's main conclusion in return and risk with examples as follows:

2.1 Return and risk of two-asset portfolio

（1）Two-asset portfolio return

$$E(aR_A + bR_B) = aE(R_A) + bE(R_B) \qquad (1)$$

a, b is weight of asset A , B respectively, R_A , R_B is return of asset A , B respectively.

（2）Two-asset portfolio variance (risk)

$$Var = a^2\sigma_A^2 + b^2\sigma_B^2 + 2ab\rho_{AB}\sigma_A\sigma_B \qquad (2)$$

This variance is formed by two parts: (1) $(a^2\sigma_A^2 + b^2\sigma_B^2)$ is the sum of variances of A and B two assets as the weight with the square of every assets. It reflects an impact of every asset's respective risk over the combination risk; (2) $2ab\rho_{AB}\sigma_A\sigma_B$ (covariance item) is the risk of portfolio influenced by two assets' mutually affects and common movement. The size of this kind of influence is reflected by ρ_{AB}(correlation coefficient). When A,B two assets are not correlated perfectly $(0<\rho_{AB}<1)$，investment combination of minimum risk can be found; When A, B two assets are negatively correlated $(-1\leq\rho_{AB}<0)$, investment combination can reduce the investing risk more.

Therefore, so long as the assets returns are not completely positively correlated, portfolio can reduce the risk of investment; this is the risk dispersion effect caused by portfolio.

2.2 Return and risk of N-asset portfolio

（1）N-asset portfolio return

$$E(R_p) = \sum_{i=1}^{N} X_i E(R_i) \qquad (3)$$

X_i is the weight that asset i takes up the asset portfolio, R_i is return of asset i.

（2）N-asset portfolio variance(risk)

$$Var = \sum_{i=1}^{N} X_i^2 \sigma_i^2 + \sum_{i=1}^{N}\sum_{\substack{j=1 \\ j \neq i}}^{N} X_i X_j \rho_{ij}\sigma_i\sigma_j \qquad (4)$$

As the same to two-asset portfolio, part I is a contribution to the portfolio's variance that every asset's own variance does, reflecting the risk state of every asset and its impact on the portfolio's risk; part II (covariance item) is the contribution to the portfolio's variance caused by each asset's mutual interaction and mutual influence. ρij is the correlation coefficient between asset i and asset j.

Formula (4) is a summation of N2 item, among them part I takes up N items and part II takes up N2-N items. When N is bigger, the covariance item (Part II) should be far greater than the variance item (Part I). Therefore, when there are more assets projects in the asset portfolio, the interaction and influencing each other among the assets is the main risk source of portfolio. That is to say, increasing the assets figure, portfolio can reduces greatly, and even dispels the specific risk that each asset causes, i.e. non- systematic risk, finally. But the risk caused by interaction among all assets, i.e. the systematic risk can not be dispelled with the increase of N. The systematic risk refers to the whole uncertainty that will exert an influence on all returns of the assets; it is the result of whole economic situation and the political situation change.

Generally speaking, if want to reduce the risk effectively, 10 kinds of assets is necessary; 15 kinds of assets are better quantity. But does not say it is the better that assets are the more. Further increasing of assets items can only increases the difficulty of management and trade expenses, but not reduces the risk effectively. [1]

3. Application of portfolio theory in controlling supply chain crisis

Today, the market competition is no longer a competition between enterprises and enterprises, but a competition between the supply chains. This is accepted by more and more enterprises already. Supply chain cooperation and supply chain alliance become the strategic choice that a lot of enterprises use for replying the market competition in recent years. It can not only obtain scale merit, but also can maximize favorable factors and minimize unfavorable ones, enable each enterprise to give play to one's own relative advantage, obtain one's own no or relatively weaker ability at the same time. We can say, supply chain cooperation is a kind of two-win or multi-win cooperation, and is enterprise's inevitable choice in the environment that modern science and technology develop violently, and market competitions become fierce. However, supply chain cooperation also is fragile. Once supply chain rupture, the losses caused to enterprise will be very serious. In 2003, according to Gartner Group's (U.S.A.) prediction, there is one in every five enterprises will be influenced for the reasons that supply chain is cut off in various forms. In these influenced enterprises, 60% will end up with going bankrupt. In addition, the transition on the commercial mode of a lot of enterprises has caused them to the change of the supply chain risk situation. For example, 'simplify measure', 'out sourcing' and reducing suppliers have become an overall trend, and all these will make supply chain more and more delicate.

Supply chain is formed by a lot of nodal enterprises which are all independent economic subjects. As rational people of economy, it is their instinct and excited to chase one's own interests biggest. Usually, key enterprises will be in the surging position in supply chain cooperation, but if it can't give consideration to the interests of other nodal enterprises and make them satisfied, they would change direction and cooperate with other enterprises for the economic reason. Thus bring crisis to the supply chain.

What is called supply chain crisis? It means in the course of supplying chain operation, uncertain major accidents influence the stability of supply chain and even lead supply chain system to disintegrate seriously, thus may leave enormous loss and damage to the products, service, fund and reputation in the whole supply chain. Why does the Supply chain crisis produce? Besides factor of interests' distribution, there are a lot of other factors. We can divide and summarize them as two classes of the external risk and endogenous risk. Among them,

The external risks include: (1) Policy risk; (2) Legal risk; (3) Industry's environmental risk; (4) Technology changes risk; (5)Natural disaster risk; (6)Market fluctuations risk, etc..

The endogenous risks include: (1) Morals risk (credit risks) of the cooperative partner; (2) Ability risk of the cooperative partner; (3) Fund risk of the cooperative partner; (4) Information transmission risk of the cooperative partner; (5) Trust crisis of the cooperative partner, etc..

According to the portfolio theory, the endogenous risks belong to non-systematic risk in the supply chain operation, caused by the supply chain structure and problem of management, and can be controlled effectively through the suppliers' combination; the external risks belong to systematic risk in supply chain operation. They are the risks more difficult for member enterprises to control. Its difficulty relates to the range of risk--the greater the range is, the greater the difficulty is.

4. Methods of controlling supply chain crisis effectively

4.1 Setting up elastic supply chain

According to the portfolio theory, so long as the returns of the suppliers are not relevant perfectly or relevant negatively, the risk of the supplier combination can be dispersed and reduced. These suppliers are usually independent. They can be the same area; also can be different areas or different supply channel. In addition, only the suppliers of a supply chain reach certain amount, the risk can be dispersed effectively. What is this best amount? It is usually relevant to the purchase scale of enterprises. But just as assets can not be too much, the suppliers we choose can not be too much either. If not, suppliers' combination can't reduce the risk. It may causes greater risk because of failure management, failure control, or increasing uncertain factor. Moreover, that too much suppliers is unfavorable to realizing purchasing scale merit.

In a word, "don't put all eggs in the same basket." Now, cutting down the supplier's quantity is becoming a trend in some large-scale enterprises. They aim to establish the partnership relation or strategic alliance with the suppliers by cutting down supplier's quantity. For example, Xerox reduces its supplier's quantity to 400 families from more than 5000; Zhongxing Telecom Co. (China) is implementing a project of "improving the concentration degree of purchasing", and its goal is to concentrate the amount of purchase of 80% on the first 50 key suppliers. But what we should pay attention to is that although these enterprises cut down their supplier's quantity, but their supplier's quantity still maintains at certain number. If is for lower costs or so-called consolidation relation, an enterprise cuts the supplier's quantity to little, even adopts 'Single Sourcing', that is to say, place all raw materials' purchase of a kind of product on a supplier, then the potential risk of its supply chain is very great. ②

After the upper suppliers (including lower distributors) reach certain amount, supply chain becomes supply net. It is an elastic supply chain (Fig. 1).

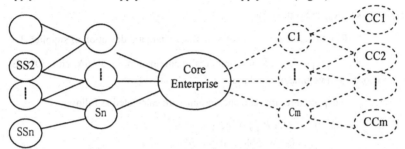

Fig.1   Elastic Supply Chain (Supply Net)

So when the upper (including the lower) nodal enterprises break away from the supply chain or other crises appear, other nodal enterprises or channels still guarantee the supply chain's operation normally. Certainly, at this time, enterprises should make a self-examination; look for the problem existing in supply chain management; take measures in order to prevent the further enlargement of the supply chain crisis.

4.2 Looking for the efficiency front of suppliers combination

The portfolio efficiency front theory points out: Investors seek the high return, but avoid the risk; on the basic of analyzing expected return, risk and relevance of investment combination, we can delineate the front of efficiency out, which includes investment combinations of realizing optimum equilibrium between risk and return; investors select the corresponding assets combination from the front of efficiency according to risk endurance and other restraint. We can infer that different supplier's combination it is, different efficiency it is. So, in order to find an optimum or effective supplier's combination, enterprises must be able to describe the expected return ratio and risks of each supplier and their combination quantitatively, and delineate out the efficiency front curve of a supplier's combination on this basis. Here, expected return ratio is the return ratio that a enterprise obtains from a supplier, can be expressed with the return rate of the purchase cost; The risk refers to the intensity that various uncertain accidents make the supplier expected return ratio to deviate from the average return. We can use the Level Analytic Approach, Fuzzy Analytic Hierarchy Process (Fuzzy-AHP) etc. to carry on comprehensive analysis to each supplier's possible morals risk, cut-off risk, ability risk (or performance risk), fund risk, etc.; then, estimate the probability of various expected return ratio; finally, use 'mean value - variance law' to calculate E (R) and σ.

The following is the analysis on the efficiency front of two-supplier combination and N-supplier combination.

(1)Efficiency front of two-supplier combination

Suppose as follows:

●E (R_A) =5%, $σ_A$ =6%

E (R_A): the return ratio of supplier A; $σ_A$: standard deviation of supplier A.

●E (R_B) =9%, $σ_B$ =7%.

E (R_B): the return ratio of supplier B; $σ_B$: standard deviation of supplier B.

●The proportion of the suppliers' combination is 50%A and 50% B according to volume of purchase.

Then, the expected return ratio and variance are calculated as follows:

$$
\begin{aligned}
E(aR_A + bR_B) &= aE(R_A) + bE(R_B) \\
&= 0.5 \times 5\% + 0.5 \times 9\% \\
&= 7\%
\end{aligned}
\tag{5}
$$

$$
\begin{aligned}
Var(aR_A + bR_B) &= a^2 σ_A^2 + b^2 σ_B^2 + 2abCOV_{AB} \\
&= a^2 σ_A^2 + b^2 σ_B^2 + 2ab ρ_{AB} σ_A σ_B
\end{aligned}
\tag{6}
$$

In formula (6), COVAB =E (AB) - EAEB, is covariance of return ratio of supplier A and B; ρAB is the correlation coefficient of return ratio of supplier A and B, reflecting the mutual effect of change of A and B two suppliers' return. The relation between COVAB and ρAB is:

$$
ρ_{AB} = \frac{COV_{AB}}{σ_A σ_B}
\tag{7}
$$

$$
Var(aR_A + bR_B) = 0.5^2 \times 0.06^2 + 0.5^2 \times 0.07^2 + 2 \times 0.5 \times 0.5 \times 0.1357 \times 0.06 \times 0.07
$$

$$
=0.00241
$$

If cov_{AB}=0.057% , then $ρ_{AB}$=0.1357,

Standard deviation, $σ_P = \sqrt{Var(aR_A + bR_B)} = 4.91\%$

By same means, we can get every E (R) and σ of A, B two-supplier combination, which is made up in a random proportion according to the volume of purchase. All these suppliers' combinations form a supplier combination set. Regarding σ as abscissa, E（R）as ordinate, copying out all group data on the coordinate, we can get a curve which connects A and B (Fig. 2):

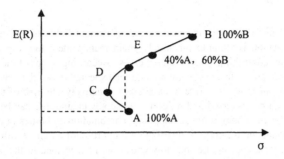

Fig.2 Efficiency front of two-supplier combination

Different points on the curve ACEB represents a A,B two-supplier combination of different allocation proportion according to volume of purchase (for example, E represents a proportion of 40%A and 60%B). Enterprises can choose the points appropriately according to their need, but the line segment CEB is the efficiency front for making up a suppliers' combination, i.e. under the situation with certain risk, expected return is the highest; or under the situation with certain expected return, the risk is the lowest.

(2)Efficiency front of N-supplier combination

$E(R)$ and σ of every N-supplier combination can be calculated with formula (3), formula (4) respectively. N suppliers can form a lot of combinations; the set that these suppliers' combinations make up is an area on a plane (Fig. 3).

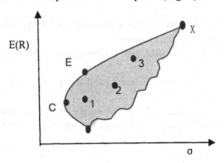

Fig.3 Efficiency front of N-supplier combination

In this area, point 1 may be the combination formed by 10 suppliers; point 2 may be the combination formed by 15 suppliers, and so on. Enterprise can choose its favorable set in this area arbitrarily. However, the curve CEX is obviously the efficiency front of the supplier' combination. Comparing with the within area of shade, supplier's combinations on CEX curve have higher expected return ratio on the same risk, or have lower risks under the same expected return ratio.

5. Conclusion

Although the portfolio theory is based on the investment field, its risk analysis and risk control method is suitable for supply chain management too, especially very meaningful for controlling supply chain crisis. According to portfolio theory, if suppliers chosen are up to certain amount and the expected return that enterprise win from them are not relevant perfectly or relevant negatively, the risk of the supplier combination can be dispersed and reduced, and supply chain crisis can be controlled effectively. The composition of the suppliers' combination embodies in different of suppliers' amount and different of distribution proportion of purchase volume among different suppliers. The supplier quantity choice will be decided to the scale of the enterprise purchases, and the proportion of purchases can be optimized through the operation method and tool. On the basic of analyzing the supplier's expected return and risk, calculating the E(R) and σ of every kind of suppliers ' combination, enterprise can get different points on the coordinate. All these points form a set of supplier's combination. The front of efficiency only includes a small part of the possible supplier's combination, i.e. the curve above the left of the set. The supplier's combinations on the efficiency front curve are the best choice for enterprises.

References

1. P.L Song, "Study on the modern portfolio theory", *Guizhou finance and economics institute journal*, 2000 (3),P14-17 (in Chinese)

2. Y.G Cao, *Securities investment study*, Beijing University Press, 1993, P119-136(in Chinese)

3. Y.H Liang, "Research on crisis forewarns index system of supply chain", *Information magazine*, 2006(5), P24-25 (in Chinese)

4. Stauffer, "Risk: the weak link in your chain", *Harvard Management Update*, March 2003

5. Formation Workshop, "Enterprise and supply chain risk", *Management &Continuity Forum*, America, Feb 19, 2003

6. Alain Halley, Jean Nollet," The supply chain: the weak link for some preferred supplier", *The journal of supply chain management*, summer, 2002, P39-47

Network Niche of E-business Enterprises

Cequn Lou, Xiaoxi Yang

Information Management Department, Huazhong Normal
University, Wuhan, 430079, China
llcqd@yahoo.com.cn

Abstract. This paper uses the Niche concept of Ecology to analyze the role and functions of e-business in network. It discusses the network niche of e-business enterprises in the aspects of network function, network information resources, network technology resources and network customer resources.

1 Introduction

Ecological theory has been applied to human society in many fields to form new branches of ecology, such as education ecology, administration ecology and industrial ecology and so on. In the same way, we can learn from the ecological concepts and methods to explain the problems in the development of network. In 1999, the United States Department of Commerce published the report of "emerging Digital Economy". This report makes a link between ecology and network and puts forward the concept of "Internet ecology". Till now, some Chinese scholars have begun the research of network ecology. According to the statistic, Tian Zhengyu put forwarded the words of "network ecology" earliest in China. In 1998, he wrote in the paper of "network ecology": network clouds around us as the forest. Every time running the "enginery" and climbing up the network, I will inspect for the new generation of eco-system and new lives while walking through the network jungle. [1] In this paper, "Network ecology" is only a vivid metaphor but not defined or explained exactly. In 2000, Zhang Qingfeng discussed the concept of "network ecosystem" in the paper of "The theory of ecological network". He wrote in the paper:" All the social systems which affect the development of network constitute a network development environment. When we use the perspective of link and development to analyze the interaction and mutual influence between networks and network environment, the network ecology has been formed". [2] Many Chinese scholars research more in the aspects of network ecological systems, network ecological crisis, ecological balance of Network but less in the aspect of the theory of network niche. This paper will explore the theory of network niche in concept and its dimensions. We will also analyze the network niche of e-commerce enterprises from the overall perspective.

Please use the following format when citing this chapter:

Lou, C., Yang, X., 2007, in IFIP International Federation for Information Processing, Volume 251, Integration and Innovation Orient to E-Society Volume1, Wang, W. (Eds), (Boston: Springer), pp. 17-25.

2   The Concept of Network Niche

Niche is an important ecology concept which doesn't have a unified definition currently. The definition of niche put forwarded by Whittaker in 1975 is more influential. He believed that niche means the position of time and space, functions of every species in the communities. In other words it means the relative position between a species and other species.

According to the concept of niche and the characteristics of network ecosystem, we define network niche as the specific locations of network activity participants in the network environment.

Network activity participants are individuals and social organizations which participate in the activities of computer network. They are the most active elements of network ecosystem which corresponds to concept of animals of natural ecosystems. Specifically speaking, the types of network activity participants include the government, enterprises, other organizations and individuals. Network activity participants can be classified in different ways according to different standards. For example, according to the area standard, they can be divided into political, economic, education, life, entertainment and other related participants. According to whether for the purpose of profit, they can be divided into non-profit and profit participants. In this paper, according to whether participate in the production of network resources, we classify network activity participants into network resources producers, network resources consumer and network resources transmitters. Producers produce and provide network resources as information content, network technology and other network resources. Consumers consume these network resources. Transmitters transmit network resources between different participants. The roles of network resources producers and consumers are not fixed. They will change under different conditions. For example, e-government participants are network resources producers when they issue public information and news, while they are network resources consumers when they use the software and network technology or take up the network server space.

Network eco-environment is the whole of all the other elements which impact on the network activity participants directly or indirectly.[3] It includes hardware infrastructure, network software, network information, network policies and regulations. Hardware infrastructure is the basis of network ecosystem, which is equivalent to the soil of the natural ecosystem. The entire network resources must depend on the hardware infrastructure. Software and network-related laws and regulations are very important to the normal operation of the network ecosystems. They are equivalent to the plants of natural ecosystem to create air. Without software technology, it is impossible to present diversified network information content or to realize all the modern information services. Network information content which bases on the hardware, software, the legal foundation is equivalent to nourishment of natural ecological system. It makes network activity participants communicate and interact with each other. Leaving the network information content, networking activity participants break the relations and the network ecosystem can't exist anymore.

In ecology, scholars study the status of life-form from the aspects of function, nutrition and space. And they put forward the dimensions of functional niche, nutrition niche, and space niche and so on. Similarly, we can analyze network activity participants from the two dimensions of network function niche and network resources niche. Network function niche reflects the role, social function, duty and authority of network activity participants. [4]

Network resources niche reflects the situation of network activity participants in production, demand, occupancy and utilization of network information, network technology and network customer resources, and other resources. Network resources niche can be subdivided into network information niche, network technology niche and network customer niche. Network information niche reflects the situation of network activity participants in production, demand, occupancy and utilization of network information. Network Technology niche reflects the situation of network activity participants in production, demand, occupancy and utilization of network technology. Network customer niche reflects the situation of network activity participants in production, demand, occupancy and utilization of network customer resources.

3   Network Function Niche of E-commerce Enterprises

Different network activity participants have different status and roles in the network. Network function niche of e-commerce enterprises reflects the status and function of e-commerce enterprises.

3.1 Realizing the economic function of the network and promoting the formation of the network economy

Network has a variety of functions, such as the function of science, economy, education and entertainment. The economic function of network means that we can perform economic activities and create value through the network. Network performs the main economic function by exchanging economic information, producing social communication, trading all kinds of commodity, controlling economic activities. E-commerce enterprises help to accomplish this function: Firstly, e-commerce enterprises disseminate and collect economic information through the network to realize economic information exchange. Secondly, e-commerce enterprises cooperate and interact with upstream and downstream firms and clients by network to realize social production and communication functions. Thirdly, the e-commerce enterprises carry out marketing and payment online and to achieve all kinds of commodity trading. Fourthly, network promotes government to adjust and control e-commerce enterprises activities to realize function of economic activities regulated.

Broadly speaking, the network economy refers to an economic form which takes the Internet as the core, telecommunications networks, communication networks and enterprise networks, a series of networks as the foundation, the network industry as the leading power and which produces, exchanges, distributes and consumes commodity by network. E-commerce is an important component part of network economy. It started earliest among all the network economy activities. E-commerce can promote the exchange of economic information and services. It also promotes the development of the network finance. For example, the development of e-business provides the new service areas and styles for the financial industry. Correspondingly, financial services content will meet the demands of e-commerce and provide relevant information support. It brings new opportunities for financial institutions, particularly in the small and medium-sized banks and emerging financial services institutions. Financial industry must adjust the services content and method to meet people's demands to let them take financial activities regardless of time and place restrictions. In this sense, it is an inevitable trend of the development of e-commerce, online banking, online payment, online personal financial management, Internet insurance agency services, online insurance quotations, online claims management, online stock trading, online investing, and online financial information services, and other electronic finance.

It shows that the development of e-business can promote the performance of network economic activities and perfect the network economy form. Although e-commerce activities are related to a wide range of activity participants, e-business enterprises play a key role in the e-commerce activities. Therefore, e-business enterprises have powerful functions in the formation and development of network economy and should not be underestimated.

3.2 Promoting the production of information resources and the development of e-government

Network information resources include network information content and network information technology. E-commerce enterprises can produce large amounts of business information. Activities such as internal information exchange, electronic advertising, and products development by using network, transactions between partners of supply chain, electronic financial services, electronic tax and other activities will bring a lot of information. In the information, a considerable portion is open in the network, such as the basic information of enterprises, products information, bidding information, service information, etc. The information can be used by other network activity participants. Therefore, e-commerce enterprises can promote the production of network information resource. E-commerce is a business activity in essential, and its mandate does not include the development of new network technology. However, as the development of networks and e-commerce, network technology has become the key to the success of e-commerce. Therefore, e-commerce enterprises should attach great importance on the development and application of new network technology. Some enterprises have developed network information system to meet the needs of enterprises. However, , there are often many drawbacks in this process of self-development, such as lack of staff expertise, development of the network information system not meeting the needs of corporations, development costs being too high. Under such circumstances, professional network technology companies began to flourish. These network technology companies provide support of professional network technology; develop new technology constantly to meet the needs of e-commerce enterprises. While e-commerce business enterprises do not have developed these new technologies, their demands on technology stimulate the development of new network technologies.

Promote the development of e-government. E-commerce enterprises promote the development of e-government through e-commerce activities in two aspects: promote government information technology and applications through e-commerce B2G, and fulfill the effective management and services of e-commerce through the development of e-government.

Online procurement is an important way of government procurement. It is also a natural trend of development of procurement. Online procurement saves cost for the government and improves the efficiency of the procurement center. It also achieves the principles of open, fair and competition in government procurement. Therefore, to achieve e-procurement, we must strengthen information technology to lay the foundation for the launching of e-government. The majority of business activities are conducted online after the realization of e-commerce. Business activities information will be transferred and exchanged online. It will be inefficient if the government departments use the traditional approaches to manage e-commerce activities. E-government can manage e-commerce enterprises easily and quickly. Industrial and commercial administrative departments can set up a special website to facilitate consumers' reporting on detrimental enterprises, inform the enterprises to correct by the way of electronic orders, electronic documents.

Online pricing departments issue electronic orders about the products pricing authority, the scope of price fluctuations, and install early warning systems. When the price is not in keeping with the provisions of the pricing department, the system will automatically feedback price information to the department of management. Commodity inspection departments will receive EDI implementation. The users can declare check by computers and the telephones. Commodity inspection departments will receive data and then input it into the computer system automatically. It accelerates the pace of the process of declaring check and also reduces input errors resulting from the duplication.

4   Network Information Niche of E-commerce Enterprises

Network Information Resource is an important and indispensable component in e-commerce activities. It is one part of the e-commerce activities to process and use network information resources. Network Information Resources have formed the normal operation environment in the e-commerce activities. However, network information is accessed and used by different network activities participants. Competition between network activities participants and different e-commerce enterprises exists. Therefore, e-commerce enterprises should optimize their network information resources niche from the following three aspects.

Firstly, network information niche of the e-commerce enterprises is reflected in their requirement of the content of network information. Network information resource varies in content. It includes not only scientific information, technical information, economic information, but also education information, policy and regulations information, medical information, price information, entertainment information, tourist information and so on. E-commerce enterprises use network to perform economic activities. Therefore, E-commerce enterprises mainly access and use network information about economic management. This information is used to analyze the situation of production, marketing and service needs to meet current customers' requirements about products. For example, enterprises can access customers' preference information to design and produce products of different functions. In the activities of e-commerce, it requires that enterprises should access feedback and demanding information at real time, predict market changes accurately, make timely adjustments and business decisions in time and improve customer satisfaction. E-commerce activities demand more credit information than others. Credit information is the evaluation about the enterprises' credit by customers and has an important impact on the e-commerce enterprises. Customers generally use two methods to get credit ratings information about e-commerce enterprises. The first way is to establish accreditation through the third party. For example, customers learn about the company's quality certificates by the state government's relevant departments. The second way is to get information through advertise in various comprehensive websites to improve enterprises' images. [5]

Secondly, the network information niche of e-commerce enterprises is reflected in the quality requirements of network information. E-commerce activities require accurate and reliable information. If e-commerce enterprises can not obtain information about national economic policies, regulations, raw materials supply of upstream enterprises, customers' demand and purchase behavior and credibility accurately by the network, it will disturb the normal development of e-commerce enterprises or lead economic loss of enterprises. However, in networks, dissemination and production of information are not stipulated. The quality of information appears uneven because of lack of standard restrictions. Therefore, when an e-commerce enterprise accesses information through networks, it should first establish reliable information access channel, in another words, it should determine to access information from which website. It is believed that to judge the accuracy and reliability of information, we should evaluate the credibility of the owners of the website. If the owners have authority, information released by their websites will be mostly high in the degree of accuracy and reliability. For instance, information on the web sites of government is all subject to strict scrutiny and almost has no mistakes. Information of this type should be regarded as the ultimate basis of e-commerce enterprises. Some personal websites information, without qualification or certification, will need to be checked stringently.

Thirdly, network information niche of the e-commerce enterprises is also reflected in the order of using network information. Network information can be shared. It won't make conflicts when e-commerce enterprises and other network activity participants use the same information at the same time. However, if other e-commerce enterprises pre-empt some network information, the value and effectiveness will be greatly weakened to the enterprises that reuse the information. In addition, network information is modified frequently. It requires e-commerce enterprises access information on the network timely. Therefore, e-commerce enterprises need to obtain information resources rapidly and seize beneficial niche of network information.

5   Network Technology Niche of E-commerce Enterprises

To launch various electronic service activities online, there must be network information technology to support correspondingly. Different needs in type and properties of technology exist in different network activity participants. E-commerce enterprises will optimize their niche of network technology from the following two aspects.

Firstly, network technology niche of the e-commerce enterprises is embodied in network technology types. E-commerce activities will apply to a variety of technologies, such as network information dissemination technology which can promote and display their products, network information retrieval technology which can help customers to check the information they need, network information exchange technology to communicate with cooperation partners and customers. The most obvious difference between e-commerce and other electronic services is the use of network payment technologies. Whether for traditional transactions, or the emerging e-commerce, payment is an important part of transaction. The difference is that e-commerce payment process stresses on the means of electronically payment, which is an important component of e-commerce. [6] Therefore, E-commerce enterprises demand more on the use of network payment technology while other participants demand less. In e-commerce activities, network security technology has the most prominent status. Because e-commerce activities involve large amounts of confidential business and financial control issues. Information about customers must be protected or it will bring huge loss to enterprises and customers. Compared with other network activities, e-commerce activities require network security more strongly. Without protection of network security technology, e-commerce activities can't be carried out. Network security technologies occupied by e-commerce enterprises include identity authentication technology, virus protection technology, data encryption technology and firewall technology. These technologies can protect e-commerce information and network security of funds transfer, and realize e-commerce functions fully. [7]

Secondly, network technology niche of the e-commerce enterprises is reflected in requirements of network technology performance. Network technology performance affects the e-commerce activities at all levels. For e-commerce activities, technologies with good performance should have the following three features: (1) Secure and stabile operations. This should be taken into account at first. Secure and stable operation of the network technology can support e-commerce activities in a normal way, solve the internal errors and prevent external intrusion. (2) Powerful functions. Network technology should be able to meet the needs of the e-commerce activities. In some cases, the use of network technology can also develop services can not be realized in real life, improve user satisfaction. (3) High level of system compatibility. Network technology should have a high degree of compatibility to avoid conflict e caused by version mismatch of equipment or software and achieve the communication with customers.

6   Network Customer Resource Niche of E-commerce Enterprises

Network customers are individuals or organizations which use network to take part in various social activities. Network customers can be divided into five main types according to different purposes. The first type of purpose is to use the network information for study. These customers are mainly individuals and their activities are usually reading news, cultural knowledge and technology knowledge. They usually have better information technology and learning capacity. The second type is to entertain online. These customers are mainly individuals too. The third type is to complete various tasks, such as administrative work or data processing. These customers are generally in the form of organizations, including the government, enterprises and other organizations. The fourth type is to communicate in real-time through network. Customers of this type can be either individuals or organizations. The fifth type is to perform business and use the network for various transactions. Such customers are enterprises, organizations, or individuals.

Customers of e-commerce enterprises are mainly the fifth type, including upstream and downstream enterprises who take part in e-commerce activities online, government departments, organizations and individuals who purchase online. Judging from the current situation, B2B and B2G develop rapidly. Upstream and downstream enterprises and government departments are the main customers of e-commerce enterprises. But with the development of B2C e-commerce, A large number of families and individuals also participate in the activities of the network and make the network customers resources increasingly abundant.

However-commerce enterprises of different types and different sizes should develop, possess and use different customer resources by strengthening customer relationship management to establish, maintain and expand their network customer resources niche. E-commerce enterprises can take advanced network technology to segment markets according to their products, network market position in order to define customer troop properly. Interface of the enterprises' web site should be friendly to give customers convenient use. System pages demonstrated to customers should be accessible to communication between the system and customers allow customers involved in the product design in order to attract clients get their interests, highly satisfy personalized products and form network customer resources niche. E-commerce enterprises should acquire individual customer information such as gender, age, occupation, loving and so on by building customer files. It is helpful for understanding customers' consumption trends. The files should be updated according to time and situation by network information technology. Enterprises can take advantage of powerful network to provide after-sales service. Enterprises can meet customers' demand by establishing of self-service platform.[8] (Such as an online chatting room, etc.) To enable customers exchange information about products function or shortcomings, these methods can stabilize customers, maintain network customer resources niche. It is necessary to hold the old customers, stimulate potential demand, and constantly open up new markets to attract new customers in order to expand its network customer resources niche.

References

1.Z.Y Tian. "Network Ecology", *Software world*, No. 2, 1998: p.130-131.
2.Q.F Zhang. "Research on Network Ecology", *Information and Documentation Services*, No.4, 2000: p.2-4.
3.Rafael Capurro. Towards an Information Ecology [A]. International seminar "Information and Quality"[C] 1989.[EB/OL]. [2007-3-2]. http://www.capurro.de/nordinf.htm
4.C.Q Lou. Approach on Information Niche Theories, Document, Information & Knowledge, No. 9, 2006: p.23 – 27.
5.Vicki L. O'Day, Bonnie A. Nardi. *Information Ecologies: Using Technology with Heart* [M]. MIT Press 2002.
6.B. Hu. "On E-commerce Application Implementation Technologies". *Computer knowledge and technology*, No. 20, 2006: p. 63.
7. MacBride, Sean: Many Voices One World: Towards a New More Just and More Efficient World Information and Communication Order; Report of the International Commission for the Study of Communication Problems. New York, NY: UNIPUB 1980.
8.Guotai Chi. "Strategies of Customer- Relationship Management in Electronic Commerce Environment", *China Soft Science*, No.7, 2002: p.52-56.

Mining XML Frequent Query Patterns

Cheng Hua[1], Hai-jun Zhao[1], Yi Chen[2]

1 Guangdong Electronic Business Market Application Key Laboratory,
Guangdong University of Business Studies. #21, Chisha Road, Haizhu
District, Guangzhou, Guangdong Province. 510320, P.R.C.
huacheng@gdcc.edu.cn
WWW home page: http://gdec.gdcc.edu.cn
2   Ricoh Software Research Center (Beijing) Co., Ltd.

Abstract. With XML being the standard for data encoding and exchange over Internet, how to find the interesting XML query characteristic efficiently becomes a critical issue. Mining frequent query pattern is a technique to discover the most frequently occurring query pattern trees from a large collection of XML queries. In this paper, we describe an efficient mining algorithm to discover the frequent query pattern trees from a large collection of XML queries.

1   Introduction

With the increase in XML applications such as e-business transactions, XML middleware systems, effective and efficient delivery of XML data has become an important issue. Regular path expression (RPE) is a common feature of XML query languages, and processing RPE queries can be expensive since it involves navigation through the hierarchical structure of XML, which can be deeply nested.

Mining frequent sub tree is a technique to discover the most frequently occurring sub trees from a large collection of relevant information, and it has been widely applied in domains like bioinformatics, web mining, and structured-based document clustering, and so on. In [1, 2, 3], some discussions have been given on mining frequent query pattern. In this paper, we will describe an efficient mining algorithm to discover the frequent query pattern trees from a large collection of XML queries.

The rest of the paper is organized as follows. Section 2 discusses some concepts used in mining query patterns. Section 3 describes our approach to mine frequent query patterns efficiently. Section 4 shows how the discovered query patterns can be exploited in caching. We discuss the related work and conclude in Section 5.

Please use the following format when citing this chapter:

Hua, C., Zhao, H., Chen, Y., 2007, in IFIP International Federation for Information Processing, Volume 251, Integration and Innovation Orient to E-Society Volume1, Wang, W. (Eds), (Boston: Springer), pp. 26-34.

2 Preliminaries

In this section, we first define the concept of a query pattern tree which forms the basis of the XQPMiner and XQPMinerTID. Then we explain why the simple tree matching technique is not applicable in finding frequent query patterns for XML data. Finally, we give a formal definition of the query pattern mining problem.

2.1 Query Pattern Tree

For each XML query q_i issued, we can extract related information by transforming the XML query into XML algebra[4]. This information includes the result that users want, the filtering conditions applied and the XML files involved in the query. Such information can be represented in the following form:

q_i{*resultPattern*; *predicates*; *documents*}

where resultPattern is the result schema pattern; predicates is the filtering conditions used in the XML query; and documents is the XML data files involved in this query.

Note that this transformation only includes the paths or patterns of the original schema instead of the restructured part. For example, given the following XML query in XQuery [5] syntax:

Q_1: for $b **in document**(book.xml) /book
     where some $a **in** $b/author **satisfies** $a/last/data()="Buneman"
   return
   <result>
        <book>{$b/title,$b/author,$b/price}<book>
   </result>

Q_1 can be expressed using the algebra proposed in [4] as follows:

v(result)(v(book)($\in$($b/title,$b/author,$b/price)($\sigma_{\$a/last/data()="Buneman"}$($\phi_{\$a=\$b/author}$
($\phi_{\$b=/book}$($s$(book.xml)))))))

After resolving the path expressions involved in the query, Q_1 relevant information is extracted below:

Q_1{ *resultPattern* ={/book/author, /book/title, /book/price},
     predicates={/book/author/last/ data()="Buneman"}, documents={book.xml}}

Some preprocessing is necessary. For example, substituting parent with the actual parent node or its binding variable. After extracting the path expressions, we will obtain three types of label: element tag name, wildcard *, and relative path //. The wildcard "*" indicates any label (tag) in DTD; and the relative path "//" indicates zero or more labels(descendant-or-self). Here, we use the same notations as those in XQuery[4] and XPath[6]. According to the binding variable relationship, the pattern tree can be easily constructed by combining *resultPattern* and *predicates* by extracting the path and ignoring the constants. Note, when adding the path(s) of *predicates* to *resultPattern*, if the content of the path(s) is already contained in *resultPattern*, the path(s) will not be added. Take Q_1 for example, the content of path "/book/author/last/" is contained in *resultPattern*, so this path will not be added to *resultPattern*. Formally, a pattern tree is defined as follows

Definition 1 (*Query Pattern Tree*): A *query pattern tree* is a rooted tree QPT=<V,E>, where V is the vertex set, where one distinguished node of V is the root denoted as *root*(QPT), and E is the edge set. For each edge e = (v₁, v₂), node v₁ is the parent of node v₂. Each vertex v has a label with its value in {"*","//",tagSet},where the tagSet is the set of all element and attribute names of a DTD of the context. v's label is denoted as v.label.

For simplicity, we use label to represent a node. The query pattern tree QPT₁ of Q₁ can be represented as:

 <book>

  <title></title>

  <author></author>

  <price></price>

 </book>

The corresponding graph representation is shown in Figure 1(a).

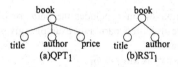

Figure 1: The Query Pattern Tree For Q1 And A Root Subtree.

Definition 2 (*Rooted Subtree*): Given a query pattern tree QPT=<V,E>, a rooted subtree RST=<V',E'> of QPT is a subtree of QPT that satisfies the following conditions:

- *root*(RST)=*root*(QPT)

- V'⊆V, E'⊆E

One of rooted subtrees of QPT₁ is shown in Figure 1(b).

Let *T* be a tree, the size of T is defined by the number of its nodes |T|.

2.2 Tree Pattern Matching

In general, a tree T=<V, E> matches another tree T'=<V', E'> if there exists a mapping φ which satisfies:

- *root*(T')=φ(*root*(T)) and ∀v∈V, ∃v'∈V',s.t. v'=φ(v),where v.label=v'.label.

- φ preserves the parent-child relation: if (v1,v2)∈E, then (φ(v1), φ(v2))∈E'

we say that T is a subtree of T' or T is contained in T'.

Unfortunately, this definition is not applicable to our problem here because of the presence of wildcards "*" and relative path expressions "//". For instance, when comparing two trees T1 and T2 in

Figure 2, it is obvious that the path "book/section/figure/title" in T2 can match the path "book//title" in T1, because "//" in "book//title" can be zero or more labels between book and title. It is the same with "book/section/figure/image" and "book//image". Hence the tree T2 can match T1. In other words, T2 is contained in T1, which is written as T2 ⊆ T1. One might try to expand those non-deterministic paths to deterministic paths such as expanding the path "book//title" to "book/section/figure/title". But this is only feasible when the XML DTD (schema) is a DAG. The method fails for a DTD with cycles.

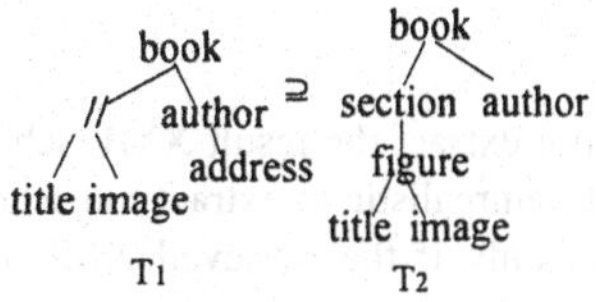

Figure 2: An Example Of Pattern Tree Containment

Expanding "//" remains crucial. This is because without the context information, one cannot tell whether a path is contained in "//" or not. For example, while it is clear that the path "/book/section/figure/title" is contained in "/book//title", we are not sure if the path "/book/section/figure/" is contained in "/book//title". The reason is that the former two paths share the same leaf. A more complicated example of query pattern QPT is given in Figure 3. We cannot merge the two child nodes "//" under node "book" because node "title" and node "image" may not share the same parent node. Thus we have RST$_1$ and RST$_2$ are contained in QPT while RST$_3$ is not contained in QPT by simple tree matching.

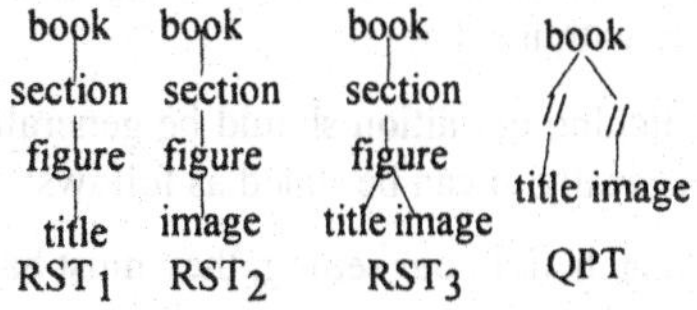

Figure 3: A Complex Query Pattern

We will expand a node "//" in QPT from XML schema as follows. Assuming the node "//" to be expanded has a child n. The expansion is straightforward if no cycles exist in XML schema. When a cycle exists and one of the expanded paths is root/.../p/n where n's parent p has a child that points back to p's ancestor, we'll introduce a node "//" between p and n. Consider Figure 4 as example. The XML schema includes a cycle, and the QPT to be expanded is "part//num". By straightforward expansion, we'll have "part/subpart/num", "part/subpart/part/subpart/num" and so on. By using the "//"node, we can concisely represent it as "part/subpart//num". After such expansion, we add context information to the QPT and do not introduce a cycle in QPT.

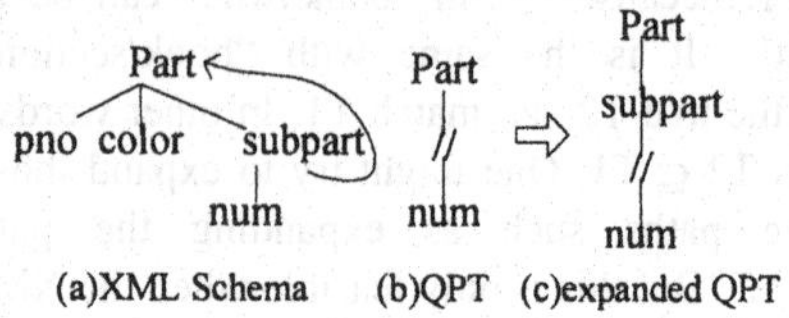

(a)XML Schema   (b)QPT   (c)expanded QPT

Figure 4: An Example Of Path Expansion

One may wonder why not extract the result XML schema and mine it? There are two reasons. One is that it's unrealistic to extract the schema online. Another reason is that this method effects only if the retrieved XML data is static. For dynamic changing XML data, it will fail.

To decide whether one pattern tree is contained in another, the exact tree matching cannot be naively used because of the existence of wildcards and relative path. By analyzing the relationship among labels and paths, we can derive that any node matches a node with label "*", and, on the other hand, it is contained in a node with label "//". Thus, the path "/book/*/figure" is contained in the path "/book//figure", while "/book/section/figure/title" is contained in "/book/*/figure/title". Note that the notion of containment here consists in the structure containment not in the extent. So our definition is different from [1].

Based on the above discussion, we can infer that the labels in the two pattern trees satisfy the partial order relationship$\leq$:

- Given label l, $l \leq l$, i.e., a node with label l matches with a node with the same label; Hence, we have $* \leq *$ and $// \leq //$.

- $l \leq * \leq //$,i.e., a node with label l matches a node with label * and a node with label * matches a node with label //.

Therefore, the tree matching definition should be generalized. To decide if a RST is contained in a QPT, basically, it can be stated as follows:

(1)   root nodes are matched. In our setting, they must have the same label.

(2)   If node $w \in$ RST is matched with node $v \in$ QPT, it satisfies:

   a) $w.label \leq v.label$

   b)   each subtree of w is contained in some subtree of QPT

The corresponding procedure will be given in later section.

2.3 Frequent query pattern mining problem

After transforming a set of XML queries $\{q_1,\dots,q_N\}$ into query pattern trees $D=\{QPT_1,\dots,QPT_N\}$, mining the frequent query pattern means to discover the frequent rooted subtrees (RSTs) in the query pattern trees. A natural approach is to divide the queries into different categories according to the XML data files that are involved.

Given a rooted subtree RST, RST matches a query pattern tree QPT in D, or RST occurs in D, if there exists a QPT that contains RST. The total occurrence of RST in D is denoted as Freq(RST), and its support rate is denoted by supp(RST)=Freq(RST)/|D|. For a positive number σ, RST is σ-frequent in D if supp(RST)≥σ. Hence, the query pattern mining problem can be stated as:

Frequent Query Pattern Mining Problem:

Given a query pattern tree database $D=\{QPT_1,\dots,QPT_N\}$, and a positive number $0<\sigma\leq1$ called the minimum support, find all σ-frequent rooted subtrees F such that $\forall RST \in F$, supp(RST)≥ σ.

For instance, consider the example in Figure 5. The RST occurs in two of query pattern trees and thus is frequent with respect to this database with supp(RST)=2/3 and Freq(RST)=2.

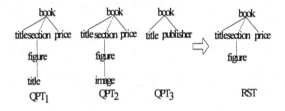

Figure 5: An Example Of Frequent Rooted Subtree

3   Discovering Frequent Rooted Subtrees

In this section, we propose an efficient algorithm for discovering the frequent query patterns. In our frequent pattern mining setting, the dataset of transactions D is a set of pattern trees. Each transaction $t \in D$ is a labeled directed pattern tree extracted from a XML query. Given a minimum support *minSupp*, we would like to find the frequently occurred rooted subtrees(RSTs) in at least *minSup**|D| transactions.

The main framework of our algorithm QPTMiner is shown in Figure 4. The notation RST^k denotes a k-edge rooted subtree; F_k a set of frequent k-edge rooted subtree; and C_k a set of k-edge candidate RST. Edges in the algorithm correspond to items in traditional frequent itemset discovery. Given a set of QPTs, QPTMiner initially enumerates all the rooted subtrees of every QPT; and put them in a candidate set C_k, and counts the frequency for each of these candidates. Next, QPTMiner drops those RSTs that do not satisfy the minimal support requirement.

```
Algorithm:QPTMiner(D,minSupp)
Input:    D—pattern tree transaction database
minSupp—the minimum support
Output: the set of all frequent RST sets
(1) { F_i =φ| i = 1, ..., n};
(2) for (k = 1, k++, k <= n)
(3)     read C_k from database;
(4) for each QPT_i in D
(5)     S_i=enumerate(QPT_i)
(6)     for each RST_i^k in S_i
(7)       for each candidate RST^k∈C_k do
(8)         if Contains( RST_i^k , RST^k) then
(9)           RST^k.count++;
(10)      else
(11)            C_k← RST^k
(12)            RST^k.count = 1;
(13) for (k = 1, k++, k <= n)
(14)     F_k={RST^k∈C_k|RST^k.count ≥minSupp*|D|};
(15)     save C_k to database;
(15) return {F_i| i = 1, ..., n };
```

Figure 6: Algorithm To Find Frequent Rooted Subtree

We compute the frequent pattern trees in an incremental way. After being computed, the frequent query pattern RST^k and their count RST^k.count is maintained in a database (C_k in the algorithm), and every time when we have to re-compute the frequent pattern trees, we read previous result from the database. In this way, previous result can be reused and the computation cost minimized.

The support of each candidate is counted based on the query pattern tree matching definition in section 2, the Contains algorithm can be constructed to compare two trees recursively from root to leaf to decide whether a RST is contained in a QPT. Due to the space limitation the detail of Contain algorithm is not included in this paper, interested reader also can find it in [1].

4   Conclusion

In this paper, we have described a schema-guided mining approach to discover frequent rooted subtrees from XML queries. This approach allows us to enumerate only valid candidates RSTs. We have also developed a tree pattern containment algorithm that takes into account the relative path "//" and wildcare "*" when matching RSTs with query pattern trees.

Future work includes investigating how frequent query patterns can be applied to the problem of view selection. By incorporating user information, the discovery of frequent query patterns will reflect the user preferences and requirements. This is especially useful in designing data warehouses for XML.

References

1. L. H. Yang, M. L. Lee, W. Hsu. *Mining Frequent Query Patterns in XML. 8th Int. Conference on Database Systems for Advanced Applications* (DASFAA), 2003.

2. L. H. Yang, M. L. Lee, W. Hsu. *Approximate Counting of Frequent Query Patterns over XQuery Stream*, (DASFAA), 2004.

3. Yi, Chen. *Discovering Ordered Tree Patterns from XML Queries*, PAKDD, 2004.

4. S. Boag (XSL WG), D. Chamberlin, MF. Fernandez, D. Florescu, J. Robie, and J. Simeon. XQuery 1.0: An XML Query Language, *W3C Recommendation* 23 January 2007, http://www.w3.org/TR/2007/REC-xquery-0070123/.

5. P. Fankhauser, M. Fernández, A. Malhotra, etc. The XML Query Algebra, *W3C Working Draft* 04 December 2000,.

6. http://www.w3.org/TR/xpath.

A Fuzzy Negotiation Model with Genetic Algorithms

Dongsheng Zhai, Yuying Wu, Jinxuan Lu, Feng Yan
School of Economics and Management, Beijing University of Technology,
Beijing, China, 100022
zhaidongsheng@bjut.edu.cn hlbao@bjut.edu.cn
lvjinxuan@emails.bjut.edu.cn yanfeng@bjut.edu.cn

Abstract. An offer in a fuzzy negotiation model is rejected or accepted by acceptability based on fuzzy set theory and membership functions. Since different issues have different effect on negotiators, the combined concession in the multi-issue negotiation for negotiators and negotiation agents and genetic learning mechanism are adopted to update their beliefs about incomplete information. The fuzzy negotiation model with genetic algorithms is more practical than the traditional negotiation model.

1 Introduction

Automatic negotiation and transaction on the internet is becoming more popular with the development of computer technology and e-commerce, and more and more people accept it as a new way of doing business. The negotiation and transaction on the internet can save a lot of human resources and material resources than the traditional negotiation and transaction. Especially automatic negotiation, which does not need a fixed place to negotiate with many participators [1] [2], can reduce side effect of the traditional negotiation and transaction.

The task of negotiation can be delegated to a software agent [3][4] in order to save users' time on activities which are either routine or demanding in e-commerce [5]. Some experts predict that there will be paradigm shift in e-commerce due to the emergence of agent [6], and many people are focusing on agent in recent years. [7] There are bilateral and multi-lateral negotiations according to the number of negotiators; there are single issue and multi-issue negotiations according to the number of issues concerned in negotiations. Here we focus on the bilateral multi-issue negotiation, because it is more difficult than bilateral single issue negotiation and it is a basic tool for multi-lateral multi-issue negotiation.

But due to complexity of e-commerce negotiation's and negotiation's processing is difficult to control, common negotiation model is difficult to be

Please use the following format when citing this chapter:

Zhai, D., Wu, Y., Lu, J., Yan, F., 2007, in IFIP International Federation for Information Processing, Volume 251, Integration and Innovation Orient to E-Society Volume1, Wang, W. (Eds), (Boston: Springer), pp. 35-43.

implemented. There are many works on theory of automatic negotiation of e-commerce [8][9], but there are few works on programming of automatic negotiation of e-commerce to apply in real e-commerce negotiation. [10][11]Many people are developing multi-agent system by genetic algorithms [1][3][5], but few are applying in automatic negotiation as a learning mechanism.

TOPSIS [12][13] (Technique for Order Preference by Similarity to Ideal Solution) is a classical multiple criteria decision making (MCDM) method. The negotiators can either accept or reject the offers depending on their utility [6][7]. If the negotiator's utility is higher than a specified value, he may accept the offer. If his utility is lower than the specified value, he may reject the offer. But there are many uncertain factors in negotiation. First, negotiators' preferences (or weights) are uncertain and dynamic. It is difficult to get exactly negotiators' preferences. Secondly, the evaluation of the solution is uncertain, which makes utility functions inaccurate. [14] So people always do not accept or refuse the offers definitely but at a certain degree in the business transaction. Considering these uncertain factors, we should measure the degree of acceptance or rejection of the negotiators for the offer by fuzzy numbers [13]. Therefore we evaluate the acceptability by membership function based on the fuzzy set theory [15][16].

There are various learning mechanisms in automatic negotiations such as Bayesian learning, case based reasoning and genetic algorithms [3]. Genetic algorithms [1] are useful for optimization and Rubenstein Montano and Malaga [17] states a genetic algorithms negotiation mechanism for searching optimal solutions for multiparty multi-objective negotiations. Genetic algorithms based on negotiation agents were used in the dynamic concession of bi-lateral negotiation [18]. Genetic algorithms are inspired by natural evolution, i.e. selection, reproduction, crossover and mutation. The basic principles of selection are means to select an optimal from initial populations of feasible solutions for a fitness function. Genetic algorithms for negotiation denote a set of feasible offers of the negotiation agent as a population of chromosomes. The fitness of a chromosome or a feasible offer is evaluated through the fitness function.

First, we provide a fuzzy negotiation model of e-commerce, which we state in our paper [19]. Secondly, we give a better fuzzy negotiation with genetic learning mechanism. Thirdly, we simulate the fuzzy negotiation model by genetic algorithms.

2   A Fuzzy Negotiation Model of E-commerce with Genetic Algorithms

Here we adopt the monotonic concession protocols as our negotiation protocols. [20] Agents start by assigning certain initial solutions from the feasible solution space to the negotiation variables [21]. An agreement is reached if one agent matches (or exceeds) what the other one asked for; otherwise the negotiation proceeds to the next step. The negotiation continues to another round if neither agent matches or exceeds the other's expectation. An agent is not allowed to offer the other agent lower prices than it did in the previous round, and it means that the agent has to increase at least one issue at one time as a counteroffer. If neither agent concedes at a certain step, then the negotiation ends with either an agreement or a deadlock. [22][23]

The advantage of the negotiation using the monotonic concession protocols is that it is similar to the real negotiation process, and it guarantees rapid convergence or stops the negotiation promptly when it is not convergent. Here we set a critical value λ to decide if an offer is acceptable to the negotiator, i.e. the acceptability of the negotiator.

The offer from one agent is a vector $(x_1, x_2, \cdots, x_n)$, where x_i (i=1,...,n) is the value for the i issue of the negotiation. Its membership function $v(x_i)$ is the acceptability for the value x_i, so the agent's offer can be represented as a vector $(v(x_1), v(x_2), \cdots, v(x_n))$, where $0 \le v(x_i) \le 1$ (i=1,...,n). Suppose w_i (i=1,...,n) is the weight for i issue of the negotiation, the relative importance of i issue for the negotiator, where $\sum_{i=1}^{n} w_i = 1$, the negotiator's acceptability for the offer is represented as $\sum_{i=1}^{n} w_i v(x_i)$

We take normal membership function as the acceptability for both seller agent and buyer agent, $v(x) = e^{-\left(\frac{x-a}{b}\right)^2}$ where a>0, b>0. Suppose the membership function of price is $v(x) = e^{-\left(\frac{x-a}{b}\right)^2}$, where a>0, b>0, a is the negotiator's most acceptable price, which can be its initial offer, and b is the negotiator's sensitivity for price.

When b's value is smaller, the sensitivity is smaller. The negotiator's acceptability is less sensitive to the price with smaller b's value when price varies in a bounded area; and vice versa. Suppose membership functions of the buyer and the seller both are normal distribution for convenience, and the left side is for the buyer and the right side is for the seller.

We set a critical value λ. When both negotiators' acceptability for the agent's offer exceeds or equals the critical value, the negotiation ends with a solution; otherwise the negotiator will exit the negotiation without a solution. We can set a critical value for the offer too. When the acceptability of both negotiators reaches the critical value, the negotiation can make an agreement.

Genetic algorithms are inspired by natural evolution, i.e. selection, reproduction, crossover and mutation. The basic principles of selection are means to select an optimal from initial populations of feasible solutions for a fitness function. Genetic algorithms for negotiation denote a set of feasible offers of the negotiation agent as a population of chromosomes. The fitness of a chromosome or a feasible offer is evaluated through the fitness function, and it is a combination of both seller's and buyer's acceptability. The fittest chromosome is a tentative solution for next round negotiation or a new offer.

The fitness function is a combination of both seller's and buyer's acceptability, the negotiation ends when both negotiators' acceptability reaches their target values rather than setting the iterative times. The genetic algorithms are as follows and flow chart of genetic algorithms is shown in Figure 1. choose an initial populationdetermine the fitness of each individualperform selection repeat perform crossover perform mutation determine the fitness of each individual perform selection until some stopping criterion applies.

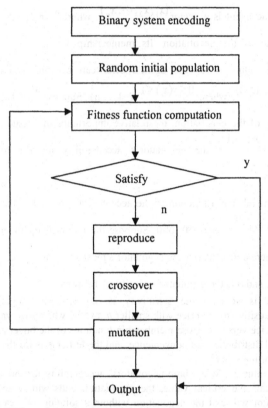

Fig 1 Flow chart of genetic algorithms

3 An Example

In the e-commerce, the buyer and the seller always negotiate about goods or service. Here we give a simple example to demonstrate the process of negotiation.

Suppose both the buyer and seller negotiate about four issues of goods, i.e. price, quality, transportation and service. Suppose the price for goods ranges from ¥10 to ¥14 per item, and the quality, transport and service are rated into 5 levels in Table 1 Negotiation issues.

Table 1 Negotiation issues

Price C	Quality Q	Transportation T	Service S
10	4	4	4
11	3	3	3
12	2	2	2
13	1	1	1
14	0	0	0

Suppose the membership function of each issue is normal distribution, and the weight of each issue is the same. They are ω_c =0.6, ω_q =0.2, ω_t =0.1, ω_s =0.1 respectively.

We know price is the key issue for both buyer and seller. We set the critical values of both buyer and seller for price is 0.6 and the sensitivity for each issue is 3.

Buyer's membership function for all issues are as follows: membership function for price is $v(x) = e^{-(\frac{x-10}{3})^2}$; membership function for quality is $v(x) = e^{-(\frac{x-4}{3})^2}$; membership function for transportation is $v(x) = e^{-(\frac{x-4}{3})^2}$; membership function for service is $v(x) = e^{-(\frac{x-4}{3})^2}$.

Seller's membership function for all issues are as follows: membership function for price is $v(x) = e^{-(\frac{x-14}{3})^2}$; membership function for quality is $v(x) = e^{-(\frac{x}{3})^2}$; membership function for transportation is $v(x) = e^{-(\frac{x}{3})^2}$; membership function for service is $v(x) = e^{-(\frac{x}{3})^2}$.

When acceptability of both buyer and seller for counteroffer exceeds λ =0.6, the offer is an acceptable offer. Suppose the sensitivity of both buyer and seller for time is the same and if one negotiator does not accept the counteroffer, he will reduce the acceptability for his own offer by 10%. Suppose the initial offer of buyer is (10,4,4,4) and the initial offer of seller is (14,0,0,0).

In the end, we can get the offer（12,2,2,3）as a solution. The membership functions of buyer and seller for the offer both reach 0.6. The buyer's acceptability is 0.6*0.641+0.2*0.0.641+0.1*0.641+0.1 *0.895=0.6664 and the seller's acceptability is 0.6*0.641+0.2*0.641+0.1*0.641+0.1*0.368=0.6137. (Table2 and Table3)

Table2 Seller's offer

membership / seller's offer	seller	buyer
（14, 0, 0, 0）	1	0.189

(13, 1, 1, 1)	0.895	0.368
(12, 1, 1, 1)	0.743	0.532

Table3 Buyer's offer

membership / buyer's offer	seller	buyer
(10, 4, 4, 4)	0.189	1
(11, 3, 3, 3)	0.368	0.895
(12, 3, 3, 3)	0.532	0.743
(12, 2, 2, 3)	0.666	0.614

We can see the buyer and seller reach an agreement at the offer (12,2,2,3). We know the fuzzy negotiation model is similar to the practical negotiation and the process of negotiation is similar too.

4 Genetic Algorithms Parameters

There are four issues to negotiate in the example, so we take four sections of genes to represent four items price, quality, transportation and service, their codes are shown in Figure 2. The difference between maxima and minima for each issue equals 4, at least three bits are needed in binary code for each issue, so the coding length for four issues is 12. Suppose the population size is 20, probability of crossover is 0.95 and probability of mutation is 0.05.

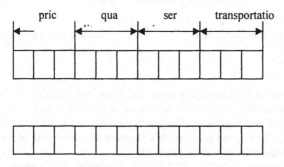

Fig 2 Binary code of negotiation

The initial offer or the first generation population of chromosomes is generated randomly, so simulations of negotiation process will change randomly. The final negotiation round of one simulation may differ from that of another simulation greatly, but the final offers of buyer agent and seller agent, and the acceptability of buyer agent and seller agent vary a little when buyer agent and seller agent reach an agreement, if we suppose that the ending condition for negotiation is both negotiators' acceptability reaches their target values. The final negotiation round of simulations may vary a little, but the final offers of buyer agent and seller agent, and the acceptability of buyer agent and seller agent in one simulation may differ from that in another simulation greatly, if we set the iterative times. The simulation result with target acceptability value is better than that with preset iterative times, and it is more practical.

The fitness function is a combination of both seller's and buyer's acceptability, the negotiation ends when both negotiators' acceptability reaches their target values rather than setting the iterative times. The fitness function can take various forms, and the fitness function of simulations is seller's acceptability multiplied by buyer's acceptability.

5 Simulation

The initial offers or the first generation population of chromosomes are generated randomly, so one simulation with the same preset acceptability may differ from another simulation greatly in iterative times, but final offers of buyer agent and seller agent and final acceptability of buyer agent and seller agent will vary within preset errors when they reach an agreement, because the ending condition of negotiation process is both negotiators' acceptability reaches their target values. The negotiation result is insensitive to the selection of first generation population and it is an advantage of genetic algorithms. One simulation output of negotiation is shown in Figure 3, the negotiation ends in 107 round. The final offer is (12.857, 4.0, 4.0, 2.286), seller agent's acceptability is 0.6256 and buyer agent's acceptability of buyer is 0.6144. From the simulation result, both negotiators are satisfied with the final result, and genetic algorithms are practical learning mechanism in bilateral negotiations.

```
100111111101 offer(12.286,4.0,4.0,2.857) accepability of seller=0.5239295396955331 accepability of buyer=0.7222629148316078
100111111101 offer(12.286,4.0,4.0,2.857) accepability of seller=0.5239295396955331 accepability of buyer=0.7222629148316078
100111111101 offer(12.286,4.0,4.0,2.857) accepability of seller=0.5239295396955331 accepability of buyer=0.7222629148316078
100111111101 offer(12.286,4.0,4.0,2.857) accepability of seller=0.5239295396955331 accepability of buyer=0.722629148316078
100111111101 offer(12.286,4.0,4.0,2.857) accepability of seller=0.5239295396955331 accepability of buyer=0.7222629148316078
100111111101 offer(12.286,4.0,4.0,2.857) accepability of seller=0.5239295396955331 accepability of buyer=0.7222629148316078
100111111101 offer(12.286,4.0,4.0,2.857) accepability of seller=0.5239295396955331 accepability of buyer=0.7222629148316078
100111111101 offer(12.286,4.0,4.0,2.857) accepability of seller=0.5239295396955331 accepability of buyer=0.7222629148316078
100111111101 offer(12.286,4.0,4.0,2.857) accepability of seller=0.5239295396955331 accepability of buyer=0.7222629148316078
100111111101 offer(12.286,4.0,4.0,2.857) accepability of seller=0.5239295396955331 accepability of buyer=0.7222629148316078
100111111101 offer(12.286,4.0,4.0,2.857) accepability of seller=0.5239295396955331 accepability of buyer=0.7222629148316078
100111111101 offer(12.286,4.0,4.0,2.857) accepability of seller=0.5239295396955331 accepability of buyer=0.7222629148316078
107's chromosome
101111111100 offer(12.857,4.0,4.0,2.286) accepability of seller=0.6256145571497915 accepability of buyer=0.6143752542006342
101111111100 offer(12.857,4.0,4.0,2.286) accepability of seller=0.6256145571497915 accepability of buyer=0.6143752542006342
101111111100 offer(12.857,4.0,4.0,2.286) accepability of seller=0.6256145571497915 accepability of buyer=0.6143752542006342
101111111100 offer(12.857,4.0,4.0,2.286) accepability of seller=0.6256145571497915 accepability of buyer=0.6143752542006342
101111111100 offer(12.857,4.0,4.0,2.286) accepability of seller=0.6256145571497915 accepability of buyer=0.6143752542006342
101111111100 offer(12.857,4.0,4.0,2.286) accepability of seller=0.6256145571497915 accepability of buyer=0.6143752542006342
101111111100 offer(12.857,4.0,4.0,2.286) accepability of seller=0.6256145571497915 accepability of buyer=0.6143752542006342
101111111100 offer(12.857,4.0,4.0,2.286) accepability of seller=0.6256145571497915 accepability of buyer=0.6143752542006342
101111111100 offer(12.857,4.0,4.0,2.286) accepability of seller=0.6256145571497915 accepability of buyer=0.6143752542006342
101111111100 offer(12.857,4.0,4.0,2.286) accepability of seller=0.6256145571497915 accepability of buyer=0.6143752542006342
101111111100 offer(12.857,4.0,4.0,2.286) accepability of seller=0.6256145571497915 accepability of buyer=0.6143752542006342
101111111100 offer(12.857,4.0,4.0,2.286) accepability of seller=0.6256145571497915 accepability of buyer=0.6143752542006342
101111111100 offer(12.857,4.0,4.0,2.286) accepability of seller=0.6256145571497915 accepability of buyer=0.6143752542006342
101111111100 offer(12.857,4.0,4.0,2.286) accepability of seller=0.6256145571497915 accepability of buyer=0.6143752542006342
101111111100 offer(12.857,4.0,4.0,2.286) accepability of seller=0.6256145571497915 accepability of buyer=0.6143752542006342
101111111100 offer(12.857,4.0,4.0,2.286) accepability of seller=0.6256145571497915 accepability of buyer=0.6143752542006342
101111111100 offer(12.857,4.0,4.0,2.286) accepability of seller=0.6256145571497915 accepability of buyer=0.6143752542006342
101111111100 offer(12.857,4.0,4.0,2.286) accepability of seller=0.6256145571497915 accepability of buyer=0.6143752542006342
```

Fig 3 Output of genetic algorithms

6   Conclusions

In traditional E-commerce negotiation, both negotiators always accept or reject an offer by a specified value. We give the fuzzy negotiation model based on genetic learning mechanism and evaluate the acceptability based on fuzzy set theory and membership functions so that the automatic negotiation is similar to the practical situation of negotiation. We adopt the monotonic concession protocol as our negotiation protocol and state the combined concession in the multi-issues negotiation for the negotiators and adopt genetic learning mechanism so that its negotiation outcome is more exact. This protocol is simple, so it is easy to implement automatically. The example shows the fuzzy negotiation model is reasonable and feasible and it is similar to the real negotiation process. The fuzzy negotiation model used here is the normal distribution. Other more complex distribution need further study. We hope that fuzzy multi-issue negotiation model of e-commerce can be applied in real business transaction.

References

1 Samuel P.M.Choi, Jiming Liu, Sheung-Ping Chan. "A Genetic Agent-based Negotiation System". *Computer Networks* 37, 2001, 195-204.

2 Ren-Jye Dzeng,Yu-Chun Lin. "Intelligent Agents for Supporting Construction Procurement Negotiation". *Expert Systems with Applications* 27,2004, 107-119

3 Raymond Y.K. Lau, Towards Genetically Optimised Multi-Agent Multi-Issue Negotiations, Proceedings of the 38th Hawaii International Conference on System Sciences, 2005, 1-10

4 F. Bergenti, A. Poggi, An Agent-based Approach to Manage Negotiation Protocols in Rexible CSCW Systems, Proceeding of.4th International Conference on Autonomous Agents, Barcelona Spain, 2000, 267–268.

5 Raymond Y.K. Lau, Maolin Tang, On Wong, Towards Genetically Optimised Responsive Negotiation Agents, Proceedings of the IEEE/WIC/ACM International Conference on Intelligent Agent Technology (IAT'04), 2004, 1-7

6 W. C. Stirling. Social Utility Functions–Part 1: Theory, IEEE Transaction Systems, Man, Cybernetics. C, Applications and Reviews, vol. 35, no. 4, 2005 522–532

7 W. C. Stirling, R.L. Frost . Social Utility Functions–Part 2: Theory, IEEE Transaction Systems, Man, Cybernetics. C, Applications and Reviews, vol. 35, no. 4, 2005 533–543

8 Y.Y Wu, J.X Lu, "A Fuzzy Negotiation Model of E-commerce", Journal of *System Science and Information,* 2006, Vol.4, No.1, 33-37

9 S.L Zhao, G.R Jiang, T.Y Huang. An Analysis Model to Agent Ability Report Deception in Multi-agent Cooperation, Proceedings of 2005 International Conference on Management Science & Engineering, 2005

10 S.L Zhao, G.R Jiang, T.Y Huang. The Deception Detection and Restraint in Multi-agent System, Proceedings of 17th IEEE International Conference on Tools with Artificial Intelligence, 2005

11 D.S Zhai, J.X Lu, Y.Y Wu, "A Program of Automatic Negotiation in E-commerce", Journal of *Information and Decision Science*, 2006, Vol.1, No.1, 7-11

12 Sheng-Hshiung Tsaur, T.Y Chang and C.H Yen, "The Evaluation of Airline Service Quality by Fuzzy MCDM", *Tourism Management*, 2002 (23), pp.107-115.

13 M. Bo, F. Wei, A Negotiation Model Based on Fuzzy Multiple Criteria Decision Making Method, Proceedings of the Fourth International Conference on Computer and Information Technology, CIT'04, 2004, 1039 – 1044

14 C.-B. Cheng, C.-C. H. Chan, and K.-C. Lin, Intelligent agents for e-Marketplace: Negotiation with Issue Trade-offs by Fuzzy Inference Systems, Decision Support System.

15 Y.X Meng, B. Meng. An Agent-based Negotiation Support System with Fuzzy Multi-objective Decision-making Method, Proceedings of ICSSSM '05. 2005 International Conference on Services Systems and Services Management, 2005, 1141 - 1144 Vol. 2

16 Lai. K.R. Chung Hsien Lan. Development of an Assessment Agent to Promote the Learning Effectiveness in a Computer Supported Collaborative Learning Environment, Proceeding of Fifth IEEE International Conference on Advanced Learning Technologies, 2005. ICALT 2005. 354 – 358

17 Bonnie Rubenstein-Montano, Ross A. Malaga, A Weighted Sum Genetic Algorithm to Support Multiple-Party Multiple-Objective Negotiations, IEEE Transactions on Evolutionary Computation, Vol. 6, No. 4, 2002, 366-377

18 Ravindra Krovi, Arthur C. Graesser, William E. Pracht, Agent Behaviors in Virtual Negotiation Environments, IEEE Transactions on Systems, "Man, and Cybernetics-Part C": *Applications and Reviews*, Vol. 29, No.1, 1999, 15-25

19 Y.Y Wu, J. Lu, F. Yan, A Fuzzy Negotiation Model of e-Commerce and Its Implementation, Technology Management for the Global Future, PICMET 2006 Proceedings, Vol.3, 9-13 July, Istanbul, Turkey, 1180-1185

20 Z.Ren*,C.J.Anumba,O.O.Ugwu. The Development of a Multi-agent System for Construction Claims Negotiation. Advances in Engineering Software 34,2003, 683-696.

21 Wei-Po Lee. Towards Agent-based Decision Making in the Electronic Marketplace: Interactive Recommendation and Automated Negotiation. Expert Systems with Applications 27, 2004.

22 Chun, A., Wai, H., & Wong, R.. Optimizing Agent-based Meeting Scheduling through Preference Estimation. Engineering Applications of Artificial Intelligence, 16, 727–743

23 Chang-Shing Lee,Chen-Yu Pan. An Intelligent Fuzzy Agent for Meeting Scheduling Decision Support System. Fuzzy Sets and Systems 142,2004, 467-488

A Group-Based Trust Model in Peer-to-Peer Environment

Fen Xu, Yajun Guo,Qin Wang

Department of Computer Science, Huazhong Normal University, Wuhan
430079, Hubei,China, xufen5460@tom.com

Abstract. The open and anonymous nature of peer-to-peer system makes it easy to be attacked and abused by some malicious nodes, so it is very important to establish a perfect trust mechanism in peer-to-peer environment. In this paper, we propose a novel group-based trust model in which the trust relationships between entities are divided into trust relationship in group and trust relationship between groups. This model deals with these two kinds of trust relationships in the different way and improves trust value calculation method. The model can get more real trust value at the small price, and the advantages of the model are simple structure and high reliability.

1 Introduction

With the continuous development of peer-to-peer technology, distributed computing, electronic commerce, file sharing and instant messaging have been widely used. Peer-to-peer users directly establish interconnection and share resources. Peer-to-peer has been a new focus in Internet application.

At present, peer-to-peer can be classified into three categories according to the network structure. The first category is a purely decentralized peer-to-peer system, such as Gnutella [1] and Freenet [2] and so on. All nodes must play the role of searching resource and downloading. The second category is a hybrid peer-to-peer system, such as Napster, MSN, and BT file sharing and so on. Its searching function can be implemented in the centralized directory server, but downloading is still in peer-to-peer way. The third category is a super-node network architecture system, such as KaZaa (one of the most popular file sharing system currently). It is the organic combination of the purely decentralized peer-to-peer system and the hybrid peer-to-peer system. These super-nodes unlike the server in the hybrid peer-to-peer are transparent in function. Even if some fail, the whole network will not be affected.

Please use the following format when citing this chapter:

Xu, F., Guo, Y., Wang, Q., 2007, in IFIP International Federation for Information Processing, Volume 251, Integration and Innovation Orient to E-Society Volume1, Wang, W. (Eds), (Boston: Springer), pp. 44-50.

Although peer-to-peer network structure is with dynamic property and convenience, there are serious security issues. Good trust model is the key to assuring high quality service which is provided by the network. At present, there are a lot of research on the trust model based on peer-to-peer environment and mainly can be divided into the following categories [3, 4]: Digital signature model. This method doesn't pursue the credibility of nodes, but emphasizes the credibility of the data. Take file sharing application for example, when downloading is completed every time, the user judges the authenticity of the data. If the user trusts the authenticity of the data, makes a signature for the data. The data obtains the more signatures, the authenticity is higher. However, this method can only be applied for data sharing application, and can't prevent mass fraud, namely, malicious group of nodes all make signatures for inauthentic data. Currently popular file sharing applications are using this method [5]. PKI-based [6] trust model. There exist a small number of central nodes which are responsible for the supervision of the entire network and announce illegal nodes in the regular time. The legitimacy of central nodes is guaranteed by certificates issued by the CA. This kind of system usually relies on the center and has scalability and single node failure etc. issues, such as many servers [7] of eDonkey. Global credibility model. This kind of model obtains the global credibility of nodes by using mutual satisfaction iteration among the neighbor nodes. Local recommendation-based trust model [8, 9]. A node obtains the credibility of a certain node by asking for limited other nodes in this kind of system.

These models respectively have their advantages and disadvantages. In this paper, the basic idea of constructing the model is based on the local recommendation trust model. Trust value calculation method is improved in this model, so we can get more real trust value at the small price.

2   A group-based trust model

In this paper, we propose a novel group-based trust model based on the third categories super-node network structure (as shown in figure 1). This model can be used to deal with trust relationship between the entities in peer-to-peer environment and help peer-to-peer entities make trust choice. Select a node whose performance is the optimal as a super-node in each group of nodes. Some information of nodes in this group is stored in super-nodes. There is a lot of this kind of groups in the whole peer-to-peer structure, and super-nodes in each group are connected in the form of the pure peer-to-peer structure in the overall structure. This model divides the trust relationships between entities into trust relationship in group and trust relationship between groups which are dealt with in a different way. This model can evaluate the trust relationship between the entities more accurately, thus can solve security issues more effectively in peer-to-peer environment.

2.1   Implementing process of the model

Group is a set of node members which have certain relationships, and can be organized according to different principles. The principle of organizing group in this model is the set of members which transact frequently, so there are transaction histories among all members of the group. In this process, when node u requests for transaction with node v, it is necessary to know the trust value of node v at first. Two cases are discussed here.

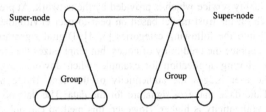

Fig. 1. Group-based peer-to-peer structure

(1) If node u and node v belong to the same group, the trust value of node v is calculated by node u using trust value calculation method in group. According to the trust value, node u judges whether transacts with node v. Update local records according to the results of the transaction at last.

(2) If node u and node v belong to the different group, the trust value of node v is calculated by node u using trust value calculation method between groups. According to the trust value, node u judges whether transacts with node v. Update records in the super-node according to the results of the transaction at last.

Implementing process of the whole model is shown in figure 2.

2.2   Trust value calculation

The trust value calculation of the model is divided into calculation in group and calculation between groups. The trust value of node v calculated by node u is $TV_{u,v}$ which is a discrete value between 0 and 1. The results of evaluation are more near to 1, namely, the node obtains the more satisfactory services, or the opposite.

● **Trust value calculation in group**

The trust value in group is calculated by using time based past transaction as well as peer recommendations.

The time based past transaction value of node v calculated at node u is denoted as $PT_{u,v}$ which is defined as follows:

$$PT_{u,v} = 1 - \frac{1}{\max[\{\mu_s ST_{u,v} - \mu_u UT_{u,v}\}, 0] + 1} \qquad \dots \ (1)$$

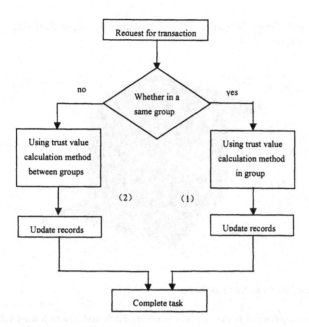

Fig. 2. Implementing process of the model

Where $PT_{u,v}$ is the past transaction value of node v calculated by node u based on past transactions, $ST_{u,v}$ is the successful transaction between node u and node v, $UT_{u,v}$ is the unsuccessful transaction between node u and node v. Both μ_s and μ_u are positive numbers depending on the time, and respectively represent the corresponding weights of $ST_{u,v}$ and $UT_{u,v}$. The weight μ_s is defined as:

$$\mu_s= \begin{cases} h & t_s \leq 1 \\ m & 1 < t_s \leq 2 \\ 1 & t_s > 2 \end{cases} \quad \ldots (2)$$

μ_u is defined similarly. This mapping function assigns low, medium, or high weights based on the last transaction time. The time t_s and t_u are defined as:

$$t_s = \frac{t - st_{u,v}}{\Delta t} \qquad t_u = \frac{t - ut_{u,v}}{\Delta t} \qquad \ldots (3)$$

Where t is the current time, $st_{u,v}$ ($ut_{u,v}$) is the time of last successful (unsuccessful) transaction, Δt is the threshold time.

The graph of the past transaction evaluation against successful and unsuccessful transactions is shown in the figure 3. 'h', 'm' and 'l' are given the values 3, 2, and 1 respectively, and μ_s and μ_u are randomly assigned one of these values in every calculation of $PT_{u,v}$. The graph shows fluctuations when $ST_{u,v}$ and $UT_{u,v}$ have roughly the same values, but when $ST_{u,v}$ is considerably larger than $UT_{u,v}$, $PT_{u,v}$ approximates to 1.

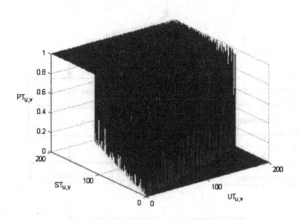

Fig. 3. Time based past transaction evaluation

Suppose the number of nodes is n in the group. Each node owns a trust value of any other nodes it transacts with before. When any node obtains peer recommendations, the trust value of the node is calculated by using the following formula.

$$PR_{u,v} = \frac{\sum_{k=1}^{n-1}[TV_{u,k} * TV_{k,v}]}{n-1} \qquad \cdots (4)$$

Where $PR_{u,v}$ is the peer recommendations trust value of node v calculated by node u, $TV_{u,k}$ is the trust value of node k calculated by node u, and $TV_{k,v}$ is the trust value of node v sent by node k.

Suppose that node u wants to calculate the trust value of node v, then $TV_{u,v}$ is calculated by the following equation:

$$TV_{u,v} = (1-\lambda) * PT_{u,v} + \lambda * PR_{u,v} \qquad \cdots (5)$$

Where λ is a constant which is between 0 and 1. For nodes just joining the peer-to-peer network or without any thought, users are more willing to believe that the recommendation information of the other nodes, so the value of λ can be set larger. For some opinionated nodes, they prefer to trust their own judgment, so the value of λ can be set smaller, generally we can set λ 0.5.

Update the local records based on the results of the transaction at last.

● **Trust value calculation between groups**

Suppose that there are n nodes in the group in which the performance of super-node is optimal. Super-node has higher power and memory compared to other nodes in the group. Taking storage efficiency into account, the size of group should be small. For the calculation of trust, super-node cyclically broadcasts a request in a group. In response, all group member nodes forward their $\overrightarrow{TV_{sn}}$ trust value of other member nodes to super-node. The trust vector of super-node is defined as:

$$\overrightarrow{TV_{sn}} = (TV_{sn,1}, TV_{sn,2}, ..., TV_{sn,n}) \qquad \qquad ...\ (6)$$

Where $TV_{sn,k}$ is the trust value of node k. It is calculated by the following equation:

$$TV_{sn,1} = \frac{\sum_{k=2}^{n} TV_{k,1}}{n-1} \quad , ..., \quad TV_{sn,n} = \frac{\sum_{k=1}^{n-1} TV_{k,n}}{n-1} \qquad ...\ (7)$$

This trust vector is saved in the super-node and updated in the cyclical time.

When node u requests for transaction with node v, and node u and node v belong to the different group, the trust value $TV_{u,v}$ is calculated by the following formula:

$$TV_{u,v} = TV_{sn_v,v} * \theta_{sn_v,sn_u} \qquad \qquad ...\ (8)$$

Where sn_u is the super-node of node u, sn_v is the super-node of node v, θ_{sn_v,sn_u} is the trust weight between super-node sn_v and super-node sn_u.

3   Performance analysis

The real-time performance of the trust value. When trust value is calculated in this model, time-based past transaction evaluations are considered. Time is set in order to give larger weights of the trust evaluation for recent transactions. For the historical trust value, the recent behavior is more concerned, because the recent behavior can reflect the credit records of the node in the most recent period, thus real-time performance of the trust value is guaranteed. And adding the time factor can also reflect the easy-destruction-hard-construction performance [10] of the credit.

The accuracy of the trust value. When the node calculates the trust value, it not only considers transaction histories of the local records, but also asks for recommendations of members in the group. If small numbers of nodes fail, it doesn't have too much effect on the entire trust value calculation, so the reliability of the model is greatly improved. Because the local stores are only transaction records participated in by their own, and recommending to other nodes is more reliable, thus making the accurate judgment to the trust value is guaranteed.

The integrity of the trust value. Trust values are stored in the node itself in this model and need not other nodes participate in the management, so it prevents the trust value from being altered, forged or deleted by malicious nodes, thus the integrity of the trust value is guaranteed.

The calculation efficiency of the trust value. Selecting a set of nodes among which transactions are very frequent constitutes a group in this model. The advantages are that these nodes are worth trusting at first which can be drawn based on transaction experience, otherwise, it will not frequently transact with them. And these members whose relationships are close are easier to provide effective information. A node only needs to access to the set of nodes in the group, it can better judge the trust value of the node which wants to transact, so the communication is less and the efficiency is higher.

4 Conclusions

In this paper, we propose a novel group-based trust model based on the super-node network architecture. The structure of this model is very simple. The model is very easy to be accepted by users and can suit for many kinds of peer-to-peer application environment. The trust relationships between entities are divided into trust relationship in group and trust relationship between groups in the model. For the different trust relationship, we use the different calculation method to assure the real-time performance, accuracy, integrity and calculation efficiency of the trust value. In future, we will make much more specific definition and description for this model such as updating strategy of the trust value and so on. We will also incorporate intrusion tolerant intelligence in this model, so that nodes are able to detect false information sent by any malicious node.

References

1. Distributed System for Information storage and Searching Model Description, http://www.gnutella.co.uk/liberary/pdf/paper final gnutella english.pdf.
2. I. Clark, O. Sandberg, B. Wiley, T. Freenet Hong, A distributed anonymous information storage and retrieval system, *Proc. of the Workshop on Design Issues in Anonymity and Unobservability*, Berkeley, CA, July 2000,311-320.
3. W. Dou, H.M. Wang, Y. Jia, A recommendation-based peer-to-peer trust model , *Journal of Software*, 2004, 15 (4), 571-583.
4. F. Cornelli, E. Damiani, S. D. C. Vimercati, *Choosing reputable servents in a P2P network*, in: Proc. of the 11th International World Wide Web Conference Hawaii, ACM Press, May 2002, 376-386.
5. K. Albrecht, AR. Clippee Ruedi, *A large-scale client/peer system, Technical Report*, TR-410, Swiss Federal Institute of Technology, 2003.
6. SD. Kamvar, MT. EigenRep Schlosser, Reputation management in P2P networks, Proc. of the 12th Int'l World Wide Web Conf Budapest, ACM Press, 123-134.
7. J. Altman, PKI Security for JXTA overlay networks, Technical Report, TR-I2-03-06, Palo Alto: *Sun Microsystem*, 2003.
8. A. Abdul-Rahman, S. Hailes, A distributed trust model, *Proc. of the 1997 New Security Paradigms Workshop*, ACM, September 1997, 48-60.
9. M. Blaze, J. Feigenbaum, J. Ioannidis, The role of trust management in distributed systems security , *Secure Internet Programming: Issues in Distributed and Mobile Object Systems*, volume 1603 of Lecture Notes in Computer Science, July 1999, 183-210.
10. Y. Zhong, Y. Yu, *Dynamic Trust Production Based on Interaction Sequence Technical Report*, CSD-TR 03-006, Dept. of Computer Science, Pudure University, 2003.

An Optimization Handover Scheme Based On HMIPv6

Feng Lu [1], Jianjie Wang [2]

1 Wuhan University of Technology, Wuhan,430070, Professor,E-mail:lufengwut@163.com.

2 Wuhan Univesity of Technology, Wuhan,430070, E-mail: seven_810717@163.com.tel:13407173506

Wuhan University of Technology jianhu A-106#,430070

Abstract. The process that mobile node still maintains its connectivity when moved from one access router (AR) to another access router is called handover. The handover technology is one of the most important technologies for the quality of real-time operation. In order to reduce the handover delay, Fast Mobile IPv6 (FMIPv6), Hierarchical Mobile IPv6 (HMIPv6) and Fast Hierarchical Mobile IPv6 are studied. Then, an optimization method based on HMIPv6 is advanced. On the basic of mobile anchor point (MAP), this scheme introduces the concept of regional anchor point (RAP) with the purpose of reducing the binding update messages between mobile node and home agent (HA) or correspondent node, thus lowering the handover delay.

1   Introduction

The rise of wireless communications and computer technology promotes the rapid development of the society on the direction of high-tech and information technology, which make people become more and more dependent on network. The integration technology for mobile communication technologies and wireless network satisfies people to visit internet at any time by mobile terminals and realizes dynamic link between mobile terminals and Internet, and achieves to maintain a seamless connection with Internet without reconfiguration network terminals, even without disruption of the network conversation.

The mobile IPv6(MIPv6) protocol, based on IPv6, has provided support for those mobile network users.Its working principle is shown in Fig.1.①An MN detects that it has moved to a new subnet when it roamed[1]. Then it may use either stateless or stateful address auto-configuration to form one or more care-of addresses. ②The association made between the home address and the care-of address is known as a binding, and binding update (BU) is sent to HA and CN. Its HA and CN will store BU in their binding cache once they obtained the BU and send a binding

Please use the following format when citing this chapter:

Lu, F., Wang, J., 2007, in IFIP International Federation for Information Processing, Volume 251, Integration and Innovation Orient to E-Society Volume1, Wang, W. (Eds), (Boston: Springer), pp. 51-57.

acknowledgement (BACK) to MN. ③The HA uses the neighbor advertisement (NAdv) to intercept the data packets intended to MN, then encapsulates and forwards them to the care-of address by tunnels. ④The data packets are directly sent to care-of address by routing extension header of home address included in data packets, which can prevent forming triangular routing between CN and MN due to HA.

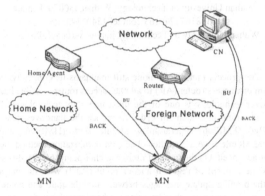

Fig.1. IPv6 working principle

2   Handover methods of mobile IPv6

In mobile IPv6, MN registers its care-of address to HA after it leaves home address, and constructs a bidirectional tunnel with HA. Then the data groupings communicating with CN will be forwarded by HA. But this kind of bidirectional tunnel leads to serious grouping latency, the protocol advanced a method for routing optimization, namely, any CN which communicates with MN and has the foundation of mobile IPv6 can maintain a cache to bind the MN care-of address. Therefore, MN can communicate with CN directly, reducing the handover latency. The MN will perform the handover process of MIPv6 when it moves from one IPv6 network to another IPv6 network.

The MIPv6 handover technology can be divided into three categories: the first is smoothness handover (also called low grouping handover). Its characteristic is almost not to loss any grouping, which is used to the text transmission business not sensitive to latency and allowing poor performance. The second is fast handover (also called low latency handover), which requires MN' process of handover fast and the grouping latency as low as possible. At present, it's mainly applied to more and more real-time multimedia business on Internet, which can abide grouping loss on some degree, but more care about the latency and handover wobble. The third is seamless handover, which merges the virtues of the former two, and implements low latency and low grouping loss handover, so it's the ultimate objective.

2.1 Mobile IPv6 fast handover

The model of fast Mobile IPv6 (FMIPv6) based on MIPv6 accelerates the handover by increasing set of message mechanisms[2], such as router solicitation for proxy (RtSolPr), proxy router advertisement(PrRtAdv), handover initiate(HI), handover Acknowledgement(HACK), fast binding update(FBU), fast binding Acknowledgement(FBACK), fast neighbor advertisement (FNA) and so on. FMIPv6 allows MN to obtain the information of new AR and its subnet proxy when it stays on its old AR. Therefore, it can anticipate new care-of address, which can reduce the latency for configuring care-of address by some operation after handover.

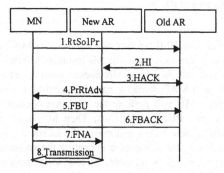

Fig. 2. Principle of fast handover

Simultaneously, MIPv6 requires MN to set up a tunnel between the old AR and the new AR when it has attained the new care-of address. In this case, MN can still receive the grouping sent from CN on the period of handover. The grouping will be intercepted by the old AR and forwarded to the new AR through the tunnel. The new AR firstly cached the grouping before it receipted the MN' advertisement and won't forward the new care-of address until the MN sends advertisement indicating it truly moves to the AR. The process of fast handover is shown in Fig.2.

2.2 Hierarchical mobile IPv6

The model of hierarchical mobile IPv6 (HMIPv6)[3] is an amelioration of MIPv6 that imports a function entity—mobile anchor point (MAP, which is a router in any layer of HMIPv6). Then the care-of address in MAP domain is divided into link care-of address (LCoA, which is a temporary address conserved in a MAP)[4] and regional care-of address (RCoA, which is a MN' MAP address conserved between HA and CN). When MN moves in the same MAP, its RCoA doesn't change, so it only needs to register a new LCoA to MAP. The MAP updates its couple of address [RCoA, LCoA] in the binding cache and intercepts the MN' RCoA data packets sent to its own domain, then forwards them to MN' LCoA through tunnel. Its network configuration is as shown in Fig.3.

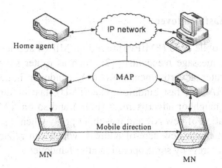

Fig.3. Network configuration of HMIPv6

The handover process of HMIPv6 has two instances: ①MN moves in the same MAP domain, namely micro-movement. In this instance, MN just needs to register the LCoA and not change its RCoA, so MN doesn't need to rebind to HA and CN. ②MN moves in different MAP domains, namely macro-movement. When moving to a new MAP domain, MN will perform the detection operation, and obtain two care-of addresses by AR: RCoA and LCoA. Then MN sends a binding update message which produces new RCoA and makes the LCoA as its original address. Ensuingly, MAP returns a BACK message indicating the registration successful or not. After MN received the BACK message, the following operation is just like MN moving in a common IPv6.

3. Optimization handover method of HMIPv6

Based on the above description on the working principle of FMIPv6 and HMIPv6, it is easy to conclude that FMIPv6 makes MN anticipate the care-of address produced after handover, which reduces the latency related with matching care-of address after moving. Meanwhile the tunnel set up between the old AR and the new AR degrades the data packets loss rate because of handover. But FMIPv6 doesn't consider the alternation of a great deal of binding messages when registering update. On the other hand, HMIPv6 has solved the problems, such as reducing the link efficiency and network throughput and increasing the handover latency, produced by handling a large number of update messages for HA and CN. But it ignores that the using of MAP increased the grouping transmission router between MN and CN and also adds the handover latency at some degree. Otherwise, HMIPv6 only applies to MN moving in the same MAP. Aimed at tackling the shortcomings of FMIPv6 and HMIPv6, the paper, coming from the purpose on reducing the number of registering update messages and degrading handover latency, advances an optimization scheme based on HMIPv6.

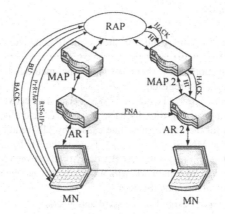

Fig.4. Handover process in different MAP of the same RAP

The optimization scheme is based on HMIPv6, combining some neighboring MAP domains to form a bigger domain, so a new function entity is introduced – regional anchor point (RAP)[5-8]. It acts as a temporary HA just like MAP, but its management area is broader than MAP'. When MN moves in this model, its care-of address consisted of three parts: link care-of address (MN' temporary address which conserved in MAP domain), regional care-of address (MN' temporary address conserved between MAP and RAP domain) and local care-of address (MN' address conserved between HA and CN). When it moves in the same MAP domain, MN keeps its regional care-of address and local care-of address as the same as before, but changes its link care-of address. On this time, MAP acts as MN' HA and intercepts the IP data packets sent to HA or CN. Then these data packets will be forwarded to MN' link care-of address by tunnel. Those operations are totally transparent to the MN' HA, CN and RAP. When MN moves in the same RAP but different MAPs, RAP acts as MAP' HA and MAP acts as RAP' mobile node. Here, MN' local care-of address still keeps invariability but its link care-of address and regional care-of address both changed. We can operate fast hierarchical handover in this layer handover. Fist of all, MN directly sends an RtSolPr to RAP. Once RAP receives the RtSolPr message, it returns a PrRtAdv to MN as soon as possible and matches a new regional care-of address and link care-of address with MN. In order to maintain communication between the old and the new link, MN needs to send fast binding update message to RAP. After that, RAP forwards the information of care-of address to the new MAP through AR and sends HI information. Ensuingly, MAP sends HI information to the new AR, which will detect the validity of link address continuously, then send HACK message to the new MAP. Once the new MAP obtained the HACK message, it quickly sends HACK message to RAP. Hence, a bidirectional tunnel is set up between the new AR and RAP. After MN obtains the connection information sent from the new AR, it will send a fast neighbor discovery message to the new AR. At this moment, the new AR can forward data groupings to MN. Figure 4 shows its handover process.

4. Performance Analysis

During the process of network handover, the mobile IP handover delay formula is:
$$T_{handoff} = T_{md} + T_{reg} \cdots\cdots\cdots\cdots\cdots\cdots\cdots\cdots\cdots\cdots\cdots\cdots\cdots\cdots\cdots\cdots\cdots\cdots\cdots(1)$$
T_{md} is mobile detection delay (here, we take the method of ESC, Eager Cell Switching), and T_{reg} is MN registered delay.

Assuming that T_{Mp}、T_{MAPp}、T_{RAPp}、T_{Hp} respectively represents the registration packet processing time by MN, MAP, RAP and HA; T_{MMbu} and T_{MMba} respectively stands for the link latency time caused by MN sending BU to MAP and MAP returning BA to MN. Similarly, T_{MHbu}/T_{MHba} is the BU/BA delay time between MN and HA, and T_{MRbu}/T_{RMba} is the BU/BA delay time between MAP and RAP.

When MN moved in a network without RAP, the movement from MAP1 to MAP2 is a macro-movement, on this time,
$$T_{reg} = T_{Mp} + T_{MMbu} + T_{Mp} + T_{MAPp} + T_{Hp} + T_{MMba} + T_{MHbu} + T_{Mhba} \cdots\cdots\cdots\cdots\cdots\cdots(2)$$
Hence,
$$T_{handoff} = T_{md} + T_{Mp} + T_{MMbu} + T_{Mp} + T_{MAPp} + T_{Hp} + T_{MMba} + T_{MHbu} + T_{MHba} \cdots\cdots\cdots\cdots\cdots(3)$$

When MN moved in the same RAP but different MAPs, the movement from MAP1 to MAP2 is a micro-movement, on this time,
$$T_{reg} = T_{Mp} + T_{MMbu} + T_{Mp} + T_{MAPp} + T_{MMba} + T_{MAPp} + T_{MRbu} + T_{RAPp} + T_{RMba} + T_{MAPp} \cdots\cdots\cdots(4)$$
Hence,
$$T_{handoff} = T_{md} + T_{Mp} + T_{MMbu} + T_{Mp} + T_{MAPp} + T_{MMba} + T_{MAPp} + T_{MRbu} + T_{RAPp} + T_{RMba} + T_{MAPp} \cdots(5)$$

Compared (3) with (5), we can easily draw a conclusion that, aside from the same parts, (3) has its own unique parts of $T_{MHbu} + T_{MHba} + T_{Hp}$, but (5) has peculiar parts of $T_{MAPp} + T_{MRbu} + T_{RAPp} + T_{RMba} + T_{MAPp}$. Although the latter has one more handover process than the former, the HA will deal with numberless BU and BA at the same time, and the frequent BU and BA will lead to HA overload, even information block. That is to say, T_{MHbu} and T_{MHba} account for a big proportion throughout the process of handover. The improved HMIPv6 is through two times handover to alleviate the burden of HA, therefore reduce handover latency.

5. Conclusion

Although the ameliorative HMIPv6 has decreased the handover latency in a bigger area and reduced the management of registering update message between HA or CN and MN in greater degree, it also increases the hidden security troubles among MN, MAP and RAP. They must include authentication and integrity protection and have a capability of preventing replaying attack. Lack of any protection will make malicious node to imitate arbitrary legitimate nodes, even a MAP or a RAP. Any attack of those kinds will exert bad influence on the communication between MN and CN. Though there are still some problems on MIPv6 handover in one way or another, it can be true that with the development of technology and the depth of research, the handover latency and wobble will gradually disappear and eventually achieve a seamless handover.

Acknowledgments

This research was supported by the International Science and Technology Cooperation Project of the Ministry of Science and Technology under Grant No. 2006 DFA73180.

References

1. MegerianS, KoushanfarF, PotkonjakM, etal. Worstand best case cover agein sensor networks, *Mobile Computing, IEEE Transactionson,2005*,4(1):84~92
2. Pack S, Choi Y. Pre-Authenticated fast handoff in a public wireless LAN based on IEEE 802.1x model. In: *Proc. of the IFIP TC6/WG6.8 Working Conf. on Personal Wireless Communications 2002.*
3. Kong Xian-song and Jia Zhuo-sheng, Technology of Handover In Mobile IPv6. *Computer Engineering and Design*, Vol.27, No.8, Apr.2006.
4. Zhang Hong-hai, Hou Jennifer. Maintaining coverage and connectivity in large sensor networks. International Workshop on Theoretical and Algorithmic Aspects of Sensor, *Adhoc Wirelessand Peer to Peer Networks*, Feb.2004.
5. Yu-Ben Miao, Wen-Shyang Hwang, Ce-Kuen Shieh. A transparent deployment method of RSVP-aware applications on UNIX [J]. *Computer Networks*, 2002,40:45-56.
6. Ren Lan-fang, Zhou Hua-chun ,Qin Ya-juan and Zhang Hong-ke, Study of Adap-tive Handover Delay Optimization for Mobile IPv6, *Journal of Beijing Jiao tong University*, Vol.30 No.5, Oct.2006.
7. Nicolas Montavont and Thomas Noël, Handover Management for Mobile Nodes in IPv6 Networks, *IEEE Communications Magazine*, August 2002.
8. Sun Wei-feng, Yang Shou-bao and Chen Yang, QoS Context Transfer Based Seamless Handover Method for Mobile IPv6, *Mini-Micro Systems*, Vol.27, No.11, Nov.2006.

Risk Assessment of Virtual Enterprise Based on the Fuzzy Comprehensive Evaluation Method

Gang Liu, Jiao Zhang,Wangmin Zhang and Xian Zhou
School of Business, Hubei University, P.R. China, 430062

Abstract. For the organizational specialty of a virtual enterprise, the enterprise faces more complicated risk management problems than those in the traditional enterprise. So, to analyze the main affecting factors about the risk and to assess deeply the level of risk management for a virtual enterprise have their important and realistic significance. Based on the aspect of life cycle, this paper divides the cycle of a virtual enterprise into four periods, which are recognition period, construction period, operation period, and termination period. After that, this paper analyzes the possible risks that occur in each period and establishes a set of risk indicator system. According to these, the paper constructs a risk assessment model based on the fuzzy mathematic theory, then adopts this model to evaluate the project risks of virtual enterprise, and testifies its effectiveness through an example finally.

1 Introduction

Along with the integration of world economy and the revolution of the information technology, the competition between the enterprises' external markets becomes more intense. In order to response the market opportunity in time, meet the market demand and obtain more market shares, many enterprises make the virtual enterprise as a realistic choice for a new organization form. Virtual enterprise can help the enterprise response the market flexibly. However, it also contains many risk factors inevitably. Risks and opportunities coexist in virtual enterprise, and the success of risk management ensures the successful operation of virtual enterprise. Therefore, the risk management of virtual enterprise now becomes the focus of people's attention.

Nowadays, scholars in and abroad have done some researches on risk of virtual enterprise. References [1-2] mainly proposed relative risk management measures in

Please use the following format when citing this chapter:

Liu, G., Zhang, J., Zhang, W., Zhou, X., 2007, in IFIP International Federation for Information Processing, Volume 251, Integration and Innovation Orient to E-Society Volume1, Wang, W. (Eds), (Boston: Springer), pp. 58-66.

terms of the systematic analysis of risk factors in virtual enterprise, and focused on how to supervise its risks effectively and timely. But risk analysis is only the basis of risk management and risk supervision is only the part of risk control too. The focus of risk management about virtual enterprise is risk assessment. There are also many scholars have done some effective researches on risk assessment of virtual enterprise from different aspects, reference [3] constructed a set of index system which adapted to the risk assessment of virtual enterprise based on analyzing the main factors that should be considered in the process of risk assessment. Then it gave index value and assessor's subjective sensation value, and introduced the fuzzy and multi-attributed decision based on the expected value to get the prior order of the synthetic choice about the virtual enterprise's solutions. According to the character of having project as the organization model, considering the influence from the project time factor to the whole risk, reference [4] adopted a model called PERT to construct the risk assessment model of virtual enterprise based on the correspondence of the end time in a process and the fuzzy description by the process to the risk level.

This paper connects the risk factor of virtual enterprise with its life cycle, and recognizes the risk factor of virtual enterprise during its different developing phases with detailed analysis. After that, it establishes a series of indexes which adapt to assess the risk factor of virtual enterprise in terms of its lifecycle. It refers to the application circumstances of fuzzy method which can be used in risk problems of virtual enterprise, so it adopts the fuzzy mathematics theory to establish a model to evaluate the risk of virtual enterprise. Finally, it uses the fuzzy comprehensive evaluation method based on the risk factors to appraise the risk of virtual enterprise, and testifies its effectiveness through an actual example.

2 The basic concept of virtual enterprise and its life cycle theory

The concept of "Virtual Enterprise" was firstly put forwarded by Iacocco Institute of Lehigh University in American in the report of "China's Manufacturing Industry Development Strategies in the 21st Century" [5]. The virtual enterprise can adjust the strategy in order to adapt to the changed market timely, and can integrate all the advantages of the enterprises to reach "win-win". So the idea of "Virtual Enterprise" is greatly praised as soon as it was put forward. At present, there is no clear and agreeable definition of virtual enterprise, many scholars think it is equal to the dynamic alliance, and consider it is a temporary enterprise union which is formed by several enterprises in order to seize and take advantage of rapidly changing market opportunities through information technologies. Once the market opportunities do not exists, the enterprise union will disorganize [6-7].

The virtual enterprise emerges when the market opportunities exists and it self-disorganizes when the opportunities disappears. So the life cycle of virtual enterprise is obvious. After researches and conclusions from several relevant references [8-9], this paper considers that it is suitable to divide the virtual enterprise's construction and operation into four periods, which are recognition, construction, operation and termination period. The recognition period is the start of enterprise. The main tasks in this period are the recognition, evaluation and selection of the market opportunities. Main contents of construction period include recognition and selection of the partners, designation of the organizational operation model, establishment of interest/risk institution and designation of the information system. Main contents of operation period include the distribution and coordination of tasks, cost control, performance monitoring, risk management and credit management. In termination period, along with the disappearing of opportunities and the separating of partners, the virtual enterprise corrupts. Main contents of termination period include the terminal recognition and disposal of checking out.

The life cycle of enterprise is shown as figure 1:

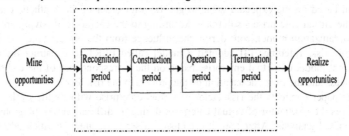

Fig. 2, The life cycle of enterprise

3   The index system of virtual enterprise's risk assessment

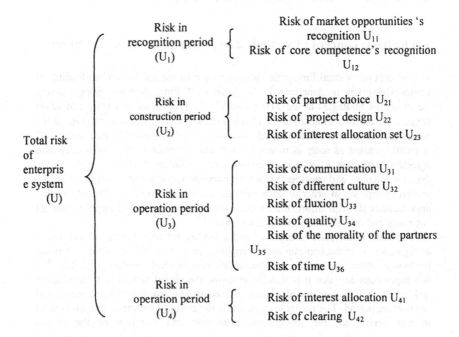

Fig. 2, the virtual enterprise's internal risk assessment system

The risk of virtual enterprise is brought by two parts generally. The first is from external factors, such as political risk, market risk, finance risk, etc. These are called external risks which enterprises can not control.

The second is the risks leaded by the enterprise's activities which can be controlled through proper strategies, it is internal risk. This paper recognizes the internal risks based on the virtual enterprise's life cycle, and constructs the virtual enterprise's internal risk assessment system that is shown in figure 2.

Figure 2 divides the index system of an assessment of inner risk into 3 layers, and considers the risks in recognition period, construction period, operation period and termination period synthetically. Each layer has its own sub-index.

3.1 Risk in recognition period

(1) Risk of market opportunity recognition, which means that the core enterprises misunderstand the low-valued market opportunity as the promising market opportunity because of collecting inaccurate information or choosing wrong analysis tools.

(2) Risk of core competence recognition, which means the risk that the core enterprise assesses its own core competences highly or lowly so that it leads to a wrong choice in the realization of the market opportunity.

3.2 Risk in construction period

(1) Risk of partner choice, which means the loss caused by the improper choice of partner, and it leads to the virtual enterprise to change partner or disorganizes in the midway.

(2) Risk of cooperate project design, which means unreasonable task allocation or improper resource integration, and it leads to higher operation cost or the loss caused by the partner who can not finish the task in time.

(3) Risk of interest allocation set, which means the interest allocation solution set by the core enterprise is unreasonable, and it leads to the loss of the partners' enthusiasm or the quit of the partner in the midway. Hence it leads to the risk of the virtual enterprise's disorganization in the midway.

3.3 Risk in operation period

(1) Risk of communication, which means the alliance members' insufficient communication, it leads the dislocation of process assignment or causes other losses.

(2) Risk of different culture, which means the different culture background, it leads to the confliction which makes the virtual enterprise disorganize in the midway.

(3) Risk of fluxion, which means the partners can join or leave the organization freely as the virtual enterprise is an open organization, and this fluidity may lead to the project shelved or disorganized, it is also disadvantage to the knowledge accumulation.

(4) Risk of quality, each partner's policy and level of quality may be different, if one's quality has problem, it will affect the whole product's quality.

(5) Risk of the morality of the partners, which means the result of a possibility that each member uses its advantages to get self-benefit maximized might harm the others.

(6) Risk of time, because the starting time of information processing is inflexible to each member, the member may not finish the task in the planning time.

3.4 Risk in termination period

(1) Risk of interest allocation, which means the interest allocation is unreasonable or the law affairs may be caused by not executing the allocation plan.

(2) Risk of settlement, as the virtual enterprise is composed by a contract made by the enterprises in alliance, and sometimes the ownership is not determinate, so it may cause law affairs during the financial settlement period.

4   Fuzzy comprehensive evaluation model based on risk factors

Risk assessment is the process to evaluate the possibility of a recognized risk and its loss, so that the enterprise will be able to take effective measures to prevent and control it. It is known that the external risk is uncontrollable, so this paper only assesses the internal risks of virtual enterprise based on its life cycle.

In the risk assessment system that it has been constructed above, the referred assessment indicators are hard to be accurate and numerical. Therefore, this paper adopts the fuzzy comprehensive evaluation method based on the risk factors to evaluate the project risk of virtual enterprise [10-11]. The basic idea is to solve the above 4 determined factors, and then to integrate the risk factors to get the total system factors. According to the standard of probability classification, if the happened probability from a pre-designed rule is less than 30%, the happened probability of the risk is pimping. While, if it is more than 70%, the happened probability of the risk is great. So it is generally believed that if the total factor is above 70%, the virtual enterprise's project has a higher risk and a low risk if it is less than 30% and between them the project has a middle risk.

According to the definition of risk, risk R is not only the function of the incident probability P of risk events, but also the function of the consequence C of it. This point is easier to be understood that, although something is of great probability, it costs little expense if it happens, so it is of low risk. On the contrary, something happens occasionally, but it costs much if it occurs, so it is risky. This relationship can be described as a function of $R=f (P, C)$. Let P_f be the probability of the event fails, P_s be the probability of the event succeeds, C_f be the influent degree of the failed event and C_s be the influent degree of the success event, then the risk function can be described as follows:

$R_f = 1 -$ unhappened probability of risk event $\times$ the probability of its consequence

$$= 1 - P_s C_s$$
$$= 1 - (1 - P_f)(1 - C_f)$$
$$= P_f + C_f - P_f C_f.$$

In those, R_f is the risk factor.

4.1 The determine of P_f

Since this system is a hierarchical structure system, it can be analyzed by analytic hierarchy process[12] to determine the influent degree of each factor to the failure of the project. Let A_i be the subsystem i, $A_i = (a_1, a_2, ..., a_n)$, and n is the number of the factors in the subsystem i.

Let $B = (b_1, b2, b3, b4, b5) = (0.1, 0.3, 0.5, 0.7, 0.9)$ be the magnitude of assessment for each factor. It is determined by experts. For example, the experts consider that a_i belongs to b_j. Let e_{ij} be the total number of the experts who consider a_i belong to b_j divided by the total number of attended experts. ($i = 1, 2, ..., n, j = 1, 2, 3, 4, 5$). So the failed probability is as follows:

$$P_f = \sum_{i=1}^{n} \sum_{j=1}^{5} (a_i e_{ij} b_j) = AEB^T$$

4.2 The fuzzy comprehensive evaluation method of C_f

For the estimation to the influent degree of the risk event's consequence has great uncertainty, so the C_f is estimated by the fuzzy comprehensive evaluation method.

(1) Establishment of the set of factors

The set of factors is a set of indexes composed by each index of predetermined assessment objects, so, according to the assessment index system above, the assessment index set is as follows:

The first layer of index set: $U = \{U_1, U_2, U_3, U4\}$

The second layer of index set: $U_i = \{U_{i1}... U_{in}\}$ (U_{in} is the *nth* factor in U_i)

(2) Determination of the assessing set

The assessing set is the set composed by total assessment which might be done by the assessors to the assessed objects. According to the influent degree of failure, the set can be divided as V={lower, low, middle, notable, high}, and it is given the value of V={0.1, 0.3, 0.5, 0.7, 0.9}

(3) Determination of the weight of each factor

The weight is the important degree of one index in the whole index system. This system is a hierarchically structural system, so the determination of the weight of each factor can be done by the analytic hierarchy process. Comparing with each two factors can obtain the compared matrix, then, by the solution of the eigenvalue of this matrix, the weight set can be gotten. The effectiveness of the weights though the coherence verification can be ensured. By using the analytic hierarchy process, the weight set of the first subsystem A={A_1, A_2, A_3, A_4} can be found, and the weight corresponding to each subsystem factor is A_i={a_{i1}, ...,a_{in}}, here i is from 1 to 4, n is the number of the factors corresponding to each subsystem.

(4) The fuzzy comprehensive evaluation method

By using the method of Delphi and consulting with the assessment set V to evaluate U_{in}, the fuzzy comprehensive evaluated matrix R_i in each subsystem is solved. The synthetic assessment matrix for factors in the *ith* subsystem is $H_i = A_i R_i$ ={ h_1, h_2, h_3, h_4, h_5 } (i=1,2,3,4). By normalizing H_i to be $\bar{h}_i = h_i / \sum_{j=1}^{5} h_j$, the $\bar{H}_i = (\bar{h}_1\ \bar{h}_2\ \bar{h}_3\ \bar{h}_4\ \bar{h}_5)$ is gotten. So the influent degree to the failure of a project in the virtual enterprise cab be expressed by

$$C_f = \bar{H}V^T = 0.1h_1 + 0.3h_2 + 0.5h_3 + 0.7h_4 + 0.9h_5 .$$

4.3 Calculation of risk factor R_f

According to $R_f = P_f + C_f - P_f\,C_f$, the risk factor R_{fi} of each subsystem is found out. As this system is a two layer of hierarchical structure, so the total risk factor R_f can be determined by the summarizing of the risk though the follow formula after solving each subsystem's risk factor:

$$R_f = \sum_{i=1}^{n} R_{fi} A_i$$

R_{fi} is the risk factor in the *ith* subsystem, A_i is the weight of the *ith* subsystem.

5 An example

One virtual enterprise plans to use fuzzy comprehensive evaluation method based on the risk factors to evaluate its project's risk. Taking the risk in construction period as an example, there are 10 experts to evaluate the probability of risk of partner choice, risk of cooperate project design, risk of benefit allocation, according to the assessing set V. After the statistic classification, the result is gotten as follows:

$$E_2 = \begin{bmatrix} 0.1 & 0.7 & 0.2 & 0 & 0 \\ 0.1 & 0.3 & 0.5 & 0.1 & 0 \\ 0.2 & 0.6 & 0.2 & 0 & 0 \end{bmatrix}$$

$A_2 = (0.4\ 0.3\ 0.3)$ is determined by the analytic hierarchy process, then the failed probability in the constructed period is calculated as follows:

$$P_{f2} = A_2 E_2 B^T = 0.344$$

The fuzzy assessing matrix of the influent degree to the failed result of each risk in the construction period is gotten by the experts scoring method as follows:

$$R_2 = \begin{bmatrix} 0.1 & 0.4 & 0.2 & 0.3 & 0 \\ 0.2 & 0.2 & 0.3 & 0.2 & 0.1 \\ 0.2 & 0.4 & 0.3 & 0.1 & 0 \end{bmatrix}$$

The weight of each factor in this period $A_2 = (0.5\ 0.3\ 0.2)$ though analytic hierarchy process, so the synthetic assessment matrix $H_2 = A_2 R_2 = (0.15\ 0.34\ 0.25\ 0.23\ 0.03)$ in the period is gotten, and then the influent degree $C_{f2} = H_2 V^T = 0.43$ in this period is also found.

Such the risk factor in construction period is $R_{f2} = P_{f2} + C_{f2} - P_{f2}C_{f2} = 0.63$.

By using the same method the risk factor $R_{f1}=0.55$in recognition period, $R_{f3}=0.49$in operation period, and $R_{f4}=0.34$ in termination period can be found. The weights in the first layer of subsystem A=$(0.3\ 0.2\ 0.3\ 0.2)$ though analytic hierarchy process can be found too. So the total risk factor of the virtual enterprise's project is as follows:

$$R_f = \sum_{i=1}^{n} R_{fi} A_i$$
$$= 0.55 \times 0.3 + 0.63 \times 0.2 + 0.49 \times 0.3 + 0.34 \times 0.2$$
$$= 0.506$$

According to the assessment rule above, the total risk factor of the virtual enterprise's project is between 0.3 and 0.7, so the risk of this project is belong to the middle degree.

The above fuzzy comprehensive evaluation method model based on the risk factors makes the enterprise's risk become measured, and helps the decision maker very much. It is benefit for decision maker to find where the key risk is and to take efficient measures to reduce the risk loss.

6   Conclusion

Aiming at the character of complexity, fuzziness and uncertainty, this paper proposed the fuzzy comprehensive evaluation model based on the risk factors. From the above example, the fuzzy comprehensive evaluation method based on the risk factors can estimate the total risk degree of the virtual enterprise's projects, and get an intuitional measurement value which can help the decision maker a lot. Compared with other assessment methods, this one is simple and easy to be understood.

However, the method in this paper also has its limitation. For example, it can't give a detailed explanation about the core of the risk factor to the virtual enterprise's risk. So after the decision-making of using the risk factor assessment method, it still needs to do fine-analysis to the virtual enterprise's project risk to find out where the key risks are, and then to take effective measures to avoid and control the risk loss.

References

1. W.D. Feng and J.Chen, Study on Risk Analysis and Monitoring within Virtual Enterprises, *Chinses Journal of Management Science*, 05, (2001).

2. D.M. You and W. Pen, Study on Risk Monitoring in Virtual Enterprises, *Journal of HuNan Economic Management College*,10, (2003).

3. Z.b. Zeng, Y.L. Li and j. Shu, Risk Appraisal Based on Fuzzy Multi-Attribute Decision for Virtual Enterprise Formation, *Computer Engineering and Applications*, 4,(2006).

4. M. Huang, F.E. Li and X.W. Wang, PERT Based Risk Evaluation Model for Virtual Enterprise, *Journal of Northeastern University (Natural Science)*,9(9) , (2005).

5. R.N. Nagel etc, *21st Century Manufacturing Enterprise Strategy*, Iacocco Institute, Lehigh University, Bethehem(1992).

6. G. Martha, H.R. Karlene, Risk Mitigation in Virtual Organizations, *Organization Science*,10(6):704-721(1999).

7. Y.L. Wang, The 21st Century Oriented Production Model and Its Management, *Journal of XiAn JiaoTong University*, 1-4, (1997).

8. Z.m. Li, G. Du and Z. Li, Risk Recognize Index Systemand and Evaluation Model in Virtual Enterprises Based on Life Cycle, *Journal of Xidian University(Social Sciences Edition)*,3(2) ,(2006).

9. Z.B. Zhao, Analysis on the life cycle and risk management of virtual enterprise, *Technoeconomics & Management Researc,h* 3, (2003).

10. Zhao H.f., QiuW.h., WangX.z., Fuzzy Integrative Evaluation Method of the Risk Factor . *Systems Engineering-Theory & Practice*, 1997, 17(7)

11. J. Li, Application of Fuzzy Integrative Evaluation Method to Risk Management of Virtual Enterprises, *Industrial Engineering Journal*, 5(3) , (2004).

12. L.F. Wang and S.B. Xu, *An introduction to the analytic hierarchy process*, China Renmin university press, Beijing(1996).

Network Externality Products C & Competition Strategy: An Experimental Economics Approach

Geng Zhou, Jiaofei Zhong, Han Zhou and Yu Chen
Information school, Renmin University of China
100872 Beijing, China
hxk191@163.com

Abstract: Based on the theory of Complexity Adaptive System (CAS) and methods of experimental economics, using Multi-Agent-Based Simulation, we build a model of the network externality product market with the platform Netlogo3.1.2, analyze the macroscopic consumers' behavior, find out the important aspects that influence the spreading of products and the proper strategies of enterprises during this process and make a prediction of the China's instant messenger software market.

1. Introduction

Network externality is an essential rule of network. It has been a vital aspect in the construction of network since network was born.

In the IT industry, by taking advantage of network externality, a large number of enterprises (like Microsoft, Tencent and many web2.0 websites) succeeded through high-speed growth and hold their position with enormous profit unthinkable for enterprises in other fields, while by failing to make use of it, an even larger number of enterprises lost their chance forever. Since the spreading of network externality products is dynamically complex, using the theory of Complexity Adaptive System (CAS), multi-agent modeling and experimental economics methods to analyze the procedure has a special significance. Through the single-product-market model, we find that the 3 aspects of network externality, information circulation rate and initial number of users have an obvious impact on the spreading of network externality products and we also explore the proper occasion to release advertisements. And through the two-products-model, we explore the effect of random factors, and the strategies to fight against adverse situation. Finally, we make a prediction of the fractionized China's instant massager market.

Please use the following format when citing this chapter:

Zhou, G., Zhong, J., Zhou, H., Chen, Y., 2007, in IFIP International Federation for Information Processing, Volume 251, Integration and Innovation Orient to E-Society Volume1, Wang, W. (Eds), (Boston: Springer), pp. 67-79.

2. Research background

2.1 Network externality

Network externality is also called the "network effect". If the value of a product to a user is decided by the total number of users, we say this product possesses the property of "network externality". This kind of "externality" has a tight relation with the scale of network: the few members in a network not only have to bear the high cost of operating, but also can commute information with only a few people; as the network grows the cost for every user decreases and the scope of communication is broadened, so that every user gains a higher value.

The Metcalfe law describes the effect: the value of a telecommunications network is proportional to the square of the number of users of the system (n^2). [1]

2.2 Agent-based modeling

ABM (Agent-based modeling) is widely adopted in the research of complex adaptive systems comprising of large number of active agents such as society, economics, and environment. Network externality product market is a typical complex adaptive system. A network externality product comes into a market, spreads among the customers, competes with its competitors until winning or washed out. This is a typical complex procedure in a complex system. ABM is eligible in analyzing such problems.

3. Objective of research

Use multi-agent modeling, theory of Complexity Adaptive System(CAS), and experimental economics methods to simulate and analyze the procedure of spreading of the network externality products, so as to demonstrate and explore the economical law, study the macroscopic behavior of consumers and the strategy of enterprises, find out the important aspects that influence the spreading and proper strategy to adopt to promote the spreading; use the conclusions gained from these to analyze and predict the China's instant massager software market.

4. Descriptions of the model

4.1 Platform

Operation system: Windows XP, Stimulation software: Netlogo 3.1.2, Statistics software: Excel 2003.

4.2 Structure of the model and agent behavior rule

We made two models: a single product market model and a two products market model.

In both models we uses a two dimension environment to simulate the real market, forming a virtual commercial environment with more than 1000 agents (simulate the consumers) and a number of advertisements.

The rule in the model fall into 3 parts: motion rule, influence rule, buying rule.

(1)Motion rule: every agent choose a random direction to move, the length of one step is a random number between 0 and the maximize number set according to the real market.

(2)Influence rule: Assume that the value of the network is in direct proportion with number of user agents (Metcalfe law); the influence from advertisements to agents and between agents increases as the network and network externality grows (certainly a more valuable network has a stronger impact).In both model, influence from buyers and advertisements to potential buyers will raise their "buying value"; in the two products market model, influence from advertisements to buyers will cause them to evaluate the opportunity cost and the switch cost when altering product.

(3)Buying rule: assume that there are already initial users when the model runs and all other agents are potential buyers (or potential users of free product) who can afford the cost. When a potential buyer contact with buyers and advertisements, it is influenced (as in the influence rule) and when the "buying value" reaches a certain value set according to the real market, the potential buyer will buy the product and turns into a buyer.

In the simulation of two products market, assume that there are two kinds of products competing with each other; they are similar, but not compatible with each other; and potential buyers choose only one of them. After a potential buyer buys a product, he is influenced by the advertisements, and will change product if he weighs opportunity cost and the switch cost and finds that he can gain more value by using the other kind of product.

4.3 Figure of the concept model

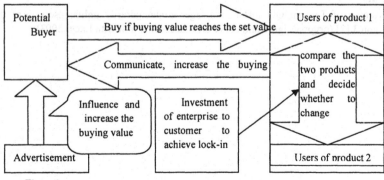

Figure1:

5. Analysis <1>: Single product market.

The time and number in the model has no fixed units, they can be day/ten
days/month/year and hundred/thousand/million according to the real market, and in
the qualitative analysis here we care more about the proportion.

We will simulate a single product market (no competitors) here, aiming at
studying the macroscopic behavior of the consumer and reaching the basic
conclusions about the network externality product market. The results are as follows:

5.1 Description of the curve of the growth in the number of users.

Set the total number of agents as 1000, initial users as 10, value of network
externality as 10(highest value in this model), see figure 2:

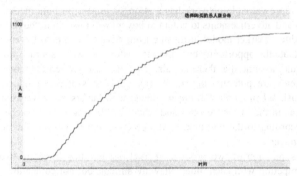

Figure2

From the curve, the number of users (buyers) goes through a period of
accumulating, then it reaches the critical number, so that the value of the network is
fully embodied and the influences from buyers and advertisements to potential
buyers increase obviously, which then results in a time of rapid growth. When the
market is nearly fully occupied, the growth rate decreases. At last the market is fully
occupied.

Case:

Number of Tencent QQ instant massager contemporarily online users is as the
figure3 [2] (original figure and curve draw according to it with Excel 2003):

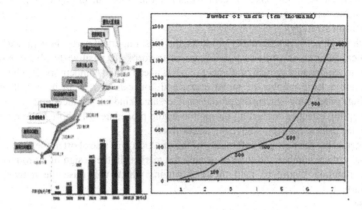

Figure3

It's easy to find that the number of QQ instant massager users is in the period of rapid growth, the critical number of high-speed growth is about 5 million.

Since there can't be an unlimited growth in the market of instant massager, it is can be predicted that after a short time of rapid growth, the increase rate will fall and the market will meet its bottleneck for the first time.

5.2 The effects of network externality

Set the total number of agents as 1000, the initial users as 10. The result is

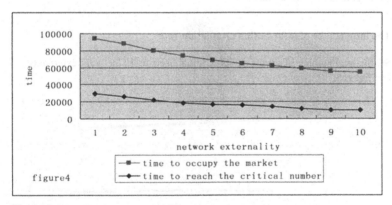

Figure4

By changing the value of the network externality (from 1-10) only, we see an obvious decrease in the time to reach the critical number and the time to occupy the market. There exists a faster growth in the high network externality markets than the low ones. The network externality of the product will form an efficient positive feedback between the growth in number and the growth in value of the network. And the market with higher network externality will make it earlier than the lower ones.

Often the result of strong positive feedback is that only one winner enjoys most of the profits of the market.

Competition strategy:

1. For the high network externality products, the most important part is how to reach the critical number as early as possible so as to form the positive feedback and achieve an exponential growth in number of users ahead of the competitors. It'll help if there are a large number of initial users, and you can have them by excellent marketing, purchasing enterprise producing the same kind of products and so on. Also adopting effective marketing during the whole procedure will shorten the time to reach the critical number. Above all, attack first.

2. By increasing the network externality of the products will also shorten the time to reach the critical number and time to occupy the market. In the design of a product, enough attention should be paid to the functions which will raise the network externality.

Case:

According to the "2006 brief report on China IM" [3], the first three IMs used most are QQ (80.1%), MSN (7.7%), Tencent TM (1.6%). Study shows that the IM industry ranks the third in the five industries which have the highest convergence. [4] We can see that Tencent QQ has monopolized the IM market. The Internet-based QQ was developed by Tencent Company in 1999.2, and by its high network externality register users of QQ grows rapidly. Tencent Company also combines it into several other correspondence platforms such as cell phone, which increase the network externality. Today QQ already has more than 580.5 million ID registered.[5] Besides, another reason for Tencent's success is that Tencent is a forerunner. It concentrates on IM very early and so gained the advantage of attacking first, thus achieved rapid growth the earliest.

5.3 The importance of information circulation rate

Set the total number of agents as 1000, initial users as 10, network externality as 10. See **figure5**:

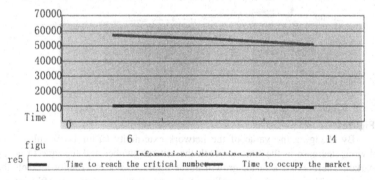

Figure5

When setting the information circulating rate as 2 (4% of the highest value in the model), there is no such a period that the number of users grow rapidly. On the contrary, the figure is linear. See **figure 6:**

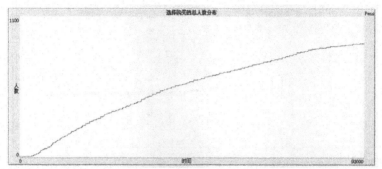

When the information circulating rate is extremely low, the information of buyers can not spread, thus they can't influence the potential buyers, therefore the growth of the value of the network can't be sensed by the potential buyers, and so the effect of network externality is quite low.

As the technique of correspondence improves, the rate of information circulation rises. By changing the value of information circulation rate (from 5~50) only, we see a decrease in the time to reach the critical number and to occupy the market. In fact, a higher information circulating rate decreases the time for the customers to evaluate and accept the product, and turn them into buyers quickly.

Competition strategy

1. It's better for enterprises to choose mediums which provides high information circulation rate such as the Internet and seriously consider introducing the product first in areas where the fundamental establishments related to information circulation rate are well-developed.

2. It will also help if the enterprises increase the information circulation rate themselves like building a product website or a search engine.

5.4 The effect of initial number of users

Set the total number of agents as 1000, network externality as 10 and the information circulation rate as 50. The result is **figure7:**

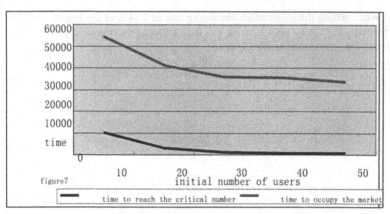

Figure7
    By changing the value of initial users (from 5~50), we see an obvious decrease
in the time to reach the critical number and to occupy the market. This is because the
number of initial users is related directly to the time to reach the critical number.
    Competition strategy:
    Finance permitting, the enterprises should try hard to increase the initial number
of users. Proper marketing strategy such as free edition, discount, binding with other
products and excellent public relation will help. Purchasing enterprises producing the
same kind of products will also help.

5.5 Appropriate occasion to advertise

    We find that to stop advertising after the users have reached the critical number
has little influence on the exponentially growth and the time to occupy the market.
This is because after the critical number is reached, the influence from orally
spreading and the behavior of buying increase greatly, and this kind of influence
outweighs the influence of advertisements.
    We know that few advertisements are put out to propagandize the basic function
after the users of cell phone, telegrapher, BP reached the critical number.
Competition strategy:
    After the high network externality product goes into the period of rapid growth,
it is proper to lessen the advertisements on the basic function, and put the precious
fund more on the value-added service so as to achieve a better lock-in (a higher
swatch cost) on the buyers to increase the profit.

6. Analysis <2>: Two product market.

    There will always be competitors. The purpose of using this model to simulate a
market with two network externality products(or enterprises) competing with each
other is to go even nearer to the real market, and study the strategy of enterprises and
behavior of consumers on a higher stage. Assume that the two products are

similar(no essential difference) but not compatible with each other; and that the finance ability of the two enterprises are the same; the two products goes into the market at the same time.

6.1 The influence of random factor

Let both enterprises put out the same amount of advertisements and take no other action of competition.

Set the total number of agents as 1200, network externality as 10, and initial number of users as 10(both 5). The result is **figure8**: (both of two curves represent the number of the buyers)

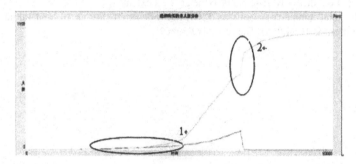

Figure8:

In ellipse 1, in the beginning there occurs a small distinction in the user number, and then this small distinction made one product reach the critical number earlier and consequently resulted in a rapid growth. In ellipse 2, the high value resulted from a large network of the product was fully realized. This value easily outweighs the value of the other product's network and the switch cost of the users of the other product so that the winning product attracted many users of the competitor's product. Those who changed their products along with the new buyer gave the number of the winning product "a big leap". At the same time, the losing of users caused a collapse of the competitor's product: the decrease of users and the decrease of value of the network formed a strong negative feedback which deprived the failing product of its users in no time.

Through experimenting many times, we found that competing in the same environment with no competition strategy besides advertisements, both enterprises could win, and the possibilities are almost the same. This shows the power of the random factor: there are some random factors in the market that influence the numbers of the early buyers of the products, and the distinction caused by this will provide one product a chance to reach the critical number earlier, thus resulting in an rapid growth and occupation of market.

Competition strategy:

1. Random factor of the market will cause a distinction in number of early buyers. If left unnoticed, the distinction will cause one product to reach the critical number of users earlier and make it the winner.

2. It's advisable to be highly sensitive with the number of users and take actions to reach the critical number as early as possible whether you are lagging behind.
3. The high network externality product market is usually a market with the winner seized the majority and achieves monopoly, while others—if not fail completely—share the rest small part. Therefore, if an enterprise finds its adversary reaches critical number first and the gap between them can't be filled up quickly, it's time to consider seriously retreating from the market.

6.2 fighting back

Let the enterprise which lags behind take actions so that it may exceed its adversary.
Both put out their advertisements to the greatest extent.
Set the total number of agents as 1200, network externality as 10, and initial number of users as 10(both 5). The result is **figure9:**

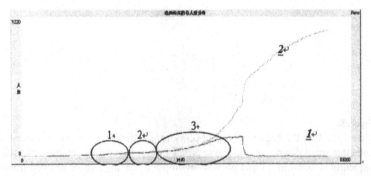

Figure9:
After the two products were introduced into the market, there exists a distinction in numbers of users in ellipse 1 caused by random factors, then enterprise *2* sensed the situation and raised its investment (includes two parts: the investment on buyers of enterprise *2*'s product aiming at achieve lock-in; the investment on buyers of enterprise *1*'s product aiming at helping them overcome the switch cost and make them change product.). We see shakes in ellipse 3 which shows that the new investment worked and caused some decrease in the users of product 1 by drawing them to the other side. Also the investment slowed the increase of new buyers of product 1 down by attracting the potential buyers who could be the buyers of product 1 if no action was taken. The result is enterprise *2* reached the critical number earlier and occupied the market. The adoption of action in time filled up the adverse gap and saved enterprise *2*.
Competition strategy:
1. During the spreading of high network externality products, once lagging behind, enterprise should take action to eliminate the gap immediately and achieve solid lock-in as early as possible. In the beginning, it's wise for enterprise to put more resource into increasing the number of users, and prepare enough funds for the following fierce battle to attract consumers.

2. The importance of critical number will certainly make it the main battlefield. It's possible to take actions early and fight the adversary back successfully. Also it's a must to hold the favorable situation and enlarge the gap.

3. Although it's possible to fight back in the real market, even after the adversary reached the critical number, the amount of investment needed is no doubt an astronomical number. It would be a heavy burden for the enterprise even if affordable. So the beginning is always the most important part, and it's better to take the first battle as the decisive battle.

4. The finance ability is crucial. If an enterprise don't have the advantage of first action, and the finance situation is not so well, it should consider the situation seriously before stepping into the market. While any enterprise which occupies the network externality market will find the investment worthy due to the strong lock-in and monopoly.

7. Prepare for the decisive battle in the fractionized instant massager software market in China

In the following part, we will analyze and predict the coming fractionized instant massager (IM in short) software market in China.

7.1 Comprehensive instant massager software market

Typical products in this market are Tencent QQ, MSN, Sina UC and so on. The Tencent QQ have already taken the majority of the market (>70%). Thanks to the high network externality of the IM, the large number of users of QQ gives the network enormous value and this high value resulted in a strong lock-in of users. In the conventional way of operating an IM product, any other enterprises which attempt to offset the switch cost and the opportunity cost for users to give up QQ so as to attract them to their side will meet a high investment and the fierce counterattack of Tencent Company. It can be predicted that in the near future the Tencent QQ will hold its favorable profitable position.

7.2 Website instant massager software market

Website IM deals mainly with the online correspondence between website members, websites and members, buyers and sellers and so on. In this new field, the TQ [6] have gained the advantage of first action. "An investigation on the representative websites of 10 open industry and the evaluation of the whole IM show that 83% of the website which adopt IM as their sales platform chose TQ as their instant massager."[7] By now the website IM software market is not fully developed, it is still in the period of accumulating early buyers as shown in the early area in the figures above. The new enterprises should come in the market quickly and competing with TQ in attracting consumers if they are to gain a favorable situation

with a comparatively low cost. While for TQ it will be a major concern how to reach
the critical number early.

7.3 Enterprise instant massager software market

Enterprise IM deals mainly with the online correspondence of management,
communication, dealing and so on inside the enterprises and between the enterprises.
There are already some kinds such as the Sametime of IBM, the ActiveMassager of
Hengchuang Company. There is none which gained the advantage of first action.
However the potential enormous profit of this market has attracted much attention.
Once the technique and commercial condition is ready, there is sure to be a severe
campaign.

There is another trend that should not be ignored: just because no enterprises
have gained advantage of first action and the information system of enterprise is a
high cost investment, there is a greater chance for the many kinds of new enterprise
IM to realize interlinking with each other (While in other IM markets this
interlinking is rare.).If so, the situation of the winner taking the majority share as
shown above may not occur. The compatibility of products will result in a market
carved up by a number of enterprises which have similar shares.

7.4 Instant massager software for particular group of people.

The "xiaonei" massager serves as a perfect case in this market. Aiming at college
student has won it 3 million users. [8] Another "PPme" commercial massager calls
itself "the working IM made especially for the people professional in lights." so as to
attract consumers of that industry. Obviously these IM have obtained much
inspiration from the success of web2.0.

There are several trends:
1. The professional aiming and the comparatively few potential users would make
the spreading of the product more like the single product market above. That is, one
enterprise goes in and occupies the market in a short time before the competitors
come.
2. The professional aiming gives this kind of IM some advantage when competing
with traditional comprehensive IM in certain professional areas and thus helping it
attract many buyers back (these users chose the comprehensive IM because there
were no other IMs before). This will cause a decrease in value of network of the
comprehensive IM and provide a chance to break the monopoly of the Tencent QQ
3. The problem of not being interlinked will be even more serious with the kinds of
IMs growing. Also it will be extravagant running several IMs on one computer. So
it's an important question whether these IMs will re-combine to form a totally new
standard of the industry and a new vast correspondence network based on it. If the
interlinking is realized, the market will not follow the form of development of the
two-product market model as above. (Because we assumed that the products are not
compatible.)

7.6 Welcome the time of open source instant massager software.

The P2P software sever provider—DianShi software company in Shenzhen have boldly released its ANYQ IM to enterprises for free in an open source way. This product is reputed as a million of investment, a large number of users and distributed organized. There is no doubt that this action will influence the market deeply: because the ability of interlinking with other IM, the users enjoy the value of the whole network so that the company will not have to worry about the attack led by competitors as shown in the two-product market model and even realize the development form similar to the single-product market model!

Moreover the open source ANYQ have the potential to have a larger network than any of the other products which is not open source and this larger network may be a new revolution in the IM software market.

8. Sum-up

Based on experimental economics method and multi-agent modeling, this essay analyzed the spreading of network externality product market, demonstrated and explored the behavior of macroscopic consumers and the important aspects which influence the procedure as well as the strategy of the enterprises; predicted the future of China's fractionized IM software market. This research also shows the advantage of experimental economics method over traditional way in dealing with dynamic procedures. This model can still be improved to simulate the market with detailed data of consumers and advertisements.

Reference

1. http://en.wikipedia.org/wiki/Metcalfe%27s_law
2. http://adver.qq.com/dctx_04.shtml 2007-5-17
3. http://down.iresearch.cn/Graphs/Content/8842.html
4. China Internet Industry Survey Report http://report.internetdigital.org/
5. http://www.tencent.com/about/history.shtml
6. http://qtt.tq.cn/
7. http://it.sohu.com/20060913/n245324149.shtml Sohu IT
8. http://xiaonei.com/pages/im.jsp

Analysis of the Supply-demand Value Chain in the B2B E-business

Guoliang Ge

Department of Information Management, HuaZhong Normal University,
Wuhan 430079, China
geguolian70@163.com

Abstract. Value chain is a basic method and framework to understand enterprise behavior and guide competition conduct. In the B2B E-business, traditional value chain changes greatly under the influence of information technology. So, in the paper, B2B E-business's influence on traditional value chain was analyzed, and similarities and differences between physics value chain and virtual value chain are compared. The relationship of participate partners in the transfer process of virtual value chain was investigated using collaboration-deal model. At the base of that, the model of enterprise value network based on value chain integration and transfer process was established. Finally, IPR-PN model based on Petri network was established, which achieved the simulation of value chain transfer.

1   Introduction

Business deal of business to business (B2B) and that of business to consumer (B2C) via network are called E-business. From the latter half of 1999, upsurge of E-business occurred in USA, which is called the third phase of network industry, it is a real E-business epoch. In 2005, the gross of E-business deal was 49000 hundred million dollar; in 2006, the gross reached about 99000 hundred million dollar, which showed a promising foreground. So, the task of studying B2B E-business, helping enterprise find the field that can impel value increment by value chain analysis methods, and exploring the integration approach of "Click+Brick" is pressing.

Professor Porter in the book- competition advantage proposed the conception of value chain, which provided a basic method and framework to understand the enterprise behavior and guide competition. To analyze the cost and value of business deal in different phase, Porter distinguished business deal into the basic and assistant deal, which was designed into framework of value chain analysis.

Value chain is employed to support common stratagem analysis, at the same time, it is a efficient tool for information systems management; which can help system

Please use the following format when citing this chapter:

Ge, G., 2007, in IFIP International Federation for Information Processing, Volume 251, Integration and Innovation Orient to E-Society Volume1, Wang, W. (Eds), (Boston: Springer), pp. 80-87.

development staff identify information technology that brought the enterprise strategic chance [2-3]. With the advent of E-business, value depends greatly on the data, information, knowledge and so forth. Virtual value chain becomes the tool that analyzes the change E-business brings in enterprise management. The application of value chain model in information system was extended into virtual value chain [4-6], as a result, the study on value chain also developed into virtual value chain from the physical value chain. In the virtual value chain, the value is not only achieved by physical value of real product, but also information.

Understanding the influence information technology brings on the value chain, modifying physical value chain to exert potential of information technology greatly will promote to achieve the E-business further [7-8]. The phenomenon was regarded in developed countries universally.

2   Influence of B2B E-business on traditional value chain

Porter's value chain model can be considered as a typical value chain model, which includes nine kinds of enterprise business. The business deal can be distinguished into basic and assistant deal. The model of value chain can be expressed in figure 1.

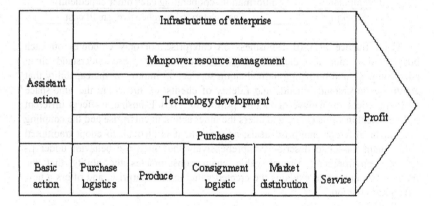

Fig.1 Porter's value chain model

Porter's model aims at manufacture enterprise. Value deal focus on the materiel flow, for example, acquirement of raw materials, manufacture, distribution, installation and so on. In B2B E-business, the enterprise achieves the business deal via electronical means. B2B E-business brings the enterprise some influences, they are: ① changing the traditional approach of stocking, distribution and after service; ② altering the produce manner and bringing traditional industry revolution; ③ shortening the tach of value chain; ④ innovating the value.

The influence the B2B E-business brings on basic and assistant action of traditional value chain was described in table 1.

Table1   Influence of B2B E-business on basic and assistant action of traditional value chain

Action	Influence of B2B E-business
Stock logistics	Relation with provider is fast, cheap, credible
Produce logistics	Increasing the relation in enterprise; promoting clients to participate in produce; responding to change fleetly
Consignment logistic	Relation with clients is fast, cheap, credible
Market distribution	Decreasing cost, developing market, closing further with clients
Service	Fast and cheap service; more relation channel with clients, stable clients
Enterprise infrastructure	Oblate Organization Structure，gradual disappearance of intermediation，the whole organization became external oriented
Manpower resource management	Internet cultivation and tool of employment
Technology development	Relating with other enterprises, sharing information, cooperating each other expediently
Stocking	Fast, cheap, comprehensive, small cost

The influence of B2B E-business on enterprise not only embodies on each business deal ,but also the followings: ① helping enterprise understand client adequately, (), and providing individuation service; ② improving the capability that enterprise understands clients, and fidelity of clients. ③ breaching the time-space limit for client to achieve economic profit. So, B2B E-business affects different business deal in value chain; and alters the inner action in enterprise and the coupling relation in different enterprise deals; as a result, it is difficult to adopt traditional value chain model to describe comprehensively the enterprise behavior under E-business environment. Virtual value chain consummates the ability that the traditional value chain explains the created value in an enterprise, and offers a new strategical creation.

3   Virtual value chain

3.1 Connotation of virtual value chain

Rayport and Sviokla presented the concept of virtual value chain in 1995[6]. Any enterprise competes each other in two different worlds: one of the worlds is a real world that manager can look and feel. The other is a virtual world that information forms, which creates the E-business that creates new value. The new information world is called "market space". The two worlds develop value creation action via different value chain. The foregoing creates value by physical value chain, for example, stocking, product, distribution and so on. The latter creates value by virtual value chain, for example, collection of information, organization, integration, choice and so on.

It is necessary to analyze market for understanding the virtual value chain further. A market holds three parts: principal part (surrogate), product and process. Principal part of market is purchaser, bargainor, agency, and other groups (for example, government, protection organization of consumer); product is the exchanged materials; the exchange between the market principal part and other market organization is called process, which includes choice of product, produce, market research, inquirement, order, payment and consumption. The three parts may be real (off-line) and digital (on-line). The range physical value chain and virtual value chain work in marker can be expressed in figure 2.

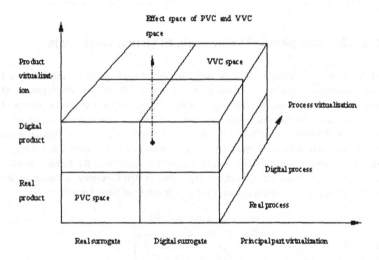

Fig.2 Effect space of PVC and VVC

Analyzing figure 2, it can be found that virtual value chain is a result of product virtualization, principal part virtualization, process virtualization; furthermore, the effect range of virtual value chain will increase with the increment of digitalization of product, principal part, process.

3.2 Comparison between virtual value chain and physical value chain

From figure 2, we can find that virtual value chain and physical value chain have a lot of differences on product, principal part, and process. To understand distinctly the characteristic of virtual value chain, table 2 compared their characteristics from the aspects such as economy principle, management content, process of value increment, information effect and so on.

Table2. Comparison between virtual value chain and physical value chain

Comparison item	Physical value chain	Virtual value chain
Economy principle	Degression of marginal profit	Increase of marginal profit

Management content	Real product	Digital product
Process of value increment	Action is continuous	Action is not continuous
Information effect	Assistant factors	Creation of value
Agency	Physical agency	Degression of traditional agency, rise of information agency
Role of clients	Accepter of product	Participator of producing
Focus	Manufacture, service, and the sensed kernel value	Information communication

4 Transfer from physical value chain to virtual value chain

B2B E-business is developing rapidly, the range that digital product refers is expanding, and various information agency is developing vigorously. With the development of informationlization, information technology is adopted more and more widely in process of enterprise operation, the status of virtual value chain is becoming more and more important in value creation. Therefore, some problems refer to the transfer process from physical value chain to virtual value chain are showed. Of course, the transfer is not unrestrained; it is reason is that any E-business under healthy operation condition depends on the balance between virtual value chain and physical value chain. Application of B2B E-business is expending, the transfer from physical value chain to virtual value chain can be expressed into figure 3.

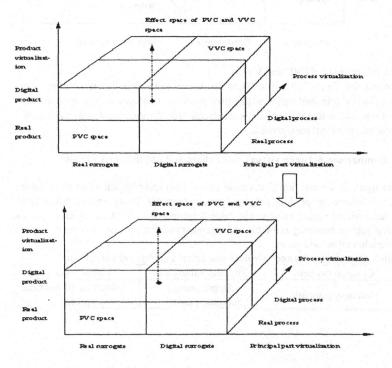

4.1 Participant entity

In virtual value chain, value is created using the contact between member, material provider, operator, and user, which is a participant entity in transfer from physical value chain to virtual value chain. Their relation can be described via cooperation-deal competition model (for example figure 4). The model is put forward based on five kinds of competition model with adding the competition model between cooperator and alliance, at the same time, equality and virtual characteristic of E-business enterprises is referred. The model analyzes the participants that correlate with enterprise such as provider, consumer, cooperator, alliance, competitor, invader, and replacer from three respects such as deal, cooperation, industry and so on. The cooperation deal tactic of virtual value chain transfer is established on the basis of cooperation-deal model.

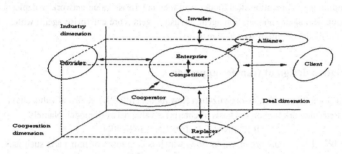

Fig.4 Cooperation-deal model in value chain transfer

4.2 Transfer approach

The basic rules of physical value chain are standardization, volume-produce, popular-communication; however, that of virtual value chain are oriented client, one-to-one communication, it is a unification between produce system and communication system. In the process of transition, the builder must improve the flexibility of communication in order to form an efficient communication channel. The provider will alter the stratagem depends on standardization produce greatly, consider the individuation demand of clients, and improve the flexibility of produce and logistics. The operator must renovate constantly system to make product and communication meet the client oriented demand. The transfer approach can be expressed into figure 5.

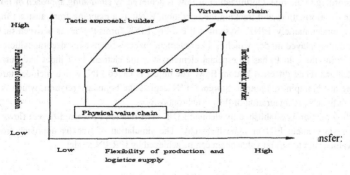

➤ Builder; builder develops, organizes, manages all kinds of content and conception; and distributes them. Managing market efficiently, and integrating different provider chain using the least friction and the fastest velocity are its kernel craftsmanship, which increase the capability of value creation.

➤ Provider; provider offers content, component, product, sub-system, user service and user instruments. They not only consider the builder as a distributor but also a virtual business entity.

➤ Operator; the operator answers for the real commodity flow, and runs electronic information infrastructure and so forth.

➤ User; user keeps contact with builder each other.

Builder, provider, operator and user can be modeled by multi-agent system. Beginning from inner value chain in enterprise, the value network is created by expending the cooperation-deal model; and then enterprise value network is depicted by adopting deal agent, cooperation agent, industry agent, core enterprise agent, which will form the model of enterprise value network.

4.3 Simulation design of transfer approach

The formalization define of trans-organization flow model (IPR-PN) in virtual value chain is formed by Petri network tool on the basis of enterprise value network model. Namely:

$$IPR\text{-}PN=\{T, P, TOKEN, LINK, PIN\}$$

Where IPR- PN is trans-organization flow, which is composed of four parts such as T, P, TOKEN, LINK; T ={TI, TO, TF}; T is a transfer object in a Petri network, which is a set that holds the disposition of input resource and action of produce output. TI is an input object, which depicts the characteristic of input data. It includes one or more objects, which represent the business entity. TO is an output object that depicts the logistic relation of different action. TF is the operation of action, which describes the deal of input object. Because of hierarchy of flow, T also denotes IPR—PN in next hierarchy; as a result, T holds two basic kinds: system and processor. P is position element in the Petri network. It denotes an occurrence or a field; at the same time, it also denotes resource in the field. PP denotes locale or event. P has two basic kinds: Channel and Store. Element T holds TI, TO, TF; and it and P form the network framework of flow. TOKEN is a set composed of all kinds of token. TOKEN holds enough information; it is an information carrier of flow model, which includes the involved factors that leads to change of flow. The factors include raw material, product, staff, tool, equipment, data and so on. When it flows in the network composed of element T and P, TOKEN will change according to the rule. Optimization of flow is achieved by simulating approach of flow, the change of information, and tracking the operation. LINK is a mapping from abstract flux to sub-flow model, namely, LINK: System→ IPR—PN. LINK forms the nexus between super stratum and underplayed model, which is a key element that can achieve the decomposition of hierarchy in the flow. In P, has an especial element; it is the element P of input and output flow, which can relate different bottom flow. The object is called PIN, which includes three kinds; they are Inputpin, Outputpin, Storepin. PIN depicts the boundary relation, which is a key element to achieve integration of flow synchronously.

Sub-flow relation is established by element LINK. The relation between different flows is established via element PIN in same hierarchy. The simulation of transfer approach from physical value chain to virtual value chain can be achieved by IPR-PN model.

5 Conclusion and future development

Value chain is a basic method and framework to understand enterprise behavior and guide competition conduct. In the B2B E-business, traditional value chain changes greatly under the influence of information technology, and the changes are analyzed in the paper. The connotation of virtual value chain in B2B E-business is represented, the similarities and differences of physical value chain and virtual value chain is compared, the transfer approach and steps from physical value chain to virtual value chain were investigated, which can provide the application of B2B E-business in an enterprises with novel ideal.

The model of value chain for enterprise study focus on function department, the process of resource flow is similar to the process of value increment in different department in enterprises. However, with the drastic development of global competition and the fast change of consumer demands, the management pattern that focus on occupation craftsmanship based on labor and specialization cooperation is facing serious challenge, separate deal can not create satisfactory value for consumer. Integrating all action orderly can create approving value for consumer. In B2B E-business, enterprises need cooperation greatly. As a result, the recombination of trans-origination operation flow is necessary, which is a motif need be investigated in the further.

References

1. Michael. Porter. *Competitive Advantage*[M]. Huaxia Publishing House, 1997;
2. Jeffrey F.Rayport & John J.Sviokla. "Exploiting the Virtual Value Chain"[J].*Harvard Business Review*, Sep—Dec, 1995;
3. Prahalad.C.K.and Hamel.G."The Core Competence of the orporation"[J].*Harvard Business Review*, 1990;
4. Q. Yang, X.T Wang & S.J Hu. "Strategic Alliance---- New Ideas of Enterprise Development". *Management Modernization*, 2001, (1);
5. L. Chen, W.X Xu, T.X Liu. "On Economic Essence of Virtual Enterprises" [J]. *Chinese Management Science*, 2000, (11);
6. X.B Song, J.L Yu. "Technology Innovation& Concept Innovation" [J]. *Enterprise Management*, 2001,(1);
7. S.G Wang. "Virtual Enterprises based on Global Supply Chain". Journal of *Management Engineering*, 1999, (5);
8. X.Y Chi. "Review of Value Chain Research& Development"[J] . *Foreign Economic& Management*, 2000, (1);
9. J.X Shen. "Value Chain Management Pattern of New Economic Era: Virtual& Vertical Integration"[J]. *NanJing Social Sciences*, 2002, (11);
10. H.L Lan. "Analysis& Acknowledgement of Core Specialty"[J]. *Enterprise Management*, 2000, (3);
11. R.H Lin , H.A Li. "Network Organization---- A New Organizational Model of More Environmental Adaptability"[J]. *Nankai Management Review*, 2000, (3).

An Intergrated Data Mining and Survival Analysis Model for Customer Segmentation

Guozheng Zhang1 Yun Chen2

1College of Business, Houzhou Dianzi University, P.R.China, 310018
(E-mail: guozhengzhang@gmail.com)
2School of Public Economy Administration, Shanghai University of finance
& economics, P.R.China, 200433
(E-mail: chenyun@mail.shufe.edu.cn)

Abstract. More and more literatures have researched the application of data mining technology in customer segmentation, and achieved sound effects. One of the key purposes of customer segmentation is customer retention. But the application of single data mining technology mentioned in previous literatures is unable to identify customer churn trend for adopting different actions on customer retention. This paper focus on constructs a integrated data mining and survival analysis model to segment customers into heterogeneous group by their survival probability (churn trend) and help enterprises adopting appropriate actions to retain profitable customers according to each segment's churn trend. This model contains two components. Firstly, using data mining clustering arithmetic cluster customers into heterogeneous clusters according to their survival characters. Secondly, using survival analysis predicting each cluster's survival/hazard function to identify their churn trend and test the validity of clustering for getting the correct customer segmentation. This model proposed by this paper was applied in a dataset from one biggest china telecommunications company. This paper also suggests some propositions for further research.

1 Introduction

Over the past decade, there has been an explosion of interest in customer relationship management (CRM) by both academics and executives (Werner Reinartz, Manfred Krafft, And Wayne D. Hoyer, 2004). Organizations are realizing that customers have

Please use the following format when citing this chapter:

Zhang, G., Chen, Y., 2007, in IFIP International Federation for Information Processing, Volume 251, Integration and Innovation Orient to E-Society Volume1, Wang, W. (Eds), (Boston: Springer), pp. 88-95.

different economic value to the company, and they are subsequently adapting their customer offerings and communications strategy accordingly. Currently research demonstrates that the implementation of CRM activities generates better firm performance when managers focus on maximizing the value of the customer (Gupta, Sunil, Donald R. Lehmann, and Jennifer A. Stuart, 2004). A deeper understanding of customers has validated the value of focusing on them. Customer segmentation is one of the core functions of CRM. Customer segmentation is the base of how to maximize the value of customer (Yun Chen, Guozheng Zhang, et al., 2006). Both researchers and managers need to evaluate and select customer segmentations in order to design and establish different strategies to maximize the value of customers.

Generally, customer segmentation methods mostly include experience description method, traditional statistical methods, and non-statistical methods (Per Vagn Freytag, et al, 2001, Lei-da Chen et al., 2000, E. H. Sub et al., 1999). Non-statistical methods mainly are arisen application of data mining technology in segmentation (Agnes Nairn, and Paul Bottomley, 2003, Verhoef P.C, et al., 2003, Jon Kleinberg, et al., 2004). Jaesoo Kim etc (2003) researched the application of ANN in tour customer segmentation. Fraley, C. and Raftery, A.E (2002) researched the application of clustering approaches in customer segmentation. These literatures use single data mining technology analyses single business issue, and have got some good effectives. But these applications have one obvious big shortages: One of key purpose of customer segmentation is customer retention, previous segmentation methods may be able to position which segment need more care, but it is unable to identify customer churn trend for take effective actions for different customers segments.

The purpose of this article is to propose a new customer segment model.The new customer segment model is called Intergrated Data Mining and Survival Analysis Model for Customer Segmentation. Its effectiveness lies not only in that it identifies key customer segments, but also in that it is able to predict the customer hazard/survival probability (churn trend). Enterprises can make effective customer retention action based on hazard/survival probability (churn trend) of each customer segment. And after segmentation, each customer's hazard/survival probability (churn trend) in one segment is approximately same level, so when calculating customer value, we can use the customer retention rate instead of single customer's hazard/survival probability.

2 Intergrated Data Mining and Survival Analysis Model

2.1 Model Architecture

The intergrated data mining and survival analysis model proposed by this paper contains two key components: Customer Clustering and Churn Trend Identification. They are two indiscerptible parts of the model. Figure 2 shows the architecture of this model.

In Customer Clustering phase, using data mining clustering arithmetic cluster customers into heterogeneous segments according to their survival characters. And in Churn Trend Identification phase, using survival analysis predicting each segment's survival/hazard function to identify their churn trend and test the validity of clustering. Finally, getting the correct customer segmentation.

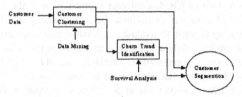

Figure1 Integrated Data Mining and Survival Analysis Model for Customer Segmentation

2.2 Model Implementation Steps

The method consists of cluster technology and survival analysis, as shown in figur1. The customer character for clustering is extracted according to industry and customer behavior attributes. Take the telecommunication industry as example, customer's communication hours, times and expense in recent several months are widely used for churn forecast and they are explainable exactly. So this paper uses these behavior attributes as segmentation variables in empirical analysis.

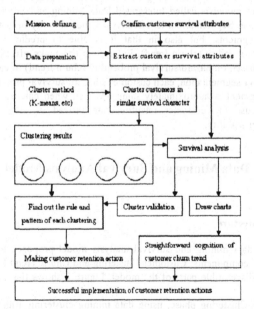

Figure2 Customer Segmentation based on survival character

2.3 Steps

(1) Mission defining. Confirming customer attributes for mission.

(2) Data preparation and Data extraction. Extracting necessary customer behavior attributes from data warehouse.

(3) Clustering. Using data mining clustering methods such as K-means to cluster customers based on similar hazard/survival possibility.

(4) Appending a new attribute: Cluster Number. After clustering, each customer has a new attribute named Cluster number, its necessary for survival analysis.

(5) Survival analysis. It just needs three necessary attributes: Months with Service, Customer Number and Clustering Number. Survival analysis have two purpose: ①Segmentation's quality can be measured by homogeneity in subdivisions and heterogeneity among subdivisions（Wedel M, Kamakura W A, 2000）. It can make comparer between different clusters to test clustering performance and help getting the correct customer segmentation. ②Drawing survival function curve for straightforward cognition of customer churn trend.

(6) Find out the rule and pattern of each clustering.

(7) Successful Implementation of customer retention action

3. Empirical Analysis

A china telecommunications company, which throngs more and more customers, but on the other hand, strives with stronger competition, is our studying case.

3.1 Data selected and filtering

The company wants to make decision to satisfy customers, and prevent customer churn. In collaborate with the company, it supplies with us the research data. Customer data are selected and filtered, and deleted some insignificant records, such as register without transaction records. In the end, we select 1000 records from data warehouse, each record including256 attributes.

Attributes list as follow: customer's basic information(name, gender, register date), churn flag, customer's transaction records from first month to sixth month after register （such as total numbers each month, total fee, the number of calling in and calling out each month, fee in every month, roaming about each month, the number of note, the number of calling in and calling out in working day, the number of transactions in one net and the time, the number of transactions among nets and the time）, the number of customers' consultation, etc..

In the selected dataset, 27.4% customers occur with churn among all customers, namely 72.6% shares with our service. In this paper, we don't list all of attributes, a part of attributes have been listed as showed in table1.

Table 1: customers' behavior attributes

Attributes	Explains	Attributes	Explains
Tenure	Months with service	Total_Times_1	Total number of transaction in first month
Age	Age in years	Total_Times_2	Total number of transaction in second month
Marital	Marital status	Total_Times_3	Total number of transaction in third month
Address	Years at current address	Total_Times_4	Total number of transaction in fourth month
Ed	Level of education	Total_Times_5	Total number of transaction in fifth month
Employ	Years with current employer	Total_Times_6	Total number of transaction in sixth month
Retire	Retired	Total_Duration_1	Total duration in first month
Gender	Gender	Total_Duration_2	Total duration in second month
Reside	Number of people in household	Total_Duration_3	Total duration in third month
Fields Name	description	Total_Duration_4	Total duration in fourth month
Churn Flag	churning flag	Total_Duration_5	Total duration in fifth month
Total_Disc_Fee	Total discount in the past six months	Total_Duration_6	Total duration in sixth month
		...	
		...	

3.2 clustering customer based on similar survival character

A K-means cluster analysis was performed. According to former literatures with the prediction in customers churn, we selected and filtering 196 attributes to cluster, and omitting some of attributes, like worthless attributes or inapplicable in K-means, especially like sparse datum (Pang-Ning Tan, Michael Steinbach, Vipin Kumar, 2006). Generally, the parameter must be appointed in the beginning with K-means. Now according with advanced experience, the parameter K is set as 2-6. The studying uses the software of SPSS, the result finally arrived at four clustering .Parts of clustering results as showed in table2

Table2 clustering results

Customer ID	Churn flag	Cluster ID	Number of customers in each cluster
1	1	cluster2	
2	1	cluster4	
3	0	cluster4	Cluster1 :194
4	0	cluster2	Cluster2 :264
5	1	cluster3	Cluster3 :269
6	0	cluster2	Cluster4 :273
7	1	cluster4	
8	0	cluster1	
...	...	...	

3.3 Verifying the clustering

The aim to estimate the survival and hazard function help us obtain customer survival/churn information. Necessary variable: Months with service, Churn flag, Customer ID. Firstly, these cluster were been pairwise compared. As showed in table3, their difference is distinct (all sig. <0.10, almost all sig. <0.05). And we get survival function(churn trend) , as shows in Figure3.

Table3 Pairwise Comparisons

Cluster ID	Compared cluster ID	Wilcoxon (Gehan) Statistic	Sig.
1	2	18.640	.000
	3	37.154	.000
	4	2.949	.086
2	1	18.640	.000
	3	5.515	.019
	4	9.222	.002
3	1	37.154	.000
	2	5.515	.019
	4	27.229	.000
4	1	2.949	.086
	2	9.222	.002
	3	27.229	.000

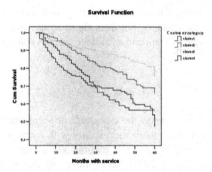

Figure3 survival function

4 Management Applications

With the analysis to all kinds of features, we can find the rule and pattern as showed in Table4, and in the end find relevant market tactics.

Table4 cluster features

class	
1	More fees, more long-distance transactions, highest churn
2	Normal fees, second lowest churn
3	Little transaction each month and more note, lowest churn
4	More transactions each month, more call in and less call out, second highest churn

Clustering1: these customers share important similar features, such as more fees,

more long-distance transactions and highest churn. As these customers expend more, and their expectation is high, we must hold up them with more resource, so as to decrease the churn. And as showed in Figure3, the churn trend is much quicker in the beginning phase that latter phase, so firms must adopt retention actions as soon as possible.

Clustering2: generally, these customers hold average expenditure each month, and every numeric displays equilibration, not higher or lower. The churn is low comparatively. Relatively, these customers satisfy with the company's service, and they hope to share with the company's service. The company must launch into appropriate resource to hold them, for they are the foundation of the customers.

Clustering3: these customers' expenditure is lowest comparatively, and the probability of churn also is also lowest comparatively. They satisfy present services provided with the company, but contribution is lower than average level. Company needn't distribute any resource on them.

Clustering4: these customers have more spending, with more call in and lower call out. They are valuable customers, but their churn is also high. Company must allocate some resources to retain them and encourage them to call out more.

5 Conclusions

A key role of marketing is to identify the customers or segments with the greatest value-creating potential and target them successfully with corresponding marketing strategies to reduce the risk of these high lifetime value customers defecting to competitors (Andrew Banasiewicz, 2004). Segmenting customer is the basic work of data mining according to known historic segmentation information. The training data used to construct segment forecast mode can be historic data or exogenous data that gain from experience or survey.

For an enterprise, how to use data mining, and how to practice enterprise's tactics should we use in determine segmentation? To answer this question, this paper proposes a Integrated Data Mining and Survival Analysis Model for Customer Segmentation. The model proposed by this paper has expanded the simple application of single data mining technology in customer segmentation, it can guide for more complex applications of data mining in CRM. The model clusters customers into heterogeneous clusters with similar churn probability, each clustering have its unique churn trend, so enterprise can make retention action according to this. And via observe the sharp of survival function curl, enterprises can get straightforward cognition of customer churn trend.

Effective segmentation can help companies increase revenue by acquiring and retaining high value customer at low cost. It can also help in aligning cost-to-serve to customer value, perhaps reducing overall marketing, sales and service costs. The model proposed by this paper is testing in the telecomm industry; it may be used in other industry such as finance service etc. Therefore, the future researches may focus on testing this model in other service industry.

Acknowledgements

The Research is supported by the Young Teacher Research Start-up Project "Research of Customer Lifetime Value Management System Basded on Data Mining Technology" of Houzhou Dianzi University under the grant No: Y021507037.

References

26. 1. A. Nairn, and P. Bottomley (2003), Cluster analysis procedures in the CRM era, *International Journal of Market Research*, Vol. 45 Quarter 2
27. 2. A. Banasiewicz, Acquiring high value, retainable customers, *Database Marketing & Customer Strategy Management*, 2004, Vol. 12, 1, 21–31
28. 3. E. H. Sub, K .C. Noh, C .K.Suh (1999), Customer list segmentation using the combined response model, *Expert Systems with Applications*, 17(2): 89-97
29. 4. C. Fraley, and A.E. Raftery(2002), *Model-Based Clustering, Discriminant Analysis, and Density Estimation*. Journal of the American Statistical Association 97:611-631.
30. 5. G. Sunil, D.R. Lehmann, and A.S. Jennifer (2004): *Valuing Customer Journal of Marketing Research*, , 41 (February), 7–18.
31. 6. JR. DW. Hosmer, and S. Lemeshow(1999), *Applied Survival Analysis: Regression Modeling of Time to Event Data*, New York: John Wiley & Sons,.
32. 7. K. Jaesoo et al.(2003): Segmenting the market of West Australian senior tourists using an artificial neural network, *Tourism Management*, 24(l):25-34
33. 8. J. Kleinberg, C. Papadimitriou, P. Raghavan (2004): *Segmentation Problems, Journal of the ACM*, Vol. 51, No. 2, March, pp. 263–280.
34. 9. L.D. Chen, K.S. Soliman, E. Mao, M. N. Frolick (2000): Measuring user satisfaction with data warehouse: an exploratory study, *Information & Management*, 37(3): 103--110.
35. 10. P.N. Tan, M. Steinbach, V. Kumar (2006). *Introduction to Data Mining*, Posts & Telecom Press, pp310-320, Beijing.
36. 11. P.V. Freytag, et al(2001), Business to Business Market Segmentation Industrial Marketing Management, 30(6):4 73486
37. 12. Y. Chen, G.Z. Zhang, D.F Hu and S.S. Wang (2006), Customer Segmentation in Customer Relationship Management Based on Data Mining, *Knowledge Enterprise: Intelligent Strategies in Product Design, Manufacturing, and Management*, Volume 207, pp.288-293
38. 13. P.C. Verhoef, P.N. Spring, J.C. Hoekstra , The commercial use of segmentation and predictive modeling techniques for database marketing in the Netherlands, *Decision Support Systems*, 2 003,34(4):471-481
39. 14. M. Wedel, W.A. Kamakura and U. Bockenholt (2000): Marketing data, models and decisions, *International Journal of Research in Marketing* 17(2-3) 203-208.
40. 15. W. Reinartz, M. Krafft, and W.D. Hoyer(2004), The Customer Relationship Management Process: Its Measurement and Impact on Performance, *Journal of Marketing Research*, 293 Vol. XLI (August), 293–305)

Related Problems of the Vocational Qualification Standard for Online Financial Marketing

Haijun Zhao

Senior Economist of the Guangdong Provincial E-Commerce Key
Laboratory of Guangdong University of Business Studies, and Secretary-
General of China Electronic Commerce Association Securities Information
Broadcast Committee

Abstract. The prosperity of the Chinese financial market and the development of financial information technology have given rise to a new occupation, "online financial marketing". However, in our higher education, no special course system for "online financial marketing" has been set up, and our vocational education also lacks a set of scientific vocational qualification standard for "online financial marketing". This paper attempts to solve this problem. On the basis of analyzing the scientific connotation, vocational category and social demand of "online financial marketing" and defining the principles for formulating the vocational qualification standard for "online financial marketing", this paper puts forward the basic framework of the vocational qualification standard for "online financial marketing".

1 Introduction

Online financial marketing is a compound phrase. To comprehensively understand the concept and disciplinary connotation of "online financial marketing", to clarify the objects of online financial marketing, and to fully understand the responsibilities of and qualifications for the occupation of online financial marketing, we must analyze the phrasal structure of "online financial marketing".

"Online financial marketing" is a phrase composed of three basic words, "online", "finance" and "marketing". As "online" and "finance" can form "online finance", and "finance" and "marketing" can form "financial marketing", "online" and "financial marketing" can form "online financial marketing", and "online finance" and "marketing" can form "online financial marketing". Therefore, "online financial marketing" has two meanings, financial marketing with "online network" as the marketing tool and marketing with "online finance" as the marketing object. The former refers to the process of

---

Please use the following format when citing this chapter:

Zhao, H., 2007, in IFIP International Federation for Information Processing, Volume 251, Integration and Innovation Orient to E-Society Volume1, Wang, W. (Eds), (Boston: Springer), pp. 96-106.

successfully introducing financial products and services to consumers by using online technologies to conduct online market survey, online promotion and publicity of traditional financial services; the latter refers to all-directional introduction and promotion activities specially for financial products and services based on online technologies. The marketing objects of the former include all the financial products and financial services, with their marketing method being "online marketing" ; the marketing objects of the latter are high-tech financial products and services with modern online information technology as the means, including online banking, online securities, online fund, online futures and online insurance etc., with their marketing method including not only "online marketing" but also traditional marketing.

Therefore, the disciplinary studies of online financial marketing shall not only include financial marketing with "online network" as the marketing means, but also marketing with "online finance" as the marketing object. Both financial marketing with "online network" as the marketing means and marketing with "online finance" as the marketing object are basic categories of the studies on financial e-commerce. We can call the combination of the two the discipline of online financial marketing. That is to say, the discipline of online financial marketing is a special learning of online marketing of financial products and services and marketing of online finance. As to the disciplinary attributes, according to the *Catalogue of Undergraduate Specialties of Regular Institution of Higher Education*(Ministry of Education ,1998) [1], the discipline of online financial marketing is an inter-disciplinary science of finance (020104), marketing (110202) and information management and information system (110102). More accurately, it is an interdisciplinary subject of finance (020104) and e-commerce (110209 W), a specialty outside the catalogue approved by the Ministry of Education. We can say that it is an applied branch discipline of finance or an applied branch discipline of e-commerce.

2   The Occupational Category of Online Financial Marketing

Like the information industry, e-commerce is an industry that can be intersected with any industry in the national economy and form a new field in this industry. The intersection of e-commerce and finance forms a new field of financial e-commerce. The driving business of financial e-commerce is online financial marketing, which is the soul and foundation for financial e-commerce. Though there is classification of the occupation of online financial marketing in Classification and Dictionary of Occupations in the People's Republic of China [2] and national standard GB / T 6565-1999 Occupational Classification and Codes [3], in reality, online financial marketing has indeed become a new industry branch and a new occupation. In recent years, almost all the big securities companies, fund management companies, big commercial banks and insurance companies have set up an e-commerce department of online marketing department. In their recruitment announcements, the position of "online marketing" has the largest demand. Meanwhile, with the great development of financial informatization and cyberization, and online finance, online financial marketing will become a very important occupational position, and the cause of online financial marketing will provide the society with thousands of new occupational posts. The high-tech marketing measures of online financial marketing, while promoting the innovation and development of the financial cause, will also quickly create a new wealthy group because of its special speed of market opening and online proliferation effects. This wealth gathering effect, in turn, will further elevate the social status of online financial marketing talents and thereby accelerate the process of professionalization of online financial marketing.

3   Occupational Demands of Online Financial Marketing

3.1 Social demand for the occupation of online financial marketing

As a new marketing means in the financial industry and a new occupation in the field of e-commerce, online financial marketing has started to display its boundless charms. For example, the Agricultural Bank of China started the online fund direct sale service in April 2006 [4], thus becoming the first large-scale state-owned commercial bank to open online fund sales service. Seven companies participate in the online fund direct sale platform of the Agricultural Bank of China, Guotai Fund, Fuguo Fund, Changsheng Fund, Dacheng Fund, Changxin Fund, Penghua Fund and Zhonghai Fund. The varieties of participating funds include over 30 open-ended funds from money fund, guaranteed fund, bond fund, index fund and leverage fund to equity fund. By the end of last July, the number of new fund transaction customers via this system had surpassed 11 thousand. In the beginning of September, the Agricultural Bank of China also united with 7 fund companies to hold online fund direct sale demonstration meetings in Shanghai and Shenzhen etc. Selling funds online and staging road shows on the spot are typical and comprehensive online financing marketing operations.

From the above case, we can see two modes of online financial marketing—passive marketing and active marketing. To set up an online fund direct sale platform and develop online fund service are passive online financial marketing. To stage road shows of online fund service or to further conduct online road shows and to promote online fund service are active online financing marketing. What passive marketing needs are online financing talents versed in technology, that is, the talents for building and developing the online financial platform, while what active marketing, as the continuation and expansion of passive marketing, needs are financial marketing talents and online marketing talents versed in business. "Online finance" adds wings to financial business. Plus active marketing, "falconers" come into being, who will make modern financial business "soar as it likes above the global village". The total amount of financial business will also rapidly increase in the form of geometric growth. The rapid growth of modern financial business will inevitably bring about a large amount of demand for professionals in online financial marketing.

3.2 Demand of skills for the occupation of online financial marketing

From the above analysis, we can see that online financial marketing talents are compound talents integrating multiple knowledge skills including financial business knowledge, online information technology, marketing skills and skills in using online tools. A qualified online financial marketing talent shall not only master the basic theories of finance and financial market, but also are familiar with all kinds of financial products, financial tools and financial services in the financial market, be able to not only conduct information resource planning of online financial marketing management and system platform construction, but also guarantee the financial security and information security of online financial services, not only grasp the basic theories and methods of marketing but also have practical ability in marketing, and not only be able to skillfully use all kinds of online tools to conduct marketing but also have the working ability to guide customers, cultivate customers and retain customers. The author has listed some basic qualities that a qualified online financial marketing talent shall have in the following table.

Table 1 Basic Skills that an Online Financial Marketing Talent Shall Command

Knowledge in financial business	Online information technology	Marketing skills	Use of online tools	Other knowledge and skills
Grasp the basic knowledge of finance and financial market	Have the basic skills in information resource planning, and be able to skillfully conduct information resource planning of online financial marketing management	Grasp the basic theories and methods of marketing	Be familiar with and skillfully use such common online promotion tools as google, yahoo, sohu and website title to conduct website and business promotion	Grasp the basic knowledge of consumption psychology and behavior finance
Be familiar with all kinds of financial products, financial tools and financial services including banking business, monetary market, capital market, foreign exchange market, futures market, derived market, gold market and property right market	Be familiar with and can adeptly use such modern online information and communication technologies as the internet, broadcasting and TV networks, telecommunication network and mobile communication network, and construct online marketing platforms	Have the basic skills in market survey, market segmentation and market development, be able to independently conduct analysis of financial marketing environment, formulate financial marketing strategies, and conduct financial marketing performance evaluation and regulation management	Be able to skillfully use multiple information channels such as e-mail, e-magazine, online fax, short message, WAP web and blog to conduct financial marketing activities	Customer training skills for transmitting financial knowledge and guiding financial consumption
Be familiar with the basic business processes of banking	Be familiar with the management processes and service processes of	Be familiar with and grasp CRM system, do well in customer management work	Know the volume of flow of large portal websites, selectively publish online	Basic skills to help customers to manage

business, securities business, fund business, bond business, futures business and insurance business	such online finance as online banking, online securities, online fund, online futures and online insurance	and have basic skills in database marketing	advertisements, or have reciprocal links, or join in narrow ad league, publish narrow ads, or use functional software to conduct pushing-based marketing	finance or provide customers with financial management consultation services
Understand related financial policies and financial laws and regulations	Be familiar with basic online formation security technologies and ensure the information security of online financial services	Grasp such basic marketing or promotion techniques as advertisement promotion, price promotion, service promotion and channel promotion, and have the practical ability in marketing	Such publicity reports as focus media and digital broadcasting	Emotional quotient to maintain close relationship with customers

4 The Urgency of Developing and Formulating the Vocational Standard for Online Financial Marketing

The occupation of online financial marketing demands compound talents with both modern financial business ability and online marketing skills, and it is difficult to cultivate such talents and the cultivation cycle is relatively long. However, the reality is that almost no finance specialty, marketing specialty or e-commerce specialty in each institution of higher education across China has set up the course of "online financial marketing" ; whereas the present situation is that the online financial marketing industry has emerged and displayed the tendency for rapid development. Currently every financial institution develops online financial services. The lack of online financial marketing talents has become the bottleneck for the development of the modern financial service industry. There have been frequent reports in the media about the fact that large-scale financial institutions fail to recruit suitable online financial service talents. Therefore short-term vocational skill training becomes an inevitable solution.

In order to ensure the quality of the vocational training of online financial marketing and cultivate qualified practical talents, it is particularly urgent to develop a set of scientific and reasonable "vocational qualification standard system for online financial marketing" . This shall arouse sufficient attention of related experts, scholars, the state administrative departments of the finance industry, in particular, the financial e-commerce industry, and related industry associations.

5   The Basic Framework of the Vocational Standard for Online Financial Marketing

Vocational qualification standard is standardized requirements on the working ability and level of practitioners on the basis of occupational classification and the activity contents of an occupation (type of work). Vocational qualification standard occupies the most important position in the whole national vocational qualification system and plays a guiding role. It will directly guide the direction and contents of vocational education and skill training and the key points and rules for conducting evaluation and assessment of students. It plays a vital role in the human resource development strategies of the national economy. The vocational qualification standard system must be a measurement system of uniform knowledge and skills with common characteristics of an industry that not only meets the objectives of the labor market and enterprise development but also meets the actual needs of modern economic development. It is the necessary foundation for the establishment of a national vocational qualification certificate system. Online financial marketing, as a new occupation born under the conditions of modern online information technology, must have its own set of qualification standard system if it is to be included into the uniform national vocational qualification certificate system.

The principles for formulating the vocational standard for online financial marketing shall accord with the general principles of national vocational standard compilation: with occupational activities as the orientation, occupational skills as the core. With occupational activities as the orientation is to plan the boundary and content scope of necessary knowledge and skills of practitioners of an occupation with the occupational behavior characteristics, behavior contents and general behavior patterns of online financial marketing as the main thread; with occupational skills as the core is to study out the levels of practitioners of the occupation and their corresponding skills and operation abilities with the occupational technical characteristics, technical contents, technical grades and application ability demands as the review targets.

According to the above principles and following *Technical Regulations on Formulating National Vocational Standard* [5], the following basic framework is proposed for the vocational qualification standard for online financial marketing:

(1)Title of the occupation

"Online financial marketer" is used for professionals engaged in the occupation of online financial marketing

(2) Definition of the occupation

An online financial marketing master is a compound business talent who has received uniform training from an authoritative training system and passed the assessment and evaluation, can use online information technology to conduct financial business publicity and service promotion, and can conduct online sales and management activities of financial products and services including e-finance or online finance, and a professional engaged in operation and management who commands comprehensive financial knowledge and operation and management ideas, operation methods and realization measures of financial e-commerce and can provide informatization and cyberization business services or management services for a certain link or the whole of a financial institution.

(3)Occupation levels and basic standards

Online financial marketers have three levels, with their titles and standards being respectively:

1) Online financial marketing member: have general basic financial knowledge, be able to use basic online marketing tools and independently complete the publicity and service promotion of financial business and the online marketing of financial products and services including e-finance or online finance.

2) Online financial marketing master: have solid financial theoretical basis, be able to take an overall view of the situation of financial market and the development direction of online information technology, be familiar with online finance technology, be able to develop the information resource planning and system construction of online financial marketing, be able to skillfully use modern online marketing tools to conduct financial marketing, be able to solve the general technical difficult problems in online financial marketing and difficult problems of customer services, and be able to guide and train online financial marketing members.

3) Senior online financial marketing master: have profound financial theoretical knowledge, command the financial innovation forefront and the development forefront of online information technology, be versed in online financial technology, be able to lead the information resource planning of an financial institution and the system development and platform construction of online financial services, be able to develop and formulate online financial marketing strategies and conduct the master planning and coordination of online financial marketing, be able for smoothly solve the technical difficult problems in online financial marketing and difficult problems of customer services, be able to smoothly use cutting edge online information technology in the practice of online financial marketing and conduct financial project innovation, and be able to conduct systematic technical training on online financial marketing.

(4)Requirements for registration for an examination:

1) Online financial marketing member: students registering themselves for this level of examination must have a degree of junior college.

2) Online financial marketing master: students registering themselves for this level of examination must have a bachelor's degree or have a degree of junior college and have worked in a related post for over 1 year, or have obtained the vocational qualification certificate for an online financial marketing member

3) Senior online financial marketing master: students registering themselves for this level of examination must have a master's degree or have a bachelor's degree and have worked in a related post for over 1 year, or have a degree of junior college and have worked in a related post for over 3 years, or have obtained the vocational qualification certificate for an online financial marketing master.

(5)Training requirements

People registered for examinations shall participate in the special training held by a local training institution recognized by the online financial marketer certification administration authority and complete the whole course of training according to regulations. The contents and methods of training include: lessons (lectures and case discussions), exercise (homework and experiments), practical operation (practices and papers) and commercial salons etc.

1) Training term

Online financial marketing member: the training takes about 1-2 months (120 class hours), including about 36 class hours of lectures and abut 84 class hours of exercise and practical operation (completed by students with self discipline).

Online financial marketing master: the training takes about 1-2 months (120 class hours), including about 60 class hours of lectures and case discussions and abut 60 class hours of exercise and practical operation (completed by students with self discipline).

Senior online financial marketing master: the training takes about 2-4 months (240 class hours), including about 100 class hours of lectures, case discussions and commercial salons and abut 140 class hours of practices and project design (completed by students with self discipline).

2) Training teachers

A special teacher team selected, trained and determined by the online financial marketer certification administration authority according to the general requirements of the vocational training objectives of online financial marketing.

3) Equipment for training places

Audio-visual classrooms, e-commerce applied experiment platforms, online financial service experiment platforms and online examination systems that meet the standards stipulated by the educational department.

(6) Appraisal requirements

To acquire a vocational qualification certificate for online financial marketing, one must pass the examination and appraisal of the online financial marketer certification administration authority or its authorized organization. Senior online financial marketing masters, online financial marketing masters and online financial marketing members must pass online written examination. Besides, senior online financial marketing masers shall complete a stipulated project design and oral defense for their paper and online financial marketing masters shall also complete stipulated paper for the specialty.

1) Online financial marketing member

Those who have one of the following qualifications can acquire a vocational qualification certificate for an online financial marketing member: ① be registered for and pass the systematic training of the online financial marketer certification administration authority or its authorized organization, and acquire a course completion certificate for an online financial marketing member; ② have a bachelor's degree and have worked in a post of online financial marketing for over 1 year or have a degree of junior college and have worked in a post of online financial marketing for over 2 years, and file an application with the online financial marketer certification administration authority or its authorized organization for a certificate of an online financial marketing member and pass the examination.

2) Online financial marketing master

Those who have one of the following qualifications can acquire a vocational qualification certificate for an online financial marketing master: ① be registered for and pass the systematic training of the online financial marketer certification administration authority or its authorized organization, and acquire a course completion certificate for an online financial marketing master; ② have acquired a vocational qualification certificate for an online financial marketing member and have worked in the post of the occupation for over 2 years, and file an application with the online financial marketer certification administration authority or its authorized organization for the certificate of an online financial marketing master and pass the examination; ③ have a bachelor's degree and have worked in a post of online financial marketing for over 2year or have a master's degree and have worked in a post of online financial marketing for over 1 years, and file an application with the online financial marketer certification administration authority or its authorized organization for a certificate of an online financial marketing master and pass the examination.

3) Senior online financial marketing master

Those who have one of the following qualifications can acquire a vocational qualification certificate for a senior online financial marketing master: ① be registered for and pass the systematic training of the online financial marketer certification administration authority or its authorized organization, and acquire a course completion certificate for a senior online financial marketing master; ② have acquired a vocational qualification certificate for an online financial marketing master and have worked in the post of the occupation for over 3 years, and file an application with the online financial marketer certification administration authority or its authorized organization for the certificate of a senior online financial marketing master and pass the examination; ③ have a master's degree and have worked in a post of online financial marketing for over 3 years, and file an application with the online financial marketer certification administration authority or its authorized organization for a certificate of a senior online financial marketing master and pass the examination.

(7)The proportion table for vocational skill examination

Table 2 The Proportion Table for the Examination of Knowledge and Skills of the Online Financial Marketing Occupation

Online financial marketing knowledge module	Level	Prop-ortion	Online financial marketing skill module	Level	Proportion
Basic knowledge of finance	Necessary for online financial marketing members	1/6	Successful employment of ordinary online marketing tools	Necessary for online financial marketing members	1/2
Financial market, financial products, financial tools and financial services	Necessary for online financial marketing masters	1/6	Flexible employment of advanced online marketing tools	Necessary for online financial marketing masters	1/3
Financial projects and financial innovation	Necessary for senior online financial marketing masters	1/6	The information resource planning and system design of online financial marketing	Necessary for online financial marketing masters	1/6
Basic knowledge of online information	Necessary for online	1/6	Information resource	Necessary for senior online	1/6

and e-commerce	financial marketing members		planning of online financial marketing and the project management of online marketing platform development	financial marketing masters
Theories of online economy and financial e-commerce	Necessary for online financial marketing masters and senior online financial marketing masters	Online financial marketing masters 1/6; senior online financial marketing masters 1/6	The monitoring and control of online security	Necessary for senior online financial marketing masters 1/6
Laws and regulations, honesty and integrity, and moral codes	Necessary for all the levels of online financial marketing talents	1/6	Diagnosis and repair of technical failures in the online marketing system	Necessary for senior online financial marketing masters 1/6

Note: The proportions in the table reflect the proportions of each type of knowledge and work content or the related knowledge of occupational functions in training and examination

6 The Association Strategies for the Formulation of Vocational Standard for Online Financial Marketing

The above basic framework is a sketchy conception intending to start further discussion. The study and formulation of a vocational standard shall not stop at the attention of a scholar from the academic perspective. People of this occupation, the business organizations of this occupation and their administrative departments shall pay more attention to it from the perspective related with their own interests, the interests of the units and industry administration. The state labor and social security department shall perform its administrative duties according to related administrative laws and regulations, operate from a strategically advantageous position, and pay attention to it from the perspective of standardizing the vocational training market. In fact, it is basically industry associations that preside over the study, formulation, issuing and implementation of overseas standards and international standards. For example, the internationally current "Chartered Financial Analyst (CFA)" certificate and training and certification standard was designed and developed by the Association for Investment Management and Research (AIMR), The International Commercial Art Designer (ICAD) certificate and training and certification standard was designed and developed by the International Commercial Art Designer Association (ICADA), etc.

In our country, due to the remaining influence of the planned system, related laws and regulations proclaim that "the labor and personnel administration departments of the State Council shall, together with the related departments in charge of an industry, study and formulate the scope of vocational qualifications, occupational (specialty and type of work) classification, vocational qualification standard and the measures for degree authentication, qualifying examination, expert assessment and skill appraisal." The related industry associations are excluded from the power of studying and formulating vocational qualification standards, so much so that *Classification of Occupations in the People's Republic of China* also has such a stipulation: the title and definition of a new occupation shall be determined by the Ministry of Labor and Social Security after the demonstration of experts. Under the present new technology and competition conditions, in particular, after our country's accession to the WTO, new industries, new trades and new occupations are emerging. If the title and definition of a new occupation is determined by the Ministry of Labor and Social Security, it will affect and lag behind the development and social demand of new occupations. It is a historical necessity for related industry associations to assume the duties and responsibilities for developing and formulating the standards for new occupations, which also accords with the big direction of the reform of government administrative systems. In this respect, the China Electronic Commerce Association has taken the lead and made a good initiative. It formally published "Certification Standard for Chinese Electronic Commerce Professional Managers (trial implementation)" in the form of No. 1 document of CCCEM[2005] in May 2005, which has exerted wide influence in the society. At the same time, the association has cultivated a large number of qualified Chinese electronic commerce professional managers for the construction of the national economy. Such a measure shall also be adopted for the development and formulation of the vocational standard for online financial marketing so as to make the new occupation of online financial marketers serve the development of our national economy rightfully and with high quality as soon as possible.

References

1. "Ministry of Education of china: Catalogue of Undergraduate Specialties of Regular Institution of Higher Education (1998)" .
http://jwc.qfnu.edu.cn/Article/wxfg/jywx/199803/19980329113934.htm
2. Working Committee of the State Occupational Classification and Vocational Qualifications: *Classification and Dictionary of Occupations in the People' s Republic of China*, China Labor & Social Security Publishing House, Beijing,May (1995)
3. State Bureau of People's Republic of China for Quality and Technical Supervision: *Occupational Classification and Codes*—State standard GB / T 6565-1999, (March 1, 1999)
4. Tao Li, "The Agricultural Bank of China Launches Online Fund Direct Sale", China Business *Times*, (September 10, 2006)
5. "Ministry of Labor and Social Security of the People' s Republic of China", *Technical Regulations on Formulating National Vocational Standard*, (July 2001).

Internet Virtual Money Under Chinese payment Enviromnent and It's efficiency analysis

Haishan Tian, Kuanhai Zhang
Payment and Settlement Institute,
School of Economic Information Engineering,
Southwestern University of Finance and Economics,
St.55 Guanghuacun,Chengdu, P.R.China, Zip code: 610074,
tianhs_t@swufe.edu.cn, zhangkh_t@swufe.edu.cn

Abstract. The development of e-Commerce needs suitable online electronic-payment and settlement arrangement. In China, most online virtual commodity and service providers adopt a new payment and settlement solutions which is named "Webcoin" by this paper. In this paper we analyze the China's online and offline payment environment, explain the reason why the Webcoin come into being now, give the definition of the Webcoin, present the Webcoin's characteristics, and introduce the concept of payment friction coefficient to discuss the efficiency of the Webcoin as a payment instrument on virtual commodity and service.

1 Introduction

A new type of online payment mode have been adopted more and more by most online e-Commerce companies in China since 2002[1], such as "Q coin" adopted by Tencent Company, "U coin" adopted by Sina.com, and so on. In this paper we call all this kind of payment mode Webcoin. This mode is suitable to the payment and settlement environment in China now, and fits the characteristics of the online products especially the virtual commodity and service. Because of the use of Webcoin, the online companies in China succeeded in conquering the online flexible payment problem and make huge profits[2]. What's Webcoin? How can it make this achievement? Why does it emerge and grow up in China? This article analyses the present environment of the payment and settlement in China, explain the advantage of Webcoin to be online micro-payment for virtual properties, and through the analysis of the payment friction coefficient to show the importance of the Webcoin to the virtual commodity and service.

Please use the following format when citing this chapter:

Tian, H., Zhang, K., 2007, in IFIP International Federation for Information Processing, Volume 251, Integration and Innovation Orient to E-Society Volume1, Wang, W. (Eds), (Boston: Springer), pp. 107-114.

Webcoin is not an electronic-payment products, it is a micro-payment mode that is used to charge intangible goods online in China's web companies . In China, there are many companies which had been issuing their own "coin" which circulated and was used for buying the product provided on their own websites, i.e. the "Q coin" issued by Tencent company(www.qq.com) which is a leading Internet company in China, the "Baidu coin" by Baidu company(www.baidu.com) which is a leading Internet search engine company in China, the "U coin" by Sina company(www.sina.com.cn) which is a primary Internet portal in China, the "santa point ticket" by Santa company(www.santa.com) which is a leading online game company in China, the "star coin" by Super Star Digital Library(www.ssreader.com) which is a leading online library in China. Customers buy the Internet company's "digital cash" through lower cost payment instruments or payment channels such as cash, bank card, telephone, and Internet bar. The amount of money that they pay for Webcoin is recorded in a particular virtual account set up by the company. When customer purchases something in the Internet company's web, the value of relative virtual account is deducted. For example, customers can get the "Q coin" in book store by cash, and then they can buy the virtual commodity and service provided by qq.com using this account.

2 The relationship between the virtual commodity and service and payment environment

The virtual commodity and service is those low value intangible goods which is provide by Internet companies for online customers such as online games, the download of phone ring, the video and audio products online, the photos and pictures viewing, online books and magazines reading, online consultancy, web show like QQ show, web pets breeding, and so on. The main characteristic of those products is the low price, that is probably 0.01 cent or even lower, the second characteristic is the large number of the virtual commodity and services that can be shared by all users, the third one is the large number of potential customers whose age is young and their income is low, and the last one is that the value-add-in of those products is very large; it can bring large profits to those web companies. On the other hand, the virtual commodity and service is pure digital product, it can distribute to customers online, and the cost of transportation is very low. Under the effect of the network externality and the zero margin cost of those products, the market of the virtual commodity and service is very large [1].

The key role of the development of the virtual commodity and service is the payment and settlement arrangement. The potential huge number of customers, the lower price of the products and high frequency of the payments, all these need a low cost and efficient way for payment. But there are many payment barriers in online exchange in China, especially in virtual goods online, and the micro-payment also encounters the cost pitfall [5]. Therefore, it is very important to find a flexible and creative payment system that is suitable to the Chinese e-Commerce and electronic payment environment.

3 Background of payment environment in China

The payment environment in China now mainly serves for traditional economy [6]. The payment organization consists of central banks, commercial banks and other financial organizations which are engaged in clearing and settlement. The payment system consists of RTGS(Real Time Gross System) and DNS(Deferred Net System) which interconnect the banks and other payment and settlement organizations. The detail payment system consists of banks, post office and clearing house. The payment instruments include check, bill exchange, casher's check and bank card. The payment and settlement environment is dominated by banks and is suitable to traditional economy, It does not support e-Commerce fully.

Although there were online payment and e-payment methods in China since 2000, most people still like to pay with cash that time. The willing of using bank card (debit cad or credit card) is not strong, because the customers worried about that the information of their card exposed on the Internet [7]. Moreover, whenever the customer using bank card, the web companies also were dependent on banks to deal with customer's account and settlement, for the regular payment way using bank card is through the gateway of banks. The additional major problem is that most potential customers who are middle school students and have not bank cards for themselves [8].

In general, the main problems for the online payment in China are as follows:
- The period of payment and settlement is too long for customers to pay their online services.
- The fee charged to customer or to web companies is high. So it is not suitable to micro-payment.
- The payment method is not designed for online payment, and there are many trade arguments.
- Lack of standard of charge fee, lack of unified online payment and settlement standard, and lack of online payment organizer and arbitrator.

As known to all, people can not see each other on Internet, they don't want go to bank for just a micro-payment as well, so the paper bills or checks which were treated on the bank's counter is no longer in effect yet, even cash. The fund transfer which is depend on bank's account is also unavailable because of expensive fee compared the price of virtual good and service, for example the fund transfer fee is at least more than 1 yuan RMB for each deal. Even using card also brings expenditure such as communication fee, handling fee and commission charge. Generally the efficiency and cost of payment structure now in China is not suitable for online payment, especially for online virtually goods. So the web companies have to explore creative ways for online payment.

To overcome these payment problems, Internet companies took a series alternative way in the early stage, such as:
- Free policy, to allure customer, waiting proper time to charge.
- Charge by year or month, or charge for membership.
- Through telecommunication Companies such as China Mobile to charge customers, then web company settlements with Telecommunication Company at schedule time.
- through the third party institute such as payment website like alipay.com or

network banks. The main payment instrument is bank cards in China.

The first method adopted is not the market solution, after all no company can develop well without having steady and continuous profit or revenue. The market practice also proved this is not a long term solution. If people are used to have these services for free, it is very difficulty to charge them later. The change of consume habit can not be in effect in short time and may make company in trouble. The second way is in effect for the customers who favor the company very much and faithful to it. However, the way is lack of flexibility, and is not good for marketing. It can not subtract the vast potential customers and lose them at last. Furthermore, the most of the potential customers of the virtual good provider online are students and young people whose income is lower than $200, so the second way is not good for enlarge the market share. The third and forth way mention above increase the business procedures, the Telecommunication Company will get their own profit from the sum of money which paid by customer, even majority of the amount (i.e. 60%). Therefore, the cost of the last two ways is so high that limit the fast pace grown of web company.

4 Webcoin and it's characteristics

The Webcoin emerged in 2002 from Tencent Company in China can overcome and reduce these payment barriers. It is a prepaid payment mechanism. It presents the amount of money that customer have paid to web companies for future purchases. The Webcoin is not a real coin or money of the real world, it is just a number in the Internet company's account and represents the customer's right to purchase commodity or service online. In fact, it is similar to the telephone card.

People can get the Webcoin through several channels online or offline such as bookstore or Internet bar by cash, or network bank by bank card. While people buy the Webcoin, the money is transfer from customer to web company, then the customer gets the right to consume the products that the company provide, and the company guarantees the customer's right and their money security. If customer buys something on the web, the number in the virtual account is deducted. When the number is zero or lower than the product's price, customer is noticed to buy Webcoins to refill the account. Different companies have their own Webcoin and give them different names, in this paper we call all of them Webcoin.

The advantage of using Webcoin in virtual commodity and service on line is make use of the financial facilities such as bank card, bank account, telephone bank, network bank, as well paper currency. It can be sold by store, booth, gas station or Internet website. It not only fits into the environment of payment in China, but also the consumer habits in China. It seems simple and easy, but it avoids the kind of limits to high payment cost and other problems mention above. It is a suitable payment mode in the payment environment in China. Besides, as for the Webcoin is stored in computer, it is easy to put into use for many purposes such as marketing statistics and product price marks[10].

Due to the role of payment instrument in the virtual world and the function of price mark of intangible goods, i.e. a T shirt in the "QQ show" of QQ.com website is marked 1.5 "Q coin", it is paid by Webcoin also, some experts in China think that the Webcoin will act as the currency in the virtual world. Furthermore, considering the potential huge market of the intangible market, these experts also think the Webcoin will bring an impact on fiat paper currency and lead to inflation in the real world.[11] Through the analysis above, we think the Webcoin is a warrantee just like a receipt or voucher after customer had bought something, it's not the real money, it can not buy anything except the virtual goods provided by this web company who has issued the Webcoin in its own website. In the other hand, the Webcoin can not be exchanged back to paper currency. So, we do not think that the Webcoin is fiat money, it can not influent the issuing amount of real world currency, it cannot lead to inflation as well.

The Webcoin payment mode promotes the web company fast grown. For example, the register user of QQ.com which is the first web company to use Webcoin is over 570 million by the end of 3rd quarter of 2006[2]. The revenue from the Internet service-add-in paid by Webcoin is reach 0.49b Yuan RMB in the 3rd quarter of 2006, increase by 139 % comparing with last year. The rest web companies include Baidu.com, 163.com, Shenda.com, Sina.com.cn, Sohu.com, Wangfangdata.com, Ssreader.com, and so on, all adopt or plan to adopt the Webcoin payment mode. The table below figures out the part of web companies which had their own Webcoin solutions.

Table 1. Part of web company's Webcoin solutions

website	Webcoin name	Price (RMB)
QQ.com	Q coin	1Q coin/1 yuan
Sdo.com	Sanda point ticket	0.5 -2point /1 yuan
Baidu.com	Baidu coin	1 Baidu coin/1 yuan
Sohu.com	Hu coin	1 Hu coin /1 yuan
Sina.com.cn	U coin	1 U coin /1 yuan, by bank card 3 U coin/6 yuan, by phone
163.com	POPO coin	10 POPO coin /1 yuan
Kingsoft.com	K coin	100 K coin /1 yuan
Ssreader.com	Star coin	1 Star coin/1 yuan

5 Webcoin's efficiency analysis

Webcoin raised the payment efficiency and reduced the payment cost remarkably. Suppose there are three participants in the web market, the customer, the web company, and the agency which provide payment service. First of all, we define the payment friction coefficient simply like this:

Payment friction coefficient＝cost of payment/total revenue *100%

Obviously, Payment friction coefficient presents the influent of payment environment on web trade. If the coefficient is big, the efficiency is low, vice versa.

The payment mode on the web in China in the early stage is shown in Fig.1. The agency for payment is telecommunication companies such as China Mobile. The procedure is as below:

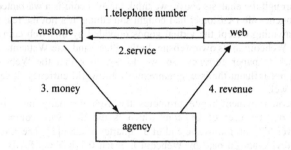

Figure.1. payment mode early stage in China

The procedure is like this: customers give their mobile phone numbers to a web service company which then transfer user's information to a agency company (such as a telecommunication company), the latter checks this number and verifies whether the customer can pay the service from the users account through the agency, if the check is through, the amount of money will be deductedt by the agency from the user's account. Finally, the agency settlement with web company in agency. In this circle, the agency will keep 40% to 60% from the total amount received from customers. The payment friction coefficient is about 50%. Hence, the efficiency of payment at early stage is low. For example, if Customer buys 3 "U Coin" through telephone, he pays 6 yuan RMB. The agent company gives the web company 3 yuan RMB also, (Fig.1).

If the web company adopt Webcoin mode, suppose there is an agency company to deal with the Webcoin card sales, the procedure circle will be changed like Fig.2. The difference with the Fig.1 is that agency sale Webcoin card to customer, and then customer opens or refuels an account which is kept in the web company. Now customer can consume by their Webcoin. Because of the Webcoin card is issued by the web company, so the discount is range of 10% to 15%. Therefore, the payment friction is less than 15%, it means that payment mode in Fig.2 is more efficient than that in Fig.1. The Tencent Company's QQ card carries out like the way of fig.2.

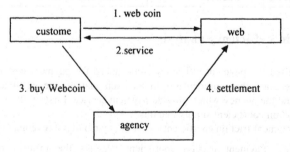

Figure.2. Webcoin payment model with agency

Moreover, if the web company sales Webcoin by oneself, the payment friction coefficient can be reduced to a very low level. The Tencent Company's Esale is the way like this. The procedure circle can be shown in Fig.3 as below:

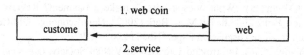

Figure.3. Webcoin payment model without agency

From the analysis above, we can find the Webcoin mechanism can reduce the payment friction coefficient, and raise the payment efficiency remarkably.

6 Conclusions

Payment model should be matched the payment environment and the demand of the market, or there will be payment friction between them. The main function of the Webcoin which is a micro-payment mechanism, a prepaid payment mode, a customer's right to get correspond amount of virtual commodity or service, is introduce in to reduce the friction between the Internet service providers and the particular payment environment in China, where the payment situation now does exist much friction. Webcoin is also can be thought to be a number in the virtual account, it is easy to put into use for many purposes such as marketing statistics and product price marks. But it's not real money and no any impact on real world monetary so far.

Considering the potential huge market of the online virtual commodity and service, it is very important to research and find better ways to pay. The practice of the Webcoin in China is proved that the Webcoin is suitable to China's payment environment, which promotes the web companies fast grown. Therefore, it is very important to research and make use better of this payment mode in China.

References:

1. iResearch Consulting Group (2006), *2006 Report of Research on Internet Payment in China*.http://www.tencent.com/ir/pdf/news20070516a.pdf
2. Zhangguang Wu (2006), Virtual Currency and Electronic Commerce, *Finance and Economics,* Issue 12, 2006, pp86-87.
3. Lei Zhang (2007), The Essence of Internet Virtual Currency and Regulation, *Commercial Times,* Issue 4, 2007, pp56-57.
4. James C. McGrath (2006), Micropayments: The Final Frontier for Electronic Consumer Payments, Payment Cards Center, Federal Reserve Bank of Philadelphia, discussion paper-June.2006
5. Haizhong Chang (2007), Study on the Evolutionary of Financial Ficticiousness, *Journal of Guangdong University of Finance,* Issue 1, 2007, pp66-71.
6. Kuanhai Zhang, Jing Zhang (2006), Analysis and Research of Third Party

Payment, *Proceedings of The 3rd Sino-US E-Commerce Advanced Forum*, Nankai University, Tianjin, June 3-5, 2006

7. Qiping Jiang (2006), Will Virtual Currency Lead to Inflation? *China Internet Weekly,* Issue 40, 2006, pp68-69.

8. David Humphrey, What does it cost to make a payment? Review of Network Economics, Vol.2,2003.06Jan Marc Berk (2002), New Economy, Old Central Bank? Tinbergen Institute Discussion Paper, No. TI 2002-087/2

9. Tao Yang (2006), Interrogatory to Law of Virtual Society, *Government Legality,* Issue 24, 2006, pp4-7.

10.   Bin Li (2007), The Phenomenon of Q-coin: the crisis of virtual currency, *China Society Periodical,* Issue 3, 2007, pp42-43.

11.   Jinbing Ding (2007),Guard against the Risks of Virtual Currency, *Finance and Economics*, Issue 1, 2007, pp26-27.

12.   Connel Fullenkamp, and Saleh M. Nsouli (2004), Six Puzzles in Electronic Money and Banking, *IMF working paper* No.WP/04/19

13.   Timo Henckel, Alain Ize, & Arto Kovanen (1999), Central Banking Without Central Bank Money, IMF Working Paper: WP/99/92

14.   Cornelia Holthausen, and Cyril Monnet (2003), Money and Payments: a Modern Perspective, European Central Bank working paper No.245

15.   Qiping Jiang (2005), Personalized Virtual Currency, *China Internet Weekly,* Issue 31, 2005, pp60-62.

16.   Shaowei Li (2006), Three Potential Risks caused by Virtual Currency, *Electronic Business World*, Issue 10, 2006, pp38-40.

17.   Zhangxi Lin (2006), The Internet and E-commerce in China – Identifying Unique Research Focuses, a presentation at SobrIT, Helsinki University of Technology, October 19, 2006.

18.   Chenghe Liu (2004), Challenge of Electronic Currency Laundry, *Netinfo Security,* Issue 7. 2004, pp23-25.

19.   Frederic Mishkin (1999), Monetary economics, Beijing: Chinese Renmin University Press, 2005.

20.   Qinghong Shuai, and Kuanhai Zhang (2005), Analysis of electronic commerce payment principle, *Chinese Finance Computing,* Issue 4, 2005, pp85-88.

21.   Daniel D. Garcia Swartz, Robert W. Hahn, and Anne Layne-Farrar (2004), The Move toward a Cashless Society: A Closer Look at Payment Instrument Economics, AEI-Brookings Joint Center Working Paper No.04-20

22.   Zhanbo Wang (2007), Virtual Currency Appeal to Supervision, *China Computer User,* Issue 7, 2007, pp12-14.

23.   Guofu Yu (2006), Internet Virtual Money and Inflation, *China Computer User,* Issue 44, 2006, pp57-58.

24.   Kuanhai Zhang (2004), *On-line payment and settlement and electronic commerce,* Chongqing University Publishing House, 2004.

25.   Kuanhai Zhang, Haishan Tian (2005), Effects of transaction circulating rate and currency issue quantity under the circumstance of using e-money, The Proceedings of ICEC2005, Xi'an, August 14-16, 2005.

An Analysis on the Implementation of Electronic Supply Chain in International Trade

Hanlin Chen, Lingxiang Kong

The business school, Hubei University, Wuhan, 430062, China

luckhl@yahoo.com.cn

Abstract. The advancement of information technology has allowed firms that participate in supply chain management to share information across organizational boundaries. An innovative transaction process which is electronically supported may lead to efficiency gaining and cost reducing, at the same time it enhances the operational effectiveness. The implementation of electronic supply chain in international trade improves coordination between buyers and sellers and increases transaction efficiency by raising the operational effectiveness. The paper gives us a rough introduction of electronic supply chain. Then it shows us the process of international trade in which an effective electronic supply chain is implemented. Finally, a case study about Dell is brought out to show how to implement E-supply chain in international trade.

1 Introduction

Fewer than 10 years ago, the purchase of a product, using some modes of transport to reach the shopping destinations, selecting the product physically, and then paying for the purchase. Today, many consumers, be they at home, at work, or at some other locations, can go online 24 hours a day, seven days a week, and select and purchase a great assortment of products over the Internet while doing their "shopping". Indeed, it is now possible, in many instances, to buy books, videos, and CDs online as well as to order food from a supermarket or a restaurant in an electronic manner, and have the items delivered afterwards to the desired destinations.

Information technology (IT) allows a greater amount of data to be distributed with increased accuracy and frequency along the supply chains, and for their activities to be synchronized. As a result, the firms in supply chain are able to efficiently coordinate their business decisions and activities and become integrated (Frohlich, 2002[1]; Sahin&Robinson, 2003[2]). A tightly integrated supply chain leads to superior performance and improved competitiveness for each firm in the supply chain (Frohlich, 2002[1]), and many innovative firms have adopted SCM and its integrating mechanisms as a top strategic priority.

Please use the following format when citing this chapter:

Chen, H., Kong, L., 2007, in IFIP International Federation for Information Processing, Volume 251, Integration and Innovation Orient to E-Society Volume1, Wang, W. (Eds), (Boston: Springer), pp. 115-125.

In supply chain management, much of the past debate had centered on the ability of the supply chain to be either "lean" (Womack&Jones, 1996[3]) or "agile" (Goldmanetal, 1995[4]). Lean supply chains on the one hand focus on doing "more with less' by reducing waste through inventory reduction, lean manufacturing, and a just-in-time approach. A lean approach is said to be suitable for markets characterized by predictable demand, high volume and low requirements for product variety. Agile supply chains, on the other hand, are designed for flexibility, emphasizing the supply chain's ability to respond rapidly to changes in demand, both in terms of volume and variety. The market conditions in which companies with agile supply chains find themselves are characterized by volatile demand and high requirements for variety (Christopher, 2000[5]).

Some supply chain scholars also have championed various complementary perspectives in order to resolve problems in collaboration and information sharing, including optimization-, simulation-,and multi-agent-based. Prior research focused primarily on optimization-based techniques and mathematical modeling of operational aspects of information sharing (Maturana&Norrie, 1997[6]). Management Science/Operations Research (MS/OR) researchers have used this approach extensively to identify optimal solutions forgiven situations subject to specific assumptions. This approach is strong in addressing focused sets of problems, such as inventory management, logistics optimization, and production scheduling. Simulation-based approaches allow dynamic modeling of behaviors of supply chain firms with varying degrees of constraints and policies, dealing with diverse contingencies caused by supply and demand uncertain ties. However, they can not generate the design itself, and can only run models with pre-specified parameters and conditions (Harrison, 2001[7]).

The advent of electronic commerce is enabling the world to move closer to the realization of a single, borderless market and is driving the increasing globalization of not only businesses but also supply chains. Indeed, the importance of global issues in supply chain management has been emphasized in several papers (cf. Kogut and Kulatilaka, 1994; Cohen and Mallik, 1997; Nagurney et al., 2003[8]), Recently, Dramatic advances in IT have enabled supply chains to integrate various functions into their total processes within e-business settings (Cagliano, Caniato, &Spina, 2003[9]; Vakharia, 2002[10]). The scholars are paying more attention on supply chain in the setting of electronic commerce, because electronic supply chain is becoming more important. The implementation of electronic supply chain can reduce cost greatly especially in international trade. Now the little research on electronic supply trade is mainly theoretical, and there is little research on the practical area. This paper will present the implementation of electronic supply chain in international trade.

The paper's organization is as follows: Section 2 gives us a definition of electronic supply chain and discusses the electronic global market. Section 3 briefly outlines an electronic trading framework, in which electronic supply chain is implemented. Section 4 focuses on the case study about Dell and compares its electronic supply chain with its traditional supply chain. Section 5 will do a summary about the article and give some advice on the research of electronic supply chain.

2 Electronic Supply Chain and a Global Electronic Market

The advancement of information technology has allowed firms that participate in supply chain management to share information across organizational boundaries, bringing about substantial performance increases. For example, the collection of sales information at the point-of-sale and the sharing of that information via an electronic data interchange have lowered costs in the ordering processes.

2.1 The Growing Importance of Electronic Supply Chain

Firms today increasingly consider supply chain management (SCM) to be a major vehicle to gain a competitive advantage in turbulent markets. While firms have traditionally acted as sole economic entities in the market, they have begun to form strategic alliances with other firms, integrating their business processes, and consolidating their resources. According to the Global Supply Chain Forum, SCM is defined as:

"The integration of key business processes from end user through original suppliers that provides products, services, and information that add value for customers and other stakeholders."(Lambert & Cooper, 2000)

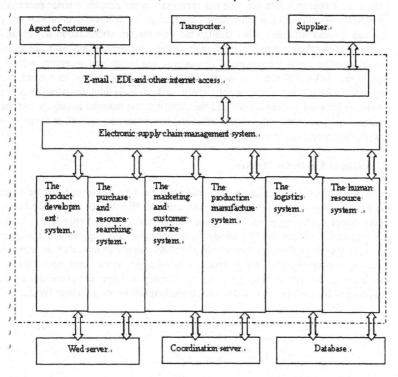

Figure. 1. The frame of electronic supply chain management: from Guan Shurong [11]

Electronic Supply Chain (ESC) is a functional network chain structure pattern consisting of the suppliers, manufactures, and distributors, which integrates the key business processes from raw materials purchase, middle products and final products manufacturing to the ender users'comsuming through controlling the information flow, the physical flow and the fund flow. It is an organizational connection network which provides the end users with the products and services.

ESC is mainly realized through conforming electronic commerce and supply chain. The conformity angle contains the entire organization flow, such as product development design, purchase and resources search, marketing and the customer service, the production manufacture and the daily arrangement, the logistics supply, the manpower resources and so on.

Through the clarifying states of the related content about electronic supply chain management, this article gives us the brief framework of the electronic supply chain management system, as it is shown in figure 1. From the figure we can see that the agent customer, the transporter and the supplier can exchange their information through E-mail, EDI and other international access without visiting the partners physically. Electronic supply chain management system concludes the subsystems of the product development, the purchase and resource searching, the marketing and customer service, the production manufacture, the logistics and the human resource. This is the company's intranet. The enterprise can coordinate his interior processes through the system, and the subsystems are managed by different departments, they also can connect with each other through the web servers, coordination servers and database. Using the electronic supply chain system, the departments also can know the information about the products' production, marketing and inventory without face to face talking. It can improve the efficiency of the company. In a word, the implementation of electronic supply chain system is helpful to coordinate the purchases between the enterprises and the suppliers, the material managers and the transport companies, the sales organization and its wholesalers, as well as company's daily activities and customer services.

2.2 A Global Electronic Market

SCM has gained importance in the marketing field as being one of the main marketing processes that has a positive influence on shareholder value. And lately, International marketing place have gained importance for electronic supply chain management. For example, Wildemann et al. presented some application examples for international marketing place within electronic supply chains, such as using e-auctions, online-brokers, e-catalogues, or e-freight stock exchanges for e-procurement, e-logistics, and customer relationship management. Lancioni et al. have argued hat companies do not use the Internet much for supply chain issues.

A B2B eMarketplace - Supply Chain

Figure. 2. Electronic marketplace supply chain: from the view of Grieger [12]

Fig.2 gives us a detailed supply chain in electronic market place. We could see that in international trade process the major buyers and the major suppliers can contact with each other and do most of their businesses through the internet. For the major buyers, they can carry on this procurement such as a product search, shopping cart feature, purchase order automation, automation of approval process and so on. For the major suppliers, they also can finish these applications, such as product catalog management, inventory availability, product configuration, automation of purchasing process, order trading service and so on. For the small-medium enterprises, they also can do market transactions through the wed browser. It can reduce the trading cost largely.

3 The Implementation of E-supply Chain in International Trade

Supply chain scholars have championed various complementary perspectives in order to resolve problems in collaboration and information sharing. (Maturana & Norrie, 1997). Lancioni et al. surveyed 1000 US firms that were members of the Council of Logistics Management regarding their application of Internet technologies within their supply chains. They found that Internet adoption had increased from 1999 to 2001, moving away from indiscriminate use of Internet-related processes towards more focused, strategic applications and the development of precise and measurable goals. Their study, ''Strategic Internet Trends in Supply Chain Management'', shows that beyond cost reductions, the use of electronic supply chain increases productivity and profits for participating firms. The Internet

allows firms to customize service solutions for their customers, which enhances the
overall value and competitive position throughout the supply chain network.

The international trade process includes looking for the trade partners,
purchases, goods transportation and track, payments and post-sale services. We will
explain how electronic supply chain is implemented in international trade process, as
follows.

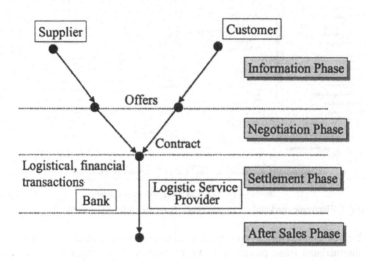

Figure. 3. Phases of market transactions: comparison of Schmidan Lindemann [13] and
Scharl [14].

3.1 Looking For the Trade Partners

Looking for the trade partners is the first step for developing international trade. In
the traditional way, the buyers or the sellers have to pay the extremely high price, for
seeking the appropriate trade partners. But looking for the trade partners using the
electronic commerce may save much manpower and many physical resources,
without limitation of time and location. On one hand, the enterprises can provide
supply and demand information about the related products and the services to the
potential customers in the world by establishing their own websites or drawing
support from the related electronic commerce platform of international trade,
attracting correlated customers to do business with each other. On the other hand, the
enterprises may search for all kinds of economy and trade information on the internet,
seeking the ideal trade partners. With the development of electronic commerce, the
role of "the Guangzhou trade fair" was weakened in some content. The domestic
importers and exporters may find the overseas trade partners without going abroad.

The overseas customer may also easily find the most ideal Chinese Import and export Enterprises.

3.2 Electronic Purchases

The electronic purchase is trying to realize the enterprises' electronic purchase of the products, the raw materials, the unproductive products and the services by the purchase process on the internet. It may simplify the distribution, reduce the cost and improve the efficiency. A completely developed electronic purchase system should be able to automate the purchase process. Present electronic purchase software may be divided into 3 categories. The first one is buyer desktop purchase system. It may help the enterprise staffs to carry on the purchase through the table computer. The second is buyer central purchase management. It helps manager and the buyer to manage the purchase process, analyze transaction information and manage the suppliers. The third is sellers' application software. It helps the manufacturers and distributors to sell products through the network. It usually includes the electronic catalogue, the electronic transaction order and so on.

3.3 Electronic Transportation and Track

Generally the electronic transportation and the track establish the intranet of foreign trade transportation through the ports. Electronic data interchange (EDI) is being used in booking shipping space, handling containers and ships, tracking the cargos, transmitting documents, finance and settlement. With the application of merchandise tracking system on internet, the customers and their trade partners can directly get inquire about the information of the cargo's conditions, get the transportation and commercial partners' information which reduces the time of cargo stock and the time of the cargo customs clearance, and speeds up the trade distribution. The electronic management of foreign economy and trade transportation widens the electronic commerce by the operation process of trade chain. United Package Service Company (UPS) is a typical case, which carries out "The entire process supervision". Namely, it is using the company's automotive packages tracking system to monitor the packages during the entire delivering process.

3.4 On-line Payments

On-line payments in the international trade is extremely convenient for the intangible products, such as software, music, film and consult services, which can be directly transmitted on internet. It may save many personnel's expenses. At present, there is not any domestic enterprise that can completely realize the on-line payment in international trade, which needs to overcome the technical and security problems. The on-line payment requests electronic finance. The E-bank will be established ultimately. So the domestic and foreign banks are adjusting their own strategies to meet the increasingly high requests of a bank in the electronic international trade. Now there are banks which developed totally depending on the development of intranet. With the increasing development of network security technologies, the on-line payment' superiority will be displayed more obviously in the international trade.

3.5 Electronic Post-sale Services

The electronic post-sale services mean that Internet is used in the post-sale service to collect the information of the customers and the products and store them into the database. Putting the information about the product literatures, technology reports and ordering on the internet not only makes the post-sale service personnel save time to deal with more complex matters and manage the customer relationship, but also provides the new business increase for the enterprise and promotes customers' satisfaction and loyalty.

3.6 Transactions Management Network

The activities of international trade involve many government departments as well as the finance, the insurance, the transportation and other service sectors. The management of international trade transactions includes the related market laws and regulations, the taxation collection, the declaration and the transaction dispute arbitration. In the traditional operation process, the enterprises must alone deal with each related department which surely spends massive manpower, the physical resources, and takes the massive time. Electronic business makes the international trade transactions achieve network management paperless. The engaged enterprises can directly handle with the banks, the insurance companies, the taxation departments and the transportation companies to manage the related electronic bills and the electronic documents through internet, which has greatly saved the time and the expense in transaction process.

4 A Case Study: Dell Corporation's Electronic Marketing

This section highlights a short case study about Dell Corporation that describes implementation of electronic supply chain in international trade.

An important success for Dell Corporation is that Dell successfully applies the internet to the company management. The following is the organization network which starts from the suppliers to Dell Corporation, then arrives the customer. That's Dell's supply chain which is established based on the network and the modern technology.

From the following chart, we can see that, compared with the traditional supply chain, there are main two differences: (1) There is no wholesalers and retailers in the supply chain established by Dell. Dell Corporation as the manufacture sells its products to the customers directly. Dell's proud of its selling philosophy----directly selling the computers to the users, removing the retailers' profits and saving the money for the consumers. (2) There is a new distribution level: "the agent server".

They neither provide the products to the customers; nor purchase the products from Dell Corporation. They only provide the services and the supports to the customers. This is the inevitable result of Dell Corporation "outside contracting approach". It enables Dell to provide the high quality post-sale services to customers; at the same time it also enables Dell to avoid facing the problem of "the excessively huge organizational structure".

By this way, the components suppliers, Dell Corporation and the agent servers constituted a "virtual" enterprise. They improve their coordination and achieve the optimized resources disposition through electronic data exchange. Simultaneously, they also reduce the costs; provide the high quality products and the services for the customers. Dell Corporation succeeds in realizing "Virtual integration" between the suppliers and the customers, and forming an effective supply chain.

At present Dell's approximately one third technical support works and over 70% order inquiries are carried out on internet. Website "www.dell.com" accepts about 40,000 emails each month. About 90,000 files are downloaded by users each week and global order inquiries are approximately 100,000 pieces. Over 40,000 enterprises, government departments and the organizational customers have adopted the DELL special user services in the world, dealing with all the businesses with the Dell on line. Because of the cost reduction and the improvement of the productivity, they may save expenditures as high as several million US dollars every year.

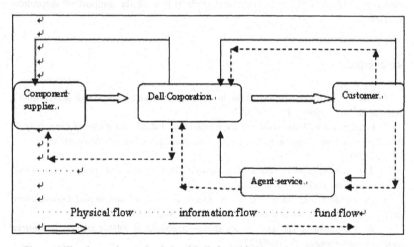

Figure.4. The electronic supply chain of Dell: from Liu Hongqiang [15]

5 Conclusions

This paper has introduced the definition of supply chain and induced the essence of electronic supply chain. ESC is an organization network, which integrates the key business processes. It provides the mutual connection in the activities and processes of providing the products and services to the end users. Then, the paper gives us the implementation of ESC in international trade. The international trade process includes looking for the trade partners, purchases, goods transportation and track, payments and post-sale services. The paper gives a detailed implementation of ESC, such as the electronic purchase, on-line payment and so on. Finally, there is a case studying about Dell. Dell is a successful example. It uses the electronic supply chain to sale his products to the world, propagandizing products and receiving the orders on-line. After a detailed analysis of Dell's electronic supply chain, we could get the results that the implement of ESC in Dell Corporation have improved the efficacy and improve its performance greatly.

Transaction processes in international trade are complex and, as a consequence, often inefficient. From the analysis of ESC we can know that the application of ESC in international trade leads the international trade become paperless and electronic. The suppliers and the buyers can both realize automation, which is a great advantage in trade. In today's global markets, having an effective ESC can be a source of superior advantage. It can save a lot of time and money for the traders.

This paper presents the implementation of ESC in international trade from the practical perspective. The benefits brought by ESC are visible. But the building of the electronic supply chain system needs information technology and money costs. Maybe it cannot be taken by the small and medium enterprises. So it's better to do some survey about the small and medium enterprises, and the benefits from the implementation of ESC in international trade still need the support of theoretical research.

References

1. M. T. Frohlich, "E-Integration in the supply chain: barriers and performance", *Decision Sciences*, 33(4), 537–556 (2002).

2. F. Sahin and E. P. Robinson , "Flow coordination and information sharing in supply chains: review, implications, and direction for future research", *Decision Sciences*, 33(4), 505–537(2003).

3. J. P. Womack and D. Jones, *Lean thinking: Banish waste and create wealth in your corporation*, New York: Simon and Schuster (1996).

4. S. Goldman, R. Nagel and K. A. Preiss, *competitors and virtual organizations: Strategies for enriching the customer*, New York: Van Nostrand Reinhold (1995)

5. M. Christopher, "The agile supply chain—competing in volatile markets", *Industrial Marketing Management*, 29, 37–44(2000).

6. F. P. Maturana and D. H. Norrie, "Distributed decision-making using the contract net within a mediator architecture", *Decision Support Systems*, 20, 53–64(1997).

7. T. P. Harrison, "Global supply chain design [Special issue: supply chain management]", *Information Systems Frontiers*, 3(4), 413–416(2001).

8. A. Nagurney, J. Cruz and D. Matsypura, "Dynamics of global supply chains upper networks" ,*Mathematical and Computer Modelling,*37, 963–983(2003).

9. R. Cagliano,F. Caniato and G. Spina, "E-business strategy: how companies are shaping their supply chain through the Internet", *International Journal of Operations & Production Management*, 23(10), 1142–1162(2003).

10. P. Press, Amsterdam and A. J. Vakharia, "The Netherlands E-business and supply chain management", *Decision Sciences*, 33(4), 495–504 (2002).

11. S. R. Guan , W. Zhang and X. Y. Huang, "An Effective Way to Optimize Business Supply Chain: E-SCM", *Journal of Northeastern University* (Social Science), Jan., Vol 16, No.1 (2004) (in Chinese).

12. M. Grieger, "Electronic marketplaces—an overview and a call for supply chain management research", In: Stefansson G, Tilanus B, editors. Collaborationin logistics, connecting islands using information technology. Proceedings of the 2001 Nordic Logistics Conference (Nofoma). Go¨tebor: Chalmers University of Technology (paper23) (2001).

13. S. B. Schmid and M. A. Lindemann, "Elements of a reference model for electronic markets", 31st Hawaii International Conference on System Sciences (*HICCSS*-31). Hawaii, USA: IEEE Computer Society Press.193–201 (1998).

14. A. Scharl, "Evolutionary Web development", *Applied computing*. London: Springer (2000).

15. H. Q. Liu, *Dell's marketing*, the economy and science press, Beijing, 3, 65-84, 208-209(2003) (in Chinese)

Research and Design of Multimedia NSS for E-Commerce

Hanxiao Shi ,Guiyi Wei

Computer and Information Engineering College, Zhejiang Gongshang
University, Hangzhou, 310035, China
hxshi@mail.zjgsu.edu.cn

Abstract. As the Internet has become mainstream, so has Electronic commerce (EC) become an important part of conducting business. NSS facing EC will be a very important subsystem during the process of EC development. This paper introduces the current research situation about NSS, stresses on the whole system architecture and key technologies, sets forth solution scheme about some important problem, such as multiparty cooperation text technology and inter-stream synchronization. Our goal is to develop a NSS prototype and to test its feasibility in simulation environment. It also creates a user-friendly interface for Graphic User's Interface (GUI). The implementation prototype system demonstrates excellent performance.

1 Introduction

With the great development of Internet and EC, trade mode will have a thorough change. A business transaction consists of three main phases, namely searching for potential business partners, negotiating about contract conditions and finalizing the business contract, and fulfilling the contract. Negotiation in traditional as well as in electronic commerce is a complex communication process. In the networking environment, the process of business negotiation will be an online mode in stead of the traditional face-to-face mode. The research on EC-oriented negotiation support system (NSS) is an aid for EC, as well as a new explorer for the development of NSS. This project is very important in the domain of EC and related business.

Apparently, improvement of network infrastructure is a base to implement online NSS. We propose an interaction platform over audio-video based on multimedia technology, and present a function mode of multiparty cooperation text technology (MCTT) and third party authority technology, which can realize effective E-Contract. Otherwise, take advantage of NSS, to give better service to any negotiators. As a result, the research of EC-oriented NSS can realize visible negotiations in different place. In a word, it saves the negotiations cost, enhances the negotiations efficiency.

Please use the following format when citing this chapter:

Shi, H., Wei, G., 2007, in IFIP International Federation for Information Processing, Volume 251, Integration and Innovation Orient to E-Society Volume1, Wang, W. (Eds), (Boston: Springer), pp. 126-133.

This paper has a deep research on multimedia technology, MCTT, negotiation server design and so on, proposes a whole negotiation flow structure, implements a multimedia-based NSS.

2 Related Work

Negotiation is a decision process in which two or more parties make individual decisions and interact with each other for mutual gain. NSS has introduced advanced computer-information technology and decision support system (DSS) theory into the domain of negotiation collision; it provides some question-solution tools [1-3] for any negotiators through many sides of technology and theory, such as computer-human interaction, operation research, DSS, behavioral science, psychology, and so on.

In general, NSSs have the following basic features[4]: (1) a formalism to describe the negotiation activity in terms of choices and outcomes, (2) a way to generally characterize the associated outcome probabilities, and (3) a methodology for processing the model to evaluate the expected values of choice alternatives. NSSs normally assist negotiators to assess situations, generate and evaluate options, and implement decisions. However, most NSSs do not consider the generation of contracts, which we consider to be the primary aim of negotiation in ecommerce, as an outcome of negotiation process. For example, NEGOTIATOR [5] seeks to guide negotiators to move their individual goals and judgments to enhance the chance of achieving a common solution. It supports problem adaptation through information sharing, concession making, and problem restructuring. However, NEGOTIATOR only helps the negotiators make decisions without any support to other entities involved in negotiation, such as contracts. INSPIRE (InterNeg Support Program for Intercultural Research) [2] is a Web-based prototype for supporting inter-cultural as well as intra-cultural negotiations. It can conduct negotiation anonymously, evaluate the goodness of an offer, and review the history of a negotiation. INSPIRE supports the communication among negotiators by exchanging messages, but we propose direct interactions among different entities with Web services.

Recently, researchers are developing negotiation protocols for agent automation in e-commerce environments. Bartolini et al. [6] develop an agent-based software framework for automated negotiation, aiming for reuse. Tamma et al. [7] further propose negotiation protocols to be expressed in terms of shared ontology among agents. However, they only showed an example protocol for English auction in the paper with rule-based axioms and did not detail their negotiation process support and management environment. Neither did they present Web services implementation frameworks that support both human and programmatic users as in this paper. Griffel et al. [8] present an application of contract negotiation by mobile agents. A contract is represented as an object that can be accessed by the negotiation parties. Each party has the opportunity to change or insert clauses. They only provide a conceptual view of their approach, without any supporting formal model.

Gradually NSS based on web and E-commerce become to a research focus, there are not a few researches on this domain. References [2, 9, and 10] show CBSS and

INSPIRE (Carleton University) which have referred to some related researches. These references propose some specifics about these NSS: (1) Provide a simultaneous distribution negotiation; (2) Have a real-time multiparty interaction; (3) Provide a structural negotiation procedure; (4) Provide some security functions, such as identity recognition, data secrecy. Reference [11] proposes an evolution computation method in electronic business negotiation, which makes use of negotiation agents to select a best negotiation strategy from strategy-base according to enterprise targets and benefits.

Reference [12] proposes a NSS model based on B2B mode – Negoisst, which supports negotiators to do complicated E-Negotiation. It has three main functions: auto-questioning, intelligent negotiation agents, negotiation support. Multi-negotiation and file management are implemented by communication technology and information system.

3   Analysis and Design of Multimedia NSS

3.1   Work Flow of Negotiation Support Systems

Negotiation support systems do not automate the negotiation process but provide IT support for complex negotiations, leaving the control over the negotiation process with the human negotiators. There are several participators during a negotiation, and each of them is a decision maker, they analyze and judge the situation of negotiation, and make decisions. From the decision-supporting view, the process of negotiation can be considered as a decision-making process of negotiators, and it can be divided into 4 stages: conceptualizing negotiating problem; expressing negotiating problem; problem solving; analyzing the solving plan. Negotiating process starts from conceptualize negotiating problem till analyzing the solving plan in theory, and go along step by step. However, the feedback and circle in fact is much more complex than this, during which multimedia and cooperation text technology are used. During the process of negotiation, participators reach an agreement on problems need to negotiate, and this is a necessity to farther the negotiation. The negotiate model is shown in Figure. 1.

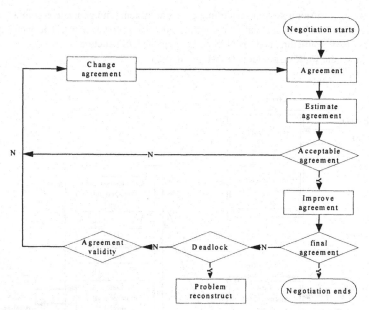

Figure. 3. A negotiation system model

3.2   Function Models of NSS

This is a net-based NSS, written in Java and implemented in a client – server architecture. This system contains several function models as follows:

(1) User management model: including user registration, user information modification, etc
(2) Client to client audio and video interaction model: simulating face to face communication, and all this data transfer without the server.
(3) Character interaction model: supplying traditional network communicating tool, and keep all the interaction information on the server if needed.
(4) Cooperation text edit model: realizing online user's synchronous and asynchronous data interchange.
(5) Data communication management model: supporting all the communications between clients (negotiators) and server.
(6) E-contract management model: after editing and conforming the cooperation text, an e-contract will be created based on this. Realizing e-contract interchange on Internet.

3.3   System Architecture

NSS facing EC will be a very important subsystem during the process of EC development, the client access the website by web browser, download the client of NSS, and connect the server after installing. Besides, the system supply mutual supports with some models like Internet information service system, electronic identity identification system, electronic payment system, and generate e-contract as a part of EC archives, to realize e-contract interchange on Internet. The web part adopts the B/S structure, and the NSS part adopts the C/S structure.

The whole working model is shown in Figure. 2.

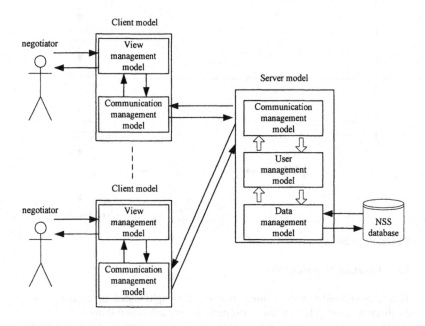

Figure. 2. System architecture of NSS

At the client side, system can be divided into two models: communication management and view expression; At the server side, system includes communication management model, user management model, and data management model. The communication management model is responsible for the information interchange between client and server, and the key part of it is a communication protocol, through this protocol, the data flow between client and server fulfill all kinds of functions like encode and decode, complete control orders, transfer data. The user management model plays a center role in supervising communication models and harmonizing the information interchanging between different users. The data management model is responsible for the data interchange between database, and reading, storing, SQL querying etc.

4 Key Technologies of System

4.1 Multiparty Cooperation Text Technology

Real-time cooperation text editing system (like Grove [13] and Reduce [14]) is a very important part during the applications of computer supported cooperative work (CSCW), it allows a group of cooperators from different places to edit shared files at the same time. It has such characteristics as (1) rapid response; (2) distribution; (3) highly concurrent; (4) consistency. In order to reach the goal of rapid response, full-copy structure is frequently used to deal with shared files in cooperation editing system, which means copy shared files to every participator. This structure allows operations to be executed locally, and then spread to other participator, the response time is very short. However, some problems may be raised under this structure, an arithmetic of concurrent control is needed to keep the consistency of files.

This system adopt mark method to realize MCTT [15], through marking the shared files, it will hide the changed part, no matter how many operations have been executed before. This assures the file under operation is exactly the same one the moment before the operation works, to realize the maintenance of operation process

4.2 Synchronization of Audio and Video Stream

A system supporting audio and video communication based on H.323 protocol. After collecting and encoding, audio and video data arrive the receiver through Internet, and store to each play-buffer after decoding. The inter-stream synchronization is controlled by media synchronization between these buffers.

During a multimedia system, there are many media streams, the independent stream is named main-media stream; and during playing, those who depend on this stream are named sub-media stream. Main-media stream plays at a normal speed, to keep synchronization, the sub-media stream may need to jump or pause. During multimedia communication system, considering our ear is relatively more sensitive to sound pause, repeat and playing rate adjustment, audio stream is usually regarded as the main-media stream, and other streams including video are treated as the sub-media stream, to realize the synchronization by adjusting playing time. As the main-media stream, audio adopts G.723.1 encode standard, and the sub-media stream, video adopts H.263 encode standard. When the Internet is unobstructed, it can assure the video and audio stream transfer with the settled rapid, the delay is basically fixed, the jitter is small, and the space between audio and video in both sender and receiver keeps the same: that means media data are almost integrated. When the Internet is blocked, the inter-media asynchronism may exist, and some technologies must be taken to realize the synchronization. In this system, time stamp in RTP package head is used to solve this problem. The detail algorithm is aimed at optimizing and dealing with sub-media stream (mainly video data) comparing with the main-media stream. Tv: the time stamp of video frame arrived, Ta: the time stamp of audio frame now, Td: the tolerance of audio frame asynchronism.

```
VideoFrameArrived:              //video frame arrive
    Tv=getVideoFrameTime ();        //get the time stamp of video frame now
    if ( Tv < Ta - Td )
        Video data package lag, so to drop;
        else if (Tv > Ta + Td )          // ahead of time;
        {
                VideoFrameWaitNum + + ;   //the number of pending package in buffer plus 1
        }
        else
            play(v);          // the audio and video are synchronous, play video.
```

The process of audio stream is relatively simple, as soon as audio data arrive, the audio device plays them as well as system needs to check video data. If video frame is not null at same time, video data is played as mentioned above.

5 Summaries

In this paper, we have introduced the concept and development of NSS through laying out some representative works and some researches on NSS. We have also pointed out their respective merits and shortcomings based on comparison and analysis. In the meanwhile, we have designed a NSS's work flow and some function models. At last, we have brought forward the system realization architecture of NSS, and discussed some key technologies, such as multiparty cooperation text technology, inter-media synchronization, and so on. By simulating experiment in intranet, this system realized online-negotiation with multimedia integration, offering each negotiator a kind interface and multi-choices of assistant function. And after a period of testing, this system works well. In some degree, it meets the real-time need of NSS, and has some important significance in promoting the development of china EC.

Acknowledgement

The authors wish to thank the support of Zhejiang Provincial Education Department for Scientific Research Fund under grant Number 20061078 and the Natural Science Foundation of Zhejiang Province, P. R. China for the National Science Fund under grant Number Y105356. We would also like to thank our referees for their helpful comments and suggestions.

References

1. M.M. Delaney., "An Empirical Study of the Efficacy of A Computerized Negotiation Support System (NSS)", *Decision Support Systems*, 20(3), 185-197 (1997).

G.E. Kersten and S.J. Noronha, WWW-based Negotiation Support: Design, Implementation and Use, *Decision Support Systems*, 25(2), 135-154 (1999).

3. Y.W.S. Stanley, C.B. Huang and J. Hammer., A Replicable Web-Based Negotiation Server for E-Commerce, *IEEE Thirty-third Hawaii International Conference on System Sciences* (HICSS-33), 212-221 (2000).

4. InterNeg, For and about Negotiations (2000), http://interneg.carleton.ca.

T.X. Bui and M.F. Shakun, Negotiation Processes, Evolutionary Systems Design, and Negotiator, Group Decision and Negotiation, 5, 339- 353 (1996).

5. C. Bartolini, C. Preist, and N.R. Jennings, Architecting for Reuse: A Software Framework for Automated Negotiation, *Proceedings of the 3rd International Workshop on Agent-Oriented Software Engineering*, 87–98 (2002).

6. V. Tamma, M. Wooldridge and I. Dickinson, *An Ontology-Based Approach to Automated Negotiation*, Proceedings of the Fourth International Workshop on Agent-Mediated Elctronic Commerce (AMEC-2002), 219—237 (2002).

7. F. Griffel, M.T. Tu, M. Münke, M.M. da Silva, M. Merz. and W. Lamersdorf, *Electronic Contract Negotiation as An Application Niche for Mobile Agents*, Proceedings of the First International Enterprise Distributed Object Computing, 354 – 365 (1997).

8.G.E Kerstern, Negotiation Support Systems and Negotiation Agents, Modèles et Systèmes Multi-Agents pour la Gestion de l'Environement et des Territoires, *Cemagref ENGREF, Clermont-Ferrand*, France, 307-316 (1998).

9. Y. Yuan, R.B. Suarga and N. Archer, A Web-Based Negotiation Support System, *International journal of electronic markets*, 8(3), 13-17 (1998).

10.Y.A. Salem and A.A. Al-Fahoum, An Evolutionary Computation Approach to Electricity Trade Negotiation, *Advances in Engineering Software*, 36(3), 173–179(2005).

11.M. Schoop, A. Jertila and T. List, Negoisst:, A Negotiation Support System for Electronic Business-to-Business Negotiations in E-Commerce, *Data and Knowledge Engineering*, 47(3), 371-401 (2003).

12. C.A. Ellis and S.J. Gibbs, *Concurrency Control in Groupware Systems*, Proceedings of 19th ACM SIGMOD Conference of Management of Data, 399- 407 (1989).

13.C. Sun, X. Jia, Y. Zhang and D. Chen, Achieving Convergence, Causality-Preservation, and Intention-Preservation in. Real-Time Cooperative Editing Systems, *ACM Transactions on Computer-Human Interaction*, 5(1), 63-108 (1998).

14. X.Y Wu and N. Gu, A Concurrency Control Method Based on Document Marking, *Journal of Computer Research and Development*, 39(12), 1663-1667 (2002).

Two kinds of Online Retailers' Price Competition on B2C Market

Hao Fu[1], Jieyao Ding[2], Leilei Liu[2]

1 Hao Fu, Herbert A.Simon & Reinhard Selten Behavioral Decision
Research Lab, School of Economics and Management,
Southwest Jiaotong University, ChengDu 610031, China
86-28-87600895; 13808177037; Haofu12@126.com

2 Jieyao Ding, Leilei Liu, Herbert A.Simon & Reinhard Selten
Behavioral Decision Research Lab, School of Economics and
Management, Southwest Jiaotong University, ChengDu 610031,
China

Abstract. Using game theory as research tool, this paper investigates deeply on price competition behavior between Multi-Channel Retailers (MCRs) and Pure Online Retailers (Dotcoms) on e-commerce market, elicits four kinds of market structures. Furthermore, it gives out perfect equilibrium prices as well as market scale under each condition of market structure. On this basis, two related propositions and two related conclusions are pointed out. First, it gets MCRs' and Dotcoms' critical prices. Secondly, as the penetrate rate of e-business increasing, two kind retailers' perfect prices will decrease, and there exists a stable relationship between the ratios of speed declining.

1. Introduction

At the beginning of Internet arisen, basing on the cognitive of Internet information technology's characteristic, people hold that on the e-business market, through investing even less than on traditional economic, consumers can search and face with more suppliers which may leads competition among suppliers. As a result, the consumers can get a lower price. In terms of economics, comparing with traditional off-line trade mode, e-business possesses higher market efficiency and lower market friction, reduces trade and search cost effectively, and consequently decreases suppliers' monopoly profit [1,2]. The so-called "free-friction trade hypothesis" which can be tested directly through comparing price level on e-business market attracts many researchers doing theoretical and empirical studies on comparing price competition between online retailers and off-line retailers [3]. It can be concluded that existent researches on modeling the price competition between traditional retailers and online retailers have been developed sufficiently [4].

Please use the following format when citing this chapter:

Fu, H., Ding, J., Liu, L., 2007, in IFIP International Federation for Information Processing, Volume 251, Integration and Innovation Orient to E-Society Volume1, Wang, W. (Eds), (Boston: Springer), pp. 134-146.

However it is noticeable that, recent years, along with online market's expanding, more and more traditional retailers enter into B2C market. As multi-channel retailers (MCRs), they compete directly with pure online retailers (Dotcoms). But there is little research on the price competition between these two kind of online retailers within online market's internal. In existing references, an important analytical model and empirical analysis paper investigate on price competition between MCRs and Dotcoms based on Hoterlling model [5]. As the author said, their "analytic model is based on Hotelling's linear city framework and is limited by its assumptions. Relaxing some of the assumption can make the model richer, albeit more complex". Moreover, Friberg [6] gave out a more general model about price competition between MCRs and Dotcoms, and did relevant empirical researches. But in his research work, the effect of e-business's penetrate rate (equal to number of Internet users/total population) on price competition is not taken into consider. Therefore, regarding two kind of retailers internal e-business market as research object, based on Friberg [6,7] and Cheng Yun's [8]modeling methodology about price competition between traditional off-line retailers and pure online retailers, this paper makes further development and generalization in order to get a more clear recognize on price competition between MCRs and Dotcoms.

According to O'keefe and McEachern's[9] consumer's decision making model, when consumers are conscious about the imbalance between ideal consuming and practical consuming, they face with channel choosing problem " where to buy" after decide what goods to buy for the purpose of offsetting this imbalance. Therefore, we suppose that: in the era of e-economic, when consumers who can purchase online choose their shopping mode (where to buy), there are two layers for them to make choice:1) purchase online or off-line; 2) if choose purchase online, then weigh the two online purchasing channels: MCR and Dotcoms. So researching on consumers' decision making between two online purchasing channels, this paper boosts existed results from working over price competition between traditional retailers and online retailers into two kind of retailers' competition in online market internal.

2. Hypothesis

Basing on previous statement, we first divide retail market into two parts: traditional off-line market and e-business online market. Then by setting up game model, compartmentalize market share among off-line channel and on-line channel respectively. Further, do more game analysis on price competition between MCRs and Dotcoms. In short, this paper divides the retail market into the following structures (figure 1):

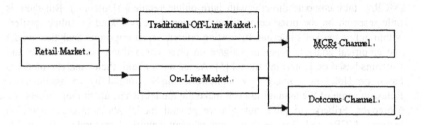

Figure. 1 Channel Division for Retail Market

According to consumers' choices—online/offline and different parameter relationships, various market structures are built. Consumers who choose purchasing online will make second layer choices—MCRs or Dotcoms. Concretely, when $\theta_e \geqslant \theta_t$ (θ_e, Utility consumers gain when they purchase online; θ_t, Utility consumers gain when they purchase off-line), there are $v(1-\hat{\theta})$ (v degree of e-business is actualized; θ critical evaluate value of consumers who choose e-business) consumers who choose purchase online; when $\theta_e < \theta_t$, there are $v(1-\theta_e)$ consumers who choose purchase online. For simple, under these two conditions, this paper analysis further on price competition between MCRs and Dotcoms.

For the consumers who surely purchase online (online consumer), there are two kinds of online retailers –MCRs and Dotcoms on e-business market, therefore they have to choose purchasing channel from MCRs and Dotcoms.

Suppose utility function that online consumers choose MCRs or Dotcoms

$$U(\theta) = \begin{cases} \theta - P_m - t_m\theta \\ \theta - P_d - t_d\theta \end{cases}$$

1) θ, consumer's evaluation on commodity ($0 \leq \theta \leq 1$), utility that consumer gains when purchase a commodity. Meanwhile hypotheses is θ uniformity distributed on [0, 1].

2) P_m, commodity's price when consumer purchases on MCRs,

P_d commodity's price when consumer purchases on Dotcoms.

3) t_m, commodity's opportunity cost coefficient when consumer purchases on MCRs ($0 < t_m < 1$);

t_d, commodity's opportunity cost coefficient when consumer purchases on Dotcoms ($0 < t_d < 1$);

Therefore, consumers' critical value evaluations on MCRs and Dotcoms are respectively

$$\theta_m = \frac{P_m}{1-t_m}; \qquad \theta_d = \frac{P_d}{1-t_d}$$

Next, we analysis different market structures formed by price competition between MCRs and Dotcoms based on the value of θ_m and θ_d.

3 Division of market structure

3.1 When the number of online consumer is $v(1-\hat{\theta})$,

3.1.1 When $\theta_m \geq \theta_d$ ($\theta_e = \theta_d$)

Here, the consumer whose critical evaluation value is θ_m or on the right of the axis can choose both MCRs and Dotcoms which means $v(1-\theta_m)$ consumers can choose either way. For these consumers, when they choose MCRs, it is necessary that

$$\theta - t_m\theta - P_m \geq \theta - t_d\theta - P_d,$$

that's $(t_d - t_m)\theta \geq P_m - P_d.$

Therefore, when $t_d - t_m > 0$, the consumer whose value evaluation is between $((P_m - P_d)/(t_d - t_m), 1)$ will choose MCRs, and the consumer whose value evaluation is between $(\hat{\theta}, (P_m - P_d)/(t_d - t_m))$ will choose Dotcoms.

When $t_d - t_m < 0$, the consumer whose value evaluation is between $(\hat{\theta}, (P_m - P_d)/(t_d - t_m))$ will choose MCRs, and the consumer whose value evaluation is between $((P_m - P_d)/(t_d - t_m), 1)$ will choose Dotcoms.

Concretely, because $\theta_m \geq \theta_d$, $P_m/(1 - t_m) \geq P_d/(1 - t_d)$, then $(P_m - P_d)(1 - t_m) \geq (t_d - t_m)P_m$

When $t_d - t_m > 0$, $(P_m - P_d)/(t_d - t_m) \geq \theta_m$, here critical evaluation of the consumers who choose MCRs finally is $\check{\theta} = (P_m - P_d)/(t_d - t_m)$. Price competition in MCRs and Dotcoms form the market structure as follows,

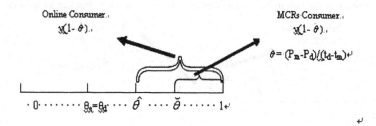

Online Consumer.   MCRs Consumer.
$v(1-\check{\theta})$. $v(1-\check{\theta})$.

$\check{\theta} = (P_m - P_d)/((t_d - t_m)$

· 0· · · · · · · $\theta_e = \theta_d$· · · · $\hat{\theta}$ · · · · $\check{\theta}$ · · · · · · 1

Figure. 2. Market Structure One Formed from Price Competition Between MCRs and Dotcoms

when $t_d - t_m < 0$, $(P_m - P_d)/(t_d - t_m) \leq \theta_m$, here consumers who choose MCRs finally is empty which means MCRs's market share is zero. We focus on analysis of competition between MCRs and Dotcoms in online market and this condition is excluded from our research area, so we don't take it into consider.

Market Structure One:

Under the condition that the number of online consumer is $v(1-\hat{\theta})$, $\theta_m \geq \theta_d$, when and only when $t_d - t_m > 0$, there exists a market structure that MCRs and Dotcoms coexist. Then, there are $v(1-\check{\theta})$ consumers choose purchasing on MCRs, and there are $v(\breve{\theta}-\hat{\theta})$ consumers choose purchasing on Dotcoms.

3.1.2 When $\theta_m<\theta_d$ ($\theta_e=\theta_m$)

Here, the consumer whose critical evaluation value is θ_d or on the right of the axis can choose both MCRs and Dotcoms which means $v(1-\theta_d)$ consumers can choose either way. For these consumers, when they choose MCRs, it is necessary that

$$\theta-t_m\theta-P_m\geq\theta-t_d\theta-P_d$$

So that $\quad$ $(t_d-t_m)\,\theta\geq P_m-P_d$

Therefore, when $t_d-t_m>0$, the consumer whose value evaluation is between $((P_m-P_d)/(t_d-t_m),1)$will choose MCRs, and the consumer whose value evaluation is between $(\hat{\theta},(P_m-P_d)/(t_d-t_m))$ will choose Dotcoms.

When $t_d-t_m<0$, the consumer whose value evaluation is between $(\hat{\theta},(P_m-P_d)/(t_d-t_m))$ will choose MCRs, and the consumer whose value evaluation is between $((P_m-P_d)/(t_d-t_m),1)$ will choose Dotcoms.

$\because \theta_m<\theta_d \therefore P_m/(1-t_m)<P_d/(1-t_d) \therefore (1-t_d)\,P_m<(1-t_m)\,P_d$

$P_m-P_d<(\,t_d\,P_m-t_m\,P_m)+(t_m P_m-t_m P_d) \quad (1-t_m)\,(P_m-P_d)<(t_d-t_m)\,P_m$

So that: when $t_d-t_m>0$, that $(P_m-P_d)/(t_d-t_m)<\theta_m=\theta_e$

Because at this time, the number of consumer who choose Dotcoms is $(\hat{\theta},(P_m-P_d)/(t_d-t_m))$, it has been proved before that $\hat{\theta}>\theta_e$ so it is not taken into consider.

Price competition in MCRs and Dotcoms form the market structure as follows

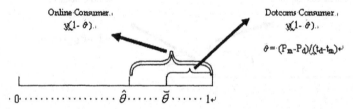

Figure. 3. Market Structure Two Formed from Price Competition Between MCRs and Dotcoms

Market Structure Two:

Under the condition that the number of online consumer is $v(1-\hat{\theta})$, $\theta_m<\theta_d$, when and only when $t_d-t_m<0$, there exists a market structure that MCRs and Dotcoms coexist. Then, there are $v(\breve{\theta}-\hat{\theta})$ consumers choose who purchasing on MCRs, and there are $v(1-\breve{\theta})$consumers who choosing purchase on Dotcoms.

3.2 When the number of online consumer is v (1-θe),

3.2.1 When $\theta_m \geq \theta_d$: ($\theta_e = \theta_d$)

Here, theconsumer whose critical evaluation value is θ_m or on the right of the axis can choose both MCRs and Dotcoms which means v $(1-\theta_m)$ consumers can choose both purchasing way. For these consumers, when they choose MCRs, it is necessary that

$$\theta - t_m\theta - P_m \geq \theta - t_d\theta - P_d,$$
$$\text{that's } (t_d - t_m) \theta \geq P_m - P_d.$$

Therefore, when $t_d - t_m > 0$, the consumer whose value evaluation is between $((P_m-P_d)/(t_d-t_m),1)$ will choose MCRs, and the consumer whose value evaluation is between $(\theta_e ,(P_m-P_d)/(t_d-t_m))$ will choose Dotcoms.

When $t_d - t_m < 0$, the consumer whose value evaluation is between $(\theta_e, (P_m-P_d)/(t_d-t_m))$ will choose MCRs, and the consumer whose value evaluation is between $((P_m-P_d)/(t_d-t_m), 1)$ will choose Dotcoms.

Concretely, because $\theta_m \geq \theta_d$, $P_m/(1-t_m) \geq P_d/(1-t_d)$, then $(P_m-P_d)(1-t_m) \geq (t_d-t_m)P_m$

When $t_d - t_m > 0$, $(P_m-P_d)/(t_d-t_m) \geq \theta_m$, here critical evaluation of the consumers who choose MCRs finally is $\breve{\theta} = (P_m-P_d)/(t_d-t_m)$. Price competition in MCRs and Dotcoms form the market structure as follows

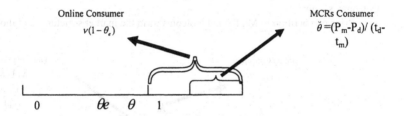

Figure. 4. Market Structure Three Formed from Price Competition Between MCRs and Dotcoms

When $t_d - t_m < 0$, for $\theta_m \geq \theta_d$, then $P_m/(1-t_m) \geq P_d/(1-t_d)$.

So $P_m - P_d \geq t_d P_m - t_m P_d = (t_d P_m - t_d P_d) + (t_d P_d - t_m P_d) = t_d (P_m - P_d) + (t_d - t_m) P_d$

Because $t_d - t_m < 0$, $(P_m-P_d)/(t_d-t_m) \leq P_d/(1-t_d)$, that's $\breve{\theta} \leq \theta_d = \theta_e$, therefore value evaluation $(\theta_e ,(P_m-P_d)/(t_d-t_m))$ of consumers who choose MCRs is empty one and it will be not taken into consider.

Market Structure Three:

Under the condition that the number of online consumer is v $(1-\theta_e)$, $\theta_m \geq \theta_d$, when and only when $t_d - t_m > 0$, there exists a market structure that MCRs and Dotcoms coexist. Then, there are v $(1-\breve{\theta})$ consumers who choose purchasing on MCRs, and there are v $(\breve{\theta} - \theta_e)$ consumers who choose purchasing on Dotcoms.

3.2.2 When $\theta_m < \theta_d$ ($\theta_e = \theta_m$):

Here, the consumer whose critical evaluation value is θ_d or on the right can choose both MCRs and Dotcoms which means $v(1-\theta_d)$ consumers can choose both purchasing way. For these consumers, when they choose MCRs, it is necessary that

$$\theta - t_m\theta - P_m \geq \theta - t_d\theta - P_d,$$

Still that $(t_d-t_m)\theta \geq P_m-P_d$.

When $t_d-t_m >0$, the consumer whose value evaluation is between $((P_m-P_d)/(t_d-t_m),1)$ will choose MCRs, and the consumer whose value evaluation is between $(\theta_e,(P_m-P_d)/(t_d-t_m))$ will choose Dotcoms.

When $t_d-t_m <0$, the consumer whose value evaluation is between $(\theta_e,(P_m-P_d)/(t_d-t_m))$ will choose MCRs, and the consumer whose value evaluation is between $((P_m-P_d)/(t_d-t_m),1)$ will choose Dotcoms.

$\because \theta_m<\theta_d \quad \therefore P_m/(1-t_m) <P_d/(1-t_d) \quad \therefore (1-t_d)P_m< (1-t_m)P_d$

$P_m- P_d<(t_d P_m- t_m P_m)+(t_mP_m-t_mP_d) \quad (1-t_m)(P_m-P_d)< (t_d-t_m)P_m$

(a) when $t_d-t_m>0$, that $(P_m-P_d)/(t_d-t_m)< \theta_m$;

(b) when $t_d-t_m<0$, that $(P_m-P_d)/(t_d-t_m)> \theta_m$.

When $t_d-t_m >0$, evaluation cluster $(\theta_e, (P_m-P_d)/(t_d-t_m))$ of consumers who choose Dotcoms is empty.

Price competition in MCRs and Dotcoms form the market structures as follows

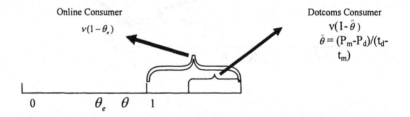

Online Consumer
$v(1-\theta_e)$

Dotcoms Consumer
$v(1-\breve{\theta})$
$\breve{\theta}=(P_m-P_d)/(t_d-t_m)$

$0 \qquad \theta_e \quad \theta \quad 1$

Figure. 5. Market Structure Four Formed from Price Competition Between MCRs and Dotcoms

Market Structure Four:
Under the condition that the number of online consumer is $v(1-\theta_e)$, $\theta_m<\theta_d$, when and only when $t_d-t_m <0$, there exists a market structure that MCRs and Dotcoms coexist. Then, there are $v(1-\breve{\theta})$ consumers who choose purchase on Dotcoms, and there are $v(\breve{\theta}-\theta_e)$ consumers who choose purchase on MCRs.

4   Game analysis under four market structure

Using backward induction, we deduce two kinds of retailers' optimum prices and equilibrium solutions as follow:

The demands of consumers who choose purchasing channels of MCRs and Dotcoms are respectively:

$$D_m = v(1-\frac{p_m-p_d}{t_d-t_m}); \qquad D_d = v(\frac{p_m-p_d}{t_d-t_m}-\hat{\theta})$$

Profit functions are:

$$\pi_m=(P_m-C_m)D_m; \quad \pi_d=(P_d-C_d)D_d$$

Perfect price are respectively:

$$p_m^* = -\frac{1}{3}(-c_d-2c_m-2t_d+\hat{\theta}t_d+2t_m-\hat{\theta}t_m)$$

$$p_d^* = -\frac{1}{3}(-2c_d-c_m-t_d+2\hat{\theta}t_d+t_m-2\hat{\theta}t_m)$$

Therefore, equilibrium solutions are as follows:

$$\theta_m^* = -\frac{1}{3}(-c_d-2c_m-2t_d+\hat{\theta}t_d+2t_m-\hat{\theta}t_m)/(1-t_m)$$

$$\theta_d^* = -\frac{1}{3}(-2c_d-c_m-t_d+2\hat{\theta}t_d+t_m-2\hat{\theta}t_m)/(1-t_d)$$

$$\tilde{\theta}^* = \frac{-c_d+c_m+(1+\hat{\theta})(t_d-t_m)}{3(t_d-t_m)} \qquad D_m^* = \frac{v[c_d-c_m-(\hat{\theta}-2)(t_d-t_m)]}{3(t_d-t_m)}$$

$$\pi_m^* = \frac{v[-c_d+c_m+(\hat{\theta}-2)(t_d-t_m)]^2}{9(t_d-t_m)} \qquad D_d^* = -\frac{v[c_d-c_m+(2\hat{\theta}-1)(t_d-t_m)]}{3(t_d-t_m)}$$

$$\pi_d^* = \frac{v[c_d-c_m+(2\hat{\theta}-1)(t_d-t_m)]^2}{9(t_d-t_m)}$$

Similarly, perfect price and equilibrium solution of structure two are:

$$p_m^* = -\frac{1}{3}(-c_d-2c_m+t_d-2\hat{\theta}t_d-t_m+2\hat{\theta}t_m)$$

$$p_d^* = -\frac{1}{3}(-2c_d-c_m+2t_d-\hat{\theta}t_d-2t_m+\hat{\theta}t_m)$$

$$\theta_m^* = -\frac{1}{3}(-c_d - 2c_m + t_d - 2\hat{\theta}t_d - t_m + 2\hat{\theta}t_m)/(1-t_m)$$

$$\theta_d^* = -\frac{1}{3}(-2c_d - c_m + 2t_d - \hat{\theta}t_d - 2t_m + \hat{\theta}t_m)/(1-t_d)$$

$$\tilde{\theta}^* = \frac{-c_d + c_m + (1+\hat{\theta})(t_d - t_m)}{3(t_d - t_m)}$$

And , perfect price and equilibrium solution of structure three are:

$$p_m^* = -\frac{1}{3}(-c_d - 2c_m - 2t_d + \theta_e t_d + 2t_m - \theta_e t_m)$$

$$p_d^* = -\frac{1}{3}(-2c_d - c_m - t_d + 2\theta_e t_d + t_m - 2\theta_e t_m)$$

$$\theta_m^* = -\frac{1}{3}(-c_d - 2c_m - 2t_d + \theta_e t_d + 2t_m - \theta_e t_m)/(1-t_m)$$

$$\theta_d^* = -\frac{1}{3}(-2c_d - c_m - t_d + 2\theta_e t_d + t_m - 2\theta_e t_m)/(1-t_d)$$

$$\tilde{\theta}^* = \frac{-c_d + c_m + (1+\theta_e)(t_d - t_m)}{3(t_d - t_m)}$$

Last, perfect price and equilibrium solution of structure four are:

$$p_m^* = -\frac{1}{3}(-c_d - 2c_m + t_d - 2\theta_e t_d - t_m + 2\theta_e t_m)$$

$$p_d^* = -\frac{1}{3}(-2c_d - c_m + 2t_d - \theta_e t_d - 2t_m + \theta_e t_m)$$

$$\theta_m^* = -\frac{1}{3}(-c_d - 2c_m + t_d - 2\theta_e t_d - t_m + 2\theta_e t_m)/(1-t_m)$$

$$\theta_d^* = -\frac{1}{3}(-2c_d - c_m + 2t_d - \theta_e t_d - 2t_m + \theta_e t_m)/(1-t_d)$$

$$\tilde{\theta}^* = \frac{-c_d + c_m + (1+\theta_e)(t_d - t_m)}{3(t_d - t_m)}$$

5 Discussion

Basing on four kinds of MCRs and Dotcoms coexist market structures and each equilibrium solution confirmed by two-step game analysis, we can deduce other useful results including necessary condition of Nash equilibrium. As for the core of this paper—price competition between online sales channels MCRs and Dotcoms on e-business market internal, we can make conclusions through comparing two kinds of retailers' perfect prices in each market structure. Results are showed in Table1.

In order to simplify the condition $P_d^* < P_m^*$ showed above, we introduce parameter s which stands for e-business market's scale. Obviously, s is between [0, 1], and there exists relationships among four kinds of market structures:

$$s = \begin{cases} v(1-\hat{\theta}) & \textit{market structure } 1 \textit{ and } 2 \Leftrightarrow \hat{\theta} = 1 - \dfrac{s}{v} \\ v(1-\theta_e) & \textit{market structure } 3 \textit{ and } 4 \Leftrightarrow \theta_e = 1 - \dfrac{s}{v} \end{cases}$$

Then we can unify the condition $P_d^* < P_m^*$ of four kinds of market structures

$$C_d - C_m < (2-s/v)\,(t_d - t_m)$$

Come to following propositions:

Proposition 1: In the competition of e-business market that two kinds of online retailers coexist, four factors together decide the price of two kind online retailers:

retailers' cost C_m and C_d, , other cost parameters t_m and t_d that consumers perceive when they purchase from two kind of retailers, e-business market's scales and e-business penetrate rate v. When two kinds of retailers' cost difference is lower than a critical value $(2-s/v)\,(t_d - t_m)$, prior retailers' price is lower than the latter's. When the difference between costs that coefficient consumers perceive when they purchase from two kind of retailers is higher than a critical value $(C_d - C_m)v/(2v-s)$, prior retailers' price is lower that the latter's.

Prove:

From $C_d - C_m < (2-s/v)\,(t_d - t_m)$ and relationship between t_d and t_m of four market

Table 1 Competition Relationship Between MCRs and Dotcoms on E-Business Market

Market Structure	Relationship of Parameter	$p_m^* - p_d^*$	Condition that Dotcoms's price is lower that MCRs's price
1	Online Market Scale $v(1-\hat{\theta})$, $\theta_m \geq \theta_d$, $t_d > t_m$	$-\dfrac{c_d - c_m + (1+\hat{\theta})(t_m - t_d)}{3}$	C_d- $C_m < (1+\hat{\theta})(t_d - t_m)$
2	Online Market Scale $v(1-\hat{\theta})$, $\theta_m < \theta_d$, $t_d < t_m$		C_d- $C_m < (1+\hat{\theta})(t_d - t_m)$
3	Online Market Scale $v(1-\theta_e)$, $\theta_m \geq \theta_d$, $t_d > t_m$	$-\dfrac{c_d - c_m + (1+\theta_e)(t_m}{3}$	C_d-$C_m < (1+\theta_e)(t_d$-$t_m)$
4	Online Market Scale $v(1-\theta_e)$, $\theta_m < \theta_d$, $t_d < t_m$		C_d-$C_m < (1+\theta_e)(t_d$-$t_m)$

structures, we can find that:

1) Under all four market structures, there is: when Dotcoms's cost $C_d < C_m + (2-s/v)$ $(t_d - t_m)$, Dotcoms's price is lower than MCRs's.

2) Under all four market structures, there is: when other parameters except price that consumer' perceive when they purchase on Dotcoms $t_d > t_m + (C_d - C_m) v/ (2v-s)$, Dotcoms's price is lower than MCRs's.

3) Under market structure 1 and 3, when e-business market scale $s < v(2-(C_d - C_m)/(t_d - t_m))$, Dotcoms's price is lower than MCRs's. Under market structure 2 and 4, when e-business market scale $s > v (2-(Cd-C_m)/(t_d - t_m))$, Dotcoms's price is lower than MCRs's.

4) Under market structure 1 and 3, when e-business penetrate rate $v > s/(2-(C_d - C_m)/(t_d - t_m))$, Dotcoms's price is lower than MCRs's; Under market structure 2 and 4, when e-business penetrate rate $v < s/(2-(C_d - C_m)/(t_d - t_m))$, Dotcoms's price is lower than MCRs's;

Finish.

Proposition 2: As e-business penetrate rate increasing, two kind retailers' perfect prices decrease and there is a stable relationship of ratio of decline speed; in market structure 1 and 3, the difference increase; and in market structure 2 and 4, the difference decrease.

Prove:

Market Structure 1:

$$p_m^* = -\frac{1}{3}(-c_d - 2c_m - 2t_d + (1-\frac{s}{v})t_d + 2t_m - (1-\frac{s}{v})t_m) = -\frac{1}{3}(-c_d - 2c_m + (1+\frac{s}{v})(t_m - t_d))$$

$$p_d^* = -\frac{1}{3}(-2c_d - c_m - t_d + 2(1-\frac{s}{v})t_d + t_m - 2(1-\frac{s}{v})t_m) = -\frac{1}{3}(-2c_d - c_m + (1-\frac{2s}{v})(t_d - t_m))$$

$$p_m^* - p_d^* = -\frac{1}{3}(c_d - c_m + (2-\frac{s}{v})(t_m - t_d))$$

Then

$$\frac{\partial p_m^*}{\partial v} = \frac{(t_m - t_d)s}{3} * \frac{1}{v^2} \le 0; \qquad \frac{\partial p_d^*}{\partial v} = \frac{2(t_m - t_d)s}{3} * \frac{1}{v^2} \le 0; \qquad \frac{\partial (p_m^* - p_d^*)}{\partial v} = \frac{(t_d - t_m)s}{3} * \frac{1}{v^2} \ge 0$$

Market Structure 2:

$$p_m^* = -\frac{1}{3}(-c_d - 2c_m + t_d - 2(1-\frac{s}{v})t_d - t_m + 2(1-\frac{s}{v})t_m) = -\frac{1}{3}(-c_d - 2c_m + (1-\frac{2s}{v})(t_m - t_d))$$

$$p_d^* = -\frac{1}{3}(-2c_d - c_m + 2t_d - (1-\frac{s}{v})t_d - 2t_m + (1-\frac{s}{v})t_m) = -\frac{1}{3}(-2c_d - c_m + (1+\frac{s}{v})(t_d - t_m))$$

$$p_m^* - p_d^* = -\frac{1}{3}(c_d - c_m + (2-\frac{s}{v})(t_m - t_d))$$

Then

$$\frac{\partial p_m^*}{\partial v} = \frac{2(t_d - t_m)s}{3} * \frac{1}{v^2} \le 0; \qquad \frac{\partial p_d^*}{\partial v} = \frac{(t_d - t_m)s}{3} * \frac{1}{v^2} \le 0; \qquad \frac{\partial (p_m^* - p_d^*)}{\partial v} = \frac{(t_d - t_m)s}{3} * \frac{1}{v^2} \le 0$$

Market Structure 3: similar with market structure 1.

Market Structure 4: similar with market structure 4.

Finish.

6 Conclusion

This paper is based on model (Friber [6,7]; ChengYun et al.[8]) that focuses on price competition problem between traditional off-line market retailers and pure online retailers, and develop it further into considering the price competition behavior of both Multi-Channel Retailers (MCRs) and Pure Online Retailers (Dotcoms) on e-business market. Furthermore, we calculate perfect equilibrium price of two kinds of e-business retailer under four types of market structure, introduce parameters that indicate the scale of e-business market, and discuss characteristic of the changes about pricing strategy and perfect price that belong to these two kinds of retailer.

This research not only consummates price competition behavior of double-channel retailers on e-business market academically, but also provides theoretical foundation for further empirical research on e-business market pricing. Admittedly, we do not include other factors such as price competition behavior of MCRs's offline part and traditional offline retailers. It is worthy studying further on this part.

References

1. J.Y. Bakos, "Reducing Buyer Search Costs: Implications for Electronic Marketplaces", *Management Science*, 1997,43(12):1613-1630
2. J.Y. Bakos, "The Emerging Role of Electronic Marketplaces on the Internet", *Communications of the ACM*, 1998,41(8):35-42
3. S. Balasubramanian, "Mail versus Mall: A Strategic Analysis of Competition between Direct Marketers and Conventional Retailers", *Marketing Science*, 1998,17(3):181-195
4. M.D. Smith, J. Baily, & E. Brynjolfsson, "Understanding Digital Markets: Review and Assessment", In: E. Brynjolfssom & B. Kahin(Eds). *Understanding the Digital Economy*. MIT press.2000
5. X. Pan, V. Shankar, & B. Ratchford, "Price Competition Between Pure Play vs. Bricks-and-Clicks e-Tailers: Analytical Model and Empirical Analysis". *Advances in Applied Microeconomics*, 2002,11:29-61
6. R. Friberg, M. Ganslandt, & M. Sandström, "E-commerce and Price-theory and evidence", Working Paper, *Stockholm School of Economics,* 2000
7. R. Friberg, M. Ganslandt, & M. Sandström, "Pricing Strategies in E-commerce: Bricks vs. Clicks", Working Paper, *Stockholm School of Economics*, 2001
8. Y. Chen, H,C, Wang, H.Z. Shen, "Study on the Price Competition between E-commerce Retailer and Conventional Retailer", *Theory and Practice of Systematical Engineering*（in Chinese）, 2006（1）：P35-41
9. R.M. O'keefe, & T. McEachern, "Web-based Customer Decision Support System", *Communications of the ACM*, 1998,41(3):71-78

Research on the Interoperability Architecture of the Digital Library Grid

Hao Pan

Department of information management , Beijing Institute of
Petrochemical Technology, China, 102600
bjpanhao@163.com

Abstract. With the rapid development of the digital libraries, Interoperability
is the problem to realize the real information sharing and eliminate the digital
information islands. In this paper, the character and requirement of digital
library interoperability is discussed. As the limitations of the current
technologies in the realization of the large-scale digital library interoperability
on the Web, the architecture of the digital library interoperability is put
forward based on the Grid technology, and the working process of the digital
library Grid is presented. Using the Grid technologies, the high performance
OAI federated search service is realized.

1 Introduction

With the quick development of the information technology, people's working,
learning and life style have been greatly influenced by the Internet. At the same time,
library information enterprise has come to a new phase-DL (digital library), after
being through traditional library and automatic library phase. A DL can discover,
manage and publish digital information in an effective way in order to provide a
simple and convenient digital information querying platform for groups of
individuals. Many countries have developed their own digital library one after the
other, such as NSDL [1], NCSTRL [2], DLI2 [3]. As different libraries take different
technology, platform, protocol and architecture according to its different objective
and running manner, it is an impending problem in the field of the DL
interoperations that how to integrate these libraries with different infrastructure and
technology in order to exchange information and share documents between different
DLs, finally to build a big virtual DL, to provide uniform and convenient services for
global users.

Present solutions to the DL interoperability, such as distributed search
technology [4], metadata collection technology [5], middleware technology, cannot
solve the problem of large scale DL interoperability on the Internet in an appropriate

Please use the following format when citing this chapter:

Pan, H., 2007, in IFIP International Federation for Information Processing, Volume 251, Integration and Innovation
Orient to E-Society Volume1, Wang, W. (Eds), (Boston: Springer), pp. 147-154.

way [6]. In order to have real DL interoperability, we need to solve the problem from the beginning of the DL architecture design and implementation. This article makes it by offering architecture of the DL interoperability based on Grid technology, which uses the character of resource sharing of the Grid technology to support OAI service.

2   The Outline of the DL Interoperability

2.1 The Character of the DL Interoperability

DL is a network based magnanimous database, which has massive and different types of information   such as text, images, video, audio, automation, etc. The characters of a DL are as follows:

1. Heterogeneity. Platform heterogeneity, information source heterogeneity and metadata heterogeneity embody the heterogeneity of a DL.   The electronic information resources in a DL are always heterogeneous in the form of resource storage format, service mode offering, access interface and data transport protocol.

2. The physical distribution of the digital resource. The resource of a DL is physically distributed in the network. It is a great challenge to provide service for the user over the tremendous digital resources of the DLs in the WEB.

3. Autonomy. Almost all the digital libraries distributed over the Internet are autonomous information systems. It means they manage and maintain their own resources and services, They also manage their access method and authorization independently.

4. Openness. You can enter or logout an interoperated DL at any time.

2.2 The requirement of the DL interoperability based on metadata harvesting

Many DL projects use distributed searching method. It unites many DLs to provide a single service interface for the users, and thus to implement the DL interoperability. However, this method is only suitable for a DL which has less nodes (e.g. number of nodes <20) because it uses real time searching method. When there are so many nodes (like more than 100), it becomes very difficult to perform a mass distributed searching over the Internet. The good thing is, metadata harvesting method can solve this problem very well. This method is based on OAI/PMH [7] infrastructure. It can offer a uniform querying service for the users by transforming all metadata from different DLs to one format and store them into the metadata depository.

The OAI-PMH offers a technology to support the organizational evolution of digital cultural content creation and collective services to access cross-domain collections. It is an attempt to build a "low-barrier interoperability framework" for archives containing digital content. It allows Service Providers to harvest metadata from Data Providers. The Open Archives Initiative's Protocol for Metadata Harvesting (OAI-PMH) was created to facilitate discovery of distributed resources. The OAI-PMH achieves this by providing a simple, yet powerful framework for metadata harvesting. Harvesters can incrementally gather records contained in OAI-PMH repositories and use them to create services covering the content of several repositories. The OAI-PMH has been widely accepted, and until recently, it has mainly been applied to make Dublin Core metadata about scholarly objects contained in distributed repositories searchable through a single user interface.Figure gives the metadata interoperability architecture based on OAI-PMH.

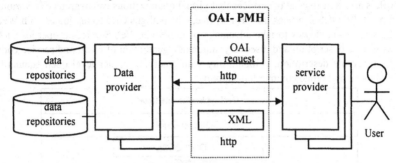

Fig.1. The metadata interoperability architecture based on OAI-PMH

Primarily, there are two kinds of roles in OAI infrastructure: data provider and service provider. Data provider is to provide and distribute the metadata while service provider collects the metadata from multiple data providers and provides querying service to the end users. Service provider communicates with data provider via OAI-PMH protocol. OAI-PMH protocol, whose metadata uses XML format, is based on HTTP protocol to transport data, which makes it widely used in the Web environment and enables information exchange between distributed heterogeneous resources.

    In order to effectively implement the metadata discovery, harvesting and indexing service, appropriate architecture to support these operations and high performance servers are required. At the present, all the metadata discovery,, harvesting and indexing jobs are centralized on one or several given servers, which makes the performance and the reliability extremely poor [8]. As the scale of the DLs interoperability enlarges continuously, it will get harder to expand the solution. In this paper, Grid technology is introduced to enhance the reliability and the scalability of the service and the performance of the metadata harvesting and indexing service.

3 The Grid technology

Grid computing is a solution for resource sharing and problem solving in the dynamic and heterogeneous virtual organization, which made the Internet into a tremendous super computer to realize the computing resources, storage resources, data resources, information resources, knowledge resources, equipment resources, etc [9]. The basic character of Grid computing is resource sharing .

3.1 Open Grid service architecture

OGSA is the most widely used Grid architecture at present. The need for integration and interoperability has led to the design of the open Grid service architecture, which offers an extensible set of services that virtual organizations can aggregate in various ways [10]. OGSA defines the Grid service, which aligns Grid technologies with Web Services technologies to take advantage of important Web Services properties such as service description and discovery, automatic generation of client and service code from service description, compatibility with emerging higher level open standards and tools, and broad commercial support.

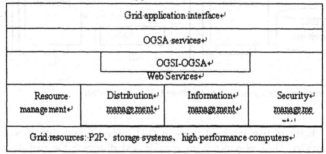

Fig.2. open grid service architecture

In OGSA, every resource is represented by a Grid service, which defines standard mechanisms for creating, naming, and discovering persistent and transient Grid service instances [11]. It provides location transparency and multiple protocol bindings for service instances and supports integration with underlying native platform facilities, which can solve the problem of interoperability among the heterogeneous grid facilities and provides the virtual service. Fig.2 describes the OGSA, the digital libraries interoperability can be realized by using the service of resource discovery, resource distribution, and resource accessory provided by OGSA.

3.2 The advantage of the Grid digital libraries

The Grid technology which supports the large scale resource sharing has the advantage in the respect of heterogeneous platform compatibility and system harvesting. The DL interoperability and the Grid computing have many similar characters, such as distribution, heterogeneity, autonomy. Therefore, the Grid technology can be used to solve the problem in the DL interoperability.

1. The heterogeneity of the resource. Two aspects of the resource heterogeneity are solved in the Grid technology, firstly, the heterogeneity of different resources, such as the computing resources, the storage resources; secondly, the heterogeneity of the structure of the same resources. The DLs interoperability can solve the resource heterogeneity using the Grid technology.

2. The sharing of the resources. The aim of the Grid computing is to realize the

resource sharing, and eliminate the information Isolated island and the knowledge Isolated island [12]. Using the Grid technology, the DL interoperability can be enhanced, and the resource sharing can be realized.

3. The autonomy of the resource. The resources in the Grid belong to different organizations. The resource owners can manage and control their resources absolutely. The Grid systems cannot control these resources. The DLs interoperability also requires solving the autonomy and sharing of the resources.

4. The individuality of the service. The Grid provides the intellectual and individual services for the users. The DL also provides the individual services for the users, and realizes the information formulation and the initiative pushing of the information.

4 The architecture of Grid digital library

4.1 The architecture of digital library based on the Grid technology

To solve the interoperability of the digital library based on the metadata level and the service level, the architecture of DLs interoperability based on the Grid technology is proposed, Fig.3 gives the architecture.

The architecture of Grid digital library contains 3 layers. The base layer is the data layer, which is made up of the DLs distributed on the different regions, as the data provider of the DLs interoperability, the data layer provides the metadata that data format is decided by OAI-PMH protocol to form the Metadata Repository based on the OAI-PMH protocol; the top layer is the application layer of the virtual digital libraries, which provides the united service interface, and provides the data retrieval service and data query service; the middle layer between the data layer and the application layer is the Grid layer, which shields the distribution and the heterogeneity of the base layer, and provide the united service interface for the application layer by the way of metadata discovery, harvesting and indexing.

4.2 The principle of the digital library Grid

The digital library Grid realizes the shielding of the distribution and heterogeneity of DL and the metadata discovery, harvesting and indexing of the digital libraries distributed on the different places, and provides the generous information service for the users. There are three layers in the architecture of DL grid, the application layer, the grid layer and the data layer. The application layer is to provide the generally query interface to the readers, the readers start a query not knowing how and where to get the data. The data layer contains the heterogeneous DL, every DL in the data layer realize the function of the DP of the metadata. In the grid layer, the metadata is collected by the metadata harvesting point to the metadata generally harvesting point, which provides the unified metadata to the application layer.

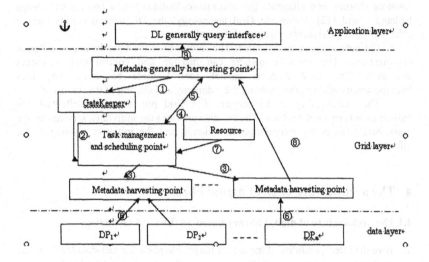

Fig.3. the interoperability architecture of digital library Grid

The working steps of the digital library Grid in the Fig.3 is as follows.

1. The metadata generally harvesting point initiates the harvesting duties, the DL Grid initiates the Gatekeeper procedure of providing working assignment.

2. The Gatekeeper procedure builds the duties according to the duty requiring, the task and resource distribution is carried on by the task management and scheduling point.

3. The task management and scheduling point carries on the metadata harvesting jobs.

4. The task management and scheduling point provides the condition information of the task for the metadata generally harvesting point.

5. The metadata generally harvesting point submits the request of duty canceling.

6. The DL distributed on different regions provides their own metadata for the metadata harvesting point.

7. In the procedure of the metadata harvesting, if there is breakdown on one harvesting point, the duty management and scheduling point will transmit its harvesting code to other points using Grid FTP to guarantee the advancement of the metadata harvesting.

8. After the metadata harvesting works, the metadata harvesting point sends the metadata to the metadata generally harvesting point, and the corresponding metadata is store on the metadata repository.

9. After the metadata generally harvesting works, the metadata is stored on the metadata repository, the generally query interface can be provided for the user, which send the request to the corresponding metadata repository, and collect the query results, and submit the results to the user.

5 Conclusions

The aim of the digital library interoperability is to unite the isolating DLs over the Internet, to provide the united and virtual information provider to the user, and to realize the information resource sharing of the global digital libraries. According to the requirement of the large scale digital library interoperability and the advantage of the Grid technology on the aspect of resource sharing, the architecture of the digital libraries interoperability is proposed, which unites the Grid technology and the OAI/PMH protocol, realizes the high performance metadata discovery, harvesting and indexing. As the Grid can make fully use of the idle resources over the Internet, the cost of the digital library interoperability can be greatly reduced. The digital library interoperability can also realize the metadata redundancy and enhance the reliability of the service using the idle resource over the Internet.

References

1. C. Lagcne and W. Hoehn, Core services in the architecture of the national digital library for science education (NSDL), *Proceedings of the Second ACM/IEEE Joint Conference on Digital Libraries* 201~209(2002).
2. B.M. Leiner, The NCSTRL approach to open architecture for the confederated digital library,
http://www.dlib.org/ dlib/december98/ leiner/121einer.html.[2003-02-05].
3. Digital Libraries Initiative Phase2, http://www.dli2.nsf.gov/. [2005-12-12].
4. B. Matthias, M. Sebastian, W. Gerhard and Z. Christian, Challenges of Distributed Search Across Digital Libraries.
http://www.mpi-inf.mpg.de/~czimmer/papers/delos05.pdf. [2005-04]
5. M. Zhang, D.Q. Yang and S. A. Wang, An Architecture Supporting Metadata and Service Interoperability in Digital Libraries, *Computer Science*, 22(4), 482-487(2004).
6. C. Leonardo, C. Donatella and P. Pasquale, A service for supporting virtual views of large heterogeneous digital libraries, *7th European Digital Library Conference*, 362-373(2003).
7. S. Hussein, Introduction to the open archives initiative protocol for metadata harvesting, *Proceedings of the Second ACM/IEEE-CS Joint Conference on Digital libraries* (2002).
8. D. David and F. Muriel, Open Archives Initiative – Protocol for Metadata Harvesting Practices of cultural heritage actors.
http://www.oaforum.org/ otherfiles/oaf_d48_cser3_foullonneau.pdf.[2003-9].
9. F. Ian, K. Carl and T. Steven, "The anatomy of the grid: enabling scalable virtual organizations", *International Journal of Supercomputer Applications*, 15(3), 200-222(2001).
10. F. Ian and K. Carl, et al, The physiology of the grid: an open grid services architecture for distributed systems integration, open grid service infrastructure WG.
http: //www. Gridforum.org/ogsi-wg/drafts/ogsa-draft.pdf.htm. [2004-12-9].

11. F. Ian, "Grid computing: concepts, applications, and technologies". http://www.mcs.anl.gov/~foster.htm. [2004-12-18].

12.B. Fran,F. Geoffrey and H. Tony, *Grid Computing: Making the Global Infrastructure a Reality* (Wiley & Sons Ltd, 2003).

The Research on Enterprise Manufacture Integrated and Collaborative Commerce System

Hechao Wang [1], Huijuan Shang[1], Wensheng Liu[2]

1 School of Management, China University of Mining and Technology, Xuzhou, 221008, China

2 Information center of Xu Zhou Cigarettes Factory, Xuzhou, 221000, China

wanghechao@sina.com, liuws@xzjyc.com.cn

Abstract: Global optimization and fast response ability in market cannot be simply achieved by computer automation without considering systematic application integration. The manufacturing enterprises need integrated platform and the coordinated commercial support platform to improve its whole productivity, flexibility, competitiveness and the ability in emergency management. This paper presents an e-commerce project at Xuzhou Cigarettes Factory with Jiangsu cigarette industrial group. We introduced the current information-based situation of the Xuzhou Cigarettes Factory with Jiangsu cigarette industrial group, identified the key problems and bottlenecks in the enterprise's management, and proposed the solution for enterprises' manufacturing integration and collaborative commerce. Our solution could be referred and used for information construction in manufacturing enterprises.

1. Introduction

As the informationize manufacture industry develops deeply, it is the enterprises' research and practice hot-spot that improving enterprises' productivity rate, flexibility, changeable management ability, and quick response ability to the market need by the construction of manufacture integrated and collaborative commerce platform. Based on the case of application of Ecommerce project of the cigarette industrial group of Jiangsu Xuzhou Cigarettes Factory, this thesis researches on the enterprise manufacture integrated and collaborative commerce system.

Please use the following format when citing this chapter:

Wang, H., Shang, H., Liu, W., 2007, in IFIP International Federation for Information Processing, Volume 251, Integration and Innovation Orient to E-Society Volume1, Wang, W. (Eds), (Boston: Springer), pp. 155-166.

2. The Current Information Situation About Xuzhou Cigarettes Factory.

The Xu Zhou Cigarettes Factory built on 1939, which is one of the large-scale Chinese tobacco industry key enterprises. Now it has staff and worker more than 2,000 people, has 550,000 boxes cigarettes production scale and 800,000 boxes cigarettes production ability. It's fixed assets original value amounting to 1,700,000,000 Yuan. It possesses a leaf silk high expansion system silk production line which is first one in our whole country and has international leading level. It also has a scientific and perfect quality control system. It considered being a profession "digitalization tobacco enterprise" experimental build unit and demonstration unit. Xu Zhou Cigarettes Factory has been determined as one after another" the nation-wide tobacco profession key enterprise of 10% of technical reformation", " 36 profession key enterprises " and " profession informative advanced enterprise " , becomes the main force of Chinese tobacco industry.

As an advanced Information construction enterprise in tobacco industry, Xu Zhou Cigarettes Factory has already successively been put into effect ERP system , Office Automation System , country bureau production Information projects such as managerial decision making management system , CRM system , financial affairs system It has been put into effect systems in the field of enterprise manufacture automation making silk production line collection charging system, the flake production line for assembling charging system, electric power air-conditioning control system etc; It has established the overhead warehouse of raw material automation formula , and has assisted in the field of logistics automation to expect that the overhead warehouse and the robot automation distribution system , attachment the overhead warehouse and so on; each system runs fine and has brought the important effect for managing the enterprise manufacture.

Though Information construction in the industry starting is earlier, some Xu Zhou Cigarettes Factory construction information system was build in order to be fit unlike business purpose , these systems' usage platform , program develop language and information transfer standard diversity, causing enterprise inside resource not able to cooperate effectively, some phenomenon, as certain dissipation and running efficiency has not highly brought out , the realization not product a link in enterprise manufacture integration, the business administration does not have an effective information analysis system tier. It doesn't has a effective closed cycle taking form between down-stream enterprise, and has no way to change the data into useful information. The inherent potential of enterprise is not brought into full play, and in certain degree.

3. The Urgent Need Of Putting Enterprise Fabrication Integration And Collaborative Commerce System Into Practice For Xuzhou Cigarettes Factory

Owing the understanding of urgent need industry competes and oneself develop, know urgency and necessity that the project builds!

（1） Industry competition urgent demand enterprise acceleration construction fabrication integration and Collaborative Commerce system.

Being accompanying prompt tobacco enterprise dilation's is that product quantity straight line rises, the market is control by seller rather then buyer. Some companies have to close for an bad management. At present, the whole national tobacco industry already develops from the amounts dilation to the brand, to quality.

More direct competition depends on of the opening to the outside world that is tobacco produces also already opens to the foreign merchant: Already allow foreign capital tobacco to enter China with joint investment form. At present only the channel not open to the outside, and it difficultly to hold such condition. The cigarette has as fleetness consumer goods, but replacement , this consume manufacture , supply of material , marketing have proposed that very highly demand of characteristic to cigarette to be to need "to depend on amounts , coming to develop markets depending on being satisfied with in time". Except the abundance guarantee supply of material, returning back to the channel smoothness such that swear to be authorized for dispatch of , be delivered goods, retail broad spreading point , in short , to be needing to ensure that the consumer all can buy in any moment , any place. Marketplace competing in altitude is out of stock otherwise, in a single day under the situation, may there is somebody being equivalent to your place right away immediately. But need to reach this one target, Xu Zhou Cigarettes Factory "can't be separated from IT absolutely", need to create integrated coordination business system owing to enterprise more.

（2） Puts enterprise fabrication integration and coordination business system into practice is an Information tobacco industry desire for development.

Tobacco Monopoly Administration has suggested three big Information construction targets in 2003,that is system integration , resource integrate , information shares. Then it made three uniting clear further afterwards , has been big industry information system uniting a network , uniting platform , uniting a data base, and concentrating on planning and putting three into practice， Namely: The cigarette produces managerial decision-making management system, Office Automation System, Electronic Commerce system. Xu Zhou Cigarettes Factory should puts enterprise fabrication integration and coordination business system into practice as soon as possible, and preparation the industry produce managerial decision making management system and electron business system carrying out integration.

Support "integrated inside and coordination outside" enterprise creates integration and meets the need of business system accords with the Information desire for development of industry, the energy and industry system realize "system integration, resource integrates, information enjoys ".

Request putting enterprise fabrication integration and coordination business affairs into practice being Xu cigarette informationize planning.

(1) Facing population development strategy administration needs.

Core business of enterprise develops: marketing, R&D, manufacture, logistics need supported with Collaborative Commerce affairs platform.

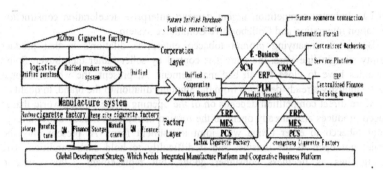

Figure.1 Support Platform

(2) Facing the needs of information strategy plan-------digitization tobacco.

"Digitization tobacco" idea , whose purpose are links , each technological process with informationize transfixion tobacco industry production management control each , information changes complex and volatile tobacco being not bad the quantization data , passes numerical analysis , development of estate provides the basis making policy to every enterprise even entire. Austerity developing and facing according to enterprise is real; Xu Zhou Cigarettes Factory must realize enterprise digitization, concrete doctrine: Procedure of production digitization, fabrication is equipped with digitization, design digitization, manage digitization.

(3)The manufacture that faces enterprise is integrated into demand.

Xu Zhou Cigarettes Factory's condition at present is:

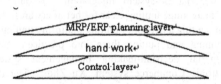

Figure. 2 Relationship Layer

Enterprise production program system high when go up, cause scene to become dark box;, function of auto machine does not get integration, forming automatic isolate lan inland produce bottleneck.

Producing organization construction and business process repeat, is unhappiness, conducted efficiency is low, need to carry out the business process of the science and organization construction that optimizes to form efficiency;

Now lack effective information communication and integration between each system implemented, it is serious that piece cuts apart, can not manage for that data resource carries out effective integration;

Information collect is not put into effect in the line and detecting equipment mass , the mass process control does not perfect , quality analysis does not prevent an off-test product from flowing into a marketplace on timely , unable secondary headstream;

Online and detection equipment quality information collection has not been implemented, the process control of quality is un-sound, quality analysis is not prompt, can not prevent from fountainhead that rejected product flows in market;

The process that has not realized major production process is trailed, can not trace back the source that product quality problem produces, can not accomplish the meticulous management in process;

Need to establish enterprise therefore to make integrated system, connect the planned same workshop schoolwork control of upper levels of management system on-the-spot , solve the control layer on-the-spot and the management level of upper levels join , the information that realize production to control layer, the automatic layer of commodity circulation and ERP system share , the science and promptness that realizes the degree layer of middle tone melt , meticulous melt. Accept production actual data feedbacks to ERP system, again instructing the production of the management system of upper levels to give the process of arriving control layer(PCS); About company know the control equipment on-the-spot and the platform of business management, realization data have no seam connection with share.

（4） The business that faces market cooperates with demand.

Through manufacture integrated construction, Xu Zhou Cigarettes Factory must control its' inside industrial operation management form bottom— — production manages execution — the systems such as ERP and CRM — — decision-making system to support system to realization the data flow of two-way. It is a good internal data foundation for Collaborative Commerce construction establishes. But found enterprise cooperate with commercial system still need establish E-business systematic commodity circulation management system etc. between the upper-lower enterprise that closely related with enterprise. With raising knowledge shares degree and enterprise innovation ability between close enterprise behaviors, it is so unceasing to raise enterprise competitive ability.

Through the construction of collaborative commerce, Xu Zhou Cigarettes Factory will reduce enterprise cost by further using IT , which can promotes the level of business management and raises the core competitiveness of enterprise .

In a word, manufacture integration and melt in collaborative commerce platform for Xu Zhou Cigarettes Factory is imperatively, is extremely urgent!

As the advanced enterprise of tobacco profession informative construction, Xu Zhou Cigarettes Factory grasps the opportunity that promotes enterprise to develop with IT , implements the project " enterprise manufacture integration and collaborative commerce system" , quests of the development way in such hard competitive environmental develops the collaborative commerce practice experience with valuable accumulation.

4.The Construction Of Xuzhou Cigarettes Factory Manufacture Integrated And Collaborative Commerce

4.1 Construction target

Taking tobacco profession informative application as background, it takes Xu Zhou Cigarettes Factory overall development strategy as guidance , managing system through optimizing process and organization transform and establishing the tobacco supply chain of " integrate product , supply and marketing ";

By establishment support enterprise the integrated E-business platform of "internal integration, external cooperate with ", and supplementing leading decision-making support so raises enterprise operation efficiency, it can promote the level of business management strengthens enterprise core competitiveness.

4.2 Project content

Demand has made clearly, how to satisfy the above demand? Especially according to integration, how to be founded? What system this platform should include as well as what function may realize manufacture basically to integrate with cooperates with business?

According to the analyze about Xu Zhou Cigarettes Factory enterprise manufacture integration with collaborative commerce system comprehensive build table , the major content that determines this project construction is with establishment " internal integration , external cooperate with " integration melts , E-business platform is key, include some following aspects specifically:

Firstly , manufacture integration platform: Build demand around enterprise key business application system, integrate when carrying out the systematic product life management system , manufacture execute system ,supply chain management system on ERP systematic foundation to realize the application of enterprise key business; Revolve around enterprise decision-making support system is shared and integrated for efficiency into the data demand of optimization, establishment enterprise data center, realization enterprise data integration, establish enterprise decision support system on this foundation.

Secondly, integrate in collaborative commerce platform: On the platform of completing enterprise internal manufacture integration, informative application expands outward to enterprise supplier and customer layer , realizes the electron between " supplier - Xu Zhou Cigarettes Factory - tobacco company " to melt trade, promote enterprise external business to cooperate with.

Thirdly, network sustain and apply safety: Integrate and cooperate with the efficient safe operation of commercial system for that effective support enterprise makes , need to reform for that original network carries out upgrade , and establish reliable network, application and the further raisings such as information safe system enterprise garden district net and the communication quality with profession net and internet, ensure that systematic success runs.

4. 3 Construction scheme

Xuzhou Cigarette Factory manufacture integration with collaborative commerce system is under the guidance of the enterprise informative frame of overall planning (as Fig.3 shows), and on based the analyze foundation for enterprise present informative present situation put forward. From this program frame, we may find out that the informative support system of Xuzhou cigarette factory overall program may divide into 4 levels. It ensures Xuzhou Cigarettes Factory realizes business process innovation with two parts, and melts in coordination the technical guarantee of E-business.

4 levels: Since outside, it is divide into ´internal network layer, data layer, application systematic layer and decision-making layer from the most basic internal network layer to the application level of E-business, above of those 4 levels, it is the specific application of E-business;

Two parts: Overall manufacture integration consists of enterprise internal and external resource and the integration of internal resource are integrated. Internal resource integration part is the information on the integrated foundation of enterprise key business application system to share, integration, the integration part of internal and external department resource is in internal resource integration, on the application system as well as portals , electronic business platform foundation that joins enterprise two ends specify melt in coordination E-business application.

Network layer: network layer is the basic platform that enterprise internal information resource to share, and the essential condition of IT application system. It is a key point for realizing enterprise melts in coordination the of E-business. Xuzhou Cigarette Factory has established relatively perfect network environment, and established good foundation to implement this project.

Data layer: Data layer covers the demand for service of cigarette industrial enterprise for entire application systematic and enterprise decision-making service. In this project, will found cigarette enterprise data platform, establish enterprise data center, and establish foundation for future enterprise development.

Apply layer: Application systematic construction will combine goal process, carries out unified construction on unified program foundation. This project take the enterprise resource planned management system that had been completed (ERP) and customer relation manage (CRM) as foundation, the further construct management system of supply chain management (SCM) and manufacture execute system (MES) and product life management system (PLM) and decision-making support system and the E-business platform that melts in coordination wait for that core has systematic application.

Decision-making layer: Xuzhou cigarette factory decision supporting support platform (DSS) takes the data center of establishment as core, data warehouse (Data Warehouse) technology as basic, with OLAP and Data Mining tool carries out the supplementary leading decision-making support of enforcement for means system.

5. Application System Construction

5.1Manufacture execute system

(1) Software structural design.

It is the various advantages that combine domestic and international production to manage software to develop the overall objective of this system, foster strengths and circumvent weaknesses, make system reach really practical degree under existing network soft hardware condition. Production manages software the Dot Net and COM/DCOM/COM+ that has Microsoft frequently with application configuration, CORBA of object management organization (OMG) and solar tiny system company (SUN Microsystems Inc) J2EE. Since the structural model of Microsoft is more mature, this systematic overall structure may be considered with the structural model of Windows DNA or Dot Net adopts the software structure of B/S or fake B/S for foundation. Following Fig.4 shows:

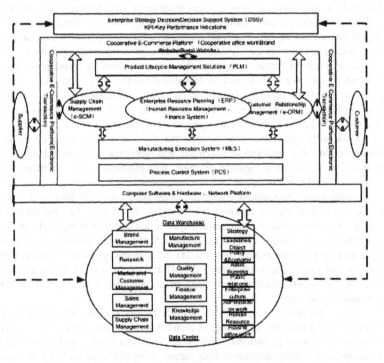

Figure.3 Overall Information Technology Planning Framework

Specific, realize the data communication of long-distance customer and application server as well as WWW server using the agreements such as Http and TCP/IP. WWW server communicates through COM assembly /Web Service and the COM assembly agreement of /Web Service of Microsoft. It can makes user monitor the development processing and long-distance visit on-the-spot in customer end using standard webpage browser real time to control the data on-the-spot, in order to make the purpose of reaching telemonitoring and monitoring come true. The system designed according to the above goal, this system consist of operating the WWW server in local server , the server of Web Service , relation database, and of operating on data server ,such as data collection server and database of real time, of operating on customer end browser, as well as the data collection software composition on-the-spot of real time.

(2) Systematic function design

This system refers to MES (manufacture execute system) model, systematic overall function configuration shows as Fig.5. The core of the system is production distribute management, realizing the real time management of the workers, equipments and stock, monitoring production process and offering analyze function about production to system.

■ **Production disposition**

The product brand and stock catalog may get from the basic data management system of ERP system; Product constructer technology route may obtain from ERP systematic technology management subsystem; ERP systematic equipment management system included the basic dates such as equipment situation and equipment relationship.

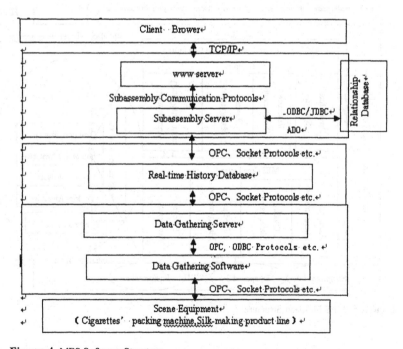

Figure. 4 MES Software Structure
■ Resource management

This modular manages person and thing (raw material, supplement material and spare parts) , the productions such as equipment resource, which in order to guarantee production going on normally.

(1) staff manage

Offer staffs' state data information, including staffs' basic information and turn out for work, and the information such as business ability, the work of guiding various post people according to the change of people qualifications, working pattern and demand for service, in order to develops employee biggest subjective activity. Suggest realize the human resource management system in ERP, realize the integration and share the functions of human resource of ERP and MES on this foundation.

(2) Equipment management

Equipment management offers equipment basic data information as well as equipment working ability information, offer real time and the accuracy of basis and emphatic planned dispatching for planned dispatching.

System carries out flexible statistical analysis inquiry for the information such as the equipment operation state, fault, repair and task of real time in the aid of in various charts. At the same time, system realizes equipment information analysis in deeper level in the aid of in SPC statistical analysis control picture.

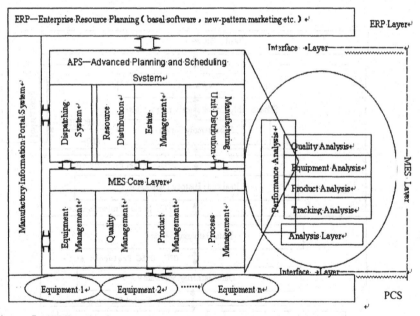

Figure. 5 MES Function Structure

■   Production management

This modular is the key modular of this system, divides into some following son modules:

(1) Production plan queues and is given:

Through the terminal on-the-spot, communicate production in time to workers of field work schoolwork plan and production schoolwork work sheet (the list of production processing、 the list of working central work sheet) , the information such as schoolwork procedure and schoolwork quality standard.

■   Commodity circulation is managed

According to the detailed production plan, systematic automatic generation raw material and supplement material collar material application. They are delivered to ERP systematic tobacco management system and supplement material management system; Guide the production of the stocks such as stem silk and slice silk, guide expansion silk manage. In that way, the system can raise accuracy and the efficiency of commodity circulation, as well as production efficiency.

■   Task execution track

By metering the condition of production plan going on Real time land, it is easy for produce management department to adjust production in time. It can trail to produce unit, workshop and the production planned executions such as factory level.

■   Statistical inquiry and analysis

The way that offers various form and graph to melt wraps the product of line for making silk thread and roll to carry out inquiry statistics and analysis. Through the data collection systematic or handwork record on-the-spot of real time enter way, to each related production the production that people offer workshop has information real time, as well as workshop production has information record (include producing to plan record information, workshop schoolwork record information and machine schoolwork record information) inquiry interface. Inquiry rank includes workshop level, production unit level and equipment level.

■   Quality management

After analyzing and appraising the production process for workshop, it can reflects selected production process information to operation and administrator in different levels management units (workshop, unit and machine) ,such as product quality, equipment efficiency, stock consumption, equipment load ability and comprehensive capability index.

■   **Production process and production trace back**

However it can not embody the character of MES system completely and the production management function only through tracing back to the process of making silk and roll bale, or getting the production management information such as output, brand and batch. At the same time, it can not carry out further use the MES system if we don't analysis trail information for these production processes completely.

■   **Data collection**

Through the data system of the packing shop, it finishes the data receiving of the connecting machine, the output of the packer, the auxiliary materials consuming, and the equipment operation conditions, it offers basic data information, which will be calculated in the online production cost system in the future, and also is the basis that examines the workshop to ERP system..

5.2 Melt in e-commerce platform in coordination.

In coordination with the commercial concept, the purpose of the enterprise's information construction is not merely the inside resources of the management enterprises, it also needs to set up one unified platform, bring the customer, supplier, the retail trader and other cooperative partners into the enterprise's information-based administrative system, make all of enterprises data integrate to a information management platform, and offer to the users with an unified user's interface, implement a series of chaining of the high-efficient sharing and business of information. "Work in coordination with

The Melt in e-commerce platform in coordination is shown in the following figure 6:

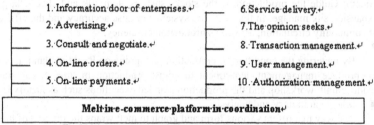

1. Information door of enterprises.   6. Service delivery.
2. Advertising.   7. The opinion seeks.
3. Consult and negotiate.   8. Transaction management.
4. On-line orders.   9. User management.
5. On-line payments.   10. Authorization management.

Melt in e-commerce platform in coordination

Fig.6 Melt in e-commerce platform in coordination

6   Conclusion

After more analysis research in detail, we may approximately understanding the present situation of Xuzhou Cigarette Factory informative construction At present, the project is being implemented smoothly as planned. It must be a fundamental change to the operating mechanism and management system while bringing remarkable direct economic efficiency. Then has a profound influence to enterprise's development.

References

1. Zhu Guan Zhou, "Chinese ERP market's situation report",*PC World*,2002(2)

2. HongTao, "Advanced e-bussiness study course," *Economic Management Press*,2003(4)

3. Xue Jian, "The thinking of Chinese enterprise in conformity with ERP" ,*The industrial journal of higher junior college of Chong Qing*,2003,(12)

4. Liu NaXin, "The comparative analysis of the management software of ERP using in the enterprise", *Problem and study*2003,(12)

5. SUN Shudong ,DENG Weimin , XIE Guiliang. "Job shop management system based on cost control" . *China Machine Engineering*, 2001, 12 (3):322 - 324 (in Chinese)

e-Market Benefit—Findings from Chinese Main Websites Case Studies

Honghong Qing

College of Computer Science and Information Engineering,
Chongqing Technology & Business University, Chongqing, P.R.China,
400067
Qing.lily@163.com

Abstract. e-Market is on the agenda both in research and in practice and there is a rather broad research field. This paper examines current case studies in order to seek the e-Market benefit and some directions for future research. All data collection in this paper comes from the websites of Alibaba.com and Taobao.com, 2004-2006. The case studies provide an insight on the benefit businesses can gain from e-Market which not only improve business' survival environment but also enhance business' competitive advantage.

1 Introduction

Marketers have been using electronic tools for many years, but the Internet and other information technologies created a flood of interesting and innovative ways to provide customer value. e-Marketplace is based on traditional market with information technology. The Internet and other technologies affect traditional market in three ways. First, they increase efficiency in established marketing functions. Second, the technology of e-Market transforms many marketing strategies. Finally, it has fundamentally changed consumer behavior through a power shift from firms to mouse-holders. The Internet also serves as an efficient marketing planning tool for both secondary and primary data collection. e-Business is important, powerful, and unstoppable. But what is it, exactly?

In e-Marketplace, e-Business is conducted on computers ad the Internet with continuous optimization of a firm's business activities. With digital technologies, computers and the Internet can store and transmit data in digital formats so that e-Business can implement the business' strategies and attract and retain the right customers and business partners. While e-Market flows from the organization's overall e-Business strategies and selected business models. It permeates business processes, such as product buying and selling. It includes digital communication, e-Commerce, and online research, and it is used by every business discipline.

Please use the following format when citing this chapter:

Qing, H. 2007, in IFIP International Federation for Information Processing, Volume 251, Integration and Innovation Orient to E-Society Volume1, Wang, W. (Eds), (Boston: Springer), pp. 167-178.

e-Market and e-Business era are both changing the way businesses look at globalization and competition. Organizations are rushing to adopt some kind of e-Market strategy. In many organizations, information is now accessed via corporate web-servers, so the web browser is a universal user interface for the corporation databases. The Internet has made it possible for business to gain access to an information infrastructure larger than that owned by any major corporation. But how much does the Internet help business gain benefit in its operations and practices?

This paper is to explore the benefit of business in e-Marketplace, based on the result from Report on the Survival and Development of e-Market in China 2004-2006 (RSDEB) [1]. From 2004 to 2006 a questionnaire survey of Chinese companies was carried out within the framework of RSDEB project among other things on their use of Internet. The questionnaire covered 3628 firms with between 10 and 500 employees. The selection was based on several different criterions such as size, region, branch and so on.

The paper provides an analysis of a series of case studies of Chinese businesses which are active e-Market users. The discussion is based on RSDEB and the case study addresses the pre-conditions for e-Market success and strategic effects resulting from its use. The paper includes presentation of the background of the literature reviews, participants, research method, and analysis of e-Market benefits according to the results of RSDEB.

2 Background of the participants

2.1 The Present Situation of e-Markets

At a World Internet Centre symposium in Silicon Valley in 2000 one session focused on the topic: "B2B e-marketplaces and the future of e-commerce: what path will it take?"

In business, everyone started with great expectations and predicted a path that e-market would lead to great success. Buyers expected to reduce costs by automating processes and, at the same time, increase visibility. Suppliers expected to increase sales by being hot-wired to a purchasing chain – a new sales channel – just a mouse click away.

In China, the e-Marketplace, Alibaba.com was set up in 1999. It was eye-catching. At the very beginning, Alibaba.com had its clear business model with the purpose of becoming the biggest and most active e-Marketplace in the world. Up to July, 2001, it had 730,000 members from 202 countries and regions of the world. Everyday more than 1500 businessmen register for membership of Alibaba.com. In 2006, Alibaba.com had gained more than ￥2bn. Obviously, this model – providing firms e-Marketplaces, local or regional, horizontal or vertical, and the opportunity to think about joining e-Markets – will help more and more firms to get their desired benefit.

2.2 Literature Review

e-Market researches are extensively made. Since 1989 the research area "e-markets" is a relevant topic for the CCEM Competence Centre Electronic Markets at the Institute for Information Management, University of St. Gallen. An overview of the previous work and a detailed analysis of the theoretical framework can be found in [13], [14], [15], [16].

The current research of e-Market is targeted at the four sites: e-Market infrastructure   (Ashish Arora,   Gregory Cooper,   Ramayya Krishnan   and Rema Padman, 2000;)[17], e-Market innovation(Qiuli Qin, Zhao Xi, Jingyan Chen,2001)[18], e-Market model (Prithviraj Dasgupta, Louise E. Moser and P. Michael Melliar-Smith, 2005;)[19] and e-Market evaluation(Qizhi Dai and Robert J. Kauffman, 2006;)[20].

In China, scholars pay attention to e-Market and does research concerned. Zhu [2] presents the three modes of e-Business from e-Market management perspective. They are: (1) e-Market controlled by seller means that the suppliers create their webpage a products catalog by themselves to attract more buyers and reduce the transaction costs. (2) e-Market controlled by buyers means that the buyers create webpage and put their products on e-Market by themselves to attract more suppliers and reduce the transaction costs. (3) e-Market controlled by intermediary means that e-Market play the role of digital intermediaries [5, 6].

Liang et al. [9, 10] proposed that a successful e-Market provides the users with transaction opportunity, transaction verifying and transaction executing. For example, demand and supply information can be aggregated and disseminated, and buyers and sellers can be matched in e-Markets, and to make transaction at the marketplace for increasing transaction efficiency and reducing transaction costs for both parts. He states that intermediary e-Market provides the platform for small and medium sized enterprises which can't establish their own company website, and for large enterprises which realize the integration of interior ERP/MRP/MIS/CRM with exterior exchange markets.

Jiang [7] presents that the greatest advantages of e-Market are improving efficiency, reducing transaction costs. The platform integrated the different suppliers and purchasers into the e-Market, which has greatly facilitated finding products and the selection of suppliers who can more easily promote their products. This not only reduces the cost of sales, but also can handle inventory and make an inventory of assets.

Yan et al. [8] explored the mechanisms for building reliable transaction between sells and buyers under the environment of e-Market. A theoretical framework of e-Market is proposed for reliable transaction system includes credit control, credit appraisal, credit obligation, credit feedback and cooperation criterion.

In summary of literature found, although prior work in this field has substantially contributed to our understanding of the role of e-Market in China, but more case studies need to be conducted to find companies how to get benefits via the process of practical transaction in an e-Marketplace.

2.3 A Case

The Report on the Survival and Development of e-Market in China 2004-2006 (RSDEB) [1] reports that from 2004 to 2006 a questionnaire survey of Chinese companies was carried out within the framework of RSDEB project on their use of Internet. There are 3628 businesses participating in this study. These participants were selected from the websites of Alibaba.com and Taobao.com etc [11, 12]. Businesses which had been involved in an earlier survey research project designed to establish the profile of Chinese businesses using the Internet. The questions designed for the study involve the following aspects: business sectors; the services and products they provided; staffing; turnover (in RMB$); number of years they have been using the Internet; investment plan; and the key reasons expressed for their ongoing Internet use.

The sample was deliberately chosen from a variety of business sectors, so that the existence of the non-manufacturing sector could be investigated. This is important to further research and the formulation of future research questions.

3 Research method

The survey study was designed to collect quantitative data and made no provision for interaction with the participants, with the result that any important issue not covered directly by the questionnaire would be missed. While such an approach is ideal for capturing larger samples' attitudes and activities, it is realized that a deeper insight into the dynamics of Internet use would be helpful to understanding current and future activities within the non-manufacturing business sector. So in order to understand the implications of business Internet use, some more focused methodology was clearly needed.

The case studies were designed as a series of interviews and site visits. Where site visits were not feasible, owing to distance or time factors, the questionnaire on-line were carried out instead. Interviews and discussions were recorded as a series of field notes and subsequently transcribed into more detailed accounts and figures, which were then verified with the case study participants for accuracy. The interviews were carried out by using a set of open-ended questions as guide to avoid drifting from research foci. The survey mainly covers the following parts:

> i. Gathering information on the background of each company, its director, and the role played by the director/management in adopting Internet use;
>
> ii. Asking participants to provide examples of how their firms have gained benefits from e-Market;
>
> iii. Attempting to identify the integration between existing internal application systems and e-Market;
>
> iv. Examining each organization's way of using e-Market to support traditional business activities.

4 Results and analysis

The data analysis process involves identifying patterns in the participants' answers to the open-ended questions. The main points made by participants are consolidated and the information and results from a survey study conducted prior to the case studies are incorporated, which makes it possible to assess the validity of the dominant patterns recurring in the 3628 cases. For example, the answers from the majority of participants all indicate that there is need to use e-Market to support human communication.

4.1 e-Market as a communication medium

Most of the 3628 firms take the key function of e-Market as a medium for human communication. These firms see the e-Market succeed in providing what the telephone or fax services cannot offer – asynchronous communications, overcoming time and geographic limitations and multimedia transmission. Cost savings is also regarded as a key reason for using e-mail, although most does not take into consideration set-up and ongoing costs. Being able to transfer electronic documents is suggested by some participants as very important, because neither the telephone nor the fax services can do this as easily as e-mail does.

In Figure1 below it can be seen that the firms use e-Marketplace to do their business from 1999 to 2006. If these results are compared with Figure2, it can be seen that the extent of implementing business on E-Marketplace has increased. That means that more and more firms are using the new technology and are trying to gain an understanding of whether e-Market, for example, is a medium for increased contact in the market. Replacing paper-based communication between firms and their vendors/customers is also high on their list of priorities.

Though it is not long since the businessmen are engaged in the e-Marketplace, they are curious to find the value of e-Business and make good use of it. According to a survey (see Figure1 below), 1999, only 1% of businessmen used e-Marketplaces to do their business. In 2003, the percentage went higher. Up to 2006, the number of e-Businessmen of the first half of the 2006 was the same as that of the whole year 2005.

At the same time, there is much difference among firms in their choosing e-Marketplace. As is shown in Figure2, the number of e-customers both Alibaba.com and other websites served, was growing in 1999. As time goes by, more customers prefer to choose Alibaba.com. It shows that e-Businessmen have a clear knowledge of e-Market. They choose e-Marketplace for their business development based on their own characteristics and other factors.

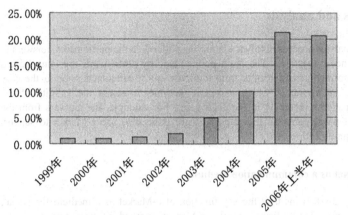

Figure.1. Firms on e-Market (%)

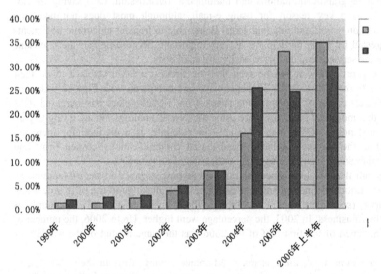

Figure.2. Website used (%)

4.2 Promoting management on e-Market

The extent to which firms put effort into e-Business process development can be seen in Figure3 below. The results show that during recent years businesses focus more on the management and organization development to improve e-Business process than other.

According to the result of the interview, both external forces in the form of customers and competitors as well as internal requirements to improve efficiency in the organization are the driving forces behind the changes.

Some firms have changed their information systems. The interview shows that most of the firms focus on e-Market issues and many firms are at present involved in making major changes in reform of their management. There may be many reasons behind the need for changing the information systems. Changes in business operations may, of course, require changes in information systems, but the rapid development in e-Market area also provides possibilities for increased management. New applications and new computerized approaches can influence the firm management.

When firms have made larger change to meet the e-Business process and organization on e-Market, the firms' managements are largely the basis for change.

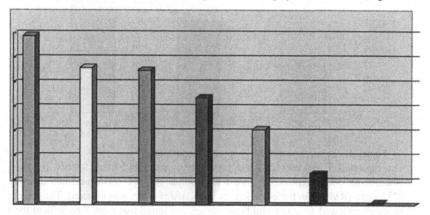

Figure.3. Changes for firms' management

4.3 Benefits from e-Market

e-Market benefit can be measured in a variety of ways. In this study, it can be measured in change of financial turnover and investment since adopting e-Market. Figure4 shows the firms' turnovers on e-Market in 2005. Figure5 shows that the firms have made change in the investment.

To the question whether there was sufficient return directly resulting from e-Market that they could cover their connection costs, participants from small businesses gave answers of either "no" or "barely". So, it is confirmed to some extent that small businesses were not reaping significant short term benefits. However, most of the participants saw that online purchases and transactions were only one way e-Market could be used to support their businesses. As most of the participants were using e-Market as a communication medium, the ways e-Market supported their business operations were similar to common communication services like traditional way, but more easily and efficiently. Even those who admitted gaining short term benefits (particularly direct benefits) were aware that such benefits were only marginal, and often circumstantial. Most participants said that indirect benefits were keeping them connected to e-Market. As more businesses start to trade via e-Market, most participants believe it is still much cheaper to access the global marketplace in this way, prior to setting up serious business relationships. It seems that the positive trend of e-Market business development was what kept the participants connected to the e-Market. Most participants believed not having an e-Market presence (most referred to an e-mail address and a Web page) will soon become a competitive disadvantage.

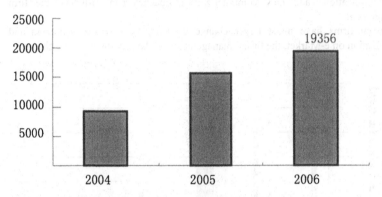

Figure.4. Average Invest of the Firms on e-Marketplace

The figures 4,5 indicates that businesses show more and more interest in doing business on e-Marketplace. Figure 4 shows that in 2004, e-Businessmen invested 9233 yuan (RMB$) in the e-Market. In 2006, 19356 yuan was invested. The project group interviewed 10 successful businessmen and found that more than 90% of their business was done on e-Marketplaces. The most amount reaches 0.7 million yuan in the e-Business. Figure 5 shows that in 2004 most e-Businessmen only invested a few thousand yuan, but in 2005 and the first half of 2006, they invested more than 10000 in their e-Business.

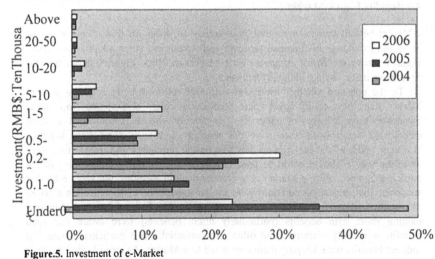

Figure.5. Investment of e-Market

4.4 Industry and product specificity

The figure 6 shows that when the businesses enlarge their investment in e-Business, e-Marketing is becoming multiple and united. In the e-Business model, business marketing and promotion has changed from comparatively exclusive to inclusive. E-business information of every kind is issued through internet. Thus e-Marketplace provides firms and users special and personalized e-Marketplace so that the competitive businesses can use the new tools in their competition with each other.

As for how e-Market is used in business operation, it becomes obvious that industry and product specificity have influenced them in using e-Market to support their business operations. It is observed that if the firm has more customers and business partners using e-Market, it is itself more willing to use e-Market for its business. There seems to be a "peer encouragement" effect in this case, particularly if all parties have convincing evidence that they are, indeed, better off. In terms of industry and product dependency, those firms which belonged to e-Market-spawned businesses were relying on e-Market more than firms from other business sectors. Figure6 shows the firms' activities on e-Market. Apart from the fact that these firms were more "e-Market literate", they had actually experienced first-hand the ways in which e-Market has improved the effectiveness and efficiency of their business relationships. Such improvements made them more competitive and this kept the advanced e-Market user exploring the e-Market for assistance in further aspects of their business dealings.

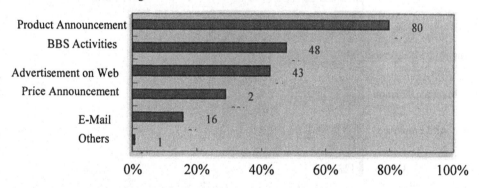

Figure.6. Activities on e-Market

In China, more vertical websites that focuses on a business are springing up. In the survey, at least more than 200 specific websites in 25 fields of business have been set up now. As Figure 7 shows, more than 10 businesses have their business operation in a considerable scale.

The effect of product (or service) specificity related to e-Market use can be measured by investigating how much the customer would be satisfied with an electronic version of the actual "thing". Our findings lead us to believe that if the usefulness of the product or service is preserved or enhanced when delivered in digital form, then the business itself, its customers and business partners would tend to use e-Market more. For example, group of e-Market spawn businesses often use e-Market to deliver their products (e.g. software or Web page design), not only because the electronic version was better than its physical counterpart, but also because this saves time and costs (service enhancement). This is why the specific websites attract most users, including firms and customers.

As benefit in the e-Marketplace is going up, more and more industry group attaches importance to enhancing their e-Market. Figure8 shows the firms' plan of investment in 2007 for similar reasons. Other participants were using e-Market as improving management, such as a document transfer medium etc.

No.	2005 Business Volume (¥)	Special Website
1	Under 5 million	90
2	5-10 million	75
3	10-50 million	10
4	Above 50 million	5
Total		180

Figure.7. (2005 Business Volume on Special Website)

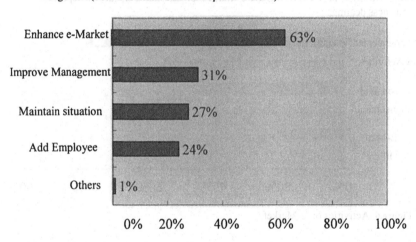

Figure.8. Plan of E-Business in 2007

4.5 Integration for e-Business systems on e-Market

In the questionnaire firms are also asked to state the extent to which sectors were specially grouped for different functions. The interviews also show that to the extent they have IT specialists these often have the role of operations sectors. Literature on e-Market and strategic advantage often stress that longer term benefits can only be realized with well-planned integration of business functions in an inter-organizational or sector-wide manner. But the findings indicate that at present there is little integration between e-business systems and e-Market among this group of early adopters. Among the participants, internal IS functions such as accounting, customer and inventory management were still operating independently of e-Market. For this group of companies, there was a gap between inter-organizational and internal IS activities. Although all firms were using e-Market for information exchange with their customers, none has reached the integration so that messages through e-Market, such as orders, could be processed by its internal system automatically.

The results of our studies, in fact, suggest the process of integrating e-Business systems with internal application systems among businesses is likely to differ from the conventional ones. IT enables business transformation to start with local business functions within the organization, then expands to inter-organizational and, finally, to sector-wide transformation. Although this does not explicitly state that the different stages are sequentially connected, it is implied by examples showing organizations passing through these stages sequentially.

5 Conclusion

The overall result from the study indicates that among those who have been online for about two years, there is evidence that e-Market has been providing benefit to its adopters. The study provides evidence that the most crucial issues affecting ongoing e-Market use within businesses are management's commitment and perception of benefits. Most firms are still using e-Market as a communications medium in addition to the telephone and facsimile, although advertising and marketing are also driving Internet use.

When compared to traditional internal application systems, e-Market offers a tool on which users can build their business processes. Therefore, user input and ways of use will determine how much benefit one can get out of e-Market. This leads us to believe that businesses that use e-Market will eventually create the difference between firms which has a positive attitude towards e-Market use and those having a negative view of this e-marketplace.

We admit that there are many other factors in both dimensions which have not been explored in this study. Yet, the outcome from this study helps to focus future research efforts on this topic. We hope the outcome of this study will help to focus current and future initiatives by governments and international bodies in helping Chinese firms to become beneficiaries of e-Market. Our future research will further investigate the types of benefit gained from e-Market and whether these are sensitive to organizational context.

References

1. Alibaba Group and Chinese Journal of EB World (2006): Report on the Survival and Development of e-Business in China 2004-2006

2. Z Zhu, The study on vertical application model B2B e-Marketplace (University of International Business and Economics, Bei*jing, 2005)*

3. S Poon and Swatman PMC, A longitudinal study of expectations in small business internet commerce. *International Journal of Electronic Commerce* 3(3), 21–33. (1999)

4. S Poon, Business environment and internet commerce benefit, *European Journal of Information Systems* (2000) 9, 72–81.

5. J.P.Bailey and J.Y.Bakos, An exploratory study of the emerging role of electronic intermediaries, *International Journal of Electronic Commerce 1(3),7-20(Spring 1997).*

6. J.Y.Bakos, Reducing buyer search costs: Implications for electronic marketplaces, *Management Science 43(12), 1676-1692(December 1997)*

7. Jiang Yubin, A B2B E-procurement Model based on Intermediary Website, *Shanghai Management Science 6,41-44(2005)*

8. Yan Zhonghua, Guan Shixu and Mi Jianing, The theoretic Study about the Confidence Mechanism of B2B Based on System, *Technoeconomics & Management Research 5,89-89(2003)*

9. news.ccidnet.com, http://chat.ccidnet.com/art/5169/20070118/1004617_1.html

10. cio.ccidnet.com, http://industry.ccidnet.com/pub/html/industry/zhuanti_jsp/index.htm

11. Alibaba.com,(2004-2006),http://www.alibaba.com

12. Taobao.com,(2004-2006),http://www.taobao.com

13. Himberger, A., Der Elektronische Markt als Koordinationssystem, Thesis, University of St. Gallen, Switzerland, (1994)

14. Krähenmann, N., Ökonomische Gestaltungsanforderungen für die Entwicklung elektronischer Märkte, Thesis, University of St. Gallen, Switzerland, (1994)

15. Langenohl, T, Systemarchitekturen elektronischer Märkte, Thesis, University of St. Gallen, Switzerland, (1994)

16. Schmid, B, Elektronische Märkte, Wirtschaftsinformatik, Vol.35, No.5, 465-480. (1993)

17. Ashish Arora, Gregory Cooper, Ramayya Krishnan and Rema Padman , IBIZA: E-market Infrastructure for Custom-built Information Products, *Information Systems Frontiers*, Volume 2, Number1 65-84 (2000)

18. QI Qin, Zhao Xi, Jingyan Chen, The Innovation of E-marketing Combination Tactics, *Lecture Notes in Computer Science*, Volume 2105/2001 (2001)

19. Prithviraj Dasgupta, Louise E. Moser and P. Michael Melliar-Smith , Dynamic Pricing for Time-Limited Goods in a Supplier-Driven Electronic Marketplace, *Electronic Commerce Research*, Volume5, Number2,267-292 (2005)

20. Qizhi Dai and Robert J. Kauffman, To be or not to B2B: Evaluating managerial choices for e-procurement channel adoption, *Information Technology and Management*, Volume7, Number2 109-130 (2006)

Development of China C2C E-commerce
from the Perspective of Goods Delivery

Hongjiao Fu, Youbei Huang and Xuxu Wei

Deptartment of Economic Information Management, School of
Information, Renmin University of China, Beijing 100872, P.R. China
fuhongjiao@263.net, yopey@263.com, weixuxu2005@263.net

Abstract. As one of the key applied forms on Internet, C2C E-commerce has
been growing at a very high speed in China in recent years. Starting from the
perspective that C2C E-commerce consumers pursue low price while retailers
try to decrease the cost, by using the methods of sampling survey and case
study, the paper will discuss issues about goods delivery cost, delivery time
and delivery quality in C2C E-commerce and compare them with B2B E-
commerce. According to the result of research, the paper predicts the future
development trend of China C2C E-commerce.

1 Introduction

The importance of E-commerce has been accepted by more and more people in
various circles. The emergency of China C2C E-commerce mode is marked by the
establishment of EBay China Inc. in 1999 and its development is very rapid. With
the improvement and maturing of the environment, the transaction volume of China
C2C E-commerce has quickly increased in recent years. In 2001, the transaction
volume of China C2C E-commerce market was merely RMB 400 million. It reached
up to RMB 13.71 billion by 2005 with a CAGR of 142.0% [1]. Today China's C2C
E-commerce market is dominated by three major players: Taobao
(www.taobao.com), EBay China (www.ebay.com.cn), and Paipai (www.paipai.com).

When the issues of credit and safe online payment become the public's focus,
some problems emerged in goods delivery that affect online consumers' behaviors
without being noticed. The problems of credit and safe e-payment prevent some
consumers from getting into field of E-commerce. To the consumers who use E-
commerce, after crossing the threshold of "credit and safety", they must face another
big problem i.e. goods delivery. It is clear that the issue of goods delivery affects the
number of consumers who would participate in E-commerce. Starting from the
perspective that C2C consumers pursue low price while retailers try to decrease the
cost, the paper will discuss issues about delivery cost, delivery time and delivery

Please use the following format when citing this chapter:

Fu, H., Huang, Y., Wei, X., 2007, in IFIP International Federation for Information Processing, Volume 251, Integration
and Innovation Orient to E-Society Volume1, Wang, W. (Eds), (Boston: Springer), pp. 179-186.

quality in C2C E-commerce and compare them with B2B E-commerce by using the methods of sampling survey and case study. Through comparison and analysis, the paper discusses the future development trends of C2C E-commerce in China.

The data used in this research came from 107 survey questionnaires we sent out and in-depth interviews with related retailers and consumers. The survey consists of a survey of C2C consumer and a survey of C2C retailer. The targets of the survey are located in seven cities including Beijing, Shanghai, Guangzhou, Qingdao, Chengdu, Hangzhou, and Harbin.

2 Related concepts in C2C E-commerce

Some concepts related to C2C E-commerce will be involved in this paper, so we will explain them in this section.

2.1 Structure of goods price

Currently, goods price of C2C E-commerce consists of two parts: retail price and delivery cost. Retail price has same meaning as it in traditional business which refers to sale price of a good. Delivery cost refers to the cost that needs to be paid to the company who delivers goods for consumers. The main delivery entities in China are China Post and express delivery companies. The sum of the retail price and delivery cost is called purchase price paying to the retailer by the consumer.

2.2 Auction way of the goods

There are two ways for consumers to purchase goods online including "fixed price" and "auction price". "Fixed price" means the retailers sell the goods in a regular price and no bargaining. "Auction price" means the retailers offer the starting price and price bid increment when they sell the goods. The consumers input the lowest price they want or input the highest price they can accept then waiting for the processing of the auction system. When the auction is finished, the consumer who bid the highest price will take the good.

2.3 Ways of goods delivery

Now the ways of delivering goods in China C2C E-commerce include: Regular Mail, EMS and Express Delivery. "Regular mail" refers to delivering the goods in the form of an ordinary parcel or print design through China Post from the retailer to the consumer. "EMS" refers to Express Mail Service through China Post mainly by airplane to speed the delivery up. Depending on the distance, the mail or parcel will be sent to destination from one day to seven days. "Express Delivery" refers to the express delivery service offered by other express delivery companies except China Post. They have their own networks and mainly are private companies, such as ZJS (www.zjs.com.cn). There are about one thousand express companies in China now.

2.4 Logistics distribution system of E-commerce in China

There are three ways of logistics distribution in current China E-commerce [2]: (1) Establishing their own distribution channels and facilities to deliver goods by themselves. The E-commerce companies set up storage centers and distribution centers where online consumers are densely populated. (2) Entrusting the third party professional logistics distribution institutions to deliver goods. (3) Cooperating with chain department stores and China Post EMS to complete goods delivery together.

3 Study on goods delivery of China C2C E-commerce

Goods delivery has a great effect on operation cost of E-commerce companies. Most C2C E-commerce consumers are scattered group. Their orders are random and scattering that leads to small delivery batch and high delivery cost. Now "goods delivery" has become top-four problem of "the most untrustable issue of C2C online shopping" after goods quality, sellers' credit and payment [1]. Next this paper will discuss China future development tendency of C2C E-commerce from the perspective of goods delivery cost, delivery time and delivery quality.

3.1 Delivery cost

According to the related report [1], 78.4% of online consumers choose C2C website to shop for the reason of "relatively cheap price". By the end of 2006, the young people between 18 and 24 years old account for 35.2% of all Internet users. Main consumers of C2C E-commerce are those young people [3]. However, most of them earn a low or no income, so pursuing cheap price is their main intention of online shopping. In fact, when consumers shopping on C2C websites, they usually find that most goods always have similar purchase prices as traditional stores. Sometimes the price is even a little higher than offline shopping. Why this happens? The main reason is that online shopping has extra delivery cost.

Current C2C online transactions are mainly cheap goods and the profits of these goods are very little. If adding delivery cost into the purchase price, the consumers will not take the advantage of favorable prices of online shopping, so they naturally hesitate when making online shopping decisions.

3.1.1 The analysis of goods delivery cost of B2C E-commerce

As mentioned above, there are three ways of distribution adopted by E-commerce Company. The first way is mainly used in large or medium-sized companies. Taking the famous B2C website Joyo.com as an example, in March of 2002, it established Beijing Century Joyo Express Delivery Service Corporation, supplying the services including "home-delivery" and "cash on delivery" in some large cities of China [4].

Meanwhile, Joyo.com also uses the second and the third way. Joyo delivers goods by China Post in the places where no their home delivery service. However, according to postage standard of regular post service, the more goods consumers buy, the higher the delivery cost is. Sometimes delivery cost might be over one hundred RMB or exceed the value of the good itself. Such high postage restricts consumers' enthusiasm of online shopping. To solve this problem, Joyo chose to cooperate with China Post to reduce the postage since November of 2002. For a regular mail within mainland China, no matter how many goods, it only costs RMB 5. If buyers spend more than RMB 99 at one time, then they don't need to pay delivery fee [4].

In fact, like Joyo.com, most B2C E-commerce websites have preferential delivery charge. Such as Dangdang.com, it charges free when consuming over RMB 99 one time [5]. The free level of Bertelsmann (www.bol.com.cn) is even as low as RMB 38 [6]; 2688 website offers free delivery service in most cities of China [7]. The decrease of delivery cost stimulates consumers to shop on such websites.

3.1.2 The analysis of goods delivery cost of C2C E-commerce

C2C E-commerce retailers are individuals. Mostly C2C retailers sell small amount of goods with high frequency and disperse destinations. As a result, C2C retailers haven't enough power to setup their own delivery teams, or sign a long-time contract with China Post or delivery companies. In most cases, they would choose the second or third method for delivery, so the delivery fee must be in accordance with China Post or delivery companies, so the delivery cost is high and hard to reduce.

We samples retail price and delivery cost of different kinds of goods in different C2C online shops. According to our investigation data, we can get the relationship between delivery cost and retail price, shown as Fig.1. Through calculation and analysis, we get a cubic polynomial $Y=4\times10^{-11}X^3-10^{-6}X^2+0.0101X+9.9404$. Here X represents retail price and Y represents delivery cost (regular mail).

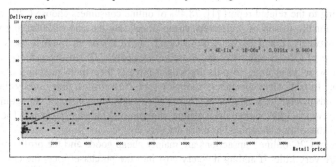

Figure.1. The relationship between delivery cost and retail price

Through colligated analysis of all the data above, we can get the delivery costs with different retail price region, as shown in Table 1.

Table 1. The regular mail of different retail price（regular mail）

Retail price	0-15 Yuan	16-50 Yuan	50-300 Yuan	300-500 Yuan	500-5000 Yuan	Above 5000 Yuan
Delivery cost	5 Yuan	6-8 Yuan	8-10 Yuan	10-20 Yuan	20-35 Yuan 35-50 Yuan	

Here, we advance the concept "Peijiabi", which refers to the rate of delivery cost and retail price. As shown in Fig.1, the slope of this cubic curve is "Peijiabi". We can see that the higher the retail price is, the smaller the slope is. Then we conclude that the "Peijiabi" of goods with high retail price is small and vice versa.

In the questionnaires, we investigate consumers about "Peijiabi". 35% of consumers will choose to give up shopping online if "Peijiabi" beyond 0.5. When the rate is between 0.1 and 0.4, 23% will choose to compare the price with the goods nearby then make the decision. As the rate is smaller than 0.1, only 2 % will abandon. We can conclude that because of the high delivery cost, the market share of C2C E-commerce has shrunk greatly. Due to low retail price, the "Peijiabi" of small-ticket items is often high. Those data confirm that the delivery cost is the key factor to influence small-ticket commodity sales online.

3.1.3 The effect of delivery cost on C2C E-commerce

At present, the goods delivery costs are centralized mainly between RMB 5 and 20. The delivery cost almost equals to retail price for goods cheaper than RMB 20. This phenomenon slacks down the price advantage of C2C E-commerce and reduce enthusiasm of shopping online. However, small-ticket goods sell well now with two reasons: (1) many consumers are still suspicious of C2C E-commerce; they usually buy some small-ticket items at the first time; (2) there aren't the goods nearby consumers want. But E-commerce platform collect many sellers who come from the whole country even the whole world, so buyers are easier to find the items they like.

However, with economic globalization and growing up of E-commerce, no matter online or offline, the goods choices for consumers will be more. Moreover, B2C E-commerce companies can cooperate with distribution companies to reduce the cost by signing long-term agreement. Obviously, if C2C companies can't lower their delivery cost, the development of C2C E-commerce will be restricted hugely.

3.2 Delivery time

The E-commerce consumer must wait for receiving goods after making an order. According to the survey from CNNIC [8], many people think the biggest problem is "channels not flowing easily thus taking too much time to send goods", 21.6% of online buyers think that delivery time needs to be shorten. During our interviews with C2C consumers, we find that almost half of them give up shopping online due to long delivery time that they can't bear.

3.2.1 The Analysis of goods delivery time in China

Different delivery methods lead to different length of delivery time. Regular mails usually need one or two weeks depending on the distance from sending place to receiving place and don't supply home-delivery service. EMS and express delivery need less time. Goods can arrive at the same day if sending place and receiving place in the same city. If they are in different cities, it depends on whether it is a provincial capital, small-medium cities or remote district. Usually EMS needs two to seven days, while express delivery needs one to three days.

3.2.2 Goods delivery time of C2C E-commerce

In our survey, most consumers think regular mail and EMS take too long time, so they would choose express delivery service. 16.7% of consumers choose "The main delivery way is express delivery when shopping on C2C website". They all express that they choose express delivery just for getting their items as quickly as possible.

However, the common price is RMB 10 per kilogram through express company; the minimum charge of EMS is RMB 20. Such expensive delivery fees make many consumers lose the interests to shop on C2C website.

3.2.3 Goods delivery time of B2C E-commerce

Unlike C2C E-commerce, B2C retailers have their own distribution teams. Except regular mail and EMS, their express delivery includes home-delivery service and urgent home-delivery service. For regular mail and EMS, both B2C and C2C rely on China Post, so there is no difference in delivery time. But urgent home-delivery service of B2C equals with express delivery in C2C. In fact, urgent home-delivery service needs to pay extra RMB 10 to 15 which consumers are not willing to pay. Home-delivery service time is between regular mails and express delivery in C2C. In Beijing or Shanghai, home-delivery service requires 12 to 24 more hours than C2C express delivery. In other places, home-delivery service needs 1 to 6 days or more.

3.2.4 The effect of delivery time on C2C E-commerce

We know from above analysis that the delivery time of C2C has more advantage. However, home-delivery service in B2C only charges RMB 5, which is lower than express delivery in C2C. If delivery times are same, especially to consumers in Beijing and Shanghai, the advantage of C2C delivery time isn't obvious.

3.3 Delivery quality

The feature of E-commerce determines that goods delivery needs a certain time. When goods come to consumers at last, the quality may slip up due to mistakes in the delivery process. Both sides of transaction couldn't control this. According to the related report [8], the unpleasant experiences caused by delivery issues take 22.5%, 24.3%, and 14.7% separately in Taobao, EBay, and Paipai.

3.3.1 The analysis of goods delivery quality in current C2C E-commerce

During delivering process, damage of goods is easiest-to-appear. In our survey, many consumers complained that frangible goods, such as glass, are easy to be damaged. which also make baneful influence on goods delivery. They also said some deliverers are unethical and sometimes exchange valuable goods like cell phones. Retailers can only complain to express companies or post office. Maybe they can get compensation, but it is hard to regain all money.

If delivery mistakes can't be avoided, both sellers and buyers should get compensation. But on the community forums of Taobao, EBay and Paipai, many consumers complain that sellers reject to compensate when goods are damaged. Meanwhile, many C2C retailers complain that post office or express companies also reject to compensate when goods damaged. Thus, it's very important to issue related bylaws to avoid these things to happen.

In fact, most C2C retailers belong to a small capital business. When they can't get compensation, it is natural for them to assume the loss with consumers, even reject to compensate consumers. This situation makes bad influence on retailers and blows the passion of consumers to shop on C2C website.

3.3.2 The analysis of goods delivery quality in current B2C E-commerce

At first, B2C E-commerce companies have their own delivery team or a long-term cooperation with the third party logistics distribution express companies. Once mistakes occur in delivery, it's easy to find person in charge and compensate according to relevant provisions. Secondly, B2C E-commence websites have their own provisions about after-sale services. Once there are qualities issues in delivery, consumers can claim for compensation according to relevant provisions.

In C2C E-commence, retailers often reject or require consumers to bear delivery fees when consumers ask for return of goods. However, B2C E-commence websites have correlative return sales policy. For example, Joyo makes detailed explanation: "Joyo.com promises that they will supply return service with whole refund if the goods and packaging keep the original state within 15 days from receiving day"; "for the returned purchase due to goods quality or other causes of Joyo, delivery fees and payment for goods are returned to consumers together." [9]

3.3.3 The influence of goods delivery quality on C2C E-commence

The delivery quality is the instable and unpredictable factor in C2C E-commence. After consumers accept goods retail price, delivery fee and delivery time, delivery quality will directly influence their satisfaction degree and the enthusiasm to C2C.

So besides packing goods more scrupulously, C2C retailers should actively contact with express delivery companies with good reputation. For those large scale C2C retailers, they should sign contracts with a fixed express delivery company which can reduce delivery fees and make delivers more responsibly.

4 Conclusion

According to above investigation and analyses, we can conclude that B2C E-commerce gains more advantages over C2C E-commerce in reducing delivery cost and delivery time, and in improving delivery quality. However, most consumers are inclined to shop on C2C websites rather than B2C websites. The main reasons for that can be summarized as follows: (1) China B2C E-commerce is still under-developed. The market scale is far smaller than that of C2C. From our survey we found that the reason of consumers not choosing to shop on B2C websites is because many consumers know little about those websites and their preferential terms of delivery fees; (2) generally, retail prices on C2C E-commerce websites are lower than B2C websites, and the types of goods sold on C2C websites are much more than those sold on B2C websites. As consumers can't find what they need nearby or on B2C websites, they seem to resort to search and purchase the goods on C2C websites.

However, from the perspective of economizing, both B2C and C2C E-commerce retailers will try to reduce cost and lower the price to attract customers. If consumers know well about C2C and B2C E-commerce, and goods prices are similar, the delivery cost will be the deciding factor. According to the above analysis, B2C E-commerce has more advantages in delivering cost.

In most cases, prices of goods sold on B2C E-commerce websites are higher than those on the C2C E-commerce websites. For customers, the biggest concern now is the purchase price, including retail price and delivery fee. Sometimes there are few differences between B2C E-commerce with higher retail price and lower delivery fee and C2C E-commerce with lower retail price and higher delivery fee. Considering the credit and the guarantee of high quality goods of B2C E-commerce companies, consumers are more likely to shop on a B2C E-commerce website. Thus, in order to get a certain market share, C2C E-commerce websites will need to lower retail price or reduce the delivery cost. Some large-scale retailers would like to imitate management pattern of B2C E-commerce companies, making a contract with a local post office or an express delivery company to reduce delivery cost. But for small-scale retailers, they have to cut price further. If the goods prices are close to, even lower than the cost price, the retailers will choose to withdraw from C2C E-commerce market. Therefore, from the perspective of retailers, the development of C2C E-commerce will be hindered and the market share will shrink.

Fortunately, it is clear that C2C E-commerce would not disappear. In the future, C2C E-commerce websites will sell unique goods which are customized and not easy to produce on a large scale, such as signature of a movie star, a book published 100 years ago, etc. These goods satisfy the individual needs of consumers. They will not think too much and even ignore delivery fees when buying. In other words, the C2C E-commerce websites will concentrate on individualized goods, while the best sellers or popular goods will be sold on B2C E-commerce websites which are superior in both price and delivery fee.

Reference:

1. Shanghai iResearch Co., ltd., 2005 China C2C *Ecommerce Research Report*, 2006.
2. L. Zhao, R.X Cai and Y. Cui, "Analysis on logistic distribution of E-commerce", *Industrial Technology Economy* , 9, 45-46(2006).
3. China Internet Network Information Center (CNNIC), The 19th Survey Report on Statistical Reports on the Internet Development in China, Jan 2007.
4. Http://www. joyo.com.
5. Http://www.dangdang.com.
6. Http://www.bol.com.cn.
7. Http://www.365ebuy.com/Merchant_Page/2688.htm.
8. China Internet Network Information Center (CNNIC), 2006 online shopping report of China C2C E-commerce, 2007.
9. Delivery time, delivery fee standard and return policy, http://www.joyo.com/help. [2007-4-23].

Research on the internal cause and correlative factor of virtual enterprises

Hu Yi

School of economics, Huazhong Normal University,
152 Luoyu Road, wuhan, P.R.China, 430079
hy197105@126.com

Abstract. This paper makes use of a vertical integration model to explain virtual enterprises, analyses respective characteristics of virtual operation and internal integration, probes into the correlative factors of virtual operation. The paper points out that virtual operation and internal integration are two parallel ways which enterprises may choose to expand their organization. Virtual operation urges exterior market to become perfect, so may overcome the problem of market failure. Virtual operation can construct a relatively perfect exterior market, also uses existing exterior market efficiently, so enterprises are able to control market and transaction through virtual operation. But effective virtual operation is restricted by many conditions. The correlative factors of virtual enterprises includes the interior conditions of enterprises and exterior conditions from the dimensionalities of micro-environment and macro-environment. Therefore, along with the changes of market, environment, competition and enterprises' strategy, being agile and taking dynamic integration or virtual operation should be the best policy of enterprises' organization.

1 Introduction

Nowadays the advantage of virtual enterprises and virtual operation has been proven by lots of theory and practice. In the theory of competition and cooperation[1], the competition among enterprises has experienced antagonistical competition, tolerant competition and cooperative competition. Since the market environment is changeable, the cooperative competition among enterprises, which can be formed through organizing alliance to resist market risk, broadening market space, and complementing mutual advantage can swell competitive advantage of enterprises. In the strategic mode of virtual operation enterprises can share and exchange information to reduce costs of trading, harmonizing and management, can broaden

Please use the following format when citing this chapter:

Yi, H., 2007, in IFIP International Federation for Information Processing, Volume 251, Integration and Innovation Orient to E-Society Volume1, Wang, W. (Eds), (Boston: Springer), pp. 187-193.

cooperative scope of enterprises external, and can accomplish complex cooperation with the characteristic of close coupling of cooperation. Moreover, cooperation appears as shared knowledge and resources. Knowledge is one of the most important factors of production, and its feature of cumulative results in ability shortage of individual enterprise in changeable market. Resource partaking of capital, technology, market, information and management can remedy shortage of resources. As mentioned above, cooperative competition of virtual operation brings about its strategic advantage. In the theory of transaction cost[2], market or enterprises is a mode of resource allocation, and there is transaction cost in either of them. With complication of trading, transaction cost will be added continuously. However, enterprises can interiorize its trading to reduce transaction cost, which can acts as the main mode of resource allocation. The expansion of enterprise size will add transaction cost such as management costs to turn enterprises as hyper-marketing contractual organization operating virtually. To a certain degree, virtual enterprises, a kind of contractual organization, can remedy imperfection of contracts to resist market risk. These theories demonstrate the functions of virtual operation enough.

The virtual operation has brought the change of the enterprises' form. Charles P. Kindleberger[3], one of the founders of theory of monopolistic advantage, even already no longer regarded the modern TNC as the single manufacturer in the traditional microeconomics. He thought that the modern TNC was the unified firm by no means, it was the loose agglomerations of profit centers which were composed by the local certain profit centers in different countries. The view manifested the trend of enterprises' network and virtual organization.

However, so far the study on the internal cause and correlative factors of virtual enterprises is deficient. Why do enterprises implement virtual operation? What are the conditions of virtual operation? This paper will make some theoretical analysis on the internal cause and correlative factors of virtual enterprises in virtue of a vertical integrated model.

2   A model to explain virtual enterprises and virtual operation

A vertical integrated model is built to analyze the internal cause of virtual enterprises in this paper.

Consider a partial market with supplier A and enterprise B, supplier A provides raw material X which enterprise B needs, quantity of X is the x, production cost is $C(x)$, and $C(0) = 0$. Enterprise B pays $\omega(x)$ to purchases X, and $\omega(0) = 0$. Then the total profit function of supplier A is

$R_A = \omega(x) - C(x)$

In order to enhance the production efficiency, enterprise B is willing to make irreversible investment K to buy and use the specific equipment, the cost of investment K will be k, and investment K would determine the total management return of enterprise B, the total profit function of B is

$R_B = P(x, k) - \omega(x) - k$

Then under the perfect condition, the best outcome is causes the total profit maximization of B and A.

$$\Pi = P(x, k) - \omega(x) - k + \omega(x) - C(x) = P(x, k) - C(x) - k$$
$$\frac{\partial P(x, k)}{\partial k} = 1$$
$$\frac{\partial P(x, k)}{\partial x} = \frac{\partial C}{\partial x}$$

Under the best condition the marginal value of investment is equal to the marginal cost of investment, and the marginal value of X was equal to the marginal cost of X produced by supplier A.

Because of imperfect market, the opportunism behaviors like hold-up are supposed between supplier A and enterprise B. After enterprise B makes investment K, supplier A requests the enterprise B pay more to purchase X, therefore the new negotiations have carried on. Enterprise B has to pay more to purchase X because investment K is irreversible and k becomes sunk cost. Thus, profit target of enterprise B is

max R_B=max [P (x, k) −ω (x)]

And profit target of supplier A is

max R_A=max [ω (x) −C (x)]

According to the Nash equilibrium,

$$\max_{\omega(x)} [P(x, k) - \omega(x)][\omega(x) - C(x)]$$

The result is that

$$\frac{\partial P(x, k)}{\partial x} = \frac{\partial \omega}{\partial x} = \frac{\partial C}{\partial x}$$
$$\omega(x) = \frac{[P(x, k) + C(x)]}{2}$$

It shows that the total payments of enterprise B to supplier A is one half of the sum of total repayment of enterprise B and total cost of supplier A, that is to say that enterprise B and supplier A divides equally the total income if production achieved equilibrium.

Now considering the investment scale of enterprise B, substitutes ω (x) , enterprise B attains the profit is

$$R_B = P(x, k) - k = \frac{[P(x, k) - C(x)]}{2} - k$$

Because enterprise B can forecast this result, it will choose an investment scale to maximize own profit, that is

$$\frac{\partial P(x, k)}{\partial k} = 2$$

Thus according to Nash bargaining solution, the marginal value of the investment made by enterprise B should achieve two times of the capital marginal cost. As compared with the best investment, investment according to the Nash equilibrium is insufficient definitely, and will affect the production of X at the next stage. The market failure causes effective investment insufficient Therefore in order to obtain the more return by optimizing investment, enterprise B will implement the vertical internal integration and enter the realm of X's production.

In above model, one side of upstream and downstream enterprises has the opportunism behavior, another side has incentive to implement the internal integration to gain the greater return. But in fact, the internal integration is one kind of choice for manufacturer to overcome the opportunism behavior. If specific management behavior except internal integration can guarantee the transaction quantity and price, the manufacturer also may enable the investment to achieve most superior.

Virtual operation is one of such management behaviors, it introduces establishing long-term cooperation relationship, concluding service agreement, setting up strategic alliance, outsourcing and so on, has formed correlative dependence and reciprocity between the transaction sides, causes a side of transaction to have the tremendous influence to opposite side even control opposite side, thus it plays the role which guarantee the transaction performed smoothly. In other words, manufacturer may obtain assuring contract through virtual operation. Daniel F. Spulber[4] has already proven: If the contract is reliable and has guaranteed, the enterprise holds or does not hold the specific property rights, all can realize the investment efficiency optimization, namely under this condition property rights are neutral. Therefore, virtual operation can replace internal integration in theory.

Reviewing the American Enterprises' development, Ford Motor Company, once was the model of internal integration management, since 1980's transformed the former internal integrated organization, and used more and more exterior transaction contracts to replace the internal organization. All manner of virtual operation and activities may show in practice that: enterprises are possible to obtain the very good economic efficiency equally even though they do not hold the property rights of certain assets. Virtual operation urges exterior market to become perfect, so may overcome the problem of market failure.

3   An analysis of respective characteristics of internal integration and virtual operation

Through above analysis, both virtual operation and internal integration can guarantee the inside or outside contracts, increase profits of enterprise. The form of modern enterprise's organization more and more tends toward diverseness and variety. Modern enterprise may use internal integration behavior to enhance the enterprise ability, also may adopt virtual operation to strengthen own capability to conclude and fulfill the contract by virtual market.

Enterprise adopts internal integration behavior, carries out specific investment, sets up more complicated organization, implements the common control and coordination by unified management system, so it obtains stronger transaction ability by possessing more internal resource.

Enterprise uses virtual operation, concludes and implements sorts of assuring contracts and strategic agreements, integrates interior and exterior resource, achieves sharing and controlling exterior resource, so it gains more management resource through guaranteed contracts.

Thus it can be seen, the internal integration and virtual operation all are the ways of enterprise to enhance transaction ability and strengthen competitive advantage.They are also two approaches of enterprise to expand its organization. The way of internal integration would form a relative integrity of enterprise's organization, but the way of virtual operation would form the loose structure of enterprise's organization(virtual organization).

The superiorities of virtual operation to internal integration are: virtual operation ɩ ealize interior and exterior resources of the enterprise sharing and optimizing, rɩ e business risk by lessening specific investments and overcoming orɡ zation's rigidity, and virtual operation can help firms to enhance ability to conɩ de and fulfill transaction contract as more exterior assets and resources of firms ɔould be used in key business's activities. Certainly, virtual operation is inferior to internal integration in controlling transaction contract.

Internal integration behavior takes out interior market and uses it, but virtual operation establishes perfect exterior market(virtual market) and uses it. Interior market and exterior market have each own characteristic. Internal integration improves semifinished products and factors trade through constructing interior market, spurs exterior market to become perfect; virtual operation colligates exterior and interior market, increases efficiency of transaction. Although virtual operation does not have the absolute right to control the transaction contract, it has the flexibility actually to choose the manner and object of contract.

Each kind of enterprises cultivate their own competitive advantage depended on constructing and using interior market and exterior market. The conducts to construct market change structure of market, including constructing exterior and interior market, establishing a new market and alter estate of existing market, shifting a imperfect market to a perfect market. The conducts to use market utilize all sorts of market, including using exterior market, virtual market and interior market, making use of perfect market and imperfect market. Virtual operation can construct a relatively perfect exterior market(virtual market), also use existing exterior market efficiently, so enterprises are able to control market and save transaction cost through virtual operation.

4 The study on the correlative factors of virtual enterprises

In order to develope rapidly, enterprises should use more exterior resources with the aid of other enterprises by virtual operation. But effective virtual operation is restricted by many conditions. The study on the correlative factors of virtual operation is the key to do basic work and virtual operating scientifically. The correlative factors of virtual enterprises includes the interior conditions of enterprises and exterior conditions from the dimensionalities of micro-environment and macro-environment.

The interior conditions of virtual operation consist of the competitive advantage of structure, the competitive advantage of ability, informationalization of enterprises and harmony of innovation and control competence. In the competitive advantage of structure, the competitive advantage theory of Porter[5] expatiates orientation of enterprises in the chain of value and make use of the three principles of competitive advantage and the relevance theory of enterprises to enhance competitive advantage of enterprises, so as to improve virtual operation. The competitive advantage of ability lays stress on important effect of nuclear abilities in virtual operation. The conformity of nuclear abilities guarantees success of virtual operation, only the enterprises with some nuclear abilities can be received as virtual members by other enterprises. In addition, the strategy transformation from multielement to refocusing reflects the strategic demand of change of market environment and business process reengineering of enterprises, which is the inevitable choice of enterprises to meet the competitive advantage of ability. Informationalization of enterprises can benefit their nuclear competitiveness to operate virtually, can favor cooperation with virtual partners to develop cooperation advantage, and can profit informationalization and management innovation of enterprises to better virtual operation. The adaptive business process based enterprises should look beyond the traditional enterprises and marketplaces through collaborative interactions and dynamic e-business solution bindings. The harmony of innovation and control competence can guarantee rational operation of enterprises, so does virtual operation. The harmony of innovation and control competence can improve nuclear abilities of enterprises; so, the "degree" in virtual operation and all kinds of its manifestation should unify competitiveness of innovation and control dynamically.

Exterior conditions can be divided into credit, national informationalization, logistics, and legal environment. Credit can reduce transaction cost to remedy market risk which is resulted from incompleteness of contracts and uncertainty of market, can eliminate information asymmetry to enhance operation efficiency of enterprises so as to guarantee virtual operation. Virtual operation is based on credit and enterprise may give more credit to other enterprises through virtual operation. National informationalization provides a platform for virtual operation, besides, development of information industry, popularization of network and development of electronic commerce and electronic government administration are the indispensable conditions, these conditions can improve the management and exchange of information in each enterprise and among enterprises. Logistics provides the channel of shared information and resources for virtual operation, supply chain management should build the coordination mechanism between upstream and downstream enterprises to guarantee virtual operation by effective logistics, both informationalization and logistics are inter-determined. Legal environment guarantees smooth virtual operation, which impenetrate the whole process of virtual operation. Along with the rapid development of virtual operation, a great deal of legal problems emerged. The legal environment is the safeguard for virtual operation, whole process of virtual operation including the market opportunity recognition, the partner enterprises choice, negotiations with partner, conclude and fulfill the contract, needs correlative legal.

The enterprises carry out virtual operation restricted by interior and exterior conditions, therefore, along with the changes of market, environment, competition and enterprises' strategy, being agile and taking dynamic integration or virtual operation should be the best policy of enterprises' organization.

5 Conclusion

In term of above analysis, virtual operation and internal integration are two parallel ways which enterprises may choose to expand their organization. Virtual operation urges exterior market to become perfect, so may overcome the problem of market failure. Virtual operation can construct a relatively perfect exterior market, also can use existing exterior market efficiently, so enterprises are able to control market and transaction through virtual operation. But effective virtual operation is restricted by many conditions. The correlative factors of virtual enterprises includes the interior conditions of enterprises and exterior conditions from the dimensionalities of micro-environment and macro-environment. Therefore, along with the changes of market, environment, competition and enterprises' strategy, being agile and taking dynamic integration or virtual operation should be the best policy of enterprises' organization.

References

1. N. Rackham, L. Friedman and R. Ruff, *Getting Partnering Right: How Market Leaders are Creating Long-term Competitive Advantage* , McGraw Hill Publications, New York(1996),.

2. R. H. Coase, "The Nature of the Firm", *Economica.* 4, 386-405(1937).

3. C. P. Kindleberger, "The 'New' Multinationalization of Business", *ASEAN Economic Bulletin.*, 5, 113-124(1996).

4. D. F. Spulber, *Market Microstructure: Intermediaries and the Theory of the Firm* , Cambridge University Press, New York,(1999).

5. M. Porter, *Competitive Advantage* , Free Press, New York(1985).

6. R. Jaikumar, "Post Industrial Manufacturing", *Harvard Business Review,* 86, 69–76(1986).

7. S. J. Grossman and O. Hart, "The Costs and Benefits of Ownership: A Theory of Vertical and Lateral Integration", *Journal of Political Economy* ,94, 691-719(1986).

Mobile Agents Integrity Research

Huanmei Guan[1,2], Huanguo Zhang[2,3], Ping Chen[1], and Yajie Zhou[1]

1 Computer Center, Wuhan University, Wuhan 430072, China
hmguan-wh@163.com

2 College of Computer, Wuhan University, Wuhan 430072, China
liss@whu.edu.cn

3 The State Key Laborary of Software Engineering, Wuhan University,
Wuhan 430072, China

Abstract. Mobile agents are an important technology in e-commerce systems and offer new possibilities for the e-commerce applications. This paper examines some mobile agent integrity protocols and proposes a new protecting protocol of mobile agent integrity. It can defend most known attacks, provides encryption transmission and route secrecy of mobile agents.

1 Introduction

Mobile agents are an important technology in e-commerce systems and offer new possibilities for the e-commerce applications. They can provide very flexible approach for information gathering on prices and assets available from the hosts they visit. They can create new types of electronic ventures from e-shops, e-auctions to virtual enterprises and e-marketplaces. Such systems are developed for diverse business areas, e.g., contract negotiations, service brokering, stock trading and many others([1]) .

Mobile agent systems have many advantages over traditional distributed computing environments: require less network bandwidth, increase asynchrony among clients and servers, and dynamically update server interfaces, and introduce concurrency and so on ([2]). But certain applications have a need for protection of security of the mobile agents. In the mobile agent systems the agent's code and internal state autonomously migrate between hosts and could be easy changed during the transmission or at a malicious host site. A malicious host may expose, modify, insert, delete or truncate data the agent collected from other previously visited servers to benefit itself ([3, 4]).

The integrity of an agent means that its code and execution state can not be changed by an unauthorized party or such changes should be detectable. The general goal is to protect the results within the chain of partial results from being modified ([5, 6, 7]). To protect integrity some protocols have been proposed in different

Please use the following format when citing this chapter:

Guan, H., Zhang, H., Chen, P., Zhou, Y., 2007, in IFIP International Federation for Information Processing, Volume 251, Integration and Innovation Orient to E-Society Volume1, Wang, W. (Eds), (Boston: Springer), pp. 194-201.

papers. This paper will examine some protocols and extract general methods from these protocols. As result of this examination the paper will proposes a new integrity protocol for mobile agents. It can defend most known attacks, provides encryption transmission and route secrecy of mobile agents.

The rest of this paper is organized as follows. Section 2 describes related work. Section 3 describes the notations and security properties. Section 4 proposes a new integrity protocol for mobile agents. Section 5 gives security analysis of this protocol. Finally, conclusions are drawn in section 6.

2 Related work

Forward Integrity denotes the integrity of the partial results. Yee ([8]) defines the notion of weak forward integrity in the following mode "if a mobile agent visits a sequence of servers S_1, S_2, ..., S_n, and the first malicious server is S_m, then none of the partial results generated at servers S_i, where $i < m$, can be forged". In their scheme, an agent and its originator maintained a list of secret keys, or a key generating function. The agent used a key to encapsulate the collected offer and then destroyed the key. However, a malicious host may keep the key or the key generating function. When the agent revisits the host or visits another host conspiring with it, a previous offer or series of offers would be modified, without being detected by the originator.

Karjoth ([9]), et al. proposed a notion of strong forward integrity where an attacker S_m can not forge any of partial results generated at server S_i, where $i < m$, even by colluding with one (or more) other visited server S_j, where $j < i$. In the their scheme, A chain O_0, O_1, O_2, ..., O_n is an ordered sequence of encapsulated offers such that each entry of the chain depends on the previous and the next members. This dependency is specified by a chaining relation. Their scheme could resist the modification attack but could not prevent two colluders truncation attack. In this attack, a host with the agent at hand colludes with a previously visited host to discard all entries between the two visits.

Cheng ([10]), et al. proposed a data collection protocol that prevents two colluders truncation attack in a free roaming agent. The protocol is to require an external party, typically the preceding visited host, to co-sign the agent migration. Therefore, two colluders are not sufficient to affect a truncation attack. Their scheme can also be generalized to prevent the L ($L \geq 2$) colluder truncation attack. The co-signing mechanism But it could not prevent more than L colluders truncation attack.

Darren Xu ([11]), et al. proposed a scheme uses "one hop backwards and two hops forwards" chain relation as the protocol core to implement the generally accepted mobile agents security properties. This scheme can defend most known attacks. But if itinerary of mobile agents is protected, it difficult to find the second host forward.

3 Notations and security properties

Table 2. The Notation Used in This Paper

Notations	Meaning
(I_A, C_A, S_A, D_A)	I_A is A's identity, C_A is A's code, S_A is the state of A and D_A is A's data
$S_0 = S_{n+1}$	ID of the originator
$S_i, 1 \leq i \leq n$	ID of the host i
T	ID of the trusted third party
o_0	A secret possessed by host S_0. It can be regarded as a dummy offer and is only known to the originator
$o_i, 1 \leq i \leq n$	An offer from host S_i
$O_i, 0 \leq i \leq n$	An encapsulated offer (cryptographically protected o_i) from host S_i
$O_0, O_1, ..., O_n$	The chain of encapsulated offers from the originator and host $S_1, S_2, ... , S_n$
h_A	The agent integrity check value
$h_i, 0 \leq i \leq n$	Message integrity check value associated with O_i
$r_i, 0 \leq i \leq n$	A random number generated by host S_i
$(KD_i, KE_i), 0 \leq i \leq n$	A private/public key pair of host S_i
(KD_T, KE_T)	A private/public key pair of T
$Enc_{KE_i}(m)$	A message m asymmetrically encrypted with the public key KE_i of host S_i
$Dec_{KD_i}(m)$	A message m asymmetrically decrypted with the private key KD_i of T
$Sig_{KD_i}(m)$	The signature of host S_i on a message m using its private key KD_i
$Verif(\sigma, KE_i)$	A signature verification function for signature σ and public key KE_i
$H(m)$	A one-way collision-resistant hash function
$A \rightarrow B: m$	A sending a message m to B

An agent is defined as $A = (I_A, C_A, S_A, D_A)$ where I_A is the identity, C_A is the code, S_A is the state and D_A is the data of the agent. Both I_A and C_A are static while S_A and D_A are variable.

Digital signature and encryption need a working public key infrastructure. Each host S_i has a certified private/public key pair (KD_i, KE_i). The transmission of mobile agents is encrypted. An agent's route information is secret. The main technique is to require a trusted third party.

Assume that an agent has visited an undetermined number m of hosts, $m \leq n$. An agent is captured by an attacker. This attacker possibly is the host S_{m+1}. Some hosts excluding S_m may collude with the attacker. Let i range over 1, ..., m. Mobile agents security properties based on the assumptions:

- Verifiable Forward Integrity: The trust third party T can verify the offer o_i by checking whether the chain is valid at O_i.
- Data Confidentiality: Only the originator can extract the offers o_i from the encapsulated offers O_i.
- Non-repudiability: Host S_i cannot deny submitting o_i once it has been received by originator S_0.
- Forward Privacy: None of the identities of the creator of offer o_i can be extracted.
- Strong Forward Integrity: None of the encapsulated offers O_k, where $k \leq m$, can be modified.
- Insertion Resilience: No offer can be inserted at i unless explicitly allowed, i.e., S_{m+1}. It is not possible for S_{m+1} to insert more than one offer even if S_{m+1} collude with some specific L hosts.
- Deletion Resilience: No partial result O_k can be deleted by any S_i, with $k <$ m. It is not possible for S_{m+1} to delete more than one offer even if S_{m+1} collude with some specific L hosts.
- Truncation Resilience: Truncation at i is not possible.
- Itinerary Secrecy: Only the originator and the trusted third party T know a mobile agent's migration route. Truncation at i is not possible even if some specific L hosts collude with S_i to carry out the attack.
- Secure Transmission.

4 The Protocol

4.1 Agent at the originator S_0:

$$S_0: \quad O_0 = Sig_{KD_0}(Enc_{KE_0}(o_0, r_0))$$
$$h_0 = Sig_{KD_0}(H(O_0), Enc_{KE_T}(S_1))$$
$$h_A = Sig_{KD_0}(H(I_A \| C_A))$$

$$S_0 \rightarrow T: h_0$$
$$S_0 \rightarrow S_1: Enc_{KE_1}(I_A \| C_A \| S_A \| D_A), h_A, O_0$$

4.2 Agent at host S_1:

$$S_1: \quad Dec_{KE_1}(I_A \| C_A \| S_A \| D_A)$$

$$Verif(h_A, KE_0) \overset{?}{=} true$$

$$O_1 = Sig_{KD_1}(Enc_{KE_0}(o_1, r_1))$$
$$h_1 = Sig_{KD_1}(H(O_1), Enc_{KE_T}(S_2))$$

$$S_1 \rightarrow T: h_1$$
$$S_1 \rightarrow S_2: Enc_{KE_2}(I_A \| C_A \| S_A \| D_A), h_A, \{O_0, O_1\}$$

4.3   Agent at host S_i:

$$S_i: \quad Dec_{KE_i}(I_A \| C_A \| S_A \| D_A)$$

$$Ver(h_A, KE_0) \overset{?}{=} true$$
$$O_i = Sig_{KD_i}(Enc_{KE_0}(o_i, r_i))$$
$$h_i = Sig_{KD_i}(H(O_i), Enc_{KE_T}(S_{i+1}))$$

$$S_i \rightarrow T: h_i$$
$$S_i \rightarrow S_{i+1}: Enc_{KE_{i+1}}(I_A \| C_A \| S_A \| D_A), h_A, \{O_k \mid 0 \le k \le i\}$$

4.4   Agent at host S_n:

$$S_n: \quad Dec_{KE_n}(I_A \| C_A \| S_A \| D_A)$$

$$Ver(h_A, KE_0) \overset{?}{=} true$$
$$O_n = Sig_{KD_n}(Enc_{KE_0}(o_n, r_n))$$
$$h_n = Sig_{KD_n}(H(O_n), Enc_{KE_T}(S_{n+1}))$$

$$S_n \rightarrow T: h_n$$
$$S_n \rightarrow S_{n+1}: Enc_{KE_{n+1}}(I_A \| C_A \| S_A \| D_A), h_A, \{O_k \mid 0 \le k \le n\}$$

4.5   Agent at host S_{n+1} ($S_{n+1} = S_0$):

$$S_{n+1}: \quad Dec_{KE_{n+1}}(I_A \| C_A \| S_A \| D_A)$$

$$Ver(h_A, KE_0) \overset{?}{=} true$$

$S_{n+1} \rightarrow T: \{h_k' = H(O_k) \mid 0 \le k \le n\}$, T verifies the forward integrity and returns results to host S_{n+1}

4.6   At the trusted third party T:

$$T: \quad Verif(h_i, KE_i), \text{ recover } H(O_i), Enc_{KE_T}(S_{i+1})$$

$$\mathrm{Dec}_{\mathrm{Kd_T}}(S_{i+1}), \text{recover } S_{i+1}$$

$$\text{Receive } h_0', h_1', h_2', ..., h_n'$$

$$h_k' \overset{?}{=} H(O_k), (0 \le k \le n)$$

To begin the protocol, the originator S_0 randomly generates r_0. Host S_0 encrypts a dummy offer o_0 and r_0 using its own public key KE_0. Host S_0 signs this encrypted value to construct a dummy encapsulated offer O_0. Next, Host S_0 calculates a hash value h_0 from O_0, and encrypts S_1 using T's public key KE_T, and then signs them. Host S_0 also computes a hashed value h_A from I_A and C_A. h_A is the certified agent integrity checksum. Host S_0 encrypts this agent using it's the next host's public key KE_1. Finally, Host S_0 sends h_0 to the trusted third party T and the agent migrates to the first host S_1.

When the agent arrives at host S_i, S_i verifies h_A in order to ensure the identity I_A and code C_A were not modified by any malicious hosts. Host S_i randomly generates r_i. Host S_i encrypts o_i and r_i using the originator's public key KE_0. Host S_i signs this encrypted value to construct an encapsulated offer O_i. Host S_i calculates a hash value h_i from O_i, and encrypts S_{i+1} using T's public key KE_T, and then signs them. Finally, Host S_i sends h_i to the trusted third party T and the agent migrates to host S_{i+1}.

When the agent returns host S_{n+1} ($S_{n+1} = S_0$), S_{n+1} verifies h_A again. Host S_{n+1} computes a hash value h_k' from O_k ($0 \le k \le n$), then sends h_k' to the trusted third party T and requests T to verify the forward integrity.

The trusted third party T receives h_i, recovers $H(O_i)$ and S_{i+1}. The chain of hash $H(O_0)$, $H(O_1)$, $H(O_2)$, ..., $H(O_n)$ is an ordered sequence. $S_1, S_2, ..., S_n$ is the agent's route information.

T receives h_k' ($0 \le k \le i-1$). It compares h_k' with $H(O_k)$, so as to ensure O_k was not altered. Then T returns results to host S_{n+1}.

5 Security Analysis

Here we analyze how the protocol achieves the security properties.

♦ Verifiable Forward Integrity: The trust third party T fulfills the forward integrity for each host S_i.

♦ Data Confidentiality: If the encryption scheme is secure, only the originator S_0 can decrypt $\mathrm{Enc}_{KE_0}(o_i, r_i)$ to extract o_i. The trusted third party T and other hosts cannot gain o_i.

♦ Non-repudiability: Each host S_i signs its offer o_i by its private key KD_i. If the signature scheme is secure, host S_i cannot repudiate O_i.

♦ Forward Privacy: The host identity S_i is encrypted using the trust third party T's public key. Only T can extract the identity of S_i. T saves the agent migrate route.

♦ Strong Forward Integrity: Suppose the attacker leaves O_m intact but changes O_k to O_k', where $0 \le k \le m-1$. S_{n+1} will calculate h_k' from O_k' and send h_k'

to T. In the trusted third party T, Since h_k' not equal $H(O_k)$, T will report this attack to S_{m+1}.

♦ Insertion Resilience: Suppose the attacker leaves O_m intact but inserts a O_k' before O_k, where $0 \le k \le$ m-1. Following similar reasoning as in the above analysis, S_{n+1} will calculate h_k' from O_k' and send h_k' to the trust third party T. Through comparing h_k' with $H(O_k)$, T will find this change. Therefore no offer can be inserted in the chain of encapsulated offers.

♦ Deletion Resilience: Suppose the attacker leaves O_m intact but deletes O_k, where $0 \le k \le$ m-1. S_{n+1} will calculate h_k' from O_{k+1} and send h_k' to the trust third party T. Through comparing h_k' with $H(O_k)$, T will find this change.

♦ Truncation Resilience: Suppose the attacker leaves O_m intact but deletes O_k, where $0 \le k \le$ m-1. S_{n+1} will calculate h_k' from O_{k+1}. Similarly, T will find this modify. In the other words, if the T is secure, Collusion attack is infructuous.

♦ Itinerary Secrecy: Only the originator and the trust third party T know a mobile agent's migration route.

♦ Secure Transmission: The transmission of mobile agents is encrypted.

6   Conclusions

This paper examined some protocols and gives security requirements in mobile agent systems. As result of this examination the paper will proposes a new integrity protocol for mobile agents. It can defend most known attacks, provides encryption transmission and route secrecy of mobile agents.

Acknowledgement

This research is Supported by the National Natural Science Foundation of China (60673071)

References

1. A. Corradi, M. Cremonini, R. Montanari and C. Stefanelli, Mobile Agents Integrity for Electronic Commerce Applications, *Information Systems* Vol. 24, No. 6, pp. 519-533 (1999).
2. D.B. Lange and M. Oshima, Seven Good Reasons for Mobile Agents, *Communications of the ACM*, 1999, 42(3): 88–89.
3. W. Jansen, Countermeasures for Mobile Agent Security, *Computer Communications*, 2000, 23(17): 1667–1676.
4. S. Fünfrocken, Protecting Mobile Web-Commerce Agents with Smartcards, *First International Symposium on Agent Systems and Applications* (ASA'99)/Third International Symposium on Mobile Agents (MA'99), Palm Springs (1999).
5. D. Westhoff, et al, *Protecting a Mobile Agent's Route against Collusions*, Proceedings of SAC'99, San Antonio: Springer-Verlag, 1999: 215–226.
6. M. Giansiracusa, Mobile Agent Protection Mechanisms and the Trusted Agent Proxy Server (TAPS) Architecture,
(2003). http://www.isi.qut.edu.au/research/publications/technical/qut-isrc-tr-2003-010.pdf.

7. P. J. Hardjono and J. Seberry, Fundamentals of Computer Security, *Springer-Verlag*, Berlin (2003).
8. B.S. Yee, *A Sanctuary for Mobile Agents*, Proceedings of Secure Internet Programming: Security Issues for Distributed and Mobile Objects, Berlin: Springer-Verlag, 1999: 261–273.
9. G. Karjoth, N. Asokan, and C. *Gülcü, Protecting the Computation Results of Freeroaming Agents*, Proceedings of the 2nd International Workshop on Mobile Agents (MA '98), Stuttgart: *Springer-Verlag*, 1998: 195–207.
10. J.S.L. Cheng and K.W. Victor, *Defenses against the Truncation of Computation Results of Free-roaming Agents*, Proceedings of the 4th International Conference on Information and Communications Security, Singapore: Springer-Verlag, 2002: 1–12.
11. X. Darren, *An improved free-roaming mobile agent security protocol against colluded trunation attack*, Proceedings of the 30th Annual International Computer Software and Applications Conference (2006).

An Empirical Research of Factors Influencing the Decision-Making of Chinese Online Shoppers

Hui Chen[1] and Yuanzhi Li[2]

1 Economic & Management School, Beijing University of Posts & Telecommunications. No. 10, Xitucheng Street, Haidian District, Beijing. chen-hui@vip.sina.com.

2 Economic & Management School, Beijing University of Posts & Telecommunications, liyuanzhi2008@163.com

Abstract. As the number of Chinese online shoppers increases, it becomes increasingly important to understand their decision-making processes. The factors that influenced the purchasing behaviour of 190 online shoppers were studied. Our research showed that the ease of use of a website, the quality of product information provided the entertainment value and perceived trust all greatly enhanced the satisfaction of online shoppers and significantly influenced their buying intentions.

1 Introduction

E-commerce is developing rapidly in China. By June 2006 it was estimated that 30 million Chinese citizens had made online purchases and the number of regular online shoppers had grown by 50% compared to the same period of the previous year. According to a report issued by CNNIC[1], transactions on the B2C market in the second quarter of 2006 totalled 907,400,000 RMB Yuan (about 113,200,000 dollars), up 6.2% against the first quarter and up 72.1% against the same period of the previous year.

E-commerce is a relatively new business mode. The factors, which influence the buying intentions of online consumers, are different to those that influence traditional consumers. Some foreign studies have already looked into the decision-making of online shoppers, but, so far, Chinese researchers have paid little attention to this field. China's unique social-cultural environment along with the recent rapid development of Chinese E-commerce markets combine to provide

Please use the following format when citing this chapter:

Chen, H., Li, Y., 2007, in IFIP International Federation for Information Processing, Volume 251, Integration and Innovation Orient to E-Society Volume1, Wang, W. (Eds), (Boston: Springer), pp. 202-210.

Chinese online shoppers with their own particular characteristics regarding their decision-making. This study empirically assesses the factors that influence the decision-making of Chinese online shoppers.

2 Conceptual Framework

Studies into online shopping decision-making may use either purchasing behaviour or buying intention as dependent variables. This research uses buying intention as the dependent variable.

On the basis of previous research [2,3], factors relating to the individual consumer, to the product being purchased and to the retail website were identified as being those which influenced the buying intention. Factors relating to the individual consumer include: attitude, sense of control, perceived risks, previous experiences, self-confidence, creativity, cultural background and demographic characteristics. Factors relating to the product include: the product type, price and perceived quality. Factors relating to the retail web site include the interface design of the website, the size and reputation of the company, the ease and speed of use of a website, and the frequency with which information on the website is updated.

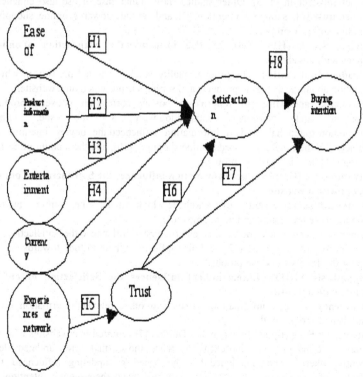

Fig.1. Research Model

Concentrating on B2C e-commerce, we took into account the current state of Chinese online shopping and the results of previous studies. This study focuses on factors that relate to the online shopping websites themselves and to factors that relate to the individual consumer. Factors relating to the online shopping websites include ease of use, product information, and entertainment and currency. The individual factors are the trust of consumers in the retail website and Experience of network. The factors relating to the retail websites and to Experience of network are independent variables. Trust and consumer satisfaction with the retail websites are mediate variables. The buying intention of the consumer is used as the dependent variable in the construction of the research model (Figure 1).

2.1 Definitions and Hypotheses

2.1.1 Website Factors

Ease of Use. The ease of website navigation, organizational structure, clear pricing and simple purchase procedures.

Several studies have reported a positive relationship between ease of use and consumer satisfaction [4, 5]. Other studies showed that ease of use also enhanced consumer trust [6], shopping intention [7] and attitude towards online shopping [8]. In this work, we propose:

Hypothesis 1 (H1): Ease of Use influences the Satisfaction of online shoppers with a website.

Product Information. The product quality, stock levels and the way in which information about the available products and services is presented on a website.

Syzmanski and Hise [4] reported a positive correlation between product information and consumer satisfaction with a web site. Other studies demonstrated that product information influenced the buying intention of consumers [9], their attitude towards online shopping [10], and the amount of online shopping [11]. In this work, we propose:

Hypothesis 2 (H2): Product Information influences the Satisfaction of online shoppers with a website.

Entertainment. Elements of a website which make the online buying experience more interesting and more enjoyable.

Other researchers have shown that entertainment influenced the satisfaction of consumers towards a website [12], and also influenced their attitude towards online shopping [8]. In this work, we propose:

Hypothesis 3 (H3): Entertainment influences the Satisfaction of online shoppers with a website.

Currency. Product information, prices and other relevant information on a website is updated promptly.

Studies by Fogg [6] and by Chen and Dhillon [7] reported that websites with up to date information are more trusted than those that are updated less frequently. Other studies concluded that the speed of updating influenced the satisfaction of consumers with a website and influenced their buying intention. In this work, we propose:

Hypothesis 4 (H4): Currency influences the Satisfaction of online shoppers with a website.

2.1.2 Individual Factors

Experience of network. Previous experience of using the Internet, frequency of use and degree of computer literacy.

Korgaonkar and Wolin [13] reported that experienced online shoppers were more likely to play down security issues and seek information, convenience, and economic value whilst Ward and Lee [14] found that online experience increases search proficiency. Yang and Huang [5] found that experienced online shoppers focused less on security issues but more on reliability, personalization, and ease of use. Finally, the Pew Foundation [15] found increased levels of online shopping and spending amongst experienced Internet users. In this work, we propose:

Hypothesis 5 (H5): Experience of network influences how much an online shopper will Trust a website.

Trust. The degree of confidence that the consumer has in the Internet in general and in the reliability and sincerity of the shopping website in particular.

It was found [16], that if a consumer trusted a particular website they would search for product information from that website more frequently and they would be willing to provide the necessary personal data to the web site in order to make a purchase. We also believe that if a customer trusts a particular website, they will be more likely to use and make purchases from that website in the future.

In this work, we propose:

Hypothesis 6 (H6): Trust in a website influences the Satisfaction with the website.

and

Hypothesis 7 (H7): Trust in a website influences the buying intention.

Satisfaction. Degree of contentment. How happy the consumer is with the shopping experience.

Sutton and Hallett [17] proposed that past experiences influence future actions. The satisfaction of online consumers with a website will influence the current buying intention and will influence their future use of that website and subsequent buying intentions. In this work, we propose:

Hypothesis 8 (H8): Satisfaction with a website as a mediate variable influences the buying intention.

3. Research Methods

3.1 Object

According to the Statistics Report on Chinese Internet Development [1], students make up 36.2% of all Internet users in China. Hoffman and Novak [16] found that online shoppers were mainly composed of highly educated young people with high incomes. Accordingly, all of our subjects had received a university or above level of education. Many of the subjects were still university students and all of them had previous experience of using the Internet. 193 questionnaires were distributed and collected, 190 (98.4%) of which were included in this study. 55.3% of the subjects were male and 44.7% were female.

3.2 Procedure

The two websites (website A and website B) used in this research study were real-life commercial websites rather than simulated sites. Both of the chosen websites sold a similar range of products that related to the everyday needs of the subjects. The subjects were instructed to buy articles such as books and CD's and given a fixed budget to carry out their purchases. The testing procedure was conducted in a computer laboratory in which each computer was configured identically. Each subject completed the test procedure independently. The subject were told to decide which products they would like to purchase and to spend about 15 minutes browsing the first website for the appropriate product information. After 10 minutes rest period, the subject was told to repeat the search procedure on the second website. The subjects were then told to make a comparison between the two websites and to decide which one they would choose to make their purchases. After making their purchase decisions, each of the subjects was asked to fill in a questionnaire relating to their browsing and purchase experiences on the chosen web sites. The subject's required about 45 minutes to complete the whole test procedure.

In this study, the subjects were asked to state which website they preferred to make purchases from and to then complete questionnaires which were used to evaluate their buying intention. The online shopping exercise gave us useful insights into factors relating to website design and provided the subjects with a recent online buying experience to call upon when filling in the questionnaire.

3.3 Measurements

The measuring indices of the major variables studied in this work were adapted from those used recently in the research literature. All of the questionnaires used 5-point Likert scales. Measuring questionnaires included: Ease of Use, 4 items, as developed by Lynch and Ariely [18]; Entertainment: 4 items, as developed by Paul [19]; Currency: 4 items, as developed by Fogg [8] ; Product Information: 4 items, developed by Paul [19]; Trust: 4 items, developed by Joey [20]; Buying intention: 3 items, as developed by Chen and Wells [21]; Satisfaction: 5 items, measurement procedure developed for this work. Experience of network; 15 items, measurement procedure developed for this work.

4. Research Results

4.1 Questionnaire Reliability Analysis

Alpha (Cronbach α) coefficient is used to test the internal reliability of the measuring questionnaire. "Ease of use", α=0.7237, "Product information", α=0.6992, "Entertainment", α=0.6542, "Currency", α=0.7014, "Experiences of using network", α=0.6845, "Trust", α=0.7123, "Satisfaction", α=0.7846, "Buying intention", α=0.7645. Generally speaking, it is acceptable when alpha value is higher than 0.6.

4.2 Path Analysis

Path analysis of SPSS 11.5 was used to verify our research model and hypotheses. The data obtained from the completed questionnaires supported most of our hypotheses.

H1, H2, H3, H5, H6 and H8 were supported by the results of the data analysis.

Ease of use, product information, entertainment, and trust all influenced the satisfaction of online shoppers with a website. Experience of network influenced trust. The satisfaction of online consumers with a website significantly influenced their buying intention.

Hypotheses H4 and H7 were rejected. Currency did not have a definite influence over consumer satisfaction. Trust did not have a definite influence over the buying intention.

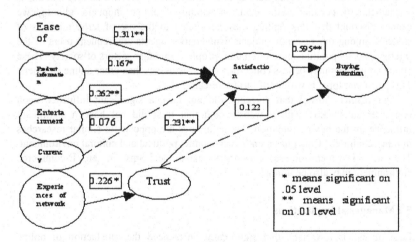

Fig .2. Result of Path Analysis

5. Discussion and Managerial Implications

5.1 Discussion

Hypotheses H1, H2, H3, H5, H6 and H8 were supported by analysis of the completed questionnaires.

Our results supported the findings of of previous research into the buying habits of online consumers. Paul [19] postulated that easily navigable web pages, clear organizational structure, and simple purchasing procedures were necessary to satisfy the needs of online consumers. Syzmanski and Hise [4] demonstrated a strong positive correlation between product information and the satisfaction of online consumers. Coyle and Thorson [12] also showed that entertainment had an influence on a consumer's satisfaction with a website. A consumer's satisfaction with a website had a strong influence on their ultimate buying intention.

Hypotheses H4 and H7 were rejected after analysis of the completed questionnaires.

We found that currency did not have a definite influence over consumer's satisfaction. This finding opposed our hypothesis H4 and was in contradiction to the results of Paul [19]. Whilst well developed in a number of economically advanced countries, e-commerce is a recent phenomenon in China and still something of a novelty. In a separate study [22], we found that many consumers browse and shop online to satisfy their curiosity.

We discovered that trust did not have a definite influence over the buying intentions of consumers. This went against our hypothesis H7. We believe that this is a characteristic peculiar to the decision-making of online shoppers, although we cannot discount that this finding may be related to the use of large numbers of students among our research subjects. University students are frequent users of the Internet and shop online more often than people from other sectors of society. These young consumers may be less concerned with trust issues than other online shoppers. This particular topic is worthy of further research.

Our results showed that currency did not have a significant influence upon consumer satisfaction with a website and that trust did not have a significant influence on the buying intention. These findings are opposite to similar researches in other countries. China has a unique economic, political and cultural environment. The way in which Chinese consumers make decisions in an E-commerce environment may also be unique.

5.2 Managerial Implications

Ease of use is a variable that significantly influenced the satisfaction of online shoppers. The two web sites used in this study did not differ greatly in terms of interface design, product category and distribution system, yet 74.7% of the subjects chose to make their purchases from website A. Website A possessed a practical guide system, had detailed product descriptions and had a straightforward method for making purchases. Website A was rated much more user-friendly than website B. Online retailers should strive to improve the ease of use of their websites and to increase the quality of the services they offer in order to ensure the satisfaction of their consumers and obtain a favourable buying intention. Online retailers must also aim to get repeat business from existing consumers and market themselves to attract new consumers.

Product Information also had a positive influence on the satisfaction of online shoppers. In particular, consumers expect to have complete and up to date product specifications to enable them to compare different products and different brands. Web sites that accommodated the information needs of consumers were evaluated more favourably.

Entertainment had a significant impact upon the satisfaction of online shoppers. We found that the subjects were attracted to extraneous design elements not directly related to the purchasing process. One method of increasing the average time spent on a general retail website is to include peripheral elements, such as high-resolution graphics, music and humorous characters. Entertainment enhances the browsing experience of low involvement shoppers.

Trust is an important factor in determining the satisfaction of online shoppers with a website. Our research was unable to verify a direct link between trust and the buying intention, although we did find that trust influenced satisfaction, which subsequently influenced the buying intention. Our subjects voiced concerns relating to Internet and credit card security, spam, identity fraud and the misuse of personal data. Given our finding that trust has a large influence on the satisfaction of online shoppers with a website, it is clear that online retailers must work hard to create and maintain trust in their business.

In conclusion, increasing numbers of Chinese citizens are choosing to make online purchases and E-commerce is making increasingly important contributions to the Chinese economy, yet the decision making behaviour of Chinese online consumers may be different to those from other countries. Thus, businesses wishing to be successful in the Chinese E-commerce market are advised to take into account the particular needs of Chinese consumers. The unique decision making behaviour of Chinese consumers, both online and offline, is deserving of further study.

References

1. CNNIC. *Statistics Report on Chinese Internet Development in 2006*, People Posts & Telecommunications Press, Beijing(2006).

2. H.R. Li, K. Cheng, G. Martha and C. Russel, The Impact of Perceived Channel Utilities Shopping Orientations and Demographics on the Consumer Online Buying Behavior, *Journal of Computer-Mediated Communication*, 5(2),108-109 (1999).

3. V. Swaminathan, E. Lepkowska-White and B.P. Rao, Browsers or Buyers in Cyberspace? An Investigation of Factors Influencing Electronic Exchange, *Journal of Computer Mediated Communication*, 12(1), 77-79 (1999).

4. D.M. Szymanski and R. T. Hise, e-Satisfaction: an initial examination, *Journal of Retailing*, 76(2), 309-322(2000).

5. Z. Yang, R.T. Peterson andL. Huang, Taking the pulse of internet pharmacies, *Marketing Health Services*, 21(2), 4-10 (2001).

6. B.J. Fogg, J. Marshall, 0. Laraki, A. Osipovich, C.Varma, N. Fang, J. Paul,A. Rangnekar, J. Shon, P.,Treinen and M. Swani, What makes web sites credible? A report on a large quantitative study, *Persuasive Technology Lab*, 11(1), 61-68(2001).

7. S. Chen and G.. Dhillon, Interpreting dimensions of consumer trust in e-commerce, *Information Technology and Management*, 4(2-3), 303-318(2003).

8. S. L. Jarvenpaa, and P. A. Todd, *Electronic Marketing and the Consumer. Edited by R. S. Peterson.* Thousand Oaks, CA: Sage Publications(1997).

9. N. Donthu, Does your web site measure up?, *Marketing Management*, 10(4), 29-32(2001).

10. L.R. Vijayasarathy andJ.M. Jones, Print and internet catalog shopping: assessing attitudes and intentions, *Internet Research*, 10(3), 191-202(2000).

11. S. Bellman, G.L. Lohse and E.J. Johnson, Predictors of online buying behavior. Association for Computing Machinery, *Communications of the ACM,*42(12), 32-38(1999).

12. J.R. Coyle andE. Thorson, The effects of progressive levels of interactivity and vividness in web marketing sites, *Journal of Advertising*, 41(3), 65-77 (2001).

13. P.K. Korgaonkar and L.D. Wolin, A multivariate analysis of web usage. *Journal of Advertising Research*, 39, 53-68(1999).

14. M.R. Ward and M.J. Lee, Internet shopping, consumer search, and product branding, *Journal of Product & Brand Management*, 9(1), 6-20.22(2000).

15. Pew Foundation. http://www.pewintemet.org/reports.[2007-1-7].

16. C.C Hoffman and CT.P. Novak, Marketing In hypermedia computer-mediated environments, *Conceptual foundations Journal of Marketing*, 60(3), 50-80(1996).

17. S.R. Sutton and C. Candhallett, Understanding seat-belt intentions and behavior: a decision^êmaking approach, *Journal of applied Social Psychology,*(l9), 1310-1325(1989).

18. J. G.. Lynch and D. Ariely, Wine online: search costs affect competition on price, quality and distribution, *Marketing Science* 19 (Winter), 83-103(2000).

19. S. Paul, Factors that affect attitude toward a retail web site, *Journal of Marketing Theory and Practice* 2005 (Winter), 40-51, (2005).

20. F. Joey and George, Influences on the intent to make Internet purchases, *Internet Research Electronic Networking Applications and Policy*, 12(2), 165-180(2002).

21. Q. Chen and W. D. Wells, Attitude toward the site, *Journal of Advertising Research,*40(5), 27-37(1999).

22. H. Chen and Y.Z. Li, *The research of motivation of online shoppers* (in press) (2007).

Research on Selection of theThird-Party Logistics Service Providers

Huimin Zhang[1], Guofeng Zhang[2], ,and Bin Zhou[1]

1 Henan University of Technology, College of Management, Zhengzhou
450052, P.R.China, zhm76@126.com,
2 Henan Business College, Department of Business Management

Abstract. At present, the supply chain is the last field, which can make enterprise reducing cost and improving flexibility. How to construct the supply chain successfully has received much attention and logistics outsourcing has become common among large manufacturers. The information age and globalization are forcing companies to place a premium upon collaboration as a new source of competitive advantage, so companies are facing significant challenges to evaluate and select appropriate third-party logistics (3PL) providers. This paper will choose a set of indicators, construct a framework for performance measures and introduce an evaluation method which proceeds as follow: (1) choosing principal components applying principal components analysis; (2) ranking the 3PL providers applying grey relational analysis.

1 Introduction

Since competition is no longer between organizations but among supply chains, effective supply chain management has become a potentially valuable way of securing competitive advantage and improving organization performance. In order to make core business outstanding and improve efficiency, more and more large manufacturers outsourced their logistics. Being the most important mode of logistics outsourcing, the third-party logistics services have become an important option for large manufacturers to develop supply chain strategies. 3PL providers offer such companies a broad range of services, both in domestic and in international markets.

According to a recent report from Datamonitor, the global spend on 3PLs in 2005 finished at $227.2 million, fueled by increased trade between Asia and the U.S [1]. The third-party logistics providers continue to see strong demand for their services, although operational efficiency can be the differentiator between long-term success and being put on the block.

On the other hand, large quantity of third-party logistics providers come into the world and inevitably the bad become mixed with the good. It is important to both

Please use the following format when citing this chapter:

Zhang, H., Zhang, G., Zhou, B., 2007, in IFIP International Federation for Information Processing, Volume 251, Integration and Innovation Orient to E-Society Volume1, Wang, W. (Eds), (Boston: Springer), pp. 211-221.

3PL providers and users of their services to facilitate the development of corporate supply chain strategy. The 3PL industry continues to evolve, executives considering the use of such services are faced with many puzzles, whose key is how to evaluate and select the appropriate 3PL providers.

2 Evaluation System Construction

A performance evaluation system will be of great interest to manufacturers and distributors with potentially high costs and delays across complex operations, or to enterprises recognizing the need to reduce costs and improve levels of customer service. These systems are designed to enable management to pay attention to deriving business benefits in areas such as improvements in delivery reliability, increased levels of greater flexibility, customer responsiveness, reductions in operational costs, effective asset management.

Selecting performance indicators is the premise of 3PL provider's evaluation, comprehensive and reasonable indicator system is the key of ensuring correct performance evaluation. Indicator system construction should follow the rules: all sidedness, versatility, comparability and operability. Many researchers have adopted several components or multiple dimensions to evaluate the performance of 3PL. For example, Xuefen Ma suggested evaluating 3PL's performance from four aspects: development potential, logistic technology, logistic equipment and level of service [2]. Two surveys [3, 4] identified the following as significant outsourcing functions: transportation, warehousing, freight consolidation and distribution, labeling, packaging, inventory management, traffic management and fleet operations, freight payments and auditing, order management, carrier selection, rate negotiation and so on. These functions can be divided into four categories: warehousing, transportation, customer service, and inventory and logistics management. Evaluation framework can be constructed on the foundation of these four categories.

The traditional evaluation system pays much attention to cost cutting and the evaluation system commits itself to earn a profit. The evaluating indicators always deal with delivery reliability, delivery costs, management efficiency and so on. But the environment of competition today is a departure from yesterday. Firstly, the environment is filled with uncertainty and the demands of customers diversified day by day. Enterprises must become more flexible to meet individualized demand. Secondly, increasing attention is devoted to suppliers' social responsibility with a particular focus on environmental protection, fair and legal use of natural resources. Green supply chain management is emerging to be an important approach for enterprises to improve performance. We should think highly of environmental performance when evaluate 3PL. Thirdly, information technology develops rapidly. To implement 3PL, real-time information flow is essential. IT links members of a supply chain, such as manufacturers, distributors, transportation firms, and retailers, as it automates some element of the logistics workload, such as order processing, order status inquiries, inventory management, or shipment tracking. So the evaluation system must pay enough attention to flexibility, environment protection, information sharing.

2.1   Flexibility

Nowadays, the environment's rate of change is more rapid than at any previous time. Enterprises have continuously devoted their efforts to keeping flexible or agile in order to maintain a competitive advantage over its rivals. Agility is firstly used in manufacturing industry. The manufacturing environment has undergone several transitions, from the craft industry, to mass production, and now the newest paragon, agility. Agile-based competition is destined to displace mass-production based competition as the norm for global commerce [5]. Flexibility can be regarded as a critical compete factor. Being flexible means having the capability to provide products/services that meet the individual demands of customers [6].

More or less the same, we can evaluate the flexibility or agility of enterprises in service trade. A 3PL service provider with flexibility is one whose processes are designed to respond effectively to unanticipated change. Flexibility of 3PL provider can be measured from response capability to quantitative change of demand, time response capability, capability of adopt new technology, capability of expanding and so on. These indicators aid in monitoring the capability of a process to respond to unanticipated change.

2.2   Environmental Management

Today, competition has intensified and globalized, many governments impose standards that set the lower boundary of customers' expectations regarding environmental compliance, which results in higher pressure and drivers for enterprises to improve environmental performance. Environmental issues in construction typically include soil and ground contamination, water pollution, construction and demolition waste, noise and vibration, dust, hazards emissions and odors, wildlife and natural features demolition, and archaeological destruction [7]. Environmental pollution is a serious problem, it is reported that road vehicles are responsible for more than 25% of Britain's greenhouse gas emissions, according to the government's Transport White Paper, 24000 people each year die prematurely due to air pollution.

With the increasing acceptance of ISO 14001 environmental standards, there is a greater role for enterprise in organizational environmental practice. Many enterprises take up measures to improve environmental performance, but these control and management appear to be very qualitative. So we should select the quantitative indicators to evaluate 3PL service providers' environmental performance. These quantitative approaches are useful for indicating, reducing and mitigating pollution level.

2.3   Information Communication

A supply chain is dynamic in nature and involves the constant flow of product, cash and information between different stages. It is the coordination or integration of the activities of all the members of a supply chain. Modern information technology, through its power to provide timely, accurate, and reliable information, has led to a greater integration of modern supply chains than possible by any other means [8]. Timely and accurate information communication can highly improve the forecast precision of management and the flexibility to unanticipated change, so we should pay enough attention to information activity when measure the level of cooperation among the members. We can evaluate the information activity from four aspects: informatization level, information accuracy rate, ratio of information activity in time and information sharing level.

By measuring performance across several business areas using a set of performance indicators, for example: financial, non-financial, customer, operational, leading and lagging, it is possible to coordinate and optimize supply chain performance to achieve strategic competitive advantage. Performance measurement systems provide significant impact when used to support a program to monitor key performance indicators that have been aligned to critical business issues. They will reduce decision-making cycle times by notifying key decision-makers through workflow or event management, to initiate corrective action before problems escalate into major issues. This is often difficult to achieve when existing management information systems fail to provide real time performance data.

On the basis of the discussion above, the paper selects 17 indicators from 5 aspects, refers to table 1.

3   Evaluation Method

After the construction of evaluation system, an appropriate method may be used to evaluate and select 3PL providers. In this paper, the evaluation method can divide into two stages: firstly, choose principal components applying principal components analysis, then rank the 3PL providers applying grey relational analysis. The specific steps proceed as follow.

3.1   Principal Components Analysis

Principal components analysis [9]–[11] (PCA) is a way of identifying patterns in data, and expressing the data in such a way as to highlight their similarities and differences. Since patterns in data can be hard to find in data of high dimension, where the luxury of graphical representation is not available, PCA is a powerful tool for analyzing data which transforms a number of correlated variables into a smaller number of uncorrelated variables called principal components. The main advantage of PCA is that once you have found these patterns in the data, and you compress the data, by reducing the number of dimensions, without much loss of information.

3.1.1 Standardized process of raw data

The larger the target value the better:

$$y_{ij} = \frac{x_{ij} - \min x_{ij}}{\max x_{ij} - \min x_{ij}} \qquad (1)$$

The smaller the target value the better:

Table 3. Indicator system for 3PL provider's evaluation

Indicator classification	Indicator	Quantitative description of indicator
X_1: Transportation activity	X_{11}:Transportation cost	Transportation cost/the value of goods delivered
	X_{12}:Correct transportation ratio	Times of correct transportation /total times of transportation
	X_{13}:Delivering loss rate	Value of delivering loss/ inventory value delivered
X_2: Warehousing activity	X_{21}:Inventory turnover rate	Cost of goods sold/average inventory
	X_{22}:Inventory defection rate	Value of inventory defection/ total inventory value
	X_{23}:Warehousing cost per ton	Warehousing cost/ average inventory
	X_{24}:Warehouse utilization rate	Inventory level/storage capacity
X_3: Information activity	X_{31}:Information accuracy rate	Times of accurate information activity / total times of information activity
	X_{32}:Ratio of information activity in time	Times of information activity in time/total times of information activity
	X_{33}:Information sharing level	Given through benchmarking
	X_{34}:Informatization level	The level of hardware and software, given through benchmarking
X_4: Environmental performance	X_{41}:Pollutants released	Pollutants released/quantity of goods delivered
	X_{42}: Energy consumption	Energy consumption /quantity of goods delivered
X_5: Flexibility	X_{51}:Response capability to quantitative change of demand	Quantity delivered according to buyer's rectification/quantity rectified on buyer's demand
	X_{52}:Time response capability	Times of adjusted delivering on buyer demand /times of delivering with schedule adjusted
	X_{53}:Capability of expanding	Kinds of new service/ kinds of service
	X_{54}:Response capability to consumer's change	Number of new client/number of client lost

$$y_{ij} = \frac{\max x_{ij} - x_{ij}}{\max x_{ij} - \min x_{ij}} \qquad (2)$$

The closer to the target value the better:

$$y_{ij} = \frac{1}{1 + OB - x_{ij}} \qquad (3)$$

OB: the target value

3.1.2 Calculate the covariance matrix

After the Standardized process of raw date, we get a matrix, and then calculate the covariance matrix of the matrix. Covariance is always measured between 2 dimensions. If we have a data set with more than 2 dimensions, there is more than one covariance measurement that can be calculated. For an n-dimensional data set, we can calculate $\frac{n!}{(n-2)*2}$ different covariance values and put them in a matrix.

3.1.3 Calculate the orthorhombic eigenvectors and eigenvalues of the covariance matrix

Since the covariance matrix is square, we can calculate the eigenvectors and eigenvalues for this matrix. These are rather important, as they tell us useful information about our data. By this process of taking the eigenvectors of the covariance matrix, we have been able to extract lines that characterize the data.

$$\lambda_1 \geq \lambda_2 \geq \cdots \geq \lambda_i \geq \cdots \geq \lambda_n \geq 0 \qquad (4)$$

$$u_j = (u_{11}, u_{12}, u_{13}, \cdots u_{ij} \cdots u_{54}) \qquad (5)$$

λ_i : The ith eigenvalue of the covariance matrix

u_j : The jth eigenvectors of the covariance matrix

3.1.4 Calculate accumulative variance' contribution ratio of eigenvalue

Once eigenvectors are found from the covariance matrix, the next step is to order them by eigenvalue, highest to lowest. Then calculate the contribution ratio.

$$E = \frac{\sum_{i=1}^{m} \lambda_i}{\sum_{i=1}^{n} \lambda_i} \qquad (6)$$

m : The minimum integer when $E \geq 85\%$

3.1.5 Choosing principal components

Choose certain principal components, from large to small, let $E \geq 85\%$.

$$y_k = \sum_{j=1}^{n} u_{kj} X_j \qquad (k = 1, 2, \cdots, m) \qquad (7)$$

y_k : The kth principal component

3.2 Grey Relational Analysis

Grey relational analysis was pioneered by Deng Julong in 1984, which aim at analyzing the relationships among things [12]. GRA, in fact, might be reckoned as a contrasting way, in wholeness, equipped with reference for contrasting. Differing from the traditional mathematical analysis, GRA provides a simple scheme to analyze the series relationships or the system behavior, even if the given information is few.

In the former part of the paper, we have got the principal components which can be taken as the input of GRA. What follows are the steps needed to perform a GRA on a set of data.

3.2.1 Standardized process of principal components

According to the algorithm of principal components, calculate and standardize the principal components.

3.2.2 Establish the reference series for GRA

The series consist of the best dates of the principal components after standardized process above.

$$y^0 = (y^0{}_1 \ldots y^0{}_j \ldots y^0{}_m)$$

3.2.3 Calculate the grey relational coefficient

The algorithm on grey relation coefficient is as follows:

$$\xi_{ij}(y^0{}_j, y_{ij}) = \frac{\min\limits_{i}\min\limits_{j}\left|y^0{}_j - y_{ij}\right| + \rho\max\limits_{i}\max\limits_{j}\left|y^0{}_j - y_{ij}\right|}{\left|y^0{}_j - y_{ij}\right| + \rho\max\limits_{i}\max\limits_{j}\left|y^0{}_j - y_{ij}\right|} \qquad (8)$$

ρ : distinguishing coefficient, $\rho \in [0, 1]$, usually, $\rho = 0.5$

3.2.4 Establish the weights of indicators

We can take the variance contribution ratio as weights, refers to Table 3.

$$W = (w_1, w_2, w_m)$$

3.2.5 Calculate the monolayer Grey Relational Grade

$$\gamma_i = \sum_{k=1}^{m} w_k \xi_{ik} \qquad (9)$$

According to the value of grey relational grade, the 3PL provider can be ranked.

4   Case Studies

In order to illustrate the evaluation method, the paper selects a manufacturer whose products are quick-frozen foods and its five 3PL providers. The indicators used are those which are listed in table 1 and the indicator value is listed in table 2. The paper evaluates the performance and gives the numerical value for every indicator, then ranks these 5 enterprises according to their performance, MATLAB7.0.1 being the computational aids.

Table 2. The raw data of indicators for 5 enterprises

Indicator	A	B	C	D	E
X_{11}	0.10	0.12	0.28	0.20	0.09
X_{12}	0.98	0.99	0.97	0.95	0.85
X_{13}	0.10	0.01	0.20	0.03	0.05
X_{21}	1.90	3.55	3.50	4.00	2.50
X_{22}	0.08	0.01	0.13	0.04	0.02
X_{23}	2.40	4.20	3.50	1.50	4.00
X_{24}	0.78	0.95	0.70	0.90	0.88
X_{31}	0.85	0.70	0.65	0.95	0.99
X_{32}	0.12	0.40	0.25	0.89	0.99
X_{33}	1	5	6	8	9
X_{34}	2	6	5	7	9
X_{41}	0.10	0.01	0.20	0.03	0.02
X_{42}	0.35	0.12	0.30	0.20	0.19
X_{51}	0.62	0.85	0.80	0.70	0.98
X_{52}	0.58	0.90	0.88	0.59	0.97
X_{53}	0.01	0.12	0.08	0.02	0.05
X_{54}	0.18	0.05	0.41	0.11	0.48

The raw data in table 2 are standardized and the covariance matrix is calculated, then the orthorhombic eigenvectors and eigenvalues of the covariance matrix are also calculated. The paper chooses 3 principal components to model according to $E \geq 85\%$. These 3 principal components are listed in table 3, eigenvalue, variance contribution ratios and accumulative contribution ratios are also calculated.

Table 3. The contribution ratios and eigenvectors of eigenvalue

Eigenvalue	1.3723	0.7144	0.4542
Variance contribution ratio	46.81%	24.37%	15.49%
Accumulative contribution ratio	46.81%	71.88%	86.67%
u_{11}	0.0223	-0.0245	0.0057
u_{12}	-0.1008	0.0366	-0.0832
u_{13}	0.1152	0.0065	-0.0114
u_{21}	0.0789	0.0701	0.0151
u_{22}	0.1183	0.0281	0.0360
u_{23}	0.0433	-0.1384	-0.1868
u_{24}	0.1197	0.0368	0.0190
u_{31}	0.1353	-0.1258	-0.0564
u_{32}	0.1860	-0.0310	0.0423
u_{33}	0.1378	0.0216	0.0861
u_{34}	0.1331	0.0345	0.0993
u_{41}	0.1283	0.0044	0.0073
u_{42}	0.1134	0.0945	0.0897
u_{51}	0.0582	0.0885	0.1699
u_{52}	0.0038	0.1456	0.2243
u_{53}	-0.0301	0.1677	0.1456
u_{54}	0.1894	-0.0301	0.0038

The principal components can be expressed as follows:

$y_1=0.0223X_{11}+0.1008X_{12}+0.1152X_{13}+0.0789X_{21}+0.1183X_{22}+0.0433X_{23}+0.1197X_{24}+0.1353X_{31}+0.1860X_{32}+0.1378X_{33}+0.1331X_{34}+0.1283X_{41}+0.1134X_{42}+0.0582X_{51}+0.0038X_{52}-0.0301X_{53}+0.1894X_{54}$

$y_2=-0.0245X_{11}+0.0366X_{12}+0.0065X_{13}+0.0701X_{21}+0.0281X_{22}-.1384X_{23}+0.0368X_{24}-0.1258X_{31}-0.0310X_{32}+0.0216X_{33}+0.0345X_{34}+0.0044X_{41}+0.0945X_{42}+0.0885X_{51}+0.1456X_{52}+0.1677X_{53}-0.0301X_{54}$

$y_3=0.0057X_{11}-0.0832X_{12}-0.0114X_{13}+0.0151X_{21}+0.0360X_{22}-0.1868X_{23}+0.0190X_{24}-0.0564X_{31}+0.0423X_{32}+0.0861X_{33}+0.0993X_{34}+0.0073X_{41}+0.0897X_{42}+0.1699X_{51}+0.2243X_{52}+0.1456X_{53}+0.0038X_{54}$

From the expressions above we can see that y_1 pay more attention to ratio of information activity in time, information sharing level and response capability to change of consume; y_2 pay more attention to time response capability and capability of expanding; y_3 pay more attention to response capability to quantitative change of demand, time response capability and capability of expanding.

According to algorithm 8, we get the grey relational coefficients, ρ =0.5, shown in table 4.

Table 4. Grey relational coefficient

Coefficient	A	B	C	D	E
ξ_{11}	0.3333	0.5182	0.5301	0.7021	1.0000
ξ_{12}	0.3333	0.4199	0.4736	1.0000	0.4829
ξ_{13}	0.3333	0.4169	0.5012	1.0000	0.9188

At last, grey relational grade is calculated, refers to algorithm 9.

$\gamma_1 = 0.2889$, $\gamma_2 = 0.4095$, $\gamma_3 = 0.4412$, $\gamma_4 = 0.7273$, $\gamma_5 = 0.7281$

Optimally selected schemes are as follows:

$E \succ D \succ C \succ B \succ A$

5   Conclusion

This paper integrates PCA with GRA, chooses principal component with PCA and takes them as key indicators which leave the complex for the easy, then takes the key indicators as the input of GRA and ranks the 3PL providers according to the value of grey relational grade. PCA is a powerful tool for analyzing data, PCA can reduce the number of dimensions and find the key factors influencing performance easily, without much loss of information. Moreover there also exists uncertainty of less date, incomplete information and devoid of experience in 3PL providers evaluation, GRA is a useful tool to deal with such grey system.

The evaluation framework presented in this article improved previous evaluation system; it can help management evaluate outsourcing logistics services in new competitive situations. Using this framework and the factors essential to quantify outsourcing, we have established a set of indicators for 3PL provider selection. It is worth mentioning, the indicator system is flexible and different enterprise may select different indicators. But the indicator selected should be easy to quantify for example by using benchmarking and the information systems should provide real time performance data. Overall, this study provided additional insight into the growing field of 3PL evaluation. Clearly, the field has ample space to grow in terms of research and practice.

References

1. Purchasing (September 21, 2006); http://purchasing.com.
2. X. F. Ma, Y.Y. Liu, S.D Sun., X.L. Wu. Evaluation and Selection of TPLs in Supply Chain Management, Computer Engineering and Applications, 3(2), 2003, pp.7-9.
3. E. Rabinovich, Outsourcing of integrated logistics functions, International Journal of Physical Distribution and Logistics Management, 29 (6), 1999, pp.353-373.
4. H.L. Sink and C.J. Langley, A managerial framework for the acquisition of third-party logistics services, *Journal of Business Logistics*, 19 (1), 1997, pp.121-136.
5. S. L Goldman, R. N. Nagel, and K.Preiss, *Agile competitors and virtual organizations* (Van Nostrand Reinhold, New York, 1995).
6. Gunasekaran, C. Patel, E. Ronald, McGaughey, A framework for supply chain performance measurement, *Production Economics* Vol 87, 2004, pp. 333-347.
7. S. Coventry and C. Woolveridge, *Environmental good practice on site* (Construction Industry Research and Information Association, United Kingdom, 1999).

8. M. M. Naim, The book that changed the world. *Manufacturing Engineer*, No.2, 1997, pp.13-16.

9. W. W. Guo, D. L. Massart, C. Boucon, C. S. Jong, Feature selection in principal component analysis data. *Chemometrics and Intelligent Laboratory System*, Vol 61, No.1, 2002, pp.125-130.

10. Z. Sheng, S. Q. Xie and C.Y. Pan, *Probability Theory and Mathematical Statics* (Higher Education Press, Beijing, 2001).

11. Z. F. Yuan, J.Y. Zhou, *Multiple statistical analysis* (Science Press, Beijing, 2002).

12. J. L. Deng, The theory and methods of socio-economy grey system, *Social science in China* No.6, 1984, pp.47-60.

Looks Can Cost; Especially On A Small Screen

James Grant[1], Kathy Lynch[2], and Julie Fisher[3]

1. Faculty of IT, Monash University, Victoria, Australia
2. University of the Sunshine Coast, Queensland, Australia,
Kathy.Lynch@usc.edu.au
3. Faculty of IT, Monash University, Victoria, Australia.
Julie.Fisher@infotech.monash.edu.au

Abstract. Today, the average consumer is comfortable browsing a web site using a desktop, laptop or kiosk computer. However, this is changing a rapid rate as more and more consumers access the same web content using a small screen device such as a mobile phone or personal digital assistant (PDA). Regardless of the consumers' expertise with the mobile device, the experience is becoming frustrating as they try to navigate their way through web content that has been designed for a large screen; a design that results in cumbersome layout, slow-loading images and 'off-screen' navigation points when viewed on a small screen device. The result is dissatisfaction on part of the consumer, and possible loss of revenue for an e-business enterprise. The main objective of this paper is to highlight several techniques and technologies that are currently available that can assist in displaying 'user-friendly' web pages regardless of the screen size of the device.

1   Introduction

With the growing number of public wireless networks that offer broadband access, and wireless-enabled mobile devices, it is becoming common to access the Web using a mobile device. In exchange for their mobility, small mobile devices lack the common design characteristics of standard desktop computers - such as large screens, millions of colours, full keyboards, and high processing power. Many web applications have been designed to harness the characteristics of these desktop computers, however when presented on a small mobile device they can quite often be difficult or awkward to use, inhibiting the effectiveness and usability of the mobile web environment. Furthermore, these small mobile devices are often expected to perform similar functions and provide a similar functionality to other

Please use the following format when citing this chapter:

Grant, J., Lynch, K., Fisher, J., 2007, in IFIP International Federation for Information Processing, Volume 251, Integration and Innovation Orient to E-Society Volume1, Wang, W. (Eds), (Boston: Springer), pp. 222-232.

computing devices, and in particular, it is expected that these small devices are able to display usable and accessible web content [1].

A small mobile device is used in a unique computing context; the style and length of interaction by the user are somewhat different to a desktop or laptop computer. The mobile device is designed to be used for short and frequent periods of interaction throughout the day or night to allow the user to quickly perform the tasks they want with minimal effort. Consumers become efficient with environments that are familiar to them [2]: the web is no different. When a prospective customer views an e-business web site, the 'view' should be easy to use regardless of the viewing device. However, accomplishing this 'one' view can be both complex and expensive in terms of development, and more importantly, in terms of loss of the mobile e-customer.

2. Background

Nielsen and Morkes [3] state three major features of user behaviour when reading online text; these can bed summarised as:

- users scan the pages, trying to pick out a few sentences or even parts of sentences to get the information they want;
- users prefer text to be short and to the point, and do not like long, scrolling pages;
- users dislike anything that seems like marketing hype preferring factual information.

Of these three features, the first and second are of relevance here, and are critical to designers of effective web sites. We can readily assume that Nielsen and Morkes [3] were referring to online reading of text on normal computer screens, which at the time of the publication were commonly 15" CRT screens. A study conducted by Jones et al. [4] found that there was a 50% reduction of user effectiveness when using a web interface on a small screen (screens of today on small mobile devices are commonly smaller today than in 1999- which is when the paper was published), therefore, one could argue that if the study was re-run in 2007, the findings would be similar, or possibly even a higher level of dissatisfaction.

Despite the usability constraints placed on mobile devices, users are currently able to access websites on small screen, web-enabled mobile devices. In an attempt to overcome usability constraints, there are a number of techniques and technologies which re/format the presentation of generalist web information in order to display readable and usable content on a small screen device. The following sections present an overview of these technologies and techniques.

2.1 Techniques for Manually Coding Multi-format Web Content

Techniques used to create web content in a number of formats include manually redesigning a site in a specialist mobile programming language, for example, Wireless Mark-up Language (WML), Cascading Style Sheets (CSS) and extended Hypertext Markup Language (XHTML).

2.1.1 Wireless Mark-up Language (WML)

A mobile device displaying a WML page has the ability to organise the web content into a logical structure even though the display area is very limited. WML is a tag-based language that was created for devices that are "hardware-constrained, narrow band [...] with limited input/output capabilities" [5, p.17]. Having a similar structure to HTML, WML is based on the Extensible Markup Language (XML), which is a tag-based markup language that gives the programmer the ability to describe data using their own tags. Due to data transfer limitations there is a need to make file sizes small; WML reduces file size as it allows its developers to specify all text and navigational structure of a site structure whilst automatically catering to the specific needs of portable devices such as small screens, limited processor speeds and slower text input [6, p.66].

Websites coded with WML can be split into a series of sub-pages or 'cards', and placed into collections of similar data or 'decks' [7]. This structure allows the user to quickly navigate through the content without having to wade through design related 'space', such as large graphical navigation bars. Upon launching a WML page, the key elements of the site are downloaded and sorted into decks for the user to explore. Schiller [8] describes each card as containing one unit of user interaction, such as an array of data entry boxes, or a logical group of information, such as a short list of phone numbers [8, p.345].

WML is a simple solution to creating low-bandwidth web content on small screen mobile devices. However, viewing a WML page on a standard desktop computer would be very plain with little interaction when compared to its counterpart desktop HTML version. As such, any organisation wanting to implement a WML version of their e-business services needs to code the 'mobile version' separately from general web content, and therefore duplicating design, development and maintenance processes [9].

2.1.2 Cascading Style sheets (CSS) and Extendible Hypertext Markup Language (XHTML)

CSS is a style sheet language used to describe the presentation of a document written in a markup language. CSS has various levels and profiles. Each level of CSS builds upon the last, typically adding new features. Profiles are typically a subset of one or more levels of CSS built for a particular device or user interface. It is within profiles where instructions can be set for various screen sizes [10].

XMHTL has the same depth of expression as HTML, but a stricter syntax; XHTML is the successor to HTML. It was specifically developed for the new devices that are being developed from the standard desktop computer, and is convergence with mobile, telecommunication devices. An XHTML web page can theoretically be faster and made to run more easily on miniaturized devices than comparable HTML web page sizes [11].

2.2   Technologies for Automatically Coding Multi-format Web content

In addition to the manual techniques for creating web content for small screen devices, there are commercial products and techniques that enable web pages designed for desktop viewing to be viewed reasonably well on a small screen mobile device. One such example is, automatic 'clipping' of visual page content to reduce bandwidth and visual load. There are also a number of commercial products which can be installed on a mobile device, for example Power Browser, which will extract the textual content of a web page and semantically summarise it into an 'information tree' that can be browsed by the user [12]. SmartView is a program that follows a different model of data management; it takes a virtual snapshot of the webpage as if it were to be displayed on a desktop sized screen so the user can 'zoom out' to view the entire page structure and 'zoom in' to read individual pieces of text [13].

2.2.1 Web clipping

Palm™ developed a set of drivers that allows web content to be downloaded in such a way that it is quickly accessible to PDA-like devices. A applications using these drivers are known as 'Web clipping' applications [14]. Web clipping operates on two levels, first, when displaying the page to the user for the first time, the source code is completely scanning and all the 'static data' is extracted. This static data includes graphics, logos, photographs and unnecessary text. These data are stored in the devices cache. On subsequent visits, the static content on the webpage is displayed locally from the device's memory, and only the dynamic content will be updated from the Web [15]. Not only does web clipping conserve the resources of the device by caching data locally, it also increases the speed that a page can be downloaded as less data is required to be transferred to the device.

2.2.2 Page summation

Buyukkokten et al [9] found that web content not created using WML and viewed on a small screen has excessive amounts of vertical and horizontal scrolling. Further research conducted by Buyukkokten [12] produced a tool that allows users to access the web content via their mobile device. This tool not only ignores the page's graphical elements, but also its text formatting style, therefore, presents the page's content as a summary of textual information. Being similar to web clipping technology, the entire page's source is scanned for certain content, and is processed by the small screen mobile device before anything is displayed on screen. That is, instead of displaying the traditional format of a web page, only the headings, sub-headings, the body text, and link anchors of the pages are displayed.

2.2.3 Page adaptation

Chen, Ma and Zhang [13] devised a solution to overcome limited screen size without disrupting the structure of a webpage using a relational 'zooming' method called page adaptation. They developed a piece of software called SmartView that can be installed on a small screen mobile device in order to translate incoming web documents. Through page adaptation techniques, SmartView allows the user to view a miniaturised version of an entire webpage as it would be seen on a desktop computer. The miniaturised version image of the website is divided into visual thumbnails of layout information and data. Each thumbnail contains a section of the webpage, such as a navigation bar, image or textual article. The user is able to select a thumbnail, and zoom in, enabling the content to be readable from the small screen.

A drawback of this model is that parsing such high amounts of visual information results in high resource use.

3. The Research

A study was designed to explore a number of techniques frequently used to display content on small screen mobile devices. Several web sites were selected for viewing by volunteer participants using an iPAQ™ 4150 PDA. The page creation techniques explored where:

- *Flat-form (No different to desktop design - HTML)* relate to website design that has generally be developed for the desktop user, and therefore assumes that users will be using an average screen size of 1024 x 768 pixels.
- *Thin-form (CSS/XHTML)* may contain an element that reformats a desktop web page to fit into a PDAs limited screen size when the user to specifies they are using a mobile device.
- Wireless Application Protocol-enabled *(WAP-enabled)* relate to websites written specifically for mobile devices by rewriting the code using Wireless Markup Language (WML) as signified by the use of a .wml file extension.

One goal of the study was to evaluate the design of websites rather than the information management behind the site, therefore, sites that were user driven, contained forums or chat areas, were not considered. Furthermore, pages that required third party software such as web clipping, page summarisation or page adaptation, were not be considered as they require the use of commercial software that is generally not packaged with a PDA or similar device.

3.1   The Selected Websites

A range of websites were chosen to allow the exploration between those websites which were designed specifically with mobile devices in mind, and those that did not. Five web sites were selected for the study (see Table 1); all are the types of websites you might expect a typical PDA user might want to access when mobile. Three out of five of the selected sites for the study were sites specifically designed for mobile devices and were available on the web in two formats; desktop and PDA format. The other two sites were chosen for a comparison and selected due to their generally good web design for viewing on a large screen.

Table 4. Websites used in the study.

Site	Business	Archetype	URL
National Australia Bank	Bank	Flat form	http://www.national.com.au
NineMSN	News	Flat form	http://www.ninemsn.com.au
The Age	News	Thin page	http://www.theage.com.au
Qantas	Airline	WAP	http://www.qantas.com.au
Modern Sci-Fi	Magazine	WAP	http://www.scifi.com

3.2 Participants

A call for expression of interest in the study was disseminated using the global email system of an organization, and various internal mailing lists. This call returned twenty responses. It was decided that only participants who had reasonable computer skills and were web 'savvy' would participate in the study, therefore, a short survey collected selection criteria data, of which 17 of the 20 potential participants qualified.

Prior to conducting the study, additional participant data was collected. This included PDA ownership (8 participants: 47%), type of PDA owned (88% owned a Hewlett Packard™, 12% owned a Palm™). The participants who owned a PDA were also asked what they used it for: their usage was as follows:

25 % for diary/calendar
24% for note-taking
17% for surfing the web
17% for games
17% for storing/transferring files

3.3   Questionnaire

The primary data gathering tool of the study was a nine question Likert-type questionnaire (see Table 2). The users were asked to place a mark on a scale for each statement, ranging from "strongly agree" (5) to "strongly disagree" (1), or "not applicable" (null) if they believed the question was not relevant. The questions were based on Shneiderman's *Golden rules for interface design* [16 pp 74-75], and Nielson and Molick's *Usability Heuristics* [13]. The quantitative questions were followed with two general qualitative questions. The same questionnaire was used to evaluate each of the three websites.

Table 2: Questions, Q1-9 used a Likert-type scale, Q10-11, were open-ended

	Question:
1	Upon using it, I quickly understood the purpose and motive of this site."
2	I was easily able to return "home" if I needed to
3	The visual design of the site was consistent
4	The site is intuitive and I did not require instructions on how to use it
5	The clarity of the text was clear and easy to read."
6	The sites navigational tools were apparent and easy for me to use
7	I felt that color added value, or would add extra value to the site."
8	The textual information was categorised in a logical order."
9	I consider this site to be easy to use."
10	Was there any part of the interface that encumbered your use of the site?
11	Optional comments:

4. Results and findings

Descriptive tests of mean score and standard deviation (Table 3) were calculated on the data to highlight the participants' perceptions of recognised design features of the site.

Table 3: Interface usability: Mean and Standard Deviation

		National Flat form	NineMSN Flat Form	The Age Thin-page	Qantas WAP	Sci-Fi WAP
1. Clearly defined purpose	m	3.35	3.41	4.59	4.35	4.12
	sd	0.86	1.00	0.51	0.70	1.22
2. Ability to return 'home'	m	2.24	2.76	3.29	4.59	3.24
	sd	1.03	1.15	1.49	0.80	1.30
3. Consistent visual design	m	3.35	2.53	4.47	4.24	4.12
	sd	1.12	1.18	0.52	0.56	0.99
4. Intuitive design	m	2.71	3.29	4.53	4.12	3.76
	sd	1.05	0.92	0.62	0.49	1.09
5. High clarity of text	m	2.18	3.06	4.47	4.18	4.29
	sd	0.81	1.14	0.62	0.39	0.99
6. Apparent navigational tools	m	1.88	2.41	3.82	3.76	3.12
	sd	0.86	1.00	1.07	1.25	1.45
7. Colour used for value	m	2.71	3.06	3.59	3.18	3.06
	sd	1.16	1.03	1.23	1.13	1.03
8. Logical organisation	m	2.65	2.94	4.35	4.06	3.88
	sd	1.06	0.90	0.61	0.83	0.93
9. User Satisfaction	m	1.59	2.12	4.47	4.24	3.65
	sd	0.62	0.70	0.62	0.75	1.32

1. Clearly defined purpose and motive: For each website used in the study, the majority of participants "strongly agreed", or "agreed" that they understood the purpose and motive of the given website. The users believed that The Age website (thin page archetype), had the most clear purpose and motive. All participants either "agreed" or "strongly agreed" that The Age was the quickest to be understood, whereas the users believed that NineMSN had a purpose that was much slower to be understood with 47% of the users responded with "unsure" or "disagreeing" that they quickly understood it. The majority of users "agreed" with each other about a website's ability to be quickly understood. However, the Sci-fi website had the most dispersed results, with 53% of the users "strongly agreeing" and 24% of the users "disagreed" or "strongly disagreed".

2. Ability to return 'home': Mobile devices generally do not allow multiple browser windows, so the user must follow a single path of navigation; therefore it is important that the user is able to return to the interface's 'home' without having to restart the browser. The Qantas website (WAP-enabled archetype) provided a home link on each page back to the main menu: 71% of users "strongly agreed" and 23% "agreed" that they were easily able to return 'home' when using the Qantas website, only 6% disagreed. In comparison, The National Bank website (Flat-form archetype) provided a home link on the desktop version of the website, but as it does not translate well to browsing using a PDA, making it difficult to return to the main index of the website, with 77% of users "disagreed" or "strongly disagreed" that they were able to return 'home' if they needed to.

3. Consistent visual design: Over 85% of users for each Qantas, National Bank and Sci-fi websites "agreed" that they contained a consistent visual design. When reviewing The Age web site, 47% of the users "strongly agreed" and 53% "agreed" that the visual design of The Age website was consistent. NineMSN website (flat form archetype) was the lowest scoring site with 59% of participant responses claiming that the design was inconsistent.

4. Intuitive design: PDAs have a limited number of possible user interactions, so the interface should be designed to minimise incorrect user actions. The Age and Qantas websites had the majority of positive user responses. In addition, The Age had the highest percentage (59%) of users stating that the website contained an intuitive design. The National Bank website had the highest number of users (71%) stating that the web site did not have an intuitive design.

5. High clarity of text: The Age, Qantas and the Sci-fi websites had the majority of users stating that the text on the site was easy to read. In contrast however, 71% of the users thought that the text on the National Bank website was difficult to read.

6. Navigational tools: The Age, Qantas and the Sci-fi websites had similar results in that 65% or greater of responses stated that the site's navigation tools were apparent and easy to use. The two flat form archetype sites (National Bank and NineMSN) scored poorly, each having 75% users "disagreeing" or "strongly disagreeing" that the website's navigational tools were apparent and easy to use, with the National Bank website rating the worst.

7. Value of colour: The Age website scored highly, with 65% of users agreeing or strongly agreeing that colour added value to the website. The response for the Qantas and NineMSN websites was significantly lower, with each site having 35% of users stating that colour did not add extra value to the website. The National Bank website scored the lowest with 41% stating that the use of colour did not add value to the site.

8. Logical organisation of content: The Age website scored the highest in this question with 94% of the users "agreeing" or "strongly agreeing" that its content was logically structured. The Qantas and Sci-fi websites each scored highly with both having over 76% of the users "agreeing" or "strongly agreeing" that the textual information was categorised in a logical order. This was followed by NineMSN then the National Bank.

9. User Satisfaction: When taking into consideration the previous results, predictably The Age website was perceived as the most easy to use with 94% of the users agreeing or strongly agreeing that it was easy to use. This was closely followed by the Qantas website, then the Sci-fi website. The NineMSN website was perceived as not easy to use (82%). The National Bank website was the least easy to use with no participant stating that it was easy to use, 6% stating that they were unsure, and an overwhelming 94% stating that is was not easy to use.

According to the aggregate of the responses from the participants, The Age (Thin page archetype) was the most 'usable' website due to its consistently high mean score across all categories. On the other hand, both NineMSN and the National Bank (Flat form archetypes) generally scored low across all categories. Qantas and Sci-fi (WAP-enabled archetypes) were generally middle-ranked (see Table 4).

Table 4: Usability of the selected sites (and corresponding archetype

	Website
Most usable	The Age (Thin page)
	Qantas (WAP-enabled)
	Sci-fi (WAP-enabled)
	NineMSN (Flat form)
Least usable	National Bank (Flat form)

5. Conclusion

A key goal when designing web sites for mobile devices, and in particular for e-business, is to allow the user to be able to access information quickly and easily. Effective interfaces should give a sense of control, be apparent to the user, and allow the user to "quickly see the breadth of their options, grasp how to achieve their goals, and do their work" [17].

Kim and Albers [18] believe that many web design guidelines will often consider a PDA as a portable computer, and the screen to simply be a "miniature computer monitor" [18, p.194]. This outlook can be somewhat problematic when attempting to effectively display text on a mobile device that has limited input and display space when compared to a desktop computer. While users may inherently adopt similar text browsing habits on a PDA as they do for a desktop view, however, additional 'rules' should be applied to a PDA due to the vast physical differences between display a document on a desktop to that of displaying on a small screen device.

The study presented details the views of typical PDA users relating to their preference in relation to a website's presentation on a PDA. The results of the study show that users prefer simplistic interfaces that require minimal interaction, such as those presented in flat form and WAP-enabled website archetypes. The comments given by the users suggest that they prefer websites which follow the standard form of a website with vertical scrolling rather than the 'deck and card' style of WAP-enabled pages. While WAP-enabled sites are designed specifically for mobile devices, thin page sites more closely mirror the interfaces we commonly associate with on a desktop computer screen.

However, the use of a web-formatting technology to display the same sourced content appealing on any device does not guarantee that the website is 'user-friendly'. Careful designing of the site, regardless of the display device, must be taken seriously.

"Usability rules the web. Simply stated, if the customer can't find a product, then he or she will not buy it" [19, p.10].

(Note: The National Bank, Australia, have since addressed the problems with viewing their website on small screen mobile devices, therefore, if the study was conducted today, the results for the National Bank would be more positive.)

References

1. Preece, J., Y. Rogers and H. Sharp (2002). Interaction Design -- beyond human computer interaction. USA, John Wiley and Sons.

2. Cooper, A. (1995). About Face – The essentials of user interface design. IDG Books Worldwide, California, USA.

3. Nielsen, J, and Morkes (1997). Concise, scannable and objective: How to write for the Web. Accessed on April 2003, from http://www.useit.com/papers/webwriting/writing.html

4. Jones, M, Marsden, G, Mohd-Nasir, N, Boone, K, and Buchanan, G. (1999). Improving Web interaction on small displays. In Proceedings of the Eighth International World Wide Web Conference (pp. 1129-1137). Toronto.

5. Mann, S. (2000). Programming Applications with the Wireless Application Protocol: The complete developer's guide. USA, John Wiley & Sons, Inc.

6. Bulbrook, D. (2001). WAP: A beginner's guide. Berkley, California, Osbourne

7. Buchanan, G, Jones, M, Thimbleby, H, Marsden, G, and Pazzani, M. (2001). Improving mobile Internet usability. In Proceedings of the Tenth International Conference on World Wide Web (pp. 673-680). Hong Kong: International conference on World Wide Web.

8. Schiller, J. (2000). Mobile Communications. Harlow, UK, Addison-Wesley.

9. Buyukkokten, O, Kaljuvee, O, Garcia-Molina, H, Paepcke, A, and Winograd, T. (2002) Efficient web browsing on handheld devices using page and form summarization. ACM Transactions on Information Systems. 20 (1), 82-115.

10. Wikipedia (2007a) http://en.wikipedia.org/wiki/Css Accessed April 2007

11. Wikipedia (2007b) http://en.wikipedia.org/wiki/XHTML Accessed April 2007

12. Buyukkokten, O. (2004). Power Browser. Accessed on November 2004 from http://www-diglib.stanford.edu/~testbed/doc2/PowerBrowsing/

13. Chen, Y, Ma, W. Y. and Zhang, HJ. (2003). Detecting Web Page Structure for Adaptive Viewing on Small Form Factor Devices. In Proceedings of the twelfth international conference on World Wide Web (pp.225-233). Hungary: WWW 2003.

14. Palm. (2000). Wireless Enterprise Applications for Mobile Information Management. Accessed on April, 2003, from http://www.palmos.com/dev/tech/webclipping/wireless.pdf

15. Freire, J, Kumar, B, and Lieuwen, D. (2001). WebViews: accessing personalized web content and services. In Proceedings of the International World Wide Web Conference (pp. 576-586). Hong Kong: International World Wide Web Conference.

16. Shneiderman, B. (1998). Designing the User Interface. Addison-Wesley, USA.

17. Togazzini, B. (2003). First Principles. Accessed on September 2003 from http://www.asktog.com/basics/firstPrinciples.html

18. Kim, L, and Albers, M. (2001). Web Design Issues when Searching for Information in a Small Screen Display. In Proceedings of the 19th annual international conference on Computer documentation (pp. 193-200). Mexico.

19. Nielsen, J. (2000). Designing Web Usability. USA, *New Riders Publishing*.

The Information Architecture for Website Design

An Empirical Study of B to C E-commerce Websites in China

Jin Nie[1], Huiling Hao[2]

School of Information Management, Whuhan University, 430072, Hubei,
P.R.China
1 jinnie@whu.edu.cn
2 haohuiling0223@163.com

Abstract: Information Architecture is an important part of web page design, which includes page layout, classification, navigation system and search system. Effective information architecture enables E-commerce website to attract more visitors and customers. For E-commerce websites navigating consumers successfully is the key to keep the sales records. The paper applied the information architecture theory to analyze two B to C E-commerce websites in China and discussed the improvement for future webpage design.

1 Introduction

With the fast growing of E-commerce transactions in China, Chinese E-commerce websites have been developing rapidly. Online shopping and transactions become part of people's daily live. Since the primary goal of E-commerce site is to connect users to products, the basic requirement of website is to help consumer locate the items they want and begin the ordering process online. This is the major difference between online shopping and traditional on site shopping. The information provided on the websites and its arrangement will directly affect customers' shopping decisions.

The traditional merchandise distribution strategy in store has been changed to the information layout strategy of merchandise online. Regular counter displaying of goods and services are replaced by product pictures or some multi-media navigation systems [1]. For online stores the effective marketing strategy is to provide sufficient goods or service information on web and direct consumers to the merchandise they need. Here implementing information architecture in the website design will be an efficient method to structure information so people can find it and use it successfully.

The following of the paper will present the main theory of IA, and apply the theory to analyze two online stores website interface construction. The research method is to search the same merchandise on two websites, and compare the process

Please use the following format when citing this chapter:

Nie, J., Hao, H., 2007, in IFIP International Federation for Information Processing, Volume 251, Integration and Innovation Orient to E-Society Volume1, Wang, W. (Eds), (Boston: Springer), pp. 233-240.

and results of the search. We evaluated the navigation and searching procedures with the IA theory. Based on our finding provide some improvement suggestion for each online stores website arrangements.

2 Theories of website information architecture

Information Architecture is: "First: individual who organizes the patterns inherent in data, making the complex clear; Second: a person who creates the structure or map of information which allows others to find their personal paths to knowledge." This is the definition by Richard Saul Wurman who was first person coined the term. Wurman views architecture as the science and art of creating an "instruction for organized space [2]." It involves the design of organization, labeling, navigation, and search systems to help people find and manage information more successfully. Information architecture is the term used to describe the structure of a system, i.e the way information is grouped, the navigation methods and terminology used within the system [3]. Originally, the theory is applied in the architecture of text information. Due to the rapid rise of the Internet, network information has been growing explosively. When people face massive information, they also have difficulties on how to choose and get effective information. At this point, information architecture emerged.

On the web, IA is a combination of organizing a site's content into categories and creating an interface to support those categories [4]. It composed with the following parts [5]:

(1) Organization system. Divide information in different categories and based on the characteristics of the content, targeting customers with diversified interests. According to Wurman[6][7], there are five ways to organizing information: Location(organize information on the characteristics of location), Alphabet(organize information according to their alphabetical order), Timeline(organize information chronologically), Category(organize information by different categories) and Hierarchy(organize information according to a hierarchical relationship (eg. importance)).

(2) Labeling system. Create a unified labeling program for each specific group of contents of information.

(3) Navigation system. Set up the web browser to help users map out the information the need.

(4) Search system. Help people develop retrieval expression matching related documents to meet users' information requirements.

The goal of information architecture is to achieve the best searching results through web construction. IA is characterized by its practice; not by its research [8]. In the following part of the paper we are going to apply the theory to analyze two E-commerce websites in China and discuss the feature design and future improvements needed for each site.

3 The Searching Case

The sequence of shopping for most people is: first, decide what commodity to buy; second, set the price; third, decide the quality and function of the merchandise. For online shopping the website should present the feature and function of each product clearly and accurately to help consumers search them on the net. We chose MP3 as the merchandise for searching study. Other specific product requirements are: price not higher than RMB500; Color screen with multimedia function; volume no less than 1GB. The selected websites are D1 convenience website (http://www.d1.com.cn) and Yixun website (http://www.icson.com). There are three kinds of strategies to be implemented in information contents arrangement: navigation layout, classification and search engine layout. We focused on the three kinds of layout study of the two websites. For each search we use the same computer operation system, same network speed, the exactly same individual to conduct the search activities. We also count the time on each searching practice and based on the searching speed to find out the right MP3 product to conduct our analysis. We finish our search in November 2006.

3.1 Search plan 1 -- navigation bar

The navigation part is usually on the top of the websites. It can provide direct access to each kind of product by linking with catalog. Using navigations will help users to narrow down the scope of commodity they are looking for.

(1)D1 convenience website (http://www.d1.com.cn)

Click navigation link to the digital product area, there are several search bars in the linked webpage. For different digital products (MP3, MP4, mobile storage, computer accessories, digital accessories, etc.), we use different search methods and options, as is shown in figure 1. Users can choose MP3 by different options (by price, by time, etc.). 40 results returned on the website and in which 37 meet the requirements.

Fig. 4. Search bar of mp3 in D1

(2)Yixun website(http://www.icson.com)

"MP3"→return 90 goods in 10 pages→look through one by one→succeed

3.2 Search plan 2 –classification directory

The search program of organization system is to search through the list of the commodities by classification.

(1) D1 convenience website (http://www.d1.com.cn)

Digital products → digital music → MP3 player → linked to the page of plan 1(navigation bar)

(2)Yixun website(http://www.icson.com)

Digital video and music device → MP3 player → linked to the page of plan 1(navigation bar)

3.3 Search plan 3—search engine

The search engine inside the website can be used to search for a specific product. Key in the key words of the merchandise, the searching result will be pop up on the screen.

(1) D1 convenience website (http://www.d1.com.cn)

Run full text search using different combinations of key words "MP3, video, 1G" and results are:

①enter "MP3"→ 1452 results automatically classified into 8 types→ digital products→succeed

②enter "MP3, video"→44 digitals, 7 books→succeed

③enter "MP3, 1G"→64 MP3, 6 MP4→succeed

④enter "MP3, 1G, video"→2 MP4→too expensive

The user has found that some MP4 have the same function as MP3 which have been put into different classes. What cause this problem?

(2) Yixun website(http://www.icson.com)

Repeat the same steps as in D1, but only when entering "MP3" the searching result will pop up.

Another problem appears. "iPOD Monopoly" (iPOD is a kind of MP3 which is produced by a company named APPLE) is in the directory of "MP3". "MP3 player" and "iPOD Monopoly" belong to two different categories. So if user clicks "MP3 player", there will be no information about iPOD. But if keyword "MP3" is directly entered in the search engine, information about iPOD will be chosen.

4 Analysis of the cases with the theory

After series of tests, the effect of IA in these websites can be figured out. Most of the search processes succeeded, but some spent much time while some are efficient. And there are still some failed cases. Table 1 presents the searching result we recorded in November 2006.

Table 1. The search results comparison

Website	D1 Convenience Website	Yixun Website
Navigation bar	yes	yes
Main category	yes	yes
Sub category	yes	no
Main search engine	yes	yes
Sub search engine	yes	no

Order of goods	yes	yes
Search plan1-navigation bar	Succeed, 30sec	Succeed, 2min
Search plan2-classification directory	Turn to plan 1	Turn to plan 1
Search plan3-search engine	3 succeed (less than 1min), one fail	1 succeed(1.5 mins) , 3 fail

As is shown on the table, both of them have navigation layout, classification layout and search engine layout. But the quality of those designs directly leads to the results. D1 has several advantages: first, the amount of successful cases is larger; second, D1 spent much less time in all examples; third, design of D1is more meticulous with series of main systems and sub systems.

(1) Directory

Implementing IA theory there are different ways to organizing information. Both websites apply taxonomy which is proper with the characteristics of products. Taxonomy agrees with people's general logical thinking habit. Meanwhile, when search target is not clear or keywords are inaccurate, application of this method can improve search efficiency.

But when user hit the navigation bars or the classification links in Yixun, he has reached the bottom of the category level. There is no further search directory available. In the theory of organization system design, the depth and breadth of classification should be adequate and poised. The level of product directory in Yixun is so superficial that users can not continue to narrow the scope of search. They have to browse a large quantity of mixed information, spending a lot of time on unrelated commodities.

(2) Classification and label

The critical part of organization system is taxonomy. Scientific organization and labeling systems will increase the efficiency of users' search. Each label should represent one kind of information to help users understand the classification of information. So the labels on the websites will directly influence the extent of users' understanding of information.

①Yixun separates "iPOD" from other MP3s and creates different labels. This is not an accurate way of sorting information which is classified by neither brand nor function. The two labels may cause users' misunderstanding of iPOD and MP3. In our cases users do not care about the brand of MP3s, as long as the products meet with the requirements about price, volume and video. However, Yixun's design will directly separate information from iPOD when users start navigation. Therefore, the rate of recall is not assured.

②Ambiguous labels of MP3 and MP4. User's goal is to search for a MP3, so it is obvious that user only search goods under the MP3 directory. But when keywords "MP3" are used to search goods, results contain MP4 which belong to another sort, but fully meet with the requirements. The reason why MP4 are searched out is that MP4 is the upgraded product of MP3 which embodied all the functions that MP3 has, so when full-text retrieval is done, some describes of MP4 include keywords "MP3" and these products are selected out.

The root of this error is the discrepancy between user's knowledge structures and websites'. Each user's knowledge structure is different, so does their understanding of MP3 and MP4. Some users will treat one product as MP3 while another may regard it as MP4. If the websites only organize and label the information according to their own understanding, conflicts of concept understanding will appear.

(3) Search engine

Search engine provides users with a search scheme different from classification or navigation. It is one of the important tools of search system that can help users quikly find things which have specific descriptions and cannot be displayed in navigations or directories. Search engine can satisfy user's special search requirements.

①User enters the same combinations of keywords into the search engines in the homepages of the two websites. All these plans in D1succeed within 1minute, but only one has results in Yixun(table 1).

②When user has implemented the search command in the homepage of D1, the results will be automatically classified for user to narrow the search scope. But Yixun shows only one page and user cannot eliminate or abstract the information.

③D1 supplied different sub search engines based on different types of goods. In our case, user can limit all kinds of functions of MP3 (price, volume, FM, brand, etc.) at one time without narrowing the scope step by step. To search for other products, such as jewelry, there is another sub search engine (including price, material, brand, type, etc.). Yixun dose not have anymore search engines except for the one in homepage.

Yixun's search system is too simple. First, the keywords dictionary is not rich, and search function is not efficient. When entered more than one keyword, Yixun can not find the location of the goods. That is not because Yixun does not have this product but its search system is too simple that the brief combination of keywords can not be recognized. Second, the design of the search engine can not move further, so it dose not have the function to filter information based on results of last step.

(4) Targeting and navigation bars

E-commerce websites must be designed focusing on the requirements and tastes of users [9]. D1 has better consideration on different levels of users' demands. It devises the navigation bars from two different aspects to make comprehensive classification. The first is the previously mentioned navigation bar classified according to the function; the second is another navigation bar in accordance with different types of users whose demands for goods will be different. These goods are typed based on gender, age, occupation and season (Christmas Day, Children's Day, New Year and other special plate, etc.). Two classifications methods may fit users' different search habits.

5 Suggestions

Based on the analysis, we generated the following suggestions:

(1) If the definition of two products is hard to distinguish, organized them into the same category, create unified retrieval formula and increase the limited indicators for each good. This will avoid missing in search. For the two websites we should put MP3 and MP4 into the same classification catalog, using unified logo "MP3 and MP4". Adding the keywords of commodity's description into catalog, not only volume, price, and also whether supporting video format, whether there are affiliated functions (such as photo browser, text browser, etc.)

(2) Enhancing the sub-directories for each kind of product. In the general directory "MP3" should be one of the sub directories based on the performance of MP3 (Brand, volume, etc.). Sub-directory can help user narrow down the types of goods in their search. For example, when all MP3s with volume bigger than 1G are listed, user can also limit price selection in current search, and people can find the products satisfy both obtain conditions. The sub-directory level should be suitable

which is neither too shallow nor too deep. Cognitive psychologists Miller said that the symbols amount or the block size which people can preserve and deal effectively with in a short memory is 5-9, generally limited to 7. So the depth should be ensured that users will not be forced to click more than 4.5 layers to reach the target information [10].

(3) The list of commodities should be arranged in a user friendly way, not in random order. Random array will make user feel that information is fragmented and lose the interest to go on. So whenever results are returned, products should be automatically put in order according to some manner such as time, price and so on. For example, search results are listed with the order that prices from high to low. The arrangement will not influence the normal operation, but make the results more acceptable. In addition, the website should provide other ranking methods for customers to make the selections.

(4) The design of the directory should be extensible. Both websites we studied in this paper are small and medium-sized E-commerce websites. For small and medium sized business websites possess relatively less commodities, so it is not necessary to classify the goods into more detail. Sometimes, too exhaustive categories will bring about reverse effects. But considering the amount of goods will increase in the future, the designers must make sure that the structure can adjust to changes. By the time not only the quantity of commodities increases, but also the frame of commodity classification changes. So the information structure should be designed to facilitate the expansion and modifications from the very beginning. For example, now MP4 products have not become prevail in the market and are very alike with MP3, so gathering them into one catalog is more helpful for users. With the technology development, MP4's functions become more powerful, and the differences between them are gradually obvious. At that time, we should consider whether or not to separate them into two category lists.

(5) Search engine is a very powerful tool in the search process. But as for the theory of search system, designers should be careful when making decision on whether the website really needs a search engine [11]. There are two things need to be thinked ahead: Dose the website have enough contents and will the search engine divert resources from more useful navigation systems? Yixun is a small website which has relatively less information. Navigation and organization system are effective enough to help users make quick selection. Search engine may not fit in this situation. In addition, plan 3 has indicated that the current search engine in Yixun is not efficient and replacing it with navigation and organization system may increase efficiency.

(6) Future work. The research result may be not accurate as we predicted since the research was based on two websites and the testing time is limited. We need to conduct further detailed research on a more broad data collection and analysis basis.

Reference.

1 L. R. Gan, "Examination & Analysis of Information Architecture of E-commerce Websites", *Journal of Information Theory and Practice*, 2005, 28(6), pp.605-608

2 Wuman Richard Saul, Bradford Peter, *Information Architects*, Zurich, Switzerland: Graphis Press, 1996. ISBN: 2-85709-458-3.

3 Lain Baker, 2005, "what is information architecture?"www.steptwo.com

4 Heather McNay, Information Architecture-Visual Displays, Professional Com-munication Conference,2003, p.104

5 W. T. Jia, Y. W. Ding, "Brief Introduction of IA in China", *Library Work and Research*, 2006(4), p.10

6 Y. H. Rong and Z. P. Liang, "An Approach to Information Architecture (IA)", *Journal of the China Society for Scientific and Technical Information*, 2003, 22(2), p.231

7 Mark Fischetti, "Five Rules for Mapping Information so Others Can Find Their Way;" http://www.fastcomany. com/online/10/blue-print.html

8 Karl Fast, "The Confluence of Research and Practice in Information Architecture", *Bulletin of the American Society for Information Science and Technology*, 2006(June/July), p.27

9 Q. H. Liu, W. H. Liu and J. B. Mou, "On the Information Architecture and the Website Construction of Information Literacy Tutorials", *Journal of Qingdao Vocational and Technical College*, 2006,19(2), pp.67

10 L. Li and G. J. Qi, "Analysis of the Development of Information Architecture in Accordance with Yahoo's Classified Catalogue", *Journal of Information Theory and Practice*, 2006,29(2) , p.1

11 Peter Morville and Louis Rosenfeld, "Information Architecture for the World Wide Web", *O'Reilly*, December 01, 2006

Research on Indexing Systems for Enterprise Credit Evaluation in B2B

Jinbing Ha[1], Yingjie Wang[2]

1 School of Economics and Management,Nanjing University of Science and
Technology,Nanjing 210094, huwenbin@nuaa.edu.com,
2 School of Economics and Management,Nanjing University of Science and
Technology,Nanjing 210094,qyx0955@sina.com

Abstract. Electronic commerce depends on credit system much more than traditional commerce. Credit problem becomes the bottleneck in the development of electronic commerce. Since it is the research basis and object for wholly credit evaluation, how to design the Indexing system of enterprise credit evaluation in B2B is very important. The paper tries to establish the Indexing system with consideration the characteristic of online business and online transactions. Hypoteses for enterprise credit evaluation for B2B are discussed. The indexing system of enterprise credit evaluation in B2B is developed including Offline Static Indexes and Online Dynamic indexes. The two factors which impact on online evaluation weights are then proposed.

1   Introduction

1.1 Related Research

Traditional credit evaluation Indexing systems include "5C" Indexing system, "5P" Indexing system and LAPP Indexing system. Traditional credit evaluation methods include 5C and the comprehensive evaluation which based on 5C method developed and widely use [1].Generally key factors are the following five indexes: Character, Capital, Capacity, Collateral, and Condition. 5P means Personal, Purpose, Payment, Protection, and Perspective。 5P reclassify 5C elements, but lack of quantitative analysis [2]. LAPP means Liquidity, Activity, Profitability, and Potentiality [3].However, in china the enterprise credit evaluation and management is still at an early stage, the research was relatively small.

Since 1990s, along with the rise and popularity of e-commerce, Enterprise credit management theory and credit evaluation to be further developed. Viktor proposes the collective credit in the network environment and the concept of personal credit,

Please use the following format when citing this chapter:

Ha, J., Wang, Y., 2007, in IFIP International Federation for Information Processing, Volume 251, Integration and Innovation Orient to E-Society Volume1, Wang, W. (Eds), (Boston: Springer), pp. 241-250.

and gives the quantitative method. Dong Huynh and others made a business credit evaluation model called FIRE. Mui's research emphases on the credit evaluation model in electronic business transactions. The Web-based online reputation management system is a reputable management tool that the number of e-commerce websites use of. It helps to build the online trust. Reputation Research Network makes the reputation management system as a major study object, conducted a series of studies. R. A. Malaga points that the existing reputation management system has six aspects problem, and proposed a number of solutions. C. Dellarocas identified two types of the system fraud: feedback unfair and sellers of discrimination behavior, and made subject to two mechanisms: controlled anonymity and cluster filtering, to eliminate or reduce the negative influence. C. Dellarocas takes the eBay's reputation management system as example, through establishing the mathematical model to analyze the economic efficiency of the reputation management system.

And there is still a certain gap between home and abroad. Above all kinds of domestic and foreign enterprises credit evaluation research, credit evaluation mainly through financial ratio analysis, that the selection of a number of financial indicators allocated to different weights and through the various methods of scoring indicators, hence the reputation of the enterprise credit. These credit evaluation methods are not fully applicable for our enterprise credit evaluation in B2B.

1.2 Importance of Enterprise Credit Evaluation in B2B

In the world of e-commerce to flourish, bring opportunities for Chinese enterprises to enable them to face challenges. It is relatively easy to establish a hard environment, while improving the soft environment is difficult.

Compared with the traditional business, e-commerce on the credit requirements are higher, and the development of e-commerce must enhance credit. Online transactions have B2B, B2C and C2C three models. B2B model which is the best development in online transactions, because of the relatively high amount of the transaction, the risks are great. there was an urgent need to establish a scientific and effective Indexing system of Enterprise credit evaluation in B2B.

2   Hypotheses for Enterprise Credit Evaluation in B2B

This paper established Indexing system of enterprise credit evaluation in B2B (shown in the Fig.1) has two hypotheses:

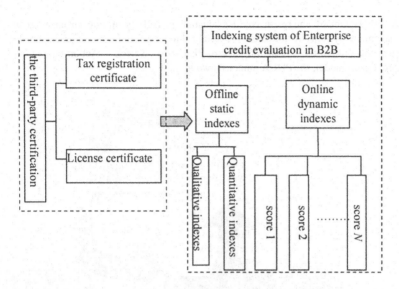

Fig.1. Indexing system of enterprise credit evaluation in B2B and two hypotheses

1) B2B website itself has a good reputation;
2) Online enterprises through third-party certification in the field.
In this paper we suppose B2B website itself has a good reputation, the information provided is true and effective. Second, to assess the situation before the credit evaluation should verify the legitimacy and authenticity of online business. In this Indexing system of Enterprise credit evaluation in B2B, through third-party certification provided by the Registry to obtain registration information, the virtual environment is real enterprises, and enterprises in the Indexing system of Enterprise credit evaluation in B2B as a hypothesis for online transactions.
The third-party certification according to in basic information submitted online request enterprise fax business license and certification of the authorization of attorney. Through local Business Information Inquiry System ask the enterprise made real and the registration of Companies to register relevant information. Through check the tax registration certificate and license certificate given to prove authenticity. Not through third parties authentication, the business will not have access to accredited enterprise credit evaluation in B2B system.

3 Indexing system of Enterprise Credit Evaluation in B2B

Indexing system of enterprise credit evaluation in B2B is on-line business credit management system. It followed the establishment of the general management system to improve the circulation pattern: Plan-- Do --Check -- Action continuous improvement model, the PDCA model shown in the Fig.2.

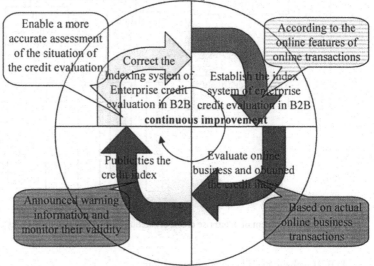

Fig.2.PDCA model of enterprise credit evaluation in B2B

Indexing system of enterprise credit evaluation in B2B in which continuous improvement model, the corresponding steps: Plan--According to the online features of online transactions, established the Indexing system of Enterprise credit evaluation inB2B; Do--based on actual online business transactions, using the Indexing system of Enterprise credit evaluation in B2B evaluate online business and obtained the credit index; Check--publicities the credit index and monitor their validity. At the same time, announced warning information; Action--According to a specific implementation, correct the Indexing system of Enterprise credit evaluation in B2B that enable a more accurate assessment of the situation of the credit evaluation. This paper will be the establishment of Indexing system of enterprise credit evaluation in B2B in offline state enterprise and online transactions for both state examination considerations. The following two sections will be selected on two categories of indexes.

4 Offline Static Indexes to Enterprise Credit Evaluation in B2B

4.1 Offline Static Qualitative Indexes

Offline static qualitative indexes main line of business as a true indicator of the operating entity of society tour inspected the main external factors and the quality of enterprises.

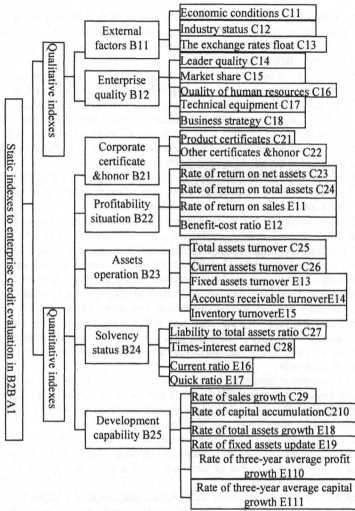

Fig.3.static indexes to enterprise credit evaluation in B2B

1) External factors

In the development process, external factors have an important role to play. The Indexing system inspected by the main external factors, including economic conditions, industry status, the exchange rate float.

2) Enterprise Quality

Besides external factors, enterprise quality is more important factor affecting Enterprise credit evaluation in B2B. The main indexes of the quality of the enterprise system include leader quality, market share, quality of human resources, technical equipment, and business strategy.

4.2 Offline Static Quantitative Indexes

Quantitative indexes of Enterprise credit evaluation in B2B need to consider static line is the corporate certificate honor, profitability situation, assets operation, solvency status and development capability [4]. Static indexes to enterprise credit evaluation in B2B is shown in Fig.3.

1) Corporate certificate and honor. The target selected for the honorary certificates to enterprises is the accumulated operating offline credit extended to the Internet.

(1) Product certificates. It provides online transactions a certificate to the product including the product quality, specifications and other information. (2) Other certificates &honor. In other areas, the honor or certificates (such as bank accounts to prove that open an account, certificate awarded by the website) can upload to the Internet and be the reference information.

2) Profitability situation. The main indexes used to measure the profitability of the business are rate of return on net assets, rate of return on total assets. Suggestions indexes are rate of return on sales, and benefit-cost ratio.

3) Assets operation. Assets operation indexes reflect not only on business enterprises in using various resources efficiently, but also show that the level of asset management [5]. Bad enterprise operating may lead capital to tension. It will impact the repayment of principal and interest for loans to enterprises. The major indexes for assets operation are total assets turnover and current assets turnover. Suggestions indexes are fixed assets turnover, accounts receivable turnover, inventory turnover.

4) Solvency position. Solvency is the core capability of business credit evaluation. Solvency can be divided into short-term solvency and long-term solvency. The key indicators of Solvency position that used to measure assets and liabilities, including liability to total assets ratio, times-interest earned. Suggestions indexes are current ratio, quick ratio.

5) Development capability. The inspection focused on the growth and sustainable development of business. The growth is the foundation for sustainable development; and sustainable development is the objective requirements of enterprises [6]. No development, there is no future, let alone credibility.

The main indexes for measuring development capability include rate of sales growth, rate of capital accumulation. Suggestions indexes are rate of total assets growth, rate of fixed asset update, rate of three-year average profit growth, rate of three-year average capital growth.

In the Indexing system, offline B2B Online static indexes it is difficult for SMEs to obtain , but the Indexing system will target its consideration, because they can be full-line static indexes, a true understanding of operation and development situation and can be a good illustration of the extent of the online business's credit.

5 Online Dynamic Indexes to Enterprise Credit Evaluation in B2B

Online dynamic indexes suggesting that these criteria are objective formed in the course of online trading, mainly selected delivery, transport, payment, service and reference. Two different online dynamic indexes are proposed for the seller & buyer. Online dynamic indexes as in the Fig.4:

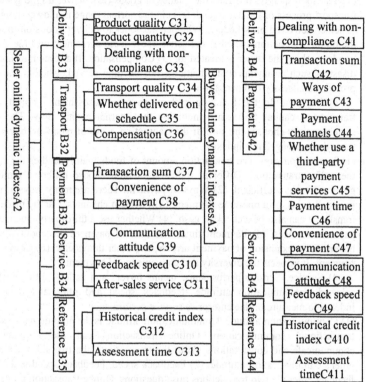

Fig.4. Online dynamic indexes to enterprise credit evaluation in B2B

1) Delivery. In the Indexing system it selects product quality, product quantity and dealing with non compliance three indicators to be evaluated.

(1) Product quality. It mainly indicates whether the seller in accordance with the agreed terms of the Internet to provide the same quality, the same specifications of products, whether the defects, and so on. (2) Product quantity. It means whether agreement with the number of Internet-related cases. If the seller deliberately reduced number of goods with no explanation, and not given the compensation package, which can be regarded as violations, it could greatly affect the index of the Enterprise credit evaluation in B2B. (3) Dealing with non-compliance. At the point of delivery, if goods default (the goods quality or quantity have problem, cancellation of transactions, etc.), how to dealing with these problems.

2) Transport. Transport of goods mainly reflects whether the transport of merchandise on time and the quality of delivery, compensation, and so on.

It needs to be pointed out that in online transactions, most transport is through third-party logistics companies to provide, but the transport of merchandise situation some extent reflect the seller's credit behavior.

(1) Transport quality. It means the quality of goods (expensive, fragile goods) in the transport process of the damage, defects in the normal range is allowed to ignore. (2) Whether delivered on schedule. Whether the seller to deliver goods on time is after the online transactions whether the seller obeys lease agreement on time and makes goods reaching the buyer is located to. (3) Compensation. If a force majeure (natural disasters such as unexpected situation), not on time served, whether the seller to provide satisfactory compensation.

3) Payment. In the Indexing system, payment assessment's object is online transactions capital flows, not including the internal capital flow. The Indexing system mainly chooses the sum of the transaction, ways of payment, payment time, these three-pronged test indexes.

(1) Transaction sum. The transaction amount of funds mainly studies the amount of the online transaction. Different industries should choose different standards for given different coefficient. (2) Ways of payment. There are many ways of payment, in installments, or a one-time payment. (3) Payment channels. Can be made by bank transfer, it can also be a check or cash. (4) Whether use a third-party (such as paypal) payment services. (5) Payment time. The time of payment see about whether the buyer has an extension of payment arrears, and other things else. (6) Convenience of payment. It inspects the diversity and convenience of payment.

4) Service. Service performance means buyers and sellers' attitude, the paper selected communication attitude, feedback speed and after-sales service three indexes to measure online enterprise service performance.

(1) Communication attitude. Communication attitude is the attitude between the two transactions' communication. Online transactions can use the network to communicate and consultations. After the transactions, the two sides evaluate each other's communication attitude. (2) Feedback speed. Feedback speed is the speed of feedback after the two transactions raise questions. Online transaction process on the parties to the transaction may raise product characteristics, means of transport, form of payment and other questions. At this time feedback speed will become an online transaction indexes. (3) After-sales service. After goods sold, how about after-sales service, were offered technical support, maintenance and other after-sales service.

5) Reference. Reference mainly refers to data that provide information as reference while online transaction happening.

(1) Historical credit index. A credit history index party to the transaction is the current credit index, the credit evaluation results of the current Indexing system. (2) Assessment time. The time that Online business to participate in the Indexing system of Enterprise credit evaluation in B2B means whether or not to pay on time online credit evaluation system, and long-term honesty and trustworthiness. In this paper online business that participates in evaluating the credit of enterprises are willing to deal honestly. Therefore into online business credit evaluation system more time, the corporate credit rating higher.

6 The Two Factors Impact on Online Evaluation Weights

After online transactions, according to the performance of the other parties to the online transaction in the transaction process and after the transaction, the other side assesses its credit evaluation points. At the same time, the valuators credit index will affect the credibility of their evaluation; online credit evaluation time distance will also affect the validity of the evaluation.

Therefore, when concentrate the dynamic index score, it should also consider two factors that influence online transactions parties credit evaluation.

1) The valuators credit index. The valuators credit index is the last score in Indexing system of Enterprise credit evaluation in B2B. This reference is a reflection of the credit valuators' credit degree. The higher credit index valuators got the more credibility the evaluation is. So valuators credit index to some extent reflected the valuators credit index credible.

2) Online credit evaluation time distance. Online credit evaluation time distance will also affect the validity of evaluation. Evaluation of a short time, that is relatively new credit evaluation will be better able to explain the recent evaluation of the enterprise credit, This assessment is more effective; evaluation of the long time show an earlier time enterprise credit, the evaluation of the effectiveness is poorer than new credit evaluation.

References:

1. C. Gomez and A. Careening, "Business credit scoring", *Journal of Business Credit*, Mar 2001,103,3.

2. S. Standifird , "Reputation and ecommerce: eBay auction and the asymmetrical impact of positive and negative ratings", *Journal of Management*, 2001,27(3):279-295

3. P.Resnick, R.Zeckhauser,E.Friedman and K. Kuwabara, "Reputation systems",*Communicationsof the ACM* ,2002,43(12):45-48.

4.E.I.Altmam, F.Varetto, "Corporate Distress Diagnosis: Comparisons Using Linear Discriminant Analysis and Neural Networks (the Italian Experience)", *Journal of Banking and finance*, 1999(18):505-529

5.E. I. Altman,R. G. Haldeman, P. Z. Narayanan, "Analysis: A New Model to Identify Bankruptcy Risk of Corporations", *Journal and Finance*, 1997(1):29-54

6.J. Ohlson, "Financial. Rations and the Probabilistic Prediction of Bankruptc", *Journal of Accounting Research*, 1980(2):109-130

7.S. Viktor, Grishchenko, "Redefining Web-of-Trust: reputation, recommendations, responsibility and trust among peers", Ural State University, Institute of Physics and Applied Mathematics, 1999,159-166

8. T. Dong Huynh, Nicholas R. Jennings, Nigel R. Shadbolt. "FIRE: An Integrated Trust and Reputation Model for Open Multi-Agent Systems", *School of Electronics and Computer Science*, University of Southampton,UK,2001.147-151

9.Lik Mui, "Computational Models of Trust and Reputation: Agents, Evolutionary Games, and Social Networks", *Electrical Engineering and Computer Science*, 2002(6):112-124

10.M. Fisher, "What is the Right Supply Chain for Your Product", *Harvard Business Reviews*, 1997(4):112-116

11.S.Standifird, "Reputation and e-commerce: eBay auction and the asymmetrical impact of positive and negative ratings", *Journal of Management*, 2001,27(3):279-295

12.P. Resnick, R. Zeckhauser, E. Friedman and K. Kuwabara, "Reputation systems", *Communications of the ACM* ,2002,43(12):45-48.

13.J. H. Cui, "China's e-commerce development of the credit system to explore", *modern shopping malls*, No. 471 overall, 2006 (6): 134-135

14.J. Zhen, "China's e-commerce credit system construction", *Dalian Maritime University Journal*, Volume 5, No. 2, 2006 (6) : 73-76

15.J.Wang and G. Wu, "Electronic assessment of goodwill", *agricultural information network*, 2006 (4) : 66-68

16.Z. H.Yan, S.X. Guan and J.N. Mi, "Based on the model of B2B e-commerce trust theoretical research", *research management*, Volume 25, No. 2, 2004 (3) : 76-81

17.W. Yang, "Research on Enterprise Credit System and Design, South China University of Technology", *a master's degree thesis*, 2004 (3)

18.Y. Yan, "E-commerce trust management realized", *Wuhan Institute of Science and Technology Journal*, Vol 16, No. 6, 2003 (12) : 90-94

19.G. Q. Yu and G.X.Song, Tourism means of e-commerce trust building and economic issues to explore, 2005 (11) : 118-121

Knowledge Sharing Network Based Trust Management for Agent-Mediated E-Commerce

Jing Lei[1,2], Xixiang Zhang[1] and Bao'an Yang[1]

1. Glorious Sun School of Business& Management, Donghua University,
Shanghai 200051,China

2 Shanghai Business School, Shanghai 2000235, China

leijing1289@sina.com

Abstract. The efficiency of e-commerce can be increased through the usage of intelligent agents which negotiate and execute contracts on behalf of their owners. The knowledge of trust to secure interactions between autonomous agents is crucial for the success of agent-mediated e-commerce. Building a knowledge sharing network among peer agents helps to overcome trust-related boundaries in an intelligent environment where least human intervention is desired. Based on this network, this paper proposes a trust management model integrating external trustworthiness ratings from other peer agents and the internal assessment of past experiences with the peer node. Knowledge of trust is developed over time through learning from prior business interactions and problems related to peer agents' dishonesty can be solved.

1 Introduction

With the development and popularity of e-commerce, intelligent agents are being employed to automate time and resource consuming tasks such as service discovery, service selection, contract negotiation, business execution and quality of service reviews. The efficiency of e-commerce can be increased through the usage of intelligent agents, but problems concerning trust for automated interactions still represent a major obstacle for the adoption for agent-mediated e-commerce.

In the literature for trust-aware multi-agent networks, trust is defined as "a particular level of belief of an agent that the other agent will act or intend to act beneficially" [1]. Thus, trust implies a long-term future vision based on past reputation and previous performance.

The management of trust in distributed environments is widely studied among researchers. At present, the most widely used trust management model in distributed environments is the reputation-based model built on knowledge sharing network. Reputation is "the expectation about an agent's behavior based on observations of its

Please use the following format when citing this chapter:

Lei, J., Zhang, X., Yang, B., 2007, in IFIP International Federation for Information Processing, Volume 251, Integration and Innovation Orient to E-Society Volume1, Wang, W. (Eds), (Boston: Springer), pp. 251-258.

past behavior" [1]. Generally, a reputation system receives, aggregates, and provides ratings about participants' past behavior. The ratings help participants decide whom to trust, encourage trustworthy behavior and deter dishonest people from participation [2]. eBay [3] and taboo [4] are successful examples of a reputation system. In eBay, partners are rated by each other after the completion of a transaction. A central registry which stores these global ratings for each agent is openly accessible. This simple approach has its weakness when applied to unsupervised automated e-commerce environments. It is easily attacked by dishonest agents via inserting arbitrary number of fake ratings into the central registry. In multi-agent networks, only the individual trustworthiness judgment of one agent for another can fulfill the demand for security [9].

Other decentralized models based on knowledge sharing network [5, 6] are proposed for trust management in distributed systems. In these models, agents query about the trustworthiness of peers to interact with by sending broadcasts to collect advices from neighboring peers, regardless of the credibility of these peers. This method is not just inefficient, but also gives continued opportunities for dishonest peer agents to damage and influence the reputation network, because it does not consider the credibility of the knowledge sharing peers.

Through literature review, we have investigated the shortcomings of existing trust management models when applied to the autonomous agent-mediated e-commerce. Then, in the rest of the paper, we will extend the existing models which use knowledge sharing network to better incorporate both internal and external knowledge sources. The trust inference is based on the individual settings of each agent. Credibility of knowledge sharing peers is considered. Knowledge of trust is developed over time through learning from prior business interactions and problems related to peer agents' dishonesty can be solved. A book buying example is chosen to demonstrate the application of our model and verify the model's effectiveness. Finally, we close this paper with some conclusions and future work about the model.

2   Proposed trust management model

2.1   The knowledge sharing network and the model elements

In this section, we introduce our model for the management of trust between autonomous agents in agent-mediated e-commerce environments. This model is based on a knowledge sharing network (see Fig 1).

In one transaction, the *Requesting Agent*, who initiates the transaction, first locates the *Target Agent* that meets his requirements or expectations. Before the business interaction with the Target Agent, the Requesting Agent retrieves trust knowledge about the Target Agent from its individual repository which stores the knowledge extracted from past interactions. In addition, the Requesting Agent broadcasts a *TrustRequest* to all his known neighboring agents. Peer agents which have had interaction with the Target Agent may answer this TrustRequest with a *TrustResponse* and act as *Recommending Agents*. Then, the trust inference based on the diverse information sources can be carried out by the Requesting Agent.

For each peer agent with whom the Requesting Agent directly interacted, it keeps two attributes in its Trusted agents Table TT: the target agent's id *Tid* and its own perception about the trustworthiness of target agent TV_l . To prevent dishonest Recommending Agents from providing false or poor recommendations, we introduce the concept of Recommending Credibility (RC). For each Recommending Agent who has provided recommendations about other peers to the Requesting Agent, it keeps a record in its Recommenders Table RT, including the Recommender's id *Rid* and the Recommending Credibility *RC*.

The trust value TV_I and Recommending Credibility RC can be adjusted through interaction reviews. Interaction review is the key mechanism in our model to prevent dishonest recommendations. Also, knowledge of trust is learnt from interaction reviews and developed gradually over time.

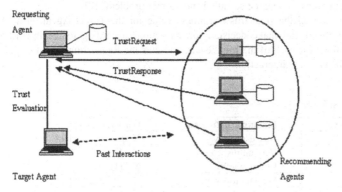

Fig. 5. Knowledge sharing network

2.2 Trust inference

After messages from several Recommending Agents being received, the Requesting Agent needs to pre-process the provided information. Different agent may define different trust value range, so the Requesting Agent have to scale the received trust values to its individual trustworthiness range using the supplied range [t_{min}, t_{max}] in the TrustResponse. If the Requesting Agent's trust value range is [0, 5], the definition of each level see Table 1. Then the received trust value t_v from the Recommending Agent can be transformed to this range using Eq.(1).

$RTV=(t_v-t_{min})*5/(t_{max}-t_{min})$ Eq.(1)

The Requesting Agent then retrieves Recommending Credibility (RC) of Recommending agents from its Recommenders Table (RT). If no credibility record exists, the Requesting Agent assigns an initial credibility value for the Recommending Agent to overcome the so called "newcomer problem" [7].

Subsequently, the TV and RC of Recommending Agents are fed into an inference engine. The summarized trust output that reflects the experience of all Recommending Agents TV_E can be calculated using Eq.(2), where n represents the total number of all Recommending Agents who responded to the TrustRequest.

$TV_E = \sum_{i=1}^{n} TV_i \times RC_i / \sum_{i=1}^{n} RC_i$ Eq.(2)

In addition, the Requesting Agent looks up its own trust record about the Target Agent in past interactions from its Trusted agents Table TT. The internal query result TV_I and the external summarized result TV_E are incorporated to retrieve the overall trust value OTV for the Target Agent. Different Requesting Agent may weigh the internal direct trust and external reputation differently on different context. In order to provide this flexibility we can multiply an internal weight W_I to the internal query result TV_I, and multiply an external weight W_E to the external summarized output TV_E. St: $W_I + W_E = 1$. The overall trust value OTV can be calculated using Eq.(3).

$OTV = TV_E \times W_E + TV_I \times W_I$ Eq.(3)

If the Target Agent is a new partner and there is no record about it in the trusted agents Table TT, the Requesting Agent assigns an initial trust value for the new Target Agent to overcome the so called "newcomer problem" [7].

Having inferred the final trustworthiness value for the Target Agent, now, the Requesting Agent can make decisions on its actions according to the interaction policies defined for each of the trust levels, and thus the Requesting Agent can now complete the business interaction.

Table 1. Trust levels

Trust level	Linguistic definition	Trust value
0	No trustworthy	X=0
1	Very untrustworthy	$X \in [0,1]$
2	Untrustworthy	$X \in (1,2.5]$
3	Medium trustworthy	$X \in (2.5,3.5]$
4	Trustworthy	$X \in (3.5,4.5]$
5	Very trustworthy	$X \in (4.5,5]$

2.3   Business interaction review

After the interaction with the Target Agent is completed, an interaction review is carried out by the Target Agent to evaluate the Target Agent's actual performance by measuring the degree of fulfillment of the contract criteria which he negotiated with the Target Agent prior to their business interaction.

We make use of the modified Commitment methodology [8] for the performance evaluation. The evaluation of the overall performance is achieved by assessing the following two factors:

1. The commitment to each criterion of the contract C_k range [0,5]
2. The importance of each criterion I_k, range [0,5]

The overall actual performance of the Target Agent in the interaction ITV (Instance Trust Value) can be expressed with the following expression where m represents the number of all criteria:

$ITV = \sum_{k=1}^{n} C_k \times I_k / \sum_{k=1}^{n} I_k$ Eq.(4)

Then, the ITV, which represents the actual performance, can be used to adjust the trust value of the Target Agent and to measure the accuracy of recommendations provided by Recommending Agents, and then the Recommending Credibility of

Recommending Agents can be adjusted. Frequent interaction reviews may bring overhead to agents, a review can be taken after every nth interaction.

2.4 Trust and credibility adjustment

After business review, the trust value of the Target Agent can be updated with the ITV value in the Trusted agents Table TT.

The adjustment of the Recommending Credibility value is achieved by measuring the accuracy of the given opinions in prior business interaction. The accuracy of a recommendation AC [0, 1] can be calculated using Eq (5):

$$AC=1-|RTV-ITV|/5 \qquad Eq (5)$$

The recommendation is more accurate, AC value is more close to 1. The Requesting Agent reinforces the RC value for opinions close to the actual performance and penalizes the RC value for opinions differing from the actual performance. A tolerance value ε is introduced to determine whether the RC value needs to be increased or decreased. If $1-AC<\varepsilon$, then the RC value should be increased, otherwise the RC value should be decreased.

Additionally, it is necessary to construct separate functions for the tasks of trust credibility reducing and increasing to simulate human behavior where trust is difficult to build and easy to lose [10]. Firstly, we make the following definitions: $RC_{max}=5$, $RC_{avg}=\sum_{i=1}^{n}RC_i/n$, and n is the number of the Recommending Agents.

For the task of credibility increasing, a bell-shaped function can be used, it increases the agent's credibility value slowly if the existing credibility is relatively low or high but increases of the credibility value strongly if the existing credibility is medium[9]. The recommendation is more accurate, the increase is more significant. We use the following function for credibility increasing, see Eq (6).

$$\Delta RC^+=RC_{new}-RC=AC\times (1-RC/RC_{max})\times e^{-(RC-RC_{avg})2} \qquad Eq (6)$$

$0<e^{-(RC-RC_{avg})2}\leq1$, it is a bell-shaped function and reaches its maximum value when RC is close to the average credibility value.

$0\leq AC\leq1$, $AC\uparrow$, $\Delta RC^+\uparrow$

$\Delta RC^+=AC\times (1-RC/RC_{max})\times e^{-(RC-RC_{avg})2}\leq1-RC/RC_{max} \qquad <RC_{max}-RC$,
$RC_{new}=RC+\Delta RC^+<RC_{max}$.

So the credibility increasing function is reasonable and can fulfill the above requirements for credibility increasing.

For the task of credibility reducing, an exponential function can used, it reduces the agent's credibility slowly if the existing value is already at low and medium levels but decreases the credibility strongly if the existing credibility is high [9]. The recommendation is more inaccurate, the decrease is more significant. In our model, we use the following function for credibility reducing:

$$\Delta RC^-=RC-RC_{new}=RC^2/RC_{max}\times (1-AC)\times e^{(RC-RC_{max})} \qquad Eq (7)$$

$RC\leq RC_{max}$, so $0<e^{(RC-RC_{max})}\leq e^0=1$, it decreases sharply when RC is close to RC_{max}

$0\leq AC\leq1$, $0\leq(1-AC)\leq1$, $AC\uparrow$, $(1-AC)\downarrow$, $\Delta RC^-\downarrow$

$\Delta RC^-=RC^2/RC_{max}\times (1-AC)\times e^{(RC-RC_{max})}\leq RC^2/RC_{max}<RC$, $RC_{new}=RC-\Delta RC^->0$.

So the credibility decreasing function is reasonable and can fulfill the above requirements for credibility decreasing.

The carefully defined functions for Recommending Credibility adjustment can prevent possible periodic dishonesty behavior of Recommending Agents [2].

3   Application example

To demonstrate the application of our model and verify its effectiveness, we choose the simple book buying example as the business scenario. The agent owner specifies his requirements for the book buying as in Table 2.

Table 2. The book buying example

Item	Requirement	Importance
Topic	Knowledge management in e-commerce	4.5
Price	<=$25	3
Delivery	Within 5 days	3.5

Before the agent can work, the agent owner needs to define a set of variables and policies reflecting his individual security requirements. For example, he needs to specify the tolerance value to determine whether the RC value needs to be increased or decreased. Additionally, the agent owner specifies weights used for the incorporation of internal and external knowledge. In our example, the settings are as following:

Tolerance value: $\varepsilon=8\%$

Weights for internal and external knowledge: $W_I=0.45$, $W_E=0.55$

The internal trust value is 4.2. The Requesting Agent received 4 TrustResponses from 4 Recommending Agents (see Table 3). RC values of the 4 Recommending Agents are listed aside.

Table 3. TrustResponses and RC values

Recommending Agent	Recommended Trust value and range	RC value
A1	6.5,[0,10]	4.5
A2	4.5,[0,10]	4.0
A3	0.8, [0,1]	2.8
A4	3.6, [0,5]	3.5

Using the previously defined user settings, the Requesting Agent can immediately start its trust inference.

Step 1 Information pre-processing

Transform the received trust values to range [0,5] using Eq.(1):

RTV1=3.25   RTV2=2.25   RTV3=4.0   RTV4=3.6

Step 2 Trust inference

The overall trust value OTV can be inferred using Eq.(2) and Eq.(3):

OTV = (3.25*4.5+2.25*4.0+4.0*2.8+3.6*3.5)*0.55/(4.5+4.0+2.8+3.5)+4.2*0.45

=3.65

The trust level is 4: 'Trustworthy' which allows the Requesting Agent to interact with the Target Agent.

Step 3 Business interaction review

After the business interaction, the Requesting Agent reviews the performance of the delivered goods and services. Fulfillment of each criterion is evaluated by the Requesting Agent as in Table 4.

Table 4. Commitment of each criterion

Item	Commitment	Importance
Topic	3.5	4.5
Price	5	3
Delivery	2.5	3.5

The overall actual performance of the Target Agent in this interaction ITV (Instance Trust Value) can be calculated using Eq.(4):

ITV=(3.5*4.5+5*3+2.5*3.5)/(4.5+3+3.5)=3.59

Step 4 Trust and credibility adjustment

1) Update the internal trust value:

TV_I=ITV=3.59

2) Determine whether the credibility of each Recommending Agent should be increased or decreased (Tolerance value ε=8%):

A1:AC1=1-|3.25-3.59|/5=0.932,1-AC1=0.068<ε increase credibility
A2:AC2=1-|2.25-3.59|/5=0.732,1-AC2=0.268>ε decrease credibility
A3:AC3=1-|4.0-3.59|/5=0.918,1-AC3=0.082>ε decrease credibility
A4:AC4=1-|3.6-3.59|/5=0.998,1-AC4=0.002<ε increase credibility

3) Adjust credibility values:

RC_{avg} =(4.5+4.0+2.8+3.5)/4=3.7
$RC1_{new}$=4.5+0.932*(1-4.5/5)*$e^{-(4.5-3.7)^2}$=4.5+0.049=4.549
$RC2_{new}$=4.0-4.0*4.0/5.0*0.268*$e^{(4.0-5.0)}$=4.0-0.315=3.685
$RC3_{new}$=2.8-2.8*2.8/5.0*0.082* $e^{(2.8-5.0)}$=2.8-0.005=2.795
$RC4_{new}$=3.6+0.998*(1-3.5/5.0)* $e^{-(3.5-3.7)^2}$=3.6+0.288=3.888

The results show that honest and accurate recommendations are rewarded slightly; but poor or fake recommendations are punished significantly when the RC value is already high. This strategy can prevent dishonest recommenders from cheating periodically.

4 Conclusion and future work

Following our knowledge sharing network based model, agents can reach a comprehensive decision about the trust of their business partners. By collaborating in a trust network, agents can benefit from the external knowledge shared by other peer agents. The external knowledge can be incorporated with their internal knowledge to infer trust values for various potential business partners to facilitate the selection of the best matching and trustworthy business partner. The trust inference is based on the individual settings of each agent, so it can fulfill the demand for security. Furthermore, we introduced a mechanism for preventing dishonest recommendations through Recommending Credibility adjustment based on the outcome of interaction review. Using the proposed model the agents can build up a growing trust knowledge base through learning from prior interactions.

Due to the subjectivity and uncertainty contained in the individual notions and definitions of trust, trust management demands a flexible and adjustable model. In the future work, we plan to study fuzzy inference in our trust management model.

References

1. S.Y. Stephen, Managing Trust in Distributed Agent Systems, *ATC 2006, LNCS 4158*, Springer-Verlag Berlin Heidelberg , 17-25(2006).

2. A.A. Farag, *Trust Modeling and Its Applications for Peer-to-Peer Based Systems*, PhD Thesis, Computer Science, University of Mantoba(2004).

3. eBay homepage. http://www.ebay.com.

4. taobao homepage. http://www.taobao.com.

5 E. Damiani, D. Vimercati, S. Paraboschi, P. Samarati and F. Violante, A reputation-based approach for choosing reliable resources in peer-to-peer networks, *Proceedings of the 9th ACM Conference on Computer and Communications Security* ,207-216(2002).

6 L.Xiong and L. Liu, A Reputation-Based Trust Model for peer-to-peer e-commerce Communities, *IEEE International conference on E-Commerce (CEC '03)*, 270-280(2003).

7. S. Ruohomaa , Lea Kutvonen Trust Management Survey, *Trust Management: Second International Conference,* 77-92(2005).

8. F.K. Hussain, E. Chang and T.S. Dillon, Trustworthiness and CCCI metrics for assigning trustworthiness in P2P communication, *Intl. J. Comput. Syst,* 19 (4), 95–112(2004).

9. S. Stefan et al, *Applying a Fuzzy Trust Model to E-Commerce Systems, AI 2005, LNAI 3809*, Springer-Verlag Berlin Heidelberg, 318 – 329(2005).

10.M A. Patton and A. Josang, Technologies for Trust in Electronic Commerce, *Electronic Commerce Research* ,4, 9-21(2004).

Dynamic Fair Electronic Cash Model without Trustees

Jingliang Zhang [1,2], Lizhen Ma [3] and Yumin Wang [1]

1　State Key Lab. of Integrated Service Networks, Xidian Univ., Xi'an
710071, China zjlmlz@yahoo.com.cn
2　Department of Mathematics, Ocean Univ. of China, Qingdao 266071,
China
3　Department of Physics, Ocean Univ. of China, Qingdao 266071, China

Abstract. A new fair electronic cash system is proposed based on group blind signature and secret sharing scheme. Our proposed system is dynamic: we propose a method to delete the dishonest banks that maybe attack the system, which was not mentioned in the previous literatures. Our proposed scheme does not need a trusted third party to trace users: a shop owning suspicious e-coin and the bank having issued the coin can collaborate to find the user using secret sharing scheme, however, any one of them can't trace the user alone. Furthermore, a novel e-coin tracing method is used to prevent criminal activities: under normal situation, the bank issues ordinary e-coin, while under abnormal situation such as blackmailing, kidnapping etc., the bank issues marked e-coin, and at the step of deposit, any bank in the group can recognize the marked e-coin. Also, our scheme is constructed for multiple banks as in the real life, thus it is more practical.

1 Introduction

With the popularization of internet, people are engaged in electronic commerce with high frequency. Secure and efficient electronic payment systems are significant for electronic commerce. As an important electronic payment system, electronic cash (E-cash or digital cash) develops rapidly. Chaum [1] proposed the first electronic cash system with unconditional anonymity by use of blind signature in 1982. However, this unconditional anonymity may be misused for criminal activities such as money laundering, blackmailing, kidnapping etc. [2]. From then, many fair electronic cash systems were proposed which need a trusted third party (TTP) to revoke the anonymity of the users when necessary. Figure 1 is the flow chart of a basic fair electronic cash model with multiple banks.

As a powerful tool, group signature has been widely used to design fair electronic cash system [5-9]. However, any bank in the group is supposed to be

Please use the following format when citing this chapter:

Zhang, J., Ma, L., Wang, Y., 2007, in IFIP International Federation for Information Processing, Volume 251, Integration and Innovation Orient to E-Society Volume1, Wang, W. (Eds), (Boston: Springer), pp. 259-264.

honest in the previous electronic cash systems based on group signature. But it is possible that there exist dishonest banks probably in the real life, so it is reasonable to consider that there maybe exist dishonest banks in an electronic cash system.

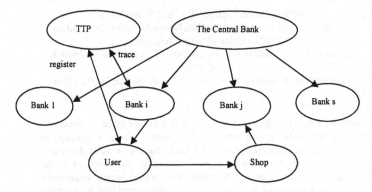

Figure 1 Fair Electronic Cash Model with Multiple Banks

In this paper we propose a member deletion method to CS97 group signature scheme [3] and according to it construct a dynamic fair electronic cash model with multiple banks: a bank can join the group, also, the group manager can delete a bank when he breaks the rules of the group. Our proposed scheme has the following properties: a user can spend his e-cash anonymously, any bank can't trace the user; there is only one public key in the group of the banks, and the length of the public key don't change with the increase of the number of the banks; given an e-cash, nobody but the Central Bank can know by which bank it is issued, which can provide anonymity for the banks; no banks including the Central Bank can issue e-cash on behalf of another bank; the previous e-cash issued by the deleted bank cannot be disclosed and it is impossible for the deleted bank to issue e-cash continuously. In particular, our scheme can realize user tracing without trustees and can prevent users from blackmailing, kidnapping etc... Figure 2 is the flow chart of our proposed model.

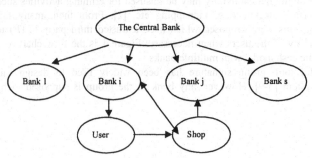

Figure 2 Fair Electronic Cash Model without Trustees

2 Dynamic group blind signature

2.1 Signature of knowledge of discrete logarithm

Besides the blind signature of knowledge of double discrete logarithm BSKLOGLOG[$\alpha \mid y = g^{a^{\alpha}}$](m) and the signature of knowledge of e-th root of discrete logarithm BSKROOTLOG[$\alpha \mid y = g^{\alpha^e}$] (m) as in LR98 [5] group blind signature, we also need the following definition:

Definition An (l +1)-tuple (c , s_1 , $\ldots$, s_l) $\in$ $\{0,1\}^k$ × Z_n^{*l} satisfying $c = H_l$ (m$\| y_1 \| \ldots \| y_l \| g_1 \| \ldots \| g_l \| g_1^{s_1} \; y_1^{c[l]} \| \ldots \| g_1^{s_i} \; y_1^{c[l]} \| \ldots \| g_l^{s_1} \; y_l^{c[l]} \| \ldots \| g_l^{s_l}$ $y_l^{c[l]}$) is a signature of knowledge of a representation of the discrete logarithms of $y_1, \ldots, y_l$ to the bases $g_1, \ldots, g_l$ on a message m, with security parameter l , denoted: SKREPLOG[$\alpha : y_1 = g_1^{\alpha} \wedge \ldots \wedge y_l = g_l^{\alpha}$](m).

We can obtain the blind one, denoted BSKREPLOG[$\alpha : y_1 = g_1^{\alpha} \wedge \ldots \wedge y_l = g_l^{\alpha}$](m), as follows:

User Round 0: User wants message m signed and sends a sign request to the signer.

Signer Round 1: For $1 \le i \le l$, generate random $2^{\lambda} \le r_i \le 2^{\lambda+\mu}$ -1, set $P_{ji} = g_j^{r_i}$ and send { P_{ji} } to the user, j=1,....,t.

User Round 2: Obtain a random permutation σ : $\{1,\ldots, l\} \rightarrow \{1,\ldots, l\}$ and set $Q_{ji} = P_{j\sigma(i)}$,for $1 \le i,j \le l$, generate random $2^{\lambda+\mu} \le a_i \le 2^{\lambda+2\mu}$ -1, and set $R_{ji} = Q_{ji} \; g_j^{a_i}$,calculate $c = H_l$ (m$\| y_1 \| \ldots \| y_l \| g_1 \| \ldots \| g_l \| R_{11} \| \ldots \| R_{1l} \| \ldots \| R_{l1} \| \ldots \| R_{ll}$), calculate c' such that $c'[i] = c[\sigma^{-1}(i)]$, send c' to the signer.

Signer Round 3: Compute, for $1 \le i \le l$, $t_i = r_i$,if $c'[i]=0$; $t_i = r_i - x$,if $c'[i]=1$, send { t_i } to the user.

User Round 4: Verify that $P_{ji} = g_j^{t_i} \; y_j^{c[l]}$, compute $s_i = t_{\sigma(i)} + a_i$,$1 \le i \le l$,output BSKREPLOG[$\alpha : y_1 = g_1^{\alpha} \wedge \ldots \wedge y_l = g_l^{\alpha}$](m) : ($c, s_1, \ldots, s_l$).

2.2 Dynamic group blind signature

The main idea is: the group manager issues the membership keys of the deleted members on a bulletin board, every group member must prove with zero knowledge that his membership key is not on the bulletin board when he signs a message. Our scheme is based on LR98 [5] group blind signature. We mainly introduce the steps of **revoke** and **sign** because the steps of **setup, join** and **open** are the same as that in LR98 [5].

Setup The group manager constructs the group's public key ($n, e, G, g, a, \lambda, \mu$).

Join A group member picks a secret key x , calculates $y = a^x$ (mod n) and the membership key $z = g^y$, obtains his membership certificate $v = (y+1)^{1/e}$ (mod n) from the group manager.

Revoke When a member is deleted, the group manager issues his membership key $z = g^y$ on a bulletin board.

Sign signer: Look up the bulletin board issued by the group manager, suppose that there are t deleted members: $z_1, z_2, \ldots, z_t$. Obtain $q \in_R Z_n^*$ and set $\tilde{g} = g^q$, $\tilde{z} = \tilde{g}^y$, $P_i^{LOG} = \tilde{g}^{a^{u_i}}$, $P_i^{ROOT} = \tilde{v}_i^{v_i^e}$, $v_1 = (z/z_1)^q, \ldots, v_t = (z/z_t)^q$, send them to U.

U: Check $v_i \ne 1$, obtain $b \in_R \{0,1,\ldots, 2^{\lambda} -1\}$, $f \in_R Z_n^*$, set $\omega = (af)^{eb}$ mod q , $\hat{g} = \tilde{g}^{\omega}$, $\hat{z} = \tilde{z}^{\omega}$, $\hat{P}_i^{LOG} = (P_i^{LOG})^{\omega}$, $\hat{P}_i^{ROOT} = (P_i^{ROOT})^{\omega}$, $v_1' = v_1^{\omega}, \ldots, v_t' = v_t^{\omega}$, $z_1' = z_1^{\omega}, \ldots, z_t' = z_t^{\omega}$, take $\hat{P}_i^{ROOT}$ and $\hat{P}_i^{LOG}$ as input, execute BSKROOTLOG and BSKLOGLOG, and execute BSKREPLOG taking $\hat{z}/v_i'$, z_i' as y_i, g_i respectively , then the signature is ($\hat{g}$, $\hat{z}$, v_1' ,..., v_t' , V_1 , V_2 , V_3), where V_1 =SKLOGLOG[$x : \hat{z} = \hat{g}^{a^x}$](m), V_2 =SKROOTLOG[$v : \hat{z}$ $\hat{g} = \hat{g}^{v^e}$](m), V_3 = BSKREPLOG[$q : \hat{z}/v_1' = z_1^{\prime q} \wedge ... \wedge \hat{z}/v_t' = z_t^{\prime q}$](m).

Open Given a signature ($\hat{g}, \hat{z}, v_1'$,..., v_t', V_1, V_2, V_3), the group manager can determine the signer by testing if $\hat{g}^{y_P} = \hat{z}$ for every group member P.

Validity of the revocation: From V_3, we obtain $\hat{z}/v_i' = z_i^{\prime q}$, that is, $\hat{z}^\omega/v_i^\omega = z_i^{\omega q}$, so $v_i^\omega = \hat{z}^\omega/z_i^{\omega q} = z^{\omega q}/z_i^{\omega q} = (z/z_i)^{\omega q}$, however, $v_i \neq 1$, thus $(z/z_i)^{\omega q} \neq 1$, this concludes $z \neq z_i$.

3. Dynamic electronic cash system without trustees

All banks form a group, the group manager is the Central Bank of the country.

Setup: The Central Bank chooses a security parameter l, and computes an RSA public key (n,e), where the length of n is at least $2l$ bits; chooses a cyclic subgroup $G =< g >$ of order n of Z_p^*; selects $a \in Z_p^*$ where a has large multiplicative order modulo all the prime factors of n; chooses an upper bound λ on the length of the secret keys and a constant $\mu >1$.The group's public key is (n,e,G,g,a,λ,μ).

A bank can obtain his certificate from the Central Bank as follows: the bank picks a secret key $x \in_R \{0,1,....,2^\lambda -1\}$, calculates $y = a^x \pmod n$ and the membership key $z = g^y$, sends (y , z)to the Central Bank, obtains his membership certificate v $=(y+1)^{1/e} \pmod n$ from the group manager.

The Central Bank need issue the deleted banks' membership keys $z_1, z_2,...., z_t$ on a bulletin board.

Withdrawal: A user U has an account in a bank B_i, U takes $u \in_R Z_p^*$ as his secret key, sends $I = g^u$ to B_i and takes I as his identity.

1 U chooses $1 \neq r \in_R Z_p^*$, $c_0 = I^r$., $c_1 = r$, f(x) $= c_0 + c_1 x \pmod q$),and chooses x_1 $\in_R Z_p^*$,computes f(x_1), $C_0 = g^{c_0}$ mod p, $C_1 = g^{c_1}$ mod p. After authenticated by B_i, U sends a withdrawal request and < x_1, f(x_1)>, C_0, C_1 to the bank and with a proof: SKREPLOG[$\gamma : I = g^\gamma \wedge C_0 = g^{C_1^\gamma}$].

2 B_i checks the validity of SKREPLOG[$\gamma : I = g^\gamma \wedge C_0 = g^{C_1^\gamma}$]and $C_0 C_1^{x_1} = g^{f(x_1)}$, then chooses X $\in_R Z_q^*$,computes $\alpha = g^x \pmod p$)and sends α to U.

3 (1) Under the normal situation, U calculates $\alpha' = \alpha^r$ and sends α' to B_i. B_i validates $\alpha' = C_1^x$, let $\beta = \alpha'$,then B_i signs U's withdrawal message m with group blind signature as the step of **sign** in section 2.2, then the e-coin is m($\hat{g}, \hat{z}, v_1'$,..., $v_t', V_1, V_2, V_3, C_0, C_1, \alpha, \beta$);

(2) Under the abnormal situation such as blackmailing, kidnapping etc., U selects $\delta \neq r$, sends $\alpha' = \alpha^\delta$ to B_i . B_i validates $\alpha' \neq C_1^x$, selects $t \in_R Z_q^*$ and computes $\beta = \alpha'$, then B_i signs U's withdrawal message m with group blind signature as the step of **sign** in section 2.2. Then the e-coin is m($\hat{g}, \hat{z}, v_1'$,..., $v_t', V_1, V_2, V_3, C_0, C_1, \alpha, \beta$).

(3) B_i stores m($\hat{g}, \hat{z}, v_1'$,..., $v_t', V_1, V_2, V_3, \alpha, \beta, x_1$, f (x_1))into his database and stores t into the tracing database of the group manager.

Pay and deposit:

1 U chooses $x_2 \in_R Z_p^*$, computes f (x_2), sends < x_2 ,f(x_2)> and m($\hat{g}, \hat{z}, v_1'$,..., $v_t', V_1, V_2, V_3, C_0, C_1, \alpha, \beta$)to the shop .

2 Shop checks the validity of ($\hat{g}$, $\hat{z}$, v_1',..., v_t', V_1, V_2, V_3) and $C_0 C_1^{x_2} = g^{f(x_2)}$, then sends m($\hat{g}$, $\hat{z}$, v_1',..., v_t', V_1, V_2, V_3, C_0, C_1, α, β)to his bank B_j.

3 B_j validates ($\hat{g}$, $\hat{z}$, v_1',..., v_t', V_1, V_2, V_3), checks if $\alpha = \beta^{t_i}$ for all t_i in the tracing database managed by the group manager. If for all t_i, $\alpha \neq \beta^{t_i}$, checks if the e-coin is double-spent via the online database of the group manager, if not, then deposits m($\hat{g}$, $\hat{z}$, v_1',..., v_t', V_1, V_2, V_3, C_0, C_1, α, β) into the shop's account and informs the shop, the shop sends the merchandise to U; If there exists some t_i such that $\alpha = \beta^{t_i}$, then freezes m($\hat{g}$, $\hat{z}$, v_1',..., v_t', V_1, V_2, V_3, C_0, C_1, α, β) and informs the shop, the shop refuses sending the merchandise to U.

Identity revocation: If the shop or B_j checks that there's something suspicious on the e-coin , such as $\alpha = \beta^{t_i}$ for some t_i, B_j sends m($\hat{g}$, $\hat{z}$, v_1',..., v_t', V_1, V_2, V_3, C_0, C_1, α, β) to the group manager, the group manager opens ($\hat{g}$, $\hat{z}$, v_1',..., v_t', V_1, V_2, V_3) using the **open** technique in the group blind signature and finds the bank B_i, sends the e-coin to B_i. B_i looks up his database and finds m($\hat{g}$, $\hat{z}$, v_1',..., v_t', V_1, V_2, V_3, α, β, C_0, C_1, x_1, f(x_1)), then B_i and the shop can recover f(x) = $c_0 + c_1 x$ by use of Shamir's secret sharing scheme with $<x_1$, f(x_1)>and $<x_2$, f(x_2)>. B_i can find U's identity by testing if $c_0 = I^{c_1}$ for every user I.

4. Analysis

Prevention of blackmailing: When a user U is blackmailed, he selects $\delta \neq r$, sends $\alpha' = \alpha^\delta$ to B_i, B_i can find the deference α^r from α^δ and gives U the marked e-coin, but, the blackmailer can't find the deference α^r from α^δ, and he is cheated successfully. Later, he can't buy back anything because any bank can identify the marked coin and freezes it. Also, the kind shop and the bank issuing the coin can identify the victim by using the **identity revocation** technique in the proposed scheme and give back the coin to the victim.

Anonymity of coins: Nobody but the Central Bank can know by which bank the e-coin is issued because of the anonymity of the group signature. However, the anonymity is conditional under an abnormal situation, i.e., the marked coin can be recognized.

Anonymity of users: A user can spend his e-coin anonymously; no bank or shop can trace the user alone without the help of the group manager because the coin is issued using blind signature.

Traceability: With the help of the group manager, the bank issuing the e-coin and the shop owning the coin can collaborate to find the user of the e-coin by use of Shamir's secret sharing scheme.

Revocation of dishonest banks: A dishonest bank can be deleted by the group manager via issuing his membership key on a bulletin board. The deleted bank can't issue e-coin continuously with his old certificate because he can't prove that his identity is not on the bulletin board; the previous e-coin issued by a deleted bank will not be disclosed because any other party can't obtain his secret key x and certificate v by his published identity z due to RSA assumption.

5. Conclusions

In this paper, we propose a fair electronic cash system with member deletion. Besides having the general functions in other e-cash systems based on group signature, our scheme can also revoke the dishonest banks without disclosing their previous data. Also, in our scheme the bank uses a novel method to issue e-coin in order to prevent from blackmailing, kidnapping etc. Furthermore, our scheme is a system without trustees and is constructed for multiple banks as in the real life, thus it is more practical.

REFERENCES

1. D. Chaum, Blind Signatures for Untraceable Payments, R. L.Rivest, *A. Sherman and D. Chaum* (Eds.): CRYPTO'82, Plenum Press, New York, 199-203 (1983).
2. B.V. Solms and D. Naccache, On Blind Signatures and Perfect Crimes, *Computers and Security*, Vol. 11(6), 581-583 (1992).
3. J. Camenisch and M. Stadler, *Efficient Group Signature Schemes for Large Groups*, *B.S.Kaliski Jr. (Ed.)*: CRYPTO'97, LNCS 1294, Springer-Verlag Berlin Heidelberg, 410-424 (1997).
4. E. Bresson and J. Stern, *Efficient Revocation in Group Signatures*, K. Kim (Ed.): PKC 2001, LNCS 1992, Springer-Verlag Berlin Heidelberg, 190-206 (2001).
5. A. Lysyanskaya and Z. Ramzan, Group Blind Digital Signatures: *a Scalable Solution to Electronic Cash*, R. Hirschfeld(Ed.): FC'98, LNCS 1465, Springer-Verlag Berlin Heidelberg, 184-197 (1998).
6. L. Chen, X.Q. Huang and J.Y. You, *Fair Tracing without Trustees for Multiple Banks*, J. Zhang, J.H. He and Y. Fu (Eds.): CIS 2004, LNCS 3314, Springer-Verlag Berlin Heidelberg, 1061-1066 (2004).
7. F.G, Zhang, F.T. Zhang and Y.M. Wang, Electronic Cash System with Multiple Banks, *Chinese J. Computers*, Vol. 24(5), 455-462 (2001).
8. S. canard and J. Traore, *On Fair E-Cash Systems Based on Group Signatures*, R. Safavi-Naini and J. Seberry(Eds.): ACISP 2003, LNCS 2727, Springer-Verlag Berlin Heidelberg, 237-248 (2003).
9. G. Maitland and C. Boyd, *Fair Electronic Cash based on a Group Signature Scheme*, S. Qing, T. Okamoto and J. Zhou (Eds.): ICICS 2001, LNCS 2229, Springer-Verlag Berlin Heidelberg, 461-465 (2001).

Customer Satisfaction Evaluation for Mobile Commerce Services based On Grey Clustering Relational Method

Jinsong Gao, Jinhui Xu, and Weijun Wang

Department of Information Management,Hua Zhong Normal University,Wuhan,430079,China
jsgaom@yahoo.com.cn xujinhui1979@yahoo.com.cn
wangwj@mail.ccnu.edu.cn

Abstract. Since mobile commerce is a new commerce mode, there is a significant meaning to research on customer satisfaction with its services. This paper evaluates the customer satisfaction with m-commerce services, which adopts ASCI model, uses AHP to identify the weight and adapts grey clustering relational method, and illustrates this method by an example. It makes an exploratory research on the application of the grey comprehensive assessment.

1   Introduction

As a new commerce mode, mobile commerce (also as m-commerce) means that any information interaction and commerce transaction is conducted via mobile network using mobile communication device such as cell phones, palm computers, portable computers and so on[1].As a new research field ,the systematical research on mobile commerce is very few in China and other country didn't start research on it until 2000[2].

Literature [3] reviewed 149 mobile commerce articles from 73 journals from 2000 to 2003 and classified them into one of the following five categories: (1)wireless network infrastructure, (2)mobile middleware,(3) wireless user infrastructure, (4)mobile commerce theory and research, and (5)mobile commerce cases and applications. Literature [4] studied the conceptualization and measurement of mobile commerce user satisfaction and pointed out that m-commerce user satisfaction could be used to evaluate whether a m-commerce system was successful and could be evaluated from four aspects: the content quality, appearance, service quality and ease of use. Literature [5] explored the consumer perception of m-commerce application. After reviewing the literature on m-commerce, we find out that the research on m-commerce service customer satisfaction is very few.

Please use the following format when citing this chapter:

Gao, J., Xu, J., Wang, W., 2007, in IFIP International Federation for Information Processing, Volume 251, Integration and Innovation Orient to E-Society Volume1, Wang, W. (Eds), (Boston: Springer), pp. 265-273.

In 1997,Kotler presents that Satisfaction is the consequence of the customer's experiences during various purchasing stages:(a)need rouse,(b)information search, (c) alternatives evaluation,(d)purchase decision, and (e)post-purchase behavior. As for the widely used customer satisfaction model such as ACSI, SWCSIC, ECSI , Kotler pointed out that An abundant literature exists validating the robustness of CSI-like models at the micro level, and have shown that customer satisfaction is a good indicator of a company's future profits in 1991.In the light of the follow-up investigation the FORTURN magazine in USA sponsored on the global top 500 enterprises, there are obviously positive association between the corporation customer satisfaction index and economical and marketing appreciation, which illustrates that if the corporation customer satisfaction index increases 1percent,the average rate of return property will rise by 11.33percent[6].As a new commerce mode, if m-commerce means to improve the customer's utilization ratio and acquire the recognition of customer, the key factor is to improve the customer satisfaction thus make them loyal. So the evaluation to m-commerce service customer satisfaction is essential. This paper adopts the American Customer Satisfaction Index Model and use grey comprehensive assessment to appreciate the m-commerce service customer satisfaction in China.

2   Grey Comprehensive Assessment

Grey system theory is proposed by professor Deng Julong by the late 1970s and early 1980s,which can resolve the indefinite problem with inexperienced and incomplete information[7].Grey assessment is a theory and method based on grey theory, which directs at special object to analyze the indices related to the object existed in a system ,then assess and describe the object using qualitative grey categories in order to form certain comparative conception and categories for the comprehensive effect and overall level of the system on a higher level.

In general, grey assessment is composed of assessment object, indices, grey category and goal[8]. In the light of assessment purpose and requirement, grey assessment can be classified into 4 categories: grey clustering assessment, grey statistic assessment, grey situation assessment and grey relational mode assessment. In the grey comprehensive assessment of practical application, several of the aforementioned categories are combined to evaluate a specific system. This paper adopts grey clustering relational method which combines grey relational mode with grey clustering method.

The basic principle of grey clustering relational method is the following[8]: firstly, use the improved whitening function of grey clustering method to compute the membership grade which every evaluated sample is affiliated to every class, then compute the grey weighted relational grade between the sample and clear comprehensive judgment, lastly, confirm the evaluated object should be classified into a grey class according to the value of the relational grades.

3   Evaluation Model of Customer Satisfaction for M-commerce Services

The steps using grey clustering relational method to evaluate is the following:

3.1   Confirm the Assessment Indices and Classes

The American customer satisfaction index model is a country-level customer satisfaction theory model which the system is the most comprehensive and the application effect is the best. Meanwhile, it is a cause-effect relationship model composed of six construct variables[9]. It measures the quality of goods and services as experienced by consumers[10] and gauges their actual and anticipated consumption experiences[11]. Fig.1 presents the model.

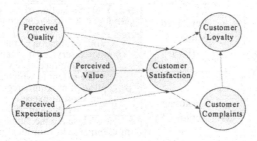

Fig.1. The American customer satisfaction index model

This paper spreads out the structural variables in Fig.1 and forms the multi-level evaluation system as Tab.1 shows.

Assessment classes adopt five-point Likert scales.Tab.2 shows the assessment standard. About PE,PQ,PV and CS, class 1,2,3,4 and 5 represent great satisfaction, satisfaction, common satisfaction, dissatisfaction and great dissatisfaction separately. For CC, they represent fewer, few, general, many, more separately. As far as CL is concerned, class 1,2,3,4 and 5 represent great loyalty, loyalty, common loyalty, disloyalty, great disloyalty separately. The value of each class adopts the decimal system which describes the indices qualitatively. As for the same reason, the third assessment standard can be summarized.

Table 1. Customer Satisfaction Indices for M-commerce Services

The first level	the second level	the third level
CUSTOMER SATISFACTION INDICES	PERCEIVED EXPECTATIONS (PE)	YOUR OVERALL EXPECTATION OF THE QUALITY OF M-COMMERCE SERVICES (PE1)
		Expectation of the extent to which m-commerce meets your personal requirements(PE2)
		Your expectation of the reliability of m-commerce services(PE3)
	Perceived Quality (PQ)	Your overall evaluation of the quality of m-commerce services(PQ1)
		Evaluation of the extent to which m-commerce services meets your personal requirements(PQ2)
		Your evaluation of the reliability of m-commerce services (PQ3)
	Perceived value (PV)	Your evaluation of the quality of m-commerce services if given the prices you pay (PV1)
		Your evaluation of the price of m-commerce services if given the quality you receive(PV2)
	Customer satisfaction(CS)	The extent to which the actual perception of m-commerce services have fallen short or exceed your overall expectation (CS1)
		How close are the actual perception of m-commerce to your ideal m-commerce services (CS2)
	Customer complaints(CC)	Official or unofficial complaints about m-commerce services (CC1)
	Customer loyalty (CL)	How likely you purchase the same m-commerce service repeatedly (CL1)
		How likely you recommend the m-commerce service to your circle of acquaintances (CL2)
		The range of price increases the m-commerce services provider adopts you can endure (CL3)
		The range of price decreases the m-commerce services competitor adopts you can resist (CL4)

Table 2. Standard of M-commerce Services

Class	PE	PQ	PV	CS	CC	CL
1	$\frac{8-}{10}$	$\frac{8-}{10}$	8—10	$\frac{8-}{10}$	0—2	$\frac{8-}{10}$
2	6—8	6—8	6—8	6—8	2—4	6—8
3	4—6	4—6	4—6	4—6	4—6	4—6
4	2—4	2—4	2—4	2—4	6—8	2—4
5	0—2	0—2	0—2	0—2	$\frac{8-}{10}$	0—2

3.2 Constructing Whitening Function

In order to make the membership existed between the whitening function and the assessment classes, the lower semi-trapezoid structure of whitening function in grey clustering method need to be improved. Three basic figures are shown in Fig.2[8].

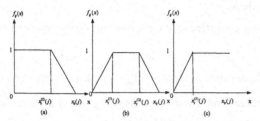

Fig.2. Three whitening function of grey clustering relational method

$x_k(j)$ represents the actual value of the index j of the kth assessment sample. In fig.2, $[x_i^{(1)}(j), x_i^{(2)}(j)]$ is the standard interval that the assessment index j is affiliated to class i. $x_0(j) = \max_i x_i^{(2)}(j), f_{ij}(x)$ is the whitening function that the assessment index j is affiliated to class i.

Three expressions can be used to calculate the three aforementioned whitening function showed in fig.2, which are as follows:

The first equation (see Fig.2a, which is applicable to the situation of $x_i^{(1)}(j) = 0$):

$$f_{ij}(x) = \begin{cases} 1, for 0 \le x \le x_i^{(2)}(j) \\ (x - x_0(j))/(x_i^{(2)}(j) - x_0(j)), for x_i^{(2)}(j) \le x \le x_0(j) \end{cases}$$

The second equation (Fig.2b, which is applicable to the situation of $x_i^{(1)}(j), x_i^{(2)}(j) \ne 0$):

$$f_{ij}(x) = \begin{cases} \dfrac{1}{x_i^{(1)}(j)} x, for 0 \le x \le x_i^{(1)}(j) \\ 1, for x_i^{(1)}(j) \le x \le x_i^{(2)}(j) \\ (x - x_0(j))/(x_i^{(2)}(j) - x_0(j)), for x_i^{(2)}(j) \le x \le x_0(j) \end{cases}$$

The third equation (Fig.2c, which is applicable to the situation of $x_i^{(2)}(j) = x_0(j)$):

$$f_{ij}(x) = \begin{cases} \dfrac{1}{x_i^{(1)}(j)} x, for 0 \le x \le x_i^{(1)}(j) \\ 1, for x_i^{(1)}(j) \le x \le x_0(j) \end{cases}$$

3.3   The Attribute Weights of Assessment Indices

Since the different contribution of each index to the assessment object, it will be unfair to adopt the equal-weight method. This paper determines attribute weights using AHP. The calculating process is as follows:

(1) Judge the relative importance of each assessment index and establish judgment matrix A.

(2) Carry out consistency test for A. The equation is expressed as follows:

$$CR = CI/RI \tag{1}$$

Where CI(consistency index) = $(\lambda_{max} - k)/(k-1)$,k represents the number of the assessment indices and RI(random consistency index) average index of randomly generated weights that can be obtained through looking up the table created by Saaty. If CR<0.1,pass the test, otherwise need to adjust the matrix A and carry out another consistency test till pass it.

(3) Calculate the eigenvector corresponding to λ_{max} (the maximum eigenvalue) of the judgment matrix A , namely, the weights of the indices are confirmed.

3.4   Calculating Grey Relational Grade

Make $y_{ki}(j) = f_{ij}(x_k(j))$,namely, the membership grade (or whitening function) of the index j of the assessment object k to the class i. If $y_{ki} = (y_{ki}(1), y_{ki}(2), y_{ki}(3), \cdots, y_{ki}(n)) = (1,1,1,\cdots,1)$,the assessment object k can be evaluated as class i, and call y_{ki} a clear comprehensive judgment.

Make y_{0i} be a clear comprehensive judgment and let it to be reference sequence, then calculate its relational grade r_{ki} with y_{ki} . The equation is expressed as follows:

$$r_{ki} = \sum_{j=1}^{n} w_{kj} \varepsilon_{ki}(j) \tag{2}$$

where

$$\varepsilon_{ki}(j) = \frac{\min_i \min_j \Delta_{ki}(j) + 0.5 \max_i \max_j \Delta_{ki}(j)}{\Delta_{ki}(j) + 0.5 \max_i \max_j \Delta_{ki}(j)} ,$$

$$\Delta_{ki}(j) = |y_{ki}(j) - 1|$$

3.5 Calculating Multi-level Relational Grade and Evaluating Comprehensively

After obtaining the relational grade of a level, relational grade of the level above it can be calculated through equation 3.

$$R_i = \sum_{k=1}^{q} w_k r_{ki} \qquad (3)$$

Where $R_s = \max_i R_i$, thus can evaluate the class of the assessment object to be s.

4 Example Analysis

As for the second-level indices PE ,PQ,PV,CS,CL and the third-level indices PE1, PE2, PE3, PQ1, PQ2, PQ3, PV1, PV2, CS1, CS2, CL1 CL2, CL3, they have same interval value of each class standard, so they have same whitening functions which are presented as follows.

The first class(Fig.2c):

$$f_{1j}(x) = \begin{cases} \frac{1}{8}x, & for\ 0 \le x \le 8 \\ 1, & for\ 8 \le x \le 10 \end{cases}$$

The second, third and forth class(Fig.2b):

$$f_{2j}(x) = \begin{cases} \frac{1}{6}x, & for\ 0 \le x \le 6 \\ 1, & for\ 6 \le x \le 8 \\ 5 - 0.5x, & for\ 8 \le x \le 10 \end{cases} \qquad f_{3j}(x) = \begin{cases} \frac{1}{4}x, & for\ 0 \le x \le 4 \\ 1, & for\ 4 \le x \le 6 \\ 2.5 - 0.25x, & for\ 6 \le x \le 10 \end{cases}$$

$$f_{4j}(x) = \begin{cases} \frac{1}{2}x, & for\ 0 \le x \le 2 \\ 1, & for\ 2 \le x \le 4 \\ \frac{5}{3} - \frac{1}{6}x, & for\ 4 \le x \le 10 \end{cases}$$

The fifth class(Fig.2a):

$$f_{5j}(x) = \begin{cases} 1, & for\ 0 \le x \le 2 \\ 1.25 - 0.125x, & for\ 2 \le x \le 10 \end{cases}$$

The whitening functions of the second-level index CC and the third-level index CC1 are contrary to the above. Namely, their whitening functions of the first class is the fifth class above, the second the forth, the third the third, ..., the fifth the first.

The actual value of each third level index can be obtained through the way of questionnaire investigation. If there are 200 valid questionnaire, the value of the third-level indices can be computed by the equal weights method. For example, if q_j represents the answer of the jth respondent, the actual value of PQ1 equal （1/200） * （$q_1 + q_2 + \cdots + q_{200}$）.

Given the actual values of the third level indices is showed in Tab.3.

Table 3. The Data of Third-level Indices of Customer Satisfaction

PE1	PE2	PE3	PQ1	PQ2	PQ3	PV1	PV2	CS1	CS2	CC1
7.3	8.6	9	5.2	6	8.2	4.5	5	7.5	5.4	3
CL1	CL2	CL3	CL4							
6.5	4.6	1.7	2.3							

Determine the weight of each index using AHP, see Tab.4.

Table 4. The Weights of the Third-level and Second-level Indices of Customer Satisfaction

PE1	PE2	PE3	PQ1	PQ2	PQ3	PV1	PV2
0.325	0.384	0.291	0.312	0.363	0.325	0.56	0.44
CS1	CS2	CC1	CL1	CL2	CL3	CL4	
0.65	0.35	1	0.32	0.12	0.3	0.26	
PE	PQ	PV	CS	CC	CL		
0.075	0.225	0.2	0.308	0.105	0.087		

Calculate the whitening functions value of the third-level indices' membership to each class. As follows:

PE: $y_{11}=$ (0. 9125,1,1), $y_{12}=$(1,0.7,0.5), $y_{13}=$(0.675,0.35,0.25),
$y_{14}=$(0.45,0.2333,0.1667), $y_{15}=$(0.3375,0.175,0.125)

PQ: $y_{21}=$ (0. 65,0.75,1), $y_{22}=$(0.8667,1,0.9), $y_{23}=$(1,1,0.45),
$y_{24}=$(0.8,0.6667,0.3), $y_{25}=$(0.6,0.5,0.225)

PV: $y_{31}=$ (0. 5625,0.625), $y_{32}=$(0.9,0.8333), $y_{33}=$(1,1),
$y_{34}=$(0.9167,0.8333), $y_{35}=$(0.6875,0.625)

CS: $y_{41}=$ (0. 9375,0.675), $y_{42}=$(1,0.9), $y_{43}=$(0.625,1),
$y_{44}=$(0.4167,0.7667), $y_{45}=$(0.3125,0.575)

CC: $y_{51}=$ (0. 875), $y_{52}=$(1), $y_{53}=$(0.75), $y_{54}=$(0.5), $y_{55}=$(0.375)

CL: $y_{61}=$ (0. 8125,0.575, 0.2125,0.2875), $y_{62}=$(1,0.7667,0.2833 ,0.3833),
$y_{63}=$(0.875,1,0.425 ,0.575), $y_{64}=$(0.5833,0.9,0.85 ,1), $y_{65}=$(0.4375,0.675, 1,0.9625)

According equation 2, the relational grade of the second-level indices to each class can be calculated, which are shown in Tab.5.

Table 5. The Relational Grade of the Second-level Indices to Each Class

Second level indices \ class	PE	PQ	PV	CS	CC	CL
1	0.9409	0.7122	04906	0.7527	0.4406	0.4670
2	0.6722	0.8445	0.7381	0.9236	1	0.5882
3	0.4116	0.8068	1	0.6750	0.6	0.6003
4	0.3723	0.5337	0.781	0.4952	0.4545	0.7373
5	0.3593	0.4497	0.5636	0.4303	0.4118	0.7483

According equation 3, the relational grade of the customer satisfaction index to each class can be calculated. The result is as follows.

R=(0.6477,0.8287,0.7355,0.5686,0.4817)

According the result, the customer satisfaction index of this example is classified into class 2, that is, satisfaction.

5 Conclusion

This paper makes an exploratory research on evaluating m-commerce customer satisfaction, which adopts ASCI model, uses AHP to determine the weight and adapts grey clustering relational method .This method is simple and easy to carry out, what is more, the calculating procedure can be realized by programming in c. By evaluating the customer satisfaction, it will help consumers to make better purchasing decisions and help service providers to understand the consumer behavior and know their strengths and weaknesses so that they can implement a serious of effective measures[12]. Despite its some advantages, this study has a key limitation. For the construct variables in ASCI model are general, it is better to combine the third-level indices in questionnaire with the practical application to be further spread out to be the forth-level indices in order to make questionnaire investigation more accurate.

References

1. Y. F. Yuan, Y. W. Wang and Z. C. Xu , *Mobil Commerce*, Tsinghua University Press, Beijing (2006).

2. W. Huang, R. D. Wang and N. Shi, "Review Study on Mobile Commerce" , *Application of Computer Research* , (1), 3-15(2006).

3. E. W. T. Ngai and A. Gunasekaran, "A Review for Mobile Commerce Research and Application", *Decision Support Systems*, 43(1),3-15(2007).

4. Y. S. Wang, Y. W. Liao, "The Conceptualization and Measurement of M-commerce User Satisfaction", *Computers in Human Behavior*, 23(1), 381-398 (2007).

5. P.Mahatanankoon, H. Joseph Wen, and B. Lim, "Consumer-based M-commerce: exploring Consumer Perception of Mobile Applications", *Computer Standards & Interfaces,* 27(4), 347-357(2005).

6. L. R. Gan, B. Ma and Y. M. Li, "Evaluation of the User Satisfaction Level on Four Famous Databases Websites", *Journal of the China Society For Scientific and Technical Information*, 23(5), 524-530(2004).

7. J. L. Deng, *The Foundation of Grey System Theory*, Huazhong University of Science and Technology Press,Wuhan (2002).

8. X. P. Xiao, Z. P. Song and F. Li, *The Foundation and Application of Grey Technology* , Science Press, Beijing (2005).

9. Q. Luo and Z. Q. Fang, "An Analysis of Common Research Model of Customer Satisfaction and Their Strengths and Weaknesses", *Journal of Guizhou College of Finance and Economics*, (6), 14-17(2002).

10. C. Fornell, M. D. Johnson, E. W. Anderson, J. Cha and B .E. Bryant., "The American Customer Satisfaction Index: Nature, Purpose, and Findings", *Journal of Marketing* , 60(4), 7–18 (1996).

11. E. W. Anderson and C. Fornell , "Foundations of the American Customer Satisfaction Index", *Total Quality Management & Business Excellence*, 11(7), 869–882(2000).

12. http://cbrc.em.tsinghua.edu.cn/ReadNews.asp?NewsID=830,2007,04,10.

Contractual Versatility in Software Business

Juhani Warsta and Veikko Seppänen
University of Oulu, Department of Information Processing Science,
P.O.Box 3000, FIN-90014 University of Oulu, Finland
juhani.warsta@oulu.fi and veikko.seppanen@oulu.fi

Abstract. This empirical study addresses the problem of how Commercial-off-the-Shelf (COTS), tailored, and Modified-off-the-Shelf (MOTS) software contracting has been approached, in practice. The focus of the study is on analyzing different contractual characterizations of the three models of software business. The empirical part of the study was completed by analyzing twelve software producing companies – eight were Finnish firms established in the Silicon Valley area in the USA and the rest were local Finnish firms with international operations. The research produced a number of practical insights for managing and developing the contracting process.

1 Introduction

The Intellectual Property Rights (IPR) with all its elements are one of the most critical issues for the development of the information technology (IT) industry. Especially now, when numerous software start-ups are entering the business as well as many established companies are forming innovative and varied kinds of research alliances and business cooperative networks, it is vital for the business to understand the assets and liabilities belonging not only to the software company itself, but to its business partners belonging to and operating in the network [1, 2]. This emphasizes the ability and knowledge to make agile and explicit use of networked software companies' proprietary rights in all situations. The IT business needs more experts that understand how to administer in concert not only the software technology issues and the application development processes, but also the legal aspects related to the whole business development.

The managing contractual issues is still more demanding when software companies enter international as well as the Internet based markets, where their main cooperative forms are resellers or agents, affiliates, selling of licenses, own

Please use the following format when citing this chapter:

Warsta, J., Seppänen, V., 2007, in IFIP International Federation for Information Processing, Volume 251, Integration and Innovation Orient to E-Society Volume1, Wang, W. (Eds), (Boston: Springer), pp. 274-281.

marketing companies, joint ventures or franchising [3]. The growing and important open source software development and its multifaceted contracting environment is not discussed in this paper as the case companies did not make any extensive use of this new phenomenon. Software contracting forms an important subject that the software company must govern in order to succeed in international competition and collaboration. The overall business environment is in constant change as the companies form and reform alliances with other companies and networks. Fast development pace of new technologies also puts extra pressure on company's legal expertise. In particular, R&D co-operation, financing and acquisitions demand for exact knowledge of the ownership, i.e. the rights to knowledge, technologies, products and associate services [1]. These will have a growing importance as IPR are forming longer and complex chains and networks of contracts in which every participant should get its justified share of the whole profit.

This paper focuses on the software company's contracting process and how the company matches this process with its software development process and business relationships. The paper is structured as follows: first we give a general view of software contracting, after that we discuss the different software business models utilized in this study. This is followed by description of the empirical research setting. Based on this empirical case material we depict what we will call the Evolutionary software contracting process. In the discussion part we relate the contractual view to the software business perspective.

2 Software contracting

The reason why software contracting is considered as a difficult task is the complexity of the software [4, 5]. The software contracting process has not been addressed directly from the perspective described in this paper in the earlier software contracting literature. Marciniak and Reifer [6] have described one of the first published software contract models. However, this model depicts only the initial stages of the whole software contracting and development process. Besides, it emphasizes the procurer's view. Even though this study of the contract negotiation is completed from the supplier's side, there are always two parties present. For the supplier it is valuable to understand the customer's intentions and behaviour in the negotiation situation.

Griffel et al. [7] discuss the generic model of contracting fitted into the Internet environment using special contracting software. They define three main phases for contracting: information phase, negotiations phase and execution phase. "A contract represents gathered information, agreed terms and conditions and steps to fulfil mutual commitments in a formal way, combined into one structured document".

Elfatatry and Layzell [8] have described a three-stage negotiation model for software services including pre-negotiation, negotiation and delivery phases where the contract is signed at the end of the negotiation phase. A more general negotiation model presented by Adair and Brett [9] contains four phases and it takes also culture into account that is notable when thinking international business operations.

3 Software business models

Building up the software company's contracting process should start from the business strategy and model that the company has selected for itself. The company has to know clearly in which business it is in, and how to run that type of business. The focal software business models relevant for this study are the Commercial-Off-The-Shelf (COTS), Tailored (bespoke) and Modified-Off-The-Shelf (MOTS) types of businesses. In all these segments customer needs are different, and thus contracts must have different contents and elements.

Rajala et al. [10] have come up with a framework for analyzing software business models that also include product development categorization. They have identified the following options for product development: project, product platform, parameterized product, core product and product family. The COTS business model corresponds with the product that is defined to focus on "the development of a single product or product family to be delivered to several customers as is" (ibid). The tailored approach again is equivalent to the project that focuses on the tailor-made software solution offered to customer's specific needs. Lastly, the MOTS business model is similar to the parameterized product with the definition of "customizable product that can be tailored to a degree". From the Williamson [12] point of view these three business models use classical contracting, relational contracting and both classical and relational contracting respectively. However, the categorization is a question of definition that is emphasized by the angle of approach used and needed in each separate study.

From the supplier's point of view it is valuable to understand the customer's environment and especially the economical valuation of the problem in the tendering and in the actual contracting situation. The procurement means a choice among several software suppliers – company's own IT department, outside experts and consultants, MOTS or COTS software suppliers – and several contracting forms. This includes the manifold field of IPR; copyrights, patents, license, etc.

4 The case and methodology

The empirical research data of this study consists of interviews of employees working in twelve SME companies developing software, addressing their experiences in different kinds of software businesses. The material gathered is mainly company managers' descriptions about the actual contracting processes and of how they see the process unfolding over time in relation to business development and different stages of customer relationships, Table 1.

This provides a picture of how the software contracting process unfolds, behaves, what contextual elements affect it, and how the whole process is being managed. Totally the empirical material comprised over 16 hours of interviews. Each of the business categories includes several companies, in order to give more reliability and material to compare the contracting processes from different types of software companies. The multiple-case approach was selected to strengthen the research base and validity of the results as the business line in focus is characterized by companies whose business situation varies [11].

Table 1. List of software companies interviewed.

Interviewee(s)	Line of business	Business mode	Employees	Founded (year)	Location, established in the USA (year)
CEO	Communications solutions software	COTS MOTS	11 - 50	1992	FIN
CEO (Co-owner), Contracts and Logistics Manager	Telecommunications software for the Internet	COTS Tailored MOTS	11 - 50	1997	FIN
Technology development director, Software development manager	Internet portal division	COTS	11 - 50	1998	USA 1998
VP of sales and marketing, COO	Internet tools and platform software	MOTS	11 - 50	1994	USA 1998/1999
CEO	Business intelligence software	COTS	51 - 100	1991	USA 1998
CEO	Mobile Internet platform	Tailored	11 - 50	1982	USA 1999
VP of Global Business Operations	Security solutions	COTS	51 - 100	1988	USA 1994
CEO and COO	Virtual communities	COTS MOTS	1 - 10	1997	FIN
CEO	Wireless Internet	Tailored	11 - 50	1997	USA 1999
COO	Data management solutions	COTS	101 - 200	1992	USA 1994
VP of R&D (Co-owner)	Engineering software	COTS MOTS	11 - 50	1989	USA 1990
CEO	Systems house	Tailored	11 - 50	1989	FIN

However, all the firms are small and fast developing, and operate in one or several business models and in a mixture of different cultures and contexts, e.g. Internet. The data was collected from small and medium size software companies in Finland, and from Finnish companies that have operations in the USA.

5 Evolutionary software contracting process

Next, most common contract forms used in the interviewed companies are briefly scrutinized. The analysis is focused on the contracting process, i.e. how and in which stage the different contracts are negotiated and what their implications for the software development and governance process are. The observed contractual structure included contracts:

1. To relieve and enable trusty *information exchange* institutions with the non-disclosure-agreements type of contracts,

2. To lay the foundation for future lasting and viable *relationship building and securing* with the framework type of contracts,

3. To secure the transfer of the *intellectual property rights* as well as other rights for the application and related material, i.e. to explicitly agree on the ownership and utilization of the software, with the license type of contracts,

4. To define the *work on specific software assignment* in detail with work-orders, project contracts and assignment contracts and lastly

5. To *maintain software*; especially in tailored and MOTS business the software companies were disposed to sign maintenance or congruent contracts to bind the customer and to secure constant and predictable future cash-flow.

The three business models have similarities as well as dissimilarities, regarding applying the software contracting processes. These divergences are further discussed and analyzed subsequently. Summing up the findings: the COTS business relied firmly on multiform licensing practices, whereas the tailored business saw the framework contract as the main contractual tool and interestingly the MOTS business employed combinations of these two previous forms, i.e. both licensing and framework contracts, Table 2. From the present study the different business models could be characterized as follows:

Table 2. The contractual elements in different business models.

Item	COTS	Tailored	MOTS
Model of business	Transaction	Relationship	Relationship
Duration of business	Short	Long	Long
Number of customers	Numerous	Few	Many
Relationship governance	Contracts	Cooperation	Cooperation with contracts
Relevance of contracts	Essential	Necessary evil	Necessary
Main contract type	License	Framework	Framework with license
Contract characteristics	Tight and gapless Fixed templates Few contract types	Relevant Negotiable templates Several contract types	Relevant Negotiable templates Several contract types
Software specifications	Own specifications	Customer's specifications	Own and customer's specifications
Software ownership	Supplier's proprietary	Customer's proprietary	Supplier's and customer's proprietary
Customer space	Global	Local	Global with partners
Marketing mode	Channel	Own efforts	Own efforts and channel
Main communication mode	Internet and channel	Face to face	Face to face, channel and Internet

- The COTS business contracts of sale resemble the Williamson type of market transactions [12]. This holds up especially with the pure COTS business, though the situation is different when business is exercised through channels with the reseller or integrator partnership.

- The tailored and MOTS business again is relationship bounded as in both cases exist or at least there is an aspiration to establish, a relationship as the joint cooperative software development process requires this in alternating density.

- The channel and other joint efforts, i.e. alliances, always require a working relationship to be viable in supplying software to the end-users. Even in some cases the MOTS type of business can be pure channel operations compared to the COTS business as the level of the tailoring and customization part of the software may vary extensively between the applications and even between the end-user's needs and requirements. Thus many times the line between COTS and MOTS business is fine and vague, as found in the analysis of data.

On the other hand, in the tailored software business the customer and the supplier are close to each other and they also strive for a long-standing relationship. In this model of business relationship it is more important to have a close working relationship and the contracts need not to be as tight as the partners (have to) depend on each other. However, this type of business is not the moneymaker - as the scaling up the business volume depends directly on the number of the employees and it is more or less culture as well as legislation dependent - compared to the possibilities of the COTS business as well as MOTS business.

The middle ground between these two business models is the MOTS business that tries to combine both advantages of the COTS and tailored businesses. Fewer contracts (i.e. customers) than in the COTS business, though more contracts than in the tailored business. Customers are better known than in the COTS business, however not so well as in the tailored business.

6 Conclusions

The software company should define from the beginning the so-called *legal plan* that it is analogous to and is included in the general *business plan*. Herein the company's contracting process, used contract templates, IPR strategy and the contract portfolio could be described. The *contracting process description* should include the issues of defined and planned processes with set owners who maintain and develop the process according to the emerging needs. Also the actors, activities as well as the resources belonging to the defined processes are clearly described.

The process plans are put in a written form so everyone in the company has the possibility to become acquainted with them and start to use and work according to these guidelines. The *IPR strategy* issue is broad and it must be done and implemented for the financier, insurance company, customer and possible acquisition perspective in mind. Further it includes issues attached to company's business operations, technology, expertise, competing technologies and competitors. The *contract portfolio* includes all the company's different contracts completed and maintained. There must be someone in charge of this portfolio and to take care of its constant follow-up. From this portfolio the different contracts can easily and clearly been found, and their interdependencies and influence on each other.

In small software companies the three basic and central issues are the price fixing, discount policy and the *utility value* of the software. The managers should understand that the *price of the application is based on the customer's value of the application, not on the production costs*. Thus the pricing starts from the customer's perspective.

When the COTS licensing is done with the end-user then it represents a pure Williamson's type of market transaction [12]. The software companies try to enter into long standing relationships with their customers making different kinds of yearly service contracts with which they bind the customer also in future. The COTS and

MOTS development, marketing, sales as well as the contracting resemble in many ways each other, as commonly the COTS application is delivered as a basis without any changes or modifications to the software itself.

The situation is the same again when the MOTS and tailored software production, delivery and marketing are compared. It depends on the MOTS software itself and its status, how large the part of the software is that the company has managed and succeeded to develop to have the common features in the fixed part of the software and what the part that the company must always customize for and after each specific customer is. This enhancement also depends on how the software developers are able to understand the problem better in order to modify and augment the application software with new features that make it easier to make the implementation project in a shorter time in the future.

Here it could be emphasized again the situation that the MOTS business combines both the COTS and tailored model resource issues. This makes the MOTS business demanding from the management point of view as in the best case the company should have *control over the tailored type of software development process as well over the COTS type of software selling process and to be able to combine these into the contracting process.*

The interviews brought up the following elements that were found to be important to be understood for a successful contracting process:

1. The line of business must be well understood.
2. The specific subject of the focal contract must be known.
3. Definition of the proprietary technology to be transferred must be done well.
4. Rights of use given to the customer or partner, including the definitions of where to use and how to use, as well as the possible rights to transfer the object of contract must be done clearly.

Other central issues are to understand what the supplier company is transferring, with what price, what are the liabilities (on both sides), what if there are delays in payments, what happens if the other party is sold, goes bankrupt or some other unexpected and undesirable events occur. The fundamental question is how in a contracting process do the business, technology and juridical issues interplay successfully. Wholly understanding and respecting each other's professionalism equally and considering the company's business success as the ultimate joint target should be the main priority. Though, this may be difficult as the experts from different disciplines easily emphasize the importance of their own domain. Even though, the importance of contracts were not unanimously acknowledged among the interviewed company managers as many times the contract drafting was seen as a nuisance delaying the business operations.

Still, clear opinions understanding and favouring were expressed that already now the business environment is changing into a more contractual direction – most of the supporting views came from companies operating in the USA – thus raising the meaning of good and effective contracts. For a software company to be competitive in global business it must have the understanding of the contractual network, i.e. what contracts to use and when. Secondly the company must also have a well-defined and smoothly operating contracting process supporting the company's other business and software development processes.

The companies should understand the importance of the relational contracting with a processual-view combined with the framework contracting with the supplement contracts that cover the life cycle of the whole contracting process that the partners live through during their cooperative business relationship.

In every case be it COTS, tailored, or MOTS business, the companies have the ambition to move from single transactions to long lasting and recurrent transactions. This is enhanced by learning, adaptation and cooperation. The companies strive to lessen needless (transaction) costs and among these, contractual issues can be found that are developed to work as smoothly and effectively as possible.

The study disclosed the concerning situation that prevails in software companies, i.e. the software companies do not have explicitly defined contracting processes even though the managers are aware of the need and importance of the fact. As already discussed the managers explained the reason; they did not have enough time to correct the situation even though it would pay back in the long run. This is especially the case among SME software companies when the companies start to move their operations abroad into a new and unknown business culture context.

References

1. H. Hertzfeld, A. Link, and N. Vonortas, "Intellectual property protection mechanisms in research partnerships". *Research Policy*, 2006. 35: p. 825 - 838.
2. R. Kemp, and C. Gibbons, "IPR indemnities in the open source and proprietary software worlds". *Computer Law & Security Report*, 2005. 21: p. 420 - 422.
3. M. Berrell, and J. Wrathall, "Between Chinese culture and the rule of law, What foreign managers in China should know about intellectual property rights", *Management Research News*, 2007. 30(1): p. 57 -76.
4. J. Bessen, "Open Source Software: Free Provision of Complex Public Goods", 2005, *Boston University School of Law and Research on Innovation*: Harpswell, ME.
5. S. Whang, "Contracting for Software Development", *Management Science*, 1992. 38(3).
6. J. Marciniak, and D. Reifer, "Software Acquisition Management", *Industrial Software Engineering Practice*, ed. F. Buckley. 1990, New York: John Wiley & Sons. 290.
7. F. Griffel, et al., "Electronic Contracting with COSMOS - How to Establish, Negotiate and Execute Electronic Contracts on the Internet". *IEEE*, 1998.
8. A. Elfatatry, and P. Layzell, "Negotiating in Service-Oriented Environments", *Communications of the ACM*, 2004. 47(8): p. 103 - 108.
9. W. Adair, and J. Brett, "The Negotiation Dance: Time, Culture, and Behavioral Sequences in Negotiation", *Organization Science*, 2005. 16(1): p. 33 - 51.
10. R. Rajala, et al., Software Business Models, A Framework for Analyzing Software Industry. 2001, *TEKES*: Helsinki. p. 76.
11. R. Yin, "Case Study Research Design and Methods", 2 ed. Applied Social Research Methods Series, Vol. 5. 1994, *Thousand Oaks: SAGE Publications*. 171.
12. O. Williamson, *The Economic Institutions of Capitalism*. 1985, New York: The Free Press. 450.
13. T. Roxenhall and P. Ghauri, "Use of the written contract in long-lasting business relationships". *Industrial Marketing Management*, 2004. 33: p. 261 - 268

Information Integration of Virtual Enterprise Based on Service-Oriented Architecture

Jun Yang [1 2], Gang Li[1], and Danxiang Ai [2]

1 Wuhan University, School of Information Management,
430072 Wuhan, China
imio2@whu.edu.cn,
www home page: http://sim.whu.edu.cn
2 Guangdong University of Technology, School of Economics and
Management, 510520 Guangzhou, China
jgxy@gdut.edu.cn
www home page: http://jgxy.gdut.edu.cn/

Abstract. The operation of the virtual enterprise requires the information sharing of the member enterprises. So it is imperative to build up a high-quality information integration platform. This paper analyzes the information integration theory of virtual enterprise. It introduces the basic concepts and methods of service-oriented architecture and brings forward the targets of the information integration in the virtual enterprise. Finally, this paper elaborates on the solution of the virtual enterprise information integration based on the service-oriented architecture.

1 Introduction

Today, we are entering an age when economy is becoming global and advanced technologies are developing rapidly. The competition among the enterprises becomes fiercer. The enterprises are facing a brand-new environment. A new kind of organization-virtual enterprise is coming into being.

However, the base architectures of the member enterprises in the virtual enterprise are different. In many cases, the member enterprises use different communication protocols and data formats. So it is difficult for the members to communicate and integrate information, which decreases the efficiency of the co-operation in the virtual enterprise. How to build up an information integration platform for the virtual enterprise has become a hot issue in recent years. However, much research on the information integration of the virtual enterprise is descriptive. There is little research on the actual organizing of the information integration

Please use the following format when citing this chapter:

Yang, J., Li, G., Ai, D., 2007, in IFIP International Federation for Information Processing, Volume 251, Integration and Innovation Orient to E-Society Volume1, Wang, W. (Eds), (Boston: Springer), pp. 282-239.

platform of the virtual enterprise. Based on the technologies of service-oriented architecture, this article discusses the information integration framework of the virtual enterprise.

The remaining of this paper is organized as follows. Section 2 gives a brief introduction on the information integration theory of the virtual enterprise. Section 3 discusses the basic knowledge of service- oriented architecture (SOA). Section 4 probes into the information integration model of the virtual enterprise based on SOA. Section 5 is the conclusion.

2 Virtual enterprise information integration

2.1 Virtual enterprise

It has been showed by Zbigniew Kierzkowski [1] that the virtual enterprise is a kind of dynamic alliance which is built up to grasp special commercial opportunities. It is composed of the core enterprise(s) and partner enterprises. There is probably only one core enterprise or there are probably several core enterprises. The number of the core enterprises depends on the scale of the virtual enterprise. To make things simple, it is supposed in this paper that there is only one core enterprise in the virtual enterprise. The enterprise which has stronger strengths in the industry acts as the core enterprise. And other enterprises in the industry which are appealed to participate in the virtual enterprise act as the partner enterprises. Both the core enterprise and partner enterprises are called the member enterprises of the virtual enterprise.

Through the information technologies, the core enterprise and the partner enterprises establish the temporary alliances to grasp the dynamic opportunities. During the co-operation, the members jointly share the benefits and risks. When the expectant goal is realized, the virtual enterprise will disappear. And when the new commercial opportunities appear, the new virtual enterprise will come forth. It has been showed by Stafford S Cuffe[2] that the greatest difference between the virtual enterprise and the traditional enterprise is that the member enterprises of the virtual enterprise need not to have the complete processes which the traditional enterprises have. What the members in the virtual enterprise should do is remaining and strengthening their core processes and outsourcing their un-core processes.

2.2 Core information processes of virtual enterprise

Essentially, the virtual enterprise is the aggregation of the core information processes of different enterprises. There are two kinds of core information processes in the virtual enterprise:

(1) The core information processes of the core enterprise. Usually, the core enterprise of the virtual enterprise is the enterprise which has stronger strengths in the industry. The core enterprise has enough resources to associate the appropriate cooperative partners to build up the virtual enterprise. The core information

processes of the core enterprise include strategic planning information process, researching and developing information process and so on.

(2) The core information processes of the partner enterprises. For the partner enterprises, their division of labor on the basis of specialization is very clear. And their core information processes are compatible and complementary. The core information processes of the partner enterprises include supplying information process, manufacturing information process, marketing information process, financing information process and so on.

All in all, the core information processes in the virtual enterprise are composed of the core information processes of the core enterprise and partner enterprises. And the core information processes of the core enterprise play a dominant role and can integrate the core information processes of the partner enterprises in the virtual enterprises.

2.3   Virtual enterprise information integration theory

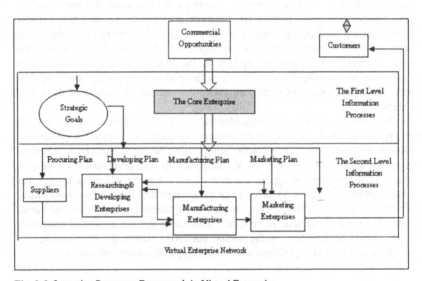

Fig. 1. Information Processes Framework in Virtual Enterprise

It has been showed by Guoqing Huo[3] that the virtual enterprise's lifecycle is following the unceasing information process integration. In the course of the information integration, every member enterprise becomes a subsystem of the whole information system. The core information processes in the virtual enterprise can be divided into two levels: the first level and the second level. The first level information processes indicate the core information processes of the core enterprise. The second level information processes indicate the core information processes of the partner enterprises. Every core information process delegates the core ability of a member enterprise. The framework of the information processes in the virtual enterprise is showed in figure1.

During the course of the establishment and the operation, the virtual enterprise centers on the core information processes of the core enterprise, searching for, optimizing and integrating the core information processes of the other partner enterprises. When the internal, external environment and the core abilities of the member enterprise change, the virtual enterprise will adjust and re-integrate the core information processes of the member enterprises. This integration theory is called virtual enterprise information integration theory.

3   Service- Oriented Architecture (SOA)

3.1   Definition of Service- Oriented Architecture (SOA)

It has been showed by Jonathan Katz [4] that service means a customer-based or user-oriented function, such as technical support or network provision. Technically speaking, service is a program or routine that provides support to other programs in reference to programming. It has been showed by N Bieberstein [5] that SOA is a kind of groupware model. Several recent investigations [6,7,8] indicate that SOA connects the services by interfaces and contracts defined in a neutral way which is independent of hardware, operating systems and programming languages. This makes the services can communicate in a uniform mode. Several recent investigations [9-13] indicate that SOA has the following characteristics:

(1) SOA is not a language or a material product. It is a kind of software architecture, which is mainly used to solve the integration problem of the different appliances on the web.

(2) Service is the core of SOA. Service is a kind of application which is encapsulated as business process. And information process is the exterior form of business process. So, it is regarded that service is a kind of application which is encapsulated as information process. In SOA, service is the core element.

(3) SOA is loose-coupling. Coupling means the relationship of different softwares, which includes relativity and dependence between the softwares. The traditional software is close-coupling. It is very difficult for the sub-systems to communicate and to be unpacked. However, in SOA, the software is loose-coupling. The service providers use the uniform definition language to define the interfaces. As long as the interfaces remain unchanged, the internal changes of some applications have no effects on the others.

(4) SOA is mutual-operational. In SOA, the users can use any function on any platform regardless of the programming languages and operating systems. This ensures the solutions based on SOA to be easily integrated.

3.2   Structure of SOA system

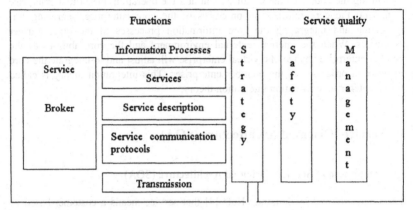

Fig. 2. Structure of SOA System

It has been showed by Wang Jian-xin [14] that SOA is an information integration system based on Internet. Its structure is showed in Figure2. SOA adopts the services-oriented software encapsulation technologies. The main elements of SOA are service-description, service-publishing, service-finding and service-calling. SOA is based XML (eXtensive Markup Language) and uses Web Services Definition Language (WSDL) to describe interfaces. The service broker is the supporter of service-finding. SOA is not only a software developing framework but also a business developing framework. It can integrate different services on different platforms.

3.3   SOA and Web Services

It has been showed by Marshall Breeding [15] that a Web service is a kind of software application which can be identified by URI (Uniform Resource Identifier). Its interface and binding can be defined, described and found as the XML-supported resources. It has been showed by H K Cheng [16] that Web Services is an important technology to realize SOA. Web Services supports XML-based messages to communicate with other software agents and can integrate the applications on Intranet, Extranet and Internet. Web Services architecture involves many layered and interrelated technologies. Figure3 shows how the Web Services technologies match SOA.

Web Services uses Web Services Flow Language (WSFL) to model the information processes, uses Web Services Experience Language (WSXL) to distribute the information processes, uses Universal Description Discovery and Integration (UDDI) to register and find the services, uses Web Services Definition Language (WSDL) to define the services and interfaces, uses Simple Object Access

Protocol (SOAP) to realize the communication between the service providers and service requesters, uses HTTP, FTP, SMTP to transmit the messages.

From the above analysis, it can be concluded that SOA is not equal to Web Services. SOA is a conception, a methodology and a model. And Web Services is a kind of concrete technology to realize SOA.

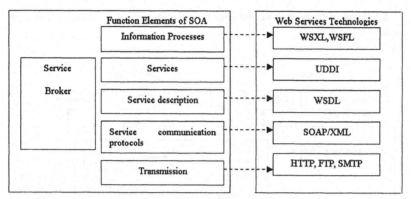

Fig. 3. Matching between Web Services Protocols and SOA

4   SOA-based virtual enterprise information integration model

4.1   Information integration goals in virtual enterprise

It has been showed by Hamid Haidarian Shahri [17] that the operation of the virtual enterprise requires the member enterprises, which come from different places and have different applications, to be able to share information instantly. So, it is imperative for the virtual enterprise to set down a high-effective information integration scheme. This scheme should realize the following goals:

(1) Reducing the reduplicate resources: It has been showed by Xu Ying [18] that the enterprise should reduce the reduplicate resources in information integration. The core enterprise needs not to offer multiform interfaces to realize the information integration. The scheme should provide a uniform definition language for the interfaces. This can dramatically reduce the reduplicate constructions.

(2) Realizing the loose coupling of integration: Virtual enterprise should make it easy to integrate different information coming from different systems.

(3) Updating the interfaces rapidly: Every member enterprise can realize the corresponding alteration automatically when any other member makes any change in the integration system.

(4) Integrating actively: Every member enterprise can automatically discover and integrate the information of any other member enterprise.

(5) Being independent of environment: It has been showed by YeYu-Feng Shahri [19] that virtual enterprise should offer an information integration model which can be applied in different systematic platforms and technical architectures.

4.2 SOA-based virtual enterprise information integration solution

4.2.1 General framework of SOA-based virtual enterprise information integration model

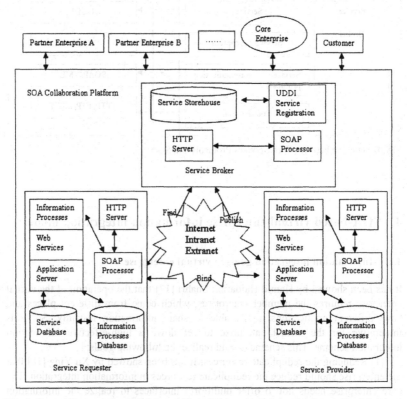

Fig. 4. General Framework of SOA-based Virtual Enterprise Information Integration Model

The member enterprises of the virtual enterprise probably have different development platforms and languages. Several recent investigations [20,21] indicate that the information integration of the virtual enterprise not only requires the members to exchange information effectively but also allows the members to deal with the remote orders and inquires etc. SOA can meet these needs. Using the widely used Web Service technologies, this paper construct an information integration model based on SOA, which is showed in figure4.

There are three principal roles in figure4: service requester, service provider and service broker. Figure5 describes the cooperation among the three roles.

(1) Service Broker: It is the supporter of service-finding. It includes a storehouse of the available services. It allows the service requester to search for the interfaces of the service providers. The service broker can receive the finding requirements from the service requesters and the publishing requirements from the service providers, and, return the corresponding responses to the requesters and providers. The service broker receives and returns the messages through HTTP. All these messages are dealt with in the SOAP processor.

(2) Service provider: It is an entity whose IP address can be found. It uses WSDL to describe and define the services and interfaces. It publishes the services by communicating with the service broker and enables the services to be accessed, received and called by the requesters.

(3) Service requester: It searches for the service(s) needed through the service broker, downloads the WSDL file(s) and calls the service(s). So, firstly, the service requester needs to set up the querying mechanism according to the information requirement. The mechanism should offer the querying conditions such as querying according to interface type and so on. Secondly, the querying conditions should be encapsulated as a SOAP request message by SOAP development tools and sent to the service broker. After dealing with the querying, the service broker encapsulates the querying results as a SOAP response message and returns it to the service requester. After receiving the response message, the service requester calls the service(s) through SOAP. Finally, the called service(s) encapsulates the service-result(s) in a SOAP message and returns it to the service requester.

In the virtual enterprise, it is not fixedly regulated whether the core enterprise or ordinary partner enterprises should act as the service requester or the provider. It should be flexibly decided according to the actual conditions. In the anterior content, we have discussed that the information integration of the virtual enterprise is the complementary integration of the core information processes of the member enterprises. So when an information process is called, the enterprise (the core enterprise or ordinary partner enterprise) who offers this information process is the service provider. And the enterprise (the core enterprise or ordinary partner enterprise) who calls this information process is the service requester.

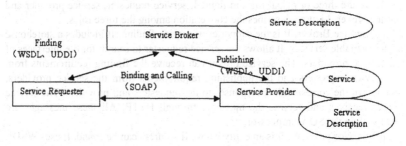

Fig. 5. The Cooperation in SOA

4.2.2 Detailed analysis of SOA-based virtual enterprise information integration solution

In the above content, we adopt Web Services technologies to construct the general framework of SOA-based virtual enterprise information integration model. This framework can realize the automatic information integration among the member enterprises. How the core enterprise, partner enterprises and customers build up the SOA platform and integrate information will be described in details in the following content. The status and functions of the core enterprise, partner enterprises and customer are showed in figure6. Figure 6 is drawn on the base of figure5. So, in order to make figure 6 be easily analyzed, the same parts as Figure5 such as the SOAP Processor and HTTP Processor are omitted.

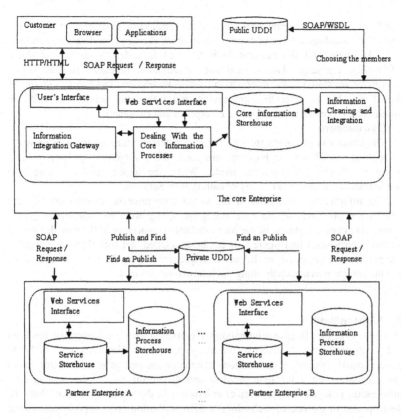

Fig. 6. Detailed Framework of SOA-based Virtual Enterprise Information Integration Model

(1) Core enterprise

The framework is built up centered around the core enterprise which leads all the members to actively establish the SOA platform. After inquiring about the information of the registered enterprises in the public UDDI, the core enterprise chooses the compatible members. The core enterprise needs to set up and maintain the private UDDI which is provided only to the members to guarantee the security and the validity of the information. The internal system of the core enterprise should be able to clean and integrate the information, so that the information read from the Web Services interfaces could be filtered before it entering the storehouse. The core enterprise should provide the customers with web-based user interfaces. And the core enterprise should analyze the request messages from the customers and send them to appropriate partner enterprises.

(2) Partner enterprises

The partner enterprises publish the interfaces of the information process applications in the form of Web Services. According to their own needs, the partner enterprises make decisions on whether they should register the services in the private

UDDI or directly integrate the services into the core enterprise. The partner enterprises build up a layer of special information exchange module between their internal system and the external Web Services in order to realize the fluent information exchange. The internal core information processes of the partner enterprises are stored in the information process storehouse. The partner enterprises should be able to offer the outsourcing and integration services of different information processes to other partner enterprises and customers.

(3) Customers

The customers communicate with the core enterprise through the web browsers or applications. When the browsers are used, the communication happens in a universal electronic commercial mode. When the applications are used, the communication happens in the way of calling Web Services.

The information integration of the virtual enterprise is centered on the core information processes of the core enterprise, along with the continuous search, optimization and integration of the core information processes of the complementary partner enterprises. From figure 6, it can be concluded that both the core enterprise and partner enterprises can be the service requesters finding the information services and the service providers publishing the information services.

5 Conclusion

How to realize the effective information integration of the virtual enterprise has been a difficult problem and challenge for many enterprises. The framework of SOA-based virtual enterprise information integration model solves the information communication and integration problem and makes full use of the existing core information processes of the member enterprises in the virtual enterprise. With the development of the related technologies, SOA will bring great opportunities to the implement and operation of the virtual enterprise. However, there are still many things to do to realize the information integration of the virtual enterprise, for example, the standard of secure message transmitting and Web affair processing should be improved. And these are our future research.

Acknowledgement

This research was supported by the grand research fund of State's Key research base of humanities and social sciences of China under Grant 05JJD870159.

References

1. K. Zbigniew, Towards virtual enterprises, *Human Factors and Ergonomics in Manufacturing* , 15(1), 49(2005).

2. S.C Stafford, Future Virtual Enterprise Strategies For the New Global Economy, *Futurics*, 29(1/2) , 46-50 (2005) .

3. G.Q. Huo, *Theory and Cases of the Integrated Management Strategies of Enterprise Information Resources*, Tsinghua University Press, Beijing(2004).

4. K. Jonathan, SOA: The Next Disruptive Force, *Industry Week*, 256(3), 41(2007).

5. N.Bieberstein, S.Bose, L.Walker and A.Lynch, Impact of service-oriented architecture on enterprise systems, organizational structures, and individuals, *IBM Systems Journal*, 44(4), 691-709(2006).

6. D.E. Cox and H. Kreger, Management of the service-oriented-architecture life cycle, *IBM Systems Journal*, 44(4), 709-726(2005).

7. S. Stephanie, SOA Is Happening-Time To Get On Board, *InformationWeek*, Feb (1127), 58(2007).

8. K. Eric, "SOA", *InfoWorld* , 9(1), 16-17(2007).

9. K. Eric and G.*Gale*, SOA: UNDER CONSTRUCTION, *InfoWorld*, 28(45),25-31(2006).

10. Charles B., SOA WORK IN PROGRESS, *InformationWeek* Manhasset,Oct 31(1062), 40-44(2006).

11. David M., SOA PLANNING: Sizing Up Your Business Processes, *InfoWorld*. Mar 28(11), 18-23(2006).

12. W. Mark, SOA: Enabler of Mass Customization, *Computerworld*, 40(47), 30(2006).

13. D. Frank, SOA evolves with information services, *Network World*, 23(42),35(2006).

14. Wang J.x., Lv X.h., Service-Oriented Information Integration Based on Web Services, *Computer Era*.2, 1-2(2006).

15. Marshall B., Introduction to Web Services, *Library Technology Reports*.May/Jun 42(3), 5-18(2006).

16. H.K. Cheng, Q.C. Tang and J.L. Zhao, Web Services and Service-Oriented Application Provisioning: An Analytical Study of Application Service Strategies, *IEEE Transactions on Engineering Management*, 53(4), 520(2006).

17. H. S.Hamid and H. S. Saied, Eliminating Duplicates in Information Integration: An Adaptive, Extensible Framework, *IEEE Intelligent Systems*, 21(5), 63(2006).

18. Y. Xu an F.Y. Xu, Research on the Supply Network Model Based on SOA, *Science and Technology Progress and Policy*. 3, 162-164(2006).

19. Y.F. Ye, "Enterprise Application Integration Scheme Based on SOA", *Microelectronics and Computer*, 23(5), 211-213(2006).

20. H. Ma and J.H. Li, Application of service-oriented architecture in dynamic enterprise application integration, *Computer Engineering and Design*, 27(13), 2507-2509(2006).

21. S.L. Yang, Y. Liu and X.J. Ma, Virtual Enterprise Solution Based on Web Services and Service-Oriented Architecture, *Application Research of Computers*, 10, 36-38(2006).

Organization Performance Model based on Evolution of Information System: Knowledge Sharing Perspective

Junling Xu

The management school of the Central China Normal University,
Wuhan, China
angelaxu03@126.com

Abstract. Information systems are advancing, even though the logic of complementarity effect is still persisting, few researches discussed how information technology boosts up multilateral cooperation effect and how information technology come into being benefit through indirect network interlink. The paper will construct a model where knowledge sharing creates indirect relation value based on information system capabilities.

1. Introduction

From a review of IS literature we identified three broad stages along which the business purpose of Information technology has evolved. During the first stage, in the past, IT was deployed largely to improve intra-organizational efficiency and effectiveness. The IS functionality was not only transaction oriented but also enabled communication between groups, decision makers and facilitated exectives'information search. Thus, other than transaction-processing systems, research on other IS such as decision support systems (DSS), group decision support systems, etc., was also conducted. Significant amount of research in the past two decades was focused at the intra-organizational level. In the second stage, deployment of IT investments to support business activity at the inter-organizational level was concurrent with the development of sophisticated IT products, which is termed as inter-organizational systems (IOS). IS literature later focused on electronic data interchange (EDI). EDI is considered to be an inflexible and transaction oriented proprietary technology where investors face large switching costs. With standardization of IS, especially with the Internet technology, more flexible Its constitute IOSs. These offer functionality ranging from automated, repetitive transactions to more collaborative and customized workplace technologies. Thus, currently investments in IOSs are aimed to not only save transaction costs, but also to enable better knowledge sharing and learning between two or more organizations. In the third stage, its are being deployed for a higher order function-that of managing interactions between different business relationships as against interactions at the dyadic level. By enabling interactions between entities spread across two or more firms, these systems such as e-markets, knowledge management systems, etc., give rise to scope or scale economies. As a result, organizations are able to offer better products to customers or reuse existing knowledge. IOSs in the stage are playing an important role in sustaining newer forms of organizational networks. This can

Please use the following format when citing this chapter:

Xu, J., 2007, in IFIP International Federation for Information Processing, Volume 251, Integration and Innovation Orient to E-Society Volume1, Wang, W. (Eds), (Boston: Springer), pp. 294-299.

guide investment in emerging technologies to not only improve benefits from relationships at a dyadic level but also at the business network level.

IT is necessary to consider the production function of information technology not limit to transact cost view while taking account of information technology functions, which helps to discuss IT operation value in organization networks based on knowledge and resource logic[1]. even though the logic of complementarity effect is still persisting, few researches discussed how information technology boosts up multilateral cooperation effect and how information technology come into being benefit through indirect network interlink. The paper will construct a model where knowledge sharing creates indirect relation value based on information system capabilities.

2. Relational Value in Inter-Organizational Networks

Increasing attention is focused on the study of business networks as organizational forms distinct from markets or firms. This is because value addition is often done jointly by business partners rather than by individual firms transacting at arms-length through market mechanisms. However, the network paradigm suggests that for organizations embedded in multiple business relationships, value can accrue because of indirect connections with other organizations through a common business entity. There are interdependencies even between those actors who are not transacting directly but may have common partners, suppliers or customers. There has been growing recognition of such interdependence effects in the literature. In a network consisting of collaborative relationships for product design and development, Eriksson et al, note that" the understanding of how technology adaptations in one relationship are contingent on adaptations in another is a key to understanding the dynamic of knowledge transfer between business relationships in a network"[4].An example of interdependencies in a business network is when a focal organization's relationship with one supplier contributes to better serving the focal organization's customers. For example in the case of Ericsson and Tokyo Digital Phone, Ericsson had to establish ties with a local Japanese firm Toshiba in order to gain necessary country-specific expertise and linguistic competence. The success of the project between them depended considerably on the success of the collaboration between Ericsson and Toshiba. The importance of information technology to manage business activities in a network context is increasingly important for good performance. We propose that as such interdependencies between firms increase, it is fruitful to explore how IS capabilities can contribute to value in business networks.

The potential to advance the theory on the value of IS in business networks can be realized by a deeper examination of the literature on value creation in business relationships. The resource-based view contends that competitive advantage results when a single firm delivers value using sustainable inimitable resources possessed and controlled by it. Whereas, the relational view suggests that"(dis)advantages of an individual firm are often linked to the (dis)advantages of the network of relationships within which a firm is embedded". This view refers to relational value as value that a firm derives by virtue of a relationship with a specific partner as opposed to relationship with alternative potential partners.

On reviewing the nature of IOSs under study and the related IS capabilities we find that IS research on business value has two main limitations. First, the theoretical bases for defining business value have predominantly a transaction cost econmomics viewpoint.Second,business value-related IS research has restricted the conception of business value at dyadic level and has not advanced it to the network level. In the next part, we develop the research model with IS capabilities as the independent variables affecting indirect relational value. We argue that knowledge sharing intermediates the effect of IS capabilities on indirect relational value.

3. Knowledge Sharing Based on Information System Capabilities

IS capabilities provide such Bus, the enterprises and their business partners, with a common platform for sharing knowledge. Literature on IT infrastructure identifies two dimensions, reach and range as leading to increased synergies across business units. However, there are few empirical studies they attempt to establish a theoretical link between IS capabilities and knowledge sharing. Therefore, we shall now conceptualize IS capabilities in terms of its three distinct facets, IS integration, IS range and IS reach. For understanding how IS integration may lead to higher knowledge sharing, we argue using the absorptive capacity viewpoint [7]. We propose that IS integration of a focal BU wth other Bus represents the absorptive capacity of the focal Bus towards these other Bus. Higher IS range implies a higher extent to which the IT portfolio represents codified rules for performing the business activities and a higher extent to which employees exposed to the IT portfolio. Thus, higher IS range can be viewed as enhancing the cognitive dimension of social capital within the enterprises. IS range can also indirectly contribute to knowledge sharing. Higher IS reach implies a richer medial for employee-to-employee connectivity and thus may enhance transfer for knowledge.

The theory on absorptive capacity views internal knowledge structures in firms as critical to the absorption, assimilation, enhancement, and application of useful external knowledge. Dyer and Singh [3] term this as partner-specific absorptive capacity. This means that combinative capabilities are nurtured within network links between organizations. This enables business units to acquire and process external knowledge. Having integrated ISs with well-defined data and application standards enables organizations to share richer knowledge across their business relationships [5]. Currently, as enterprises are implementing increasingly sophisticated IT applications to conduct business with other enterprises, higher IS integration represents a significant amount of encoding of inter-firm business rules. Thus, though empirical studies investigating the positive impact of integration on knowledge sharing are limited, there is significant qualitative evidence.

IS range and IS integration need not be considered as exclusive to an IT component also. Each IT application offers both dimensions of IS capabilities, IS range and IS integration. IS range is that which automates business activities, i.e., internal operations. Therefore, the set of IT applications and databases such as supply chain management software, CRM, etc., all are primarily designed to perform well-defined business functions. These components may measure high on IS range dimension. The second dimension is integration capability, i.e., extent of integration of applications and databases across various organizational units. This may be achieved through integration products such as middleware or web services. Thus, integration products may be viewed as measuring high on IS integration dimension but low on Is range dimension. There is not much empirical support in literature on whether IS range can lead to higher knowledge sharing .We theorize this link based on the absorptive capacity [7] and social capital viewpoints. A higher IS range signifies a higher level of absorptive capacity that helps the employees to assimilate internal information better and generate newer insights into its business activities. Having a greater IS range implies that the employees have access to rich and in-depth knowledge about their business activities. It also implies that an implicit, rich knowledge structure is imposed on the organization, which can be used to process and share knowledge and thus to create higher value. Further, when all employees have wide access to the software applications to perform their work, they develop a common cognitive frame of reference and a shared representation of the environment and business activity. This is similar to the " Cognitive dimension " of social capital that facilitates creation of intellectual capital. Therefore, higher IS range in terms of access to employees should also lead to higher knowledge sharing.

Reach refers to the extent to which employees within the ecosystem of multiple organizations are electronically connected with one another. Greater reach is characterized by increase connectivity among individuals and groups. Whereas IS range repents the sophistication of IT applications in terms of automating or facilitating internal operations in a business entity, IS reach captures the extent to which the employee-to-employee communications is supported across business unit boundaries. Dedicated, real-time, high-bandwidth information infrastructure provides a richer medium through which more complex and useful information can be transmitted. There is significant empirical support for positive effect in theoretical literature. Media richness theory supports the view that the ability of IT infrastructure to facilitate richer communication across business entities is likely to lead to greater knowledge sharing. Empirical studies found that connectivity offered by information technology is highly related to richer and more effective information sharing[6].

Though both IS integration and reach are facets of the IS capabilities of enterprises interacting with other enterprises, the two elements are distinct from a conceptual standpoint .IS reach can be viewed as facilitating unstructured coordination, while IS integration facilitates encoded, structured coordination across business units (Bus).

4.   Knowledge Sharing and Indirect Relational Value

Inter-organizational relationship literature proposes value antecedents such as knowledge sharing routines, relation-specific assets, trust, etc., that may lead to higher relational value. Significant qualitative and empirical studies strongly point to ability of IT to enhance information exchange and organizational learning. Therefore, we extend IS literature to examine how knowledge sharing may mediate the impact of IT on business value. Our overall proposition is that knowledge sharing moderates the impact of IS capabilities on indirect relational value. Prior literature richly describes how knowledge sharing is a potentially significant antecedent of relational value. For example, it is argued that a production network with superior knowledge-transfer mechanism among users, suppliers and manufacturers will be able to "out innovate" production networks with less effective knowledge-sharing mechanisms. Knowledge sharing routines refer to a pattern of inter-firm interactions that permits the transfer, recombination or creation of specialized knowledge [3]. Based on benefits such as improved innovation, knowledge sharing routines has been proposed as one of the antecedents of relational rents. Empirical literature also strongly supports the linkage between knowledge sharing and business unit performance.

We define indirect relational value as the extent to which a focal business entity's relationships with other entities, benefits the focal entity's overall business network. A related construct called business network connection refers to the influence that relationships with third parties have upon the focal relationship. A higher business network connection was hypothesized to eventually lead to higher value creation in a focal relationship. Unlike this dyadic level notion of relational value, our definition of indirect relational value views a relationship as a transmitter of benefits. Indirect relational value is a predominant outcome of business network relationships according to at least two streams of literature on organizational theory, i.e., social exchange theory and social networks. Social exchange theory suggests that in a context where organizations conduct and maintain a configuration of ongoing relationships, organizations may benefit from one relationship to the extent that it enhances the other relationships. This can happen because knowledge and solutions from a focal relationship can be re-applied to other relationships and vice versa. Social network analysis treats business entities as linked in a network. Benefits accrue to these entities depending on their structural position in the network. Since there is more than one way in which a structural position yields benefits, it is critical to understand the particular network mechanism that yields the benefits to a network entity [2]. These different types of mechanisms are closure, brokerage, prominence, contagion, etc. For example, if a network entity brokers information between multiple network entities and thus gains arbitrage, the member is said to accrue network benefits through a brokerage mechanism. Similarly if a central member inn a supply chain maintains rich and efficient relationships with other members, the central member has access to the knowledge and expertise of its partners, i.e., a closure mechanism yields benefits to the network entity. In our research context we are not interested in the brokerage benefits accruing to many particular network member but in the benefits resulting from intense, rich interactions with the network partners. These benefits could be access to new customers, acquisition of knowledge and expertise and improving coordination to improve efficiency of business operations.

The notion of indirect relational value is also consistent with the economies of scope argument in a production context. Here an organization can save on costs by reapplying its existing resources to the activities performed in other parts of the organization. Such resources are broadly labor and capital. However, in the B2B context, economies of scope can result as the Bus within the organizations learn to reapply the knowledge of the other Bus in order to derive cross-selling benefits or higher customer satisfaction. This results in faster customer acquisition or higher customer loyalty. The overall result is higher indirect relational value derived by an organization from its portfolio of relationships. Recent IS literature also indicates the benefits of transporting knowledge acquired during a particular transaction to other business activities by using knowledge management systems. Theoretical literature on alliances strongly support that knowledge sharing is positively related to indirect relational value. In the social network method, all firms in the sample are connected to each other through network linkages.

The literature review exceeds knowledge sharing and value creation relativity, moreover, the relationship of knowledge sharing based on IS capabilities dimensions are explored and workflow, society ties are also been taken in account. In the final, the paper discusses the process knowledge sharing accrues relational value. This transfer process can be seen in figure 1. Using the theoretical fondation offered by knowledge-based theories, we argue that knowledge sharing intermediates the effect of IS capabilities on indirect relational value.

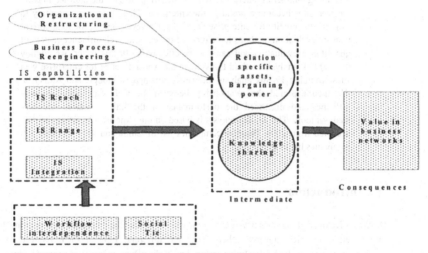

Figure1 Relational Value Model based on IS Capabilities

References

1. Amit, R., and Zott,C."Value creation in e-business". *Strategic Management Journal,* 2001, 22(6): 493-520

2. Burt.R.S.The network structure of social capital.In:Research in organizational behavior, B.M.Staw,*JAI Press,*Greenwich,CT,2000

3. Dyer, J.H,Singh,H. The relational view:Cooperative strategy and sourses of interorganizational competitive advantage. The Academy of Management review,1998

4. Eriksson, K.,and Hohenthal,J.The transferability of knowledge in business network relationships.In:Business Network Learning,J.Johanson,Elsevier Science,New York,2001.

5. Markus,K.E."Developing consensus on firm competencies and capabilities". *Academy of Management Executive*10,2000:40-51

6. Staples,S.D and Jarvenpaa,S.L.Using electronic media for information sharing activities:A replication and extension,ICIS,New Orleans,2001

7. Zahra,S.A.,and George,G.Absorptive capacity: "A review,reconceptualization and extension". *Academy of management review,*2002,27(2):185-203

Link Analysis and Web Influence Evaluation for Enterprise Websites

Junping Qiu1, Quan'e Ren2

1 College of Information Management ,Reseach Center for Chinese
Science Evaluation , in Wuhan Uninersity
jpqiu @whu.edu.cn
2   College of Information Management ,Reseach Center for Chinese
Science Evaluation , in Wuhan Uninersity
renquane @yahoo.com.cn

Abstract. As the enterprise Informatization process goes through deep, an increasing number of enterprises deploy their web sites on the internet, making the web sites become a brand of the enterprise. Thus, it is very necessary to evaluate the quality for enterprise web sites. However, almost the total current website evaluation methods have ignored the external web influence factors of quantitative evaluation and can't work effectively. In this paper, we employ the weblink analysis method to evaluate the web influence for enterprise web sites, combing 17 link analysis indicators obtained by Google and AltaVista. We then explored the relationship between the web sites type and web influence and discussed the performance of the link indicators and link analysis tools. The whole analysis is based on our experiments, using the data accepted from 2006 Top 500 companies list of China and 2006 Fortune 500 companies list in the world.

1   Introduction

Many indicators and methods have been proposed to evaluate the enterprise web sites in China and foreign countries, however, their focus are different. Few of them referred to the evaluation system of web sites link analysis and web influence [6,13]. At present, there are four typical evaluation system concerning on the electronic business web sites, such as: 5 indicators designed by Gomez, 10 indicators designed by BizRate, indicators used by the organization of CU' consumer reports online, CNNIN evaluation indicators[4], and indicators used by China Enterprise Confederation, information exchange center which belongs to China Entrepreneurs Association has launched an appraisal campaign on the web in 2005, only using standard as "Navigation clear, unmistakable link, homepage with links to columns point inflation rate of not less than 90%. " to evaluate Internal Links[2].

Please use the following format when citing this chapter:

Qiu, J., Ren, Q., 2007, in IFIP International Federation for Information Processing, Volume 251, Integration and Innovation Orient to E-Society Volume1, Wang, W. (Eds), (Boston: Springer), pp. 300-308.

From this, we divide the electronic business web sites evaluation methods into three parts: qualitative evaluation, quantitative evaluation and synthetically evaluation. The main methods of quantitative evaluation are the web traffics' indicators, often using, Alexa traffic. However, the rank is not absolutely authorities [1].

There is another quantitative evaluation method: using link analysis methods and web influence factor (WIF). Link analysis uses the webpage number of link which links to certain sites and represent its quality, this is based on these theories: if site A is linked by site B, then that means B is appreciating and using A, and the content of A and B is relevant; the more the site is linked, the bigger is the web influence. WIF measurement is based on link analysis, using WIF to represent the web influence. Therefore, we attempt to apply link analysis method and WIF measure methods to evaluate some of the typical enterprise in China and foreign countries. What's more, we explore the relationship between the type of sites and web influence.

2. Research approach

2.1 Research swatch

Because the difference exists in industry and which will influent the effect of link analysis, we define the swatch in information technology enterprises and consumable electron enterprises. The American Forrest Research company has designed a Site Need Index (SNI) to help the enterprise to decide whether they need to build a site for popular products. SNI' research results show that information technology enterprises and consumable electron enterprises hurriedly need to build their own brands and products through web sites [3, 7]. In our experiment, we selected thirty-four enterprise sites form 2006 Top 500 companies list of China and 2006 Fortune 500 companies list in the world to be our research swath. And our focus is enterprises sites in China, several foreign enterprises are used to compare with domestic web *sites*.

2.2 Indicators

In order to represent the scale and web influence of the enterprise sites comprehensively, we choose seven link analysis indicators as follows :(the website evaluated is labeled with A in this paper)

Pages Number: It represents the number of pages which are retrievable in search engines for A. It represents the scale of a website to some extent, but not necessarily represents the quality and concentration of a website.

Total Links: It is the number of pages indexed by search engines which are linking to A. This stands for the web influence of A.

Internal Links: This is the number of pages in A indexed by search engines which are linking to A itself, that is to say, it is a kind of self-link. Self-link represents the hierarchy and fullness of A's inner structure.

External links: It is the number of pages except A indexed by search engines which are linking to website A. This is the primary indicator, which is even better than total links for representing web influence.

Web Influence Factor (WIF=Total Links/Total pages) reflects the average level of pages for A that are linked. It also is the calculation way for WIF proposed by Ingwersen [5].

External Web Influence Factor (WIFe=External Links/Pages Number) reflects the total average level of Internal links of A. It is an objective indicator.

Internal Web Influence Factor (WIFs=Internal links/Pages Number) reflects the total average level of Internal links of A

3. Data Sources

3.1 Retrieval Methods and Tools

In the webometrics , there are two kind of link analysis tools. One is commercial search engines, the other is professional crawler. Because an proper tools for measuring WIF should Satisfy five conditions [10], there yet aren't any commercial search engines fits for them all.

AltaVista is often used in the research on webometrics. In fact, both Google and AltaVista are good tools to finish this task, what's more, the coverage and capacity of data in Google is better than AltaVista[12]. Thus, both Google and AltaVista are used in our experiment to eliminate and balance the uncertainty of link analysis, and improve the reliability and efficiency of the research results. In this paper, different indicators and retrieval expressions are used in different tools, as showed in table 1 and table 2

Table 1: Indicators and Query Expressions used in Google search engine, taking Haier Group for example

Indicators	Query Expressions
Pages Number: T	site: www.haier.com
Total Links: L	"www.www.haier.com"
Internal Links: S	"www.www.haier.com" site: www.haier.com
External Links: E	"www.haier.com" -site: www.haier.com
Web Influence Factor: WIF	L/T
External WIF: WIFe	E/T
Internal WIF: WIFs	S/T

Table 2: Indicators and Query Expressions used in AltaVista search engine, taking Haier Group for example

Indicators	Query Expressions
Pages Number: T	Host: www.haier.com
Total Links: L	Link: www.haier.com
Internal Links: S	S1:link:www.haier.com AND host: www.haier.com
	S2:host:www.haier.com AND link: www.haier.com
External Links: E	E1:link: www.haier.com AND NOT www.haier.com
	E2:link: www.haier.com AND NOT www.haier.com link:

	www.haier.com)
	E3:link: www.haier.com AND NOT www.haier.com host: www.haier.com)
Web Influence Factor: WIF	L/T
External WIF: WIFe	(E1+E2+E3)/3/T
Internal WIF: WIFs	(S1+S2)/2/T

The accuracy 34 Sino-foreign enterprises' name and their website URL in our swatch are showed in table 3. The experiment was done from May 1 to May 3, 2007, using a quick accessing way to eliminate and reduce errors caused by dynamic net information.

Table 3: Name and URL of the companies

Enterprise Name	Enterprise Website URL
Microsoft Corporation	www.microsoft.com
IBM Company	www.ibm.com
DELL Company	www.dell.com
Intel Company	www.intel.com
Oracle company	www.oracle.com
IBM China Company Limited	www.ibm.com.cn
Founder Electronics Co., Ltd	www.founder.com
Haier Co., Ltd	www.haier.com
Nokia Mainland China	www.nokia.com.cn
ZTE Corporation	www.zte.com.cn
Motorola China	www.motorola.com.cn
Philips China	www.philips.com.cn
Intel Company China	www.intel.com.cn
Hisense Corporation	www.hisense.com
Huawei Technologies Co., Ltd	www.huawei.com.cn
UFIDA Software CO.,LTD	www.ufsoft.com.cn
Shenzhen Skyworth Electronics Co., Ltd	www.skyworth.com.cn
TCL CORPORATION	www.tcl.com
Lenovo	www.legend.com.cn
Tsinghua Tongfang CO.,LTD	www.thtf.com.cn
Chunlan Group Corp	www.chunlan.com
Inspur Group	www.inspur.com
Konka Group CO.,LTD	www.konka.com
Panda Electronics Group Co., Ltd	www.chinapanda.com.cn
Gree Electric Appliances, Inc	www.gree.com.cn
Tsinghua Unisplendour Corporation Limited	www.thunis.com
changhong electric co., ltd	www.changhong.com.cn
Aucma co., ltd	www.aucma.com.cn
Media in China	www.midea.com.cn
BOE Technology Group Co., Ltd	www.boe.com.cn
Great Wall Technology Co. Ltd	www.greatwalltech.com
Datang Telecom Technology Co.,Ltd	www.datang.com
Oracle company China	www.oracle.com/global/cn
Cosun Group	www.qiaoxing.net

3.2 Web link data

In our experiment, we used 17 link analysis indicators to analyze the data, 7 of which is through Google, and 10 of which is through Altavista, as showed in Table 4, 5 (limited space, only display the part business' link data) :

Table 4: Data from Google search results. This was done from 19:10 to 24:10, on   May 1,2007. * represents the abnormal data, which will be discussed in part five

Oracle company	117000	1020000	116000	993000	8.718	8.487	0.991
IBM China Company Limited	21	36100	9	36100	1719	1719	4.5
Founder Electronics Co., Lt	1260	24800	1300	16400	19.683	13.016	1.032
Haier Co., Ltd	15100	66000	12300	43900	4.3709	2.907	0.815
Nokia Mainland China	3890	44100	3160	32700	11.337	8.406	0.812
ZTE Corporation	11500	45100	9420	18400	3.922	1.6	0.819
Motorola China	10900	45600	8490	22000	4.183	2.018	0.779
Philips China	384	12100	369	9170	31.51	23.88	0.961
Intel Company China *	1	10400	1	10900	10900	10900	1
Hisense Corporation	2270	14500	2120	9810	6.388	4.322	0.934
Huawei Technologies Co., Ltd	148	33100	9	33100	223.649	223.649	0.0608
UFIDA Software CO.,LTD	8850	30600	7110	9350	3.458	1.056	0.803
hen Skyworth Electronics Co.	127	4550	127	4530	35.827	35.669	1
TCL CORPORATION	3830	13100	3190	11100	3.42	2.898	0.833
Lenovo	95	6030	82	5380	63.474	56.632	0.863
Tsinghua Tongfang CO.,LTD	313	10500	306	959	33.546	3.064	0.978

Table 5: Data from Altavistasearch results. This was done from 19:10 to 24:10, on   May 1,2007. * represents the abnormal data, which will be discussed in part five

Enterprise Name	T	L	S1	S2	E1	E2	E3	WIF	WIFe	WIFs
Microsoft Corporation	27900000	92000000	243000	244000	1250000	1250000	3380000	3.287	0.07	0.009
Intel Company	8890000	31500000	26000	26000	253000	259000	884000	3.543	0.052	0.003
Founder China *	8650000	20200000	133	140	20200	20600	22000	2.335	0.0024	0
IBM	9210000	25200000	166000	167000	190000	190000	1290000	2.736	0.06	0.018
Konka Group	2910	82000	444	445	16000	16000	24800	28.179	6.506	0.153
uawei Technologies Co.,Lt	1400	63400	692	824	32500	32700	26300	45.286	21.786	0.541
Oracle China *	182000	314000	0	0	754	757	756	1.725	0.004	0
DELL Company	5900000	33800000	6600	6630	139000	140000	377000	5.729	0.037	0.001
Intel Company China	175000	752000	32800	35400	23800	23700	19200	4.297	0.172	0.195
ng Telecom Technology Co.	59400	398000	29	29	1820	1820	3630	6.7	0.041	4.882
Philips China *	57900	128000	2	2	18800	18700	27500	2.211	0.374	
IBM China	216000	612000	108000	117000	21000	21000	30500	2.833	0.112	0.521
Haier Group	114,000	834000	55	180	36800	36800	47800	7.316	31.947	0.004
Hisense Group	1,640	160000	119	120	22500	22400	33000	97.561	142.500	0.291
ZTE Corporation	770	32400	149	149	17700	17600	17400	42.078	22.814	0.194

4 Data analysis

Table 4 and Table 5 shows, use Google search and Altavista search for the enterprise links indicators specific data gap greatly. For example : the value of WIF, WIFe, WIFs of Microsoft website   were 26.655, 4.286,1.484 with Google, while with   Altavista were 3.287,0.07. 0.009. Clearly, database capacity and search mechanism of the two tools are different. If only using the original data to evaluate and rank, the conclusion wouldn't be objective. Therefore, we score each of the indicators, and then add in all indicators to gain final scores., and produce a total ranking, as showed in Table 6 ,7, 8 (Due to space limitations, only display the total ranking of the top 20 enterprise-data) :

Table 6 : rankings of enterprises site searched by Google

Enterprise Name	google Search						
	T Rank	L Rank	S Rank	B Rank	WIF Rank	WIFe Rank	WIFs Rank
Microsoft	1	1	1	1	8	19	2
Intel	3	3	3	3	14	10	16
IBM	2	4	2	4	17	14	3
DELL	5	2	5	2	9	7	17
Founder	21	13	20	12	10	9	5
IBM China	33	10	32	7	2	2	1
Haier	6	6	6	6	23	21	24
Philips China	25	20	24	18	7	6	12
Intel	34	24	34	14	1	1	6
Hua Wei	29	11	33	8	3	3	34
Oracle	4	5	4	5	16	12	8
Konka	22	21	27	15	12	11	33
ZTE	7	8	7	11	25	24	23
Hisense	17	15	16	16	20	18	15
Nokia	13	9	14	9	11	13	25
DaTang	15	30	15	25	34	29	27
Oracle China	19	25	21	33	21	33	31
TCL	14	19	13	13	27	22	22
UFIDA Software	9	12	9	17	26	26	26

Table 7 : rankings of enterprises site searched by Altavista

Enterprise Name	altavista Search									
	T Rank	Rank1	Rank2	RankB1	RankE1	RankE2	RankE3	RankIF	RanVIFe	RankWIFs Rank
Microsoft	1	1	1	1	1	1	1	19	27	23
Intel	3	3	5	5	2	2	3	18	29	26
IBM	2	2	8	8	4	4	5	12	32	29
DELL	6	6	6	6	5	5	4	23	30	28
Founder	4	4	2	2	3	3	2	27	28	21
IBM China	8	8	23	19	9	9	9	9	11	24
Haier	12	12	10	10	8	8	7	22	23	22
Philips China	15	15	20	22	12	12	10	1	3	13
Intel	10	10	3	3	13	13	11	24	26	9
Hua Wei	19	19	12	11	10	10	13	2	13	8
Oracle	5	5	19	21	14	14	16	28	34	34
Konka	17	17	9	9	6	6	6	17	15	12
ZTE	20	20	18	20	16	16	18	4	12	16
Hisense	18	18	14	15	17	17	15	5	18	17
Nokia	11	11	24	24	26	26	27	10	31	3
DaTang	14	14	7	7	7	7	8	20	21	18
Oracle China	9	9	4	4	11	11	17	13	25	15
TCL	7	7	22	13	18	18	14	32	24	27
UFIDA Software	28	28	15	16	21	21	20	31	7	5

Table 8 : total rankings of enterprises site searched by Google and Altavista

Enterprise Name	Google Search		Altavista Search	
	Total Score	Rank 1	Total Score	Rank 2
Microsoft	212	1	274	1
Intel	193	4	254	2
IBM	199	2	244	4
DELL	198	3	231	8
Founder	155	7	254	3
IBM China	158	6	221	12
Haier	153	8	216	13
Philips China	133	12	227	11
Intel	131	13	228	9
Hua Wei	124	15	233	6
Oracle	191	5	160	19
Konka	104	23	236	5
ZTE	140	10	190	15
Hisense	128	14	196	14
Nokia	151	9	157	21
DaTang	70	32	227	10
Oracle China	62	33	232	7
TCL	115	18	168	17
UFIDA Software	120	16	158	20

5 Experiment results and discussion

5.1 discussion on link analysis tools

In Webometrics study, the Altavista is the preferred search engine for researchers [8].Can we take it with other tools in the integrated use to achieve optimal results? We can answer it with Table 8 : In Ranking 1, 2 and total ranking order, the first one are both Microsoft and are consistent with the total order; while the second one is slightly different, that is IBM Corporation with Google search results, but with Altavista search results and overall rankings are both Intel Corporation; Hisense Group, in an order, are all ranked 14th in the Sort 1,Sort 2 and the total ranking ;TCL Group, Sort 1 Sort 2 and the total ranking is in turn No. 18, No. 17 and No. 18, a difference of weak. The resulting gains rough conclusions: Google web links can be as analytical tools used in conjunction with the Altavista. Although both the search results with slight deviation, they can achieve balance and comprehensive abatement through synthesizing indicators. This from another angle test our hypothesis : Altavista can make integrated use with other web link tools to achieve optimal results.

5.2 indicators and enterprises web influence

In Table 4 and Table 5, the Enterprise website with * sign can be seen, and abnormal data mainly exist in the indicators S and WIFs of all these indicators, while for indicators E and WIFe, with either Google or Altavist retrieval, the results are relative normal. Therefore, we can deduce: indicators E and WIFe is the most effective indicators of many indicators for website link analysis and its influence force evaluation.

As for the underlying factors for fluctuation of value in Table 6 and Table 7, which caused the inconsistencies of two search engines link analysis results, come from such objective reasons as the dynamic network information variability characteristics and the different search mechanisms of the search engine, simultaneously; this also reflects the availability of some enterprises websites being in question. In many literature of evaluating websites, availability is a major indicators which include the appearance ratio of webpages in search engine, the structure level of website resources and the effectiveness of internal link [14]. However, from Table 4, 5, we can see some abnormal data that produced using Google and Altavista search, such as the value is 0 or 1 of T, S. For example, the indicators T, indicators S and indicators WIFs of Intel(China) website are 1, while for IBM (China) they were respectively 21,9 and 4.5, and Huawei' S value is 9,using Google. With Altavista search, for Oracle Corporation (China), Shenzhen Skyworth Electronics Co., Ltd. and Panda Electronics Group Limited, are all 0 of S1, S2; for Philips (China), S1, S2 are 2; as for Chunlan Group Limited and Changhong Electronic Co. Ltd. , S1, S2 are 1, Great Wall Technology Co.Ltd., T is 1. These shown: without regard to search engines factors, the appearance ratio of webpages in search engine, the structure level of website resources and the effectiveness of internal link of these enterprise are not optimistic concept.

Finally, based on the assumptions of relatively availability of our retrieval and analysis tools, we can further explore the difference of some website and how such factors influence the correlation between website and its web influence , in terms of Chinese enterprises and other country enterprises, information display websites and online trading sites, and different industries type. So we can provide reference information for Chinese enterprises to optimize website construction and upgrade website influence force.

(1) Disparity exists between Sino-foreign enterprises web influence .Results from the Comprehensive rankings can be seen in this paper, selected 34 Chinese and foreign enterprises, several of the top foreign enterprises are websites, such as Microsoft, Intel, IBM, DELL, only the second one is the Founder Group, IBM Corporation (China), Haier Group, Philips (China), Intel (China), Huawei. This shows that, there is still a big gap between Chinese enterprises on the web site construction and promotion network in comparison with foreign countries. The existing causes include our late started Enterprise Informatization, infrastructure lags and other objective reasons. Furthermore, Chinese enterprises' decision-making should build awareness of the importance of websites on. From the enterprise marketing strategy, enterprises website is a integrated network marketing tools. So with an influential corporate website will enable enterprises to operate its entities into unexpected virtuous circle.

(2) Web influence depend on industries type .While the selection of samples have been taken into account the relationship between nature of the trade and its website construction ,and only selected information technology businesses and consumer electronic products enterprises, we study still found that these two field industries site also exist differences. Overall, the web influence of information technology and software products enterprises website is bigger than that of the consumer electronics business. From Table 6, 7, 8 in the rankings, we can see that the information technology or information products corporations like Microsoft, Intel, IBM, DELL, Founder, Huawei website ranks forward, but consumer electronics companies such as Haier, Konka, etc. were ranked then. So, the enterprise website building and the diffusion of different industries can take different strategies according to the characteristics of enterprises. A reasonable position of sites function is the premise to achieve perfect networks influence force for the enterprise.

(3) Web influence is relational with its function type. According to the scale and function, websites can be divided into three broad categories: information display only, online direct marketing websites, and e-commerce website[11].Information display-only website is an information carrier, the main function of which is to publish and display information (e.g. Konka Co.). If website add online orders and payment functions, it has the online marketing conditions (e.g. DELL Co.), who is on the initiative of the "linear ordering patterns." If website includes the entire business process integration of information processing systems, it is an e-commerce website (e.g. Haier Co.).

In this paper, the enterprise website link analysis and web influence evaluation showed that DELL website is better than Haier Group, and Haier Group is better than Konka Group. We presumably think that web influence and enterprises' functional types are correlated, that is, the online direct marketing enterprise website influence is better than integrated e-commerce websites and an integrated e-commerce website is better than the display of information for enterprises.

But, as for the accuracy of the results, Ronald Rousseau found that the flaw of AltaVista's arithmetic lead significant fluctuations of the search result [9]. At the same time, we may have missed some related businesses in selecting samples. What we have done is just selecting parts of business websites as representative to analyze so as to describe the problem existing. Therefore, these shortcomings and deficiencies may lead to the research errors. It suggests that it is important to reasonably understand the data results and analysis conclusions when referring to this evaluation ranking, which is also the direction we should improve.

6 Acknowledgement

This article is supported by National Natural Science Foundation of China (70673071).

References

1. Alexasir,com (January 10, 2007);http://www.alexasir.com/tech.html.
2. Cec-ceda,org (January 7, 2007); http://www.cec-ceda.org.cn/yxqywz/pxbz.htm
3. Forrester (January 12, 2007);http://www.forrester.com.
4. A.B. Huang, D.M. Zhao, "A research on the evaluation indicator system for B2C website", *Commercial Research*, 2006(1): 192-194.
5. Ingwersen. "The calculation of WEB attractiveness factor",. *Journal of Documentation*, 1998, 54,   236-243 www.//bacterio.cict.fr/backlinks.html.
6. Y.H. Li, S.J. Tang, "An evaluation on electric business website", *Library Theory and Practice*, 2006(1): 64-65.
7. Marcomconsulting (January 6, 2006);http://www.marcomconsulting.net
8. M. Thelwell, "A Comparison of Source of Links for Academic Web Attractiveness Factor Calculations", *Journal of Documentation*,2002, 58(1), 60-72.
9. R. Rousseau, "Daily time series of common single worsearches in AltaVista and Northern Light", [2007-3-2]http://cybermetrics.cindoc.csic.es/pruebas/v2i1p2.htm.
10. T. Yang, "The Webometrics Study of Twenty China Mainland Universities", *Library and Information Service*,2003(9): 61-66.
11. Z.P. Wang , *web marketing*, Wuhan: Central China normal university press, 2003.9 :P53-58.
12. J.K. Xu, "Studying by Comparison the Four Searching Engines in Common Use in the Research of Network Information Measurement", *New Technology of Library and Information Service*, 2004(11): 46-48.
13. M.Z. Yang, Y.L. Zhuang, "A summary on the theory and practice for e-business website evaluation", *Market Modernization*, 2006(2): 140-141.
14. Y. Zhang, Q.H. Zhu, "Application of Fuzzy Analytic Hierarchy Process for Enterprises Websites Evaluation", *New Technology of Library and Information Service*, 2006(6):68-71.

The Credibility of Enterprise's Website and Its Evaluation in the Customer's Perspective

Junping Qiu, Chunhui Tan

(Research Center for Chinese Science Evaluation, Wuhan University, P.R.China, 430072)

Abstract: The credibility of website is a sort of psychological feeling, in other words, a sense of trust and its intensity towards the enterprise's website produced by the customers from individual or collective perspective. The credibility of website has become a decisive factor for the website's survival and an important driving force of promotion and market expansion. Currently, the credibility of website is still at a low level. There are many factors affecting the customer's assessment of the credibility of enterprise's website. According to the website's structure and function modules, the evaluation indicator framework for the credibility of enterprise's website is divided into three level indicators, respectively: the credibility of website structure, the credibility of website service, and the credibility of E-marketing. There are a number of second-level indicators under each level indicator. Since the credibility of website is one kind of subjective psychology feeling, it can use the multi-level fuzzy comprehensive evaluation based on the expert consultation and the customer questionnaire survey to evaluate the credibility of enterprise's website. This paper finally takes a gift company website as a case study, and has carried out an evaluation of its credibility. As the evaluation of ordinary customer is obviously different from that of the expert, together with the shortcomings inherent in questionnaire survey, the evaluation of credibility of website based on customer perspective may result in deviation sometimes.

1 Introduction

Along with the trend of informationization and globalization of world economy, E-commerce is gradually moving towards a comprehensive application and permeating into various levels of socio-economics. E-commerce has developed rapidly around the world in 2006, moreover, it has become the auxiliary booster for the economic globalization. From the overall situation, the volume of trade of E-commerce

Please use the following format when citing this chapter:

Qiu, J., Tan, C., 2007, in IFIP International Federation for Information Processing, Volume 251, Integration and Innovation Orient to E-Society Volume1, Wang, W. (Eds), (Boston: Springer), pp. 309-322.

amounted to $12.8 trillion in 2006, which covered 18% of the world's total merchandise trade [1]. China has always attached great importance to the development of E-commerce, which has already become an important part in pushing forward the national economy and the social informationization. 2007 Chinese Internet Marketplaces Annual Meeting claimed that E-commerce in China has advanced by leaps and bounds, by the end of 2006, the volume of trade in E-commerce market has reached 1.1 trillion RMB, increased by 48.6% than the corresponding period in 2005[2].

Since E-commerce has notable advantages in the fields of reducing cost, improving efficiency, developing markets and improving service and so on, more and more enterprises begin to adopt this new business pattern, establishing its own website to carry out their business activities. According to the 19th China Internet Network Development Counting Report (released by China Internet Network Information Center), there are 527,728 commercial websites (including the website under top-level domain .com and secondary-level domain .com.cn) by December 31, 2006, accounting for 62.6% of the WWW websites in our country, 93.5% of which are enterprise's websites[3]. And there are even more enterprise's websites around the world.

Will enterprises be able to be successful and gain unfailing economic benefits when they built websites? This is not the case in reality. Some websites can bring extra value to enterprises, while some websites not. Then, the question is how to strengthen the business function of the enterprise website? Meanwhile, the more the enterprise websites are, the more intense the competition in E-marketing is. Besides establishing a website with exquisite pages and powerful interactive functions, are there any other important factors which enable an enterprise website outstanding in the similar industry? Of course, there is. It is the credibility of website , which though is often neglected by most enterprises.

The credibility of website is a sort of psychological feeling, in other words, a sense of trust and its intensity towards the enterprise's website produced by the customers (including individual consumers and collective consumers, also including real consumers and potential ones) from individual or collective perspective. Generally speaking, the more a customer trusts a website, the longer he would stay at this website, the greater his desire for purchasing. This is one of the reasons why the sale performance of one enterprise's website is better than others, though they all belong to the same industry and the same area. Liu and Arnett pointed out that a successful website should be attractive to customers, let them trust its reliability and provide them with information of high quality [4].

It can be said that a successful enterprise's website should be a high credibility website. The credibility of the website has become an important criterion for determining the success or otherwise of the website. And it has become the important driving factor for promoting the customer's further purchasing behavior. In fact, the customer online purchasing behavior results from the assessment result of the credibility of enterprise's website in most cases; the online shopping model is shown in Fig.1. Because of the openness and convenience of Internet, along with the improvement of the customers' professional skills, it provides convenience for customers to compare the prices before buying and bargaining and reducing risks. If the credibility of enterprise's website is not high, it is very possible for customers to visit one website from another, with one click of the mouse.

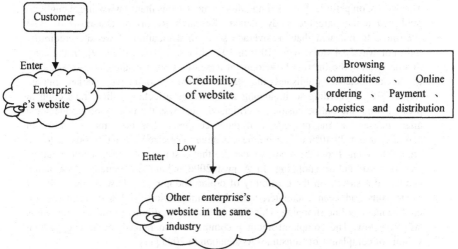

Figure.1 The Online Shopping Model Based on Credibility of Enterprise's Website

Some foreign researches have proven that credibility of website has become one of the key factors of E-commerce. In May 2005, ScanAlert, an Internet Security Corporate located in U.S., has released a survey about online customers' shopping habits entitled "A New Era of Digital Window Shopping: From Shopping Cart Abandonment to Purchase". ScanAlert found that it took average customer more than 19 hours from his first visiting a website to purchase online. And the main reason why consumers buy or abandon shopping is that consumers pay close attention to the credibility of website. ScanAlert also noted that the first value measure for consumer to purchase comparison is website credibility in general, but not the price[5]. According to the researcher Gitte Lindgaard of Carleton University in Ottawa, that users judge sites within a second, but their decision has a lasting impact. So it is essential for the websites to leave a good first impression and a good sense of trust with the browsers [6].

2   Factors affecting the credibility of website

Then, how about the specific condition of credibility of enterprise's website in customers' view?

According to a recent Cyota survey of online bank account-holders (released in May 2004), 74 percent said they were less likely to shop online due to the threat of phishing attacks[7]. The survey showed that the credibility of E-commerce in the United States fell sharply. In June 2005, A Gartner survey of 5,000 U.S. adults showed that phishing attacks grew at double-digit rates last year in the United States. Gartner analysts said most online consumers do not open e-mail from companies or individuals they do not know from prior experience. Three of every four online shoppers said they were more cautious when shopping online, and one of three reported that they bought fewer because of security concerns [8]. In December 2005, The New Competitive E-marketing Management Consultant (www.jingzhengli.cn) published a monographic study named "Research Report of Diagnosis of B2B Website". It indicated that the average score of evaluation of website credibility indicator was 50.4 (total score 100) in 102 Chinese B2B websites [9]. In the early February 2006, the Internet Development Research Center of the Chinese Academy of Social Science published the "2005 China E-commerce Market Survey Report"[10]. According to it, among many issues affecting online transaction at present, what the online customers criticized most was the quality of products and after-sale service, the proportion of these customers has been reached 43%. In addition, about 29.40% of the online customers criticized the hazardous factor of online shopping. From the report we can see that customers have suspicion about the credibility of online shopping. In August 2006, China E-commerce Association conducted a survey on the credibility of online shopping. It showed that 56.4% of participants had been encountered the fake information, 71.1% of them had no confidence in online shopping. This showed that the credibility of online shopping is still very low. The complaint about E-commerce also ranked the second in total volume of complaints of Consumer Association in 2005 [11].

Through these surveys, we can know that the overall credibility of enterprises' website is still at a relatively low level.

In the eyes of customer, what factors will affect the assessment of the credibility of enterprise website? In other words, what factors may allow website have high credibility in the mind of customer?

In June 2002, Stanford University's Persuasive Technology Lab conducted a study of over 1,600 American and European Internet users. The study highlighted various factors determining why certain Web sites enjoyed greater levels of credibility than others [12]. Study participants listed respect for the organization that created the Web site, quick responses to customer service questions, an online mention of the organization's address, the timeliness of site content, and a contact phone number as important characteristics of a credible site in addition to its overall usefulness. The same group reacted unfavorably to sites that use pop-up advertisements or fail to update copy. Broken links, poor site navigation, and links to sites perceived to be non-credible were also among the highest negative influences. Americans gave much higher credibility rankings to Web sites that offered privacy statements, sent e-mails to confirm transactions, indicated the source of site content or provided credentials for its authors.

In October 2005, the non-profit research institution Consumer WebWatch published a latest report about credibility of website entitled "Leap of faith: Using the internet despite the dangers", which had issued a survey also about credibility of website entitled "A Matter of Trust: What Users Want From Web Sites" in April 2002. As shown in the 2005 WebWatch survey[13], the factors associated with the credibility of the website are: 88 percent say keeping personal information safe and secure is very important for a Web site they visit; Being able to trust the information on a site is not far behind with 81 percent believing it very important; 76 percent think it very important to be able to easily identify the sources of information on the site; 73 percent rate knowing a site is updated frequently with new information as very important; 48 percent say knowing who owns a Web site is very important.

3   Evaluation indicator framework of credibility of enterprise's website

Generally speaking, the functions of the enterprise's website are: (1) propagating enterprise image; (2) demonstrating products and services; (3) ordering goods and services; (4) transferring accounts, payment and transportation; (5) searching and querying information; (6) managing customer information; (7) managing sales information; (8) releasing news; (9) announcing supply and demand information. Basically, these functions can be grouped into two modules: E-marketing module and website's service module. But the realization of these two function modules is rested with a certain structure of website. Therefore, from the customer perspective, the credibility of enterprise's website can be divided into three parts: the credibility of E-marketing, the credibility of website service and the credibility of website structure.

The credibility of E-marketing refers to the level of customer's psychological sense of trust about the quality of products, the product price, the advertising, the product ordering, the payment security, the logistics and distribution, the market survey and so on, which are displayed on the enterprise's website.

The credibility of website service refers to the level of customer's psychological sense of trust about the projects of service, the scope of service, the terms of service, the ways of service, the methods of contact, the information retrieval and so on, which are provided by the enterprise's website.

The credibility of website structure refers to the degree of customer's psychological sense of trust about the layout of website pages, the establishment of column, the manifesting forms of information, the visual effect, the website navigation, the page link and so on, which are used by the enterprise's website.

It can be said that the credibility of enterprise's website is affected by the credibility of E-marketing, the credibility of website service and the credibility of website structure. The credibility of enterprise's website is the combined psychological result after customer has made a comprehensive evaluation of the credibility of E-marketing, the credibility of website service and the credibility of website structure. A simple model of credibility of enterprise's website is shown in Fig.2.

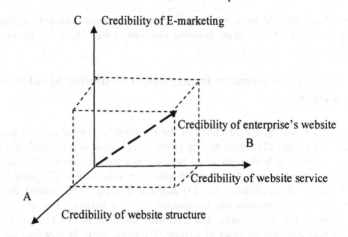

Figure.2： A simple Model of Credibility of Enterprise's Website

Therefore, when customers are engaged in online shopping, their assessment of the credibility of visiting website is the synthetic evaluation result based on the credibility of E-marketing, the credibility of website service and the credibility of website structure. In accordance with the evaluation principles, such as the combination of purposeful indicators with scientific indicators, systematic indicators with stratified indicators, comparative indicators with feasible indicators, sustainable indicators with dynamic indicators, important indicators with concise indicators, we construct the evaluation indicator framework of credibility of enterprise's website, as shown in Table 1.

Table 5.   The Evaluation Indicator Framework of Credibility of Enterprise's WebsiteKnown Results

Target indicator	Level indicator	Second-level indicator	
Credibility of enterprise's website	Credibility of website structure (U_1)	Whole layout (U_{11})	
		Outward appearance design (U_{12})	
		Navigation function (U_{13})	
		Page link (U_{14})	
		Page style (U_{15})	
		Text structure (U_{16})	
	Credibility of website service (U_2)	Enterprise introduction (U_{21})	
		Contact method (U_{22})	
		Certification prove (U_{23})	
		Search engine function (U_{24})	
		Online communication method (U_{25})	
		Information content (U_{26})	
		Individual privacy protection (U_{27})	
		Personalized information service(U_{28})	
	Credibility of E-marketing(U_3)	Product introduction (U_{31})	
		Product price (U_{32})	
		Online ordering (U_{33})	
		Payment (U_{34})	
		Credit card information protection	
		logistics and distribution, (U_{36})	
		After-sale service (U_{37})	
		Product and service complaint (U_{38})	

4   The comprehensive evaluation of the credibility of enterprise's website

The goals of the comprehensive evaluation of credibility of enterprise's website lie in: recognizing objectively the level of credibility of a enterprise's website, providing the reference of decision-making for the investors, the operators, the administrative departments, the trade associations and the consumers.

4.1 Choice of evaluation method

The credibility of website is a kind of psychological feeling for customer, although the evaluation indicator framework has been created, there are no exact figures to be used to define the specific credibility; there is only the level of credibility. In normal circumstance, it is hardly to define clearly how high the credibility of website is, it can use five grades to express the level: very high, high, normal, low, very low. But it is difficult to define the standard for each grade. From here it can be seen that the evaluation of credibility of website has the fuzziness, it can use the multi-level fuzzy comprehensive evaluation based on the expert consultation and the customer questionnaire survey to evaluate the credibility of website. So, each second-level indicator should be assessed by very high, high, normal, low, very low levels in accordance with the credibility, based on the judgment of the surveyed customers.

4.2 Determination of the indicator weight

There are many methods to determine the weight value. The usual methods are AHP, Delphi and Membership Function Method. AHP is a method commonly used in the multi-attribute decision-making and often integrates with fuzzy math to evaluate indicators. The method can turn qualitative problems into quantitative ones, handle uniformly qualitative and quantitative factors of decisions. Therefore, this article uses AHP to determine various indicators weights.

According to AHP, together with the evaluation indicator framework of credibility of enterprise's website, firstly, let experts construct the pairwise comparison judgment matrix of level indicators U1、U2、U3, then calculate the weights of U1、U2、U3 by used Eigenvalue Method and check the consistency. Assume the calculated weight coefficients of level indicators Ui(i=1,2,3) is $wi(i=1,2,3), \sum_{i=1}^{n} wi=1$ each indicators weight vector is W=(w1,w2,w3), where

Use the same method, it can calculate the weight coefficients of second-level indicators Uij（i=1,2,3; j=1,2,3 ⋯ ⋯ n, n=6 or n=8, according to the level indicators）is wij(i=1,2,3;j=1,2,3 ⋯ ⋯ n, n=6 or n=8, according to the level indicators $\sum_{j=1}^{n} wij=1$ each indicators weight vector is Wi=(wi1,wi2, ⋯ ⋯ , win）where

4.3 Fuzzy Comprehensive Evaluation steps

According to the fuzzy comprehensive evaluation method, the whole analysis step is shown below step by step.
(1) Build the evaluation indicators set:
U={U1，U2，U3}
Uij={Ui1，Ui2，⋯⋯，Uij}   (i=1，2，3；j=1，2，⋯⋯n，n=6 or n=8, according to the level indicators）
Where: U means the target indicator, Ui means level indicator, Uij means second-level indicator.
(2) Build the evaluation grade set:
V={v1，v2，v3，v4，v5},
Where: v1 means the credibility is very high, v2 means the credibility is high, v3 means the credibility is normal, v4 means the credibility is low, v5 means the credibility is very low.

(3) Construct the fuzzy judgment matrix of level indicators:

Let N participants evaluate the second-level indicators based on the evaluation set, which can calculate the level indicators' grade of membership. The fuzzy judgment matrix of level indicators is shown as follows:

$$R_1 = \begin{bmatrix} r_{111} & r_{112} & r_{113} & r_{114} & r_{115} \\ r_{121} & r_{122} & r_{123} & r_{124} & r_{125} \\ r_{131} & r_{132} & r_{133} & r_{134} & r_{135} \\ r_{141} & r_{142} & r_{143} & r_{144} & r_{145} \\ r_{151} & r_{152} & r_{153} & r_{154} & r_{155} \\ r_{161} & r_{162} & r_{163} & r_{164} & r_{165} \end{bmatrix} \quad R_2 = \begin{bmatrix} r_{211} & r_{212} & r_{213} & r_{214} & r_{215} \\ r_{221} & r_{222} & r_{223} & r_{224} & r_{225} \\ r_{231} & r_{232} & r_{233} & r_{234} & r_{235} \\ r_{241} & r_{242} & r_{243} & r_{244} & r_{245} \\ r_{251} & r_{252} & r_{253} & r_{254} & r_{255} \\ r_{261} & r_{262} & r_{263} & r_{264} & r_{265} \\ r_{271} & r_{272} & r_{273} & r_{274} & r_{275} \\ r_{281} & r_{282} & r_{283} & r_{284} & r_{285} \end{bmatrix}$$

$$R_3 = \begin{bmatrix} r_{311} & r_{312} & r_{313} & r_{314} & r_{315} \\ r_{321} & r_{322} & r_{323} & r_{324} & r_{325} \\ r_{331} & r_{332} & r_{333} & r_{334} & r_{335} \\ r_{341} & r_{342} & r_{343} & r_{344} & r_{345} \\ r_{351} & r_{352} & r_{353} & r_{354} & r_{355} \\ r_{361} & r_{362} & r_{363} & r_{364} & r_{365} \\ r_{371} & r_{372} & r_{373} & r_{374} & r_{375} \\ r_{381} & r_{382} & r_{383} & r_{384} & r_{385} \end{bmatrix}$$

Where: $r_{ijm} = N_{ijm}/N$, N_{ijm} ($i = 1, 2, 3$; $j = 1, 2, 3 \cdots \cdots n$, $n = 6$ or $n = 8$, according to the level indicators; $m = 1, 2, 3, 4, 5$) means the number that the second-level indicator U_{ij} is evaluated with the grade v_m by N experts.

(4) Calculate the fuzzy vectors of level indicators:

The rule of operation is defined as:

$S_i = W_i \cdot R_i$

$$= (w_{i1}, w_{i2}, \cdots \cdots w_{in}) \cdot \begin{bmatrix} r_{i11} & r_{i12} & r_{i13} & r_{i14} & r_{i15} \\ r_{i21} & r_{i22} & r_{i23} & r_{i24} & r_{i25} \\ r_{i31} & r_{i32} & r_{i33} & r_{i34} & r_{i35} \\ & & \cdots \cdots & & \\ r_{in1} & r_{in2} & r_{in3} & r_{in4} & r_{in5} \end{bmatrix}$$

$= (s_{i1}, s_{i2}, s_{i3}, s_{i4}, s_{i5})$

Where: S_i means the fuzzy vector of U_i; s_{im} is corresponded to the evaluation set v_m ($i = 1, 2, 3$; $m = 1, 2, 3, 4, 5$) that express the intensity of level indicator.

(5) Construct the fuzzy judgment matrix of target indicator:

$$R = \begin{bmatrix} S_{11} & S_{12} & S_{13} & S_{14} & S_{15} \\ S_{21} & S_{22} & S_{23} & S_{24} & S_{25} \\ S_{31} & S_{32} & S_{33} & S_{34} & S_{35} \end{bmatrix}$$

(6) Calculate the result of fuzzy comprehensive evaluation:
The rule of operation is defined as:

$S = W \cdot R$

$$= (w_1, \ w_2, \ w_3) \ \cdot \ \begin{bmatrix} S_{11} & S_{12} & S_{13} & S_{14} & S_{15} \\ S_{21} & S_{22} & S_{23} & S_{24} & S_{25} \\ S_{31} & S_{32} & S_{33} & S_{34} & S_{35} \end{bmatrix}$$

$$= (s_1, \ s_2, \ s_3, \ s_4, \ s_5)$$

Where: S means the result of fuzzy comprehensive evaluation; sm is corresponded to the evaluation set vm (i=1, 2, 3; m=1, 2, 3, 4, 5) that express the intensity of credibility of website. According to the biggest grade of membership principle, if s1 is the biggest, then the credibility of website is very high; if s5 is the biggest, then the credibility of website is very low.

5   Case study of the evaluation of credibility of an enterprise's website

We have conducted a customer questionnaire survey on the credibility of a gift company website located in Wuhan. First, we used AHP to calculate the weights of level indicators and second-level indicators. Then we designed the specific questionnaire according to the evaluation indicator framework of credibility of enterprise's website, demanding every participant assess each indicator with the five grades "very high, high, normal, low, very low". Considered the main consumers of gift company are young group, the questionnaire survey object is targeted at 16-35 year-old person. We have distributed 100 questionnaires and recycled 91 questionnaires, 86 of which were valid. Through counting, we obtained the following data (Table 2):

Table 2:The Counting Results of the Customer Questionnaire Survey

Level indicator	weight	Second-level indicator	weight	Evaluation grade (V) and grade of membership (rij)				
U_i	W_i	U_{ij}	W_{ij}	Very high	High	Normal	Low	Very low
				v1	v2	v3	v4	v5
U1	0.342	U_{11}	0.175	0.106	0.168	0.302	0.322	0.102
		U_{12}	0.183	0.092	0.126	0.322	0.276	0.184
		U_{13}	0.215	0.058	0.115	0.259	0.303	0.265
		U_{14}	0.234	0.094	0.132	0.276	0.258	0.240
		U_{15}	0.104	0.102	0.145	0.248	0.275	0.230
		U_{16}	0.089	0.154	0.201	0.238	0.223	0.184
U2	0.315	U_{21}	0.158	0.079	0.184	0.301	0.288	0.148
		U_{22}	0.144	0.183	0.264	0.249	0.237	0.067
		U_{23}	0.137	0.226	0.235	0.207	0.198	0.134
		U_{24}	0.101	0.076	0.103	0.231	0.248	0.342
		U_{25}	0.078	0.184	0.259	0.202	0.233	0.122
		U_{26}	0.133	0.213	0.225	0.256	0.208	0.098
		U_{27}	0.140	0.097	0.168	0.214	0.289	0.232
		U_{28}	0.109	0.146	0.205	0.238	0.269	0.142
U3	0.343	U_{31}	0.147	0.198	0.235	0.240	0.242	0.085
		U_{32}	0.138	0.201	0.204	0.216	0.223	0.156
		U_{33}	0.104	0.178	0.196	0.253	0.248	0.125
		U_{34}	0.142	0.076	0.127	0.232	0.298	0.267
		U_{35}	0.145	0.058	0.104	0.255	0.286	0.297
		U_{36}	0.132	0.188	0.197	0.244	0.248	0.123
		U_{37}	0.084	0.153	0.188	0.235	0.228	0.196
		U_{38}	0.108	0.094	0.127	0.226	0.302	0.237

According to the evaluation method and steps described above, it can be obtained:

$$S_1 = w_{1j} \times R_1$$

$$= (0.175\ 0.183\ 0.215\ 0.234\ 0.10.089)\ \bullet\ \begin{bmatrix} 0.106 & 0.168 & 0.302 & 0.322 & 0.102 \\ 0.092 & 0.126 & 0.322 & 0.276 & 0.184 \\ 0.058 & 0.115 & 0.259 & 0.303 & 0.265 \\ 0.094 & 0.132 & 0.276 & 0.258 & 0.240 \\ 0.102 & 0.145 & 0.248 & 0.275 & 0.230 \\ 0.154 & 0.201 & 0.238 & 0.223 & 0.184 \end{bmatrix}$$

$$= [0.094\ 0.141\ 0.285\ 0.281\ 0.199]$$

Similarly: $S_2 = [0.150\ 0.206\ 0.241\ 0.247\ 0.156]$
$S_3 = [0.142\ 0.172\ 0.238\ 0.260\ 0.188]$

Namely: $\mathbf{R} = \begin{bmatrix} 0.094 & 0.141 & 0.285 & 0.281 & 0.199 \\ 0.150 & 0.206 & 0.241 & 0.247 & 0.156 \\ 0.142 & 0.172 & 0.238 & 0.260 & 0.188 \end{bmatrix}$

Then:

$$S = W \bullet R$$
$$= (w_1,\ w_2,\ w_3)\ \bullet\ R$$

$$= (0.342\ 0.315\ 0.343)\ \bullet\ \begin{bmatrix} 0.094 & 0.141 & 0.285 & 0.281 & 0.199 \\ 0.150 & 0.206 & 0.241 & 0.247 & 0.156 \\ 0.142 & 0.172 & 0.238 & 0.260 & 0.188 \end{bmatrix}$$

$$= (0.128\ 0.172\ 0.255\ 0.263\ 0.182)$$

From the result, it indicates that the grade of membership of the credibility of the gift website on the evaluation set V={v1, v2, v3, v4, v5} respectively is 0.128、0.172、0.255、0.263 and 0.182. According to the biggest grade of membership principle, the v4 is used to evaluate the credibility that the credibility of the gift website is low and the customers do not trust the gift website too much.

6 Conclusions

As far as enterprise is concerned, the credibility of its website reflects the market competitive ability of the enterprise. As far as customer is concerned, the credibility of enterprise's website becomes the basis for his/her online business activity. Therefore, enterprises should strengthen the credibility of their website to win customers with high credibility.

The evaluation of credibility of website based on customer perspective may result in deviation sometimes. Firstly, there is noticeable difference between ordinary customer's evaluation and expert's evaluation. Sliced Bread Design and Comsumer WebWatch conducted a study of how industry experts rate credibility of the very same sites. The results showed that experts were far less concerned about visual appeal and more about the quality of a site's information[14]. Website credibility specialist B.J. Fogg and the Stanford Persuasive Technology Lab conducted a survey on How people evaluate a web site's credibility. 100 sites in 10 content categories were studied and a total of 2,684 people completed the survey. When asked to comment on site's credibility, the top 2 issues addressed by the survey participants were: Design Look (46.1%) and Information Design/Structure (28.5%)[15]. Secondly, questionnaire survey has the inherent shortcomings. The main abuse of a questionnaire survey is that it is possible for people to cheat. Meanwhile, the results of a questionnaire survey only reflect the "image" of a website in the eyes of customer in a certain extent, because the level of credibility of the questionnaire survey connect with various factors, such as the design of questionnaire, the method of sampling, the quantity of sample, the distribution of sample, the system error, the cost of investigation and so on[16]. So, we only studied the credibility of enterprise's credibility preliminarily. In order to get satisfactory result, further studies are needed.

Acknowledgments

This article is supported by National Natural Science Foundation of China (Item No.70673071).

References

1. 2006-2007 Annual Research Report of World E-commerce Development [DB/OL].data.chinabyte.com/494/3051994.shtml

2. "2007 Chinese Internet Marketplaces Annual Meeting" Convened Successfully in Beijing [DB/OL]. tech.sina.com.cn/i/2007-01-25/14461353756.shtml,2007-03-17

3. *The 19th China Internet Network Development Counting Report* [DB/OL].www.cnnic.cn,2007-03-17

4. C Liu, Arnett K. P. *Exploring the Factors Associated with Website Success in the Context of Electronic Commerce*[J].*Information & Management*, 2000(38): 23-33

5. Digital Window Shopping Report [OB/OL]. www.scanalert.com/pdf/DigitalWindowShoppingReport_ScanAlert_May2005.pdf,2007-03-17

6. http://www.guuui.com/browse.php?cid=155,2007-03-17

7. *Billions of "phishing" e-mails sent monthly*[DB/OL]. www.ladlass.com/ice/archives/cat_phishing_identity_theft.html,2007-03-17

8. Gartner Survey Shows Frequent Data Security Lapses and Increased Cyber Attacks Damage Consumer Trust in Online Commerce[DB/OL].
www.gartner.com/press_releases/asset_129754_11.html,2007-03-17

9. The pass of evaluation of B2B websites are less than 15% in the homeland[DB/OL].
www.b2b100.cn/strategy/2005122501.htm, 2007-03-17

10. The product quality and after-sale service had became the two great "soft rib" of online shopping [DB/OL].info.it.hc360.com/2006/02/230907130909.shtml, 2007-03-17

11. Yesong Huang. The credibility of online shopping is low, and 70% cyber acquaintances don't trust in online
shopping[DB/OL].www.pcworld.com.cn/news/1/2006/0810/133507.shtml,2007-03-17

12. What makes web sites credible? New study by Stanford University and Makovsky & Company offers some answers [DB/OL].
www.prnewswire.co.uk/cgi/news/release?id=87005,2007-03-17

13. LEAP OF FAITH: USING THE INTERNET DESPITE THE DANGERS [DB/OL].
www.consumerwebwatch.org/pdfs/princeton.pdf,2007-03-17

14. How experts evaluate web sites' credibility [DB/OL].
www.guuui.com/browse.php?cid=155,2007-03-17

15. How people evaluate a web site's credibility
[DB/OL].www.guuui.com/browse.php?cid=155,2007-03-17

16. Weijun Wang. Analysis and Comment on Study and Application of EC Websites Evaluation [J].*Information science*, 2003(6):639-642

A Dynamic Pricing Method in E-Commerce Based on PSO-trained Neural Network

Liang Peng and Haiyun Liu
School of economics, Huazhong University of Science and Technology,
Wuhan 430074

Abstract. Recently, dynamic pricing has been a common competitive maneuver in e-commerce. In many industries, firms adjust the product price dynamically by the current product inventory and the future demand distribution. In this paper, we used particle swarm optimization (PSO) algorithm to train neural networks, then introduced the PSO-trained neural network into e-commerce and presented a new dynamic pricing method based on PSO-trained neural networks. In the method, from production function principles we obtained the least variable cost, and by making the error of mean square between the actual outputs and expectation outputs minimal we got the optimal dynamic price of products. The PSO-trained neural network can simplify the rapid change of prices and can successfully set the optimal dynamic prices in e-commerce.

1 Introduction

The advancement of internet technology has enabled the establishment of electronic commerce which has made communication between buyers and sellers easy. This has resulted in the establishment of electronic price negotiation. Thus in recent years, the problem of dynamic pricing has drawn much attention. Dynamic pricing is a business strategy that adjusts the product price in a timely fashion in order to allocate the right service to the right customer at the right time. The rationale of dynamic pricing can be understood with many examples in e-commerce, such as airline tickets, new designer suits, and other marketing products associated with particular holidays etc. In all of these cases, the firm can improve its revenues by dynamically adjusting the price of the product rather than adopting a fixed price throughout the product's market life [1].

Dynamic pricing takes advantages to both buyers and sellers, some researchers have studied dynamic pricing methods [2-6]. Many ways to dynamic pricing are to change the price continuously over time by reacting to any shifts in demand

Please use the following format when citing this chapter:

Peng, L., Liu, H., 2007, in IFIP International Federation for Information Processing, Volume 251, Integration and Innovation Orient to E-Society Volume1, Wang, W. (Eds), (Boston: Springer), pp. 323-329.

characteristics. However, such a practice is often either not feasible or too costly. This paper proposed a simple and feasible dynamic pricing method which can be used for on-line price setting. The method is based on the demand sensitive model where price changes depend on the quantity demanded and the variable cost changes with the quantity of product to be sold. In e-commerce, the information is incomplete. Considering neural networks have the ability to work with incomplete data and can be applied successfully in learning, predicting, and optimization functions [7-9], we introduced neural networks into dynamic pricing in e-commerce. Because the particle swarm optimization (PSO) has the ability of evolutionary learning [10], we used the PSO algorithm to train neural networks. In this method, the optimal dynamic price was set by the PSO-trained neural network. The process of dynamic pricing is the process that the PSO-trained neural network makes the cost function minimal.

The rest of this paper is organized as follows. Firstly we introduce the PSO algorithm and neural networks simply, and then build the PSO-trained neural network in section 2. In section 3, we presented the dynamic pricing method by using the PSO-trained neural network. The paper ends with conclusions in section 4.

2   The PSO-trained neural network

2.1   Preliminaries of neural networks

Generally a neural network often includes the following:
1.   The number of layers in neural network.
2.   The number of neural units in every layer.
3.   The activation functions between layers.

By Kosmogorov Theory, under the condition of reasonable topology and right weights, a standard 3-layer neural network can approximate any continuous functions. Fig. 1 is the general topology of a neural network

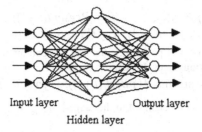

Input layer   Output layer

Hidden layer

Figure. 1. The topology of a 3-layer neural network.

The normal hidden-units were logistic units with outputs in the range between 0 and 1. The input units and context units did not do any processing-they simply passed on their input. The output unit was a linear unit. Generally, sigmoid activation function was adopted in hidden layer. The sigmoid activation function is the following:

$$f(x) = \frac{1}{1 + e^{-x}}$$

Generally, the network was trained using the error back-propagation algorithm with learning rate. The training process is to update the connection weighs and makes the network enhance learning. In this paper we used particle swarm optimization algorithm to train the neural network. After training has been completed, the neural network can record the corresponding output according to the inputs.

2.2   Particle swarm optimization (PSO)

The PSO technique was introduced by Kennedy and Eberhart. Inspired by the flocking behavior of birds, PSO has been applied successfully to function optimization, game learning, data clustering, and image analysis.

The PSO's operation is as follows. Each particle represents a possible solution to the optimization task. During each iteration each particle accelerates in the direction of its own personal best solution found so far, as well as in the direction of the global best position discovered so far by any of the particles in the swarm.

Let $\mathrm{Pr}\,esent$ denote the current position in the search space, V is the current velocity. During each iteration, each particle in the swarm is updated using (1) and (2).

$$V(t+1) = \omega * V(t) + c_1 * rand * (pBest(t) - \mathrm{Pr}\,esent(t))$$
$$+ c_2 * rand * (gBest(t) - \mathrm{Pr}\,esent(t)) \tag{1}$$

$$\mathrm{Pr}\,esent(t+1) = \mathrm{Pr}\,esent(t) + V(t+1) \tag{2}$$

where, $rand \sim U(0,1)$ is the elements from uniform random sequence in the range $(0,1)$, c_1 and c_2 is the acceleration coefficients, usually $c_1 = c_2 = 2$. ω is the weight coefficient, and $0.1 \le \omega \le 0.9$. $pBest$, the personal best position of each particle, is updated by

$$pBest(t+1) = \begin{cases} pBest(t), & if \; f(\mathrm{Pr}\,esent(t+1)) \leq f(pBest(t)) \\ \mathrm{Pr}\,esent(t+1), & if \; f(\mathrm{Pr}\,esent(t+1)) > f(pBest(t)) \end{cases} \quad (3)$$

and $gBest$, the global best position, is the best position among all particles in the swarm during all previous steps. It means

$$gBest(t+1) = \arg\max_{i} f(pBest_i(t+1)), \quad for \; any \; particle \; i \quad (4)$$

The value of V can be clamped to the range $[-V_{max}, V_{max}]$ to ensure particles in the search space.

In this paper, the variable ω is the inertia weight, this means that the value of ω is typically setup to vary linearly from maximum to minimum during the course of iterations, and ω is formulated as follows.

$$\omega = \omega_{max} - iter \cdot \frac{\omega_{max} - \omega_{min}}{iter_{max}} \quad (5)$$

where, $iter_{max}$ is the times of maximum iteration, $iter$ is the times of current iteration.

2.3   The process of training

Using PSO algorithm to train neural networks, each particle corresponds to the complete augmented weight vector that connects the neural network's input-to-hidden and hidden-to-output layers. The error of mean square between the actual outputs and expectation outputs is looked as fitness function, using PSO algorithm to seek the optimal position (or the optimal weight value) and make the error of mean square minimal. The process of training is as follows:

- Step 1: Randomly choose a swarm of particles, the maximal iteration times and the minimal error of mean square, for each particle initialize the position and velocity.
- Step 2: Let $pBest$ be current best position, let also $gBest$ be current best position among all particles.
- Step 3: Judge whether the convergence condition is satisfied, if yes, go to step 6. Otherwise, go to step 4.
- Step 4: For any particles in the swarm:
  - i.   Update position and velocity using (1) and (2).
  - ii.   Update $pBest$ using (3).
  - iii.   Update $gBest$ using (4).
- Step 5: If the convergence condition is satisfied, go to step 6. Otherwise, turn to step 4.
- Step 6: Output $gBest$.

3 Dynamic pricing by the PSO-trained neural network

Suppose a firm has to sell more than one product at a time. All products use the same factors of variable cost. The quantity to sell according to demand and pricing decision is made simultaneously. A firm sells different levels of quantities by the demand. To facilitate maximizing profits the firm will try to use a combination of inputs that will minimize its total cost of a given level of quantity demanded. The firm is employing methods dynamically, adjusting price over time based on quantity demanded. By applying principles of production function, we can use the PSO-trained neural network to get a selling price at the least total cost. From production function principles:

$$Q = f(x) \tag{6}$$

where, Q is the vector of products $q_1, q_2, \cdots, q_n$, X is the vector of input variable factors $x_1, x_2, \cdots, x_m$.

All products use the same type of variable factors, and the total number of variable factors is the same. The relationship between the quantity demanded and the output quantity of the network is as follows:

$$q_n \geq q_n^t \tag{7}$$

where q_n^t is a network output quantity at time t, while q_n is a desired output quantity (quantity demanded). The variable cost function of output quantity q_n is:

$$c_v(q_n) = f(w_m, x_m) \tag{8}$$

where w_m is a constant input unit price of x_m and the total cost $C_T(q_n)$ is:

$$C_T(q_n) = c_v(q_n) + c_F \tag{9}$$

where c_F is a fixed cost.

The following is the process of dynamic pricing by PSO-trained neural network.

➤ Step 1: Input w_m, q_n as the units of input layer in the neural network.
➤ Step 2: According to $q_n^t = f(x_n)$, compute q_n^t by using the neural network.
➤ Step 3: If $q_n \geq q_n^t$, go to step 4, else turn to step 2.
➤ Step 4: Obtain the total cost $C_T(q_n)$ by equation $C_T(q_n) = c_v(q_n) + c_F$.
➤ Step 5: Output the selling price P from $P = C_T'(q_n)$.

At the beginning of this method the difference between q_n^t and q_n is big and negative, it measures the error that the network makes. The error used to alter the input variable factors x_m in order that the network's response to the same input price w_m is better the next time around. At each alteration the difference will continue to decrease up to the point when it finds the least variable cost $c_v(q_n)$ for the quantity demanded q_n. The variable cost $c_v(q_n)$ is added to fixed cost c_F to give the total cost $C_T(q_n)$. The marginal cost $C_T'(q_n)$ is the derivative of total production cost function with respect to the level of outputs. From Marginal Decision Rule the selling price is set at the point of production when marginal cost equals marginal revenue. At this point the production cost is the minimum. Setting selling price p equal to marginal cost $C_T'(q_n)$ means that this is the minimum price the seller can sell the product, selling below this price leads to loss, and selling above this price maximizes profits. Profits are the difference between total revenues and total cost, where total revenues are the product of price and the quantity demanded.

The firm will maximize profits at the level of outputs where the slope of the profits curve is zero. Since profits are revenues less cost, the slope of the profits curve, marginal profits, is equal to marginal revenue less marginal cost. Therefore, when the firm maximizes profits where the slope of the profit curve is zero, marginal revenue will be equal to marginal cost. The profits maximizing firm is selling product at its most efficient (lowest unit cost) of quantity demanded where marginal revenue equal to marginal cost. At that level the firm will sell the product at the price which is equal to the marginal cost, which will maximize the total revenues, in other words maximizing the total profits function. For any demanded quantity q_n, $c_v(q_n)$ must be the least variable cost function. The continuous changes in demand quantity permit the continuous input substitution within the input bundle. The changes in demand quantity q_n, change the input bundle and consequently change the least cost, and consequently change the selling price p.

4 Conclusion and future work

Dynamic pricing as a changing price in a marketplace is becoming characteristic of electronic commerce. This paper presented a novel dynamic pricing method based on PSO-trained neural network. According to production function principles, the PSO-trained neural network can simplify the calculations of the least variable cost function that is the main factor in dynamic pricing. The method can set the optimal dynamic price and can be used in e-commerce with different quantities and different levels of demand at one time. In the future work, we will give numerical examples and simulation experiments.

Acknowledgement

We would like to thank the Chinese National "985" Research Project ——"Science & Technology Development and Human Culture Sprit Innovation".

References

1. S. Jagannathan, J. Nayak, K. Almeroth et al, On Pricing Algorithms for Hatched Content Delivery Systems, *Electronic Commerce Research and Applications*, 1, 264-280 (2002).
2. R. Chatwin, Optimal Dynamic Pricing of Perishable Products with Stochastic Demand and a Finite Set of Prices, *European Journal of Operational Research*, 125,149-174 (2000).
3. J. Kephart and J. Hanson, A. Greenwald. Dynamic Pricing by Software Agents, *Computer Networks*, 32,731-752 (2000).
4. K. Lin, Dynamic Pricing with Real-time Demand Learning, *European Journal of Operational Research*, 174,522-538 (2006).
5. X. J. Wang, Y. L. Chen and W. Q. Zhu, The Pricing Strategies for Agents in Real E-Commerce, WINE 2005, LNCS 3828,887-894(2005).
6. S. Netessine, Dynamic Pricing of Inventory/Capacity with Infrequent Price Changes, *European Journal of Operational Research*, 174,553-580 (2006).

7. D. Arditi, F. E. Oksay and O. B. Tokdemir, Predicting the Outcome of Construction Litigation Using Neural Network, *Computer Aided Civil and Infrastructure Engineering* ,13,75-81 (1998).
8. L.C. Jiao, *Neural Network System Theory* ,Xidian University Press, Xi an(1996).
9. S.A. Cong, *Face the MATLAB toolbox nerve network theory and the application* , University of Science and Technology of China Press, Heifei(1998).
10. J. Kennedy and R. C. Eberhart, Particle Swarm Optimization, *Proc IEEE international conference on Neural Networks* ,4,1942 -1948(1995).

Convergence Management System of Mobile Data Services

Ling Jiang[1,2], Jixin Wang[1]

1 Department of Information Technology, Huazhong Normal University,
Wuhan, China 430079
2 Engineering Research Center of Education Information Technology,
Huazhong Normal University, Wuhan, China 430079
ljiangcn@hotmail.com   wjxin@mail.ccnu.edu.cn

Abstract. To meet the mobile communication development, the necessary choice for mobile operators is to build up a convergence management system for the value-added services, which should support multiple value-added services openly. This paper introduced a new convergent management system for different mobile data services, which was developed by the author. And it focused on the development of convergent management system of mobile data services. It discussed the architecture of convergent management system and described three main management methods of typical data services.

1 Introduction

In recent years, the user number and market capacity of mobile value-added service grew rapidly, and it became the focus of all circles and many companies tried to enter to this field. In 2004, the mobile data value-added service market capacity of China was 30.8 billion yuan (RMB) with 5.3 billion (RMB) for SP market and the user number has accessed 235 million. Furthermore, after several years of development, there has been a distinctive advance in the operation idea and management mode for operators. The business mode and operation management of value-added service is also growing into maturity [1]. Nowadays the new generation mobile communication technologies such as 2.5 G (CDMA 1X, GPRS and EDGE), 3G (UMTS, W-CDMA), bring new challenges to mobile operators and SP/CPs (Service Provider/Content Provider)[2], and also bring new profitability and complex cooperation relationships. Mobile operators usually face many new challenges when introducing a new technology or entering into an uncertain service market. It, therefore, will bring great influence to service development to establish a convergence value-added service management system. At present, mobile operators also strengthen research on mobile data value-added service management platform, and they need a reliable and suitable solution.

Please use the following format when citing this chapter:

Jiang, L., Wang, J., 2007, in IFIP International Federation for Information Processing, Volume 251, Integration and Innovation Orient to E-Society Volume1, Wang, W. (Eds), (Boston: Springer), pp. 330-336.

2. Analysis of mobile data services

The development of mobile value-added service mainly depends on the carrying capacity of data channel in mobile communication networks. With main 2.5G mobile communication technologies going into commercial application, the data carrying capacity of mobile communication networks has distinct improvement. At the same time, mobile terminal manufacturers also release many kinds of new mobile phones which could support WAP, MMS, JAVA and LBS services [3]. All these cause the prosperity of mobile data value-added service. In China, after 2.5G communication network construction, mobile data value-added service started up across-the-board, increased rapidly and gained a great success. For example, with the general brand "Yidongmengwang", China Mobile puts forward MMS, WAP, STK, JAVA and other data value-added services while China Unicom comes out with MMS, SMS, STK, BREW/JAVA, WAP services under the general brand "Liantongwuxian" [4]. In all, mobile data value-added service type can be concluded as follow [5,6].

- SMS, short message service, store-forward mode.
- MMS, multimedia message service.
- Browsing service, browsing WAP websites or Internet websites.
- Download service, based on J2ME or BREW.
- LBS, Location service, GIS etc.

3. Architecture design of mobile data services management system

With rapid development of value-added service, mobile operators have an imminent management requirement for mobile data value-added service [1]. Traditionally, mobile operators usually adopt "one platform, one service" scheme where the appearing of a new service will require corresponding new value-added service platform in mobile network for third-party and new improved functions for mobile phones [4]. In fact, the shortcomings of this traditional method become more and more distinctive and then against the fast providing of new services in answer to market requirements for mobile operators. Illuminated by the IN (Intelligent Network) voice value-added service solution of one intelligent network able to support multiple services, it comes out as a problem for mobile operators how to build a mobile data value-added service convergence management platform at present [7].

Routed by this thought, the mobile data value-added service convergence management platform should provide integrated management functions and some common service support functions to all kinds of value-added services. The management functions include user management, CP and service management etc, and the common service support functions include service issuance, customization, service access control, flow control and billing etc [5]. To accomplish the above functions, a function framework of mobile data value-added service convergence management platform can be abstracted with detailed implementations shown in Figure 1.

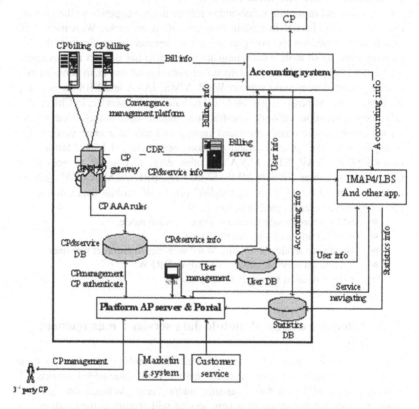

Figure. 1. Framework of mobile data service management system

It can be seen that the main function modules of mobile data value-added service convergence management platform include user management, platform portal management, CP and service management, CP gateway function, service billing, statistics and analysis, QoS and security management, PUSH service, operator management, flow control etc [3].

4. System management flow of typical data services

To describe detailed management functions, several typical mobile data value-added service management flows will be discussed as below [8].

4.1 Registration flow of value-added services

This process is shown in Figure 2.

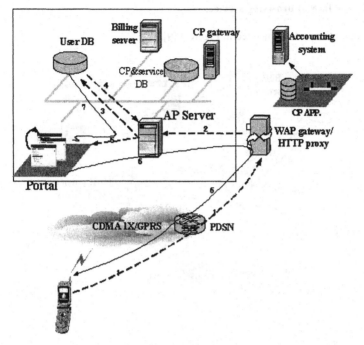

Figure. 2. User registration flow

Step 1 User accesses Internet with one-key function, and sends mapping relationship between user's IP address and IMSI to WAP gateway through the PDSN AAA server. In this way user sends his service request to the platform portal through WAP gateway (WAP 1.2 or WAP 2.0 HTTP PROXY, same hereinafter).

Step 2 Once receiving user request message, the WAP gateway makes corresponding protocol conversion (WAP to HTTP or W-TCP to TCP etc.), gets the mapping relationship between the host calling number and user IP address, and sends the request to the platform application server.

Step 3–Step 4 The platform application server (AP server) authenticates user through the user database, and returns some information from the user database as below.

- the user registers or not;
- if the user registers, what is his User Profile?

Step 5 If the user does not register, the platform application server will "inform" the portal.

Step 6 The platform portal will display the login interface. User inputs his user name and password, such as his mobile phone number, and sends his request to platform portal through WAP gateway.

Step 7 The platform portal updates the user information database through the platform application server and the user has registered successfully. He has the rights to enjoy the value-added services provided by operator's value-added service platform.

4.2 Usage flow of browsing services

This operation is demonstrated in Figure 3 [9].

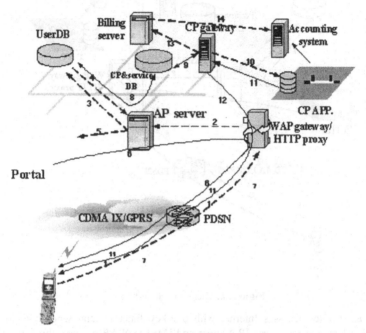

Figure. 3. Usage flow of browsing services

Step 1 User accesses Internet with one-key function, and sends mapping relationship between user's IP address and IMSI to the WAP gateway through the PDSN AAA server. In this way user sends his service request to the platform portal through the WAP gateway.

Step 2 Once receiving user request message, the WAP gateway makes corresponding protocols conversion, gets the mapping relationship between the host calling number and user IP address, and sends the request to the platform application server.

Step 3-Step 4 The platform application server authenticates user through the user database, and returns user individuated information from the user database.

Step 5 The platform application server sends user individuated information to the platform portal.

Step 6 According to user information, the platform portal makes a service list or a user individuated homepage and returns it to user.

Step 7 User selects a certain CP's service, and sends request to the CP gateway through the WAP gateway.

Step 8 As user can edit his own service list through the mobile phone, the CP gateway needs to inquire about user's service subscription information through the platform application server and returns the results.

Step 9 The CP gateway authenticates CPs through the CP and service database and discerns the legal CPs and illegal CPs. The CP gateway can filter the illegal CPs.

Step 10-Step 11-Step 12 The CP application makes response to user request and user enjoys his browsing service through the mobile phone.

Step 13 The CP gateway sends billing event to billing server.

Step 14 The billing server sends user bill to the accounting system.

4.3 Usage flow of JAVA download services

JAVA download services can be classified into three types [2,5,6,10].

- HTTP download flow. In this download mode, user uses the JAVA download client embedded in the mobile phone and accesses the download servers through HTTP protocol without the convergence management platform.
- WAP download flow. In this download mode, user uses the WAP browser embedded in the mobile phone and accesses the portal of the JAVA download services systems through the WAP gateway.
- WAP download flow through the convergence management system. User uses the WAP browser embedded in the mobile phone and accesses the platform portal of convergence management system. User can make selective download services through the CP gateway. It can be shown in Figure 4.

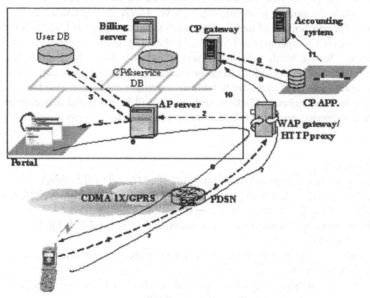

Fig. 4. Usage flow of JAVA download services

Step 1 User accesses Internet with one-key function, and sends services request to the platform portal through the WAP gateway.

Step 2 Once receiving user request message, the WAP gateway makes corresponding protocols conversion, gets the mapping relationship between the host calling number and user IP address, and sends the request to the platform application server.

Step 3-Step 4 The platform application server authenticates user through the user database, and returns user individuated information from the user database.

Step 5 The platform application server sends user individuated information to the platform portal.

Step 6 According to user information, the platform portal makes a service list or a user individuated homepage and returns it to user.

Step 7 User selects OTA to download, and sends the request to the CP gateway through the WAP gateway.

Step 8 The CP gateway sends user information and download request to the download server.

Step 9 The download server makes download content list and user select one to download.

Step 10 The download server sends the downloaded content to user (through the WAP gateway if WAP protocol used). User returns acknowledgement information to the download server.

Step 11 The service system sends user bill to the accounting system.

5. Conclusion

After several years of development, 2G value added service with SMS enters into a stable developing procedure while WAP, JAVA and BREW service has become the new hotspot of mobile data value-added service [8,10], and it is the focus of investors, operators and SP/CPs. Furthermore, mobile operators enforce the control for the whole value-added service industry chain, changing original open cooperation mode and pressing the neatening for the irregular behavior of SP. Consequently, it is necessary to build up the mobile data value-added service convergence management platform [10], which will be beneficial to accelerate the steady development of mobile data value-added service industry chain.

References

1. "Network functional model for IMT-2000[S]", *ITU-T*, Q.1711 (1999).
2. S. B. Guthery, M. J. Cronin, "Mobile application development with SMS and the SIM toolkit[M]", *McGraw-Hill Companies*, 180-182 (2002).
3. "Parameters and mechanisms for charging[S]", *ETSI*, (ETSI TR 101 734 V1.1.1999).
4. "Looking back and expectation of China mobile value-added services", *CNII*, http://www.cnii.com.cn
5. C. P. Hou, M. Song and T.Cai, "Official wireless application protocol[M]", *WAP Forum*, China Machine Press, Beijing (2000).
6. W. Z. Li, "Summarization of mobile data value-added services" . http://www.tele.hc360.com.
7. Yun. Ye, "Opportunities and challenges of 3G data value-added services" http://www.ptsn.net.cn.
8. G. A. Brosnan, "The future of mobile data services Wireless and Optical Communications". *Annual WOCC* 14 ,86(2005)
9. S. Martin, "An Expert Model on Barriers to Implement Mobile Data Services" , *ICMB '06*, .33 – 33(2006).
10. Q. Song and H. Y. Shu, "Framework of Mobile Data Service and A Download Service Platform Based On OTA", *Data Communications* (2004).

Research and application of EJBCA based on J2EE

Liyi Zhang[1], Qihua Liu[2] and Min Xu[3]

1 Center for Studies of Information Resources, Wuhan University,
430072, Wuhan, P.R.China
lyzhang@whu.edu.cn
2 Center for Studies of Information Resources, WuhanUniversity,
430072,Wuhan, P.R.China
qh_liu@163.com
3 Center for Studies of Information Resources, Wuhan University,
430072,Wuhan, P.R.China
xu19870107@yahoo.com.cn

Abstract. This article carries on the exhaustive analysis and the research of the opened source system EJBCA based on the J2EE, furthermore conducts the distribution and deployment in accordance with the required software on the Linux platform, on this basis, and builds a specific application example of EJBCA. In the end, the authors have carried on the prospect about expansion and practical application capacity of EJBCA system, hope to have the important significance of model to the independent own research and development of present domestic PKI technology and product.

1 Introduction

To ensure the confidentiality, authenticity, integrity and non-repudiation of online transmission of digital information, so that to ensure its security on the network transmission, in addition to use a stronger encryption algorithm in telecommunication transmission and other measures, it's necessary to establish a trust and verification mechanism. In other words, the parties who participate in e-commerce and e-government must have a logo that can be verified, which is the digital certificate.

Digital certificates are a proof of identity of some entities merchant/ enterprise, gateway/bank etc) in the on-line communication and the commercial transaction activity [1].It is unique, and takes together the public key of entities with the entities itself. To achieve this purpose, digital certificates must comply with the international standard of x.509 and have a reliable source. This means that we must have an authority, which is trusted by every entity in internet, responsible for the distribution and management of digital certificates, and

Please use the following format when citing this chapter:

Zhang, L., Liu, Q., Xu, M., 2007, in IFIP International Federation for Information Processing, Volume 251, Integration and Innovation Orient to E-Society Volume1, Wang, W. (Eds), (Boston: Springer), pp. 337-345.

ensures the security of online information, it is certificate authority. Its existence is the basis for the existence of e-commerce and e-government.

Now, well-known CA software are researched and developed by enterprises of foreign countries. To obtain a legal certificate from this authority, the first required is to pay the high costs of certification, the second, we don't master core technologies about the CA software, so it is inconvenience to implement the high-encrypted application, but the amount of the independent own research and development of present domestic CA software is few, and that this software all depend on the operating system platform, which using J2EE is minimal. So, it is the best way for some important government authorities、 enterprises and education department to build their own certificate authority. The OSFS of Linux and open-source project based on java provide an unprecedented opportunity for our own research on CA software. This article carries on the exhaustive analysis and the research of the famous opened source system EJBCA based on the internet of sourceforge.net, furthermore conducts the distribution and deployment in accordance with the required software on the Linux platform, on this basis, and builds a specific application of EJBCA. In the end, the authors have carried on the prospect about expansion and practical application capacity of EJBCA system, hope to have the important significance of model to the independent own research and development of present domestic PKI technology and product.

2   The basic framework of EJBCA

EJBCA is an enterprise class Certificate Authority using J2EE technology. EJBCA builds on the J2EE platform to create a robust, high performance, platform independent, flexible, and component based CA to be used standalone or integrated in any J2EE app [2].

J2EE——Java 2 Enterprise Edition, is an enterprise application solutions based on the java 2 platform.J2EE is not a product, but a range of criteria. Not only does it have all functions of the J2SE platform, but also provides the full support of EJB, Servlet, JSP,XML technology and etc, Its ultimate goal is to become an architecture of supporting for the enterprise-level application and development, simplify a series of complicated problems about the development、 deployment and management of enterprise solutions.

J2EE uses multi-tier distributed application model. This model is divided into several functional components, which are distributed with different host machines according to different layers where they are located in. These layers include client layer、 WEB tier、 business tier and data tier [3]. Business tier is also named EJB tier in EJBCA, which contains two major components——RA component and CA component, system framework of EJBCA is shown in Fig.1.

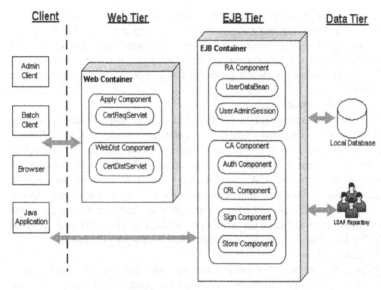

Fig. 1. System framework of EJBCA

2.1   The main components of EJBCA

Fig.1 shows that EJBCA system is mostly composed of Web component, RA component, CA component, LDAP server and database server [4].

(1) Web Component

It is mainly faced to ordinary users, and used to provide some request and services such as CertReqServlet, CertDistServlet, CertBroServlet and etc between the application server (RA component and CA component) and client browser. At the first, users receive certificates of Web component through application server. In the second, all communications between users and Web components, including some information of users and public key of browser, are encryption transmitted through encryption key of Web component. So, it is very safe to apply and transmit certificates, the process is shown in Fig. 2.

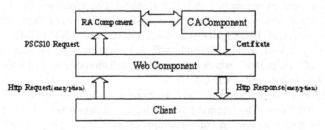

Fig. 2. The process of information transmission in EJBCA

(2) RA Component

It is also named registered authority, mostly provides some functions of user registration and auditing. RA component plays a bridging role in EJBCA. On the one hand, it transmits services of Web component's CertReqServlet and CertDistServlet to CA component; on the other hand, it transmits services of CRL and certificates which are given by CA component to LDAP and Web component.

(3) CA Component

It is the core component in EJBCA, can provide some functions such as CertDistServlet, certificate signature, certificate storage, CRL, SubCA foundation and etc. First, CA components have their own private key and public key, and then transmit certificates which are given by CA to RA component through Web component. CA also has responsibility to generate some digital certificates for all levels of administrations, such as Web components, subCA and RA. In EJBCA, types of certificate are optional. There are three types in the initialization time, ENDUSER (FIXED), ROOTCA (FIXED) and SUBCA (FIXED). In addition, users also can define their own types of certificates.

(4) LDAP Server

It provides service of catalog browsing, and charges for adding users' information and digital certificates which are transmitted by RA to servers. So, other users can receive their digital certificates through visiting LDAP server. In EJBCA, configurations of LDAP serve are optional; we can match certificates and their list to relevant LDAP servers through amending configuration files of LDAP [5].

(5) Database Server

It is a very important component in EJBCA, used to storage and manage users' information, digital certificates, diary document, statistical information and etc.

2.2   The construction of EJBCA

(1) Software installation and configuration environment variable

Download and install the relevant software Jdk 1.4.2, JBoss4.0.1 SP1, ejbca3.0.7, jce_policy-1_4_2 and apache-ant-1.6.3. System database can choose from among SqlServer, Mysql, Oracle, and etc, we use Mysql in this article. It is necessary to configure environment variables after configuring relevant software. There are several environmental variables which must be allocated: Jdk, Ant and Jboss. First, use sentences of "export" to assignment categories of Jboss, Jdk and Ant to variables of JBOSS_HOME, JAVA_HOME and ANT_HOME in the operation system of .Linux. Second, add these sentences to the tail of the document of "/etc/profile", which locate in the installation directory of EJBCA.

(2) The deployment of EJBCA

Implement the command of "ant" to compile EJBCA source code in the directory of EJBCA. The internal business logic and deployment descriptor of CA will be packaged into an enterprise application file of "ejbca-ca.ear" after running the command of "#ant deploy". Copy this file to the deployment directory of Jboss. So far, the entire CA system of EJBCA has been deployed to server of Jboss. Use sentences of "CREATE" to grant the database of Mysql. But, it is necessary to establish an own certificate authority before running the EJBCA, this is root CA. And, it must be established on the J2EE sever. First, start the server of Jboss. Second, implement the command of "#install.sh" in the directory of "EJBCA". In the installation process, CA will create three types of certificates: client administration certificate, sever certificate and certificate which is signed by root CA. Client administration certificate and server certificate locate in the directory of "P12", which is subdirectory of EJBCA directory, but the certificate of root CA locate in the letter. On the one hand, the certificate of root CA is automatically imported into the private key file of "carcerts" which locate in the Jdk security directory of "JAVA_HOME\lib\security", "JAVA_HOME" is installation directory of Jdk. On the other hand, the server certificate is imported into directory of "JBOSS_HOME\bin"; "JBOSS_HOME" is installation of Jboss. Ii is necessary for EJBCA to manage CA in SSL layer, so client needs to import the client certificate of "P12/superadmin.P12" into browsers, and then can manage CA through browsers.

(3) The configuration of Two-way SSL

The SSL protocol is a standard protocol to ensure the secure communication between the Web browser and Web server, which is developed by Netscape. It is located in the transport layer. It is seen as a standard security measure of server and web browser. The methods of configuration of EJBCA are as follows:

First, open the browser; input the address of http://localhost:8443/ejbca/adminweb; obtain the certificate of root CA. Second, add users of client and server in home page; designate the method of building private key. Third, input user names and password of client and server preserve the file of ".req" and install these certificates through the installation guide. A point worth noting is that we must award certificates to every client who can visit server and server through using root CA in the process of configuration of Two-way SSl.

3   The example of EJBCA application

In this article, authors design a demonstration example of EJBCA application, and use some specific figures of framework to display the building process of a small certificate authority. Through description of the example, authors conduct a detailed analysis of how to use the famous system EJBCA for practical application, and make it productive.

3.1   The introduction of EJBCA application example

The application example of PKI/CA is a small certificate system, which has two root CAs. One is certificate authority of china education (China IC). Its responsibility is to provide certification for a number of entities in the field of education. For example, school can certificate candidates' information in graduate entrance examination. It is not necessary to check manually students' identity. Conversely, students also can see authentication information of schools in order to avoid being taken. Another is certificate authority of Wuhan logistics (WHU ECLAB). Its main objective is to certificate entities of china special transport network, such as vehicles, drives, maintenance units. The basic framework of the application example is shown in Fig.3.

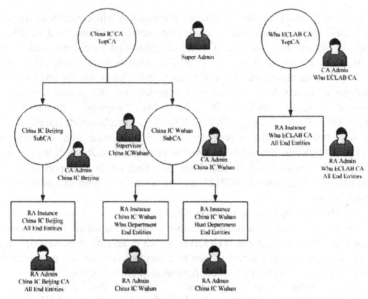

Fig. 3. The basic framework of the application

Note: In this figure, circular used to show examples of CA, rectangular used to show examples of RA

Can be seen from the Fig.3, the application example has the following characteristics:

（1）The certificate authority consists of two separate bodies, each one has a root CA.

（2）Whu ECLAB is a simple PKI, and only has a CA and a RA.

（3）China IC has two branches in Beijing and Wuhan. Therefore, each branch has a subCA; in particular, the branch of Wuhan all has businesses in the two schools of WHU and HUST.

（4）China IC education need three examples of RA to manage.

3.2　The building of EJBCA application example

We will build the system of PKI/CA from the perspective of roles. The system is divided into four roles, and is shown in Fig.4.

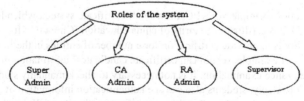

Fig. 4. Roles of the application

（1）Super Admin

He has the authority to manage the entire system. As the role of super admin, he can do some things, such as editing system configuration, managing CA, building CA admin and etc. Detailed below:

①System configuration. Set up the title, slogans and language of the top and tail of pages, the theme and the number of data of each page. Choose the item of "Enable End Entity Profile Limitations" to manage RA, and set up two items of "Enable Key Recovery" and "Issue Hardware Tokens" to "unchecked".

②Manage publisher. The publisher connects some form of certificate storage system, whose certificates will be sent to the entity. A publisher is a LDAP directory or Active directory or publisher connector of definition established. We will build two publishers:

        A、China IC LDAP
           suffix "O=China IC,C=CN"
           rootdn "CN=Manager,O=China IC,C=CN"
        B、WHU Eclab LDAP
           suffix "O=WHU Eclab,C=CN"
           rootdn "CN=Manager, O= WHU Eclab, C=CN"

③Manage CAs. Now we need to build the structure of CA. Can be seen from Fig.4, root CA of China IC will have two subCAs. One is China IC Beijing, another is China IC Wuhan. But WHU Eclab only has a root CA, it is Whu ECLAB CA. We designate that every CA all has a private key of RSA. Its length is 2,048 spaces, and it also can be valid for 10 years.

④Establish CA admin. In the PKI system, we allow the companies to manage their own certificates and RAs. We hope to have a major admin in each place. "China IC Beijing CA Admin" and "China IC Wuhan CA Admin" are administrations of China IC in Beijing and Wuhan. But "Whu Eclab in China" is an administration of Whu ECLAB in china. It is crucial that the administrators should not see each other's data, such as users, log, and etc, especially when two agencies are competitors.

(2) CA Admin

His responsibilities include managing certificate files and terminal entity files, configuring log and establishing RA admin.

(3) RA Admin

He is responsible for establishing/compiling/canceling/deleting terminal entity and seeing existent entities and their historical record. An RA only can manage the terminal entity of their own purview, so each other are transparency, as shown in Fig.5.

Fig. 5. The relation of RAs

(4) Supervisor
His responsibility is seeing entities and visiting logs.

4 Prospect

To conclude this article, the authors also consider the expansion and application capability of EJBCA. EJBCA system can be found through studying that it will have further expansion in the following areas.

(1) The improvements of encryption algorithm

EJBCA is a component –based structure. Users can develop or introduce some secret encryption algorithms to embed in EJBCA. And they also can develop their certificates and this certificates' list in accordance with the agreement of X509.

(2)The expansion of web registration mechanism

Client entities of the system are added by RA admin in the background. In fact, we can examine and certificate information through web registration mechanism when the number of users is very large [6, 7].

(3) Use technology of hardware and fingerprint recognition to certificate entities' identity

Users can use certain hardware (such as a simple encryption card) to communicate with procedures to verify identity. They also can design an identification system based on the characteristics of the fingerprint, and add this system to EJBCA as a component.

(4)The transplantation of EJBCA

EJBCA is developed on the basis of application sever of Jboss. But now a large number of enterprises and organizations all use other servers, such as IBM Websphere, BEA Weblogic and etc. So, the transplantation is a problem worth studying. The authors have utilized BEA Weblogic server to configure EJBCA, and proved its feasibility.

In summary, EJBCA is assembly simple, flexible, easy to manage. It can be applied to the security framework of e-government and e- commerce through transplantation and appropriate allocation. EJBCA is a valuable opened source system, has the important significance of model to the independent own research and development of present domestic PKI technology and product.

References

1. Z.S. Guan, *Public key infrasture and certificate authority*, Publishing House of Electronics Industry, Beijing (2002).

2. Ejbca-design. http://sourceforge.net/project/showfiles.php?group_id=39716.

3. R. Johnson and H.P. Wei , *The guile of J2EE design and development,* Publishing House of Electronics Industry, America (2003).

4. EJBCA: readm.txt.http://ejbca.sourceforge.net/do-cs/frame.htm.

5. Q. Chen and Q.S. Ling, The example of security CA——research of EJBCA, *Computer Engineering and Design* (2005).

6. X. Chen, The design and development of EJBCA, Wuhan:Wuhan University, 2006.

7. H. Zhang, Research on the Security Authentication of Electronic Commerce and the Design and Implementation of the CA Model, *Computer technology* (2006).

8. B.S. Zhou and L. Zhang, Research of EJBCA on WPKI environment, *Computer Engineering and Design* (2005).

9. T.W. Xiao,S.Y. Zhang and Y.P. Zhong, Design and Implementation of PKI/CA-based Middleware System, *Computer Engineering* (2006).

10. J.C. Li and H.L. Liu, Research on Secure Payment Protocols of Electronic Commerce, *Value Engineering* (2006).

11. L.N. Lan and X.Y. Liu, Research on Security Architecture in E-Commerce System, *China Information Security* (2007).

12. Q.H. Shuai, The Analysis of safe Certificate in E-Commerce, *Net Security Technologies and Application* (2007).

13. PKI Tutorial. http://www.cs.auckland.ac.nz/pgut001/pubs/pkitutorial.pdf.

14.   EJBCA-Architecture. http://sourceforge.net/project/showfiles.php?group_id=3971.

15.   Enterprise   Text   Message   Platform.   http://www.jrsoft. com.cn/Product/Aviation/sm s. asp.[2007-03-20].

An Efficient Mode Selection Algorithm for H.264

Lu Lu[1], Wenhan Wu[2], and Zhou Wei[3]

1 South China University of Technology, Institute of Computer Science,
Guangzhou 510640, China
lul@scut.edu.cn
2 South China University of Technology, Institute of Computer Science,
Guangzhou 510640, China
wuwenhan_2005@yahoo.com.cn,
3 South China University of Technology, Institute of Computer Science,
Guangzhou 510640, China
vivito@126.com

Abstract. H. 264 video coding standard introduces motion estimation with multiple block sizes to achieve a considerably higher coding efficiency than other video coding algorithms. However, this comes at the greatly increased computing complexity at the encoder. In this paper, a method is proposed to eliminate some redundant coding modes that contribute very little coding gain based on analysis of macroblock detail-level and texture directions. The simulation results show that the algorithm can remarkably decrease the complexity at the encoder while keeping satisfying coding efficiency.

1 Introduction

The JVT[1] (Joint Video Team) introduced a number of advanced features in H.264 or MPEG-4 AVC. These improvements achieve significant gains in encoder and decoder performances. One of the new features is multi-mode selection, which is the subject of this paper. In the H.264 coding algorithm, blockmatching motion estimation is an essential part of the encoder to reduce the temporal redundancy between frames. H.264 supports motion estimation and compensation using different block sizes ranging from 16x16 to 4x4 luminance samples, which is shown in Fig1, with many options between the two. The luminance component of each macroblock can be split by four ways: 16x16, 16x8, 8x16 and 8x8. Each of the submacroblock partitions is called a macroblock partition. If the 8x8 mode is chosen, each of 8x8 macroblock partitions within the macroblock can be further split by four ways: 8x8, Sx4,4x8 or 4x4, which are called macroblock sub-partitions. These partitions and

Please use the following format when citing this chapter:

Lu, L., Wu, W., Wei, Z., 2007, in IFIP International Federation for Information Processing, Volume 251, Integration and Innovation Orient to E-Society Volume1, Wang, W. (Eds), (Boston: Springer), pp. 346-352.

subpartitions give rise to a lager number of possible combinations within each macroblock[4].

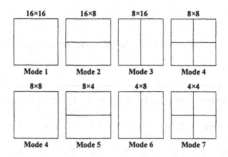

Fig. 1. Inter-prediction modes

H.264 standard uses computationally intensive Lagrangian rate-distortion (RD) optimization to choose the best block size for a macroblock[7]. The general equation of Lagrangian RD optimization is given as:

$$J_{mode} = D + \lambda_{mode} \cdot R \qquad (1)$$

where Jmode is the rate-distortion cost (RD cost) and Jmode is the Lagrangian multiplier; D is the distortion measurement between original macroblock and reconstructed macroblock located in the previous coded frame, and R reflects the number of bits associated with choosing the mode and macroblock quantizer value, Qp, including the bits for the macroblock header, the motion vector(s) and all the DCT residue blocks.

The computational complexity required by motion estimation, however, increases linearly with the number of used block types because block matching needs to be performed for each of them. In JVT reference software JM75C[5], it adopts full search method for each block type and selects the optimal block type as the final coding mode based on the RD cost function. Though it provides the best coding efficiency, the computational complexity is obviously much too high. In order to reduce the intensive computational requirement, Andy Cbang etc. proposed fast multi-block motion estimation[2]. They adopt an approach of early termination by skipping searching for mode 16x8 and mode 8x16, if the performance of mode 16x1 6 is "good enough", otherwise all coding modes will be performed. This method only considers three coding modes which are 16x16, 16x8 and 8x16 inter coding modes. Another approach, proposed by Andy C. Yu, is based on estimating block detail complexity[6]. It is an effective way judging by his simulation results, but there is more a critical factor, texture direction, which he does not think about and is also can be useful to significantly improve coding efficiency.

In this paper, we propose a method to eliminate some redundant coding modes by estimating block detail and texture direction. The paper will be organized as follows. The proposed algorithm will be described in detail in section 2. Section 3 shows the simulation and the results. Finally, a conclusion will be given in section 4.

2 PROPOSED ALGORITHM

2.1 Estimating block details

Table 6. shows the observations on how selected modes relate sequence characteristics.

sequence	Skip	16×16	16×8	8×16	8×8	Intra16	Intra4
Container	75.8	10.4	3.5	2.7	7.3	0.3	0.0
Foreman	23.7	39.9	39.9	7.3	7.6	7.3	9.3
Bus	3.5	22.0	12.1	14.4	40.5	1.0	5.5
Mobile	4.5	31.3	7.1	6.1	49.7	0.0	0.3

IPPP, 5 reference frames, CABAC, CIF Format

The choice of partition size has a significant impact on compression performance. In general, according to Tab1, large partition sizes are appropriate for homogeneous areas of the frame and small partition sizes may be beneficial for detailed areas.

We derive an approach based on summing the total energy of the AC coefficients to estimate the block detail. The AC coefficients can be obtained from the DCT coefficients of each block. The definition is:

$$E_{AC} = \sum_{u=1}^{M-1}\sum_{v=1}^{N-1}(F(u,v))^2 \tag{2}$$

From (2), EAC, the total energy of the AC components of an M×N block is the sum of all the DCT coefficients, F(u,v), except for the DC component, u = 0 and v = 0.

$$F(u,v) = c(u)c(v)\sum_{x=0}^{M-1}\sum_{y=0}^{N-1}f(x,y)\cos[\frac{(2x+1)u\pi}{16}]\cos[\frac{(2y+1)v\pi}{16}] \tag{3}$$

where,

$$c(u),c(v) = \begin{cases} \sqrt{\frac{1}{M}},\sqrt{\frac{1}{N}} & for\ u,v=0 \\ \sqrt{\frac{2}{M}},\sqrt{\frac{2}{N}} & for\ u,v\neq0 \end{cases} \tag{4}$$

According to the energy conservation principle, the total energy of an M×N block is equal to the accumulated energy of its DCT coefficients. Thus, (3) can be further simplified as

$$E_{AC} = \sum_{x=0}^{M-1}\sum_{y=0}^{N-1}(f^2(x,y)) - \frac{1}{MN}[\sum_{x=0}^{M-1}\sum_{y=0}^{N-1}f(x,y)]^2$$

(5)

where the first term is the total energy of the image intensities within an $M \times N$ block, and the second term represents the mean square intensity. Equation (6) clearly shows that the energy of the AC components of a macroblock can be represented by the variance.

Evaluating the maximum sum of the AC components is the next target. By definition, the largest variance is obtained from the block comprising checkerboard pattern in which every adjacent pixel is the permissible maximum and minimum value. Thus, Emax, the maximum sum of AC components of an $M \times N$ block is

$$E_{max} = MN\frac{f_{max}^2(x,y) + f_{min}^2(x,y)}{2} - \frac{MN}{4}[f_{max}(x,y) + f_{min}(x,y)]^2$$

(6)

Note that Emax can be calculated in advance. Then the criterion to assess the complexity of a macroblock detail is

$$r_d = \frac{\ln(E_{AC})}{\ln(E_{max})}$$

(7)

In total, 7 different block sizes are recommended by H.264 for P-frames, namely, 16×16, 16×8, 8×16, 8×8, 8×4, 4×8, 4×4 as well as SKIP, and other two INTRA prediction modes, I4MB and I16MB. However, in our complexity measurement, there are only 3 categories, which are denoted as MD16 category, MD8 category, and MD4 category, respectively.

The proposed algorithm provides a recursive way to decide the complexity of each macroblock. Firstly, a macroblock of 16×16 pixels is examined with the first piecewise equation in (7). An LDB category is given if it is recognized as being a homogenous macroblock. Otherwise, the macroblock is decomposed into 4 blocks of 8×8 pixels. Note that an 8×8 block is recognized as high-detailed if it satisfies two conditions: (a) the RB in (9) is greater than 0.7, and it is decomposed into four 4×4 block, and (b) one of its four decomposed 4×4 blocks is highdetailed as well. If an 8×8 block satisfies the first condition but not the second, it is still recognized as low-detailed. After checking all the 8×8 blocks, an MD8 category is given to a macroblock which possesses more than two high-detailed blocks, otherwise the MD4 category is assigned. Table 1 displays the relationship between the three categories in the proposed algorithm and the 9 inter-frame prediction modes. It is observed that the MD16 category covers the least number of prediction modes, whereas the MD4 category contains all the available modes. The table further indicates that the higher detailed the macroblocks are, the more prediction modes the proposed algorithm has to check.

The function of the natural logarithm is to linearize both E_{max} and E_{AC} such that the range of rd can be uniformly split into 10 subgroups. In our evaluation, a macroblock that has the $r_d > 0.7$, is considered to be a high-detailed block.

Table 2. Block categories and corresponding modes

Detail Level	Enabled Modes
LDB	16×16
MDB	16×16, 16×8, 8×16, 8×8
HDB	8×8, 8×4, 4×8, 4×4

2.2   Detecting block texture direction

It is obvious that 16×8 and 8×4 are appropriate for blocks with horizontal texture characteristics, and 8×16, 4×8 could be selected when there is a block with vertical texture direction. Texture characteristics can be estimated based on the following equations:

$$D_h = \sum_{x=0}^{M-1} \sum_{y=1}^{N-1} [f(x,y) - f(x, y-1)]^2 \qquad (8)$$

$$D_v = \sum_{x=1}^{M-1} \sum_{y=0}^{N-1} [f(x,y) - f(x-1, y)]^2 \qquad (9)$$

If $D_h > D_v$, the block tends to have horizontal texture direction. When $D_v > D_h$, the block tends to be with vertical texture direction. The maximum values of D_h and D_v are expressed as following respectively:

$$D_{h\max} = M(N-1)d^2 \qquad (10)$$

$$D_{v\max} = N(M-1)d^2 \qquad (11)$$

where d is the difference between maximum and minimum value of $f(x,y)$. In order to make a further step to eliminate redundant modes, detection of block texture direction should be performed, which uses the following equation:

$$r_h = \frac{\ln(D_h)}{\ln(D_{h\max})} \qquad (12)$$

$$r_v = \frac{\ln(D_v)}{\ln(D_{v\max})} \qquad (13)$$

If $r_h > r$, 8×16 and 4×8 will be eliminated. If $r_v > r_h$, 16×8 and 8×4 will be eliminated.

2.3   Algorithm

Step 1: Calculate r_d in the current block. If $r_d < 0.3$, go to step 2. If $0.3 < r_d < 0.3$, go to If $r_d > 0.7$, and go to step 4.

Step 2: Select 16×16 as the only enabled mode, go to step 5.

Step 3: Disable 8×8, 4×8, 4×4, and go to step 5.

Step 4: Enable all of the modes, and go to step 5.

Step 5: Calculate r_h and r_v in the current block. If $r_h > r_v$, disable 8×16 and 4×8. If $rv > rh$, disable 16×8 and 8×4. Go to step 6.

Step 6: Calculate Jmode with every enable mode, plus SKIP and INTRA. And then select the best mode.

3   SIMULATION RESULTS

To test the efficiency of our proposed method, the proposed method was integrated within JVT reference software.JM75C. Five sequences were selected for test, which were Container, Foreman, News, Mobile. Their texture characteristics are different and representative. Major parameters setting for the test is shown in Table 3.

Table 3. Major parameters setting in simulation

GOP structure	IPPP
Use Hadmard	Used
Frame Rate(HZ)	15
NumberReferenceFrames	1
InterSearch AxB	All are enable
SymbolMode	CABAC
PartitionMode	No DP
QP	30
UseConstrainedIntraPred	0
MVResolution	1/4
SearchRange	16
RateControl	Disable

Table 4 is a summary of the performance of the proposed mode selection algorithm. It is demonstrated that the proposed algorithm can save up to 28.2% encoding time as compared to JM75c. On average, there is a degradation of 0.08dB. As to compression ratio, the proposed algorithm produces an average slightly higher bit rates than H.264. The degradations and the bit differences are due to less accurate prediction in the proposed algorithm. Nevertheless, the degradations are still within an acceptable range because human visual perception is unable to distinguish the PSNR difference of less than 0.2dB.

Table 4. Simulation results of the proposed algorithm compared to JM75 in terms of PSNR, bit rate and time saved

Sequence	PSNR(db)			BITS(bit)			TIME(%)		
	JM	Proposed Agorithm	ΔPSNR	JM	Proposed Agorithm	ΔBITS	JM	Proposed Agorithm	ΔTime
Container	35.97	35.92	-0.08	189944	188712	-0.65%	279.056	226.036	-19.0%
Foreman	35.53	35.48	-0.05	577120	575432	-0.03%	281.221	211.354	-24.8%
News	36.72	36.65	-0.09	364680	367624	0.08%	280.968	201.620	-28.2%
Mobile	33.07	32.93	-0.10	4227024	4221848	-0.12%	340.858	305.639	-10.3%

4 CONCLUSION

In this paper, we propose a method to eliminate some redundant coding modes based on analysis of macro block detail-level and texture directions., which speeds up the process of multi-mode selection. The simulation results show that the algorithm can remarkably decrease the complexity at the encoder while keeping satisfying coding efficiency.

REFERENCES

1. Joint Video Team (JVT) of ISO/IEC MPEG and ITU-T VCEG, Final committee draft of Joint Video Specification (ITU-T Rec. H.264 and ISO/IEC 14496-10 AVC)[S] (2002).
2. A. Chang, O.C. Au, Y.M. Yeung, "A novel approach to fast multi-block motion estimation for H.264 video coding[A]", Multimedia and Expo, 2003. *ICME'03 Proceedings 2003 International Conference*. (2003). Volume 1, 6-9.
3. A.C. Yu, "Efficient Block-size Selection Algorithm for Inter-Frame Coding", H.264/MPEG-4 AVC[A]. ICASSP, *2004. IEEE. International Conference on Volume 3*, 17-21 (May 2004) Page(s):iii - 169-72 vol.3.
4. F.S. Yan, "Fast mode selection based on texture analysis and local motion activity", H.264/AVC [A] ICCCAS 2004. *2004 International Conference on Volume 1*, 27-29 (June 2004) Page(s):539 - 542 Vol.1
5. JVT reference software JM75c [CP]. http://bs.hhi.de/~suehring/tml.
6. A.C. Yu, Efficient Block-size Selection Algorithm for Inter-Frame Coding, H.264/MPEG-4 AVC [C]. ICASSP, 2004, *International Conference on Volume 3*, 17-21: 69-72.
7. T. Wiegand, H. Schwarz,, A. Joch, R. Kossentini, J.G. Sullivan, Rata-constrained Coder Control and Comparision of Video Coding Standards , *IEEE Trans. Circuits Syst. Video   Technol,*   Vol13   (July   2003   )   ,   pp.688-703

The Effect of Information Asymmetry on Consumer Driven Health Plans

Martin J. D'Cruz[1] & Ranjan B. Kini[2]

[1]Turku School of Economics, Turku, Finland

[2]School of Business, Indiana University Northwest, Gary, IN, US

Abstract. The healthcare industry is unique when compared to other industries in that multiple stakeholders manage healthcare services. Consumers are the ultimate users of these services; however, they have relatively little influence on their own health service choices. The industry is changing rapidly with new technologies making access to healthcare information via the Internet and other sources easier in theory. The disconnect between what consumers can learn and their ability to use what they learn results in the inability for them to truly be drivers in their own healthcare decisions. Information Asymmetry is one of the major factors that make the healthcare delivery system in the United States and other countries inefficient. The stakeholders, government, health plans, providers and employers play a pivotal role in reducing information asymmetry. Embracing Information and Communications Technology (ICT) can effectively move from an unwired to a wired healthcare delivery system and support reducing information asymmetry. For Consumer Driven Health Plans (CDHP) to succeed, consumers need information on price, quality, and cost for services. The conjecture here is that with minimization of information asymmetry, implicitly or explicitly, CDHP will drive healthcare cost down and make the healthcare market more efficient thereby reining in healthcare cost in the long-run.

1 Introduction

The health care industry is unique when compared to other industries in that healthcare services are managed by government, health plans, providers, and employers. Consumers are the ultimate users of these healthcare services; however, consumers today have relatively little influence on their own health service choices. The industry is changing rapidly with new technologies, making access to health care information via the Internet and other sources easier in theory. The disconnect between what consumers can learn and how they can use what they learn, results in this inability for them to truly be the drivers in their own health care decisions. It is believed that existence of such asymmetry in the availability of information to the consumers and other stakeholders, understood as Information Asymmetry, is one of the major factors that makes healthcare delivery in the United States (and perhaps the world)

Please use the following format when citing this chapter:

D'Cruz, M., J., Kini, R. B., 2007, in IFIP International Federation for Information Processing, Volume 251, Integration and Innovation Orient to E-Society Volume1, Wang, W. (Eds), (Boston: Springer), pp. 353-362.

inefficient. It is also generally believed that leveraging Information and Communication Technology (ICT) can effectively address this factor from an unwired to wired healthcare delivery system [1].

In this paper, a discussion of the effects of information asymmetry on CDHP products is presented. The stakeholders of this eco-system are the Government, Employers, Health Plans, Providers (hospitals and physicians), and Consumers. The discussion will identify and present the role of information asymmetry as a contributing factor to healthcare industry inefficiencies. Further, the discussion will also include the trend in the shift of health care cost to consumers with the growth of Consumer Driven Health Plans in Managed Care. The critical role of Information and Communication Technology in minimizing information asymmetry in health care industry and its influence in gaining efficiencies in health care is also presented.

2   Research

The effect of Information Asymmetry is considered one of the major factors in stifling the growth of CDHPs. Information asymmetry is defined as unequal information and the consequent role of physicians as agents for patients. It is a situation in which a few have relevant information, and the rest have little. Information asymmetry causes markets to become inefficient since not all the participants have access to the information they need for their decision-making processes. Information asymmetry is defined as a gap in knowledge between consumers and professionals regarding price and quality.   This gap of interpreting performance metrics of physicians, providers and health plans can be difficult when one party to a transaction has more or better information than the other party [2].

The stakeholders, the Government, Employers, Providers, Health Plans and Consumers recognize that healthcare cost is out of control and cannot be sustainable in the long run. Healthcare professionals and policy makers discuss healthcare information and strategies, but few suggest ideas to fix the problem. Managed Care is now considered a fad that has Plans (CDHP) costs shift to the consumer. There are already concerns regarding consumer's satisfaction with these plans, and the future is less than perfectly clear.

Consumer Driven Health Plans

To understand how Consumer Driven Health Plan (CDHP) concept was born, it helps to understand how the U.S. healthcare system has evolved over the past 50 years. For, in that evolution are lessons the society has learned with respect to healthcare consumption, management and costs.   Employer-sponsored benefits were born in the 1950s as a way for employers to attract and retain employees, and that premise holds through today. However, as American businesses continue to reel in the slumping economy of the new Millennium, how to manage what appears to be an endless cycle of dramatic healthcare cost increases, and, questioning the continuation of funding healthcare benefits moreover, is a business issue that employers large and small are taking on with a new vigor.

There has been a consensus among the stakeholders that something needs to done to reign the costs of healthcare. This involved getting consumers more engaged in the healthcare decision making process. There was consensus that healthcare costs were rising dramatically, and unlike the at-hand solutions that managed care provided in the 1980s and 1990s, there was only one viable solution to manage the new cost trends: Engage the consumer in the purchasing, pricing and utilization of their healthcare services. Defined narrowly, CDHP refers to health insurance plans that allow members to use personal Health Savings Accounts (HSAs), Health Reimbursement Arrangements (HRAs), or similar medical payment products to pay medical expenses directly, while they enjoy the protection of a high-deductible health insurance policy. High-deductible policies cost less per month than low-deductible policies, but the consumer needs to pay more upfront for medical procedures. This system of healthcare is also often referred to as "consumer directed health care" because proponents believe it gives consumers greater control over their health and health care costs.

Cardon and Showalter article identifies five main types of tax-preferred health savings accounts shown below [3]:

1. **Archer Medical Savings Accounts (MSAs):** accounts in which an individual and/or an employer can contribute pre-tax dollars to pay for most health care services. The tax advantage is the same as for employer-provided health insurance premiums. Unused monies can accumulate over time. An experiment authorized under the Kassebaum-Kennedy bill (Health Insurance Portability and Accountability Act of 1996) allowed for restricted introduction of MSAs which included the requirement of purchasing a catastrophic, (high-deductible) health insurance policy.

2. **Flexible Spending Accounts (FSAs):** like HSAs, but with no link to insurance coverage. Funds not used by the end of the year revert to the employer.

3. **Rollover FSAs:** these would allow limited rollover of FSA monies without the restrictions on insurance choices that the current HSA rules require.

4. **Health Reimbursement Arrangements (HRAs):** tax-exempt individual accounts used to pay for medical expenditures. Employers fund accounts; employee contributions are not allowed. Ownership of the accounts remains with the employer, unlike HSAs and FSAs.

5. **Medical IRAs.** This proposal would allow consumers to make penalty-free early withdrawals from their retirement plans to pay for allowable medical expenditures.

Proponents argue that most consumers will pay less for healthcare in the long run under CDHP because not only their monthly premiums will be lower, but also the use of HSAs and similar products will bring back free-market variables into the healthcare system that will encourage competition, lower prices, improved services and lower medical errors.

In its infancy stages, CDHP is manifesting itself largely in higher deductibles, higher co-payments, and reduced benefits. There is also a growing array of CDHP products being offered by all the national health insurance carriers, Blue Cross Plans, Cigna, Aetna, United HealthCare and Well Point. In addition, there is an expanding industry of niche start-up companies – early entrants such as Lemenos and Definity. These two have recently been acquired by Well Point and United Health Care respectively. In the earlier stages, CDHP was mainly focused on cost management and cost shifting. In the longer term, the goal of CDHP is to engage the consumer in a more educated process of benefits purchasing, provider selection, and management of consumption of services. One can hypothesize that such an engagement can be at least partially achieved using Information and Communications Technology (ICT).

The growing trend in the increased offering of CDHP products has significant implications to healthcare providers. With the growth of these plans, the burden of healthcare falls more on the consumer to pay for higher out-of-pocket-costs. Typically, every time a consumer spends a dollar on physicians' services, only 20 cents are paid out of pocket; the remainder is paid by health plan, employer and government referred to as the third party. From a purely economic perspective, then, user's incentive is to consume these services until their value to them is only 20 cents on the dollar. Additionally, millions of consumers such as Medicaid enrollees, Medicare enrollees who have medi-gap insurance, and people who get free care from community health centers and hospital emergency rooms, do not even pay the 20 cents. While employers are grappling with the increasing health care costs, there continues to be a shift to consumers to bear the responsibility. The shift is expected to accelerate because of the government encouragement to enroll as many as 25 percent in high deductible health plans by the end of the decade [4].

Early evidence of these CDHP products assisting consumers to reduce costs in most studies is questionable. The results thus far do suggest that CDHP could reduce the cost and spending on healthcare. The other side of CDHP raises concerns about whether reductions in cost are sustainable in the long run. Another concern is whether consumers have the information and resources to begin making rational decisions about their healthcare situation. Critics have also raised the issues of whether the consumers will compromise on the appropriate utilization of services or neglect to use the available information about quality [5].

The growth of these products makes the consumers bear a substantial portion of healthcare cost. The RAND Health Insurance Experiment [HIE] indicates that cost sharing (paying out of pocket expenditures by consumer) reduces costs by lowering healthcare utilization, but could also lead to some undesirable consequences. Cost sharing reduced the percentage of low-income adults who were associated with higher blood pressure control "highly effective care for acute conditions" by 39 percent. There were reports of less reliable use of preventive care measures such as Pep smears. However, advocates believe that shifting part of the increased cost to the consumer will turn consumers into informed consumers who will exert pressure on healthcare providers to improve the efficiency, quality of care and reduce medical errors [6].

Most economists believe that increasing the price of an item will decrease demand for the item. Health care is no different from any other good. If you increase the co-payment or coinsurance rate, people will consume fewer medical services. The RAND HIE demonstrated that higher coinsurance rates discourage medical care consumption. [6]

In general, most studies, starting with the RAND HIE study, conclude that increasing the costs (co-payments and deductibles) of health care to the patient reduces the consumption of health care, but reduces the consumption of both appropriate and inappropriate care, and the reduction is greater for low-income patients. For example, Newhouse, in summarizing the RAND study, reported that visits to physicians and hospitals decline with higher cost sharing "although for low income families such cutbacks reduced their use of beneficial as well as unnecessary services and was estimated to have increased rates of death from preventable illness" [6].

Health savings accounts (HSAs) have been a major point of contention for health care reformers. Supporters claim that HSAs can reduce health care costs by decreasing the moral hazard problem inherent when third parties—such as insurance companies or the government—pay for medical services. Opponents claim that HSAs will attract rich and healthy individuals, leaving only poor or sick individuals in the 'regular' insurance pool [7].

There has been an increase in research analyzing the actual cost and quality impact of CDHP, this new form of health care has been increasing. Researchers at the Carlson School of Management at the University of Minnesota (Stephen T. Parente), Harvard University (Meredith Rosenthal), University of Illinois at Chicago (Anthony LoSasso) and RAND HIE have examined results of these plans. The large health plans, Aetna, WellPoint, Humana and UnitedHealth Group have all provided their own independent analyses as well. Other countries with experience in this type of health plans include: China, Taiwan, Singapore and South Africa. "Research conducted by the Galen Institute has found that consumers around the world who operate under CDHP products are value conscious when it came to healthcare and more focused on preventive care" [6].

Critics of CDHP argue that the healthcare system will only burden consumers with more expenses because free-market variables can never exist in healthcare due to lack of pricing transparency, that is clearly established pricing. "Despite the theory (as expressed in the Economic Report of the President) that health insurance with higher deductibles will lead to consumers shopping around for health services (based on price and quality), the reality of inadequate information in the marketplace about health care quality and prices precludes the workability of a 'consumer-choice' type of model" according to Gail Shearer, director of health policy analysis for Consumers Union, to the Joint Economic Committee of the U.S. Congress in February of 2004 [8].

Do consumers get adequate healthcare quality and pricing information in the marketplace? The current environment makes it difficult for consumers to be well informed. Consumers are inundated with enormous amount of medical information from the Internet, medical journals, television and newspaper advertisements, websites, friends and relatives, to the extent that there is information overload. Consumers are becoming more knowledgeable and seek clinical relevant information while demanding prompt responses from the medical profession [9]. In such a situation, can consumers be capable of assuming the responsibility of making rational health care decisions? On the other hand, will the health of these consumers suffer because they elect not to seek care or adhere to medication regimens? For a long time, consumers were only responsible for a minimum payment and the Government, Employer or Health Plan paid the rest. Now, the informed consumer is expected to take charge and bring about healthcare efficiencies.

3   Information Asymmetry in Health Care

Kenneth Arrow in his seminal article recognized that Healthcare is characterized by extremely high level of uncertainty and the consumers' uncertainty about the consequences of purchasing healthcare services. Patients as consumers have this inherent inability to fully understand the effectiveness of medical treatments, and are about the remedy for their sickness or relief of pain. This makes it very difficult for consumers to learn and evaluate the quality of healthcare services. Arrow also recognized that under conditions of uncertainty, correct information becomes a valuable commodity. He further recognized that information's "elusive character" limits the marketability of both the demand and supply sides of the market. There are limits on consumers' ability to acquire information and consumers' potential to process information. This is more pronounced specifically for cases of acute illnesses where the limits on acquiring information are uncertain due to inexperience. Furthermore, consumers who are confronted with new illnesses face a very challenging dilemma as they have limited time to research and collect information. The effectiveness of many medical treatments depends on minimizing the time between the onset of illness and the start of the treatment [10].

Arrow saw the unique asymmetric nature of the information in medical markets. Arrow discusses that some market participants will be better informed than others will. "Like other commodities, it has a cost of production and a cost of transmission, and so it is naturally not spread out over the entire population but concentrated among those who can profit most from it", asserts Arrow [11]. The average consumer will experience variation in costs and benefits due to differences in income, analytical abilities and various other factors.   He concentrated on informational asymmetries between physicians and patients and comments that "Medical knowledge is so complicated, the information possessed by the physician as to the consequences and possibilities of treatment is necessarily very much greater than that of the patient, or at least so is believed by both parties. Further, both parties are aware of this informational inequality, and their relation is colored in knowledge" [11].

With the growth of the Internet, various new sources provide the potential for a metamorphosis of physician-dependent patients into better informed consumers.   The Internet will never replace physicians as patients' primary source of information on the efficacy of various medical treatments. Even for the most educated consumer with all the relevant medical information, there are barriers to consumers' abilities to process it and to make choices between treatments independently from their respective physicians. Patients tend to rely on guidance from their physicians to understand medical factors in the context of their particular medical problems and to give these medical factors their proper diagnosis in the treatment protocols.

Accessing medical information from websites, medical journals, providers, health plans relatives, and friends has been the norm for many consumers. Sometimes, consumers can challenge the physician on treatment protocols and force the physicians to be responsive in a thoughtful way. Websites such as wipricepoint.com (Wisconsin) and nhpricepoint.com (New Hampshire) that have been initiated at the state levels can be resource to a certain extent in the charge (price) and some quality indicators. With all the information available, the consumer is often overwhelmed as to what is the right treatment.

Traditional approaches for managing healthcare prices are inadequate in an environment of competition. Cognizant of the role the physician plays, the development of performance based healthcare is still at its embryonic stage according to M. Millenson [9]. With the advent of CDHP, the shift of cost to the patient is inevitable. The consumer will be more judicious with shopping for health care services related to cost and quality.   Therefore, information symmetry becomes highly relevant. In a free market situation where the doctor is primarily motivated by the profit motive, the possibility exists for physicians to exploit patients by advising more treatment to be purchased than is necessary, a supplier induced demand. Traditionally, physician's behavior is controlled by a professional code of ethics and a system of licensure. In other words, people can only work as physicians provided they are licensed and this in turn depends upon their acceptance of a code which makes the obligations of being an agent explicit or as Kenneth Arrow puts it that "the control that is exercised ordinarily by informed buyers is replaced by internalized values" [11].

So, if physicians behaved like some financial consultants or computer salesmen in the past and maximized profits without any restriction from a professional code, one would expect supplier induced demand to be a major problem. But, any system of licensure strong enough to provide the internalized values that Arrow discusses is also likely to give the medical profession power to limit the number of physicians operating. Thus, licensure and a professional code are in themselves also a source of market value. Arrows refers to this as "Supplier induced demand"[11].

Although, technology has given us more information than needed, sometimes it is very helpful, if not invaluable. There is good, solid data on the Internet that researchers can use with confidence. All of the available information can be helpful to general public with guidance. Searches for quality information have become considerably easier and quicker. In this way, information asymmetry can be reduced. Even if one thinks that one is unfamiliar with this phenomenon one usually goes through experiences in one's life when one was the victim of information asymmetry.

Here are a few examples that illustrates information asymmetry:

1. When a person is purchasing a new car, does the person feel comfortable and empowered when one starts to negotiate and haggle over price? Or, does the person feel out of control, not knowing exactly how much should one be paying for a car?

2. When a person is in their physician's office waiting to be called, one may have a list of concerns about which the person may know next to nothing. The person is highly likely a victim of information asymmetry.

3. When a person is trying to find information on a stock or a particular industry, the person may go to one's investment adviser who, for some reason may try to change the person's focus to another stock or industry. The person is not sure what to do because one is challenged with information asymmetry

Jessie Gruman, who interviewed 200 patients and families about how they used scientific information after devastating medical diagnoses, said, "I fear that the trend toward consumer-driven health care will disproportionately damage the health of the less educated and less wealthy, and that the net effect on the nation's health has already proved negative" [12]. He concluded that most patients are unable to make critical decisions about their health care in the consumer-driven model. According to Gruman some people, called "monitors," track down detailed information, while other people, called "blunters," do not want information. In Gruman's study, he commented, one blunter -- a theoretical physicist, said that he would be "insulted" if someone read fifteen papers on theoretical physics and asked him to help design an experiment, he pays his doctor to explain his choices. A "monitor," a lawyer, applied her legal research skills but could not think clearly enough to decide. People go to Internet, become overwhelmed (or overloaded), or do not understand the significance of the information. "Most health information is bad news, is stressful, and makes decisions even more difficult" [12].

According to Robert Reischauer, president of the Urban Institute and Vice Chairman of the Medicare Payment Advisory Commission, accessible information on the quality, price, effectiveness and efficiency of health-care services and providers is developing rapidly, but is nowhere near the minimum standard assumed by well functioning CDHP [13]. For example, when one goes to the physician because of a particular set of symptoms, the physician may ask a number of questions that lead to a series of recommended tests whose results then determine an appropriate treatment regime. One could select the physician to visit on the basis of price and quality but there is no guarantee that the package of tests and treatments that resulted would be the lowest cost or highest quality. The costs of the really expensive treatments would be largely unaffected.

Despite criticism leveled at the new system in 2004, a survey by the Blue Cross and Blue Shield Association found widespread satisfaction among HSA customers. "The survey found that HSA products are on par with non consumer-directed health plans (CDHPs) with 85 percent of respondents saying the product meets or exceeds expectations for controlling healthcare expenditures. The survey also revealed that 47 percent of those consumers with HSAs experienced an increase in satisfaction over the previous year, while only 27 percent of consumers with traditional health plans showed an increase in satisfaction" [7].

The proponents of CDHP, like former House Speaker Newt Gingrich, have pointed to the rise of the Internet and online comparative shopping health services as one reason they believe the CDHP model is viable. Key to CDHP's success will be the quality (and quantity) dissemination of information about health products and services [14].

In 2006, a few of the technology firms capitalized on what they believe will be a new market for comparative healthcare shopping with the growth of CDHP plans and with the goal of leveraging the Internet to enhance price transparency and quality information dissemination in the healthcare market [15].

If information asymmetry can be minimized, it will help lower prices and lead to price transparency. The use of ICT becomes critical to operationalize such a system. ICT is already heralded as an effective way to improve quality both clinical and administrative areas and save money in healthcare. Unfortunately, evaluating return on investment (ROI) for ICT remains challenging. Until a market mechanism is developed to allow all stakeholders to equitably share the benefits of ICT adoption, broad-scale adoption will not come to fruition [1].

Each of the stakeholders of healthcare delivery is an independent entity. Physician offices are completely separate from the local emergency room or hospital. The same consumer may have laboratory or imaging tests performed in multiple venues such as several physicians' offices, more than one hospital, and independent laboratories or imaging facilities. Currently, none of these systems are linked with others. ICT can assist in improving price transparency, minimize information asymmetry, reduce the price of healthcare and bring efficiency in the market information. ICT can have a tremendous impact on improving accessibility of integrated data from medical claims and providers. The goal is to let consumers of healthcare analyze comparative prices based on quality and price information related to diagnoses and treatment with improving quality. ICT can play a more significant role in health care today and in the future. We can alter the delivery of healthcare, leveraging ICT to give scalable price efficiencies and improve the dissemination of information. This can reduce information asymmetry to the consumers and justify the true price of service rendered. ICT could have significant impact on improving quality and accessibility of health care in the US while controlling the price of health spending using health information technology [16].

Strategically, ICT can help remove healthcare information asymmetry between all stakeholders in the healthcare industry and, especially between ultimate consumer and the rest. ICT makes it possible to connect and share the critical information necessary in making efficient operation of healthcare service chain. ICT will allow aggregation, consolidation, summation and differentiation of prices relating to service procedures and value of components services, and display information to consumers to make effective selection of services, providers and physicians. ICT will also allow this interchange and delivery of this information to consumers in easy user-friendly methods using web infrastructure thus empowering all services users. ICT can also empower the health care consumers to keep an ongoing dialog and report card on insurers, providers, and physicians with regard to prices and quality of their services [16].

4   Comments and Conclusions

In the above discussion, it is made clear that CDHP is here to stay. It is also true that variety of models are being tried to really put consumers in the driver seat in deciding on the true value of the healthcare services. Implicitly and explicitly several studies have shown that although it is difficult to clearly prove that CDHP will drive the healthcare costs down and healthcare market more efficient, in the long run they are expected to rein in the healthcare costs.

There are several antecedents that are necessary in making such a health care market happen.

One: The consumers of healthcare should be well informed about all the choices they have before they subscribe to any of health care services.

Two: The information consumers are seeking before or at the Point Of Service (POS) is readily available to them ubiquitously.

Three: The information is provided to the consumers regarding all relevant health care stakeholders, and is properly communicated to them through proper understandable metrics (an average individual can understand).

Four: The consumers are educated (or have an opportunity to educate themselves) about the healthcare and health care quality metrics in their decision making process.

Five: The consumers are educated about the role of different stakeholders and their role in value creation process.

Six: The consumers have a trusted place (typically on Internet) where they can post their opinions about the services they have used. These feedbacks then will become an integral part of overall quality metrics of each of the stakeholders.

One can hypothesize based on the above suppositions that the reduction in the information asymmetry among healthcare stakeholders will make the healthcare market efficient. The critical importance of ICT use as a driver in creating such information and disseminating it to the POS and simultaneously encouraging adoption and diffusion of such technology among all the stakeholders cannot be overemphasized. However, the dark side of such a system if allowed to unfold in unplanned, uncontrolled and anarchic fashion can at times be to the detriment of the very purpose it was intended, in this case information overload can become one of the negative outcome of efforts to remove information asymmetry. Issues relating information overload is outside the scope this paper and needs to be discussed separately.

References:

1. B. Middleton, "Achieving U.S. Health Information Technology Adoption: The Need For A Third Hand", *Health Affairs*, September/October 2005, Vol 25, pp.1269-1272.

2. S.M. Retchin, MD, MSPH, "Overcoming Information Asymmetry in Consumer Directed Health Plans", *The American Journal of Managed Care*, Vol 13, No 4, April 2007.

3. Cardon and Showalter, "Insurance Choice And Tax-Preferred Health Savings Accounts" , *Journal of Health Economics*, 2007, Vol: 26(2), pp. 373-399.

4. T.H. Lee, M.D. and K. Zapert, Ph.D, "Do High-Deductible Health Plans Threaten Quality of Care?", *New England Journal of Medicine* 353, no 12, pp.1202-1204, September 22, 2005.

5. G. Wilensky, "Consumer-Driven Health Plans: Early Evidennce And Potential Impact On Hospitals", *Health Affairs*, January/February 2006 Vol: 25 pp.174-185.

6. J.P. Newhouse, "Consumer-directed health plans and the RAND health insurance experiment", *Health Affairs* 2004; 23: pp.107-113 (Cited in BMJ 334:238).

7. Healthy News Service, Blue Cross and Blue Shield Association Consumer Survey Shows High Rate of Satisfaction With HSAs Cites Increased Reliance On Decision Support Tools, October 10, 2005.

8. http://www.consumersunion.org/pub/0225JECTestimonyNoSummary.pdf

9. M. Millenson, "Medical Informatics Internet, Performance-based Healthcare – The Coming Transformation of Medical Practice", *Business Briefing: Next Generation Healthcare*, October 2000, pp.28-31.

10. D.Haas-Wilson, Uncertain Times, *Kenneth Arrow and the Changing Economics of Health Care*, 2003 Duke University Press, Arrow and the Information Market failure in Health Care: The Changing Content and Sources, pp.169-180.

11. K. J. Arrow, "Uncertainty and the Welfare Economics of Medical Care", *American Economic Review* 53, pp.941-973, 1963.

12. J. Gruman, PhD, Executive Director, Center for the Advancement of Health, Keynote Address, Transforming Consumer Decision Making, Promises and Pitfalls in Consumer Decision Making, Conference, Park City, Utah, 22 September 2005.

13. "Big Issues: Consumer Choice: Can It Cure The Nation's Health-Care Ills?" *Wall Street Journal*, December 13, 2005,

14.   http://healthtransformation.net/news/cht_articles_and_op_eds/4375.cfm

15.   http://online.wsj.com/article/SB114850936291862362.html

16.   R.A. Burgelman, Dr. R. Pearl, MD and P.E. Meza, "Better Medicine Through Information Technology", *Standford Graduate Schol of Business*, October 24, 2004.

A Research on Chinese Consumers' Using Intention on 3G Mobile Phones

Matthew Tingchi Liu[1],and Zhizhong Chen[2]

1 Faculty of Management and Administration, Macau University of
Science and Technology, Avenue Wai Long, Taipa, Macau
matthewliu@must.edu.mo

2 School of Economics and Management, Tsinghua University,
100084 Beijing, People's Republic of China
Chenzz03@mails.thu.edu.cn

Abstract. With the explosion of technology development, information appliance (IA) and digital devices (DD) become more and more popular these years. And the development of the third generation (3G) mobile phone is viewed as the most potential profitable product in the next decade. However, 3G mobile phone is confronting its promotion bottleneck. By using diffusion of innovation and lifestyle theory, hence, this study aims to examine the factors influencing adopting 3G mobile phone intention. Result shows only "technology cluster" is significantly related to adoption intention among four variables examined in this study.

1 Introduction

Under the technological convergence trend, third generation (3G) mobile phone is viewed as the most potential profitable product in the next decade. Except for traditional telecommunication, consumers can do many things such as accessing to internet, receiving/sending email, watching TV, listening radio and MP3, taking photos, and even remote control appliance via 3G mobile phone.

There were many researches related to the trend of 3G mobile phone industry or product improvement in China, but very few researches were conducted about 3G mobile phone adoption process and the factors influencing the intention to adopt 3G mobile phone. If it is made clear that the key factors in the adoption process, it will do help to the diffusion and market exploration of technology-integrated products. Rogers' Diffusion of Innovation was used to research the diffusion process of the new products very often. In this study, in order to emphasize the consumers' personality traits and social characteristics, we not only adopt Rogers' Diffusion of Innovation, but also lifestyle theory in marketing field. By describing consumers' lifestyle, this research hopes to figure out the factors that influence the 3G mobile phone adoption intention and find

Please use the following format when citing this chapter:

Liu, M. T., Chen, Z., 2007, in IFIP International Federation for Information Processing, Volume 251, Integration and Innovation Orient to E-Society Volume1, Wang, W. (Eds), (Boston: Springer), pp. 363-370.

out the most important cause during bottleneck stage of 3G mobile phone diffusion processes.

2   Literature Review

2.1   Devolvement of 3G mobile phone

3G refers to the third generation of developments in wireless technology, especially mobile communications. The third generation, as its name suggests, follows the first generation (1G) and second generation (2G) in wireless communications. 3G mobile in the shape of UMTS (Universal Mobile Telecommunications System) with WCDMA (Wideband Code Division Multiple Access) as radio access technology is already a reality.

3G offers the potential to keep people connected at all times and in all places. However, there are many factors contributing to why 3G mobile do not spread. The two main reasons are technology and market.

First, the 3G mobile telecommunication licenses are not easy to get. Until August 2005, there are only 111 licenses in the whole world, strong competition exists among corporations to acquire licenses in 3G mobile. There are three main methods to release the licenses, Auction, Comparative Selection and Hybrid [1]. Auction is widely utilized in Europe for the licenses. But in mainland China, the government has not decided which method to use when selecting the mobile operators. The delay of the license distribution means the introduction of 3G will take longer.

Second, the three models in 3G telecommunication including WCDMA mainly in Europe, CDMA2000 in US, and TD-SCDMA mainly in China, attribute to the uncertainty of its development.

Furthermore, the low production of the 3G mobile handsets restrains the widespread adoption of 3G mobile. Of the several industry segments of 3G mobile, handset is always the weak one [2]. Until now, multimedia handsets developed for the new generation of networks have been not enough for customers to select and too expensive for mainstream adoption.

Last but not least, the shortcomings of 3G itself became a problem for its promotion. The disadvantage that it could not support high speed IP is an important weakness [3]. The competition from other technologies makes situation even worse as well. A main competitor is 4G a wireless service whose mobile ability is not good as 3G but has a better capacity. It could be possible that customer bypass 3G and directly adopt 4G.

2.2   Diffusion of Innovations (DOI) Mode

Diffusion of innovation (DOI) theory refers to how people adopt new idea, product, or practice, and what factors would affect this adoption process. The original diffusion research was done as early as 1903 by the French sociologist Gabriel Tarde who plotted the original S-shaped diffusion curve. Tardes' 1903 S-shaped curve is of current importance because "most innovations have an S-shaped rate of adoption" [4].

Diffusion is the "process by which an innovation is communicated through certain channels over a period of time among the members of a social system" [4]. Rogers [4] argued that it consists of four stages: invention, diffusion (or communication) through the social system, time and consequences. The information flows through networks.

Within the diffusion process, adopters could be separated into five categories: (1) innovators, (2) early adopters, (3) early majority, (4) late majority, and (5) laggards. These categories follow a standard deviation-curve, very little innovators adopt the innovation in the beginning (2.5%), early adopters making up for 13.5% a short time later, the early majority 34%, the late majority 34% and after some time finally the laggards make up for 16%.

Theory on the diffusion of innovations has been used to study the spread of new ideas and practices for over 50 years in a wide variety of settings. Most studies have been retrospective, and most have neglected to collect information on interpersonal communication networks/ device [5]. However, several studies both quantitative and qualitative have been conducted focusing on the interdependencies of organizational and technological characteristics and with the aim of generating models for intervention [6].

Rogers [4] suggested that the diffusion process will become S-shaped curve according to the speed of new product adoption. In other words, in the beginning of adoption there are few people, and when the time passes, it will be adopt by more people. During the process of new product diffusion, critical mass is an important criterion. Only after the amount of adoption people breaks through the critical mass, new product will diffuse very quickly in the society, till popular.

Thus, the content of "Diffusion of Innovation" is not only related to the diffusion process of new products, but also the characteristics of individuals will influence the diffusion process. It will be difficult to test every variable in the model because there are many variables that influence the innovation diffusion process; even the technology advancement of the industry sometimes plays a critical role during that process. According to the four elements of Rogers' DOI model, the characteristics of innovation or communication channels all related to consumers, because the characteristics of innovation should be examined by people and the uses of media also due to the behaviors of human beings. So, this study tends to investigate the factors influencing the intention to adopt 3G mobile phones.

3   Methodology

3.1   Development of Questionnaire

The questionnaire includes five parts. In the first part, we investigate whether the respondent use 3G mobile phone or not. If the answer is "No", we continually ask their further adoption intention. The answer 0 (zero) means "won't adoption", and 1 to 5 stands for levels of adoption intention; the higher the number is, the higher the adoption intention is. As to those who have already used 3G mobile phone, numbers from 6 (less than half year) to 10 (over 2 years) are on behalf of different time period used 3G mobile. Thus, we use 0-10 to present the level of adoption intention for 3G mobile phones. The higher the number is, the higher adoption intention is.

In the second part, we tested the respondents' traits of technology cluster. Because 3G mobile phones are personal technological products, we conclude seven products that are featured in high technology and individuality attributes, including PDA, notebook, digital camera, MP3, DVD player, digital video (DV) and wireless internet device after reviewing literature and technological magazines.

In third part, we collected the situation how respondents use media. We ask respondents the hours/amount per day they watch TV, listen to radio, read newspapers/ magazines, and surf internet. We tend to know respondents' media exposure degree to the communication channels.

The fourth part is about lifestyle. We adopt lifestyle scale [7], with Likert 5-points format, which was used in China for new media technology adoption research. The last part is about demographic information, including gender, age, education, personal monthly income and household monthly income. Those are factors of socio-economic status. In order to increase the face validity and avoid the confusion of items, we conducted pretest before formal survey.

3.2   Sampling

Our samples were selected from five major cities in China: Beijing, Shanghai, Guangzhou, Chongqing, and Shenzhen.

The random sampling conducted by telephone in five cities was based on the yellow pages issued by China Telecom in 2005. The subjects were focus on adults, so people who less than 18 years old, if contacted, would be interviewed further. In order to make respondents understand 3G mobile phone precisely, interviewers will explain the definition and characteristics of 3G mobile phone to respondents in the beginning. Finally, 620 respondents were interviewed, while the qualified respondents are 280 people. Therefore, the successful respondent rate is 45.2%.

4. Data Analysis

4.1 Description of respondents

Within all qualified respondents, there are 130 male (46%) and 150 female (54%). Most subjects are 26-35 years old (31%) and 36-45 years old (29%). 50% subjects have bachelor degree and 30% subjects are graduated from senior high school. 24% subjects have more than 10,000 RMB and 18% subjects have 5,000-8,000 RMB. The distribution of household monthly income centered on 10,000-15,000 RMB (24%) and more than 30,000 RMB (16%). Regarding the 3G usage style, there were 26 users (9.3%), 104 potential users (37.1%), and 150 non-users (53.6%).

4.2 Factor Analysis of Lifestyle

The lifestyle questionnaires consisted of 22 statements from Leung [7], which has been referred by many other researches. To examine the reliability of five constructs, Cronbach's alpha was computed. Although there is no precise range existing to evaluate Cronbach's alpha, Nunnally presented a rule of thumb [8], stating that alpha levels higher than 0.50 indicate internal consistency among the items of a scale.

Further, a principal-component factor analysis was performed on the lifestyle statements to assess the stability of the dimensions across. As a result, five factors emerged as our expectation, which were named as fad-chasing, life-fulfilling, pleasure-enjoying, foreign product-preferring, and media-trusting. The five factors explained nearly or above 57.039% of the total variance.

4.3 Pearson's Correlation Analysis

Socio-economic Status

As to the relationships between socio-economic variables and intention to adopt 3G mobile phone, we used Pearson's correlation analysis to verify. The relationships between intention to adopt and age, educational status, personal monthly income, and household monthly income were significant. Therefore, we could conclude that the subjects who are younger or have higher socio-economics status have higher intention to adopt 3G mobile phone.

Technology Cluster

As to the relationships between the technology cluster and intention to adopt 3G mobile phone, the result presented a positive correlation ($r=.445$). Therefore, the subjects who have high technology-cluster characteristics have higher intention to adopt 3G mobile phone. It is thus clear that people who have high technology-cluster characteristics and hence are brave in new things are relatively easy to accept 3G mobile phone.

Media Use

As to Pearson's correlation analysis of media use and intention to adopt 3G mobile phone, most mass media were not significantly related to willing to adopt but internet was ($r=.316$). Since technology products like 3G mobile phone are exposed to internet media, which are information-orientated, and the usage of internet and 3G mobile phone are both high-involved personal behaviors, exploring the internet is positively related to the adoption 3G mobile phone.

Lifestyle

The results of lifestyle variables and intention to adopt 3G mobile phone were listed in Table 5. Only life-fulfilling was significantly and positively related to intention to adopt ($r=.315$). The reason of this result may be that people who like to learn new knowledge and are hard to study are relatively familiar with product characteristics and current information of 3G mobile phone.

Table1. Pearson's Correlation of 3G use intention with socio-economic status, media use, and lifestyle

Item	Sig.	Pearson's Correlation
Age	0.029	-0.185*
Educational status	0.001	0.284**
Personal monthly income	0.001	0.287**

Household monthly income	0.000	0.313***
Technology Cluster	0.000	0.445***
Media use: TV	0.452	-.064
Media use: Radio	0.751	0.027
Media use: Newspaper	0.794	0.022
Media use: Magazine	0.070	0.154
Media use: Internet	0.000	0.316***
Lifestyle: fad-chasing	0.205	0.108
Lifestyle: life-fulfilling	0.000	0.315***
Lifestyle: pleasure-enjoying	0.085	0.146
Lifestyle: foreign product-preferring	0.501	0.057
Lifestyle: media-trusting	0.552	0.051

* P<0.05 **P<0.01 ***P<0.001

4.4 Hierarchical regression analysis

The hierarchical regression model estimates are provided in Table 6. The R-square of the whole model was 28.5%. Tests for the unstandardized β coefficient indicated that only technology cluster has significant influence on willing to adopt 3G mobile phone, but the R-square was only 6.9%. Other variables such as socio-economic variables, media use, and lifestyle did not have significant influences on willing to adopt.

Table2. Hierarchical regression model of the influence of independent variables on intention to adopt 3G mobile phone

Independent variables		Unstandardized β	Sig.
Socio-Economic	Sex	-.112	.179
	Age	-.105	.276
	Education	.003	.982
	Individual Income	.026	.817
	Household Income	.038	.721
	R^2	.163	
Media Use	TV	-.021	.807
	Radio	.009	.911
	Newspaper	.005	.951
	Magazine	-.023	.796
	Internet	.099	.298
	R^2	.190	
Technology Cluster	High-tech product-owning	.336	.001***
	R^2	.259	
Life-style	fad-chasing	-.067	.508
	life-fulfilling	.157	.113
	pleasure-enjoying	-.021	.827
	foreign product-preferring	.081	.342
	media-trusting	.030	.730
	R^2	.285	

*** P<0.001

5. Conclusion and Further Directions

5.1 Conslusion

The result showed that socio-economic status has no impact on the intention to adopt 3G mobile phones. It contradicts to many past researches [9, 10]. Combined the findings with Jeffres and Atkin's [11] study on the adoption of ISDN and Li's [12] study on the adoption of cable TV shopping, that revealed that socio-economic status doesn't have definitely correlation with the adoption of those innovations.

Technology cluster is to test the owning of other products with similar features on adoption. In this study, we raise seven products that have similar senses of technology and the claims of usages. In regression analysis, it is confirmed that technology cluster has positive and significant relationship with intention to adopt 3G mobile phones. In other words, the more someone owns products with similar features or functions to 3G mobile phones, the higher the intention to adopt 3G mobile phones.

As to the use of media dimension, the use of TV, radio, newspaper, magazines has no impact on the intention to adopt 3G mobile phones. The result is quite opposite to some past studies [13, 14]. But there are some studies pointed out that the use of media doesn't have definitely relationship with the adoption of innovation [15]. Therefore, predict the adoption of innovation by only considering the use of media is not enough, maybe it more convincing to also examine the contents that media channels provide.

Lifestyle, which describes the consumer's social and psychological traits, can be divided by five dimensions: fad-chasing, life-fulfilling, pleasure-enjoying, foreign product-preferring and media-trusting [7]. Those dimensions have no predict ability to the intention of adopt of 3G mobile phones in this study. There are 300 items in the development of AIO scale in the beginning. As time goes by, there are two major kinds of scales, including general and specific lifestyle, were developed [16]. In this study, due to the resource and time constraints, we only adopt five dimensions of general lifestyle scale which maybe not suitable to the adoption of 3G mobile phones. We might get more valued findings if taking other or some specific dimensions of lifestyle to measure.

Although the analysis in this study only revealed technology cluster has significant relationship with 3G mobile phones adopt intention, personal motive is also a critical factor to adoption of new products. Rogers also pointed out that during the diffusion process of innovation, the features of the innovation that satisfied personal needs of motives would raise the willingness to adopt, contribute to decision making and cause the adoption behaviors [4]. Thus, 3G mobile phone producers should adjust the functions of their products according to consumers' real needs.

5.2 Research Limitation and future direction

Due to time and cost limitation, this research adopt telephone interview with smaller sample size in five major cities in China. Future research may conduct larger scale survey to strengthen the representativeness. According to regression, this research found only "technology cluster" is influencing factor to willingness of adoption, and it only explains 28.5% of total variance. Therefore, future research may consider consumers' needs and characteristics of innovative products as new variables to make dimensions more complete.

References

1. K. Chen, Some approaches to the development of 3G mobile in China, *ZTE Communications*, 30, pp. 40-46 (2004).
2. S. Ming, 3G mobile: opportunity in the neck of the bottle, *China Internet Weekly*, Nov (1), pp. 13-17 (2004).
3. W. Gong, 3G mobile: slipping into the dilemma, *Business Watch Magazine*, May (1), 24 (2001).
4. E. M. Rogers, *Diffusion of Innovations* (4th edition). (The Free Press. New York, 1995).
5. Valente and Davis, *UMTS Forum Mobile Evolution White Paper*, August 2003. Article available on UMTS Forum official website
   http://www.umts-forum.org/servlet/dycon/ztumts/umts/Live/en/umts/3G_index
6. K. Kautz, and J. P. Heje, *Diffusion and Adoption of Information Technology* (IFIP, Chapman and Hall, 1995).
7. L. Leung, Lifestyles and the use of new media technology in urban China, *Telecommunication Policy*, 22(9), pp. 781-790 (1998).
8. J. C. Nunnally, *Psychometric Theory* (McGraw-Hill, New York, 1967).
9. Dutton, H. William, E. M. Rogers, and S. H. Jun, Diffusion and social impacts of personal computers, *Communication Research*, 14(2), pp. 219-250 (1987).
10. D. J. Atkin, Adoption of cable amidst a multimedia environment, *TelematicsandInformatives*, 10(1), pp. 51-57 (1993).
11. D. J. Atkin, and L. W. Jeffres, Predicting use of technologies for communication and consumer needs, *Journal of Broadcasting and Electronic Media*, 40(3), pp. 318-331 (1996).
12. S. S. Li, New Types of Non-store Shopping and Their Adopters: Examining the Factors that Influence the Intentions to Adopt Internet Shopping and Cable Television Shopping, *Proceedings of Annual Conference of the Association for Media and Communication Research*, Barcelona, Spain, 2002.
13. R. Wei, From luxury to utility: a longitudinal analysis of cell phone laggards, *Journalism and Mass Communication Quarterly*, 78(4), pp. 702-719 (2001)
14. D. J. Atkin, L. W. Jeffres, and K. A. Neuendorf, Understanding internet adoption as telecommunications behavior, *Journal of Broadcasting and Electronic Media*, 42(4), pp. 475-490 (1998).
15. C. A. Lin, Exploring personal computer adoption dynamics, *Journal of Broadcasting and Electronic Media*, 42(1), pp. 95-112 (1998).
16. D. I. Hawkins, R. J. Best, and K. A. Coney, *Consumer Behavior: Building Marketing Strategies* (McGraw-Hill, New York, 2001).

Construction of China's Publishing Enterprise Agile Supply Chain

Mei juan Zhang [1], Yun Cai [2], Xiang Hui Yang [2]

1 Zhang Mei Juan , Dr., associate professor, School of Information Management of Wuhan University, 430072 Wuhan , Hubei Province , P.R.China.   email: sqzmj@126.com

2 Postgraduates, School of Information Management of Wuhan University, 430072 Wuhan , Hubei Province , P.R.China.

Abstract: China's publishing enterprise Agile Supply Chain has its own peculiarities. The authors elaborate the significance of building the Chinese publishing enterprise Agile Supply Chain based on dynamic alliance in the current highly competitive market, and then construct and analyze three models and their characteristics. At last the authors discuss some problems deriving from the information Game, compatibility of enterprise knowledge and culture, and the administrative structure among Supply Chain member enterprises when the Agile Supply Chain comes into practice. .

1   Introduction

It's known to all that in recent years competition among the enterprises has gradually been evolved to the competition among supply chain. In the rapidly changing market environment, the competitiveness of supply chain mainly embodies in a prompt response to customer demand and turns it into a commercial opportunity.

Compared with traditional supply chain, Agile Supply Chain is an organizational strategic "alliance" which lay much stress on adapting itself to the market "dynamic" changes. It drives on the core enterprise, and with the control of logistics, capital flow, information flow, integrates suppliers, manufacturers, distributors, retailers and end-consumers to an integrated functional network chain[1]. Its main features are: (1) Market Sensitivity. This is an essential feature for Agile Supply Chain which can deconstruct and reconstruct smoothly in a timely manner so as to meet the changing market demands. (2)Process Integration. General supply chain focuses on information exchange and sharing, while Agile Supply Chain integrates business process across enterprises. (3) Network Structure. Agile Supply Chain integrate geographically dispersed

Please use the following format when citing this chapter:

Zhang, M., Cai, Y., Yang, X., 2007, in IFIP International Federation for Information Processing, Volume 251, Integration and Innovation Orient to E-Society Volume1, Wang, W. (Eds), (Boston: Springer), pp. 371-378.

enterprises based on the business process integration, supply cooperation, coordination, remodeling and distribution of interests among chain partners, rather than a single vertical "pyramid" structure.

2 The Significance of Building Publishing Enterprise Agile Supply Chain

2.1 Latest Changes of Book Consumer Market in China

With the rapid development of Chinese economy and new technologies and ideas which have been constantly introduced, the demand of reader for knowledge is of increasing diversification and customization. The fact that book consumers keep changing entirely and rapidly shows as follows: (1)Book consumer market turns from popularization to customization, needing a more variety of book distribution with less quantity and more frequency. (2)The lifecycle of book market is getting shorter. On the market-oriented production mode, one should be able to capture the market opportunities when it could meet the consumption market needs in the highest speed, which makes a new challenge for publishing enterprise Agile Supply Chains[2].

2.2 Major Problems in the Existing Publishing Enterprise Supply Chain

The publishing enterprise supply chain process mostly covers production, circulation and marketing with the aim at increasing the sales, decreasing the costs and gaining the profits. In the new marketing environment, there are some problems in the actual publishing supply chain. They are as follows.

(1) On the whole, Chinese publishing industry supply chain models can be classified into two major categories, publishing group supply chain and SMEs supply chain. The former operation is a basic administrative ties and a "pyramid" business organizational model, and its structure and function are too "rigid" and rarely adapt to the market "dynamic" nature. The latter one is the strength of enterprises mixed and lack of effective platform and linkage mechanism. So, the operation appears to be too "loose" rather than "alliance". Both of the supply chains have failed to achieve expected efficiency and to satisfy to the demands of market.

(2) The existing publishing enterprise supply chain runs by taking production rather than market as a starting point. In the case, the downstream enterprises being in a passive position usually increase their stocks to meet variable demand, which causes the growing inventory and poor response to the demand changes of readers.

(3)Information sharing mechanism and operational cooperation mechanism between enterprises don't work well.

An authoritative statistics[3] shows that in the year of 2005, the total sales of publications of the state-owned distributors are 15.798 billion lists (sheets, shares, boxes), up to 122.981 billion PMB yuan, increasing by 2.02% and 7.52% respectively in quantity and money compared with the performance last year, but the inventory grows much up by 26.9% and 39.3% respectively. The situation shows that publishing enterprise Agile Supply Chain should be built immediately to optimize and integrate resources and fit in with the changes of market.

3 Construction of Publishing Enterprise Agile Supply Chain

3.1 The Basic Principles of Construction of Publishing Enterprise Agile Supply Chain

For the majority of enterprises, including publishing enterprise Agile Supply Chains, Agile Supply Chain is a new concept. Meanwhile, as a content industry, Chinese publishing industry has its own specific characteristics. So, in order to construct successfully the publishing enterprise Agile Supply Chain in China, the following basic principles should be adhered to, apart from general principles [4] such as standardization and enterprise win-win, etc.

(1)Core enterprise (or leading enterprise) must be established in the proposed Agile Supply Chain. Without the core enterprise, the whole supply chain will be of unsubstantial operation because of no force of organization and drive. This core business generally is a strong competitor or one with certain competitive advantages.

(2)The focus concerning Agile Supply Chain Integration is business process of the product chain rather than enterprises. Only by reasonable regulation on the course of business can the enterprise integrate and utilize internal and external resources. So, all major business links and process of production should be decomposed in management from the perspective of industrial chain, and should learn about the information of operating entity with higher level of business specialization.

(3)With the core business' organization, an opening platform for information exchange and relative stability system facing a supply chain need to be established. Just like a printed circuit board, its architecture provides a slot standard and agreement between the slots link, so qualified components can be placed in slots. This assembly system of production, the use of open standards, the autonomy of "building blocks", sharing extensively common functions, Plug compatibility, allowing heterogeneous environment, the self-learning modules and self-organizing capacity, achieve reconstruction rapidly which feature Agile Supply Chain requires.

(4) The relevant publication policy should also be considered when building the publishing enterprise Agile Supply Chain. For example, the production of books in China is not allowed to run by the non-state-owned entities yet, thus, the non-state-owned entities should not be included in the publishing enterprise Agile Supply Chain.

3.2 Three Types of Publishing Enterprise Agile Supply Chain

Based on the actual situation of China's publishing industry, we have divided the publishing enterprise Agile Supply Chain into 3 types with the analysis of their characteristics from the perspective of industrial chain based on the decomposition of publishing process.

3.2.1 The Models and Features of Publishing Enterprise Agile Supply Chain Taking Publisher as the Core Enterprise

Some of the powerful publishing groups, such as the Chinese publishing Group, the Shanghai Century Publishing Group and Liao Ning Publishing Group, and other production-based book publishing enterprises could establish the publishing enterprise Agile Supply Chain taking publishers as the core enterprise, the model is shown in figure 1.

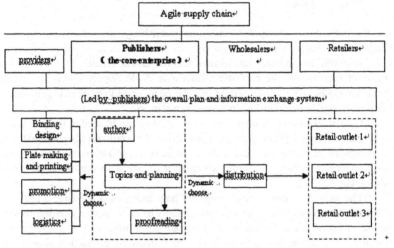

Fig. 1. the model of publishing enterprise Agile Supply Chain taking publishers as the core enterprise

These publishers could use its outstanding content production to attract resources. They could choose the right product wholesalers and retailers according to the nature of their product through contracts. They could also outsource their non-core business through contract, such as Binding design, plate making and printing, logistics, etc. in order to achieve optimal allocation of resources and to establish a strategic cooperation relationship. At the same time, they are responsible for the establishment and maintenance of the supply chain and information exchange platform.

3.2.2 The Model and Features of Publishing Enterprise Agile Supply Chain Taking Wholesalers as the Core Enterprise

The distributing groups of Xinhua Bookstore and the private wholesales have been well developed in recent years. It lays a good foundation for establishing the publishing enterprise Agile Supply Chain taking wholesalers as the core enterprise. The model is shown in figure 2.

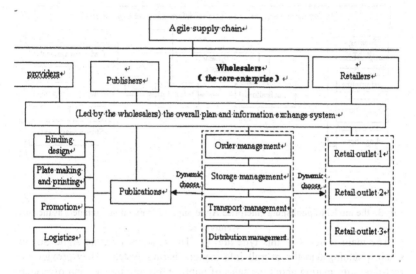

Fig. 2. the model of publishing enterprise Agile Supply Chain taking wholesalers as the core enterprise

The main features of this type of Agile Supply Chain are: (1) The wholesalers lead the Agile Supply Chain planning and the overall information-sharing system. They provide the real-time information about the distribution of publications to the other members on the chain. And they are in charge of the maintenance and management of information exchange in the entire supply chain. (2) Locating in the middle of the chain, wholesalers have the advantage of connecting the upper and lower compared with the other two types of supply chain. So the operation of this type of supply chain should be relatively easier. (3) The wholesalers select the appropriate upstream and downstream enterprises according to different publications in order to find the best and fastest way to deliver the publications to the retail outlet through various forms of dynamic alliance.

3.2.3 The Model and Features of Publishing Enterprise Agile Supply Chain Taking Retailers as the Core Enterprise

With the development of market-oriented production business model and the formation of "terminal is King" principle, the books retail terminals and large bookstores develop rapidly, such as Shenzhen Bookmall, Beijing Book Building. These retailers could and need choose their own channels and wholesalers under its own strategy, namely, to establish the publishing enterprise Agile Supply Chain taking retailers as the core enterprise. The model is shown in figure 3.

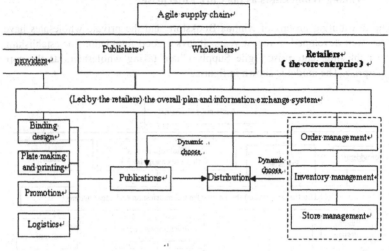

Fig. 3. the model of publishing enterprise Agile Supply Chain taking retailers as the core enterprise

The main features of this type are: (1) The retailers lead the Agile Supply Chain planning and the overall information-sharing system. They provide the real-time information about the sales of publications and the demand of readers to the other members on the chain. And they are in charge of the maintenance and management of information exchange in the entire supply chain. (2) The retailers select the appropriate upstream and downstream enterprises according to the sales of publications in order to quickly respond to book market and make every effort to achieve the ultimate goal of " seek readers for publishers , seek books for readers " through various forms of dynamic alliance

4 Issues which should be Paid Attention to when Operating the Publishing Enterprise Agile Supply Chain

4.1 The Effectiveness of Information Transfer

The immediate, accurate and complete information transfer amongst enterprises is an important node of normal operational support to Agile Supply Chain. However, as the members of the supply chain enterprises have their own independent interests and multiple purposes when joining the supply chain, the contract alone may not address differences in the conflict caused by interests. So the information transmission of the supply chain could be easily delayed and distorted. On the other hand, because of the information asymmetry in the actual information transmission process, the information senders occupy the authentic information so that the information receiver couldn't grasp, which makes the Game of information act in the process of information transfer is inevitable. That means the information senders will send information for their own benefit, and the information receivers will try to take the real messages hidden behind it.

Take the supply chain of wholesalers and bookstores for example. If the bookstore hides the demand information from wholesalers, it will cause inventory backlog to wholesalers. And if the wholesalers keep their own distribution capabilities and circulation progress as confidential information, the arrival time and the quality of books for bookstore will be affected. In other words, as for the downstream enterprises on the publishing supply chain, every enterprise is reluctant to share their information. But to the upstream node enterprises, the more the knowledge they share, the greater the profit they will get. Therefore, upstream enterprises are willing to share their information with all enterprises on the supply chain. Obviously, this information Game will affect the effectiveness in information transfer.

Building a risk sharing and incentive mechanisms based on economic interest between enterprises in the supply chain is a fundamental measure, which can reduce the information asymmetry, and can effectively prevent the negative impact of information Game. There is an incentive mechanism that the adverse side will get some compensation in order to promote the cooperation. And the balance of the information Game could be implemented by the punishment to non-cooperation betrayal [5].

4.2 The Cultural and Knowledge Coherence among Member Enterprises

Besides the complete sharing of information, the success of Agile Supply Chain also relies on the exchange of knowledge and resources between the member enterprises, which could enhance competition in the multi-joint and avoid short board phenomenon. However, the access to resources and knowledge is particularly relying on the compatibility of the strategy and knowledge of different member enterprises. In selecting a strategic partnership, if the two are at quite different levels of knowledge, the receiver is unable to accurately understand and absorb knowledge, there will be obstacles in information exchange and the dynamic union will lose its efficiency.

In addition, each business has its own unique corporate culture. In Agile Supply Chain, the compatibility of enterprise culture also has a profound impact on the success of dynamic union. The high coherence of cultural and strategy brings the high efficiency to the strategic alliance. Therefore, when choosing the member enterprises on supply chain, we should also consider the coordination of the corporate culture of the member enterprises on the same chain.

4.3 The Administrative Compatibility of the Members Enterprises

Chinese current publishing distribution system is based on administrative region. Its vertically integrated supply chain operations have gradually formed fixed groups of interest. How to break the internal structure of the interests of the system, to eliminate various practical differences, to realize the actual supply chain system based on enterprise efficiency and effectiveness itself turns out to be important issues which should be seriously taken into consideration when we are aiming at building China's publishing enterprise Agile Supply Chain and dynamic alliance.

References

1. Z.F. Wang, Supply Chain Management, *Publishing House of Electronic Industry*, Beijing, 2006, p.26.
2. Z.H. Qu, Five Changes in Chinese, *Publishing Market*, March 6, 2007; http://ent.sina.com.cn/x/2006-05-05/08561072682.html
3. China Publishing Yearbook2006. *Publishing House of China Publishing Yearbook*, Beijing, 2006), p.731
4. C.Y Gao, Analysis on the Supply Chain of Publishing Group, *A Vast View on Publishing*, 2004 (10)
5. J.N. Wu, B.L. Liu, Analysis on Supply Chain Strategic Partnership with Game theory, Logistics Technology, 2004(4)

An Empirical Study of Factors Related to Consumer Complaint Behavior

Meilian Liu [1], Feng Zhang [2]

1 Management College, Guilin University of Electronics and Technology,
Guilin Guangxi, P.R. China 541004
merryjanes@126.com

2 Management College, Guilin University of Electronics and Technology,
Guilin Guangxi, P.R. China 541004,
mlliu@guet.edu.cn

Abstract. This paper focuses on factors related to consumer complaint behavior tendency in Internet. Current literatures from home and abroad focus on how to improve consumer's satisfaction and loyalty, while there are still relatively few researches on consumer dissatisfaction and complaint behavior. Based on the analysis of consumer complaint behavior tendency in Internet, this paper discusses the factors related to consumer complaint behavior. Hypothesis test of the factors by means of structural equation model, and the model has been modified by LISREL software and has come a conclusion that some factors are related to consumer complaint behavior in Internet. The research indicates that the factors, which consist of online consumer characteristics, product characteristics, consumer attitude to complaint, customer satisfaction and shopping experience, have a positive impact on web consumer complaint behavior tendency.

1 Introduction

As early as the 1970s, the business managers and scholars have taken concerns to consumer complaint problem. With the development of E-commerce, researches on customer behavior, especially customer satisfaction and complaint behavior have appeared gradually. How to solve the consumer complaint problem properly is an effective "defensive marketing" strategy, which contributes to remain the existent customers and obtain new customers.

According to Shop.org and Forrester Study, U.S. network retail sales in 2006 will reach 211 billion increased by 20% compared to 2005. With rapid development of online retail sales, online shopping is more and more popular. However, because of open system, it is very difficult for enterprises to completely reach "zero defects". When the actual services are inconsistent with the expected service, consumers will be dissatisfied. In this case, they may choose to complain, remain silent but turn to competitors or remain silent and continue to purchase. To get valuable information about customer complaint, enterprises can realize the real need of consumers and identify the existing problems of products and services, and then persist in improving service. Therefore, to research consumer complaints and the related factors are very necessary to improve network enterprise products and services. Effective

Please use the following format when citing this chapter:

Liu, M., Zhang, F., 2007, in IFIP International Federation for Information Processing, Volume 251, Integration and Innovation Orient to E-Society Volume1, Wang, W. (Eds), (Boston: Springer), pp. 379-389.

management of customer complaints enterprises can obtain at least the following advantages. Firstly, to manage consumer complaints can be used for strategic planning and operations. Secondly, it contributes to a targeted marketing activity. Thirdly, customer satisfaction and brand loyalty can be improved.

2   Related Work Review

Researches related to consumer complaints began in the early 1970s, which were affected by the consumer conciliarism. Early studies focused on describing general consumer characteristics in different industries and summarizing complaint characteristics and methods. These researches often concentrate on such fields: The actions customers may take and the factors related to unsatisfied situation; the reasons for consumer complaints and the cost of consumer complaints.

From the end of 1970s to the beginning of 1990s, scholars began to seek for building theories and models which can explain and predict complaint behavior. Most studies focused on the following three aspects: Firstly, it was to research whether complains were related to industry competition; Secondly, whether complaints were related to consumers' perceptions to service providers or not. Thirdly, it was to analyze whether complaint intentions were related to consumer attitudes to complaints or not. By means of the gathered data from three service industries, Singh analyzed the interrelationship between customer attitudes to complaints, dissatisfaction and complaining intentions [1]. Lastly, the researches studied other factors which had an impact on complaints1 [2, 3, 4].

After the 1990s, researches on consumer complaints developed rapidly. Plymire concluded that the complaint-generation process results in a customer focused culture in which complaints are regarded as an opportunity [5]. Hansen analyzed consumer's response to the unsatisfied state and suggested that to deal with complaints properly should help prevent consumer from loss [6].

Studies from foreign countries on consumer complaining behavior such as American have gradually become mature, which focus on two areas primarily. In view of research fields, they focused on whether, when, why, how to complain and how to deal with complaints, and they put emphasis on varied methods, such as empirical research, model prediction and so on. In view of research objects, there exist both characteristics of consumer complaint studies from consumers and the importance of marketing management from enterprises perspective [7-11].

At present, the research on consumer complaints in China is still at the initial stage. Most scholars confined to the complain superficies without deeper investigation, so there were not complete and mature theories; In business domain, owing to the lack of theories guide and special cultural backgrounds, there is no enough attention though many consumer complaints exists in practical e-marketing.

Ping Zhao investigated five durables businesses by questionnaire and researched the factors related to consumer complaint which are general characteristics of Chinese consumer complaint, differences in demographic characteristics and characteristics of product itself [12]. Xiucheng Fan researched such factors of procession system for consumer complaint as the collection and analysis of complaint information, organization learning mechanism and its continuous improvement and authorization [13]. He also discussed the effect that value orientation imposed on consumer complaint. According to value orientation, consumers were divided into three groups: disadvantaged groups, individualism consumers and strong pressure consumers. The research showed that the factors related to complaint behavior are different for consumers in the same state with different value orientation [14].

3   Analysis of the Reason for Internet Consumer Complaint and Characteristics

3.1   Reason for Web Consumer Complaint

Why web consumers complain is just from their dissatisfaction with the provided products and services. Two main reasons for their dissatisfaction are product problem and service problem as well as the limitations from the Web consumer capability of their cognition products and services. It is often that consumers complain because of product problem, for example, the delivered product is not the same as the ordered, the products are damaged, and the inferiority products are regarded as superiorities. The service problems appear as such forms as: too late delivery, too many network advertisements, the complicated log process in Internet and unsafe online payments.

3.2   Complaint Type of Web Consumers

According to different complaint path, the complaint types of Web consumers can be divided into three types: direct complaint, private complaint and third party complaint.

Direct complaint refers to the Web consumers make complaints to the suppliers or service providers related to the specified transaction. Private complaint is Web consumers complain to his groups who are irrelative to the given bargain. For example, one has purchased some product in Internet, the consumer will complain to his groups by Email, bulletin board and other communication method

Contrast with the former two, third party complaint refers to Web consumers complain to objects who don't belong to his groups and are not related to the product or service providers in a transaction

3.3   Web Consumer Complaint Characteristics

Compared with consumer complaint behavior in the traditional commerce, Web consumer complaint behavior shows some new characteristics:

> Network is a main complaint channel. Because of network convenience, fast information spread and extensive spread area, Web consumers will make complaints to the purchased product and service by means of supplier service platform, BBS and QQ chat room to abreact their dissatisfaction and search for a proper solution.

> Complaint mode is diversified, but direct complaint is preferred. Web consumers pay more attention to individuation and their wish

realization compared with the consumers in traditional commerce. Once the purchased products or services are far away from their expectation, they will be dissatisfied and tend to abreact dissatisfaction by direct complaint manner.

➢ The factors related to consumer behavior are more complicated. Because of the virtual network, risky online payment and laggard distribution system compared with traditional commerce, the latent factors related to consumer dissatisfaction and consumer complaints are more complicated [15].

4   Empirical Research on the Factors Related to Complaint Behavior of Web Consumer

4.1   Method

Structural Equation Modeling is a multi-statistical analysis technology which integrates the regression analysis with factor analysis method together properly [16]. Besides estimating the factorial structure and relationship, SEM doesn't have strict limitations, so it can cope with many observable variables and potential variables, and provides possibility to analyze the structure relationship of potential variables [17]. Because web consumers complaint behavior is very complicated, to adopt traditional method such as regression analysis is not ideal, regression analysis must suppose the observation variable don't have error, while SEM allows the statistical relationship of observation variables to provide regression estimation coefficient of potential variables, so it provides opportunity from statistics supposition to confirm factors related to web consumer behavior.

4.2   Factor Supposition Related to Web Consumer Complaint Behavior

The Web consumer will inevitably encounter dissatisfied in web shopping and complaints appear. When web consumer are dissatisfied, they may propose complaints, keep silence but turn to competitor, keep silence and continue to purchase and so on. However, only to understand factor related to web consumer complaint behavior can enterprise cope with the complaint behavior effectively, and turn web consumer from dissatisfaction to satisfaction.

Hypothesis 1: Web consumer complaint attitude is related to complaint tendency

Web consumer complaint attitude will have impact on whether consumers resort to actual complaint behavior or not. The Web consumer complaint behavior could be divided into three dimensionalities: (1) whether complaint is worth? (2) Individual standard of complaint behavior. (3) The possibility of profit by complaint. The complaint tendency is relative to how serious the problem is which the web consumer perceived, the offered price, complaint cost and so on. If to complaint needs more cost than benefits, they choose not to complain. If complaint needs the specific knowledge of related service as well as the communication skill, but the consumer lack for these abilities and knowledge, then the consumer will not complain. When the Web consumer sense the enterprise will process the complaint properly, and will provide remedial treatment to not perfect product and service, they tend to complain. Here we discussed complaint manner from the three aspects of complaint cost, the skill and the complaint income.

Hypothesis 2: the individual characteristic of Web consumer is related to complaint tendency.

The young people have greater desire to express their desirability, and the web consumers who have higher educational background may have specific product and service knowledge as well as communication skill. From the viewpoint of sex, there are big differences at proposing their own opinions boldly and powerfully or claiming themselves' right between male and female. The male generally express their anger more calm than the female in the public situation. And when they are unsatisfied, the male has intense tendency to adopt complaint. Bearden's research discovered that, the race, the employment condition and the family type for the influence of the complaint behavior of consumer is not remarkable.

Hypothesis 3: Web product characteristic is related to complaint tendency.

The product type, price, quality, complexity and expected life-span of the network product, besides how serious the problem is which arose from product and service and so on both have influence to the consumers' complaint behavior. Regarding to the research of electric appliance, Bradford found the type, the price and the life expectancy of product is related to consumer's complaint behavior too [18]. When faced with problems from commodity with low price, the consumer generally don't complain directly, but will turn to the competitor next time because of lower switch cost. But for durable commodity with high price, the consumer prefers to direct complaint if he is dissatisfied to expect gains from the solved dissatisfaction problem by complaint. As for characteristic of the network product, we choose the produce or service price, expected life-span of the network product, the competition advantage of industry which the product belongs to are related to corporation image and complaint tendency. Generally speaking, the quality is included in the price, and web consumers think it necessary for corporations to maintain their image, good enterprise will attach more importance to the complaint problem thus the web consumers tend to complain. When web consumers are dissatisfied, whether the web consumers propose complaint or not is related to how intense the product competition among industries is. On condition that a greater number of competitors exist, as switch cost is low, the consumers tend not to complain, possibly remain silence but change to the competitor. Next, complaint is related to the consumer cognition of how to cope with complaint which is provided by the suppliers. If the consumers felt the enterprise can make positive response to service defaults, and can take care of consumers' complaint, then, the probability of consumer complaint is bigger [19].

.Hypothesis4: the Web consumer's satisfaction is related to complaint tendency.

Since complaint is from the Web consumer's dissatisfaction, then the relation between network satisfaction and complaint tendency is negative obviously. However, when loyal consumers for some certain brand or enterprise are dissatisfied, as long as they are not very unsatisfied, they will keep silence and continue to patronage. This paper will make a discussion between web consumer satisfaction and the complaint behavior tendency.

Hypothesis 5: On-line shopping experience is related to complaint tendency.

For consumers who experienced on-line shopping first time, when they are dissatisfied with on-line shopping, they may lose confidence in the electronic commerce, and give up online shopping; certainly they choose not to make complaint to online stores. Otherwise, they change shopping websites frequently. But for the consumer who always navigates in the shopping website, when they are dissatisfied with on-line shopping, they tend to complain to on-line store. Moreover, for those who like to chat online frequently, and web consumers possibly tend to complain in private to share their unsatisfied shopping experience with their good friends and other netizens.

Hypothesis 6: Web consumer individuality characteristic is related to Web consumer's complaint behavior tendency of Web consumer complaint manner.

Each web consumer has his individual characteristic, according to theory of planned behavior, different Web consumer shows different complaint manner [20] [21]. Therefore, we suppose that web consumer's individuality characteristic is related to Web consumer's manner to complaint, and even does have effect on web consumer's complaint tendency.

Based on the hypothesis what discussed above, we established the factor model of the web consumer complaint tendency, as show in fig.1.

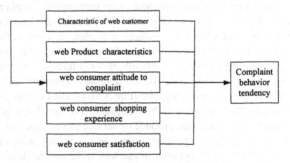

Fig.1. A conceptual model of Web consumer complaint behavior

4.3   Data Acquisition

This paper mainly focused on the customers who have experience in internet shopping by questionnaire. Most of the questionnaires have been sent out in Internet accompanied by paper questionnaire. We randomly selected 160 people, but because of incomplete and wrong information, only 152 people's questionnaires are valid. The valid rate is 95%. The average age of the people is 30 years old, 40% of which is female. From education situation, we can see that the rate of people with senior high school education background is 32%, while the proportion of college background is 25%. Population with college and even higher education background is 31%. From the view of occupation, students have a big rate is 36%. This result is accorded with the statistics report of CNNIC; there is no significant difference between them.

4.4　Variables in the Model

Six variables are involved in this model which are characteristics of internet customer, products characteristics, the attitudes of internet customer to complain, the satisfaction of internet customer, the internet shopping experience and incline of complain.

Table 1. Potential variables and number of index

Potential Variable Element	Index
characteristics of internet customer	4(age, sex, education, governable income)
products characteristics	4(price, expectable used time, product image, characteristic of industry)
attitudes of internet customer to complain	3(cost, technician, profit)
Internet customer satisfaction	3(quality of product purchased, delivery time, payment safety)
Internet shopping experience	3(time, quantity, frequency)
Complaint tendency	3(possibility of complain, reasonable of complain, change of supplier)

All these potential variables are included in 21 questions. The sample is analyzed by EFA by Lisrel 8.53. The main indexes used in research of complaint have been tested successfully by credibility analysis. The main variables are shown in the Table 1.

4.5　Test Result

In this research, we have tested Web consumer complaint tendency model by SEM. And we have established the structural model by Lisrel 8.53 software. The reliability coefficient for characteristics of Web customer, products characteristics, attitudes of Web customer to complain, Web customer satisfaction and Internet shopping experience is respectively 0.75, 0.79, 0.86, 0.88 and 0.71 respectively. It shows that the questionnaire has good credibility.

Table 2. Loadings and error of apparent variable on potential variable

Supposed Description	Loading	Error
Web customer age →Characteristic	0.6	0.82
Sex of Internet customer→characteristics	0.6	0.66
Education of Internet customer→Characteristics	0.58	0.52
Controllable income→Characteristics	0.52	0.84
Low value Products→ Characteristic of Internet Products	0.45	0.82
High value Products → Characteristic of Internet Products	0.87	0.60
Expected product life→Characteristic of Internet Products	0.66	0.62
Product Image→Characteristics of Internet Products	0.78	0.71

Industry Characteristic of Products → Characteristic of Internet Product	0.71	0.78
Complain Cost→attitudes to web consumer complaint	0.80	0.54
Benefit of Complaint→attitudes to web consumer complaint	0.62	0.34
Skills of Complain→attitudes to web consumer complaint	0.66	0.52
Quality of Product purchased→Satisfaction	0.64	0.48
Delivery Time of Product→Satisfaction Content	0.54	0.44
Safety of Payment online→Satisfaction	0.76	0.57
Time of Starting Internet shopping→ Experience of Internet Shopping	0.52	0.65
Frequency of Internet Shopping→ Experience of Internet Shopping	0.36	0.72
Times of Internet Shopping→ Experience of Internet Shopping	0.75	0.7
Possibility of Complaint→Complaint tendency	0.79	0.46
Perceived sensibility of Complaint→Complaint tendency	0.55	0.7
Supplier switch cost→Complaint tendency	0.86	0.44

In order to verify whether the suppositions are correct or not, the results are shown in table 2 and table 3 by factor analysis and path analysis. According to the supposed model, we can see that every path significance is 0.05. In this research, we choose to report 5 fit indexes to explain the model, which are X^2, NNPI, CFI, GFI, RMSEA. These parameters provide different meanings of the supposed model from different aspects. Generally speaking, if the NNPI and CFI are both above 0.9, the models have better fit. If the RMSEA is below 0.1, the model can be accepted based on the gathered data.

Table 3. Related Index Comparison of Nested Model and Supposed Model

Model	X^2	df	NNFI	CFI	GFI	RMSEA	$\triangle X^2$ ($\triangle$df)
Supposed Model	146.42	94	0.96	0.97	0.89	0.04	
Nested Model 1	151.51	95	0.95	0.97	0.90	0.04	5.09 (1)
Nested Model 2	152.45	95	0.95	0.97	0.90	0.04	6.03 (1)
Nested Model 3	162.34	95	0.94	0.97	0.89	0.05	15.92 (1)
Nested Model 4	165.56	95	0.96	0.97	0.90	0.06	19.14 (1)
Nested Model 5	172.35	95	0.96	0.97	0.90	0.06	25.93 (1)
Nested Model 6	151.58	95	0.95	0.97	0.90	0.05	5.16 (1)
Nested Model 7	150.51	95	0.94	0.95	0.90	0.04	4.09 (1)
Nested Model 8	176.65	96	0.96	0.97	0.90	0.04	30.23 (2)

Note:

Nested model 1: Based on the supposed model, the path from characteristic of Web customer to consumer complaint behavior tendency is deleted directly.

Nested model 2: Based on the supposed model, the path from characteristic of Web products to consumer complaint behavior tendency is deleted directly.

Nested model 3: Based on the supposed model, the path from attitude of Web customer to consumer complaint behavior tendency is deleted directly.

Nested model 4: Based on the supposed model, the path from characteristic of Web products to consumer complaint behavior is deleted directly.

Nested model 5: Based on the supposed model, the path from satisfaction of Web customer to consumer complaint behavior is deleted directly.

Nested model 6: Based on the supposed model, the path from experience of Web shopping to consumer complaint behavior is deleted directly.

Nested model 7: Based on the supposed model, the path from characteristic of Web customer to consumer complaint behavior is deleted directly.

Nested model 8: Based on the supposed model, the path from characteristic of Web customer to consumer complaint behavior is deleted directly and the path from attitude of web customer to consumer complaint behavior is also deleted directly.

According to results of table 3, it can be proved that the supposed model is appropriate. Except for the nested model 7, the other nested models are statistically correct. We suppose these potential variables have effect on complaint behavior tendency independently. The nested model will be inappropriate no matter any path is deleted. Therefore, the rest six suppositions we have established are proved to be true. Therefore, the result of path analysis is shown in the fig.2.

5   Conclusion and Remarks

A structural model has been established which consists of key factors related to web customer behavior, and we can come to such conclusion:

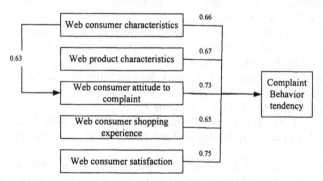

Fig.2. The factors related to web consumer complaint behavior tendency

➢   Individual diversity of web customers. Many factors are related to web consumer complaint tendency such as sex, age, education background, controllable income and independence. Contrast with the people who have higher education background and more controllable income tend to complain, the young prefer complaint to the aged.

➢   Complaint attitude is related to complaint tendency. The complain attitude of web customers can be measured by three indexes: 1) complaint cost; 2) whether complaint requires special skills; 3)

perceived increased income for complaint consumer. A more intensive attitude may cause complaint tendency.

➤   Satisfaction and complain is related to complaint behavior tendency negatively. Customers are more inclined to complain directly if they are more dissatisfied but they keep silence or switch to the competitors.

Characteristic of web products is related to complaint tendency. The more complicated is the product, the more the consumer will tend to complain. However, some related factors have been ignored such as web advertisement, value orientation, Web consumer perception and so on. What's more, how complaint come into being based on given spatial and temporal factors and environment must be further researched.

Reference

1. Singh, J. and R.E.Wilkes., "When Consumer Complain: A Path Analysis of Consumer Complaint Response Estimated" [J]. *Journal of the Academy of Marketing Science*, 1996, 24(4), pp.350-365.
2. Singh Jagdip. "Exit, Voice, and Negative Word-of-mouth Behaviors: An investigation across three service Categories" [J]. *Journal of the Academy of Marketing Science*, Winter, 1990(18), pp.1-15.
3. Beard WO, Teel J E. "Selected determinants of consumer satisfaction and complaint reports" [J]. *Journal of Marketing Research*, 1983(20), pp.21-28.
4. Fornell,Claes and BIrger Wernerfelt. "Defensive Marketing Strategy by Customer Complaint Management: A Theoretical Analysis" [J]. *Journal of Marketing Research*, 24(November), 1987, pp.337-346.
5.   Plymire, J. "Complaints as Opportunities". [J].*Journal of Consumer Marketing*, Vol. 8, 1991, pp.39-43.
6. Hansen, Scott W., Thomas L. "Powers and John E. Swan. Modeling Industrial Buyer Complaints: Implication for Satisfying and Saving Customers" [J].*Journal of Marketing*, 1997, pp.12-22
7. Sridhar Balasubramanian,Prabhudev Konana,Nirup M. Menon, "Customer Satisfaction inVirtual Environments: A Study of Online Investing"[J]. *Management Science*, 2003, Vol.49, Issue 7.
8. Isabelle Prim, Bernard Pras," "friendly" complaining behaviors: toward a relational approach" [J].*Journal of Market-Focused Management,* 1999, vol.3, pp.333-352.
9. Mustafa Jarrar, Ruben Verlinden, Robert Meersman, "Ontology-Based Customer Complaint Management" [J]. *Lecture Notes in Computer Science*, vol.2889/2003, pp.594-606.
10. McAlister, Debbie Thorne. "A content analysis of outcomes and responsibilities for consumer complaints to third–party organizations"[J]. *Journal of Business Research*, 2003 56 (4), pp.341-351.
11. Y.Cho,I. Im,R. Hiltz,J. Fjermestad ,An Analysis of Online Customer Complaints: Implications for Web Complaint Management[C].*Proceedings of the 35th Annual Hawaii International Conference on System Sciences* (HICSS'02) Volume 7,2002.
12. P. Zhao, Y.L Mo."Study on Consumer complaint Behavior in Durable Goods in China"[J].*Journal of Tsinghua university*, 2002,(2).

13. X.C Fan. "Consumer Complaint Management System of Service Corporation Oriented to Consumer Satisfaction"[J].*Chinese Journal of Circulation Economy*, 2002 (2), pp.40-44.

14. X.C Fan. "Value Oriented is Related to Consumer Complaint Tendency"[J].*Nankai Management Review*, 2002,(5), pp.11-16.

15. Z.C Li, M.L Liu. "Consumer Behavior Study in Electronic Commerce"[J] *Chinese Journal of management science*, 2002, 10(6), pp. 88-91.

16. Y. Shen, P. Zhao. "BB Model and Empirical Bayes Method Used in Complaint Behavior Tendency" [J].*Journal of Statistics Research*. 2004(11), pp.55-59.

17. J.T Hou .Structural Equation model and Its Applications [M].Beijing: *Educational Science Publishing Science*, 2004.

18. Bradford, Adelina Broadbridge, Julie Marshall. "Consumer Complaint Behavior: The case of electrical goods"[J].*International Journal of Retail & Distribution Management*, 1995, VOl 23, issue 9, pp.8-18.

19. Christy M. K.Cheung, Matthew K.O. Lee, Consumer satisfaction with internet shopping: a research framework and propositions for future research[C]. Proceedings of the 7th international conference on Electronic commerce 2005.

20. Y.G Wang, Hing-Po Lo, Y.H Yang, "An Integrated Frameworkfor Service Quality, Customer Value, Satisfaction: Evidence from China's Telecommunication Industry"[J]. *Information Systems Frontiers*, vol.6/2004,issue.4.

21. Terry L. Childersa,*, Christopher L. Carrb, Joann Peckc, Stephen Carsond. "Hedonic and utilitarian motivations for online retail shopping behavior" [J]. *Journal of Retailing*, 77 (2001), pp.511–535.

Adaptive Customer Profiles For Context Aware Services in a Mobile Environment

Mike Radmacher

Chair of Mobile Business and Multilateral Security,
Gräfstr. 78, 60054 Frankfurt am Main, Germany,
mike.radmacher@whatismobile.de,
WWW home page: http://www.whatismobile.de

Abstract. Mobile data communication generated 10 percent of the overall data revenue in Germany and between 2-3 percent worldwide [29] in 2004. This development is contradictory compared to the high investment (91.5 billion €) in networks and licenses that supported the UMTS infrastructure and thereby the mobile internet. An advertised-based revenue model [10] addresses an opportunity to increase the mobile data communication. Mobile customers and advertisers are matched based on the customer's current situation (location, time and interests). Precise customer profiles, as a requirement to overcome the information overflow, and to enable a multilateral economically reasonable matching are indispensable but the profile's quality is not given in reality. Without precise customer profiles there is no matching. With situation adaptive customer profiles the profile's quality is increasing. Its design, realization and integration into the mobile operator's infrastructure are the aim of this paper.

1. Introduction

With the beginning of the 90's the prerequisites in order to establish mobile data communication as an additional service alongside voice communication were given. 20.3 billion short messages were sent in Germany in 2005 [5]. The mobile data communication generated only 10 percent of the overall data revenue in Germany. This development is contradictory compared to the high investment (91.5 billion €) in networks and licenses that supported the UMTS infrastructure and thereby the mobile internet [10].

Furthermore, the penetration of the mobile market in Germany reached nearly 102.3% in 2006 [5] and implies a high amount of customers under multiple contracts (pre and post paid) in comparison to new customers. The stress of competition is increasing. New business models as e.g. an advertising-based revenue model shown in [10], promote mobile data communication. Mobile network operators take part in the market in an

Please use the following format when citing this chapter:

Radmacher, M., 2007, in IFIP International Federation for Information Processing, Volume 251, Integration and Innovation Orient to E-Society Volume1, Wang, W. (Eds), (Boston: Springer), pp. 390-399.

additional function as context provider. Unique features of mobile communication (e.g. location and time dependency, identity and context reference, opportunities of interaction) influence e.g. the usage of mobile services. Advertisers gain a communication channel to a customer after an opposite matching of interest. Merging customer's and advertiser's interests on the one hand, and reducing the information flow based on the high amount of information, products, services on the internet on the other hand, requires a precise image of a customer. A question that includes some of the main aspects is given [31] "To give customers exactly what they want, you first have to learn what that is. It sounds simple, but it's not". Reducing the information overflow on the fixed internet is addressed by individualization strategies as for instance recommendation techniques [24]. Amazon is using recommendation techniques typically for products while Google is using them for individualized information providing, but any kind of recommendation based on individualization is strongly dependent on an accurate customer profile.

The mobile market is seeking for differentiation by individualization or personalization. Following this path customer profiles are one key, but in most cases there is less knowledge about customer's preferences. Customers are not interested in sharing their interests or not completely sure about them [21,22]. Checking the quality of customer inputs [21] as a question of truthful statements is missing. Some disclosed personal preferences are strongly related to the benefit the customer is looking for. 94 percent of all internet customers don't disclose personal information at all. 40 percent of them disclose untruthful information [21]. Self-adaptive customer profiles can counteract this development.

This paper aims at presenting first ideas to construct a framework for designing adaptive customer profiles that means using recommender techniques to enhance customer profiles as one of the main problems instead of providing e.g. products recommendations. Furthermore it is addressing the mobile environment and presents a guideline on how to integrate adaptive customer profiles in the existing mobile network operator's infrastructure (e.g. mobile portal). Adaptive customer profiles can provide more accurate personalization and in addition advance current and future recommender mechanisms as well as individualized communication between the advertiser and customer as shown in [10]. By generating knowledge within the own mobile network, switching costs are produced which can also provide the necessary differentiation in the mobile market.

This paper is structured as follows: section 2 discusses the underlying research approach, related to the design research. Section 3 gives the first design of the framework for adaptive customer profiles, while section 4 presents a customer profile designed for a mobile environment. Section 5 visualizes a first guidance on how to integrate the mobile customer profile in the mobile network operator's infrastructure. Section 6 highlights questions of data protection and finally section 7 sums up the contribution of what we learned, and how identified questions can be addressed in more detail in future.

2. Research Approach

Based on design research, [14, 27, 28] the self-created procedure in order to answer the upcoming research questions is visualized in figure 2. Every single stage is related to the design research approach by [28].

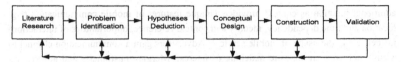

Fig. 1. Research progress related to design reseach

The procedure is separated into six stages and starts with the literature research, followed by problem identification (awareness of a problem). Hypotheses deduction and a first conceptual design (suggestions) are part of the third and forth stage. Stage five is about the construction (development) of a specific artifact and the procedure concludes with the evaluation (evaluation) in stage six.

Three main and three sub questions describe the research questions that are targeted by this paper. (Question1, also motivation) What kind of benefit do adaptive customer profiles generate from the perspective of a service provider and demander? (Question2) How to design adaptive customer profiles in a mobile environment? (Question3) How to integrate adaptive customer profiles into an existing infrastructure of a mobile network operator? (Related to Question1) How do customer profiles influence individualized service usage? (Related to Question2) What are the elements of an adaptive customer profile? (Related to Question3) How to activate still existing knowledge in companies in order to fill these profiles?

Every research starts with literature research. The areas individualized sales approach, techniques and algorithms of recommender systems and self-learning mechanism were investigated in order to profile customers in the best possible way. According to the results of the literature research customer profiles already exist in different ways. In [19] it says customer profiles were suggested as an improvement for a variety of applications. From query enhancement [16] and digital libraries [2], to the personalization of websites [12] and enhanced interpersonal communication [18]. Current trends are for the integration of customer profiling in the delivery of services for an aware environment such as family interactive TV [13], exhibitions [17], filtering of news messages [6, 23] and analyzing customers behavior while visiting internet sites [25, 26]. In [19] you will also find an overview of existing patents according to customer profiles which do not have any relation to a mobile environment and its particularities. A framework of how to design adaptive customer profiles including mobile aspects was not found through literature research as well as the idea of using recommender techniques to enhance existing customer profiles in order to advance the baseline for recommendations.

The second stage is about the problem identification. The introduction already points out that the information overflow from a customer perspective [20] and the sales approach from an advertiser perspective [9] are still not optimized fields by research. By using adaptive customer profiles, a reduction of search costs both on the customer and advertiser side can lead to differentiation and separation in the mobile commerce against the competition. The aim is to set up a framework for designing adaptive customer profiles based on existing techniques, algorithm and mechanism in order to construct a profile extensible by recommendation. Finally the integration into a mobile network operator's infrastructure is necessary.

The following hypotheses state what kind of benefits an adaptive customer profile should generate. These have to be evaluated in one of the next steps. (Hyp1) More precise customer profiles should optimize the sales approach. (Hyp2) Based on adaptive customer profiles the current recommendation mechanism might generate better recommendations. (Hyp3) An integration of adaptive customer profiles into the mobile network operator's infrastructure should support the differentiation against competition.

The conceptual design as fourth stage comprises three artifacts. (Artifact1) A framework for designing an adaptive customer profile. It is a kind of procedure and points out how to design an adaptive customer profile independent of usage driven by the idea to enhance profiles by recommendations. (Artifact2) The development of adaptive customer profile designed for a mobile environment. (Artifact3) A guideline on how to integrate the adaptive customer profile into a mobile network operator's infrastructure.

The construction includes three artifacts named above. The validation should be performed by using the architecture analysis as one method of the design research approach [28] which can test the integration e.g. into an existing infrastructure of a mobile network. Furthermore a case study is planned to get an impression of the quality improvement of recommendations. The field of transaction costs probably leads to a design recommendation to visualize the economic benefits adaptive customer profiles are providing.

3. Framework Development

Based on the literature research the following framework is a first approach combing existing, different algorithms, techniques and methods of knowledge management, recommender and self-learning systems in order to recommend profile enhancements for customer profiles. Figure 2 shows the framework, separated into two parts - customer and intermediary. The customer profile (part of the customer) is an image of customer specific information. A detailed description is given in section 4.

The intermediary (e.g. a mobile network operator) includes several components as databases, a knowledge discovery process, a recommender process, a profile generation process and a feedback process for gathering customer information, and to create an image of the customer. These components are a combination of different approaches, the literature research discovered, and additional components derived from knowledge in the area of mobile commerce.

In several distributed databases, usage specific information is saved, e.g. a service password and customer name, products bought of late and websites visited. All this information, pseudonymous stored, leads to a better understanding of what the customer is looking for.

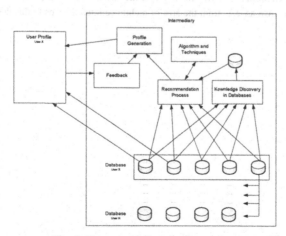

Fig. 2. Framework for adaptive customer profiles

Knowledge discovery in databases (KDD) as part of this framework indicates a process operating on distributed databases containing possible knowledge about customers. Unknown knowledge or coherence between customers and their behavior should be identified. This process aims on enhancing a customer profile without direct interaction. Knowledge discovery in databases is split up into 9 phases that can proceed as follows [11, 7]: (Phase1) Developing an understanding of the application domain and the means identifying the goal of the KDD process from the customer's viewpoint. (Phase2) Create a target data set on which discovery is to be preformed. (Phase3) Data cleaning and processing. (Phase4) Data reduction and projection. (Phase5) Matching the goals of the KDD process to data mining methods. (Phase6) Choosing the data mining algorithm(s). (Phase7) Search for patterns of interest. (Phase8) Interpreting mined patters. (Phase9) Consolidating discovered knowledge.

The recommendation process offers recommendations for customer profile enhancements. The idea behind the recommendation process includes combing well-known methods such as rule-based-, content-based-, collaborative filtering as well as hybrid systems [3, 23, 30] and further algorithms of different kinds. Results of the knowledge discovery process are also taken into account in order to enhance the customer profile. Whether an identified attribute is accurate or not is part of evaluation in the feedback process.

The customer profile (as defined in section 4) is generated based on information stored in databases as well as device specific information, the feedback process and information recommended by the recommender process.

Within the feedback process active and passive feedback [4] is differentiated. First the customer will be asked in e.g. monthly iterations if one of the recommended attributes is accurate or not. This is called the active feedback. The passive attempt is observing the customer's behavior after adding an additional preference that possibly leads to different services, information or products as part of the sales approach. If newly offered services are considered, possible profile enhancements are found. The result of the feedback process influences the profile generation process.

4. Design of an Adaptive Customer Profile

The section at hand describes the structure of an adaptive customer profile self-designed for a mobile environment. Different concepts identified by literature research [16, 2, 12, 18] as well as own aspects from the area of mobile commerce leads to this design shown in figure 3.

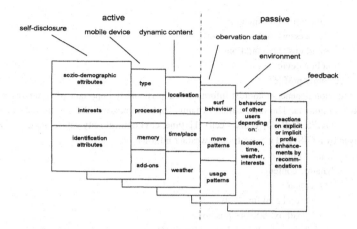

Fig. 3. Design of an adaptive customer profile

The profile consists of 6 different layers separated into 2 sections called active and passive. The active part of the customer's profile is defined as visible and accessible by the customer. In contrast, the passive part contains additional information for enhancing the active part. Information about the customer, his mobile device and dynamic situation based information is part of the active customer profile. The passive part contains observation data, information about the environment and a link to other customers in the same situation and their reaction to sales approaches.

The self-disclosure of a customer includes classical social-demographic attributes such as age, gender or interests (cinema, sports, lunch, outdoor, ..) and an identity attribute e.g. a pseudonym. The information can be stored in an xml similar notation as shown in the following example.

```
<customer profile>
  <self-disclosure>
    <socio-demographic>
      <age>25</age>
      <gender>male</gender>
    </socio-demographic>
    <interests>cine</interests>
    <id>FGhe56$%&hdf23</id>
  </self-disclosure>...
</customer profile>
```

Visualizing mobile content is strongly dependent on the mobile device a customer is using. For the Playboy magazine 65 different device profiles were stored in order to guarantee the best possible display [15]. Based on a device profile, optimal graphic rendering or an adequate distribution channel (WML, XHTML, HTML, MMS or SMS) is ensured. If a device is capable of running java applications, additional features are usable. For this purpose the active customer profile should include the following attributes: device type, memory size, processor, additional enhancements. Based on the device type, information about display, colors and resolution are derivable. Enhancements a mobile device is capable of are e.g. a flash player or the java runtime environment.

```
<customer profile>    ...
  <mobile device>
    <type>Siemens S65</type>
```

```
        <memory>64</memory>
        <processor>200</ processor>
        <add-ons>Java<add-ons>
      </mobile device >...
    </customer profile>
```

Situation dependent context information is particularly important when talking about mobile customers. The layer called dynamic content represents the current location of a customer (GPS, Cell-ID, WLAN cell) [1], time, environment (city centre, industrial zone derived by a GIS) and e.g. up-to-date weather information.

```
    <customer profile>   ...
      <dynamic content>
        <location>
          <city>Frankfurt</city>
          <postbox>60054</postbox>
          <longitude>N50°07.189'</longitude>
          <latitude>E008°39.023'</latitude>
          <place>downtown</place>
        </location >
        <time>12:23</time>
        <weather>30C</weather>
      </dynamic content>...
    </customer profile>
```

Observation data states the first information that is part of the passive profile. Observation data is information about web usage (durability, web pages sorted by categories ,...) and movement patters (which location is visited when).

Information about the environment is addressed by a separate layer of the passive profile. Hereby e.g. information about other customers at the same location and time is of importance. Amazon is a classical example from the fixed internet. A person that bought book x, also bought y and might be interested in book z. This knowledge applies to the mobile internet where a customer is maybe interested in using services others used at a specific time and place with similar profiles. Insights of this behavior, possibly derived by the process called knowledge discovery in databases, influence the recommendation of profile enhancements.

The feedback process, already described, separates the collection of insight into an active and a passive part. New profile attributes are actively communicated to the customer or questioned by the passive behavior observation.

5. Integration in a Mobile Environment

After discussing a framework for adaptive customer profile and a first design attempt of a customer profile, this section addresses how a customer profile can be integrated into the mobile network operator's infrastructure. Figure 4 illustrates the process within a mobile portal owned by the mobile network operator. The integration demonstrates how the necessary components are working together within the mobile operator's portal.

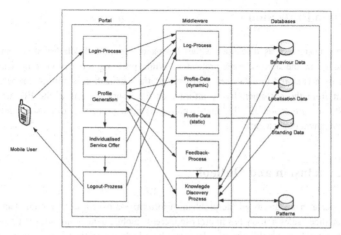

Fig. 4. Integration in a mobile environment

An already enrolled customer passes through the following process within the portal: login, profile generation, individualized service offering and logout. At every stage additional processes run in the background e.g. logging, gathering and handling dynamic and static data, feedback and knowledge discovery in databases, in order to enhance the customer profile. In the current section each stage will be discussed.

A mobile customer enters the main page of the mobile portal operated by the mobile network operator. After consent through an automatic identification process by the mobile network, a redirect is performed. A transaction pseudonym and the current location of the customer are stored in a temporal session.

The process of profile generation comprises the setup, update and storage of a customer profile. First information about the customer gathered during the login procedure (transaction pseudonym, location) is stored. Profile generation uses several sub processes (e.g. profile data as static and dynamic, feedback, knowledge discovery in databases and login), aiming at the best possible image of the customer.

Based on an always up-to-date customer profile, individualized services can be offered [8], independent of whether the idea of an advertising-based revenue model [10] is being followed or not. The baseline of every individualized service offering is an image of a customer.

The logout process finalizes the service usage. Every transaction is closed, log information is stored and potential payments are allocated.

The collection of static customer information as a transaction pseudonym, age and sex are part of the process as well as static mid-term information as hobbies (see section 4). Dynamic information is given by point of interests the customer visited, date, time or residence time. All data is pseudonymously stored in databases.

The logging process observes the following sub processes: login (date, time, location of the customer, mobile device, and pseudonym), profile generation (setup and updates), individualized service offering (service offer, service usage, usage duration, interaction level) and logout. Gathered information is pseudonymously stored in a database.

Knowledge discovery in databases is a process separated into 9 sub processes already discussed in section 4. Applied on several distributed databases, so far undiscovered insights should lead to customer profile enhancements without direct interaction.

The feedback process was already described in section 4.

6. Data Protection

Profiling customers as discussed within the paper proves difficult because it implies knowledge in the area of data protection. While profiling the customer no personal information is stored in databases. Furthermore, the localization is only performed after consent from the customer. Every information disclosure accords to the EU directive 95/46/EC on protection of individuals with regard to the processing of personal data and free movement of such data.

7. Conclusion and Outlook

The paper at hand discussed the problem of information overflow on the one hand and individualized sales approaches in order to increase mobile data communication usage on the other hand, in a mobile market described by a high penetration, competition and the absence of differentiation. Technical as well as conceptual approaches for individualization sales approaches were presented based on adaptive customer profiles. Precise customer profiles are the baseline of accurate recommendations. A proposal of a framework to design adaptive customer profiles, the construction of a customer profile for a mobile environment and a discussion on how to integrate such a profile into a platform of the mobile network operator, was part of the paper. An advertising-based revenue model [10] is able to match advertiser and customers in a better way than before.

The enhancement of the framework, the embodying of the customer profile in a mobile environment and its integration validated by the architecture analysis and a case study including complexity, hardware, response time, benefit analysis, as well as an implementation as a prototype are planned. Further discussions on data protection are necessary. According the research approach based on design research in section 2, the work this paper presented covers the first and the second stage (awareness of a problem and suggestions).

References

41.   1. A. Albers, S. Figge and M. Radmacher, LOC3 - Architecture Proposal for Efficient Subscriber Localisation in Mobile Commerce Infrastructures, *Proceedings of 2nd IEEE International Workshop on Mobile Commerce and Service, Munich*, Germany, 2005.

42.   2. G. Amato and U. Straccia, User Profile Modelling and Applications to Digital Libraries, ECDL '99, Abiteboul, S., Vercoustre, A.-M.(Eds.), 1999, pp. 184-197.

43.   3. M. Balabanović, and Y. Shoham, Fab: content-based, collaborative recommendation, Communication of the ACM, March 1997/Vol. 40, No. 3.

44.   4. R. Bulander, M. Decker, B. Kölmel and G. Schiefer, Kontextsensitives mobiles Marketing, in: B. König-Ries, M. Klein (Hrsg.): Mobile Datenbanken und Informationssysteme, in Business, Technologie und Web. BTW 2005, Universität Karlsruhe 2005, pp. 11-20.

45.   5. Bundesnetzagentur, 2006, Jahresbericht 2006. Bundesnetzagentur, Bonn.

46.   6. R. Carreira, J.M. Crato, D. Gonçalves and J.A. Jorge, Evaluating Adaptive User Profiles for News Classification, 2004.

47.   7. U. Fayyad, G. Piatetsky-Shapiro and P. Smyth, Knowledge Discovery and Data Mining Towards a Unifying Framework, 1996.

48.   8. S. Figge, Situation-dependent services—a challenge for mobile network operators, Journal of Business Research, Volume 57, Issue 12, 2004, pp. 1416-1422.

49.   9. S. Figge and A. Albers, Individualising M-Commerce Services by Semantic User Situation Modelling, Proceedings of the 7th International Conference Wirtschaftsinformatik, Bamberg, 2005.

50.   10. S. Figge and S. Theysohn, Quantifizierung IKS-basierter Marktleistungen - Analyse eines werbefinanzierten Geschäftsmodells für den Mobile Commerce, Wirtschafsinformatik 48 (2), 2006, pp. 96-106.

51.   11. W.J. Frawley, G. Piatetsky-Shapiro and C.J. Matheus, Knowledge Discovery in Databases: An Overview. AAAI, 1992, pp. 56-70.

52.   12. M. Goel, S. Sarkar, Web Site Personalization Using User Profile Information, AH2002, P. De Bra, P. Brusilovsky and R. Conejo, (Eds.), 2002, pp. 510-513.

53.   13. D. Goren-Bar and O. Glinansky, FIT-recommending TV programs to family members. Computer & Graphics, 28, 2004, pp.149-156.

54.   14. A.R. Hevner, S.T. March, J. Park and S. Ram, Design Science Information Systems Research. MIS Quarterly, Vol. 28 No. 1, 2004, pp. 75-105.

55.   15. C. Kaspar, O. von Wersch, I. Hochstatter, A. Albers, S. Figge, et al., Mobile Anwendungen - Best Practices in der TIME-Branche. Hrsg.: T. Hess, S. Hagenhoff, D. Hogrefe, C. Linnhoff-Popien, K. Rannenberg and F. Straube, Universitätsverlag Göttingen, 2005.

56.   16. R.R. Korfhage, Query Enhancement by User Profiles, Joint BCS & ACM Symposium on Research & Development in Information Retrieval, 1984, pp.111-121.

57.   17. R. Kraemer and P. Schwander, Bluetooth based wireless Internet applications for indoor hot spots: experience, 2000.

58.   18. R.J. Lukose, E. Adar, J.R. Tyler and C. Sengupta, SHOCK: Communicating with Computational messages and Automatic Private Profiles, Proceedings of WWW 2003, May 20-24, Budapest, 2003, pp. 291-300.

59.   19. B. Salem and M. Rauterberg, Multiple User Profile Merging (MUPE): Key Challenges for Environment Awareness, EUSAI 2004, pp. 196–206.

60.   20. J. Schackmann, Ökonomische vorteilhafte Individualisierung und Personalisierung, 2002

61.   21. M. Schuhmann, Individualität und Produktindividualisierung – Kundenprofile für die Personalisierung von Produkten, 2004.

62.   22. C. Shapiro and H.R. Varian, Information Rules, 1999.

63.   23. S. Singh, M. Shepherd, J. Duffy and C. Watters, An Adaptive User Profile for Filtering News Based on a User Interest Hierarchy, 2006.

64.   24. U. Spitzer, Recommender Systeme im E-Commerce. Wirtschaftsuniversität Wien, 2005.

65.   25. K. Sugiyama, K. Hatano and M. Yoshikawa, Adaptive Web Search Based on User Profile Constructed without Any Effort from Users, 2005.

66.   26. P. Srinil, and O. Pinngern, Adaptive User Profile for Information Retrieval from the Web, 2002.

67.   27. H. Takeda, P. Veerkamp, T. Tomiyama and H. Yoshikawam, Modeling Design Processes, AI Magazine, 1990, pp. 37-48.

68.   28. V. Vaishnavi and B. Kuechler, Design Research in Information Systems, AIS 2006.

69.   29. Vodafone Group Plc, Key Performance Indicators, 2006, Available:

70.   http://www.vodafone.com/assets/files/en/VOD_KPIs_20041231_2.xls, Abruf am 2005-11-01

71.   30. Y.Z. Wei, L. Moreau and N.R. Jennings, A Market-Based Approach to Recommender Systems, ACM Transactions on Information Systems (TOIS), 2005, pp. 227 – 266.

72.   31. P. Zipkin, The limits of mass customization, Sloan Management Review 42,3, 2001, pp. 81-87.

Consumer Behavior towards Continued Use of Online Shopping: An Extend Expectation Disconfirmation Model

Min Qin

School of Communication, Jiangxi Normal University, P.R. China, 330022
helenqin126@163.com

Abstract. The business-to–consumer is the most visible business type of electronic commerce. Online shopping allows companies to provide product information and direct sales to their consumers. In order to effectively drive consumers to accept electronic commerce and online transactions, there is an urgent need to understand the factors that influence consumer behavior towards continued use of online transactions. The expectation disconfirmation model (EDM) from the consumer behavior literature has been used to explain continued information systems (IS) usage behavior. This paper takes an extend EDM perspective to predict and explain consumer behavior in the online shopping context. This proposed extend EDM, incorporating the perceived risk, trust and shopping enjoyment, was empirically tested with data collected from a survey of online shopping consumers in three websites. The objective of this research is to increase the understanding of consumer online behavior for future research in e-commerce.

1 Introduction

The advantages of online shopping transactions are well known. The most common incentives for consumers to shop online are convenience, broader selections [1], competitive pricing, and greater access to information [2]. However, online sales volume still remains relatively low compared to alternative retailing forms. Lots of previous research has shown [3, 4] that obvious reasons include security and privacy concerns, lack of familiarity with the medium, and the suitability of products to be sold. Actually in the business-to-consumer electronic commerce, a consumer has the double role of the product consumer and information technology (the website system) user [5]. To the consumer in e-commerce, the website system is a full representation of the shopping. For example, some famous online shopping websites (www. amazon.com, www.buy.com, and so on) heavily depend on information system (IS) in their business strategies. A previous research [6] has shown that system use is a good indicator of the success of commercial websites. In this way,

Please use the following format when citing this chapter:

Qin, M., 2007, in IFIP International Federation for Information Processing, Volume 251, Integration and Innovation Orient to E-Society Volume1, Wang, W. (Eds), (Boston: Springer), pp. 400-407.

researchers need to combine the research streams of information systems, consumer psychology, and marketing to study and understand online consumer behavior.

The expectation disconfirmation model (EDM or expectation confirmation model) from consumer behavior literature [7, 8] posits that a consumer's repurchase intention is preceded by consumer satisfaction; whereas consumer satisfaction is directly affected by disconfirmation resulted between a consumer's pre-purchase expectations and post-purchase expectations. Bhattacherjee [9] applied this theory to the continued use of the information system, and he integrated the concept of the technology acceptance model (TAM) with the EDM to reflect the influence of a consumer's expectation of system-specific attributes on consumer satisfaction and the intention of continuous usage. From the viewpoint of information system, the EDM can reasonably explain a consumer's repurchase or continued purchase behavior.

Empirical research has indicated that the effects of online commerce on consumer behavior are not same as the traditional marketing [4]. The perceived risks, trust and shopping enjoyment associated with online shopping can influence attitudes toward online purchase, as does the perceived ease of using the website [10]. Therefore, our study will further extend the EDM to online commerce through adding some constructs. The rest of this paper proceeds as follows. The next section presents the theoretical framework, including reviewing the essence of expectation disconfirmation model, examining the constructs of perceived risk, trust and shopping enjoyment in e-commerce. An extended research model and research hypotheses are then developed in section 3, and in this section we describe research methodology. Section 4 gives data analysis and empirical results. Research findings and limitations are presented in section 5. Conclusions are given in the final section.

2   Theoretical Framework

Online shopping has been viewed as the new business model. As both the presence and operation of online shopping depend heavily on IT, they are often regarded as a type of IS [11]. To companies, online shopping commerce is their strategic information systems (IS), while to consumers, online shopping commerce is end-user of IS. This view is justified by previous literature [12, 13]. Hence, when consumers accept and use online shopping, they are accepting and using IS. In order to keep old consumers using online shopping, it is need to understand their post-adoption behavior of IS. Based on these perspectives, our study employs the theoretical constructs of EDM and perceived risks, trust, perceived enjoyment to predict and explain consumer behavior towards continued use of online shopping.

2.1   Expectation Disconfirmation Model

Since a large portion of consumer purchases are second or n-time purchases rather than initial acceptances, the study of consumer repurchase behavior continues to catch the attention from researchers [7]. The EDM explains the consumer consumption decision in the post-purchase process and constantly dominates academic research and managerial practice [8]. According to the

EDM, the consumers' post-purchase intention is chiefly determined by their satisfaction with actual use of that purchase or service. Satisfied users repurchase that product or continue accepting the service, while dissatisfied consumers stop using it subsequently. Satisfaction is viewed as the key to building and retaining a loyal base of long-term consumers. Investing in customer satisfaction is like taking out an insurance policy, and if some temporary hardship befalls the firm, customers will be more likely to remain loyal [15].

2.2   Electronic Commerce Acceptance and Continued Usage

A website is, in essence, an information system. Some prior research has reasonably validated online purchase intentions in part with the technology acceptance model proposed by Davis [16, 17], which is preeminent theory of technology acceptance in IS research. As such, online continuous purchase behavior also should be explained in part by the EDM, which is widely supported in IS post-adoption research.

2.3   Trust, Perceived Risk, and Shopping Enjoyment in E-Commerce

There are various conceptions of trust in the literature. Nevertheless trust can be described as the belief that the other party will behave in a socially responsible manner, and by so doing, will fulfill the trusting party's expectations without taking advantage of its vulnerabilities [18]. The common Trust has always been an important element in influencing consumer behavior and has been shown to be of high significance in uncertain environments, such as the Internet-based e-commerce context [19, 20]. Some previous research has proposed trust as an important element of business-to-consumer e-commerce. For example, Palmer, Bailey, and Faraj argue that building consumer trust in web retailers is essential for the growth of B2C e-commerce [21].

When engaging in an online transaction process, consumers are rightly alarmed about the different types of risks that confront them. But since risk is difficult to capture as an objective reality, the literature predominantly has addressed the notion of perceived risk, which will be defined as the consumer's subjective belief of suffering a loss in pursuit of a desired outcome [22].

Shopping can be intrinsically enjoyment, and enjoyment of the shopping experience is an important determinant of consumer behavior [18]. On the website, shopping enjoyment is positively and significantly related both to attitude toward shopping on the web and intentions toward shopping on the web [23].

3   Research methodology

3.1   An Extended Model and Research Hypotheses

A consumer's behavioral intention towards continued online shopping in e-commerce should incorporate consumer satisfaction and trust, perceived risk, shopping enjoyment. Based on the theoretical statement from EDM and attitude-related theoretical constructs influencing the online consumer behavior in e-commerce, we develop an extended research model in Fig 1.

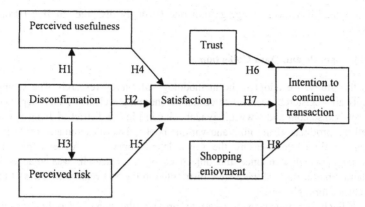

Fig. 6. An Extended Expectation Disconfirmation Model for Online Consumer Behavior

The conceptual model adopts attempts to synthesize the essence of the EDM and three important constructs in e-commerce to predict and explain a consumer's behavioral intention toward online shopping continuance. Hence, we derived the following hypotheses:

Hypothesis 1: consumers' disconfirmation will positively affect their perceived usefulness of online shopping

Hypothesis 2: consumers' disconfirmation will positively influence their satisfaction.

Hypothesis 3: consumers' disconfirmation will negatively affect their perceived risk of online shopping

Hypothesis 4: consumers' perceived usefulness of online shopping will positively influence their satisfaction

Hypothesis 5: consumers' perceived risk of online shopping will negatively influence their satisfaction

Hypothesis 6: consumers' trust will positively affect their intention to continued transaction

Hypothesis 7: consumers' satisfaction will positively influence their intention to continued transaction

Hypothesis 8: consumers' shopping enjoyment will positively affect their intention to continued transaction

3.2 Measure Development

The measure of EDM was developed on the constructs of perceived usefulness, disconfirmation, satisfaction, and intention toward continued transaction. Perceived usefulness was measured using a 4-item scale adapted from Davis et al. [24]. Disconfirmation, satisfaction and intention to continued transaction were adapted from Bhattacherjee [9], and they were measured using a 3-item scale, 4-item scale, and 3-item scale respectively. Measures for trust and perceived risk were adapted from Jarvenpaa et al. [19], both of which include three items. Shopping enjoyment was measured using a 3-item scale consistent from the previous research [25, 26]. All of the above 23 items were measured on a 5-point Likert scale ranging from one (strongly disagree) to five (strongly agree).

3.3 Sample and Data Collection

In this study, we adopted the methodology of survey research. The sampling units are registered users of three online shopping websites (www.ncgift.com, www.jxxhsd.com and www.qingyuanbook.com) in the district of Jiangxi, which sell the products of the gifts and various books. The questionnaire of 23 items was developed to measure the seven latent constructs. An electronic mail message, which explained the objectives of the research, was attached our questionnaire. Both of them were distributed to the 863 registered users of three websites through e-mail.

Each respondent was asked to provide the name of online shopping websites that he had used and had purchased the products at least one time during the last 12 months. If respondent had the online purchase experience, then they were instructed to answer all the questions from the questionnaire. Finally, 179 registered users were found to have the online shopping experience, and 156 questionnaires are complete and usable.

4   Data Analysis and Results

Table 7. Confirmatory factor analysis for convergent validity

Constr uct	Item loading	Composite reliability	AVE	Factor correlations						
				PU	DCO	PR	SE	SAT	TR	INT
PU	0.83-0.90	0.86	0.76	0.76						
DCO	0.75-0.87	0.82	0.68	0.51	0.68					
PR	0.82-0.88	0.85	0.73	-0.52	-0.43	0.73				
SE	0.74-0.85	0.81	0.64	0.45	0.36	-0.30	0.64			
SAT	0.82-0.90	0.86	0.77	0.55	0.38	-0.44	0.40	0.77		
TR	0.72-0.86	0.83	0.70	0.48	0.42	-0.39	0.33	0.41	0.70	
INT	0.82-0.91	0.87	0.80	0.58	0.37	-0.43	0.42	0.51	0.48	0.80

The seven hypotheses were tested collectively using the structural equation modeling (SEM).The data obtained were tested for reliability and validity using confirmatory factor analysis (CFA). The measurement model includes 23 items describing seven latent constructs: Perceived usefulness (PU), Disconfirmation (DCO), Perceived risk (PR), Shopping enjoyment (SE), Satisfaction (SAT), Trust (TR), Intention to continued transaction (INT).

Convergent validity is assessed using three criteria, including all factor loadings should be exceed 0.7; construct reliabilities should be exceed 0.8; and average variance extracted (AVE) exceed 0.5. As we can see from Table.1, composite reliabilities of all constructs exceeded 0.80. The CFA results indicate that all 23 items corresponding to the seven constructs had loadings value ranged between 0.72 and 0.91. The square root of AVE ranged from 0.81 to 0.87. Hence, all three conditions for convergent validity were met.

Discriminant validity assesses whether individual indicators can adequately distinguish between different constructs. The correlation matrix in Table.1 indicates that the square root of AVE of each construct (diagonal elements) was higher than corresponding correlation values for that variable in most cases, so this can assure discriminant validity.

The next step in the data analysis was to examine the significance and strength of each hypothesized effect. Examining individual paths, we can see that all paths were significant. Intention towards online continued transaction was predicted by satisfaction (0.32; $p<0.001$), trust (0.23; $p<0.001$) and shopping enjoyment (0.14; $p<0.001$), which jointly explained 68% of the variance in intention. Consumer satisfaction is predicted by disconfirmation ((0.48; $p<0.001$), perceived usefulness (0.12; $p<0.001$), and perceived risk (-0.21; $p<0.001$). It supports H2, H4 and H5 respectively. Supporting H1and H3, disconfirmation had positive effect on perceived usefulness and negatively effect on perceived risk. In summary, all hypotheses were supported.

5 Research findings and limitations

This study attempts to harmonize the essence of EDM and other consumer-related factors in online shopping to develop an extended EDM for explaining consumer's continued behavior of online shopping. From the current research model, some interesting findings can be discussed. First, trust and shopping enjoyment also are identified as two motivators of behavioral intention towards continuous use of online shopping. The effect of shopping enjoyment is much lower than both trust and satisfaction. To some extent, when consumers accept the online shopping, they pay more attention to the products themselves. Secondly, perceived risk is identified to have a direct effect on the consumer's satisfaction in this study, and its effect on satisfaction is greater than perceived usefulness. Thirdly, different from the EDM, continued use of online shopping in e-commerce may not have one motivator of satisfaction to measure.

Like most empirical research, this study is not without limitations. On the one hand, we employed consumers of three online shopping websites as the sample, and the categories of provided products are limited. The empirical results in this study may have limited to the general products. On the other hand, we do not strictly distinguish the consumers of continued using online shopping system from continued purchase the products with online shopping. The future research will make much effort on these aspects.

6 Conclusions

This paper has devoted much effort on developing an extended expectation disconfirmation model to predict and explain the consumer's continued use of online shopping. Empirical data was collected from three online shopping websites users to verify the fitness of the hypothetical model. This research findings show that a consumer's behavioral intention towards online shopping continuance is influenced by satisfaction, trust and shopping enjoyment. Perceived risk has positively effect on the consumer satisfaction. The main purpose of study is to provide the deeper understandings of consumer behavior towards continued use of online shopping.

References

1. S.L. Jarvenpaa and P.A. Todd, Consumer Reactions to Electronic Shopping on the World Wide Web, *International Journal of Electronic Commerce*,1(2), 58-88 (1997).

2. R.A. Peterson, S. Balasubramanian and B.J. Bronnenberg, Exploring the Implications of the Internet for Consumer Marketing, *Journal of the Academy of Marketing Science*, 25(4), 329-346 (1997).

3. S. Bellman, G.L. Lohse and E.J. Johnson, Predictors of Online Buying Behavior, *Communications of the ACM*,42(12), 32-38 (1999).

4. I. Maignan and B.A. Lukas, The Nature and Social Uses of the Internet: A Qualitative Investigation, *Journal of Consumer Affairs* 31(2), 346-371 (1997).

5. M. Koufaris, A. Kambil and P.A. LaBarbera, Consumer Behavior in Web-Based Commerce: An Empirical Study, *International Journal of Electronic Commerce* ,6(2), 115-138 (2001).

6. C. Liu and K.P. Arnett, Exploring the Factors Associated with Web Site Success in the Context of Electronic Commerce, *Information & Management*, 38(1), 23-33 (2000).

7. R.L. Oliver, Cognitive, Affective, and Attribute Bases of the Satisfaction Response, *Journal of Consumer Research* ,20, 418-430 (1993).

8. R.A. Spreng, S.B. MacKenzie and R.W. Olshavsky, A Reexamination of the Determinants of Consumer Satisfaction, *Journal of Marketing* ,60(July), 15-32 (1996).

9. A. Bhattacherjee, Understanding Information System Continuance: An Expectation-Confirmation Model, *MIS Quarterly*, 25(3), 351-370 (2001).

10. H.v.D. Heijden, T. Verhagen and M. Creemers, Predicting Online Purchase Behavior: Replications and Test of Competing Models, *In proceedings of the 34th Hawaii International Conference on System Sciences*, IEEE Computer Society Press, (2001).

11. L.-d. Chen, M.L. Gillenson and D.L. Sherrell, Enticing Online Consumers: An Extended Technology Acceptance Perspective, *Information & Management* , 39, 705-719 (2002).

12. S. Pant and C. Hsu, Business on the Web: Strategies and Economics, *Computer Networks and ISDN Systems* ,28(7-11), 1481-1492 (1996).

13. P. Spiller and G.L. Lohse, A Classification of Internet Retail Store, *International Journal of Electronic Commerce* ,2(2), 29-56 (1997).

14. C. Liao, J.L. Chen and D.C. Yen, Theory of Planning Behavior (TPB) and Customer Satisfaction in the Continued Use of E-Service: An Integrated Model, *Computers in Human Behavior* (2006).

15 E. W. Anderson and M. W. Sullivan, The Antecedents and Consequences of Customer Satisfaction for Firms, *Marketing Scienc,e* 12(2), 125-143 (1993).

16. D. Gefen, E. Karahanna and D.W. Straub, Trust and TAM in Online Shopping: An Integrated Model, *MIS Quarterly* ,27(1), 51-90 (2003).

17. F. D. Davis, Perceived usefulness, Perceived ease of use, and user Acceptance of information technology, *MIS Quarterly*, 13(3), 319-340 (1989).

18. P.A. Pavlou, Consumer Acceptance of Electronic Commerce: Integrating Trust and Risk with the Technology Acceptance Model, *International Journal of Electronic Commerce*, 7(3), 101-134 (2003).

19. S.L. Jarvenpaa, N. Tractinsky and M. Vitale, Consumer Trust in an Internet Store, *Information Technology and Management*, 1(12), 45-71 (1999).

20. J-M. Moon and Y-G. Kim, Extending the TAM for a World-Wide-Web Context, *Information and Management*, 28, 217-230 (2001).

21. J.W. Palmer, J.P. Bailey and S. Faraj, The Role of Intermediaries in the Development of Trust on the WWW: The Use and Prominence of Trusted Third Parties and Privacy Statements, *Journal of Computer Mediated Communication*, 5(3),2000.

22.R.A. Bauer, *Consumer Behavior As Risk Taking .In D.F.Cox (ed.), Risk Taking and Information Handling in Consumer Behavior*, Cambridge: Harvard University Press,389-398(1960).

23. S.L. Jarvenpaa and P.A. Todd, Consumer Reactions to Electronic Shopping on the World Wide Web, *International Journal of Electronic Commerce*, 1(2), 59-88 (1997).

24. F.D. Davis, R.P Bagozzi and P.R Warshaw, User Acceptance of Computer Technology: A Comparison of Two Theoretical Models, *Management Science*, 35(8), 983-1003 (1989).

25. D. Compeau, C.A. Higgins and S. Huff, Social Cognitive Theory and Individual Reactions to Computer Technology: A Longitudinal Study, *MIS Quarterly*, 23(2), 145-158 (1999).

26. M.B. Holbrook, R.W. Chestnut, T.A. Oliva and E.A. Greenleaf, Play As a Consumption Experience: The Roles of Emotions, Performance, and Personality in the Enjoyment of Games, *Journal of Consumer Research*, 11, 728-739 (1984).

Research on Anti-Tax Evasion System
based on Union-Bank Online Payment
mode

Yang Qifeng[1], Feng Bin[2], and Song Ping[3]
1-3 Economics College of Wuhan University of Technology,
Wuhan 430070, Hubei.P.R,China
Email: [1]yangqifengwhut@163.com, [2]13027154642@vip.163.com,
[3]songpingwhut@163.com

Abstract. The popularity of the e-commerce facilitates the tax evasion a lot, and the anti-tax evasion work in the e-commerce area becomes urgent. We introduced a union-bank online payment mode, which can solve many problems of existing mode such as main body status, standardization and inter-bank payment. Besides, it provides a platform for some value added services such as anti-tax evasion, anti-money laundering, credit evaluation, etc. In this mode, the transaction data is centralized so that we can carry on the investigation during the online payment process. Based on this, we designed an anti-tax evasion system utilizing the data mining, OLAP and data warehouse technologies. This system can monitor the transaction dynamically and judge the tax evasion behavior by analyzing abundant transaction data according to relevant tax law, and the knowledge in the knowledge base and expert base. Beside, it collects the tax evasion rule as knowledge in order to update itself automatically.

1 Introduction

The rapid development of e-commerce improves the flourish of the world economy and rational allocation of the worldwide resource. Meanwhile, it changes the traditional transaction mode and brings big challenge to the tax system. In the virtual market of the e-commerce, the customers can be anonymous and the sellers can conceal their address. Even the transaction can be finished without any record, and this led to many tax evasion phenomena by e-commerce.

The reason why e-commerce facilitates the tax evasion is various. Firstly, the characteristic of e-commerce makes the transaction itself difficult to be monitored. The e-commerce activities need no fixed shop, paper contract that is necessary in traditional transaction, and the goods can be immaterial such as digital product. All these characteristic will place a premium on tax evasion [1]. Secondly, the tax law of e-commerce is distempered. The problem that should all

Please use the following format when citing this chapter:

Qifeng, Y., Bin, F., Ping, S., 2007, in IFIP International Federation for Information Processing, Volume 251, Integration and Innovation Orient to E-Society Volume1, Wang, W. (Eds), (Boston: Springer), pp. 408-416.

the e-commerce activities pay the tax puzzled many countries for a long time. Some countries suggested part tax of the transaction by e-commerce should be avoided while other countries didn't think so. There is no agreement on how to impose the tax of the transaction by e-commerce. Thirdly, the revenue management of the e-commerce is disordered [2]. At present, many sellers on the net haven't registered in the administration for industry and commerce, and have no business license. This adds the difficulty of the taxation. Especially, the online payment is preferred to by the tax dodger because it reduces the cost and risk.

To solve the problem of tax evasion, we need to build an effective Anti-Tax Evasion (ATE) system with effective management mechanism. The union-bank online payment mode can provide such platform for anti-tax evasion work. On such platform, the transaction data of the whole country through online payment can be centralized, on which we can carry on the data mining so as to find out the tax evasion behavior. Based on this mode, we designed an anti-tax evasion system using data mining technology, which can improve the ability to find out tax evasion behavior a lot during the online payment process.

2 Union-bank online payment mode

2.1 Advantage of the union-bank online payment mode

Nowadays, the existing online payment mode in our country can't meet the need of favorable development of e-commerce, it's impossible to become the leading online payment mode: 1) the third party online payment platform is questioned in its main body status and business scope; the prestige of itself is not enough; and the problem of fund in float may cause system risk. So it's impossible to become the leading mode.[3,4] 2) The commercial banks can provide online payment by online bank gateway, but they all do things in their own way in the transaction procedure, interface standard and authentication mechanism. This increases the difficulty of each side and led to waste resource because of the development of multi-payment gateway and interface software. The data of information flow, capital and logistics flow referred during the e-commerce process is not normative and unified. The most pivotal issue is the distribution of benefit; it's impossible to build up the leading online payment mode based on certain commercial bank. 3) The China UnionPay is a third party online Payment Company in essence, however it succeeded in credit card electronic payment area, also faced the same problem as the third party online payment company. In this situation, it's impossible to provide the platform which can centralize the transaction data for many value added service including ATE, Anti-Money Laundering (AML), credit evaluation, etc.

The e-commerce online payment in our country faced the challenge of main body status, standardization, innovative service and inter-bank payment, so it's necessary to build up the leading online payment mode with Chinese characteristics. The payment flow chart of Union-Bank online payment mode introduced in this paper is shown in fig 1. This mode can overcome the deficiency of the existing mode, and promote the well-liking development of e-commerce by continuous innovation.

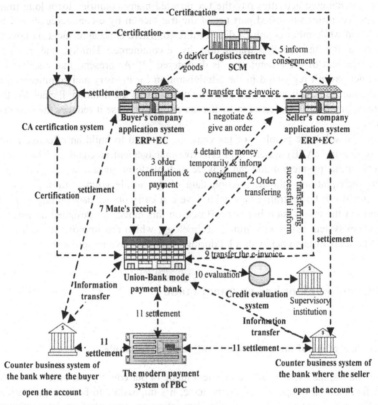

Fig. 7. Payment flow chart of the Union-Bank mode

2.2 Process of the union-bank online payment mode

The union-bank online payment mode we discussed is able to become leading mode that is just needed in our country. By the integrative connection of China modern payment system of PBC to each member commercial bank, the application system, payment gateway, network point resource and client resource can be shared, and the inter-bank payment service can be realized favorably by the extension of the payment supply chain. In this mode, the system of relevant institutions, such as buyer, seller, certification centre, logistics centre, modern payment system of PBC, mobile communication system, 315 customer association, quality surveillance office, industry and commerce administrative bureau, police bureau, can be connected and work collaboratively with unified online payment gateway, information interface standard and normal processing procedure. This will solve the chock point which blocks the development of the e-commerce effectively. By constituting national concentrating e-commerce basic data resource base building upon union-bank mode, this study takes the achievement in relevant area of domestic and international researches for reference, colligates the fruit of computer science, operations research, industry project, commercial strategy, management science, law science and so on, studies the intelligent recommend technology base on the users experience, case consequence, knowledge noumenon, prediction and early warning method, CRM,

SCM and credit evaluation method, and the innovative service regarding the online payment as hinge, in order to provide support of theory and method for the development of e-commerce economy, and create value for the online payment supplier and client.

The UBOP bank uses the "head office-branch" structure, and the UBOP platform is the national data concentration system. Participates in B2B of UBOP include: 1) Buyer's company (ERP+EC). Its main factors include goods purchase, payment, and e-check; 2) Seller's company (ERP+EC). Its main factors include goods delivery, collection, and transfer of the e-invoice; 3) Certificate Authority. It takes the charge of inspecting the legitimacy of the public key as a believed third party during the e-commerce; 4) Logistics centre. It carries on the goods delivery according to seller's order, and participate in the supply chain management; 5) UBOP centre (bank). It's the core of the online payment, and it's a special bank engaging online payment service that can take part in the settlement of PBC. Its main function is payment: both sides of the transaction should open an account which can be connected to their account in commercial bank before the online business, and then use it pay or collect money. Their extensive services include: supply chain return, quality testing complains, credit mechanism construction, etc. 6) bank where the buyer/seller open the account. The account in the commercial bank where the buyer/seller opens the account associates with the account in UBOP, and the money can be transferred between them; 7) prestige evaluation institution. It evaluates the prestige of the both parties of the transaction, Logistics Company and so on which participate in the e-commerce. This institution associates with the national quality testing department, consumers' association, and arbitration department.

3 Logical framework of ATE service system

Based on the online payment mode, the logical framework of the ATE service system can be divided into five layers: database layer, basic data resource base layer, data analysis layer, application service layer and interface layer as shown in the figure 3.1.

(1) Database layer: It is composed of abundant basic business data including user data, transaction data, tax imposition data and a history database. These provide the data support for the basic data resource layer and real-time ATE intelligent analysis and they are updated by the data import from the union-bank centre.

User data refers to relevant data of the company or customer, including the register information (register identity, register time, company or customer detail introduction, encrypted account information), use information (use time, use IP address and use aim) and credit information (times of successful transaction, times being complaint about and the credit evaluation of both sides of the transaction and union-bank).

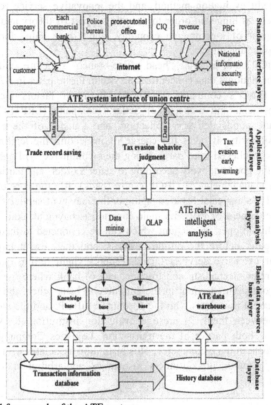

Fig.2. Logical framework of the ATE system

Transaction data includes the data relating to the transaction between the users which compounds of the transaction content (bargainers of both sides, goods information, price, paying time and paying amount), transaction process (bargain record, order of the payment and goods delivering, banks of opening account of both sides, order and invoice) and transaction result (successful or failing, failure reason, loss by the failure, complaint and the process result).

Tax imposition data refers to the relevant tax information about the transaction. It includes the transaction type, goods type, tax type, tax amount that should impose on and relevant laws.

History database is used for storing the historical data of the user information database, trade information database and capital flow database. Because these three databases will be cleaned up maybe every year, the data will be stored in history database. Certainly the history database will be clean up too, but, every 3 or 5 years. The history data finally will be sent to ATE data warehouse. Given the large amount of the information referred in ATE area, we construct the history database as a temporary buffer memory between database layer and ATE data warehouse.

(2) Basic data resource base layer: This layer stores some knowledge for data mining and suspicious transaction. By data mining, it analyzes the relation among the data from database layer so as to find some laws of these data and

provide support for the data analysis layer. It includes knowledge base, case base and shadiness base.

Knowledge Base: KB is based on the expert experience and booklore, and refreshed dynamically by the connection to the database. The basic structure of KB is hiberarchy. Its lowest layer is "fact knowledge" such as theoretical knowledge and factual data of the tax evasion, the middle layer is knowledge which controls the "fact knowledge" such as some rules and processes of the tax evasion, and the highest layer is "strategy" which controls the middle layer which we call "ATE strategies". The ATE knowledge base aims at the tax evasion area and collects the solution so as to realize the intelligence of the system.

Case Base: It collects the case in the tax evasion and ATE area, analyses the relation between them in order to extract the tax evasion methods and their representations. This will be helpful for ATE real-time intelligent analysis to judge if the current case matches the characteristic from the case base.

Shadiness Base: This stores the knowledge of the suspicious trade which can learn, adapt and update itself. The real-time intelligent analysis will obtain relevant cue from the shadiness base, and if it finds some suspicious trade, it will send a feedback report to the shadiness base.

ATE Data warehouse: The data in the database layer is independent and is classified into certain kind of information. However, the relation of them can't be reflected. Although the history database stores all the information of the three databases, it just keeps the independent structural data and won't analyze its rule. The ATE data warehouse is data integration factory oriented ATE area for decision supporting of ATE real-time intelligent analysis. All the information from database layer will flow into this warehouse and is processed here.

(3) Data analysis layer: The main function of this layer is to analyze the data form database and basic data resource base layer utilizing data mining technology. The ATE real-time analysis cleans up the data from database and basic data resource base layer, format and filtrate it through data mining, and then analyzes the feedback information and output the result to the union-bank centre. This layer clean up and convert the allopatric distributed data resource (include the database of each platform, text file, HTML file, knowledge base and so on) according to the subject heading list definition, data resource definition and data extract rule definition. Then reorganize and process the data and load them to the aim base in the data warehouse. The real-time intelligent analysis includes two modules which are OLAP (Online Analytical Processing) and Data mining. Utilizing these two powerful tools, the analysis can extract the useful information from the data for decision supporting.

Because it's necessary to carry on the operation such as Slice, Dice, Roll-up, Drill-down during the application of OLAP, we choose the cube data mode to describe the structure of multidimensional data. For instance, we can construct the cube data mode as figure 3 shows to describe the tax information. This mode is composed of one fact table and four dimensional tables. The fact table shows the tax paying situation of certain people in certain transaction and certain time. The taxpayer dimensional table lists the basic information of the taxpayer; the tax dimensional table shows the relevant tax information; data dimensional table refers to the time of the data using the combination of year, month and day; the transaction dimensional table lists the relevant transaction information corresponding to the tax. Thus these four dimensional table make up of the

Hypercube data mode, and we can carry on data analysis deeply from multi angle by this mode.

Data mining is another useful tool which is complementary with the OLAP. It carries on the knowledge discovery on the data in the data warehouse by AI and statistics analysis technology, and provides the knowledge for the user in the form of model as the foundation of tax evasion behavior judgment. Before the application of the models, we can validate them by OLAP. For example, we can construct the credit evaluation model of the taxpayer to strength the tax imposition, and construct the tax imposition elastic analysis and income prediction of the taxpayer model to make out the tax imposition task. And then validate the fitting degree of the models by OLAP.

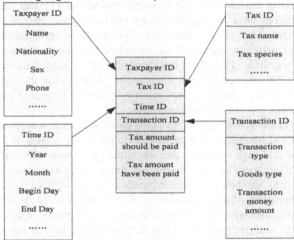

Fig.3. Tax paying information hypercube mode

(4) Application service layer: This layer mainly includes two function services: trade record saving and legality judgment of the trade behavior. When receiving the data from union-bank centre, application service layer will extract relevant information from the data and format it according to the standard format of the database, and then output it to each database. When receiving the result from data analysis layer, application service layer will display the information to the user terminal and request a decision if the result is ambiguous, and send an alarm to early warning centre if the tax evasion is ascertained. The final result is output to the union-bank centre.

(5) Standard Interface layer: This layer is the external interface integration. The trade information from the company or customer transmits to the union-bank center through Internet, and then to the ATE service system. Likewise, the ATE service system uses the interface of union-bank centre to transmit the result to PBC and National information security centre. When there is a tax evasion behavior, the ATE service system will cooperate with the other institutions and transmit information to there using this interface.

4 Key technologies

Data warehouse is the basis of the data mining and is used for supporting the decision management It is a data aggregation which is subject oriented, integrative, steady and changing continuously as the time. Compare with the traditional database that only include current fixed data mode, the data warehouse is an integrative method of distributed heterogeneous data system. It carries on the summarization and clustering of the data which is structured, half-structured, non-structured and with different source, extracts the decision supporting oriented part and loads it to the data warehouse. Thus, we can realize the uniform management of the data, and access data warehouse directly when inquiring without the need of accessing other information resource. By this, what the data mining faced is the uniform data arranged, and the processing becomes easier.

OLAP combines the concept of multidimensional database and multidimensional analysis, enables the analyzer, administer and the executer to access the information fast, conformably and interactively. The core of the OLAP is "multidimensional". For example, generally the revenue administration will consider the tax income from many aspects such as time, district and tax species which just are the "dimension". Each combination of these dimension and the tax income compose of the multidimensional array that is the basis of the OLAP analysis, and can be denoted as time, district, tax species and tax income. By all kinds of analytic action to the multidimensional array such as Slice, Dice, Pivot, Drill- down and Roll-up, the OLAP enable the decision maker to observe the data in the database from multi-angle so as to deeply understand the information hidden in the data.

Data mining is a method of extracting hidden, useful information from abundant of data utilizing artificial intelligence, advanced statistics methods, and technologies such as cluster analysis, neural net, data visualization and decision tree. [5] This information can open out the unapparent mode, trend and rule of data. The ATE system can analyze the existing data fully by data mining in order to provide evaluation and prediction. Besides, it can offer the leader layer fully decision foundation by understanding the basic information and the change of each tax resource, the influence of the main economic index to the tax resource in each district, transaction type, goods type and the tax amount that should be paid and so on.

5 Conclusion

In this paper, we introduced the union-bank online payment mode in which the transaction data is centralized at each level. Based on this platform, we designed an anti-tax evasion system as a value added service of the union-bank center. This system is able to find out the abnormal situation of the tax paying using the data mining, OLAP and data warehouse technologies during the online payment process. These are meaningful to the tax paying in the e-commerce area and strength the management of online transaction. We hope relevant criterion and law will come on fast so that the tax management of the e-commerce can have a foundation and direct to rely on.

Acknowledgements

This Research was supported by the Doctor Fund of Wuhan University of Technology under Grant 471-38650316 and the graduate student teaching reform Fund of Wuhan University of Technology under Grant 200404.

Reference:

1. Song Xiaozhong, Sun Jisheng, Suggestion to the ATE of E-Commerce in China, *Tax imposition*, 2006, No.4, pp: 9-15
2. Luo Qianzhang, Analysis of Borderline of Tax Evasion and Tax Avoidance in E-Commerce, Economic & Trade Update, Vol.4, No.49, Nov.2006
3. Zhou Xiaofan, Wu Wei, The Third Party Online Payment Platform is difficult to become popular, *Economic forum*, Dec.2006
4. Xin Yunyong, Hu Xiaohua, Online payment duplicates China Uionpay. Internet Weekly, Mar. 2005
5. Wang Tao, Xu Ping, Design of Tax Decision Supporting System based on Data Mining, *Management Sciences in China*, Vol.16, No.1, Feb, 2003
6. Qiu Ling, Discussion of ATE management in e-commerce, *Journal of Guangdong Vocational College of Finance and Economics*, No.3, 2002
7. Ran Chunyu, Gu Chuan, Chen Min, Huang Shaoluan, Design of data warehouse of tax DSS system, *Computer Applications*, No.S1, 2005
8. Fang Baorong, Wang Lei, Discussion of computer tax monitoring and control system design, *Taxation research journal*, No.06, 2000
9. Chen Dan, Mode design of tax imposition system, *Shang Hai accountant*, No.6, 2003

A Multi Psychology Accounts CSD Model for ISC Bi-Level Distribution Network

Quan Lu [1], Jing Chen [2] and Junping Qiu [1]

1 Research Center for China Science Evaluation, Wuhan University,
Wuhan, 430072, P.R.China
mrluquan@sina.com

2 Department Of Computer Science, Central China Normal University,
Wuhan, 430079, P.R.China

Abstract. The researches on Supply Chain are mainly about the conjunction mechanism and efficiency in Integrated Supply Chain to enhance its competitiveness and the cooperation between its members. But most of those belong to the standard finance field, and few about the factors of human mental or psychology. We studied the satisfaction degree models of customer with mental account based on the customer satisfaction degree (CSD) model and found they are too simplified, not reasonable and inaccurate. This paper suggests a CSD model based on multi artificial psychology accounts, which quantify exact customer psychology using cognition and artificial psychology methods, and then describes an ISC bi-level distribution network model based on this CSD model.

1 Introduction

A typical supply chain consists of three fundamental stages: material procurement, production and distribution. Procurement and production are highlighted under traditional manufacture environment. Since the early 1980s, the focus of supply chain management has been moving towards the demand side [1-3], and supply chains are becoming "demand chains" driven by the market and customers. The researches on Supply Chain are mainly about the conjunction mechanism and efficiency in Integrated Supply Chain to enhance its competitiveness and the cooperation between its members since year 2000 [4, 5], typically the researches on bi-level distribution network. But most of those belong to the standard finance field, and few about the factors of human psychology. We studied the satisfaction degree models of customer [6, 7] with mental account based on the CSD model and found they are too simplified, not reasonable and inaccurate. For example, simple mental classification in Multiple Mental Account researches of a consumer like "conservative" and "risky" is obviously not enough for a clothes supply chain system, and more accurate and

Please use the following format when citing this chapter:

Lu, Q., Chen, J., Qiu, J., 2007, in IFIP International Federation for Information Processing, Volume 251, Integration and Innovation Orient to E-Society Volume1, Wang, W. (Eds), (Boston: Springer), pp. 417-422.

effective method are needed to satisfy the customer. Our project aims to improve
the customer satisfaction level/degree and increase the enterprise's competitive
power through cognitive and artificial psychology technologies.

This paper analyzes the multi psychology accounts structure of consumers in
section 2. Section 3 presents a customer satisfaction degree model based on
artificial psychology, which quantify exact customer psychology using cognition
and artificial psychology methods. Section 4 describes a chance constrained
programming model of the ISC bi-level distribution network based on artificial
psychology. The conclusions are stated in section 5.

2   The Multi Psychology Accounts of Consumers

The optimization problem of the ISC bi-level distribution network has gone
beyond the field of traditional standard finance. Behavioral Portfolio theory [8]
and Affective Computing theory will help to its solving, from which we describe
bi-level distribution network design problem [9] under distributed multi-
manufacturer, multi-distributor and multi psychology accounts of multi-
consumer scenarios as figure 1. The decision psychology of a user is a
hierarchical structure. So the irrational optimization problem of the ISC bi-level
distribution network can be translated into one of optimizing customer demands
with multi psychology accounts.

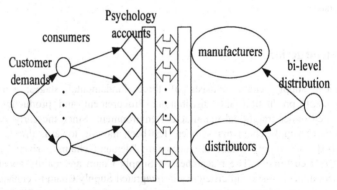

Fig. 8. An ISC bi-level distribution network model with multi psychology accounts of
consumer

3   A CSD Model Based on Multi Artificial Psychology
       Accounts

3.1   Analysis of Customer Psychology Accounts

To model customer's multi psychology accounts, the first thing we should do is
to find how many accounts there are. This can be got from history transaction
files through data preparation and clustering [10, 11].

Each user session in a user session file can be thought of in two ways; either
as a single transaction of many page references, or a set of many transactions

each consisting of a single page reference. The goal of transaction identification is to dynamically create meaningful clusters of references for each user.

Clustering algorithms are effective for this situation. We consider using a multivariate k-means algorithm [10] which calls k-means algorithm time and again to obtain transaction clusters.

K-means is one of the simplest unsupervised learning algorithms that solve the well known clustering problem. The procedure follows a simple and easy way to classify a given data set through a certain number of clusters (assume k clusters) fixed a priori. The main idea is to define k centroids, one for each cluster. These centroids shoud be placed in a cunning way because of different location causes different result. So, the better choice is to place them as much as possible far away from each other. The next step is to take each point belonging to a given data set and associate it to the nearest centroid. When no point is pending, the first step is completed and an early groupage is done. At this point we need to re-calculate k new centroids as barycenters of the clusters resulting from the previous step. After we have these k new centroids, a new binding has to be done between the same data set points and the nearest new centroid. A loop has been generated. As a result of this loop we may notice that the k centroids change their location step by step until no more changes are done. In other words centroids do not move any more.

3.2   Modeling of Customer Artificial Psychology

To illustrate the modeling of customer artificial psychology clearly, we take one cluster to consider first. Based on Cooley's user model [11] the user query and answer in user transaction file and user cognitive queries files is enhanced with cognitive psychology and the subjective expected utility is assigned. Considering the utilities for different combinations of preferences within a query a trade-off between query complexity or processing costs and an expected improvement of the query result has to be optimized. This query is processed by the database retrieval system and the results are returned to the user.

The modeling work is based on Quantification Theory I [10] and factor analysis theory. Firstly, there is a user preference value correspondence with the adjacent pair, and we call them average of the representative pairs. We can get the average value through questionnaire.

$$Y = \begin{bmatrix} y_1 & y_2 & \cdots & y_n \end{bmatrix}^T \tag{1}$$

Then we can measure the characters of the items or products like value (0-100) of cold or warm. The corresponding reactor matrix is:

$$X = [\delta_i(j,k)] =$$

$$\begin{pmatrix} \delta_1(1,1) & \cdots & \delta_1(1,r_1) & \delta_1(2,1) & \cdots & \delta_1(2,r_2) & \cdots & \delta_1(m,1) & \cdots & \delta_1(m,r_m) \\ \delta_2(1,1) & \cdots & \delta_2(1,r_1) & \delta_2(2,1) & \cdots & \delta_2(2,r_2) & \cdots & \delta_2(m,1) & \cdots & \delta_2(m,r_m) \\ \cdot\cdot & \cdot\cdot & \cdot\cdot & \cdot\cdot & \cdot\cdot & \cdot\cdot & \cdot\cdot & \cdot\cdot & \cdot\cdot & \cdot\cdot \\ \cdot\cdot & \cdot\cdot & \cdot\cdot & \cdot\cdot & \cdot\cdot & \cdot\cdot & \cdot\cdot & \cdot\cdot & \cdot\cdot & \cdot\cdot \\ \delta_n(1,1) & \cdots & \delta_n(1,r_1) & \delta_n(2,1) & \cdots & \delta_n(2,r_2) & \cdots & \delta_n(m,1) & \cdots & \delta_n(m,r_m) \end{pmatrix} \tag{2}$$

Then each case can be written in the form of reactor matrix. According to Quantification Theory I :

$$b = (X'X)^{-1}X'Y \qquad (3)$$

Now we obtain the quantification relationship of the adjective pairs and the case, with Y is a column vector in formula 1 and its value is the average of the previously evaluation corresponding to an adjective pair. Here X is the reactor matrix in formula 2. All values of b correspond with the adjective pairs can be obtained. By replacing b with its expression, we can calculate the evaluation Y of case with the help of the predictive formula

$$\hat{Y} = Xb \qquad (4)$$

Subject to:

$$r_{\hat{y}y} = \sqrt{\dfrac{\sum_{i=1}^{n} (\hat{y}_i - \bar{y})^2}{\sum_{i=1}^{n} (y_i - \bar{y})^2}} \geq 0.85 \qquad (5)$$

$\hat{Y}$ is the predicted value of a certain customer's satisfaction degree to a certain product in a certain psychology account.

3.3 A CSD Model Based on Multi Artificial Psychology and Utility Theory

Customer artificial psychology built in section 3.2 can not be used directly in ISC bi-level distribution network design. With the above foundation we propose a customer satisfaction degree model based on artificial psychology and utility theory. It can be described as following:

The customer satisfaction degree of customer i in psychology account p relative to account r as following:

$$S_{ipr} = \sum_{k=1}^{n} a_{ik} \bullet u\left(x_{ipk} - x_{irk}\right) \qquad (6)$$

Where x_{ijk} is the satisfaction value of customer i's psychology account j to character k of the product, a_{ik} is satisfaction degree coefficient: $0 \leq a_{ik} \leq 1, \boxplus \sum_{k=1}^{n} a_{ik} = 1$ and $u(x)$ is the utility function. $u(x) \geq 0$ as $x \geq 0$ and $u(x) \leq 0$ as $x \leq 0$. And x_{ij} is the predicted customer satisfaction $\hat{y}$ in formula 4.

4 A Psychology-based Chance Constrained Programming Mode of ISC Bi-level Distribution Network

The following notation is used in the model for ISC bi-level distribution network design.

Decision variables

x_{kl} = the amount shipped from manufacturer k to distribution center l.

y_{ll} = binary variables, denote whether it is a distribution center.

y_{lr} = binary variables, denote whether ship products from distribution center l to distributor r.

d_r = random variables, the demand amount of customer region r.

f_k = random variables, the production capacity of manufacturer k.

Constants

a_{kl} = unit cost of shipping from manufacturer k to distribution center l.

b_l = fixed cost of constructing distribution center l.

M_l = fixed cost of constructing distributor l.

e_{lr} = unit cost of shipping from distribution center l to distributor r.

Then we can convert the modeling problem of the ISC bi-level distribution network with multi psychology accounts into one of expected value goal programming with chance constrains according to Zhao Xiaoyu's researches [12].

Model

$$\min\left\{\sum_{k=1}^{K}\sum_{l=1}^{L}a_{kl}x_{kl}+\sum_{l=1}^{N}[b_ly_u+M_l(1-y_u)]+\sum_{k=1}^{L}\sum_{l=1}^{N}e_{lr}d_ry_{lr}+\xi\right\} \quad (7)$$

Subject to:

$$\xi=\sum_{i=1}^{l}\left(k_i\sum_{j=1}^{n}P_{ij}S_{ij}W_{(j)}\right); \quad (8)$$

$$\sum_{l=1}^{L}x_{kl}\leq f_k, k=1,2,\cdots,K; \quad (9)$$

$$\sum_{l=1}^{N}y_u=L,\sum_{l-1}^{L}y_{lr}=1,r=1,2,\cdots,K; \quad (10)$$

$$\sum_{r=1,r\neq l}^{N}y_{lr}\leq(N-1)y_{ll},l=1,2,\cdots,N; \quad (11)$$

$$\sum_{r=1}^{N}d_ry_{lr}\leq\sum_{k=1}^{N}x_{kl},j=1,2,\cdots,L; \quad (12)$$

$$x_{kl}\geq0,y_{lr}\in(0,1),\forall k,l,r_{\circ} \quad (13)$$

5 Conclusions

Customer satisfaction degree (CSD) model in ISC bi-level distribution network design problem considering customer psychology is investigated in this paper. It describes the hierarchical structure of customer psychology, presents the method to model customer artificial psychology, proposes a customer satisfaction degree model based on multi artificial psychology accounts, and then converts the optimization problem of the ISC bi-level distribution network with multi psychology accounts into one of expected value goal programming model with chance constrains, and the implementing and optimization in a real ISC bi-level distribution network of this model will be our future works.

This model covers the following features by considering customer's multi psychologies: more consistency with customer, higher customer satisfaction degree, reasonable optimization and adaptability to demanding waves under bounded rationality of customers.

Acknowledgements

This research was supported by the National Natural Science Foundation of China under Grant No. 70673071.

References

1. T. Davis, Effective supply chain management, *Sloan Management Review, Summer*, 34(4), 5-46 (1993).
2. J.T. Douglas and M.G. Paul, Coordinated supply chain management, *European Journal of Operational Research*, 94(1), 1-15(1996).
3. S. Bylka, A dynamic model for the single-vendor, multi-buyer problem, *International Journal of Production Economics*, 59(3), 297-304(1999).
4. P. H. Zipkin, Supply chain management: reflections, interpretations and predictions, *Global SCM Conference,*Berlin: Springer-Verlage Press (2002) .
5. F. Cheng, M. Ettl and G. Lin, Inventory-service optimization in configure-to-order systems, *Manufacturing and Service Operations Managemen,t* 4(2), 114-132(2002).
6. M. Friedman and L.J. Savage, The utility analysis of choices involving risk, *Journal of Political Economy*, 56(4), 279-304(1948).
7. Y.K. Ma and X.W. Tang, Decision-making methods for behavioral portfolio choice, *Journal of systems engineering*, 18 (1), 71-76(2003).
8. S. Hersh and S. Meir, Behavioral Portfolio Theory, *The Journal of Financial and Quantitative Analysis*, 35(2), 127-151 (2000).
9. J.J. Jiang etc. Optimization of the ISC Bi-Level Distribution Network with Multiple Mental Accounts, *Industrial Engineering Journal*, 8 (3), 12-17(2005).
10. Q. Lu, J. Chen and B. Meng, Web Personalization based on Artificial Psychology, *WISE Workshop on Web Information Access and Digital Library, LNCS4256*, 223-229(2006).
11. R. Cooley, B. Mobasher and J. Srivastava, Data preparation for mining World Wide Web browsing patterns, *Journal of Knowledge and Information Systems*, 1(1) (1999).
12. X.y.Zhao etc, An Optimization Model for Distribution Network Design with Uncertain Customer Demands and Production Capacity,*0-7803-8971-9/05 IEEE* (2005).

Information Overload on E-commerce

Rafael Lucian[1], Francisco Tigre Moura[1], André Falção Durão[1] and Salomão
Alencar de Farias[1]
1 Universidade Federal de Pernambuco
Departamento de Ciências Administrativas
Programa de Pós-Graduação em Administração
WWW home page: http://www.dca.ufpe.br

Abstract. In on-line purchases process, the consumer can
experience the information overload state. This paper deals about
the affective answers of the customers of e-commerce to this
phenomenon, which represents the behavior of the consumer on
influence of an exceeding number of information its capacity of
individual processing. The adopted methodology had an
exploratory-descriptive character. The first phase has used a
qualitative perspective, resulting in the construction of the scale
used in this study. The second part, a survey was conducted, and
its objective was to verify opposing theoretical relations from
searched literature. In this way, multivariate statistics techniques
had been used, with prominence in the structural equations
modeling. The conclusions had indicated that the theory of
information overload for traditional commerce is partially valid for
e-commerce and the premise that the confusion feeling is the
predictor of the satisfaction level reduction of the consumers under
influence of the information overload is deconstructed.

1 Introduction

The academy has developed an increasing and significant interest over e-
commerce on the last decade, due to the way consumers behave while facing the
diverse online shopping activities [1]. The importance given to e-commerce is
the result, mainly, of the development of commercial relations done through this
channel [2].

Internet provides comfort and commodities that are attractive to clients, such
as the convenience and agility on information search and the amount of precious
information found in a short period of time [3]. The quickness on

Please use the following format when citing this chapter:

Lucian, R., Moura, F. T., Durão, A. F., de Farias, S. A., 2007, in IFIP International Federation for Information
Processing, Volume 251, Integration and Innovation Orient to E-Society Volume1, Wang, W. (Eds), (Boston: Springer),
pp. 423-430.

communication can turn the decision making process more agile and facilitate the purchase.

Currently, companies offer a great variety of products and brands. They vary on size, shape, color, among others distinctions. Many researchers indicate that this huge amount of offer of alternatives causes on consumers the experience of information overload [4].

Information overload is defined as negative affective effect caused by the surplus of information in addition to the 'consumer's individual processing capacity [6].

This way, considering the content discussed, the problem to be investigated is defined on the question: in which way the affected responses resultant from information overload relates with consumer's behavior on electronic commerce?

The understanding of the information overload phenomena implies on a new project perspective for commercial websites. Having these answers, virtual stores will be able to manage the amount of information in a way to avoid causing negative impacts on consumers.

2   Information Overload

During the information search process, individuals are exposed to experiment the information overload state, which represents the consumer's behavior under the influence of a grater amount of information than he is capable of processing [5].

Jacoby and Malhotra [7] and Sheth [1] defines the overload state as the condition of being exposed to a plethora of information in a way that a person cans no longer process.

Previous research investigated the information overload as a negative affect experience (confusion/reduction of levels of satisfaction) caused by the huge amount of alternatives and attributes provided on the moment of purchase [5].

According to the theoretical revision made, two affective reactions are pointed as the result of information overload experience, reduction of satisfaction level [8] and confusion [5].

The e-commerce is much more than just the online shopping and selling of products. In fact, it involves the online process of development, marketing, selling, delivery and payment of products and services negotiated with clients from the interconnected global market, with the support of a worldwide network of partners [9].

The competence of the electronic commerce sites includes characteristics such as customizing of WebPages for shoppers and the configuration of products in real time [10]. The understanding of the information overload effects is particularly important on the construction of websites, since the amount of information available for the consumer on the moment of purchase is a determinant factor for the information overload experience.

The next section will discus the method adopted for this study.

3 Methodology

This study has a descriptive-exploratory character, since initially a deeper
theoretical knowledge of the constructs investigated is desired, with the
objective of describing them next in terms of purchases done through the
electronic commerce, with emphasis on the variables that are of interest of this
study.

On the first phase, exploratory, the literature is investigated, aiming the
structure of theories related to e-commerce and information overload.

The second step, descriptive, a survey was developed through the application
of questionnaires elaborated based on information gathered by the
bibliographical review and by the structuring of theoretical reference. The scales
were developed based on the literature, so that the objective of this study could
be reached.

Hair *et al* [11] states that for the use of structural equations modeling is
necessary a minimum sample of 50 respondents. This study gathered 57 valid
questionnaires.

From de desk research done, some hypotheses were developed to be tested on
this study, as can be observed on Table 1.

Table 1. Hypotheses

	Hypotheses	Source
H0	Consumers of e-commerce are not influenced by the information overload.	
H1	The information overload generates an affective response of confusion on e-commerce consumers.	Jacoby *et al* [5] Scammon [8]
H2	The information overload generates the reduction of the satisfaction level of e-commerce consumers.	Malhotra [12] Keller and Staelin [13]

The exploratory phase, which used desk research, culminated on the
elaboration of a research instrument used on this study. The next section
describes the analysis of the research.

4 Analysis and Results

The first step of the data analysis was a respondents´ profile survey. The
sample was composed by 64% of male, with average age of 35 years old and
personal average income up to 06 minimum wages.

The main products bought were books (14%), digital cameras (9%) and CD's
(9%). The purchases´ average price was US$ 240.00. Two items (Home Theater,
and notebook) were identified having their price higher up from US$ 1,000.00,
and other two (video game and LCD Television) having superior price from the
amount of US$ 1,500.00.

When questioned about the information sources, consumers had affirmed,
relating offline and online information, that they consult twice as time the first
option (friends and relatives, traditional store, printed catalogues, television
advertising, outdoors, and radio) than the second one (manufacturer's site,

salesman and research sites). This finding has contradicted the expectations. Researchers believed that the internet would be the main source of information search.

Also, the data collection instrument had measured the importance of these information sources (online and offline) in purchase decision process. Summary of this analysis can be observed in Table 2.

Table 2. Pre-purchasing Information' Sources

Information Source	Order of Importance	Information Type
Virtual Store *Website*	1°	*Online*
Manufacturer *Website*	2°	*Online*
Traditional Store	3°	*Offline*
Research *Websites*	4°	*Online*
Friends or Relatives	5°	*Offline*
Printed Catalogues	6°	*Offline*
Advertising	7°	*Offline*

The primary source of information search of daily pre-purchase is the virtual store; and the less important alternative considered in the previous moments of the purchase is the advertising (television, outdoors, and radio). Researchers believe that the reason of this result is the fact that this advertising in these specific Medias have other objectives, such as consumer mind branding fixing.

Comparing the results between the consulted sources amount, and its importance, it was observed that, although the internet is less consulted than the offline sources, it is considered as the most decisive in the electronic commerce consumers purchase decision process.

Most of the respondents (74.5%) had affirmed that they considered between 02 and 04 different alternatives during the purchase decision process. Three will be considered as the average number of alternatives in the calculation analysis.

Three attributes were identified as average during the pre-purchase. Table 3 lists the most consulted attributes informed by the respondents.

Table 3. Consult Attributes Frequency

Product Attribute	Consult Percentage
Brand	82.5%
Manufacturer	77.2%
Durability	70.2%
Size	63.2%
Color	59.6%
Weigh	57.9%
Origin	54.4%

In this analysis, it's clear that 82.5% of the consumers had analyzed the product brand before finishing the purchase.

The fact that the attributes "size" and "weight" had been analyzed by the respondents respectively 63.2% and 57.9% is an important finding. Confer to this behavior the importance that these characteristics possess, especially regarding the freightage, which is calculated based on the commodity weight.

The number of ideal information (in which the overload information experience does not occur) is between 05 and 06 [14]; therefore, the respondents of this research, analyzing all 09 information, have experienced the overload information.

The used scale was submitted to the factorial analysis technique, which objective is to analyze the internal relations between a given number of variables, and to explore the common latent factors to these items. The objective is to find a way to condense the information in a smaller number of variables (factors) with a minimum acceptable loss [11]. In order to test the scales reliability, the Cronbach's Alpha technique was done. Scales must possess the minimum reliability coefficient of 0.6 [15]. The finding indices were: KMO = 0.624; Qui-square =f 80.028; 10 Degrees of Freedom and Significance of 0.000. Table 4 represents the factor analysis results.

Table 4. Factor Analysis

Item	Factor 1	Factor 2	Alpha
I feel satisfied with my purchase	.729	-	
I'm sure I have made the right choice.	.931	-	.833
I'm happy with my choice.	.939	-	
I have felt confused during my purchase choice.	-	.519	
Between the brands I have conditions to buy, I did not make the best choice.	-	.582	
I believe I did not make the best choice.	-	.836	
If I had more information, I would have conditions of making a better choice between the options available.	-	.819	.745
I believe that more information would have caused me a bigger confusion in my choice.	-	.767	

Factor 1 is named "satisfaction" and factor 2 is named "confusion".

From the identified latent factors, a correlation matrix was developed. The *Pearson* correlation constitutes a conceptual basis for the multivariate analyses [15]. The analysis objective is to obtain a general view of the investigated variables relationship, as it's shown in Table 5.

Table 5. Correlation Matrix

Variables	Satisfaction	Confusion	Information Quantities
Satisfaction	1	-,455**	-,336*
Sig.		,001	,014
Confusion	-,455**	1	-,110
Sig.	,001		,463

It's clear that satisfaction possess negative relation with the amount of information and the confusion. This result corroborates with the information overload literature, which points to these affective responses as opposite [8].

The structural equations modeling is a statistic model which looks to explain the relationship between multiple variables. This technique examines the inter-relationships structures expressed in a series of equations, similarly to a series of multiple regression equations [11].

The structural equations modeling, according to Hair *et al* [11], can be considered as a multiple regression extension, which the most obvious difference between it and other multivariate techniques is the way of dealing with the dependent variables joints. The variables order is the most important concern in this technique. In the regression "X" causes "Y"; MES "X" causes "Y", and "Y" causes "Z", therefore, a dependent variable becomes an independent variable in the following relationship [11].

The theoretical model developed for this research is shown bellow, in figure 1.

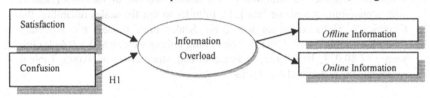

Figure 1. Theoretical Model Proposed

According to this model, the information overload is produced from the excess of online information available (manufacturer, salesperson, and search websites), and t   H2   information available (friends and relatives, traditional store, printed catalogues, TV advertisement, outdoor, and radio).

Right after identifying the model components, it's necessary to calculate the adjustments indices. These indices, also known as *fit,* indicate the model internal consistence, and they must be calculated based on the observed variables number, and the quantity N of the sample [11]. The model adjustments indices found were: CFI (0.905), and RMSEA (0.060). The summary of the calculated estimates is represented bellow, in table 6.

Table 6. Relations Between the Model Variables

Relations	Estimative	DE	Significance
Satisfaction ←→ Confusion	-0.454	0.153	0.003
Satisfaction → Information Overload	-0.979	0.188	0.000
Confusion → Information Overload	-0.988	0.201	0.000

The finding results from the analysis of structural equation modeling indicate that consumers feel less satisfied, and less confused with the information increasing.

Therefore, the null hypothesis was denied (H0). The two other hypothesis, relating information overload with confusion (H1), and satisfaction levels reduction (H2) were respectively rejected, and confirmed.

The H2 confirmation demonstrates that, as in traditional environment, virtual environment with information overload also produces reduced consumers satisfaction levels.

The main finding in this research is on the H1 rejection. Virtual consumers did not feel confused with the information increasing, but the opposite. It's possible to affirm, based on the structural equations modeling estimates, that an information overload reduces the confusion level.

Research conclusions are held in the next section.

Rafael Lucian[1], Francisco Tigre Moura[1], André Falção Durão[1] and Salomão Alencar de 429
Farias[1]

5 Conclusion

From the analysis it is possible to conclude that the information overload theory on traditional commerce is partially valid for electronic commerce.

It was confirmed that the surplus of information available generates a reduction of satisfaction level on consumers, corroborating with the literature [8].

The second and most relevant conclusion of this study refers to the inversely proportional relation between confusion and amount of information, which is contrary to most of the literature of information overload on traditional commerce [5].

This result not only indicates that e-commerce consumers feel less confused with the increase of the amount of information. It decomposes the idea that the reduction of satisfaction level occurs due to the confusion, a basic premise of information overload literature.

The analysis suggests that even the concept of the phenomena studied can be decomposed on the e-commerce perspective, since the overload definition as a negative affective effect caused by the surplus of information beyond the consumer's individual's processing capacity [5] isn't valid for virtual consumers, the word "negative" must not be avoided, since that the confusion reduction with the increase on the amount of information is a positive effect.

References

1. J.N. Sheth, B. Mittal and B.I. Newman. "Comportamento do Cliente: Indo além do comportamento do consumidor", *São Paulo*. Atlas (2001)
2. H. Miknight, V. Choudhury and C. Kacmar, "Developing and validating trust measures for e-commerce: An integrative typology", *Information Systems Research*, vol. 13, n. 3, ABI/INFORM Global (2002)
3. B. doolin, S. Dillon, F. Thompson, J. L. Corner, "Perceived Risk, the Internet Shopping Experience and Online Purchasing Behavior: a New Zealand perspective", *Journal of Global Information Management*, v. 13, n. 2, apr-jun, (2005).
5. J. Jacoby, D.E. Speller and C. "Bernning, Brand Choise Behavior as a Function of Information Load". *Journal of Marketing Research*, 11, feb. (1974).
6. J. Jacoby, D.E. Speller and C. Kohn, "Brand Choise Behavior as a Function of Information Load: Replication and Extension", *Journal of Consumer Research*, 1, 1, jun. (1974)
7. J. Jacoby, N.K. Malhotra, "Perspectives on Information Overload: Reflections on the Information Overload Paradigm in Consumer Decision Making. *Journal of Consumer Research*. Vol. 10, Iss.4. Gainesville:Mar (1984)
8. D.L. SCAMMON, "Information Load and Consumers", *Journal of Consumer Research*. 4, 148-155 (1977).
9. J.A. O'BRIEN, "Sistemas de Informações e as Decisões Gerenciais na Era da Internet",2ªed. São Paulo: Saraiva,(2004).
10. R. Kalakota, R.A. Oliver, B. Donath, "E-Commerce". *Marketing Management* 8, 3. Fall: (1999)
11. J.F. Hair, W.C. Black, B.J. Babin, R.E. Anderson and R.L. TATHAM, "Multivariate Data Analysis", 6 ed. *Prentice Hall*. New Jersey(2006).
12. N.K. Malhotra, "Information Load and Consumer Decision Making", *Journal of Consumer Research*. Vol. 10. Iss. 1. Gainesville: Jun (1982)
13. K. Keller, R. Staelin, "Effects of Quality and Quantity of Information on Decision Effectiveness", *Journal of Consumer Research*. 14, 200-213(1987).

14. P. Wright, "Consumer Choice Strategies: Simplifying vs. Optimizing", *Journal of Marketing Research*. 12, 60-7 (1975).
15. N.K. Malhotra, "Pesquisa de marketing",Uma orientação aplicada. 4 ed. *Bookman*. São Paulo (2006).

Analysis on Research and Application of China C2C Websites Evaluating Index System

Rongying Zhao [1] and Ruixian Yang[2]
1 Associate professor of School of Information Management, Wuhan
University,
Vice director of Research Center for Chinese Science Evaluation of
Wuhan University, Wuhan, 430072,China
Research Field:Knowledge Network and and Knowledge Management,
Informatrics and Scientific Evaluation, E-mail:zhaory999@yahoo.com.cn
2   A postgraduate student of School of Information Management,
Wuhan University, Wuhan 430072, China
Research Field: Information Management and Knowledge
Management,E-mail:dylis85@126.com

Abstract. Recently in China, the speed of the development of the C2C
websites has been very swift. This article is on the research actuality and the
problems of the China C2C websites, and studies the index system of China
C2C's website evaluation. Conclusions and suggestions are given by using the
index system and taking Taobao, eBay and paipai websites as example to
analyze.

1 Introduction

Electronic Commerce, E-commerce for short, in the opening network environment of
Internet, based on the application way of Browser/Client, is a new commercial
operation mode, implementing customers' shopping from network, network business
trade and online electronic payment. At present in China, according to the trading
object, the mode of the E-commerce is divided into five categories: business
organization to business organization (B2B), business organization to customers
(B2C), business organization to government administration department (B2G),
customers to government administration department (C2G)and customers to
customers(C2C).B2G and C2G is E-commerce behavior of government, not aiming
to profit, involving government stock, applying to customs and declaring dutiable
goods online, ect, have little effect on the E-commerce industry. Compared to C2C,

Please use the following format when citing this chapter:

Zhao, R., Yang, R., 2007, in IFIP International Federation for Information Processing, Volume 251, Integration and
Innovation Orient to E-Society Volume1, Wang, W. (Eds), (Boston: Springer), pp. 431-442.

B2C must be the best E-commerce mode in terms of the profit in China. Although having appeared later, B2C and C2C develop faster.

Recently new data from "China C2C online shopping in 2006" survey was released by China Internet Network Information Center (CNNIC) and iResearch-2006.The short report of China online shopping shows that the volume of trade of China C2C websites is far greater than that of B2C in 2005, and the period from 2005 to 2010 will be a period when China C2C market has a huge development. In this period, a great deal of capital and person with ability, will swarm into C2C market, and the extent of participating the online trade will be gradually deepened [5] [2]. Facing to the flourishing development tendency of China C2C market, a lot of customers will pay more attention to many questions such as transportation, payment, credit, the security of the network and so on. Faced with these Gordian knots, how to deal properly will have a function in the development of China C2C itself, and the trade of business. In this article, according to those questions above, research and discussion on China C2C websites evaluating index system are given. Through this study, it is expected that index system can evaluate the China C2C website scientifically and reasonably, with the aim to accelerate China C2C website's development healthily and swiftly.

2 Actuality and Problems of China C2C Evaluation

2.1 Actuality

So far in China many organizations and scholars have attributed to the evaluation of the E-commerce websites, especially B2B, B2C and B2G, but seldom on C2C. The research from CNNIC,iResearch, and scholars is on the subject of survey and collection of data, but not on the evaluation and application of index system. In order to adapt to the speed of the China C2C development, adopting from B2B, B2C and B2G websites' evaluating index system and considering C2C's self-identity, there will be research and discussion on China C2C website based on evaluating an index system. Using data investigated by those authoritative organizations, for analyzing three websites are chosen for further analysis and key problems are immerged.

2.2 Problems

From the analysis of research actuality above, we can identify the following problems: firstly, the research on the China C2C website evaluation is just on the stage of data investigation and collection, or data analysis, but not having integrated an evaluating index system; secondly, some evaluating indexes are not entire and comprehensive, nor forming a system and analysis of application.

3 Design of China C2C Website Evaluating Index System

Through the research actuality and problem of China C2C website evaluation, it is supposed that it is necessary to research deeply on China C2C website evaluating index system and analyze China C2C website using the index system, then concludes with the development actuality and problems of China C2C websites, using scientific method and giving constructive critique according to the problems.

3.1 Index of Evaluation

3.1.1 Network Impact

Network impact is an important index to the evaluation of the website and mainly displayed in network linking. Network linking is an essential tool to organize the information from Internet and deliver its relationship. We take "Inlink" (Inbound Link) as the index of evaluating information resource from websites. Generally it concludes number of Inlink WebPages and number of Inlink Websites [10] [9].

(1)Number of Inlink Webpages.

The number of Inlink Webpages is to describe the web information resource that points to the object we research excluding its internal links. Generally the greater the number of Inlink Webpages, the higher the usage of this website and the greater the network impact of this website. But the short-coming of this index is that if the inlink of the object we research comes from small websites, even though the number of Inlink Webpages is great, we can not tell if the website impact is also great, so when using this index, we choose number of Inlink Websites to modify simultaneously.

(2)Number of Inlink Websites.

Number of Inlink Websites is how many other inlinks pointing to the website we research, which is also used to weigh the network impact directly, not just to modify the number of Inlink Webpages as the index of evaluating index system.

3.1.2 Website Fluidity Index

Website fluidity is the most direct reflection of how the website can be used. Generally there are four indexes: the number of visiting, the number of pages visited, the average pages visited and average load time to scale the website fluidity.

(1)Number of Visiting.

The number of visiting means that how many people visit the website in a certain time. There are two ways to evaluate this index: The first one is calculating simply the number of people who visited the website, that is, in a certain time, if one person visited the website more than one time, the times will be added up. The second one is neglecting the repeat visiting in a certain time, that is, we just record one time for a certain user no matter how many times he or she visited. Compared with the first way, the second way can compute the real number of people who browse and use the website in a certain time. In this article, it takes the number of an average of million visiting who installed the Alexa as the value of the index of the number of visiting.

(2)Number of Pages Visited.

The total pages people visited in a certain time. This is the common evaluating index for all the websites, so it is also necessary here [12]. It takes the number of people installing Alexa per million as the value of this index. Because the ratio relationship between two indexes above is not directly accurate, that is to say, it may be not true that the greater the number of visiting equates with a greater the number of pages visited. One user reads one page carefully, but browses a lot of pages extensively. Thus it is more objective to take both of number of visiting and number of pages visited simultaneously as the indexes of website fluidity.

(3)Average Pages Visited.

Average pages visited means that the average number of webpages one person browses and acquires in a certain time. Webpages can either be static, or dynamic according to users' requirement. Average number of visiting and visiting time are all the indexes reflecting website's "mucosity" .However because of the different reading habit, the time users take may differ greatly even if they get the same amount of information. Moreover, many browsers will not log out spontaneously after visiting the website. At the same time, the system continues to calculate the visiting time. Obviously it is more reasonable to take average pages visited as an index to weigh "mucosity". Furthermore, through the number of visiting and the average pages visited, we can still obtain the total amount of information delivered by a website in a certain time.

(4)Average Load Time.

Average load time, an indirect index to scale website fluidity, means the time of the webpages loaded in a certain time. The more the average load time, the more the people who visited the website and the more the website fluidity. Whenever the number of the people exceeds a certain value, the burden of the server overtaking can also result in the longer load time, without taking account of technological problems here.

3.1.3 Network Visibility

The statistical report of China Internet Website Development Actuality in July,2005 shows that 84.5% network users got to know new websites depending on search engine, and 58.2% retrieved information by search engine. Therefore we can see that search engine is critical to the fact that whether the information from internet can be used by network users. Accordingly one of the important ways to enhance the rate of website usage is to make as much information as possible acquired and indexed by search engine. It is the quantity of information from a certain website which can be acquired and indexed by search engine as network visibility. We commonly take the number of webpages as measure unites [7].

3.1.4 Volume of Market Trade

As another index, volume of market trade plays a big role of evaluating websites. It is also the direct manifest of the E-commerce market's outstanding achievement. Here we take the ratio of trading volume as the "second class" index.

Consequently, the eight indexes we take in this research are number of Inlink Webpages, number of Inlink Websites, number of visiting, number of pages visited, average pages visited, average load time, network visibility, ratio of volume of market trade.

3.2   Design of China C2C Website Evaluating Index System

(1)Design with Analytic Hierarchy Process (AHP) Method

Analytic Hierarchy Process (AHP) is a useful decision-making method brought forward in 1970 by T.L.Satty, a famous operational researcher from America. This method is often successfully applied to system analysis and strategic research of economics, technology and politics. Its basic idea is to connect stable quantify with quality and process people's subjective opinion through the form of quantity. Scholars advanced a series of mark and degree methods in the process of using AHP. The earliest method is 1-9 mark and degree which is used extensively [8]. In this article, we use AHP to design China C2C website evaluating index system and mark and degree methods to calculate weight of every index.

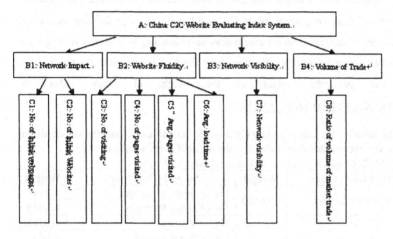

Fig.1. Design of China C2C Website Evaluating Index System

(2)Weight Calculation

Giving the value of the comparative result between two indexes at random by using AHP method [11]:

Table 1. Compare one index with the others at Random

Index	Website Impact	Website Fluidity	Network Visibility	Volume of Trade
Website Impact	1	1/2	1	1/2
Website Fluidity	2	1	2	1
Network Visibility	1	1/2	1	1/2
Volume of Trade	2	1	2	1

Using Mat LAB7.0, we got matrix A 's maximum latent root and corresponding eigenvector from table 1:

$$\lambda_{max} = 4$$
$$W_0 = [0.3162, 0.6325, 0.3162, 0.6325]^T$$

The result of the coincident verification to the eigenvector above is as follows:

$$CI = \frac{\lambda_{max} - n}{n-1} = \frac{4-4}{4-1} = 0$$

$$CR = \frac{CI}{RI} = 0 < 0.1$$

CI stands for coincidence index; RI, average random coincidence index and CR, coincidence ratio. In general, when CR $<$ 0.1, we can judge that the matrix has satisfactory coincidence. So the eigenvector corresponding with matrix A from table 1 satisfies the coincidence verification. After the further process to the eigenvector, we can get the vector of the weight of every index: W $= [0.1666, 0.3334, 0.1666, 0.3334]^T$.

Identically, we can get the weight of the second class, and figure out all the weights of every index eventually. See the result of every weight in table 2.

Table 2. China C2C Website Evaluating Indexes and Weight

First Class Index	Weight	Second Class Index	Weight
Network Impact	0.16660	No. of Inlink Webpages	0.1111
		No. of Inlink Websites	0.0555
Website Fluidity	0.33340	No. of Visiting	0.0787
		No. of Pages Visited	0.0637
		Avg. Pages Visited	0.1273
		Avg. Load Time	0.0637
Network Visibility	0.16660	Network Visibility	0.1666
Volume of Market Trade	0.33340	Ratio of Volume of Market Trade	0.3334

4   Analysis of Application

4.1   Data Source and Method

So far there is no authoritative organization to report the data of every index listed above comprehensively, thus the data source comes from different organizations. In order to keep the time of the data coincident, the time span of the data of every index is from Jan.1st, 2006 to Dec.31st, 2006.

(1)With the command of "link:" from Google and AltaVista, we got the number of Inlink Webpages of the measured object. On account of the limitation of every search engine's coverage, we chose the data whose numerical value is bigger.

(2)From Alexa,we acquired the number of visiting, number of pages visited, the number of Inlink Websites and average load time. Alexa, which was founded in Apr, 1996, is one of the most famous organizations for analysis of network fluidity and rank of websites. The data comes from "Alexa Toolbar" which is installed on the client. Owing to the fact that some data appeared monthly, the average data of 12 months is taken as the value of indexes.

(3)With the command of "site:" from Baidu,Google,Yahoo,AltaVista and AlltheWeb separately, we acquired the network visibility of measured object. Since network visibility reflects the potential possibility of the research object, we drew weight according to the ratio of usage of these five search engines and took the processed result as the value of network visibility. The way of calculation is the same as that of the first class index above. The ultimate weight of Baidu,Google,Yahoo,AltaVista and AlltheWeb is 0.4834,0.2964,0.1622,0.029,0.029[3].

(4)From iResearch survey data we obtained ratio of volume of market trade in 2006 of China C2C websites. iResearch Consulting Group, founded in 2002, is a professional market survey organization, paying attention to the economic fields such as network media, E-commerce, network games and etc.; it also studies and comprehends customers' behaviors deeply and offers market survey research and strategic counseling to network and traditional industry. iResearch Consulting Group studies market and presents reports of investigated data every year.

(5)Due to the unit difference among indexes above, all the data should be processed firstly. The detailed method is making the maximum datum of every index as 100, then computing other data proportionately, and finally, summing up correspondingly after multiplying the data which are processed.

4.2   Data Analysis

Some typical websites of China C2C are Taobao,eBay,paipai. These websites are used as examples for analysis using the index and weight above.

4.2.1 Final Rank

From the final score, we can see that Taobao website's capability is strongest, and followed by eBay and paipai. See the details in table 3.

Table 3. Data of every index, final score, and rank of three China C2C websites

Rank	1	2	3
Name of Website	Taobao	eBay	paipai
No. of Inlink Webpages (Unit: million)	19.2	103	48.9
No. of Inlink Websites (Unit: thousand)	59.051	9.983	1.505
No. of Visiting (Unit: thousand)	15.755	7.091	3.325
No. of Pages Visited (Unit: thousand)	258.027	20.318	44.414
Avg. Pages Visited	16.43	6.67	6.86
Avg. Load Time (Unit: s)	10.4	4.62	4.2
Network Visibility	48074.940	19.067	44.790

Ratio of Volume of Market Trade	65.2%	26.1%	3.5%
Final Score	100	86.51	40.28

4.2.2 Website Impact

From the data of number of Inlink WebPages,we can see eBay has the most Inlink Webpages, followed by paipai,and Taobao has the least.Fig.2(a) is the comparison of three website at this index.

From the data supplied from Alex, we can see that number of Inlink WebPages of Taobao is the most. It is almost six times more than that of eBay, and about twelve times more than paipai. Fig.2(b)describes comparison of three websites.

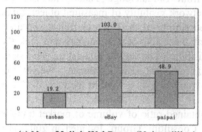
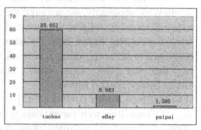

(a) No. of Inlink WebPages (Unit: million)   (b) No. of Inlink Websites (Unit: thousand)
Fig.2. Three Websites' Network Impact Comparison

4.2.3 Website Fluidity

(1)Number of People Who Visit and Number of WebPages Visited and Average Webpage per person.

Taobao is always at the first place whether viewed from the index of the number of people who visit or the index of the number of WebPages visited. Fig.3 (a) is can tell more information about these two indexes.

From the index of average WebPages per person, we can see that Taobao is still at the first place. The value of Taobao is more than double of eBay's, and the value between eBay and paipai is closed. See Fig.3 (b).

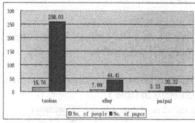
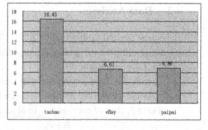

(a) No. of People Who visit and No. of WebPages people visit (b) Avg. WebPages per person
Fig.3. Three Websites' comparison on index of Network Fluidity

From Fig.4 [6], we can see that value of two indexes for three websites is different. Taobao is still the best. The difference between eBay and paipai is small, but eBay is a little better than paipai.

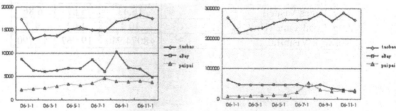

(a)Trend of number of people who visit   (b) Trend of number of pages people visit

Fig.4. Comparison of Trend on Index of Network Fluidity

(2)Average Load Time.

From the average load time, Taobao's average load time is 10.4s, the longest, and is also two times longer than eBay and paipai. The difference between eBay and paipai is small. It shows that Taobao's website fluidity is better than the others. See Table 3.

4.2.4 Network Visibility

From the search engines, we can see that the coverage capacity of Yahoo,AltaVista and AlltheWeb is better than Baidu and Google. From three websites, Taobao's visibility is the best, paipai is the next, and eBay is the worst comparatively. Table 4 can tell the details.

Table 4. No. of Search Result to Taobao,eBay and paipai website using five search engines separately

	Baidu	Google	Yahoo	AltaVista	AlltheWeb	Network Visibility
Taobao	17,300	10,800	997,000	666,000	593,000	48074.940
eBay	4	2	90	38	29	19.067
paipai	45	17	82	86	76	44.790

4.2.5 Ratio of Volume of Market Trade

The data reported from iResearch Consulting Group in Mar.2007 shows that the total volume of trade of China C2C websites in 2006 is 23 billion RMB. In China C2C shopping market, the first rank is Taobao website, whose volume of trade is 15 million and which takes up 65.2% of the whole volume of trade; the second rank is eBay website whose volume of trade declined compared with that of in 2005;the volume of trade of paipai website takes up 3.5%.After analysis, we can see that the centralization of C2C market is too high and 80% of the total volume of market trade is taken up by tabao and eBay, with Taobao taking up more than half[4].

Taobao made a quiet great progress last year and unhinged a long distance from others. There are two causes to explain this phenomenon. First, Taobao kept its élan and played down doorsill of Internet shopping. For example, in May, 2006,Taobao conducted "Taobao business city" which changed the impression of no big brand in business stores on Internet and which made customers who have brand trend more choice. Second, the basic service was absolutely for free, which offered much more opportunity for all members of society to participate. These people are not only the customers of Taobao, but they lead other people around them to be customers of Taobao. I think Taobao will continue the line of being free. See the detail ratio of volume of market trade of three websites in Fig.5.

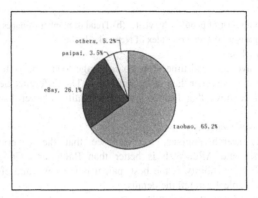

Fig.5. Volume of China C2C Website Market Trade in 2006

4.3   Result and Suggestion

(1)From data analysis of every index above we can see that Taobao is almost the first rank. I think there are several causes at work. Taobao was supported by Alibaba, which was a famous B2B website when it was founded, so many running ways are advanced. Although it is a short time since Taobao was founded, they have been able to attract a large volume of customers in China, we should learn more from it.

(2)From the analysis above, we can see the network visibility of Taobao is much better than others. Network visibility is an index to weigh the potential possibility of a website, so the bigger the value of network visibility of a website, the more the number of people who visit this website, the more the number of pages people reach, and the more the volume of market trade of a website. So other websites should learn of this from Taobao, that is, increasing the potential possibility of a website is vital.

(3)Trend of development. The data from Alexa, from Apr.12th, 2006 to Apr.13th,2007 shows that Taobao still keeps its predominance at the first place, and the difference between eBay and paipai is still small. From the time coordinate, the maximum data of every website is in October and January, which is reasonable because October and January are vacation days, then people have more leisure time to go shopping, but less in normal days [1].

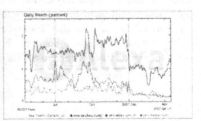

(a) Daily Reach Picture of Three Websites (b) Daily Pageviews Picture of Three Websites
Fig.6. Comparison of Three Websites' Daily Reach and Daily Pageviews

5 Conclusion

In this article we take Network Impact, Website Fluidity, Network Visibility and Volume of Trade as the first class index, use AHP method and Mat LAB software to compute the weighing of every index, and design China C2C website evaluating index system. Acquiring corresponding data from the famous Alexa and iResearch Consulting Group, we analyze the application to three websites (Taobao,eBay and paipai),and give my conclusion and suggestion.

Of course, there is also a big problem facing to China C2C website that is credit standing. Because credit standing is affected by China law and the rule of law, it cannot be solved in a short time. So future work is to survey and collect data from market carefully and study on it. I hope customers' credit standing behavior can be regulated in future.

Acknowledgement

This research was supported by the National Natural Science Foundation of China under Grant No. 70673071.

References

1. Alex Toolbar Search Result.http://www.alexa.com/data/details/traffic_details?url =www.TaoBao.com%2F.[2007-04-17].

2. China Internet Network Information Center. http://www.cnnic.net.cn/index.htm.[2007-04-13].

3. iResearch China Internet Industry Research Report. http://www.iresearch.com.cn/html/detai l_free_id_39170.html. [2007-04-13].

4. iResearch China Internet Industry Research Report 2007. http://www.iresearch.com.cn/html/

online_media/detail_free_id_42306.html. .[2007-04-16].

5. iResearch China Online Shopping Research Report 2006. http://www.iresearch.com.cn/html/Online_Shopping/detail_free_id_41269.html.[2007-04-15].

6. iResearch Consulting Group.http://www.iresearch.com.cn/html/Default.html..[2007-04-13].

7. W. Liu and D. Yu-feng, Evaluating Performance of E-Government Construction Based on Web Impact,*Journal of Information Science,* 24(11), 1705-1706(2006).

8. X.H. Ma and B.L. Liu, Application of AHP in the Construction of the Management of Information System, *Journal of Science and Technology Management Research,*(4), 193-194(2006).

9. R.R. Larson, Bibliometrics of the World Wide Web:An Exploratory Analysis of the Intellectual Structure of Cyberspace, http://www.ischool.berkeley.edu/~ray/ papers.html. [2007-08-13].

10. T.C. Almind and P. Ingwersen, Informetric Analysis on the World Wide Web: Methodological Approaches to 'Webometrics',*Journal of Documentation* ,53(4), 404-426(1997).

11. L.F. Wang and S.B. Xu, *The Theory of AHP* ,China Renmin University Press, Beijing(1990).

12. W.J. Wang, Analysis and Comment on Study and Application of EC Website Evaluation, *Journal of Information Science,* 21(6), 641-642(2003).

Study of Determinants of e-CRM in Influencing Consumer Satisfaction in B2C Websites

Rui Liu, Weijun Wang

Department of Information Management, HuaZhong Normal University,
Wuhan 430079, China

liuruiccnu@hotmail.com，wangwj@mail.ccnu.edu.cn

Abstract: This study empirically develops a model indicating the determinants of e-CRM as well as explaining the relationship between e-CRM and customer satisfaction in B2C websites. Based on the 7C model demonstrated by Rayport,J.F.&Jaworski,B.J and the Conceptual Model of Service Quality researched by Parasuraman, a theoretical framework that consists of e-CRM initiatives: context, content, customization, communication, membership, commerce, safety, customer satisfaction is further expanded. And then, this study puts forwards some suggestions to both researchers and practitioners: the function of e-CRM and the importance of customer satisfaction should be well learned; the functions of content, customization and commerce of B2C websites should be enhanced and the factors of context, membership and communication should be added when carrying out e-CRM strategy.

1. Introduction

At present, the researches on e-CRM and customers' satisfaction in China are always papers which demonstrate the two subjects respectively. Among few empirical researches in this field, a study on the relationship between service quality and customer satisfaction for general portals sorts out 4 influential factors named "ease of use" "empathy", "information quality" and "techniques of website "for general portals[1]. Besides, experts from Taiwan study on-line customer satisfaction from service quality, product quality and system quality [2] [3].

The book CRM theory design practice [4] and Customer Relationship Management [5] introduce the concept and function of e-CRM which contributes to this research.

Determinants of e-CRM in Influencing Customer Satisfaction written by Yan Liu, Chang Feng Zhou, and Ying-Wu Chen studies the relationship between e-CRM and customers' satisfaction from three factors(system quality, information quality, service quality）and two intrinsic success(responsiveness, efficiency)[6].

Zhang Cuiling [7] quotes 7C model (context/content/community/customize-tion/communication/connection/ commerce) constructed by Rayport, J.F. & Jaworski, and it introduces seven factors of CRM applied to websites for Electronic Commerce.

Previous researches can be summed as follows:

Please use the following format when citing this chapter:

Liu, R., Wang, W., 2007, in IFIP International Federation for Information Processing, Volume 251, Integration and Innovation Orient to E-Society Volume1, Wang, W. (Eds), (Boston: Springer), pp. 443-451.

(1) The theory of e-CRM has been introduces by more and more scholars and experts, some business organizations has put that into practice.

(2) CRM, service quality and customer satisfaction has been applied to on-line service of Electronic Commerce and some models have been developed for evaluating on-line service.

(3) Few researches have been done for studying the relationship between e-CRM and customer satisfaction.

2. Method

In 7C model demonstrated by Rayport, J.F. &Jaworski, B.J, community also refers that website offers BBS and allows leaving messages on-line. In fact, the two functions can be put into content as a way of representing information; thus, some other strategies of membership are added to connection and a new factor called membership is formed; besides, based on the paper Empirical Study of Influential Elements of E-satisfaction [8], the factor safety is added to our model. According to Expectation Conformation/Disconfirmation mode [9] and the Conceptual Model of Service Quality [10], a theoretical framework that consists of e-CRM initiatives: context, content, customization, membership, communication, commerce, safety, customer satisfaction is further expanded. (see Fig. 1)

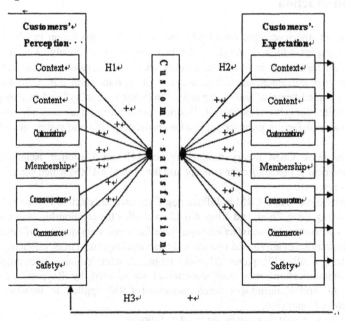

Fig. 1. The theoretical framework

This leads to the following hypotheses:

H1: customers' perception of B2C website's performances has a remarkable and positive correlation with consumer satisfaction.

H2 : customers' expectation of B2C website's performances has a remarkable and positive correlation with consumer satisfaction.

H3: customers' expectation has a remarkable and positive correlation with customers' perception.

This model was tested by means of the statistical analysis method of SPSS.A total of 51 questionnaire items were established to measure the extent to which participants gave to the perception, expectation and customer satisfaction towards e-CRM provided in B2C websites. A five point Likert scale, ranging from 1 = strongly disagree to 5 = strongly agree, was employed.

Methods used in this research include:

（1） Information investigation, acquisition work.

（2） Comparison, analysis, deduction.

（3） Survey study. Designing and using a questionnaire.

（4） Factor analysis and regression analysis. Using SPSS to test sample data.

3. Analysis

The results of Bartlett test of sphericity and Kaiser-Meyer-Olkin measure of sample adequacy are shown in Table 1:

Table 1. KMO and Bartlett's Test

Kaiser-Meyer-Olkin Measure of Sampling Adequacy.		0.858
Bartlett's Test of Sphericity	Approx. Chi-Square	2871.727
	df	276
	Sig.	0.000

Then, Reliability Coefficients is used to test customers' perception and customer satisfaction. (See Table 2)

Table 2. Reliability Analysis-Scale (Alpha)

	Factor	Item	Cronbach α
Customers 'perception	**Context**	I1- I3	0.8749
	Content	I4-I8	0.8170
	Customization	I9、I10、I17、I18	0.8281
	Membership	I11-I13	0.8292
	Communication	I14-I16	0.8176
	Commerce	I19-I21	0.8510
	Safety	I22-I24	0.8612
Customer satisfaction	**Customer Satisfaction**	I49-I51	0.6815

According to the analysis above, the entire 204 valid sample are quite fit for further analysis.

This study empirically develops a model indicating 7 determinants of e-CRM as well as discussing how customers' perception affects customer satisfaction, how customers' expectation affects customer satisfaction and how perception affects expectation. In order to avoid Collinarity in Regression Analysis, Pearson Correlation was applied. And the largest numerical value (0.562<0.75) indicated that it was fit for the Regression Analysis.

3.1 How customers' perception affects customer satisfaction

According to Parasuraman, customers' perception of service quality affects positively customer satisfaction [11]; Yi studies determinants of customer satisfaction in diverse products. It reveals that customers' perception affects positively customer satisfaction in the category of low ambiguity products [12].Former studies can lead to the following hypotheses:

H1-1: Context which customer perceived affects positively customer satisfaction.

H1-2: Content which customer perceived affects positively customer satisfaction.

H1-3: Customization which customer perceived affects positively customer satisfaction.

H1-4: Membership which customer perceived affects positively customer satisfaction.

H1-5: Communication which customer perceived affects positively customer satisfaction.

H1-6: Commerce which customer perceived affects positively customer satisfaction.

H1-7: Safety which customer perceived affects positively customer satisfaction.

Table 3 and Table 4 illustrate the coefficients of customers' perception and customer satisfaction.

Table 3. Model Summary

R	R Square	Adjusted R Square	Std. Error of the Estimate
.514(a)	.264	.238	.56770

Table 4. Coefficients（Dependent Variable: customer satisfaction）

	Beta	t	Sig.	R Square
(Constant)		8.905	.000	
context	.033	.431	.667	
content	.303	3.472	.001	
customization	.402	5.180	.000	.264
membership	.015	.183	.855	
communication	.077	1.029	.305	
commerce	.160	2.100	.037	
safety	.106	1.307	.193	

Table 5 shows that H1-2, H1-3 and H1-6 are supported after hypotheses testing.

Table 5. Results 1

Hypotheses	H1-1	H1-2	H1-3	H1-4	H1-5	H1-6	H1-7
Results	No	Supportive	Supportive	No	No	Supportive	No

3.2 How customers' expectation affects customer satisfaction

According to Yi's study, customers' expectation affects positively customer satisfaction in the category of high ambiguity products [12]; Churchill and Surprenant find out that customers' expectation affects positively customer satisfaction in nondurable assets [13]; when exploring the impact of online service quality on portal site Usage, Lin and Wu also demonstrate that customers' expectation affects customer satisfaction positively [14]. Given the researches above, we can come up to the following hypotheses:

H2-1: Context which customer expected affects positively customer satisfaction.

H2-2: Content which customer expected affects positively customer satisfaction.

H2-3: Customization which customer expected affects positively customer satisfaction.

H2-4: Membership which customer expected affects positively customer satisfaction.

H2-5: Communication which customer expected affects positively customer satisfaction.

H2-6: Commerce which customer expected affects positively customer satisfaction.

H2-7: Safety which customer expected affects positively customer satisfaction.

Table 6 and Table 7 illustrate the coefficients of customers' expectation and customer satisfaction.

Table 6. Coefficients (Dependent Variable: customer satisfaction)

	Beta	t	Sig.	R Square
(Constant)		6.655	.000	
context	.014	.146	.884	
content	.100	.800	.425	
customization	.050	.485	.628	
membership	-.059	-.571	.569	.129
communicati on	-.050	-.432	.666	
commerce	.249	1.967	.051	
safety	.077	.566	.572	

Table 7. Model Summary

R	R Square	Adjusted R Square	Std. Error of the Estimate
.360(a)	.129	.098	.61746

The results of hypotheses testing are shown in Table 8:

Table 8. Results 2

Hypotheses	H2-1	H2-2	H2-3	H2-4	H2-5	H2-6	H2-7
Results	No	No	No	No	No	No	No

3.3 How customers' expectation affects customers' perception

Spreng and Mackoy reveal that customers' expectation affects customers' perception positively [15]; Song also demonstrates that when studying the relationship between service quality and customer satisfaction for general portals [1]. These can lead to the following hypotheses:

H3-1: Context which customer expected affects positively that customer perceived.

H3-2: Content which customer expected affects positively that customer perceived.

H3-3: Customization which customer expected affects positively that customer perceived.

H3-4: Membership which customer expected affects positively that customer perceived.

H3-5: Communication which customer expected affects positively that customer perceived.

H3-6: Commerce which customer expected affects positively that customer perceived.

H3-7: Safety which customer expected affects positively that customer perceived.

Table 9 and Table 10 illustrate the coefficients of customers' expectation and customers' perception.

Table 9. Model Summary

R	R Square	Adjusted R Square	Std. Error of the Estimate
.452(a)	.204	.176	.51464

Table 10. Coefficients（Dependent Variable: customers' perception）

	Beta	t	Sig.	R Square
(Constant)		6.775	.000	
context	.239	2.662	.008	
content	.280	2.336	.021	
customization	.010	.098	.922	
membership	-.046	-.469	.640	.204
communication	.134	1.206	.229	
commerce	-.020	-.164	.870	
safety	-.100	-.776	.439	

As a result, H 3-1 and H 3-2 are supported. (see Table 11)

Table 11. Results 3

Hypotheses	H3-1	H3-2	H3-3	H3-4	H3-5	H3-6	H3-7
Results	Supportive	Supportive	No	No	No	No	No

4. Discussion

We'll discuss the results of Data Analysis from 3 aspects:

(1)Among the 7 factors we test in the model, "Customization" gets the highest Beta quotiety 0.402; the Beta quotiety of "Content" is 0.303 and "Commerce" gets the result of 0.160 which ranked 3rd.As a result, operators of EC websites should improve service quality according to the importance of the three factors.

(2)About how customers' perception affects customer satisfaction, we find out that customers' perception affects positively customer satisfaction in "content", "customization" and "commerce". "Context" which customer perceived does not influence customer satisfaction obviously. However, "membership" and "communication" which are thought to be important to customer satisfaction don't have effects on customer satisfaction. This can be explained by the Model of KANO [16]. "Membership" and "safety" can be put into the category of "Surprise & Delight" factors. These may seem to be less important but can really make the products stand out from the others.

(3)About how customers' expectation affects customer satisfaction, none of the 7 factors has impact on customer satisfaction. Reasons can be that people all give high scores to each item of the questionnaire. As a result, no matter how customers' perception changes, the expectations always remain to a higher level.

(4)About how customers' expectation affects customers' perception, "context" and "content" which customer expected affect positively on that customer perceived.

5. Conclusion

The results show that: customers' perception of B2C website's performances has a remarkable and positive correlation with consumer satisfaction from the aspects of content, customization and commerce; customers' expectation has as remarkable and positive correlation with customers' perception from the aspects of context and content; the results also indicates that the factor of customers' age has remarkable influence on website's performances which consumers perceived when shopping online.

Some suggestions can be put forward to both researchers and practitioners: the function of e-CRM and the importance of customer satisfaction should be well learned; the functions of content, customization and commerce of B2C websites should be enhanced; to be specific, B2C websites should take the following measures:

(1)Offering searching engine and BBS for consumers to retrieve information and communicate when shopping on-line;

(2)Updating the content of B2C website timely;

(3)Sending Greeting Cards or small gifts to regular customers;

(4)Offering customized goods;

(5)Offering diverse channels for ordering, payment and delivery; allowing consumers to choose the way they like;

Functions of content, customization and commerce of websites under B2C pattern should be enhanced; the factors of context, membership and communication should be added when carrying out e-CRM strategy.

Acknowledgments

This reasearch is supported by Program for New Century Excellent Talents in University (NCET) and National Social Science Foundation of China, Grant No. 06BTQ019.

References

1. B. C. Song, "Study on the Relationship between Service Quality and Customer Satisfaction for General Portals", *Hangzhou: Zhejiang University*, 25-26 (2005).

2. Y. X. Huang, "Effects of Commodity, System and Service Quality on on-line Consumers' Loyalty-an Example of 3C Internet Shopping Store", *Taiwan: Donghua University*, 44-48 (2005).

3. H. R. Ye, "A Study of Customer Relationship, Service Quality and Consumers' Loyalty-an Example of Online Shopping", *Taiwan, Dongwu University*, 22-25(2002).

4. R. Q. He, *CRM theory design practice*, Electronic Industry Press, Beijing, China (2001).

5. A. Q. Zhu, *Customer Relationship Management*, China Finance and Economy Press, Beijing, China (2003).

6. Y. Liu, C. F. Zhou, and Y.W. Chen, "Determinants of e-CRM in Influencing Customer Satisfaction", *Lecture Notes in Computer Science* 4099, 767-776(2006).

7. C. L. Zhang, "Building Customer Relationship Management Oriented Websites: A Study on the Online Flowers Shop in Taiwan", *Taiwan: Donghua University* (2005).

8. J. X. Zha, L. S. Wang, "Empirical Study of Influential Elements of E-satisfaction", *Science of Management* 19(1), 52-57(2006).

9. R. L. Oliver, "A Conceptual Model of Service Quality and Service Satisfaction: Compatible Goals, Different Concepts", *Advances in Service Marketing and Management* 2, 65-68(1993).

10. A. Parasuraman, V.A. Zeithaml, L.L Berry, "Refinement and Reassessment to the SERVQUAL Scale", *Journal of Retailing* 67(4), 420(1991).

11. A. Parasuraman, V.A. Zeithaml, L.L Berry, "SERVQUAL: A Multiple-Item Scale for Measuring Customer Perceptions of Service Quality", *Journal of Retailing* 64, 12-40(1988).

12. Y. Yi, "The determinants of consumer satisfaction: The moderating role of ambiguity in L.McAlister and M.L.Rothschild (Eds.)", *Advance in Consumer Research* 20,502-506(1993).

13. G. A. Churchill and C. Surprenant, "An Investigation into to the Determinants of Customer Satisfaction", *Journal of Marketing Research* 19, 491-504(1982).

14. C. S. Lin and S. Wu, "Exploring the impact of online service quality on portal site Usage", *Proceedings of the 35th Hawaii International Conference on System Sciences* (2002).

15. R. A. Spreng and R. D. Mackoy, "An empirical examination of a model perceived service quality and satisfaction", *Journal of Retailing* 72(2), 201-214(1996).

16. L. Yu, *Measurement of Customer Satisfaction*, Social Sciences Documentation Publishing House, Beijing, China (2003).

17. A. Parasuraman, V. A. Zeithaml, L. L Berry, "Quality and Its Implications for Future Research", *Journal of Marketing* 49, 41-50(1985).

18. Y. Yi, "The Determinants of Consumer Satisfaction: The Moderating Role of Ambiguity in L.McAlister and M.L.Rothschild (Eds.)", *Advance in consumer research* 20,502-506(1993).

19. C. S. Lin, S. Wu, "Exploring the Impact of Online Service Quality on Portal Site Usage", *Proceedings of the 35th Hawaii International Conference on System Sciences* (2002).

20. W.E. Sasser, R. P. Olsen, and D. D. Wyckoff, *Management of Service Operation: Text and Cases*, Allyn and Bacon Inc., Boston, US (1978).

21. J. E. G. Bateson, *Understanding Services Consumer Behavior. In C.A. Congram, (EA.), the AMA Handbook of Marketing for the Service Industries*, America Management Association, New York, US (1991).

22. J. Nunnally, *Psychometric theory*, McGraw-Hill Book Co, New York, US (1967).

23. J. Nunnally, *Psychometric theory 2nded*, McGraw-Hill Book Co., New York, US (1978).

The Analysis of Bullwhip Effect in Supply Chain Based on Strategic Alliance

Rui Xu, Xiaoli Li, Xiaomin Song, Gang Liu

School of Business, Hubei University, Wuhan, 430062, P. R. China,
wdxj826@126.com

Abstract. Bullwhip effect is a widespread and serious problem in supply chain management, both domestic and foreign scholars studied and came to a conclusion consistently: That the main functions that cause bullwhip effect are need forecasts, batches ordering, and fluctuations in price, rational decision-making, and time deferment and in coordination, supply chain structure. Many scholars have done quantifying study on bullwhip effect, but no one has think of the element that the ordering enterprises may magnify their demand and calculated the effect in the whole supply chain. This paper leads into the magnifying rate of market demand based on the research of Lee and Chen and others, quantifying the overstock caused by bullwhip effect in the whole supply chain, and contrast the condition under strategic alliance pattern and the condition under non-strategic alliance pattern, then testified the first pattern can bring benefits to enterprises and it is useful for saving resources, which can serve as good apocalypse for managers and entrepreneurs in supply chain.

1 Introduction

Supply chain management has being paid close attention to both by the theory boundary and the business circles. As the most important function index sign in supply chain structure and the most important performance index sign in the operation of supply chain bullwhip effect becomes the hot to be studied. It refers to the phenomenon that ultimate marketplace demand is enlarged increasingly in the process of transferring along supply chain toward the upper enterprises from the retail dealer. It was first bring about by Forrester(1958)[1] in "industrial dynamics", he listed a series of bullwhip effect examples in one book, in his opinion, bullwhip effect is caused by the constant change of organization behavior. Bullwhip effect leads to a manufacture making a production plan wrongly, enlarging stock investment, cutting down profits, reducing the standard of service, thereby brings catastrophic consequence to enterprises, many domestic and foreign scholars have done large amount of research on the cause and how to removes bullwhip effect. The

Please use the following format when citing this chapter:

Xu, R., Li, X., Song, X., Liu, G., 2007, in IFIP International Federation for Information Processing, Volume 251, Integration and Innovation Orient to E-Society Volume1, Wang, W. (Eds), (Boston: Springer), pp. 452-458.

mainly studying concentrates on the existence, the quantifying, the weakening, and the control of bullwhip effect.

For the weakening and controlling of bullwhip effect, the first step is to find out the cause and the second step is to quantify bullwhip effect. For the first step, domestic and foreign scholars found out seven functions such as demand forecasting, batches ordering, fluctuations of price, rational decision -making, time deferment and incoordination, and supply chain structure.

For the second step, there are many analysis. Wan(2002) [2] discussed the impacts of suppliers' assignment over bullwhip effect. Lu(2002) [3] certificated that the fluctuations in price or suppliers' shortsighted making price would lead to bullwhip effect. Chen adopted different forecasting technologies. At the same time, Chen(2000) [4] certificated that information share can diminish bullwhip effect efficiently, but can not eliminate bullwhip effect completely. And Chen(2000) [5] adopted the exponent level and smooth law to calculate, analysis the bullwhip effect in the two kinds of demanding patterns, and contrasted the results. Graves, Alwan and Li used time series analysis for bullwhip effect studying. Graves(1999) [6] had done this: calculated bullwhip effect when using an exponential smoothing forecast and adaptive base-stock, under the ARIMA(0, 1, 1) pattern which means unsteady demanding. Alwan(2003) [7] proved that under the AR(1) demanding pattern, using optimum forecasting method and (s, S) strategy , bullwhip effect will not happen when the neighbor term demand are negatively related. Li(2004) [8] expanded the research from peculiar time series two stage model to general ARIMA(0, 1, 1) time series many stage models, brought forward and proved that anti-bullwhip effect exists.

Their study mainly concentrates on three methods, such as system dynamics model taking Forrester(1958) [1] as a representative, autoregressive model taking Chen(2000) [4] as a representative, and Kalman filter model [9].

These study all concentrates bullwhip effect on suppliers, and have not think about the factor of demand and supply when models. For these disadvantages, this article builds a new model when leading into a market demand exaggerate rate and basing on Lee's (1997) [10] model and hypothesis. Besides, this article quantifies and contrasts the bullwhip effect under strategic alliance model and non-strategic alliance model from the whole supply chain. As a result, it proves that strategic alliance model can bring benefits to all the enterprises in supply chain.

2   The Quantifying Analysis of Lee et al

(1) Assumes in a two stage supply chain there is one supplier and i retail dealers (i= 1, 2, ..., n), retail dealers' demands area AR(1) models follow:

$$D_{it} = d + \rho D_{it-1} + \pi_{it}$$
(1)

Among the express d represents a constant, d>0; ρ expresses the relevance modulus, $-1<\rho<1$; D_{it} expresses the forecasting demand of retail dealer i at the stage t; π_{it} expresses a random variable obeying $(0, \sigma^2)$ lognormal distribution.

(2) Assumes that the retail dealers and supplier do not share information, in the condition , all the enterprises forecast their market demand independently and retail dealers adopt (s, S) ordering tactics which means that when the stock is lower than

the value s, makes stock increase to S level by ordering goods. s means the ordering point , S means the maximal stock . Assume again that the retail dealers do not have fixed cost when ordering goods from the manufacturer, then s=S. Each retail dealer's target ordering level S_{it} expresses as follow:

$$S_{it} = m_{it} + k\sigma\sqrt{v}$$

(2)

Among the express, m_{it} indicates the condition mean number, σ indicates the condition variance, and p indicates cost of being out of stock; h indicates stock cost; l indicates lead time, then:

$$m_{it} = \frac{d}{1-p}\left\{(l+1) - \sum_{j=1}^{l+1}\rho^j\right\} + \frac{\rho(1-\rho^{l+1})}{1-\rho}D_{it}$$

(3)

$$v = \frac{1}{(1-\rho)^2}\sum_{j=1}^{l+1}(1-\rho^j)^2$$

(4)

$$k = \phi^-1(\frac{p}{p+h})$$

(5)

According to hypothesis (1), suppliers' demand forecasting is:

$$Y_{it} = D_{it} + (S_{it} - S_{it-1})$$

(6)

Put expression (2) into expression (6) to get:

$$Y_{it} = D_{it} + (m_{it} - m_{it-1})$$

(7)

Put expression (3) into expression (7) to get:

$$Y_{it} = D_{it} + \frac{\rho(1-\rho^{l+1})}{1-\rho}(D_{it} - D_{it-1})$$

(8)

Put expression (1) into expression (8) to get:

$$Y_{it} = \frac{(1-\rho^{l+2})d}{1-\rho} + \rho^{l+2}D_{it-1} + \frac{(1-\rho^{l+2})}{1-\rho}\pi_{it}$$

(9)

3   The Model of this article

(1) Assumes that the factual demand during t+1 term is A_{t+1};
    (2) Assume that at the end of t+1 term the backlog of excess demand is B_{t+1}.

3.1   The Market Backlog of Excess Demand in Supply Chain under Non-strategic Alliance Model

Under this model, there is no information share, every retail dealer forecasts demand and send out their orders to the supplier independently. Since the uncertainty of marketplace, sometimes demand is greater than supplies in the whole market, and then a rational supplier often distributes a fixed rate of the each retail dealer's order. Assume retail dealer i forecasts that the supplying rate according to his order is α_i (which is a constant), then he will exaggerate his order by $1/\alpha_i$ times. Assumes that every retail dealer want to get the full amount of their forecasting demand, then they order will be:

$$D'_{it} = \frac{D_{it}}{\alpha_i} \quad (0 < \alpha_i \leq 1)$$
(10)

Because of the insharing of information, each supplier has to predicts the demands of every retailer according to their orders during the last term. So revise (9) with (10) to get supplier's demand forecasting for each retail dealer during term t is:

$$Y_{it} = \frac{(1-\rho^{l+2})d}{1-\rho} + \rho^{l+2}\frac{D_{it-1}}{\alpha_i} + \frac{(1-\rho^{l+2})}{1-\rho}\pi_{it}$$
(11)

The supplier's overall demand forecasting for every retail dealer during term $t+1$ is the total of supplier's demand forecasting for each retail dealer during term t+1 just as follow:

$$Y_{t+1} = \sum_{i=1}^{n} Y_{it+1}$$
(12)

Put expression (11) into expression (12) to get:

$$Y_{t+1} = \frac{(1-\rho^{l+2})nd}{1-\rho} + \rho^{l+2}\sum_{i=1}^{n}\frac{D_{it}}{\alpha_i} + \frac{(1-\rho^{l+2})}{1-\rho}\sum_{i=1}^{n}\pi_{it+1}$$
(13)

At the end of term t+1, the total backlog of excess demand in the supply chain is the total demand forecasting Subtract the actual demand during the term just as follow:

$$B_{t+1} = Y_{t+1} - A_{t+1}$$
(14)

Put expression (13) into expression (14) to get:

$$B_{t+1} = \frac{(1-\rho^{l+2})nd}{1-\rho} + \rho^{l+2}\sum_{i=1}^{n}\frac{D_{it}}{\alpha_i} + \frac{(1-\rho^{l+2})}{1-\rho}\pi_{it+1} - A_{t+1}$$
(15)

3.2 The Market Backlog of Excess Demand in Supply Chain under Strategic Alliance Model

Under this pattern, all retail dealers and suppliers form a strategic alliance, sharing information, trusting each other, and wielding Third-party logistics enterprises such as the distribution center for united tock and distribution.

In this condition, only supplier has to forecast the whole market demand according to the actual market information from the retail dealers. Assume that the forecasting is a AR(1) model, which has been proved right by expression (9), and the forecasting model is:

$$Y'_{t+1} = d_n + \rho_n D_t + \delta_t$$
(16)

$$D_t = \sum_{i=1}^{n} D_{it}$$
(17)

Among the express, d_n is a constant, $d_n > 0$; ρ_n is the relevance modulus, $-1 < \rho_n < 1$; δ_{it} is a random variable obeying $(0, \varepsilon^2)$ lognormal distribution.

Put expression (17) into expression (16) to get:

$$Y'_{t+1} = d_n + \rho_n \sum_{i=1}^{n} D_{it} + \delta_t$$

(18)

For both express (9) and express (18) are supplier's total demand forecasting for all retail dealers, and they are both AR(1) models, we can assume that they have equal relevance modulus, this means:

$$\rho_n = \rho^{l+2}$$

(19)

Since the marketplace facing the supplier under strategic alliance pattern is just the whole marketplace facing the retail dealers, it can be assumed that:

$$\delta_t = \sum_{i=1}^{n} \pi_{it}$$

(20)

Then under this model, at the end of term t+1, the total backlog of excess demand in the supply chain is:

$$B'_{t+1} = Y'_{t+1} - A_{t+1}$$

(21)

Contrasting (12) and (15) to get:

$$C_{t+1} = B_{t+1} - B'_{t+1}$$

(22)

(C_{t+1} is the cutting down amounts of backlog of excess demand or stock in supply chain because of strategic alliances.)

Put expression (14) and (20) into expression (22) to get:

$$C_{t+1} = Y_{t+1} - Y'_{t+1}$$

(23)

Put expression (13), (18), (19) and (20) into expression (23) to get:

$$C_{t+i} = (\frac{1-\rho^{l+2}}{1-\rho} nd - d_n) + \sum_{i=1}^{n} (\frac{1}{\alpha_i} - 1) \rho_n D_{it} + (\frac{1-\rho^{l+2}}{1-\rho} - 1) \sum_{i=1}^{n} \pi_{it+1}$$

(24)

$(1-\rho^{l+2})nd/(1-\rho)$ and dn can be understood as safety stock under strategic alliance situation, it can be understood as that supplier only have one retail dealer or he can use any retail dealer's safety stock to meet other retail dealer's access demand, then synergy effect of strategic alliance model happens, and the total safety stock must be reduced, which means:

$$d_n \leq nd$$

(25)

For:

$$\frac{1-\rho^{l+2}}{1-\rho} = 1 + \rho + \rho^2 + \cdots + \rho^{l+1}$$

(26)

So:

$$\frac{1-\rho^{l+2}}{1-\rho} nd > nd > d_n$$

(27)

Then we can get:

$$\frac{1-\rho^{l+2}}{1-\rho} nd - d_n > 0$$

(28)

For $0<\alpha_i\leq1$, so:

$$\sum_{i=1}^{n}(\frac{1}{\alpha_i}-1)\rho_n D_{it} \geq 0 \tag{29}$$

For:

$$\frac{1-\rho^{l+2}}{1-\rho}-1 = \rho+\rho^2+\cdots+\rho^{l+1} \tag{30}$$

So:

$$(\frac{1-\rho^{l+2}}{1-\rho}-1)\sum_{i=1}^{n}\pi_{it+1} >0 \tag{31}$$

According to (28), (29), (31), $C_{t+1}\geq0$

4 Conclusions

4.1 The Advantages of This Article's Model

(1) Different industries are confronted with different market supply and demand situations; even the same industry is confronted with different market supply and demand situations at different terms. The main reason of bullwhip effect is the dissymmetry of information, and the most obvious action for retails dealer is to magnify their demands. But the past scholars didn't think of this element. For this, this article's model leads into a marketplace exaggerate rate $1/\alpha_i$ $(0<\alpha_i\leq1)$, when $0<\alpha_i<1$ it indicates that the market demand is greater than supplies, down-stream enterprises exaggerates their order when sending out order to the supplier; when α_i =1, it indicates a normal buyer's market. So this article's model perfects Lee (1997) [10] and Chen(2000) [5] and others model and it is representive, it can be broadly used in different industries and enterprises, it can be used in different market conditions and has better adaptability in today's changing market.

(2) The former models all concentrates bullwhip effect on suppliers, in fact, the reduce of bullwhip effect can save the resource of the whole society, then get benefits for every enterprise in supply chain, from this point, bullwhip effect has bad effects to all enterprises in supply chain, and the past models themselves are not easy for further studies of bullwhip effect in multi-level supply chain. This article's model standing in the point of the whole supply chain, calculate the backlog of excess demand in supply chain directly, and calculate the economic benefits (resource savings) from strategic alliance model, giving the managers of supply chain a direct express and serving as a basic basis for further distribution of the benefits among all the enterprises in supply chain.

(3)The article has discussed the improvement of backlog of excess demand in supply chain by the strategic alliances model, at the same time, in the model of this article, as long as that the forecasting demands of both the most down-stream enterprise and most upstream enterprise are known, then the backlog of excess demand in the whole supply chain is able to be got. Because of these, this article's model is more simplified and easy to carry out studies of bullwhip effect in multi-level supply chain.

4.2   The Disadvantages of This Article's Model

The deficiency of this article's model is that it does not think about the effect on orders from the backlog of excess demand during, and only concentrates on the disproportion of supply and demand during a give term.

Contrasting the advantages and the disadvantage, it is obvious that this article's model is better than the farmer's models. It breaks up the limitation that only concentrates the effect on supplier, adding the magnifying element, it perfects the past models, it is innovation, it makes the model have a wider use, and supplies a new angle of view to study bullwhip effect for the later scholars, it serves good apocalypse for managers and entrepreneurs in supply chain.

Acknowledgments

This research has been supported by the key projects of bureau of science and technology of Wuhan under Grant 20064003113-31 and education department of Hubei Province under Grant 2006y073.

References

73.   1. J.W. Forrester, Industrial Dynamics, *Harvard Business Review* 36(4), 37-66 (1958).

74.   2. J. Wan, M.Q. Li, J.S. Kou, Impact of Capacity Allocation on Bullwhip Effect in Supply Chain, *Journal of Systems Engineering* 17(4), 340-348 (2002). (in Chinese)

75.   3. G.B. Lu, Q.Y. Hu, X.B. Gan, Research on Combined Pricing and Inventory Strategy, *Journal of Systems Engineering* 17(6), 531-536 (2002). (in Chinese)

76.   4. F. Chen, Z. Drezner, J.K. Ryan, D. Simchi-Levi, Quantifying the Bullwhip Effect in a Simple Supply Chain: The Impact of Forecasting, Lead Times, and Information, *Management Science* 46(3), 436-443 (2000).

77.   5. F. Chen, J.K. Ryan, D. Simchi-Levi, the Impact of Exponential Smoothing Forecasts on the Bullwhip Effect, *Naval Research Logistics* 47(4), 269-286 (2000).

78.   6. Graves, C. Stephen, A Single-item Inventory Model for a Non-stationary Demand Process, *Manufacturing & Service Operations Management* 1(1), 50-61 (1999).

79.   7. Alwan, C. Layth, Liu, J. John, D.Q. Yao, Stochastic Characterization of Upstream Demand Processes in a Supply Chain, *IIE Transactions* 35(3), 207-219 (2003).

80.   8. G. Li, S.Y. Wang, G. Yu, H. Yan, Bullwhip Effect and Validity of Production-smoothing Model, *Journal of Management Sciences in China* 7(1), 1-18 (2004). (In Chinese)

81.   9. X. Li, Y.S. Chen, How to Control the Bullwhip Effect Based on Systematic Structure Improvement, *Logistics Technology* (10), 58-60 (2006). (In Chinese)

82.   10. H.L. Lee, V. Padmanabhan, Information Distortion in a Supply Chain: The Bullwhip Effect, *Management Science* 43(4), 546-558 (1997).

Knowledge Innovation in E-business enterprises

Shaohua He [1]   Peilin Wang [2]
1 Electronic Commerce Market Application Technology,
Guangdong University of Business Studies, China,
hshua@email.whu.edu.cn
2 School of Information Management, Wuhan University,
China,
wsai_ll@163.com

Abstract. E-business is not a new topic, and many authors made many researches on this topic, such as the relationship between e-business and competitiveness, the advantages of e-business, e-business and knowledge management, e-business and management innovation, and so on. However, knowledge innovation in e-business enterprises is an ignored field. In fact, different kinds of companies at present considered knowledge innovation as the key factor for getting sustainable competitive advantage, no exception of e-business enterprises. Therefore, this paper chose knowledge innovation in e-business as its topic, and analyzed the relationship between e-business and knowledge innovation, and then explored the impact of knowledge innovation on e-business. In the end, it tried to analyze the knowledge innovation in e-business, including product and service innovation, technology innovation, and management innovation. These elements were then further decomposed.

1 Introduction

In general, e-business is the business activities on internet. When the business in a company is directly connected with the staff, customers, suppliers, and partners by intranet, extranet, and internet, various activities in those processes are e-business [1]. In the process of transforming from traditional business to electronic business, business environment is changing, the competition confronted by the company at home and abroad is increasing, and the product innovation is speeding up. Thus, in order to get the rapid response for the changing market, business crisis, and the transition to knowledge-based products/service, it is important for the companies to

Please use the following format when citing this chapter:

He, S., Wang, P., 2007, in IFIP International Federation for Information Processing, Volume 251, Integration and Innovation Orient to E-Society Volume1, Wang, W. (Eds), (Boston: Springer), pp. 459-466.

realize knowledge innovation. It is essential for the company to integrate the reserved information resources with staffs' experience by knowledge innovating to sustain its competitive advantage, so that the company can effectively explore, share, and utilize knowledge, which lead the company to understand the special knowledge it captures and know how to utilize these knowledge to develop.

As a summary, the evidence proves that e-business enterprises must depend on knowledge innovation to get the competitive advantage, and transits from business-centered and company-centered model to the customers-centered and knowledge-centered business model. Therefore, the purposes of this study are as follows.

(1) An exploration of the interrelationship between e-business and knowledge innovation.

(2) An exploration of the knowledge innovation in e-business, including product /service innovation, technology innovation, and management innovation. These elements were then further decomposed.

2   The Core of E-business Enterprises is Knowledge and Innovation

The appearance of internet and e-business changes the characteristics of the market, and leads to the appearance of new critical success factors, which change the competitive rules and influence the competitive environment. In the new business model, the competitive environment becomes boundless. As internet provides a greater marketing space for tradesmen, the limitations of space and time are more and more little. And the virtual world provided by internet leads to the products spontaneously spread all over the world. However, e-business brings uncertainty to the competitive environment at the same time. Technological change, global communication and the development of internet all reveal that the present environment is more complex and more uncertain than ever. As information technology integrating and the internet developing, the company cannot only rely on overall cost leadership, differentiation and focus provided by Michael E. Porter to competitive advantage. Knowledge becomes a new source of competitive advantage, and no exception of e-business. E-business enterprises therefore have to depend on not only cost leadership, differentiation and focus, but also on knowledge and innovation to reduce the uncertainty [2].

On the other hand, the main characteristics of e-business enterprises decide that e-business enterprises have to depend on knowledge and innovation to some extend. E-business is a new business model based on computers and internet technology, which pays more attention to knowledge and innovation than traditional business (see Table 1 [3]). And as the development of technology and the rapid reduction of the cost, there is little barrier for entering the e-business model, so that the competitors can catch up with or even exceed the company by lower cost and more advanced technology. If the company is the follower of e-business, it will lose its competitive advantage. Therefore, e-business enterprises really depend on not their rich capital but abundant knowledge resources, whose main resources of operation and risk are knowledge capital and customer relationship capital. And among those capitals in one company, knowledge capital is the leading capital, which decides the increase of customer relationship capital. Therefore, the value of the company is not its workshops, equipment or products, but its intellectual property, the degree of reliance of customers, the cooperation with partners, information infrastructure, and the innovative capacity and expertise of the staffs. In other words, the fundamental advantage of e-business enterprises is their advanced knowledge, which depends on knowledge innovation. And knowledge capture, process, integration, innovation are the strong pushes of e-business enterprises, and knowledge has become the critical factor for the development of e-business enterprises. And we can infer accordingly that the core of e-business enterprises is knowledge and innovation, and the following part will discuss the impacts of knowledge innovation on e-business.

Table 8. The Comparison of Traditional Business and E-business

	Traditional business	e-business
Assets	tangible assets	Intangible assets
Strategy	expecting	Improving the capacity of meet an emergency
Information technology	centralized	decentralized
Role of senior managers	obedience	Self-control
The process of management	application	innovation

3   Impacts of Knowledge Innovation on E-business Enterprises

The above part has inferred that the core of e-business enterprises is knowledge and innovation, and this part will discuss the impacts of knowledge innovation on e-business to prove that knowledge innovation is the key factor of e-business.

Firstly, knowledge innovation helps e-business enterprises create new ideas to start new business [4]. Considering e-business as a new business model, many pioneers have entered into this field and started different kinds of business, such as electronic retail company (for example, Amazon bookstore), electronic auction company (for example, eBAY), electronic direct distribution (for example, DELL), electronic street (for example, euyar). All of these businesses create great economical and social benefit. But these businesses are created not by accident, but by the capacity of observing the market and the sense of innovation by the pioneers. They have captured the soul of knowledge innovation-creating knowledge. As the research on knowledge innovation and e-business deepens, there are more and more people to unconsciously utilize knowledge innovation theory to start e-business.

Secondly, knowledge innovation is good for e-business to accumulate and transfer information and knowledge [5], develop new products and improve business [6], and enhance the capacity of response [7], which are critical to the development of e-business. As knowledge innovation is a cooperative innovation, use of computer and internet technology lead e-business to access to customers and suppliers. Knowledge alliance between e-business and other companies (such as distribution enterprises and banks) benefits e-business for reducing the time and cost of the research, and improving the capacity of innovation as well. For example, General automobile builds knowledge alliance with Toyota to develop manufacturing technology of automobiles, and IBM builds partnership with France telephone Co. to develop communication technology. E-business expands the customer groups, and brings large amount of out-of-order information as well. Therefore, the company has to process, organize, transfer the information, and change it into knowledge in time to improve the efficiency, which demand the use of database or knowledgebase and the tools of knowledge innovation. Through knowledgebase, e-business can directly communicate with various customers, and provide the customers with special service to meet their needs.

Thirdly, knowledge innovation builds new competitive rules for e-business enterprises [8]. In the competition of e-business, the company should not stress on how to compete in fixed rules, but pay more attention to understand and adapt the changing competitive rules. The dynamic change of environment leads to that the best practice of yesterday becomes the barriers of tomorrow, which demands the company adjust according to the change of the business and information infrastructure and learn how to utilize old knowledge and new knowledge. In one word, e-business enterprises have to develop knowledge-innovation-centered competitiveness to adapt the dynamic market in order to survive in the competition.

Fourthly, knowledge innovation helps e-business build or sustain competitive advantage. Business activities in e-business are knowledge in themselves, which are convenient to capture the internal knowledge, external knowledge, fact knowledge and workers' ideas. And the process of analyzing the information in database is in essence knowledge innovation. Therefore, the company should create the knowledge in e-business and learn from business activities. And the capacity of innovation decides the amount of value-added knowledge in business. That is to say, because different companies have different capacity of innovation, they will get different experience from similar business activities, which is mainly methodological knowledge and included in the core capacity of the company to get competitive advantage in similar business activities. For example, Dupont had deal with Dye industry, learned from it and had some creation in the field of Synthetic fiber. And finally it got the necessary knowledge on dye synthesis and its utilization, which make the company believe that they are able to solve the problem of dye coloration. Thus, the company started to develop nylon and succeeded.

In a summary, e-business and knowledge innovation are interrelated, and knowledge innovation is the key factor of e-business. E-business companies have to get knowledge innovation to get the competitive advantage, and the following part will further explore how e-business companies realize knowledge innovation.

4 Knowledge Innovation in E-business Enterprises

Although there is not a fixed definition of knowledge innovation, most authors accepts that knowledge innovation is the whole process from knowledge creation to knowledge utilization. Enterprises' knowledge innovation means applying created knowledge into the production, including products development and improvement, process innovation, service innovation, organization innovation, strategy innovation, and technology innovation as well. In e-business enterprises, knowledge innovation mainly includes products and service innovation, management innovation, and technology innovation. And this part will explore knowledge innovation in e-business by analyzing those three kinds of innovation.

4.1 Products/Service Innovation

According to Osterwalder etc. , products/service innovation is one of the important components in e-business [11] (see Figure 1). And the elements of products/service innovation cover all aspects related to the offering of the firm. Those comprise not only its products/service but the manner in which the company differentiates itself from its competitors. In other words, this includes not only the firms market scope [9] [10] - customers, geographical areas, and product segments – but also the explanations why customers will buy from this firm rather than from a competitor. Moreover, the ability to offer value for a customer demands a range of specific capabilities.

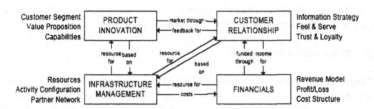

Fig. 1. The 4 Pillars Of the Business Model Ontology by Osterwalder etc. (Resources: Osterwalder, A. Pigneur, Y. An E-business Model Ontology for Modeling E-business. In the Proceedings of the 15th Bled Electronic Commerce Conference Bled, Slovenia, June 17-19, 75-91(2002))

As the cost for entrance to e-business is low, every person or company can easily enter into e-business, and similar companies in e-business provide similar products or service, which result in the fierce competition in e-business. Thus, under the condition of technology and the requirement of customers changing, e-business enterprises have to stress products/service innovation to survive and sustain. E-business enterprises are able to realize products/service innovation in two ways. One is to create new products/service, and the other is to explore new property of existed products/service. In order to realize products/service innovation, e-business enterprises have to get the interrelated knowledge on new products or service and existed products or service firstly, including whether there are similar products or service in the market or not, which are interrelated products or service, whether the company developed similar products or service, the new requirement of customers for the products and their expectations, and the cost and profit of developing the new products or service. Then, the company can create knowledge by focusing on the market and making regular research, and by participating into the projects or imitating other companies as well. The process of innovation is the process from intuitive tacit knowledge to more exact knowledge like figures, and to literature knowledge such as document or digital knowledge, and finally to utilize literature knowledge to create explicit knowledge.

4.2   Technology Innovation

Technology innovation is also one of important components of e-business. One of the premises of the development of e-business is information infrastructure, which includes internet. One of the important reasons for the development of e-business in America is that information infrastructure including internet in America builds a broad platform for e-business. Therefore, e-business enterprises have to stress technology innovation. The capacity of technology innovation is the integrative capacity by which the company creates new ideas and puts into practice. From the point of knowledge, the capacity of technology innovation is the capacity which inspires external knowledge of the company and integrates and creates knowledge to realize its value [12]. And from the point of innovation, the capacity of technology innovation is knowledge creation and inspiration in nature. And knowledge creation and inspiration depend on the improvement of innovation system and reward system. Otherwise, the inspiration of the knowledge in knowledgebase depends on its developing environment. Thus, the company has to improve its environment to get, create and inspire new knowledge for technology innovation.

4.3   Management Innovation

Management innovation is to make use of new management thoughts to promote the management innovation of e-business and build an appropriate advanced management model [13]. Management innovation should be harmony with technology innovation and new business theory. When the company starts e-business, it is difficult to carry out the traditional management theory which pays attention to division and accuracy. The company should innovate and integrate according to new requirements for safe, accurate and efficient management. The company can not ignore the coherence between management innovation and technology innovation. For example, in customized internet marketing, the company must depend on software to manage effectively. At the same time, the company depends on its products to design the best customers-oriented business solution which is based on information feedback, interactive communication and track service to realize customers' benefit and the company's revenue.

5   Conclusion

There are several reasons why academic research should be done in the area of knowledge innovation in e-business enterprise. First of all, even though many people talk about e-business, rare are knowledge innovation which is the key for the development of e-business. Executives, reporters and analysts who use the term do not have a clear idea of how to realize e-business.

The second reason why knowledge innovation in e-business enterprises is interesting to be studied is that it can be a foundation for e-business enterprises and an application of knowledge innovation theory. As product life cycles become shorter, competition global and the use of information technology are imperative, managers have to find new ways to decide in this complex environment. Managers have to understand the new opportunities offered by information technology, integrate them into their existing business models and share them with other stakeholders. The knowledge innovation in e-business enterprises we propose in this paper is a first step to facilitating management under uncertainty.

References

1. Kequn, Ch. Enterprise Management and Its Creation in the Environment of Electronic Commerce. *Journal of Anhui Agricultural University(social science edition).* 1(4), 52-54 (2002)
2. Wenwu, Z. Peilin, W. Information Risk in E-business and Its Countermeasure. *Group Economy.* 3, (2007)
3. Juan, Zh. etc. Analyzing the Development of Enterprises from the Relationship Between E-business and Knowledge Management. *China Rural Enterprise Techniques Market.* 5, 40-41(2005)
4,5,8. Wei,Ch. Delu, W. Shaoxia,Q. Knowledge Management and E-business. *Future and Development.*6, 7-8(2001)
6,7. Yang,Y. Discussion on Electronic Commerce Enterprise and Knowledge management. *Pioeering With Science & Technology Monthly.* 4, 95-96 (2006)
9. Hamel, G., Leading the Revolution, *Boston: Harvard Business School Press.* 35-36(2000)
10. Afuah, A., C. Tucci . Internet Business Models and Strategies, *Boston: McGraw Hill.* 56-71(2001)
11. Osterwalder, A. Pigneur, Y. An E-business Model Ontology for Modeling E-business. In *the Proceedings of the 15th Bled Electronic Commerce Conference Bled, Slovenia, June 17-19,* 75-91(2002)
12. Yi, Ouy.. Haichun, G. Knowledge Management Strategy in E-business Enterprises. *World Standardization and Quality Management.* 8, 37-39 (2005)
13. Yuean, X. Innovation on the Development of E-business and Its Environment. *Commercial Times.* 8, 26-28 (2001)
14. Hong, Zh. etc. A System Structure of Knowledge Management based on E-commerce at Baosteel Yichang Company. *Industrial Engineering and Management.* 2, 125-130 (2005)
15. John Flower. Internet Economic: The Coming of Digital Business Era. *Worldwide Concert Corp.* 206-228(1997)

16. M.A. Saren. A Classification and Review of Models of the Intra-firm Innovation Process. *R&D Management*. 14(1), 11-24 (1984)
17. Adamantia G. Pateli, George M. Giaglis, A Framework for Understanding and An Analyzing eBusiness Models. *16th Bled E-commerce Conference E-Transformation Bled*, Slovenia, June 9-11 (2003)

The Fuzzy Integrated Evaluation of Enterprise Information System Security Based on EC

Shaolong Zhang, Ning Zhou and Jiaxing Wu
Center for Studies of Information Resources,
Wuhan University, 430072
zhangshaolong78@yahoo.com.cn

Abstract. As enterprises increase their electronic communication in business activities through network, the security of enterprise information system based on EC becomes crucial for enterprises. This paper proposes a fuzzy integrated security evaluation method based on man-computer combined data collection and fuzzy expert evaluation in Delphi method. The method could reduce the subjectivity of expert evaluation and alleviate the difficulty of data collection and makes possible a better combination of qualitative and quantitative evaluations. Firstly, the evaluation factor and hierarchy structure of security evaluation is constructed. Secondly, according to data collected and the evaluation comment of each expert, the subjection degree matrix is constructed. Finally, a new concept of "degree of assurance" is presented for the quantificational evaluation of enterprise information system security based on. In this paper the study of the case shows that the method can be easily used and its results conform to the actual situation.

1 Introduction

Electronic Commerce is the sharing of business information, maintaining business relationships, and conducting business transactions by means of telecommunications networks [1]. The explosion of the Internet as a ubiquitous business tool has propelled the hype over fruitful electronic commerce opportunities to new heights. But while modern networking technologies such as the Internet offer new tools for making the communication and sharing of information more efficient and faster than ever before, it can significantly increase exposure to information security risks. The risks of enterprise information system based on EC come from Internet and Intranet. Leakage and invalid access of information affect not only a single user or application,

Please use the following format when citing this chapter:

Zhang, S., Zhou, N., Wu, J., 2007, in IFIP International Federation for Information Processing, Volume 251, Integration and Innovation Orient to E-Society Volume1, Wang, W. (Eds), (Boston: Springer), pp. 467-474.

but may have disastrous consequences on the entire enterprise. The security evaluation of enterprise information system based on EC is a process in which the risk factors of the system are analyzed and explained. The basic goal of the security evaluation is to control the risk in acceptability.

By the reason of the uncertainty of the evaluation factor, the fuzzy logic method is used [2]. In this paper an improved fuzzy method is proposed to solve the security evaluation. The rest of this paper is organized as follows. In section 2, an evaluation model is given for security evaluation. In section 3, a case is put forward to illustrate our method. Finally, conclusions are drawn in Section 4.

2   Construction of security evaluation model

In the evaluation of enterprise information security based on EC, we face problems such as the complication of security factors, limited history statistical data and difficulty of data collection. There is no single method to solve these problems. We need an integrated evaluation method which comprises expert evaluation, statistical information and compute technology. To construct security evaluation model, firstly evaluation factors are recognized, then data is collected through man-computer method, at last based on fuzzy subjection theory and Delphi method qualitative evaluation is transferred to quantitative evaluation.

2.1 The recognition of security evaluation factors

Before the evaluation of security, we need a investigation on security factors. Usually system security is evaluated from three aspects which are strategy, management and technology. Strategy refers strategic status and strategic decision of information system security in the enterprise. Management includes organizations and regulations to the information system security and supervision on relative people and materials. Technology refers all kinds of security technologies. But under the EC environment human is to be interactive with enterprise information system based on network, referred with the systematic methodology of "Wuli-Shili-Renli (WSR)"[3], human is the key factor to the enterprise information security. Good guidance and access control to the web users and skills of network administrator are important to security of EC. Thus when we give the recognition of security evaluation factors, human is recognized as one of the top level factors as well as strategy, management, technology which sub-factors are also recognized based on.

2.2 Man-computer combined data collection

Applied with IT technology, most security data could be automatically collected. These technologies include   computer log system, real-time scan tools and automatic audit system and so on. Using computer technology can bring benefits. Firstly it could reduce the subjectivity of expert evaluation and make the evaluation method more scientific and objective. Secondly it alleviates the human workload in data collection which not only cuts down the cost of human labor but also improves the veracity and the coverage of data collection. Some evaluation factors such as access control management and network management could be directly counted and evaluated based on automatically colleted data.

On the occasions that data could not be automatically collected by computer such as situations about training and security rules, questionnaire survey and On-the-spot investigation also could be applied.

2.3 Expert evaluation in Delphi method

The objective of most Delphi applications is the reliable and creative exploration of ideas or the production of suitable information for decision making. The Delphi Method is based on a structured process for collecting and distilling knowledge from a group of experts by means of a series of questionnaires interspersed with controlled opinion feedback (Adler and Ziglio, 1996). According to Helmer (1977) Delphi represents a useful communication device among a group of experts and thus facilitates the formation of a group judgment [4].

Based on data colleted experts make evaluations relying on their individual competence and are subjective, Delphi method is utilized to adjust the fuzzy evaluation of each expert to achieve the consensus condition of the all experts consistent.

Flowchart for the Delphi Method follows as [5]:

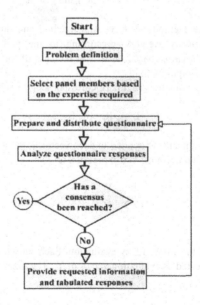

Figure 1. Flowchart of Delphi Method

2.4 Integrated Fuzzy Evaluation

The major steps of evaluation are as the following.

Step1. Construct the hierarchical structure. The top layer is the focus of the goal, and the bottom level, consists of the alternatives under evaluation. The factors and any sub-factors used to make the decision comprise the middle levels [6]. The factors is divided into s subsets which defined as $Y_1,Y_2...Y_S(Y_i \cup Y_j = \phi(1 \leq i,j \leq s\ i \neq j))$. Each subset Y_i is constructed by the factors in the next level denoted as X_{in}, so the characteristic vector of each subset Y_i is presented by the expression.

$$Y_i = (X_{i1}, X_{i2}, ..., X_{in})$$

Step2. Construct the judge set. The expert group which is composed of information system experts, enterprise manager and end users provides all the judgements of the set. Suppose the judge set has m judgements, judge set V is $V = \{V_1, V_2, ..., V_m\}$.

Step3. Build fuzzy evaluation matrix. We can construct the fuzzy reflection f: Y $\rightarrow$ F(V), Y is the whole of the factor set and F(V) is the whole of the fuzzy set in V. The reflection f means the degree of the support from the factor Y_i to each judgement in the judge set [7]. The subjection vector of Y_i to the judge set V is $R_i = (r_{ij,k})$ n*m(i=1,2,...,s; j=1,2,...,n; k=1,2,...,m). $r_{ij,k}$ is the subjection degree of factor x_{ij} to judgement V_k given by expert which meets the requirements that the range of the value is [0,1] and the count of values $\sum r_{ij} = 1$.

Step4. Estimate the normalized priority weights. The priority weight vector of subsets is presented by the expression.

$$A_i = (a_{i1}, a_{i2}, ..., a_{in}), \text{and} \sum a_{ij} = 1$$

There are several methods such as AHP method and dual correlation function method to give priority weights. According to the particularity of enterprise information system security based on EC, in the case of this paper the weights are given by experts in Delphi method.

Step5. Calculate evaluation vector B_i corresponding to subset Y_i. The calculation formula is

$$B_i = A_i \cdot R_i = (b_{i1}, b_{i2}, ..., b_{im}).$$

Weighted average means is applied to each vector B_i to take valuable information of each evaluation into account. The expression is

$$b_{ik} = \sum_{j=1}^{n} a_{ij}\ r_{ij,k} (k=1,2,...,m).$$

Step6. Calculate the whole fuzzy evaluation. Each subset Y_i is treated as a single element and B_i is treated as evaluation vector of Y_i, The fuzzy evaluation matrix is

$$B = \begin{pmatrix} B_1 \\ B_2 \\ \cdots \\ B_s \end{pmatrix}_3 =$$

Referred with priority weight vector of each subset A which is represented as A= $(a_1, a_2, \ldots, a_s)$ and $\sum_{i=1}^{s} a_i = 1$, the final evaluation $T = A \cdot B = (t_1, t_2, \ldots, t_m)$ is calculated.

2.5 Quantificational evaluation result of security

It is difficult to give quantificational result to final evaluation. To achieve a quantificational evaluation result, the degree of assurance is introduced which is denoted as G..

To calculate G, judge set V should be quantified first. For example, judgement "Very High" would be evaluated as 100. Quantified judge set $V' = \{V'_1, V'_2, \ldots, V'_m\}$.

$$G = \sum_{i=1}^{m} t_i V'_i.$$

3 The case

In this case the hierarchy structure is constructed; evaluation factors are divided into four subsets which are Strategy, Management, Technology and Human. Sub-factors and the alternatives under evaluation are shown as Tables 1 (priority weight in the brackets).

The judge set V is $V = \{V_1, V_2, V_3, V_4, V_5\}$ which shows the risk probability level. Its meaning is " V_1 Very High, V_2 High, V_3 Medium , V_4 Low , V_5 Very Low".

Table 1. Evaluation factors of the case

NO	Top factors	Sub-factors	Alternatives
1	Strategy (0.15)	Strategy status of IT department (0.5)	Information literacy of enterprise leader
			Investment of IT construction

2		Security information system construction plan and budget (0.5)	Long-term plan of information system construction
			Investment of information system construction
3		Laws and regulations (0.2)	Protection from laws and regulations
			comprehensive rules and regulations within enterprise
4		Human management (0.3)	qualifications examination of system administrator and operators
			on-the-job training
	Management (0.3)		division of privileges
5		Environment management(0.2)	firewall and router setting
			temperature and humidity control, power management, wiring management
6		Risk management(0.3)	establishment of information system backup mechanism
			preparation of emergency predetermined plan
10	Technology (0.4)	Operating system (0.2)	Legal operating system software
			system patch update
			password protection and logon privilege management
			anti-virus protection
11		Safety in transmission(0.3)	encryption in IP package
			reliable transmission in VPN
			integration in data transmission
12		Network access control(0.1)	access control of web users

13		Security audit system(0.2)	Tracing and collecting audit data including system log, firewall log
			adoption of security authentication protocol such as SSL and SET
14		Encryption key management (0.2)	creation and management of encryption key based on absolutely safe regulations
15	Human (0.15)	Human resource management(0.5)	Employment of important people
			reservation of technical personnel
16		Human education(0.5)	enterprise interior training mechanism

The experts make judgements of the subjection to the judge set V. Evaluation matrixes R1, R2, R3 and R4 are:

$$R_1 = \begin{pmatrix} 0.25 & 0.35 & 0.30 & 0.10 & 0.00 \\ 0.35 & 0.35 & 0.20 & 0.10 & 0.00 \end{pmatrix}$$

$$R_2 = \begin{pmatrix} 0.35 & 0.35 & 0.20 & 0.10 & 0.00 \\ 0.35 & 0.35 & 0.20 & 0.10 & 0.00 \\ 0.50 & 0.30 & 0.10 & 0.10 & 0.00 \\ 0.10 & 0.20 & 0.55 & 0.10 & 0.05 \end{pmatrix}$$

$$R_3 = \begin{pmatrix} 0.15 & 0.25 & 0.25 & 0.15 & 0.20 \\ 0.45 & 0.30 & 0.25 & 0.00 & 0.00 \\ 0.20 & 0.25 & 0.35 & 0.10 & 0.10 \\ 0.20 & 0.20 & 0.25 & 0.25 & 0.10 \\ 0.50 & 0.40 & 0.10 & 0.00 & 0.00 \end{pmatrix}$$

$$R_4 = \begin{pmatrix} 0.45 & 0.30 & 0.15 & 0.10 & 0.00 \\ 0.35 & 0.25 & 0.30 & 0.10 & 0.00 \end{pmatrix}$$

Calculate evaluation vector Bi

$B_1 = A_1 \cdot R_1 = (0.300\ 0.350\ 0.250\ 0.100\ 0.000)$,
$B_2 = A_2 \cdot R_2 = (0.305\ 0.295\ 0.285\ 0.100\ 0.015)$,
$B_3 = A_3 \cdot R_3 = (0.325\ 0.285\ 0.230\ 0.090\ 0.070)$,
$B_4 = A_4 \cdot R_4 = (0.400\ 0.275\ 0.225\ 0.100\ 0.000)$,

The final evaluation T is also calculated as

$T = A \cdot B = (0.32650\ 0.29625\ 0.24875\ 0.09600\ 0.03250)$

Referred with the definition in section 2.5, judge set V is quantified as $V' = \{100, 80, 60, 40, 20\}$.

The degree of assurance G=T•V'=75.765.

Suppose it defines the value G from 0 to 30 to be very dangerous, from 31 to 60 to be unsafe, from 61 to 70 to be normally safe, from 71 to 85 to be well guarded, from 86 to 100 to be perfect, The security in this case is normally safe but it need improves and reinforced.

4   Conclusion

In this paper, an integrated evaluation method of enterprise information system security based on EC is presented. Each risk factor is estimated by the experts and for calculating the quantificational security evaluation of the whole system, the degree of assurance is introduced. The case result in this paper shows that the proposed method is scientific and tally with the actual situation.

Acknowledgements

This research is supported by the Social Science Foundation of Education Department of China under Grant No.05JZD00024.

Reference

1. V. Zwass, "Electronic Commerce: Structure and Issues", *International Journal of Electronic Commerce*, Vol. 1, Nr. 1, pp.3-23, 1996..

2. J. H. M. That and V. Carr, "A proposal for construction project risk evaluation using fuzzy logic" , *Construction Management and Economics*, no.18, pp.491-500, 2000.

3.Xu Xiulin, Hu Kejin, Research of Enterprise Information Security Based on WSR Method, Network and Computer Security in China, no.2, pp.13-16, 2006.

4. The Delphi Method Definition and Historical Background 2007,
  http://www. iit.edu ~it/delphi.html, 2007-3-20.

5. The Delphi Method 2007,
  http://www.ryerson.ca/~mjoppe/ResearchProcess 841TheDelphiMethod.htm, 2007-3-20.

6. M. A. Mustafa and J. Bahar, "Project risk assessment using the analytic hierarchy process", *IEEE Transactions on Engineering Management*, vol.38, no.1, pp.46-52, 1991.

7. D. M. Zhao , " Comprehensive Risk Assessment of the Network Security", *Computer Science*, vol.31, no.7, pp66-69, 2004.

The Construction of Integrated Information Portal Based on Innovative Development ---- A Case Study of Center for Studies of Information Resources of Wuhan University

Shengli Deng,   Changping Hu
Center for the Studies of Information Resources of Wuhan University,
Wuhan,430072,China, victorydc@sina.com

Abstract. The construction of scientific research information platform is an important guarantee for innovative research. Based on scientific research oriented innovation and the change of user's need, this paper discusses the integrated function of information portal and its service orientation. On the basis of three level models and combining the construction of information portal of the center for studies of information resources of Wuhan University (CSIR), the paper constructs the integrated model of information portal for the scientific research institution and analyzes model's function and the realization process.

1. Introduction

Construction of innovative nation provides a good development opportunity for scientific research. In order to display the role of knowledge resources and based on information resources, taking the technology as the method, taking the innovation as a goal, the scientific research domain provides the information guarantee for the activities of scientific research by establishing information portal and integrating knowledge resources.

2. Background and problems

Each step of the scientific research can't leave the acquirement of information resources and obtaining abundant information is the premonition and insurance for

Please use the following format when citing this chapter:

Deng, S., Hu, C., 2007, in IFIP International Federation for Information Processing, Volume 251, Integration and Innovation Orient to E-Society Volume1, Wang, W. (Eds), (Boston: Springer), pp. 475-483.

development of the scientific research. Surrounding the technical innovation, the scientific research reflected many development trends, such as inter-organization, inter-disciplinary [1]. The scientific research has such characteristics as wide range resources sharing, open research and widespread cooperation. The concrete performances are as follows: the quantity and the importance in the network academic information resource increase day by day[2]; the scientific research's informationazation, namely "e-science", which is the important characteristic different from research environment and scientific activity in the digital age. The academic information exchange system presents the distributional, dynamical characteristics[3]. Above the new states, users need integrated and personalized information service. In the process of informationazation, the information surplus and lack of knowledge causes the scientific research institution face several difficult problems as follows [4]:

(1) How to provide the simplest information for the communication between interior and exterior of the scientific research institution?

(2) How to realize knowledge resources solidification and sharing?

(3) How to realize the fusion between the exterior resources and interior resources?

(4) How to simplify and standard the complex workflow in the institution?

(5) How to make the staff seek and use resources effectively?

Surrounding these questions, the information portals of scientific research are not only information issuing, but also provide good service for users. The portal should transform from traditional website information issuing to interactive service platform[5]. The design goal of the portal integration system of scientific research organization is to develop an opening and expandable information user platform, and integrate information resources, tools and services under unified portal to provide service[6].

3. Architecture of integrated information portal in research institution

The portal integration system of research institution is a service system which takes information issuing, operation organizing, and resources service and so on. It is a working platform for integrating and processing information. This system will carry on the organic integration of the dispersed scientific research information through the science knowledge organization system, and will provide the diverse navigation and the resources retrieval, effectively guide the user to acquire knowledge, finally realize high efficiency information sharing[7]. Based on this theory, the paper proposed three levels design thought: The first will fully demonstrate the personnel, organization information of research institution and so on, to realize the information issuing function. The second will unify the research institution routine work, operation handling to the information portal platform. The third will integrate every kind of resource and service under one interface, provide the "one-stop service" to users [8].

Based on a three-tier model, we construct a model of integrated information portal system, as shown in figure 1.

The figure takes portal system as user interface. Memory Repositories Layer includes all data and knowledge in CSIR. Data in the Repository is showed as XML format, and the design of its retrieval tools fully considers the content, metadata and the need for value-added services [9]. The knowledge administration Layer is composed with issuing platform, operating platform and knowledge service platform. Finally, demonstration Layer is responsible for transferring message to the terminal. The integrated thought of this model manifests in three aspects: resources integration, system integration and service integration [10].

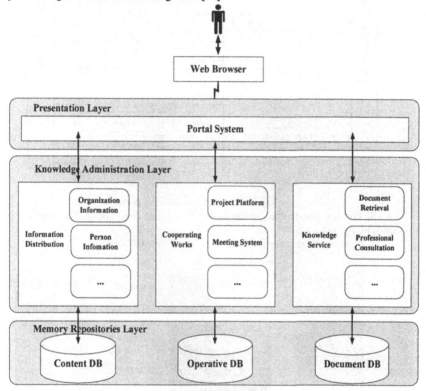

Fig. 1. Integrated system of information portal

4. A case study–integrated information portal of CSIR

According to three levels model, CSIR has established integration information portal for scientific research.

(1) The functional analysis of integrated portal of CSIR

The portal system of CSIR mainly includes the issuing platform in the front stage and management platform in the backstage. The issuing platform ought to fully integrate the information resource in the discipline domain; provide the service for the users as a unified portal. Concretely, the integrated portal of CSIR contains following three aspects: information communication; business platform; resources service. According to the above functional analysis, this paper constructs a frame as shown by figure2.

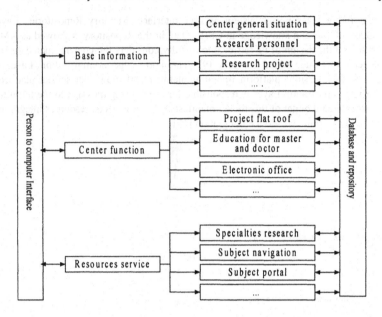

Fig. 2. Function frame of CSIR portal

CSIR Portal is constructed on the basis of the frame chart above. The interface is shown by figure3.

Fig. 3. Interface of CSIR portal

The module of "base information" fully reflects the information of teachers, achievements in CSIR. Surrounding the deployment of scientific research, users of

CSIR are divided into three aspects, which are expert user, student user and administrator. After different users enter, they can do different things such as information browse, inquire, access and search according to their own administer right.

Business organizing function is embodied in "operation organizing" module. On one hand, the operation organizing of scientific research is deployed surrounding project, users can discuss some interesting projects with each other on the project platform, set up new project and research project, but any newly founded project should be strictly examined and approved by administrators. Along with the developing of project, scientific research users intercommunicate and share the research productions through project platform; meanwhile, those productions are finally formed into document. On the other hand, CSIR plays the role of training students. Scientific research is combined with teaching. Routines are miscellaneous. The management of scientific research is implemented through the portal platform, so that work efficiency and administration ability are improved.

"Resources service" module is faced to innovative demands, offering lots of services such as specialty search, subject navigation and specialty consultation to meet the users' demand of knowledge resources by resource integration and service integration, so that scientific research is thoroughly progressed [11].

(2) Key technology

Along with the rapid development of Informationazation, the enhancement of scientific research administration and service level is very important to self-development of scientific research institution, which would affect scientific research innovation and the enthusiasm of scientific research personnel. The CSIR portal system is based on the model of MVC and Struts, combining the lucene/XML technique, which can support full-text search.

① Technical realization based on MVC+Struts

The MVC design pattern, includes three types of objects: Model is the applied object, using for storage of the state and update of the view; View is an expressional form of the model-data manifestation; Controller abstracts user interaction and the application semantics mapping, and transfer user input to the application procedure, then according to user's input and context information to choose the appropriate view for demonstrating data.

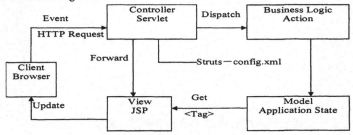

Fig. 4. MVC framework based on Struts

Struts is the MVC design pattern one kind of realization, it is a extremely outstanding application frame based on the MVC model, leaving user interface and transaction logic detached and causing the web level to be easy management and expansion, not only effectively enhanced developed efficiency of the system, but also enabled the system to have greater reusability, scalability and security. Figure 4-3 shows the realization MVC framework based on Struts.

MVC framework realization based on Struts has the following advantages:

A. When a model operates simultaneously the system can establish and use many views.

B. Because the returning data of the model does not bring any demonstrated form, thus these models can be directly applied to the interface.

C. Because an application is isolated by three-tier, therefore sometimes, as long as one tier of the application changes will be able to satisfy the changes of application.

②Based on lucene/XML technology full-text search

Lucene is not a completely full-text indexing application, while it is the full-text indexing engine tool kit, which is written with Java. It can be easily inserted into various applications aimed at the application of full-text indexing / search functions. Because XML has the characteristic of cross-platform, easy expression of the meaning, expandable, self-description and structure, content and performance separated, the emergence of XML has provided a lot of convenience for knowledge description, expression, storage and retrieval. The CSIR used the lucene/XML technology to construct the full-text retrieval system. Figure 5 is the journal literature retrieval system interface.

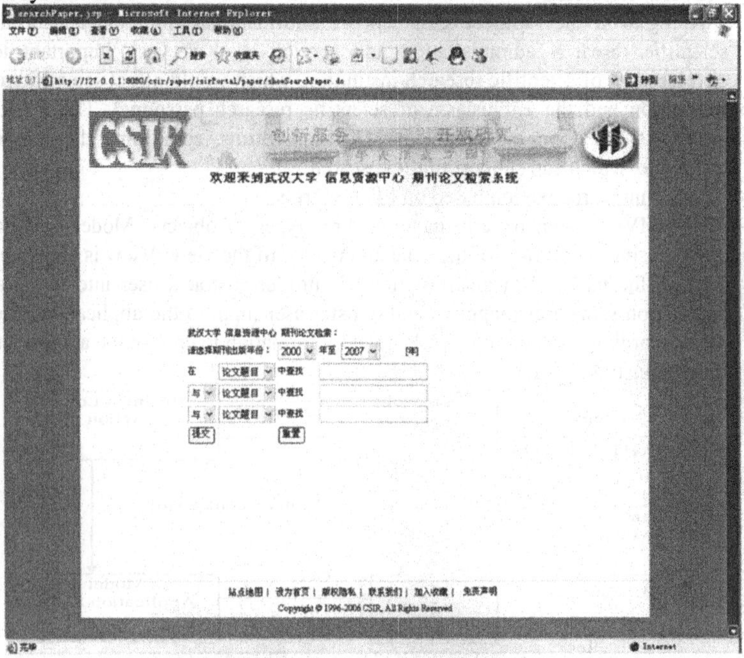

Fig. 5. Interface of periodical literature retrieval system

Each literature that includes in the retrieval system carries on the operation by XML document. The XML document is corresponding to the interface shown in figure 6

Fig. 6. Interface of Added Document

Every article input from background is written in the database by this interface. All relevant attributes of the documentation, such as author, literature title, etc. have a corresponding input frame. Submitted data is controlled by background and input to the XML file. The data corresponding to the attribute is automatically input to the label corresponding to XML file. Meanwhile, it's necessary to establish an index for the attributes to search by the interface provided by lucene as shown in figure 7, such as document title, the author, the units of the author. Meanwhile, lucene also provided logic inquiry interface that supports "and", "or", "nor", which is very easy to use.

Fig.7. Literature attributes Index based on lucene interface

5 Conclusion

CSIR has established a digital resource base and service platform through the construction of integrated information portal system. It will gradually establish a prefect digital information service system through the flexible integration of the resources, tools and systems in the application layer or user layer. Then it can effectively support knowledge application and knowledge innovation of the user. Of course, the development work of the portal is still going on and needs to be further improved. Further research is how to play the advantages of CSIR in resources and talents to upgrade information services level, which is the keystone for the portal construction in the future.

Acknowledgments

This paper is one of research results of project "The research on the system of knowledge information service of innovative nation" (number 06JZD0032) funded by Ministry of Education of the People's Republic of China

References

1. Jia jun, Xu, et al. Enterprise Information Portal. *Beijing: China Machine Press, 2004*, pp. 10-11
2. Olga Danylova, et al. Information Portal "Our School": A Case Study of IT Introduction into Education in Ukraine. *Proceedings of the IEEE International Conference on Advanced Learning Technologies (ICALT'04)*
3. Fredric Landqvist, Dick Stenmark. Portal Information Integration and Ownership misfits: A Case Study in a Tourism Setting. *Proceedings of the 39th Hawaii International Conference on System Sciences - 2006*
4. Andreas Billig, Jan Gottschick, Kurt Sandkuhl. Evolution of Web Computing Systems: Experiences from Web-Portal Projects. *Proceedings of the 2005 31st EUROMICRO Conference on Software Engineering and Advanced Applications (EUROMICRO-SEAA'05)*
5. Thomas Puschmann, Rainer Alt. Process Portals - Architecture and Integration. *Proceedings of the 37th Hawaii International Conference on System Sciences - 2004*
6. Rainer Weinreich, Thomas Ziebermayr, Enhancing Presentation Level Integration of Remote Applications and Services in Web Portals. *Proceeding of the 2005 IEEE International Conference on Services Computing (SCC'05)*.
7. HIROAKI YUASA, et al. Development of User-friendly Supercomputing Portal in Bio Research Field. *Proceedings of the First International Conference on e-Science and Grid Computing (e-Science' 05)*
8. Yongjin Zhang, Hongqi Chen, and Jiancang Xie. *Study on Intelligent Information Integration of Knowledge Portals*. 3614, 2004, pp. 1136 – 1141
9. Fredric Landqvist, Dick Stenmark, "Portal Information Integration and Ownership Misfits: A Case Study in a Tourism Setting", *Proceedings of the 39th Annual Hawaii International Conference on System Sciences (HICSS'06) Track 8, 2006*,pp. 173.

10. Hsieh, et al. An Integrated Healthcare Enterprise Information Portal and Healthcare Information System Framework. *Engineering in Medicine and Biology Society, 2006. EMBS '06. 28th Annual International Conference of the IEEE*, pp.4731-4734

11. Fengchun Zhu, et al. A Framework to Develop A University Information Portal. *Proceedings of International Conference on Information Acquisition, 2004*,pp.506- 509

3G-based Mobile Commerce Value Chain

Ting Li[1], Yong Liu[2]

1 Department of Information Management, Huazhong Normal
University, Wuhan, 430079, China
lostway@126.com
2 Department of Information Management, Huazhong Normal
University, Wuhan, 430079, China

Abstract. In recent years, due to the rapid evolution of mobile communication technologies, e-commerce has been combined with the mobile communication equipment, and a new paradigm of business – mobile commerce has appeared in business field. Nowadays, the development of 3G-related technologies further pushed the popularity of m-commerce. This paper attempts to categorize the participants in the 3G-based m-commerce value chain in B2C market and discusses its nature as well. It established a value chain in 3G-based B2C mobile market. This study can provide some fresh insight to 3G-based mobile market and help the participants in the value chain to understand better on how the value on the mobile market is delivered, which can offer them some ideas on how to make the value to be delivered efficiently on the value chain.

1   Introduction

The prevalence of the Internet has greatly changed our lives, which revolutionizes the traditional way of conducting business and gives birth to the electronic commerce (e-commerce). In recent years, due to the rapid evolution of mobile communication technologies, e-commerce has been combined with the mobile communication equipment, and a new paradigm of business – mobile commerce (m-commerce) has appeared in business field. Nowadays, the development of the third-generation (3G)-related technologies further pushed the popularity of m-commerce, which overcomes the bandwidth limitation in traditional 2G-based m-commerce.

In China m-commerce has been developed in the past several years. In fact m-commerce has a good foundation in China. According to the news released by China State Research Center, there are about 420 million mobile phone users in China by May 2006, and Deng (2006), the minister of the research center, forecasts that there

Please use the following format when citing this chapter:

Li, T., Liu, Y., 2007, in IFIP International Federation for Information Processing, Volume 251, Integration and Innovation Orient to E-Society Volume1, Wang, W. (Eds), (Boston: Springer), pp. 484-490.

will be about US $ 760 billion investments on 3G within the coming 5 years in China. He also predicts that after the full deployment of 3G in China, 3G users in China will reach 6.2 million in the first year and the number of 3G users in China will rise to 200 million in five years [1]. Obviously, there will be a huge market in the 3G-related industries in China.

Some researches have been conducted in 3G m-commerce. But few studies have been done on the value chain in 3G m-commerce. In fact 3G-based value chain in m-commerce is quite different from some other traditional value chains. First, m-commerce value chain is essentially the aggregation of the mobile communication value chain and the Internet value chain [2]. The business models and value chains of the above two industries may not completely be applied to m-commerce [3]. Second, as Kim (2007) states that most adopters and users of traditional technologies are employees in an organizational setting. They use the technology for work purposes, and the cost of mandatory adoption and usage is covered by organizations. In contrast, adopters and users of new information and communication technology, such as mobile Internet, are individuals who use it for personal purposes and the cost is normally covered by themselves [4]. Individuals become the main customers in m-commerce market, and the value chain based on business-to-customer (B2C) business model will inevitably become the mainstream in 3G-based m-commerce.

This paper attempts to categorize the participants in the 3G-based m-commerce value chain in B2C market and discusses its nature as well. It establishes a value chain in 3G-based B2C mobile market. This study can provide some fresh insight to 3G-based mobile market and help the participants in the value chain to understand better on how the value on the mobile market is delivered, which can offer them some ideas on how to make the value to be delivered efficiently on the value chain.

2. Literature Review

With the rapid development of mobile technology and application of mobile equipment in business, m-commerce has achieved success in some countries and become the focus in research in recent years. Though there are some researches on the value chain in 3G-based m-commerce, there is no agreement on the categories and the roles of the participants in the value chain in m-commerce [3]. Siau et al. (2001) state that the process of linking additional values to the end users primarily include customer, bank, mobile network operator, and other possible members [5]. Tsalgatidou and Veijalainen (2000) point out that the value chain make the participants to be involved in the activities along the value chain, which alters the value system in the traditional mobile communication industry, and undoubtedly forms new values for consumers [6].

Barnes (2002) provides a basic model of m-commerce value chain, which consists of six core processes in two main areas: content, infrastructure and services. The area of content contain three core processes: content creation, content packaging and market making, and in the area of infrastructure and services there are three core processes as well: mobile transport, mobile services and delivery support, mobile interface and applications, and the importance of the two main areas are equal. [7].

Buellingen and Woerter (2004) state that broadband mobile transmission with universal mobile telecommunications system (UMTS) will lead to some essential alteration of mobile communication visible in the expansion of the mobile value chain and build an extended mobile communication value chain. In the value chain, they generalize six key factors: nets and infrastructure, interface software, customer acquisition, transmission, content and portals, customer relation management and billing. They point out that new m-commerce value chain will increase the power of the mobile network operators by reason of controlling portal serves, which guides users and reduces searching efforts in search activities through presetting [8].

Ying and Ching (2006) categorize the participants on the 3G-based mobile commerce value chain into eleven roles: technology platform vendors, infrastructure and mobile equipment vendors, application platform vendors, application developers, content developers, content aggregators, mobile portal providers, 3G mobile network operators, mobile service providers, mobile equipment retailers and customers [3]. All these different roles are closely linked like a circle and customers stay in the center. They stress that 3G mobile network operators are the core members in the m-commerce value chain. Mobile network operators are increasingly more important, which take the functions as mediators, brokers, trustees and service providers for third parties in the value chain. The role of mobile network operators as mediators and gatekeepers is the traditional advantages in 2G m-commerce, which is natural for them to inherit these advantages in new 3G-based m-commerce. There is growing recognition of the value of contents and services in the value chain in 3G-based mobile market. Mobile phone is with the limitation of screen size and manipulation difficulty, which demands more additional mental and physical efforts [4]. Offering attractive contents and convenient services can attract customers to adopt m-commerce.

3. 3G-based M-commerce Value Chain

Based on the above-mentioned studies, we try to establish a new model of 3G-based m-commerce value chain through analyzing the key players in the value chain and investigating their relationship and respective features.

The participants of 3G-based m-commerce value chain can be generally categorized into the following 8 different roles: technology platform vendors, 3G mobile network operators, mobile equipment vendors, content providers, application platform vendors, mobile portal providers, customers, and online financial services providers.

3.1 Technology platform vendors

Technology platform vendors mainly deal with the operation and maintenance of backbone network, base stations, the infrastructure and facilitating the transmission of mobile data between mobile users and application service providers [9], and providing operating systems for smart phones and micro-browsers, which are necessary to mobile Internet services, is also the task of technology platform vendors

[6]. Technology platform vendors often charge a lot of money from patent royalty and equipment sales. For example, in China totally RMB¥250 billion has been paid abroad to the technology platform vendors in 1G network construction, while the amount has reached RMB¥500 billion in 2G network construction [1]. The huge expense on technology platform vendors is surely to raise the cost of 3G network. Currently in China, the TD-SCDMA has been promoted as the 3G standards, and Chinese enterprises own a relatively high intellectual property rights in the TD-SCDMA standards, which might lower the cost in 3G network instruction in China.

3.2 3G mobile network operators

3G mobile network operators play a key role in m-commerce value chain. No matter the general consumers or enterprise users, they need to access the bridge provided by 3G mobile network operators to enjoy or provide mobile services. Generally speaking, mobile network operators refer to telecommunication corporations [10]. In China 3G mobile network operators are mainly based on the original 2G mobile network operators, including China Mobile, China Telecom, China Unicom and China Netcom. As mobile network providers are primarily responsible for providing wireless network to ensure network quality of service and mobile location infrastructure, such as global system for mobile communications (GSM) roaming services and connection of different mobile networks.

3.3 Mobile equipment vendors

Mobile equipment vendors design and manufacture all kinds of infrastructure required for building mobile communication networks, and other devices which support Wireless Application Protocol (WAP), General Packet Radio Service (GPRS), 3G, and other communication technologies. They play important roles in promoting innovations in technology in mobile industry [10, 11]. In China, according to Byna Telecom Consulting Company's analysis, the market share has undergone a significant change in the present experimental network: Ericsson, ZTE, Huawei, Shanghai Bell and Alcatel are at first echelon, and the domestic manufacturers, such as ZTE and Huawei, are expected to take 40% to 50% share of the 3G mobile equipment market [12].

3.4 Content Providers

Content providers include content developers and content aggregators. Content developers provide, design, or produce various kinds of products or services necessary to all consumers [10]. When mobile devices become ubiquitous, content developers have to provide various kinds of content services to attract more consumers to use m-commerce model [11]. Content aggregators aggregate, integrate, re-package or distribute products or services to consumers, such as games, news and financial messages. 3G-based content providers have relatively high status in the whole value chain than in traditional 2G. When the content providers supply large volume of data and diversified information services, customers can make a comparison between 2G and 3G mobile services, and the advantages of high transmission rate in 3G market can be standout.

3.5 Application platform vendors

Application platform vendors are the middleware providers on the value chain, who are responsible for providing pre-built components, including wireless middleware and application middleware [10, 13]. Based on the content provided by content providers, application platform vendors develop the commercial use on existing mobile networks, such as the mass-broadcast robot based on short messaging service (SMS), and real-time traffic information service based on global positioning system (GPS).

3.6 Mobile portal providers

Mobile portal providers provide the gateway to access wireless networks and the first window to enjoy 3G information services. Aggregating services and information content of all kinds of properties, information index, search tools, and related services are provided to assist users in searching for desired information by mobile portal providers as well [9]. At present, mobile portals are generally provided by the combination of mobile operators (such as the BBC), application developers (such as Air Flash) and the client providers (such as Nokia, Microsoft).

3.7 Customers

Generally speaking, customers can be divided into individual consumers or enterprise users, which are both important in traditional commerce. In 3G-based m-commerce market, individuals become the main customers, and B2C business model becomes the mainstream in 3G-based m-commerce.

3.8 Online financial services providers

Online financial services providers include commercial banks, the third-party mobile payment platform companies, and safety certificating agencies. Though online financial services providers have a much less influence on the value chain, they ensure the value flow to go smoothly and safely. Their importance can not be ignored in the mobile value chain.

The 8 different roles on the 3G-based m-commerce value chain are illustrated in Figure 1. 3G mobile network operators, content providers, application platform vendors, mobile portal providers and customers are the frontline participants and main value-creators in the value chain. Content Providers, which differentiate the 3G from 2G, are the main source of the value in the value chain. When customers begin to use 3G-based products or services offered by content providers, the 3G-based m-commerce value chain begin to operate and make profits. Application platform vendors develop new software based on the contents provided by content providers. 3G mobile network operators provide the customers with value-added services, which are also based on the content providers. In this process, the amount of value rises when value flows from content providers to application platform vendors and 3G mobile network operators. Mobile portal providers offer 3G users opportunities to know and apply 3G-based services. Through mobile portal providers, 3G users can browse and retrieval different services in detail. Finally, customers enjoy the services and pay for their consumption – that is the end of value flow.

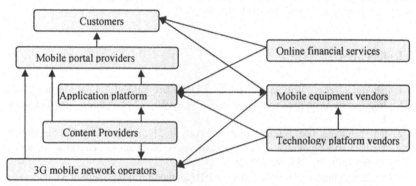

Figure 1. The 3G-based Mobile Commerce Value Chain

Technology platform vendors, mobile equipment vendors and online financial services are the main supporters in 3G-based m-commerce value chain. Though they do not create or increase the value in the value chain, they are indispensable in the value chain. Technology platform vendors provide the technology standards in the value chain. Mobile equipment vendors supply 3G-related equipments to different participants and aggregate new foundations and software developed by application platform vendors. And online financial services ensure all the participants to get their money or services from other participants in the value chain.

4. Discussion and conclusion

Based on the literature review of various studies on m-commerce value chain, a new model of 3G-based m-commerce value chain has been proposed in this study, and the 8 different participants are discussed on their roles and features in the value chain. The model illustrates the relationship of the 8 different participants in value chain. In the transforming process from traditional 2G-based m-commerce to 3G-based m-commerce, the relationships between participants in the value chain are getting more and more complex. Good cooperation is the base for the success of 3G-based m-commerce.

In 3G-based m-commerce value chain, 3G mobile network operators still hold a core position, which provide the basic networks for the entire value chain, while technology platform vendors, mobile equipment vendors and online financial services work as supporters to ensure the security and privacy of entire system. Different from traditional 2G m-commerce which are driven by technologies, 3G M-commerce is driven by contents and services. Though technologies are of great importance to the construction of 3G m-commerce value chain and to the ease of use for customers, the development of content and new services is critical for the success of 3G-based m-commerce.

Researchers and practitioners remains considering further work on integration between content supporters and technology supporters in 3G-based m-commerce value chain. There is the scope for further work on developing attractive contents or services to customers with proper technology.

References

1. Shoupen Deng, The Speech in TD-SCDMA Economical Annual Meeting 2006, http://www.ce.cn/cysc/communications/rw/200602/22/t20060222_6164863.shtml
2. C.F. Maitland, J.M. Bauer, and R. Westerveld, The European Market for Mobile Data: Evolving Value Chains and Industry Structures, *Telecommunications Policy* 26(9-10), 485–504(2002).
3. FengKuo Ying, and WenYu Ching, 3G Telecommunication Operator's Challenges and Roles: A Perspective of Mobile Commerce Value Chain, *Technovation* 26, 1347-1356 (2006).
4. Hee-Woong Kim, H.C. Chan, and S. Gupta, Value-based Adoption of Mobile Internet, *Decision Support Systems* 43, 111-126 (2007).
5. K. Siau, E.P. Lim, and Z. Shen, Mobile Commerce: Promises, Challenges, and Research Agenda, *Journal of Database Management* 12 (3), 4-13 (2001).
6. A. Tsalgatidou, J. Veijalainen, Mobile Electronic Commerce: Emerging Issues. In: *Proceedings of EC-WEB 2000 1st International Conference on E-Commerce and Web Technologies* London, Greenwich, UK, September, 477-486 (2000).
7. S. J. Barnes, The mobile commerce value chain: analysis and future developments, *International Journal of Information Management* 22, 91–108(2002).
8. F. Buellingen, and M. Woerter, Development Perspectives, Firm Strategies and Applications in Mobile Commerce, *Journal of Business Research* 57, 1402-1408 (2004).
9. N. Barnett, S. Hodges, M.J. Wilshire, M-commerce: An Operator's Manual. *McKinsey Quarterly* 3, 162-173 (2000)
10. F. Müller-Veerse, Mobile Commerce Report. Durlacher Research Ltd, http://www.durlacher.com/downloads/mcomreport.pdf.
11. H.K. Sabat, The Evolving Mobile Wireless Value Chain and Market Structure, *Telecommunications Policy* 26 (9-10), 505-535 (2002).
12. Zhangkun Yu, Equipment manufacturers will account for 40% -50% of the domestic 3G market share, http://www.byna.cn/Html/view/2006-5/9/200605090002995.html
13. R. Kalakota, and M. Robinson, *M-Business: The Race to Mobility* (McGraw-Hill, New   York,   2001).

An Approach of Personalization for Electronic Commerce Websites Based on Ontology

Weihua Dei [1],,and Ming Yi [2]

1   Dei Weihua, School of Economy & Management, Huazhong
Agriculture University, Wuhan, 430070, China
dengwhyi@yahoo.com.cn

2   Department of Information Management, Huazhong Normal
University, Wuhan, 430079, China
beiyong0415@yahoo.com.cn

Abstract Aiming at the limitations of traditional personalization approaches, this article analyzes the approach based on ontology, and proposes its practical method. This approach retains the relationships both between attributes of concepts and between concepts, providing more flexibility in matching usage profiles with current user session, which can improve the precision and coverage of the recommendation sets for personalization.

1 Introduction

More recently, Web usage mining has been proposed as an underlying approach of personalization for the e-commerce website. The goal of personalization based on Web usage mining is to recommend a set of objects to the current user, possibly consisting of links, ads, text, products, etc., tailored to the user's perceived preferences as determined by the matching usage patterns. This task is accomplished by matching the current user session against the usage patterns discovered through Web usage mining. However, related approaches mainly utilize the formal characteristics of user click behaviors (syntactic information), does not utilize the internal semantics of users' click behavior (semantic information), which can improve the accuracy and coverage of the final personalized recommendation sets.

The research on utilizing semantic information of user click behaviors focus on two sides: features and ontology. B. Mobosher, Honghua Dai, Tao Luo et al. present an approach of personalization recommendation based on integrating web usage and content mining [1]; Xin Jin, Yanzan Zhou and B. Mobasher propose a maximum entropy web recommendation system: combining collaborative and content features [2]; Mooney and Roy also propose an approach of personalization recommendation based on context Categorization [3]; Raymond J. Mooney and Raymond J. Mooney present an approach of personalization recommendation based on integrating evaluating information and context features [4]. Obviously, these approaches are all

Please use the following format when citing this chapter:

Dei, W., Yi, M., 2007, in IFIP International Federation for Information Processing, Volume 251, Integration and Innovation Orient to E-Society Volume1, Wang, W. (Eds), (Boston: Springer), pp. 491-498.

based on the content features of the e-commerce website. However, such approaches cannot capture the underlying attributes of these objects and their complex relations, for example, potentially valuable relational structures among objects such as relations between books, authors and publishers of online bookshops may be missed, if one can only rely on the description of these entities using features, and the final recommendation sets may have many limitations. Hence, a few scholars propose a new approach of personalization for the e-commerce website based on ontology, which may remedy the shortcomings of the approaches based on features [5-7]. However, they have just presented a framework about this approach, and there are many problems needed to be further researched.

2 The Process of the E-commerce Website Personalization Based on Ontology

The overall process is divided into two components: the offline component and the online component.

The task of the offline component is generating semantic usage profiles based on the e-commerce website ontology. The first step is Web usage preprocessing, which includes data cleaning, user identification, session identification and path completion. The data preprocessing ultimately results in a set of syntactic transactions. The second step is clustering the syntactic transactions to discover syntactic usage profiles. Finally, according to the e-commerce website ontology, the syntactic usage profiles will be transformed into semantic usage profiles.

The task of the online component is online recommendation. Firstly, transform the current user session into semantic one, according to the e-commerce website ontology. Secondly, match the semantic current user session against the semantic usage profiles, which may result in an extended user profiles. Finally, the extended user profiles may be instantiated to real Web objects, which may be recommended to the user. For the sake of our research, this paper assumes that the e-commerce website ontology has been constructed.

3 Discovery of Semantic Usage Profile

3.1 Discovery of Syntactic Usage Profile

Web usage preprocessing ultimately results in a set of m pageview records and a set of n user transactions.

Definition 1: $T = \{t_1, t_2, \ldots, t_n\}$, T is the set of syntactic transactions

as a result of Web usage preprocessing.

Definition 2: $P = \{p_1, p_2, \ldots p_m\}$, P is the set of pageview records as a result of Web usage preprocessing.

Definition   3:   Each   transaction

$t_i = \langle w(p_1,t_i), w(p_2,t_i),\ldots,w(p_j,t_i),\ldots,w(p_m,t_i) \rangle$ is an m-dimensional vector,

$w(p_j,t_i)$ is the weight of the pageview p_j in the transaction

$t_i, i \in \{1,2,\ldots,n\}$, $j \in \{1,2,\ldots,m\}$.

We may use standard clustering algorithms to partition T into groups of transactions that are close to each other based on a measure of distance or similarity. Such a clustering will result in a set $U = \{u_1, u_2, \ldots, u_k\}$ of clusters, where each u is a subset of the set of T. However, each transaction cluster contains thousands of user transactions, which are composed of millions of pageviews, so these transaction clusters cannot capture an aggregated view of common user profiles. Therefore, for each transaction cluster $u \in U$, we compute the mean vector to discover syntactic usage profiles.

Definition 4: $Tpr = \{pr_1, pr_2,\ldots,pr_k\}$, Tpr is the set of syntactic usage profiles , pr is a syntactic usage profile, which is defined as a set of pageview-weight pairs[8]:

$$pr = \{< p, weight(p, pr) > | p \in P\}.$$

Where, the weight of the pageview p in the usage profile pr , $weight(p,pr)$, is given by:

$$weight(p, pr) = \frac{1}{|u|} \times \sum_{t \in u} w(p,t),$$

and $w(p,t)$ is the weigh of the pageview p in the transaction profile $t \in u$.

3.2 discovery of semantic usage profile

Given the syntactic usage profile pr , we can transform pr into semantic web usage profile $spr = \{< o_1, ow_1 >, < o_2, ow_2 >,\ldots,< o_x, ow_x >\}$ by extracting instance from each pageview based on the e-commerce website ontology. Where,

o is a conceptual instance in the ontology, and ow is its weight. However, spr may potentially contains thousands of conceptual instances, we should combine the conceptual instances belonging to the same concept to reduce spr .

Definition 5: $C = \{c_1, c_2, \ldots, c_f\}$, $A_c = \{a_1^c, a_2^c, \ldots, a_l^c\}$, C is the set of concepts in the ontology, f is the total number of the concept, A_c is the set of attributes of the concept c , and l is the total number of the attribute of the concept c .

Definition 6: $spr = \{g_1, g_2, \ldots, g_f\}$, $g_i = \left\{ <o_1^c, w_{o_1}^c>, <o_2^c, w_{o_2}^c>, \cdots, <o_y^c, w_{o_y}^c> \right\}$,

$i \in \{1, 2, \ldots, f\}$. Where, g_i is the set of instances in the concept c , o^c is an instance,

$w_{o_y}^c$ is its weight, and y is the total number of instance in the concept c .

As for the concept c , we should provide a combination function φ_a for its each attribute a^c . The combination function φ_a can be represented by:

$$\varphi_a(<a_{o_1}^c, wa_{o_1}^c>, <a_{o_2}^c, wa_{o_2}^c>, \cdots, <a_{o_i}^c, wa_{o_i}^c>) = <o_{agg}, w_{agg}>.$$

Where, a_o^c is an instance of the attribute a^c of the concept c , and wa_o^c is its weight. Further more o_{agg} is a pseudo instance of a meaning that it is an instance of the attribute a^c which does not belong to a real object in the underlying ontology, and w_{agg} is its weight.

Given a set of instances, $\{o_1^c, o_2^c, \ldots, o_y^c\}$, of the concept c , the aggregated g_i and spr may be obtained by applying the combination function for each attribute in the concept c to all of the corresponding attribute instances across all instances $o_1^c, o_2^c, \ldots, o_y^c$. Table 1 is an example of the concept "Book", and the following analysis is based on it.

Table 1. example 1 of the concept of "Book"

O^{Book}	$ow_o^{c^{Bo}}$	name	author	publisher	year	genre	...
Book1	1	{name1}	{A:1}	{publisher 1}	{2001}	book→science and technology→ computer/network→ network and communication →e-commerce	...
Book2	0.8	{name2}	{B:0.6; A:0.4}	{publisher2}	{2002}	book→ science and technology→ computer/network→ network and communication→ network management	...
Book3	0.6	{name3}	{C:0.5; B:0.3; D:0.2}	{publisher 33}	{2002}	book→ science and technology→ computer/network→ database→data warehouse and data mining	...
Book4	0.3	{name4}	{D:0.6; A:0.4}	{publisher 22}	{2003}	book→ science and technology → computer/network → network and communication →network protocol	...

The combination function φ_{name} of attribute "name" is a union operation. For example, applying φ_{name} to { < { name1 } , 1>, < { name2 } , 0.8>, < {name3} , 0.6>, < {name4} , 0.3>} will generate an aggregate instance about attribute "name" { <name1, 1>, <name2, 0.8>, <name3, 0.6>, <name4, 0.3>} .

As for the attribute "author", its value contains a weighted object set. In such cases we can use a vector-based weighted mean operation. The computation method of each object's weight is given as:

$$ww'_o = \frac{\sum_l ow_{o_l}^c \times ww_o}{\sum_l ow_{o_l}^c}$$

Where, $l \in \{1, 2, ..., y\}$, y is the total number of the instance in the concept c , $ow_{o_l}^c$ is the weight of the conceptual instance, ww_o is the weight of each object (author) in the original attribute instance, and ww'_o is the weight of the aggregate object. For example, applying φ_{author} to {< { A, 1 } , 1>, < { B, 0.6; A,

0.4} , 0.8>, < {C, 0.5; B, 0.3; D, 0.2} , 0.6>, < {D, 0.6; A, 0.4} , 0.3>} will generate an aggregate instance about attribute "author" {<A, 0.53>, <B, 0.24>, <C, 0.11>, <D, 0.11>} .

$$ww'_A = \frac{1 \times 1 + 0.4 \times 0.8 + 0.4 \times 0.3}{1 + 0.8 + 0.6 + 0.3} = 0.53$$

$$ww'_B = \frac{0.6 \times 0.8 + 0.3 \times 0.6}{1 + 0.8 + 0.6 + 0.3} = 0.24$$

$$ww'_C = \frac{0.5 \times 0.6}{1 + 0.8 + 0.6 + 0.3} = 0.11$$

$$ww'_D = \frac{0.2 \times 0.6 + 0.6 \times 0.3}{1 + 0.8 + 0.6 + 0.3} = 0.11$$

As for attribute "publisher", its combination function means a union operation. For example, applying $\varphi_{publisher}$ to {< {publisher1} , 1>, < {publisher2} , 0.8>, < {publisher3 } , 0.6>, < { publisher2 } , 0.3>} will generate an aggregate instance about attribute "publisher" {< publisher1, 1>, < publisher2, 1.1>, < publisher3, 0.6>} .

As for attribute "year", its combination function also means a union operation. For example, applying φ_{year} to {< { 2001 } , 1>, < { 2002 } , 0.8>, < { 2002 } , 0.6>, < { 2003 } , 0.3>} will generate an aggregate instance about attribute "year" {<2001, 1>, <2002, 1.4>, <2003, 0.3>} .

As for attribute "genre", it contains a partial order representing a concept hierarchy among different genre values. The combination function, in this case, can perform tree (or graph) matching to extract the common parts of the conceptual hierarchies among all instances. For example, applying φ_{genre} to the example of table 1 will generate an aggregate instance about attribute "genre" {book→ science and technology → computer/network}.

Hence, aggregate semantic web usage profile $nspr$ will be formed by implying the combination functions to all attributes, which may be defined as:

$$nspr = \left\{ <o_1, nw_1>, <o_2, nw_2>, \ldots, <o_f, nw_f> \right\}.$$

Where, o is the aggregate instance of each concept formed by performing combination function, nw is its weight, which can be determined by the significance of the concept in the e-commerce website domain ontology. Therefore, table 1 can be transformed into table 2.

Table 2. example 2 of the concept "Book"

o^{Book}	name	author	publisher	year	genre	...
Book	{<name1, 1>, <name2, 0.8>, <name3, 0.6>,	{<A, 0.53>, <B, 0.24>, <C, 0.11>,	{< publisher1, 1>, < publisher2, 1.1>, < publisher3,	{<2001, 1>, <2002, 1.4>, <2003, 0.3>}	book→ science and technology → computer/ network	...

<name4,	<D,	0.6>}		
0.3>}	0.11>}			

4 Online Recommendation

In online recommendation phase, syntactic current user session should be transformed into semantic current user session $S = \{< o_{s_1}, ws_1 >, < o_{s_2}, ws_2 >, \cdots, < o_{s_f}, ws_f >\}$ firstly. Where, o_s is the aggregate instance of each concept formed by performing combination functions, ws is its weight representing the significance of the concept in the ontology. Secondly, match semantic current user session against the semantic web usage profiles by means of the semantic similarity measures [9].

As for each $nspr = \{< o_1, nw_1 >, < o_2, nw_2 >, \ldots, < o_f, nw_f >\}$, the similarity $Sim(S, nspr)$ of semantic vector s and $nspr$ lies on the semantic similarity $SemSim(s_i, nspr_i)$ of each aggregate conceptual instance:

$$Sim(S, nspr) = \sum_{i=1}^{f} \alpha_i \times SemSim(o_{s_i}, o_i)$$

$$SemSim(o_{s_i}, o_i) = \sum_j \beta_j \times Simlarity(o_{s_i}.a_j, o_i.a_j)$$

Where, α_i is the significance of concept c in the e-commerce website ontology, and β_i is the significance of the attribute a_j in the concept c .

According to the above analyses, the computation of $SemSim(o_{s_i}, o_i)$ and $Sim(S, nspr)$ can be accomplished. Therefore, as for semantic current user session S and each semantic web usage profile $nspr$, the recommendation value $Rec^o(o^{c_i}, S)$ of each aggregate conceptual instance o^{c_i} is denoted as:

$$Rec^o(o^c, S) = \begin{cases} 0, & if \ \ o^c \in S \\ nw \times Sim(S, nspr), & otherwise \end{cases}$$

Where, nw is the weight of the aggregate conceptual instance o^c in $nspr$, $Sim(S, nspr)$ is the similarity of the semantic current user session S and the semantic usage profile $nspr$ which has the conceptual instance o^c .And the extended user profile $URec(S)$ can be represented by:

$$URec(S) = \{< o^c, Rec^o(o^c, S) > \big| Rec^o(o^c, S) \geq \varepsilon\}.$$

Those aggregate conceptual instances whose recommendation value is less than a certain threshold ε will be filtered out. Then, the extended user profiles may be instantiated to real pageviews, so that appropriate pageviews may be recommended to the user for the purpose of personalization.

5 Conclusions

In this paper we have proposed an approach of the e-commerce website personalization Based on Ontology. This approach retains the relationships both between attributes of concepts and between concepts, providing more flexibility in matching usage profiles with current user session, which can improve the precision and coverage of the recommendation sets for personalization. The examples provided throughout this paper reveal how such a framework can provide insightful patterns and smarter personalization services. However, We have only provided an overview of the relevant issues and suggested a road map for further research and development in this area. One area of future work involves the study of machine learning techniques in order to discover the best way to summarize the attribute automatically. Another area of future work will be to explore use of discovered domain-level aggregates from Web usage mining to enrich the existing domain ontology for a Web site.

References

1. B. Mobasher, Honghua Dai, Tao Luo et al. Integrating Web Usage and Content Mining for More Effective Personalization. In E-Commerce and Web Technologies: Proceedings of the EC-WEB 2000 Conference, Springer, 2000.165~176

2. Xin Jin, Yanzan Zhou and B. Mobasher. A Maximum Entropy Web Recommendation System: Combining Collaborative and Content Features. In KDD'05, Chicago, 2005.21~24

3. Raymond J. Mooney and Raymond J. Mooney. Content-Based Book Recommending Using Learning for Text Categorization. In Proceedings of the Fifth ACM Conference on Digital Libraries,San Antonio, 2000.195~240

4. C. Basu, H. Hirsh and W. Cohen. Recommendation as classification: Using social and content-based information in recommendation. In Proceedings of the AAAI-98, 1998.714~720

5. H. Dai and B. Mobasher. Integrating Semantic Knowledge with Web Usage Mining for Personalization. In Web Mining: Applications and Techniques.Anthony Scime (ed.), Idea Group Publishing, 2005

6. Bangyong Liang, Juanzi Li and Kehong Wang. Web page recommendation model for the semantic web. Journal of Tsinghua Univ (Sci&Tech), 2004(9):1271~1277

7. Hongyan Pan, Hongfei Lin and Jin Zhao. Ontology-Based Personalized Recommendation system. Computer Engineering and Applications, 2005(20):176~180

8. B. Mobasher, Honghua Dai, Tao Luo, et al.Discovery of Aggregate Usage Profiles for Web Personalization. In Proc. of the Web Mining for E-Commerce Workshop (WEBKDD'00), Boston, 2000

9. B. Mobasher and Honghua Dai. A road map to more effective web personalization: Integrating domain knowledge with web usage mining. In International Conference on Internet Computing, 2003

Knowledge Processing and Service System for Digital Education based on Semantic Web

Xia Li[1], YingLong Wang[2]

1 Humanity &Social Science College, Wuhan University of Science and Engineering
Liniya_@163.com
2 Departemnt of Information Technology, HuaZhong Normal University
Wangylccnu@mail.ccnu.edu.cn

Abstract. Recent efforts in the area of learning technology have resulted in a considerable improvement in the interoperability of digital education resources. On the basis of sharing and integration of digital educational resources, knowledge Processing and service considers the Semantic knowledge extraction of metadata of educational resources, Construction ontology for educational resources, and combining the users personality characteristics, providing semantic-based personalized retrieval and delivery services. In this paper, we work out the architecture of knowledge processing and service system for digital education, then discuss the semantic representation of digital education resources, semantic mining and discovery of digital education resources and personalized knowledge delivery service.

1 Introduction

Recent efforts in the area of learning technology have resulted in a considerable improvement in the interoperability of digital education resources across different Learning Management Systems (LMS) and Learning Object Repositories (LOR) [1]. On the basis of sharing and integration of digital educational resources, knowledge Processing and service considers the Semantic knowledge extraction of metadata of educational resources, Construction ontology for educational resources, and combining the users personality characteristics, providing semantic-based personalized retrieval and delivery services

Knowledge Services is the innovation of traditional service model through computer, network and multimedia technology-based information technology, which is a brand new information service models. Knowledge Service makes use of service

Please use the following format when citing this chapter:

Li, X., Wang, Y. L., 2007, in IFIP International Federation for Information Processing, Volume 251, Integration and Innovation Orient to E-Society Volume1, Wang, W. (Eds), (Boston: Springer), pp. 499-506.

description, generation, acquisition, organization, positioning, and integration to meet the demands of users to use the information. It is closely related to two areas : knowledge-related issues and service-related issues. Dealing with issues related to knowledge of the objectives is to provide knowledge services necessary for the proper and accurate knowledge. Due to the large volume of knowledge is the source rich and complex features, it is related to knowledge modeling and knowledge base of the building. Service related to the goal is to understand user demand, which in turn service through knowledge of the operation, on the Internet in an appropriate manner to meet these demands.

Semantic Web technology is able to provide the required computational semantics for the automation of tasks related to Digital Education resources as selection or delivery [1].Ontology can play an important role in sharable semantics and concept for digital education interoperation and it can also make a knowledge base for ontology driven digital education resources retrieve and delivery

In this paper, we work out the architecture of knowledge processing and service system for digital education, then discuss the key technology involved. The paper is organized as follows: Section 2 introduces the Semantic Web and ontology, which is the key technology used for the system; Section 3 discuss the architecture of knowledge processing and service system for digital education; section 4 discusses the implementation of the key technologies in the system and provides an overview of various components of the system such as semantic representation of digital education resources, semantic mining and discovery of digital education resources and personalized knowledge delivery service; Section 5 is a brief review of related work; while conclusions are presented in section6.

2   Semantic Web and Ontology

There are a number of important issues related to the Semantic Web. Roughly speaking, they belong to four categories: languages for the Semantic Web, ontologies, semantic markup of pages on the Semantic Web, and services that the Semantic Web is supposed to provide [2].

Currently, Web content is formatted for human readers rather than programs.HTML is the predominant language in which Web pages are written. For people the html information is presented in a satisfactory way, but machines will have their problems. The semantic web representation is far more easily processable by machines. The term metadata refers to such information: data about data. Metadata capture part of the meaning of data, thus the term semantic in Semantic Web.

In computer science, the ontology could be used to build vocabulary of specific domain application that is used for a formal explicit definition of some concepts that are shared among researches. For environment of knowledge sharing, the ontology cloud be meant to *"a specification of a conceptualization"* [3]. The conceptualization is the objects, concepts and other entities that are assumed to exist in some areas of interest and the relationships that hold among them [4].

Ideally, creation of digital educational Web contents with ontological annotation should be supported by ontology-driven authoring tools and class hierarchies based on a number of underlying ontologies[2]. Digital Education resources can then be presented, edited, modified, and mixed consistently. The reality, however, is still far away from being ideal and there are a lot of further steps and efforts to make in order to move forward.

3 The architecture of knowledge processing and service system for digital education

The architecture of knowledge processing and service system for digital education is as the fig.1.The system includes two components, which are knowledge processing section and knowledge service section separately.

The section of knowledge processing consists of the following modules:

➢ Digital Resources Parsing Module: Parse resources collected by the various formats of digital education resources for a unified XML format;

➢ Knowledge Extraction Module: Extract the information about the title, disciplinary, author, keywords, such as summary metadata information from the XML documents;

➢ Ontology search module: Construct the ontology base for the digital education resources and provide the ontology driven retrieval for the user to find the required resource with correct location and information;

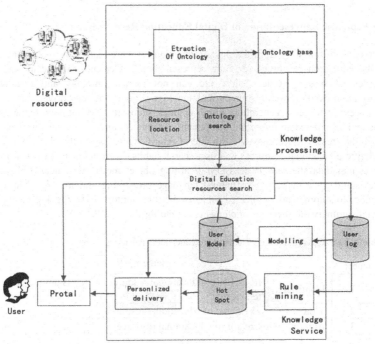

Fig. 1. The architecture of knowledge processing and service system for digital education

The section of knowledge service consists of the following modules:

➢ User modeling module: Generate and adjust dynamically the user model in term of the search requests ;

➢ Digital Education Resources search module: Parsing and Analyzing semantically the inquiry of user, such as keywords portfolio, metadata, knowledge ontology in the form of inquiries, According to the ontology Association to location the education resources meeting the required condition, and filtering and sorting the results in term of the user model;

➢ Personalized knowledge push and delivery: Achieve the initiative, Efficient knowledge Push and delivery Service According to the user model and knowledge access character of the digital education resources though various network platform;

4 The implementation of the key technologies in the System

There are mainly three key technologies in the knowledge processing and service system for digital education, which is semantic representation of digital education resources, semantic mining and discovery of digital education resources and personalized knowledge push and delivery service.

4.1 Semantic Representation of Digital Education Resources

Extraction of ontology from the digital education resources plays an important role in the education resources semantic representation.   Current mainstream search engines, such as Google, Baidu, etc can not extract ontology and metadata information from the web resources, and unable to support ontology driven retrieval resources. In the next generation search engines, metadata and ontology extraction module has become an important component of them. It can enhance the retrieval of flexibility, retrieval accuracy and the rate of return. According to the characteristics of digital educational resources and user search habits, We reference IEEE learning object metadata standard IEEE LOM (learning object metadata standard)[5], and other standards, make use of natural language processing and machine learning methods to automatically collected subjects, the title, author, keywords, Following is a brief summary of 10species of elements in ontology.

Table 1. Extraction of ontology elements for educational resources

Number	Element	
1	Identifier	Identifier of educational resource, which is unique in the world
2	Title	The name of educational resource
3	Author	Creator of educational resource

4	Abstract	Text description of the educational resource content
5	Keywords	Important descriptive word of content
6	Subject	Subject of the educational resource
7	Language	Language of the educational resource
8	Context	Main scenario using educational resource
9	Format	Technical data type of educational resource, which is used to decide the running time software required by educational resource
10	Resource Type	Concrete type of educational resources

4.2 Semantic Mining and Discovery of Digital Education Resources

Currently, the commonly used full-text index method is mainly through the text word segmentation, extracting the text contained in the feature words, to feature words for indexing projects, the establishment of words and text content of the link between indexes, the inverted index Based on the characteristics to achieve the full text word search function. However, it was found that this method the following drawbacks:

> Index files too large. Feature-based Translation indexing methods due to lack of understanding and context of broad, will introduce text in the number of message text indexing, document indexing to occupy a space too large.

> Retrieval inefficient. As the use of the word inverted index technology, With the retrieval of text and the size to the number of words and the size of the index surge, which not only affect the speed, but also the quality of inquiries and efficiency.

> Low rate of precision, high rate of repetition. Overall, such as indexing mechanism is simply to achieve a feature words and text on the link between primers, They lack the resources to the original description of semantic information (such as metadata, ontology), failed to establish friendly understanding between the three elements as "primary resources" , "ontology based indexing mechanism" and "user". it can not meet the semantic matching of user query and text content.

Based on the characteristics of the content indexing words of the aforementioned problems, we construct a "meta-data", "ontology", content and resources Association-indexing mechanism, then achieve "metadata" "ontology" and the link between digital educational resources inquiries. The model includes semantic information resources ("ontology"), to help raise resources retrieval accuracy. The same time can reduce the storage space for the occupier. The issue of resources search model involves the number of attributes resources, the need to establish an ontology driven index mechanism, hence realize the semantic mining and discovery to meet the user inquiry.

4.3 Personalized Knowledge Push and Delivery Service

Due to the differences between different users in age, sex, education, occupation, hobbies etc, the field that users are interested in is also different. Thus the results of the same search requests have different appraisal. However, the existing search engine that the service provided is the "search for" and not "user-oriented." that is, for different users to the same search requests. Search engines provide the same search result. It is hard to meet the learner's individual needs.

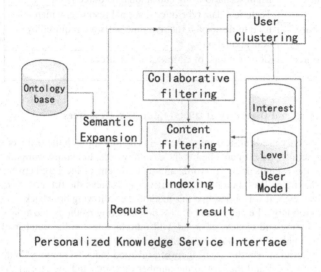

Fig. 2. Personalized Knowledge Service Framework

To address the above issues, we make use of the personalized service technology, which provide adaptive services through the collection and analysis of information of the user's interest, as the fig2 presents. At present, the realization of personalized service is mainly through the rule-based and information-based filtering technical means. The former utilizes predefined rules to filter information; the advantage is simple, direct and shortcoming is that it is difficult to ensure the quality of the rules, and the rules are of poor scalability. The latter can be further divided into content-based filtering and collaborative filtering. Content filtering is the similarity of the use of resources and users interested in, the advantage is simple, effective, the drawback is not for users interested in and users only have found similar resources with interest. Collaborative filtering is the use of user's similarity between the information to recommend information, it can discover new elements of interest for users, and the drawback is the need for user participation.

5   Relative Work

The benefits of ontologies have already been recognized in the learning technology community [6] [7]. First, the Semantic Web technologies are applied to some important learning technology standards. For example, there is an RDF Binding [8] for the IEEE Learning Object Metadata (LOM) that is a part of the regular IEEE LTSC standardization efforts. Next, in order to better define different aspects of applications in e-learning, researchers have given several classifications of ontologies [9].

In semantic web enabled e-learning domain, several approaches are currently investigated, ranging from federated or distributed learning repositories (ARIADNE [10] or EDUTELLA [11]) or learning management systems, which focus on course delivery and administrative aspects, and adaptive web-based educational systems which offer personalized access and presentation facilities to learning resources for specific application domains.

6 Conclusion

In this paper, we first have an overview of the architecture of knowledge processing and service system for digital education. Then discuss various components of the system and the key technology involved, which is semantic representation of digital education resources, semantic mining and discovery of digital education resources and personalized knowledge delivery service separately.

We plan further implementation of the knowledge processing and service system in order to construct a digital education oriented knowledge service system and utilized the semantic web technology to realized ontology driven knowledge retrieval and delivery. The final goal is to develop a user oriented system to meet the personalized user need, which can be used in education applications for querying digital education resources, and thus improving the effeteness of education systems in general.

References

1. LUISA (Learning Content Management System Using Innovative Semantic Web Services Architecture), http://www.luisa-project.eu/.
2. V. Devedzic, "Education and The Semantic Web", *International Journal of Artificial Intelligence in Education* (IJAIED), Vol.14, 2004, pp. 39-65.
3. T.R.Gruber, A translation approach to portable ontologies, Knowledge Acquisition, 1993. [Online].
4. S.Niwattanakul, M.Eboueya, D.Lillis, "Describing and Researching of Learning Resources with Ontology Model," *jva*, pp. 214-222, IEEE John Vincent Atanasoff 2006 International Symposium on Modern Computing (JVA'06), 2006.
5. Duval, E., Ed. (2002). 1484.12.1 IEEE Standard for Learning Object Metadata. June 2002
6. Sampson, D.G., Lytras, M.D., Wagner, G., & Diaz, P. (2004). "Guest Editorial:Ontologies and the Semantic Web for E-learning", *Educational Technology & Society*, 7 (4), 26-28.
7. Lytras, M., Tsilira, A., Themistocleous, M. (2003). Towards the semantic e-learning:An ontological oriented discussion of the new research agenda in e-learning, In Proceedings of the 9thAmericas Conference on Information Systems, Tampa, USA, pp. 2985-2997.
8. Nilsson, M., Palmer, M., Brase, J. (2003). The LOM RDF binding - principles and implementation, In Proceedings of the 3rd Annual ARIADNE Conference, Leuven, Belgium

9. Gasevic, Dragan; Hatala, Marek, "Ontology Mappings to Improve Learning Resource Search", British Journal of *Educational Technology*, v37 n3 p375-389 May 2006.
10. Ariadne: Alliance of remote instructional authoring and distributions networks for europe, 2001.http://ariadne.unil.ch/.
11. Edutella, 2001. http://edutella.jxta.org/.

Hierarchy Analysis Method for Management Information Systems

Xiao-xia Wang, Yuan Ling
Beijing Jiaotong University, School of Traffic and Transportation
wangxiaoxia@jtys.bjtu.edu.cn

Abstract There are many kinds of management information systems (MISs) whether in industries or in enterprises. In China, most of MISs were put into application at different time and with different demands. With the broader application of MISs, it's becoming greater important to integrate them and realize information sharing. Hierarchy analysis method gives out a general structure for the complicated integration of MISs. There are two steps for this method. (1)measure the information communication relations among MISs,(2) divide MISs into multi grade structure. For China railway industry, there are 13 kinds of big MISs, take them as an example to illustrate how to apply this method. Based on hierarchy analysis, MISs with strong connections have priority while integrating MISs. The higher the grade of MIS, the greater overall layout design priority should be given, for more information from other MISs finally reach it.

1 Introduction

China railway informationization begins early and develops in a rapid pace. In 1980s, computers were widely used in every department of railway; in 1990s, railway information technology application developed into systematization, and management information systems (MISs) for every function have been set up, including railway transport, vehicle, machine, engineering, electricity, finance, statistics and office. The real-time network system of railway transport and production was herein formed.

Experts reached a common sense on China railway informationization, which was that a rudiment frame appeared and it played a rather important role to raise the quality and capability of railway transportation and insure security of transportation. However, because of the gradual establishment of MISs, the information resources sharing is not sufficient, and the exploitation and utilization ratio is relatively low. In view of the overseas railway industry development, there is a great gap in the fields of operation and management, electronic commerce, intelligent transportation, etc.

Please use the following format when citing this chapter:

Wang, X., Ling, Y., 2007, in IFIP International Federation for Information Processing, Volume 251, Integration and Innovation Orient to E-Society Volume1, Wang, W. (Eds), (Boston: Springer), pp. 507-514.

On one hand, these problems are caused by the cosmically introduction of MISs at the very beginning of railway informationization; on the other hand, the original layout of railway MISs was based on the theory of traditional administration levels and function division, which was relatively low in view of the prediction level.

1.1 Known Results

From the aspect of economy management, there are many methods applied to MISs planning, such as critical success factors, strategy set transformation, business system planning, business information analysis and integration technology, reclaim of investment, and so on[1]. These methods were equal to apply to the micro plan of MISs in the enterprises. When they were applied to industries, such as railway, it would be too comprehensive to make an overall plan. In the fields of database, traffic and transportation plan, there also was a planning method named as cell group ranking, with the characteristic of the evident hierarchy and generally fining function. However it was rather simple from another point of view.

1.2 Our Results

Based on the informationization fruits of China railway in the past 40 years, the communication relationship among every big railway MISs are measured by applying hierarchy analysis method of general structure, and divide them into multi hierarchy structure. It resolves the problem that the emphasis of China railway informationization is not obvious, which caused by the simple enumeration of MISs, and provides decision-making support for the great-leap-forward development task of China railway informationization.

2   Method of Hierarchy Analysis of General Structure

2.1 Problem Description

Hierarchy analysis of general structure analyzes the frame of comprehensive MISs by the theory of relating matrix in gragh theory, making sure the relation among the elements within the system, and divides the comprehensive system into multi hierarchy structure. This gives out qualitative analysis on the potential relations which are not sure under the comprehensive conditions, and provides evidence for rational description[2].

There are two steps for the hierarchy analysis of general structure.

Firstly, establishes a system structure model to describe the relations among the elements within the system. The relations include cause and effect, up and down, affiliation, primary and secondary relation and aim-means relation. The generally describing method is the vector graph, in which the direct and indirect relations among elements could be measured separately by abut matrix and extendable matrix.

Abut matrix M is a boolean matrix, describing the direct influence among each neighboring elements in the vector graph. The two abut correlated elements in the matrix can be defined by two-value relation R. In the matrix, the row element is S_i, while the line element is S_j. If there is influence, it is expressed as $S_i RS_j = 1$; if there is no influence, it expressed as $S_i RS_j = 0$. When $S_i RS_j = 1$ and $S_j RS_i = 1$, S_i and S_j have strong connection.

Extendable matrix R illustrates to what extent that each nodes can be arrived at by certain routes. It is acquired by abut matrix plus identity matrix I and several other operations. If $(M+I)^1 \neq (M+I)^2 \neq (M+I)^3 \neq \cdots \neq (M+I)^{r-1} = (M+I)^r$, then extendable matrix $R = (M+I)^{r-1}$.

In matrix R, the element $r_{ij} = 1$ means that there is at most （r-1） routes reaching this node. R is also a boolean matrix, and the operations are all boolean operation which is 0+0=0, 0+1=1, 1+1=1, 0×0=0, 1×0=0, 1×1=1.

Secondly, makes sure the grade of the system structure. Builds extendable matrix R up into two son-aggregates: (1) for each element S_i, gathers all related elements that S_i may reach into one aggregate, which is called the extendable aggregate $R(S_i)$ of S_i. (2)Gathers all the elements that may reach S_i into another aggregate, named the cause aggregate $A(S_i)$ of S_i. Along each row, examines each horizontal row of extendable matrix R, all the rows that corresponding the element 1 are in the son-aggregate $R(S_i)$. Then examines each vertical line, all the lines that corresponding the element 1 are in the aggregate $A(S_i)$. In the highest grade of a multi-grade structure, no higher element reaches it, so its extendable aggregate only includes certain strong connection elements of its grade and itself. The cause agrregate $A(S_i)$ of the highest grade elements includes itself and all the elements of extendable lower grade. The qualification for S_i is the highest grade element is that $R(S_i) \cap A(S_i) = R(S_i)$. Knows the highest grade elements and scores them out of the table, then the each element of the lower grade gets, until scores out each element by the grade. Finally, the multi hierarchy structure chart can be drawn according to the result of grading, which conduces to the understanding of the grading relation and detail structure of the system.

3   Operation and Application of Method

There are 13 big MISs for railway daily operation, namely security MIS, infrastructure establishment MIS, planning MIS, personnel MIS, labor and capital MIS, statistics MIS, vehicle MIS, electricity affair MIS, power and water supply MIS, machine MIS, engineering affair MIS, finance and account MIS, transportation MIS. Takes their information communication relations as an example, expatiates the operating steps and conclusion analysis of the hierarchy analysis method of general structure.

Firstly, examines the information communication relations in every railway management function, draws the vector graph of the information communication between each MIS (Fig.1). The number 1 to 13 individually stands for security, infrastructure establishment, planning, personnel, labor and capital, statistics, vehicle, electricity affair, power and water supply, machine, engineering affair, finance and account, transportation MIS.

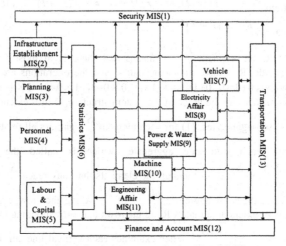

Fig. 1. The vector graph of the information communication in each MIS

In Fig.1, there exist direct and indirect influences among each MIS. For $(M+I)^2 = (M+I)^3$, the extendable matrix is $R = (M+I)^2$. The abut matrix M and extendable matrix R are as follows.

The symbol "*" in extendable matrix R does not exist in the original matrix （M+I）. It reflects the indirect relation among elements.

$$
M = \begin{array}{c}
\begin{array}{cccccccccccccc}
& s_1 & s_2 & s_3 & s_4 & s_5 & s_6 & s_7 & s_8 & s_9 & s_{10} & s_{11} & s_{12} & s_{13}
\end{array} \\
\begin{array}{c}
s_1 \\ s_2 \\ s_3 \\ s_4 \\ s_5 \\ s_6 \\ s_7 \\ s_8 \\ s_9 \\ s_{10} \\ s_{11} \\ s_{12} \\ s_{13}
\end{array}
\begin{bmatrix}
1 & 0 & 0 & 0 & 0 & 0 & 0 & 0 & 0 & 0 & 0 & 0 & 0 \\
1 & 1 & 0 & 0 & 0 & 1 & 0 & 0 & 0 & 0 & 0 & 0 & 0 \\
0 & 1 & 1 & 0 & 0 & 1 & 0 & 0 & 0 & 0 & 0 & 0 & 0 \\
0 & 0 & 0 & 1 & 0 & 1 & 0 & 0 & 0 & 0 & 0 & 1 & 0 \\
0 & 0 & 0 & 0 & 1 & 1 & 0 & 0 & 0 & 0 & 0 & 1 & 0 \\
0 & 0 & 0 & 0 & 0 & 1 & 0 & 0 & 0 & 0 & 0 & 1 & 0 \\
1 & 0 & 0 & 0 & 0 & 1 & 1 & 0 & 0 & 0 & 0 & 1 & 1 \\
1 & 0 & 0 & 0 & 0 & 1 & 0 & 1 & 0 & 0 & 0 & 1 & 1 \\
1 & 0 & 0 & 0 & 0 & 1 & 0 & 0 & 1 & 0 & 0 & 1 & 1 \\
1 & 0 & 0 & 0 & 0 & 1 & 0 & 0 & 0 & 1 & 0 & 1 & 1 \\
1 & 0 & 0 & 0 & 0 & 1 & 0 & 0 & 0 & 0 & 1 & 1 & 1 \\
0 & 0 & 0 & 0 & 0 & 0 & 0 & 0 & 0 & 0 & 0 & 1 & 0 \\
1 & 0 & 0 & 0 & 0 & 1 & 1 & 1 & 1 & 1 & 1 & 1 & 1
\end{bmatrix}
\end{array}
\qquad (1)
$$

$$R = \begin{bmatrix} 1 & 0 & 0 & 0 & 0 & 0 & 0 & 0 & 0 & 0 & 0 & 0 & 0 \\ 1 & 1 & 0 & 0 & 0 & 1 & 0 & 0 & 0 & 0 & 0 & 1^* & 0 \\ 1^* & 1 & 1 & 0 & 0 & 1 & 0 & 0 & 0 & 0 & 0 & 1^* & 0 \\ 0 & 0 & 0 & 1 & 0 & 1 & 0 & 0 & 0 & 0 & 0 & 1 & 0 \\ 0 & 0 & 0 & 0 & 1 & 1 & 0 & 0 & 0 & 0 & 0 & 1 & 0 \\ 0 & 0 & 0 & 0 & 0 & 1 & 0 & 0 & 0 & 0 & 0 & 1 & 0 \\ 1 & 0 & 0 & 0 & 0 & 1 & 1 & 1^* & 1^* & 1^* & 1^* & 1 & 1 \\ 1 & 0 & 0 & 0 & 0 & 1 & 1^* & 1 & 1^* & 1^* & 1^* & 1 & 1 \\ 1 & 0 & 0 & 0 & 0 & 1 & 1^* & 1^* & 1 & 1^* & 1^* & 1 & 1 \\ 1 & 0 & 0 & 0 & 0 & 1 & 1^* & 1^* & 1^* & 1 & 1^* & 1 & 1 \\ 1 & 0 & 0 & 0 & 0 & 1 & 1^* & 1^* & 1^* & 1^* & 1 & 1 & 1 \\ 0 & 0 & 0 & 0 & 0 & 0 & 0 & 0 & 0 & 0 & 0 & 1 & 0 \\ 1 & 0 & 0 & 0 & 0 & 1 & 1 & 1 & 1 & 1 & 1 & 1 & 1 \end{bmatrix} \quad (2)$$

Secondly, makes sure the class of the system structure. The $R(S_i)$, $A(S_i)$ and $R(S_i) \cap A(S_i)$ of this example are shown in Tab.1.

Table 1. The Extendable Aggregation and Reason Aggregation of Extendable Matrix R

S_i	$R(S_i)$	$A(S_i)$	$R(S_i) \cap A(S_i)$
1	1	1,2,3,7,8,9,10,11,13	1
2	1,2,6,12	2,3,	2
3	1,2,3,6,12	3	3
4	4,6,12	4	4
5	5,6,12	5	5
6	6,12	2,3,4,5,6,7,8,9,10,11,13	6
7	1,6,7,8,9,10,11,12,13	7,8,9,10,11,13	7,8,9,10,11,13
8	1,6,7,8,9,10,11,12,13	7,8,9,10,11,13	7,8,9,10,11,13
9	1,6,7,8,9,10,11,12,13	7,8,9,10,11,13	7,8,9,10,11,13
10	1,6,7,8,9,10,11,12,13	7,8,9,10,11,13	7,8,9,10,11,13
11	1,6,7,8,9,10,11,12,13	7,8,9,10,11,13	7,8,9,10,11,13
12	12	2,3,4,5,6,7,8,9,10,11,12,13	12
13	1,6,7,8,9,10,11,12,13	7,8,9,10,11,13	7,8,9,10,11,13

In Tab.1, the system number of the highest grade is 1 and 12, then score out the 1st and 12th line, and the systems 1 and 12 in other lines. Continually follows the search principle of $R(S_i) \cap A(S_i) = R(S_i)$. Finally, the arrange order of system structure is S={1, 12, 6, 2, 4, 5, 7, 8, 9, 10, 11, 13, 3}. According to this order, the matrix is rearranged as follows:

$$R = \begin{array}{c} \\ S_1 \\ S_{12} \\ S_6 \\ S_2 \\ S_4 \\ S_5 \\ S_7 \\ S_8 \\ S_9 \\ S_{10} \\ S_{11} \\ S_{13} \\ S_3 \end{array} \begin{array}{cccccccccccccc} S_1 & S_{12} & S_6 & S_2 & S_4 & S_5 & S_7 & S_8 & S_9 & S_{10} & S_{11} & S_{13} & S_3 \\ \left[\begin{array}{ccccccccccccc} 1 & 0 & 0 & 0 & 0 & 0 & 0 & 0 & 0 & 0 & 0 & 0 & 0 \\ 0 & 1 & 0 & 0 & 0 & 0 & 0 & 0 & 0 & 0 & 0 & 0 & 0 \\ 0 & 1 & 1 & 0 & 0 & 0 & 0 & 0 & 0 & 0 & 0 & 0 & 0 \\ 1 & 1 & 1 & 1 & 0 & 0 & 0 & 0 & 0 & 0 & 0 & 0 & 0 \\ 0 & 1 & 1 & 0 & 1 & 0 & 0 & 0 & 0 & 0 & 0 & 0 & 0 \\ 0 & 1 & 1 & 0 & 0 & 1 & 0 & 0 & 0 & 0 & 0 & 0 & 0 \\ 1 & 1 & 1 & 0 & 0 & 0 & 1 & 1 & 1 & 1 & 1 & 1 & 0 \\ 1 & 1 & 1 & 0 & 0 & 0 & 1 & 1 & 1 & 1 & 1 & 1 & 0 \\ 1 & 1 & 1 & 0 & 0 & 0 & 1 & 1 & 1 & 1 & 1 & 1 & 0 \\ 1 & 1 & 1 & 0 & 0 & 0 & 1 & 1 & 1 & 1 & 1 & 1 & 0 \\ 1 & 1 & 1 & 0 & 0 & 0 & 1 & 1 & 1 & 1 & 1 & 1 & 0 \\ 1 & 1 & 1 & 0 & 0 & 0 & 1 & 1 & 1 & 1 & 1 & 1 & 0 \\ 1 & 1 & 1 & 1 & 0 & 0 & 0 & 0 & 0 & 0 & 0 & 0 & 1 \end{array}\right] \end{array} \qquad (3)$$

$S_7, S_8, S_9, S_{10}, S_{11}, S_{13}$ forms a son-matrix whose elements are all 1, demonstrating that they have the strong circulation connection.

Finally, draws the multi hierarchy structure of information communication in MISs as Fig.2.

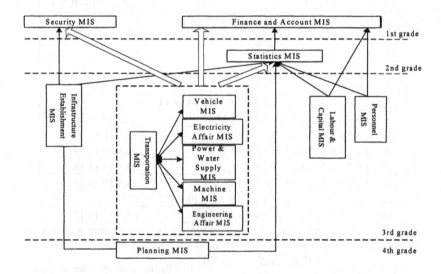

Fig. 2. The multi hierarchy structure of information communication in each operation MIS

The relation and structure of railway MISs have characters as follows: (1)The transport, vehicle, electricity affairs, electricity and water supply, machine affairs and engineering affairs MISs have strong circulation connections. (2)Security and finance MISs are the highest grade in the railway MISs, other operation MISs finally reach them. (3)Personnel MIS and labor and capital MIS are on the same grade with the same higher grade relation. Their positions and functions are relatively communicated. (4)Statistics MIS is on the second class, the daily operation information of every MISs finally reach it. (5)Planning MIS does not have MIS reach it and has the lowest grade. Therefore, the integration of railway MISs, should be based on the integration of infrastructure establishment MIS, planning MIS, personnel MIS, labour and capital MIS, statistics MIS, vehicle MIS, electricity affair MIS, power and water supply MIS, machine MIS, engineering affair MIS and transportation MIS, which have strong circulation connection, and be leaded by security MIS, finance and account MIS to make full use of their driving force.

4 Conclusion

The information communication relation and intensity among MISs can be measured by the hierarchy analysis method of general structure, separately demonstrating the strong connections between MISs. When planning MISs in a certain industry, develops and integrates MISs with strong connections first. The higher the grade of MIS is, the great prior the overall layout design should be given, for more information from other MISs reach it.

Acknowledgment

The Special Program for the Preliminary Research of Momentous Fundamental Research of Ministry of Science & Technology of China(2005CCA03900); The Program for the Preliminary Research of Momentous Fundamental Research of Ministry of Science & Technology of China(2006CB705504). "An Empirical Study on Chinese E-commerce Development of Transport Industry" （2006RC023）, Beijing Jiaotong University science fund，2006.

References

1. XUE Huacheng, *Management Information System(the 3rd edition)*, Qinghua university publishing house, Beijing，1999, pp.263.

2. LI Guogang, LI Baoshan, *Management System Engineering*, China People University publishing house, Beijing，1998, pp.107-119.

3. LIU Zhijun, Fulfill the Requirement of Tri-representation, Catch the New Historical Opportunities, Realize the Great-leap-forward Development of China Railway, *People's railway*, 2003-6-29 （1-3）.

4. LI Zhonghao, CHEN Yong, LIU Jun, China's General Situation of the Informationization Establishment in Railway and Transportation Industry in the Year of 2000, *Chinese information almanac 2001*, China，2000.

6. ZHANG Guowu, QIAN Dalin, ZHANG Xiuyuan, Traffic and Transportation Planning and Decision-making Support System, China railway publishing house, Beijing 1996, pp.163-168,186.

7. WANG Linshu, The Opportunity and Challenge Facing Railway Informationization, *Traffic and transportation systematical engineering and information*, vol.1, no.4, pp.288-293, 2001.

8. Research on Railway Information Share Demand Analysis and Frame Structure, Beijing Jiaotong University Research Report, 2003(unpublished).

Web-based Coordination for E-Commerce

XiguoZhang, GuiheWang, LiminFan
Department of Mechanical Engineering & Automation, Eastern LiaoNing
University
Dandong, 118000, P.R.China
guihewang@163.com

Abstract. As the e-commerce environment becomes more pervasive and dynamic, coordination among companies are required more frequently than ever. We give the definition of coordination as well as the model of e-commerce based on web; the communication in e-commerce is described; the function of coordination, include the architecture, execution and control of coordination is discussed. At the same time, we analyze the business process perspective and develop a coordination system based web for e-commerce, based which, the process of problem solving is analyzed.

1 Introduction

The advent of e-ecommerce has revolutionized the way that contemporary business operates [1]. With the development of the Internet, e-commerce has become more important. Dynamic e-commerce is concerned with the integrate systems across intranets, extranets, and the Internet in a dynamic fashion[2]. Equipped with advanced Internet technologies and standards, participants in dynamic e-business are able to externalize a company's business processes in a standard way and utilize business processes provided by other parties to create new applications or business flows by integrating such internal and external processes dynamically[3]. The use of Internet services lead to considerable savings time and cost for construction projects. Although, web services technology have provided a flexible deployment approach to facilitate B2B and B2C interactions[5], coordination is need frequently than ever among companies as the business environment becomes more dynamic. The required amount of information processing and communication in those cases can easily exceed a single human being's capability, especially when there are many negotiation issues and partners [6]. Therefore, systems supporting and automating business negotiations have a great potential value.

Please use the following format when citing this chapter:

Zhang, X., Wang, G., Fan, L., 2007, in IFIP International Federation for Information Processing, Volume 251, Integration and Innovation Orient to E-Society Volume1, Wang, W. (Eds), (Boston: Springer), pp. 515-522.

2   Web services for e-commerce

2.1 The model of e-commerce

E-commerce application can interact with applications of external trading partners or other internal cross-functional applications by exchanging messages [7]. Figure 1 illustrates the usage of Web services in e-commerce.

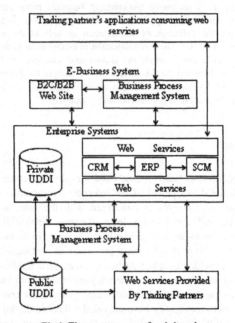

Fig.1. The e-commerce of web-based

A business process can expose its functionality as Web services and consume the functionality of other processes. Web services play an important role in enhancing business-to-consumer (B2C) and business-to-business (B2B) integration by allowing trading partners to gain access to data or business functions in the legacy systems and enterprise software systems either via Web services wrappers of these systems directly or via Business Process Management System (BPMS). An enterprise can provide Web services to its trading partners for delivering real-time data or embed its business services directly as part of partners' services to their customers. Activities in business processes can also be implemented as Web services. The BPMS uses private and public UDDI service registries to store, search, and select business partners' Web services for business process integration. Web services are used to support dynamic e-business consisting of dynamically configured business networks.

2.2 E-commerce communication

Web services are self-contained and modular applications that can be described, published, located and invoked over the web. Web services perform encapsulated business functions ranging from simple request-reply to full business process interactions, which can reduce human interaction through the embedded capability of services discovery and binding, which are standards-based and suited to build common infrastructure to reduce the barriers of business integration. The dynamic nature of Web services also opens up new opportunities for businesses, which can application in following areas:

1) Between enterprises: Web services can provide services via a standard interface to customers and business partners. In addition to exchanging plain transaction data, business process level integration with trading partners will become a real possibility.

2) Within an enterprise: Web services can accelerate the speed and reduce the cost of integration with various internal applications and systems. They also have the potential of reducing programming skill requirements and improving service asset reuse thanks to its service-oriented structure based on open standards.

3) Between an enterprise and its (internal or external)end-users: Web services can deliver a better user experience, integrate diverse content and reduce the cost of content variety to a variety of user devices due, in part, to the availability of Web services-enabled applications, data sources and devices.

2.3 Coordination definition

The first step of the system-supported coordination is to establish shared understanding of the rules of the coordination. Thus, the coordination process must be clearly defined and easily interpreted. However, defining coordination processes from scratch takes time and efforts and checking the correctness of the defined process requires expertise. The marketplace is in the best position to define coordination processes because it can accumulate know-how in designing coordination processes while supporting various transactions. The coordination processes defined and given by the marketplace have also a clear advantage in accessibility and reusability. The opponent's utility function is assumed of the following product form:

$$u = \prod_i f_i^{w_i} \qquad (1)$$

Where f_i and w_i corresponds to the utility value and weight of issue i. Note that this objective function differs from the linear combination formulation of the multi-attribute utility theory that most existing coordination system employ. Opponent's feedbacks are used to adjust the weights in order to reveal its underlying preferences. This can be achieved by comparing the changes of consecutive offers, namely:

$$R_i = \left| \frac{f_i(t) - f_i(t-1)}{f_i' - f_i'(t-1)} \right|, \qquad (2)$$

Where $f_i(t)$ and $f_i'(t)$ denotes respectively the user's and the opponent's proposed values for issue i at round t. Note that this ratio reveals the opponent's relative preference compared with the user upon issue i. A large ratio suggests that issue i is more important to the opponent than the user in a quantitative measure. Table 1 shows the weight range of categories.

Once the coordination partners agree on the coordination, an instance of the coordination process needs to be instantiated, controlled, and monitored. The coordination process can be executed and controlled by invoking and scheduling activities according to the process definition. It can also enforce the commitment of coordination partners by providing a non-repudiation mechanism. The harmonization is also the best way to execute and control coordination processes because it can provide a both-win perspective.

Table 1. The Weight Value of Categories

Categories	Weight range
Important	0.75—0.95
Less important	0.35—0.70
No important	0.10—0.30

A business coordination process is often ad hoc in nature because the relationships between negotiation partners are dynamic and the most appropriate coordination process is dependent on the specific case. The proposed Web Services-enabled marketplace architecture is a nice solution to understandability and information sharing issues and intentionally leaves internal decision and collaboration processes to the coordination partner side. However, the generation of new coordination processes and their modification are not well supported. It is often the case that at least minor changes to the given coordination process are desirable in order to accommodate company- or case specific issues. The coordination through general communication channels provides the maximum flexibility in process but the minimum codified information on the process and exchanged data. The coordination processes are in the following way:

1) The buyers and suppliers find coordination partners.

2) Partners make an agreement on the coordination process. Say a set of process $P=\{P_1,...,P_n\}$ and a set of attributes $R=\{R_1,...,R_m\}$. The attribute R_j contains patterns a_k (i.e. $R_j=\{a_1,...,a_p\}$).Each process P_i is a combination of the patters for the attributes (i.e. $P_i=\{a_1,...,a_m\}$ where $a_j \in R_j$).

3) The partners start with a coordination process which may be either one of the given coordination processes P_i or a new coordination process p_k created by the process composition tool.

4) Coordination partners perform the coordination until reaching an agreement or breaking off the coordination. Using the propriety tool, users can easily generate a new process p_k by selecting patterns for coordination process attributes $R=\{R_1,...,R_m\}$, modifying the attributes in the ready-made process.

3 The system of e-commerce

3.1 The architecture of the system

The distributed prototype system uses a J2EE based multi-layer architecture. Figure2 depicts its architecture, the prototype system consists of four tiers implemented on the J2EE platform for delivery of online information.

1) Client layer: The thin Web clients are used in the architecture. They are the Web browsers to assemble checking requests with the target server URL (Uniform Resource Locator) and send them to the server through the HTTP protocol. The checking results in dynamic HTML are also rendered at the client tier.

2) Web layer: It consists of a Web container to host all the Web components mentioned. The presentation logic of the prototype is processed at the Web layer, including the delivery of the dynamic Web content to client. Both Servlet and JSP technologies are implemented in the prototype together with Java bean.

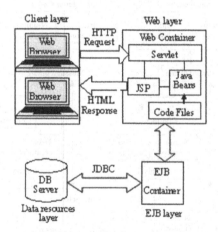

Fig.2. The architecture of e-commerce system

3) EJB layer: Enterprise Java beans are developed at this layer for responding to user requests from the Web layer through use of building rules in the knowledge base at the data resources layer. All application logic for building design support services is implemented at this layer.

4) Data resources layer: It includes a database server to hold and maintain the content of the knowledge. JDBC (Java Database Connection) is used for the connection between the EJB layer and the database server. JDBC also provides support for distributed transaction management and database access security for the prototype.

3.2 Coordination model

The traditional contract net is employed to handle coordination, which includes the inviting, bidding and awarding stages. Figure 3 shows a collaborative coordination model based on coordination and bidding. Comparing with the traditional systems, this model enables multi-contract coordinate of to improve the overall performance, resulting in a batch of contracts that are consistent and coherent to the ultimate goal—fulfilling customer orders. As shown in figure 3, a customer order is first mapped to configuration unit.

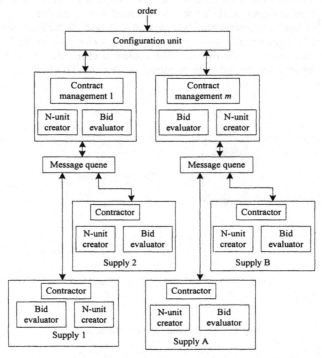

Fig.3. The coordination model

Then the system starts to find proper trading partners for individual contract Manager. Each contract unit would bid for the relevant task based on its production capability and resource availability. A separate configuration unit is used to solve the possible conflicts among individual tasks. The system employs four types of functional units: configuration unit, contract manager, information server, and coordination unit. The configuration unit is responsible for coordinating the product fulfillment process.

The contract manager is in charge of specific evaluators and manages the coordination process to reach a contract for this evaluator. The information server assists the contract manager in inviting the candidate suppliers and provides a message routing service. The coordination unit executes a certain coordination process with a supplier.

3.3 Problem Solving Process

The blackboard provides a shared data structure for knowledge sources to post solution components (e.g. new production schedules, new capacity allocations, new parties names, etc.), analysis results (e.g. resource/capacity utilization, failure records, etc.), and coordination/communication status information. It is partitioned into an arbitrary number of contexts, which corresponds to different sets of working assumptions (e.g. sets of orders need to be scheduled, available resource capacities, etc.) and different solutions. Within each context, a summary of the current state of the solution is maintained in the form of a set of "unresolved issues". An unresolved issue is an indication that a particular aspect of the current context solution is incomplete, inconsistent or unsatisfactory. For example, a request for bid still needs to be evaluated, or a promised delivery date is violated. Problem solved process is shown in figure4.

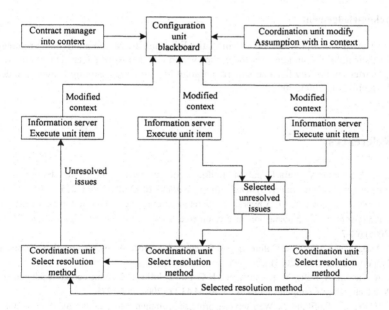

Fig.4. Flow of problem solving

All problem-solving activities within the system architecture are triggered by either the incorporation of a new event or modification of an assumption, both of which can be performed by either the end user or the unit. The module-activation service is invoked whenever there are problem-solving tasks on the agenda remaining to be executed, or initiated by units within the system. Knowledge sources serve as the primary problem solvers in the system. They communicate the real-time results by posting new information to the blackboard and modifying existing information. Each domain-level knowledge source acts primarily as a server that supports a variety of problem-solving services.

4. Conclusions

Internet and new software development technologies created new opportunities for the design and deployment of systems capable of supporting coordinators. As the business environment becomes more dynamic, coordination amount companies are required more frequently than ever, systems supporting and automating business coordination have a great potential value. The biggest advantage of the Web Services-enabled coordination is the increased size of the pool of potential partners. Through the Web Services interfaces, heterogeneous systems of trading partners can dynamically link with each other. Considering the degree of automation achieved in other business process domains, the importance of managing coordination to achieve more efficient business operations has become even higher.

Acknowledgement

The authors thank the Chairman of the Editorial Board and anonymous referees for their helpful comments on the earlier version of this work paper. This work was supported by the key Science and Technology Project from Liaoning Province under the grand No.: 2003220025.

References

1. G. Francisco, V. Rafael, and M. Rodrigo, An integrated approach for developing e-ommerce applications, *Expert Systems with Applications* 28 12 (2000) 223–235
2. L. Yu, L. Liu, and X. Li, A hybrid collaborative filtering method for multiple-interests and multiple-content recommendation in e-commerce, *Expert Systems with Applications* 26 16 (2005) 67–77
3. A. Basu, and S. Muylle, Online support for commerce processes by Web retailers, Decision Support Systems 34 4 (2003) 379– 395
4. A. Kambil, A. Kalis, M. Koufaris, and H.C. Lucas, Influences on the corporate adoption of Web technology, Communications of the ACM 43 11 (2000) 264– 271
5. H. Kreger , Fulfilling the Web services promise, Communications of the ACM 46 6 (2003) 29– 34
6. R.D. Van der Mei, R. Hariharan, W. Ehrlich, and P.K. Reeser, Performance of Web servers in a distributed computing environment, *Engineering in the Internet* 8 12 (2001) 125–134
7. E. Cohen, H. Kaplan, and J.D. Oldham, Managing TCP connections under persistent HTTP, Computer Networks 31 22 (1999) 1709–1723
8. Y. Huang and J.Y. Chung, A Web services-based framework for business integration solutions, Electron Commerce Research 34 18 (2003) 15–26

BAB-a New Ecommerce Mode in China

Xiuzhen Feng[1] and Yibin Hou[2]
School of Information, Renmin University of China
59 Zhongguancun Ave, Beijing, 100872, P.R.China
dongming3699@126.com,jiangdeshan_01@163.com,
yuanfengren@sohu.com

Abstract. Information service business becomes the predominant industry in
21st century, and eCommerce which has become the focus that all countries
and large corporation compete for is being improved and perfected ceaselessly.
Since China is very different from the west in social structure and culture
characteristic, B2B develops slowly in China [1,2]. In order to extend
ecommerce more smoothly and successfully in China, the important factor is
the reorientation and reorganization of the middle link in the actual
circumstance of China. BAB business mode made up the bottleneck problem
that restraint China's ECommerce development in a certain extent and match
the currently environment of China. The existence and participation of
intermediary will reduce risk and improve the business efficiency of
eCommerce market consumedly.

1 Introduction

In China, with the universality and development of computer and the network
technology, eCommerce develops rapidly. Numerous information technique business
enterprises, venture investment corporation etc, develop eCommerce in succession.
The development prospect of eCommerce is doubtless extremely vast, but to expand
eCommerce smoothly in the whole nation still has a lot of problem to resolve. The
existence of intermediary can reduce market risk and improve market business
efficiency, thus becomes a link between both sides in business [4,5]. BAB
eCommerce mode can effectively get the function of intermediary together, which is
a new approach to resolve the bottleneck problem especially trust and security in
extending eCommerce in China. The business mode is being explored and improved

Please use the following format when citing this chapter:

Feng, X., Hou, Y., 2007, in IFIP International Federation for Information Processing, Volume 251, Integration and
Innovation Orient to E-Society Volume1, Wang, W. (Eds), (Boston: Springer), pp. 523-532.

positively at present, and Chinabab is an eCommerce website based on BAB mode [14].

2 Pushing forward eCommerce needs suitable conditions in China.

As a new form of economy, eCommerce has its own features and needs to be support in special environment. China should create favorable conditions for the progress of eCommerce and take countermeasures to get rid of barriers and encourage its development [3].

2.1 The development of ECommerce in china

The eCommerce is a new subject developing very quickly. People generally understand eCommerce as a kind of business activity on the platform of internet. In China, eCommerce focuses on advancing B2B (Business to Business), and gives consideration on B2C (Business to Consumer) at the same time. B2B which comes into being at the earliest stage in the United States can lower the operation cost of supply chain between vendee and bargainor, reduce intermediary, cut down transaction costs, promote bargain accomplishing more easily, improve trade efficiency, so it develops quickly recently and become the mainstream of eCommerce.

Some eCommerce applications have already appeared in China, which are comparatively successful and starting gaining profit, such as alibaba. Since exterior environment of infrastructure is improved further, eCommerce gets it in gear all round and wins initial success in China.

2.2 The bottleneck problem that restrict the development of ecommerce.

The development prospect of eCommerce is doubtless extremely vast, but to expand eCommerce smoothly in the whole nation still has a lot of problem to resolve. Since China is very different from the west in social structure and culture characteristic, B2B develops slowly in China. There are a few main reasons as follows [1,2,3]:

(1) The construction of credit standing environment is lag. China's credit system has not been built completely and is not perfect enough. Under the circumstances, enterprise which does not keep its word usually makes more profit than that which keeps its word.

(2) The channel of information is not open. Business enterprises can't provide market and source information in demand mutually, resulting in the unbalance of production & sales.

(3) Enterprises have not formed market ideas fully. In china, marketplace intensive degree is not high, management is extensive, intermediate links are excessive, the efficiency of supply chain is poor and waste is more.

(4)The relative service system is not perfect. The logistics channel is obstructed, logistics distribution system is faulty, and the delivery service of on-line shopping is not rapid. On-line paying system is not perfect. A lot of companies are still accustomed to traditional payment for the sake of safety.

(5) The legal system isn't sound and lacks new market rules for eCommerce. Traditional market rules for business affairs are still put into effect.

(6) The service provided by different agencies is faulty in market.

For the characteristics of network, while reducing the transaction cost, ECommerce also brings about some problems such as the difficulty to ascertain the credit of both sides in business. These problems lower the bargain efficiency in market. In order to complete trade smoothly, effective intermediate agent need to get involved, provide relevant information about product and business credit of both sides. The participation of intermediary will improve the bargain efficiency of eCommerce consumedly.

2.3 Introduction to Electronic intermediary.

There is no unified definition of intermediary by now. Generally, we think intermediary is a professional organization which accesses market as a self-governed third-party and embarks communication、 notarization、 monitoring、 consultation on market access、 market competition、 market transaction orders、 market entanglement and others. It doesn't engage in the activity of commodity and service transaction directly [12]. Electronic intermediary is like a bridge connecting vendee and bargainor, which realizes all functions traditional intermediary has based on network. Of course, there are some new functions with Electronic intermediary.

The development of eCommerce has made some traditional intermediaries die out. At the same time, some new Intermediaries come forth [5,13]. These intermediaries are based on electronic technology and advanced management mode. They can offer more comprehensive service than traditional intermediaries do, although all of them increase the cost of value chain between vendee and bargainor [4].

2.4 Electronic intermediary can play important roles in eCommerce.

Electronic and traditional intermediaries share some common roles, such as cost reduction、 aggregation、 facilitation and market information provision. Electronic intermediaries have their own characteristics too. They are expounded as follows [6,7,9,11,12]:

(1) Aggregation

Electronic intermediaries can provide the location for potential sellers to gather together, to share some public fundaments and customers, which forms scale economy and scope economy to lower the market access cost for sellers. Further more, Electronic intermediaries break the limitation of time and space to present many kinds of commodities to buyers.

(2)Providing market information

The product price is a key factor for buyers to consider whether buy it or not. Electronic intermediaries can list the price of the same product made by different producers, where buyers can compare them by themselves. They also can narrate the quality of products.

(3)Serving as an electronic Marketplace

An electronic intermediary serves as B2B electronic marketplace where qualified members can post requests to buy or sell. An electronic intermediary provides the collection of many demands for buyers and many products for sellers effectively via the internet.

(4) Providing credit assurance

Members who want to bargain via an electronic intermediary must be qualified. An electronic intermediary must promise that buyers or sellers are legal to transact with each other.

(5) Online feedback

Buyers can communicate the quality information of product bought from producers via chat system、 BBS etc. provided by an electronic intermediary. Other buyers can obtain more information from browsing the given topics.

(6)Online Auction

Via Internet, qualified members can participate in online Auction without the limitation of time and space. Online Auction can get more people together to provide their own price for products which they like and people need not go out for bidding block.

3   The BAB mode is suitable to the development of Ecommerce in China.

3.1 It is required for the third party to get involved in overcoming the bottleneck problem.

The B2B mode which spreads currently is to describe a business enterprise to carry on bargain on modern network, which makes no difference with work performed by hand in the business mode. The eCommerce can reduce intermediary and cut down transaction cost to some extent [8]. However in China, how to build a safe and reliable trade platform for enterprises has already become an urgent problem to resolve for ECommerce. The progress of any new productivity can cause the change of production relations by all means. For the actual circumstance of China, one of importance factor is the reorientation and reorganization of the middle link.

Because there are some deficiencies in understanding information such as product quality、 price and mutual credit between both sides in the eCommerce market, in other words, information asymmetry, sometimes the completion of trade need the interposition of third party [6,11]. The more serious the indetermination of quality information is, the more intense the market demand for business intermediary is. It is not necessary that intermediary is an expert in product quality and price, or special organization in credit survey, but intermediary provides a place for numerous business enterprises and customers with shared information. The function similar to "bulletin board" is also able to play a certain role to guarantee trade credit of both sides.

It is generally believed that business intermediary is an essential element in market economy in micro-economics. Intermediary gains economy benefit depending on collecting, arranging and announcing concerned information, and becomes a link between both sides in business. Its existence can reduce market risk and improve market business efficiency.

3.2 The introduction of BAB business mode.

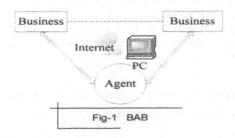

Fig.1. BAB
BAB stands for "Business-Agent-Business". BAB based on B2B is a kind of new modes for eCommerce among business enterprises. Its essence is to resolve the confidence problem among business enterprises. Its purpose is to create a reliable ecommerce environment including traffic、 fund stream、 logistics and knowledge stream, which makes up the deficiency of B2B ecommerce mode. Its trait is that the business enterprise carries on the commercial activity through a transaction platform which relies on the modern information technology、 provides overall process and all-directions service and is a high degree of integration. This platform based on the network and the computer, supported with abundant information and knowledge, put into practice by the personnel with rich experience, is a kind of whole new business mode.

The main characteristics of BAB are as follows: utilization of up to date information technology; Omni-directional and entire process commercial support including information issue and information inquiry、 identity authentication、 negotiating contracts、 payment、 logistics; Safe guarantee with man-machine union and multi- links.

3.3 The realization and function of agent

In the BAB ecommerce mode, "A" means the agent that represents business and service platform, which can also be referred to trade advisors or service advisors in the agency. The agents join the business as a third party to control the whole trade process and provide secure and reliable services for both buyers and sellers. This is a new approach to resolve the bottleneck problem about trust and security in extending eCommerce in China.

In ecommerce environment, the business agency framework includes technique support and service platform, digital authentication technique and organization, commercial bank, 3rd party logistics and 4th logistics-sustained technique and service, third party quality inspection service and enterprise credit evaluating organization and mechanism etc.

"A" is not BAB business platform itself, but is the aggregation which is assembled by BAB business platform and is made up with digital authentication system, bank, reliable logistics enterprise, quality inspection organization and enterprise's credit evaluating institution. The aggregate which bases on the responsibility taken in hand by each other and technical reliability, builds up credit system of BAB business platform, which provides the whole process and all-directions services of new ecommerce for user.

With the functions like trade processes control, risk control, business matching, resource allocation and individual recommended, members in the process can benefit from their partners, agents, etc.

3.4 BAB platform provides necessary service and fundamental condition for business enterprises in eCommerce.

BAB is different from other e-intermediaries. BAB mode bands technology means offered in network and guarantee provided by trusted Agent together. It integrates the whole process of identity authentication, information service, online payment, logistics distribution etc. It provides unified and reliable platform, and realize "three flows-in-one" (information flow, fund flow, material flow).All of these provide necessary   service and fundamental condition for eCommerce between enterprises.

BAB platform supports many business activities, such as spot transactions, barter, future transaction, resource matching, online auction, etc. It also offers digital certification, digital signature and many other mechanisms which are prerequisite in a secure eCommerce platform. Meanwhile, its particular risk controls mechanism guarantees credit of enterprises. The whole business process is harmonized and supervised by "A", which offers overall services from searching business partners to accomplishing the whole trade process for business enterprises online. This is real ecommerce trade.

Specifically, from user's perspective, they can enjoy service from BAB platform as follows:

(1) Online trading and risk control in the whole process.

By means of forming strategy cooperation partnership with CA (Certificate Authority), bank, Logistics Company, third party credit rating agency etc, it provides all-round support and risk control mechanism for online business between qualified members.

(2)Providing automatic and manual matching and promoting cooperation service for various types of business activities, such as bargaining, replacement, future transaction, online auction, lease etc.

(3) Resource matching service.

According to what the business enterprise needs, the platform can match、 collocate and integrate resource such as material, information, knowledge and the capital resources on many sides. It provides various special services with distinct characteristics to exploit the potential value fully and makes them win together.

(4) Individual recommendation service.

Making use of Web mining technique and social network analysis technique, it can dig out latent demand of enterprise and possible business partners in future thereby can carry on business matching and individual recommendation more effectively.

4 A Case Study-Chinabab

www.chinabab.cn is an eCommerce website based on BAB business mode. This project is sponsored by Development Research Center of State Council P.R China. Universities such as Renmin University of China, Tianjin University, Tongji University etc. and Enterprises have participated in the project to explore a new business mode according with the development of eCommerce in China. The project team has already built a fundamental framework by investigation、 discussion、 evolvement with theory and practice, and developed the chinabab platform in about one year. We have participated in designing and developing parts of chinabab. We'll expatiate the contents of the website and draw a comparison between alibaba and chinabab.

4.1 The contents of the website

In this website, "A" is an aggregation composed of Beijing Certificate Authority, China Merchants Bank, Guangdong Development Bank, Datian logistics, China Certification & Inspection Group etc. Via the website, "A" gathers information, financing, logistics, knowledge together to provide a trusty transaction environment. "A" provides service for the whole electronic transaction process, which are expanded next.

(A)Online Service. As a qualified member of chinabab, you can enjoy service below after logon. (1)Certificate Authority. To ensure chinabab platform safe and trusty, every member must be qualified. Members use their real names to transact with each other. Chinabab and Beijing Certificate Authority grant members a unique medium respectively, which is used to authenticate identity, sign contract. (2)Online Negotiation & Signature.Chinabab provides online video service. Most of business, negotiations, making a contract all can be completed via chinabab. To a certain extent, the service reduces business cost and enhances transaction efficiency. (3)Online payment. Cooperating with China Merchants Bank, Guangdong Development Bank, chinabab provides online payment service. However, it owns a product E-Tong to make transaction more convenient inside the website. (4) Contract inventory. Chinabab offers various business contract templates to provide references, which make sellers and buyers, sign contracts more effectively. (5) Providing logistics schemes. Cooperating with China Certification & Inspection Group, chinabab provides third-part Inspection service. The reports of inspection & logistics are evidences for payment. (6)Providing suggestions of consultants. There are many professionals in chinabab. They can provide individuation service for buyers or sellers.

(B) Network Application service about online operation.Chinabab provides point-to-point, face-to-face service for enterprises respectively, for their deficiency in the faculty of network application. The contents of service are:(1) Training employees for necessary technology and business.(2) Founding websites for enterprises freely.(3) Helping enterprises set up OA,ERP,CRM systems

(C) Offline service.The maturity of service not only includes online service,but also involves offline service.(1)Providing reports about industry trends for members regularly.(2)Organizing clientele parties such as special topic lecture、 case study conference、 project argumentation conference.(3)Business consultation service via telephone.(4)Accepting member's consignations informed by telephone

(E) E-tong. E-tong is a payment tool in chinabab system. Qualified members can open their own E-tong accounts. The account of E-tong is monitored and managed by cooperation banks. E-tong is fit for enterprises which are lack of cash temporarily. Enterprises can obtain E-tong by impawning goods、 resource. Using E-tong makes enterprises activate their assets.

With multi-faceted service, chinabab wants to achieve objectives below:

(1) Establishing a public information exchange platform. As a qualified member, you can post you requests on the website. Other members can browse them to search for their appropriate business partners.

(2) Setting up resource operation mechanism. Enterprises and relatives compose a complexity network. Based on the website, Enterprises get dispersive organizations together to form an effective industry group, which brings into play Aggregation Effect adequately.

(3) Forming a trusty transaction environment of eCommerce. Under cooperation with banks, authority organizations etc., chinabab brings many enterprises into an honest trade circumstance to fulfill their business.

4.2 A Comparison between Chinabab and Alibaba

Alibaba is a famous brand of B2B eCommerce, which is the biggest online transaction market through the world currently. In this part, we will look for the differences between Alibaba and Chinabab. These differences are presented in Tab-1 below.

Tab 1. A Comparison between Chinabab and Alibaba

Items	Chinabab	Alibaba
Business support	Beijing Certificate Authority, China Merchants Bank, Guangdong Development Bank, Datian logistics, China Certification & Inspection	Yahoo, Industrial and Commercial Bank of China etc

	Group arbitration organizations	
Settlement System	E-tong	Alipay
Logistics service	Datian logistics	No
Member authentication	Beijing Certificate Authority,	Shanghai Biz-credit Online Service Co., Ltd
Contract template	Yes	No
Online signature	Yes	No
Cargo Inspection	China Certification & Inspection Group	No

From Tab-1 above, we can conclude that chinabab concentrates on the whole process of transaction, provides logistics service and risk control to reduce cost and benefit both buyers and sellers.

5 Conclusion

It can be seen from above that BAB business mode make up the bottleneck problem that restraint China's eCommerce development in a certain extent and match the current environment of China, especially in some cases such as the enterprise which transforms to the market economy, the credit system in the process of forming, enterprise leader's actual situation, the imperfection of advisory service system. China ought to try to investigate、 explore、 carry out、 improve and perfect the implementation means of BAB business mode. BAB platform should be established by competent organization to improve business efficiency and benefit, which can extend eCommerce more smoothly and successfully in China.

References

1. H.X. Wang, S.Z. Lang and Y. Li, About Some Difficulties and Countermeasure during the Development of EC in China, *Nanjing University of Science and Technology.Nanjing* 210094.
2. Z.H. Liu and Z.L. Ge, Research on the Solutions and the questions of the Electronic Commerce Development in China. Year 2006 Graduate Paper, The Number of School:10269 ID: Zy0392010006.
3. Z. He , Features and Barriers to the Development of Electronic Business. *Commercial Research* ,156-157(2002).
4. R. Wigand and R. Benjamin, Electronic Markets and Virtual Value Chains on the information Superhighway, *Sloan Management Review* ,52-57(1995).

5. Sarkar, Mitrabarun , Brian Butler and Charles Steinfield. Cybermediaries in Electronic Marketspace: Towards Theory Building, *Journal of Business Research* ,1998(41),215-221(1998).

6. Choi,Stahl and Whinston, Intermediation, Contracts and Micropayments in Electronic Commerce, *Electronic Markets Newsletter,* 1997(4).

7. J.Y. Wang and Y. Gao, The Model of Electronic Business Intermediary, *Journal of LiaoDong University* ,5,2005.

8. C. Stephen. *Strategic Management of Electronic Commerce*, Manchester Business School, John Wiley & Sons, 2001.

9. Bailey and P. Joseph, Intermediation and Electronic Markets: Aggregation and Pricing in Internet Commerce, *Cambridge: Thesis, Technology, Management and Policy, Massachusetts Institute of Technology,* 1998

10. D.C. Croson and M.G. Jacobides, Agency Relationships and Monitoring in Electronic Commerce, *International Journal of Electronic Commerce,* (3),65-82(1997).

11. Bailey, P. Joseph and J.Y. Bakos, An Exploratory Study of the Emerging Role of Electronic Intermediaries, *International Journal of Electronic Commerce,* 1(3),7-20, (1997).

12. X.Q. Ke, Economic Analysis of Intermediaries in the Electronic Commerce Market, *Beijing:Tsinghua University,*2004.

13. M.C. Alina, A thesis submitted to the faculty of the graduate school of the university of Minnesota, Intermediation *in Electronic Commerce,* 2001.

14. http://www.chinabab.cn.

Analysis and Implementation of Workflow-based Supply Chain Management System

Yan Tu [1]and Baowen Sun [2]

1   Information School, Central University of Finance and Economics,
Beijing, 100081, P.R.China,Yolanda_tu@yahoo.com.cn
2   Department of Science and Research, Central University of Finance
and Economics, Beijing, 100081, P.R.China,sunbaowen@263.net

Abstract. Because of lack of abstraction at the stage of requirement analysis, the traditional Supply Chain Management systems are not suitable to dynamic reengineering when business needs change. This paper will combine Workflow Technologies with Supply Chain Management systems (WSCM). By decomposing work into the corresponding tasks and roles and monitoring the sequence of work activities according to a defined set of rules, we can boost efficiency, reduce cost, and optimize performance of business processes management of Supply Chain.

1   Introduction

As Internet technologies become commonplace in businesses, an emerging necessary characteristic of purchasing, logistics, and support activities is flexibility. Therefore, supply chain functions must operate in an integrated manner in order to optimize performance. However, the dynamics of the organization and the market make this challenging. In many organizations, it is likely that the sequence of work activities on business process will be changed by customers while in process, and in most cases, these change requests are difficult to manage.

In spite of the ubiquitous presence of information technology, the value that the traditional Supply Chain Management (SCM) software creates, and integration of business processes and enterprises, the challenges of implementing these applications do exist. The factors such as incompetent infrastructure, conflicting policies and standards, and changes about the sequence of work activities pose immense pressure for the organizations to move forward. The biggest challenge among them is management for the change of business processes. The issue and a potential solution we explored in this paper focus on business process management of supply chain management.

Please use the following format when citing this chapter:

Tu, Y., Sun, B., 2007, in IFIP International Federation for Information Processing, Volume 251, Integration and Innovation Orient to E-Society Volume1, Wang, W. (Eds), (Boston: Springer), pp. 533-543.

In this research, we propose a workflow-based supply chain management (WCSM) for supply chain business process definition, execution, and management. To enhance adaptability for business process reengineering, we constructed our work with three main focuses. Firstly, we define a generic workflow model (i.e. four basic control flow patterns) for design a workflow modeling subsystem. Secondly, we define a set of task status and status linkage diagram. Thirdly, we descript four kinds of task firing mechanisms to perform the desired business process according to the predefined rules. The purpose of this research is to establish a workflow-based SCM system. Further, a case study in a typical business purchase process is presented to demonstrate how the WSCM system works in the domain of procurement activities to bring benefits to organizations and purchasing managers.

The remainder of this paper is organized as followings. Section 2 introduces workflow and workflow modeling technologies, which also covers the related technologies of Petri nets and CXPN (Color Extended Petri Net). Section 3 describes the design of the workflow system architecture and management mechanism to define the workflow template involving the representation of transition (task) status, workflow pattern and token operation rules, and task firing mechanisms. Section 4 uses a typical business purchase process case as an example to demonstrate WSCM at work. The last section concludes our contributions and addresses suggestions for future researches.

2 Related Workflow Technologies

2.1 Workflow

Workflow is concerned with the automation of procedures where documents, information or tasks are passed between participants according to a defined set of rules to achieve, or contribute to, an overall business goal. Workflow Management System (WfMS) is a system that completely defines, manages, and executes workflows through the execution of software whose order of execution is driven by a computer representation of the workflow logic [1]. The main function of a WfMS is to provide procedural automation of a business process, by managing of the sequence of work activities and the invoking of appropriate human or resources associated with the various activity steps.

The benefits of workflow are promoted by the Workflow Management Coalition (WfMC) as follows:

• Improved efficiency by the elimination of many unnecessary steps;

• Better process control through the standardizing of working methods and the availability of an audit trail;

• Improved customer service through greater predictability in the levels of response to customers;

• Greater flexibility of software control over processes enabling redesign when business needs change;

• Improved processes, because focusing on processes leads to their streamlining and simplification.

2.2   Petri Nets and Color Extended Petri Net (CXPN)

The Petri nets have been widely used as a workflow modeling tool in a variety of ways such as the building, analysis, and simulation of business processes. A Petri net is a graphical and mathematical modeling tool. It consists of places and transitions, and describes the relations between them. As the names of these elements show, places refer to static parts of the modeled system. The graphic representation of Petri nets is a bipartite directed graph where places are drawn as circles and transitions are drawn as bars or boxes. Logical relations between transitions and places, i.e. between events and their preconditions and consequences are represented by directed arcs. In a complex system, a consequence of an event is a condition of other events. The validity of a condition in the modeled system can be represented by presence or absence of tokens in the appropriate place in the net. The number of token represents the number of resources [2].

In our research, we extend the classical Petri nets. This extension specifies that each transition has a value (color) which refers to specific status of task. For example, if task is executed and its state is changed from "suspend" to "run", the value (color) of transition will change automatically from "8" to "5". We call it the color extended Petri nets (CXPN).

3   Workflow-based Supply Chain Management System Framework

3.1   Three-tier WSCM System Architecture

In our research, we build a WSCM for supply chain management environment as shown in Figure 1. The system architecture is defined as three-tier model for increasing of the security of data communication and the system performance [3].

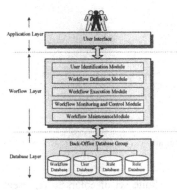

Fig. 1. Three-tier WSCM System Architecture

3.1.1 Application Layer
The application layer provides a graphical user interface between the user and the workflow kernel. The interface allows an authorized user to build workflow

templates, to define workflow instance, to provide input to information forms, to interact with workflow layer, and so on.

3.1.2 Workflow Layer

The workflow layer includes a user identification module (it is used to identify user's role and the corresponding authority), a workflow definition module (it is used for the business process designer to define the workflow), a workflow execution module (its functions include interpretation of the workflow template definition, creation of workflow instances and management of their execution, including start/ready/run/ submit/suspend/resume/abort/done, etc.), a workflow monitoring and control module (its functions include supervisory and management for workflow execution), and a workflow maintenance module (it can add, delete and modify any workflow template and its relevant tasks to enhance execution performance).

3.1.3 Database Layer

The database layer provides several of back-office databases. The relevant data are stored in these databases. These data include workflow information, user information and the role model data, etc. At runtime, the system can access its associating information in these databases.

3.2   Workflow Management Mechanism

3.2.1 The Representation of Transition (Task) Status

During the execution of workflow instances, transition (referring to one task) status may change. The status linkage diagram is shown in Figure 2.

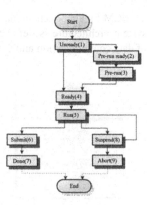

Fig. 2. Status Linkage Diagram

In CXPN, we use a finite set of colors to represent the set of transition status. The different color (different element from the color set) is corresponding with its own state. Here we use the different integer value to represent its corresponding color as shown in Table 1.

Table 1. The Representation Rules of Transition Status

Status	No.	Status Transition	Rules Description
Unready	1	Unready–Ready	All of its preconditions are fulfilled.
		Unready–Pre-run ready	Its constraint relationship is met and pre-transition is started.
Pre-run ready	2	Pre-run ready–Pre-run	Its partial pre-transitions (but not all) give the results.
Pre-run	3	Pre-run–Ready	All of its pre-transitions give their own results and all of its preconditions are fulfilled.
Ready	4	Ready–Run	It runs according to a defined set of rules.
Run	5	Run–Submit	It ends to run correctly and submits the final result to system.
		Run–Suspend	It receives the message "Suspend" or exception occurs.
Submit	6	Submit–Done	It stores the associated data into database.
Done	7	Done–End	Workflow is end.
Suspend	8	Suspend–Run	It receives the message "Resume" or exception has been handled successfully.
		Suspend–Abort	Exception is no way to handle.
Abort	9	Abort–End	Workflow is end.

3.2.2 The design of the Workflow Pattern and Token Operation

In our research, we define four basic control flow patterns: sequence pattern, parallel pattern, selection pattern and repetition pattern. We can construct the complex workflow model by using these basic patterns [2, 4].

To ensure the correct execution of business process, the rules of token operation should be defined accurately and the color (value) of corresponding transition (task) state should be modified dynamically in real time. Moreover, during the firing of a transition the appropriate number of tokens is removed from the input places and added to the output places. The number of added and removed tokens in a place depends on the nature of logical relations between the given place and its neighboring transitions. During the execution of workflow instances, the sequence follows the rules of token operation and the rules of task status transition that we mentioned earlier in the Table 1. The processes are illustrated by the following four basic CXPN-based workflow pattern and their associated rules.

（1）Sequence pattern. For the sequence pattern in workflow model, the associated rules to control workflow execution are that when the transition is fired and ended to execute, all of the tokens in its all of input places are removed and its all of output places add the corresponding tokens. The associated state changes from 'ready' to 'submit' and color (value) is modified from '4' to '6' as shown in Figure 3.

Fig. 3. Sequence pattern

（2）Parallel pattern. For the parallel pattern in workflow model, the associated rules to control workflow execution are that when the transition with AND-split is fired and ended to execute, all of the tokens in its all of input places are removed and all of output places of its corresponding transition with AND-join are added the tokens whose number is equal to the number of parallel branches. The associated state modification and the rules of token operation are the same as that of sequence pattern. It can be seen in Figure 4.

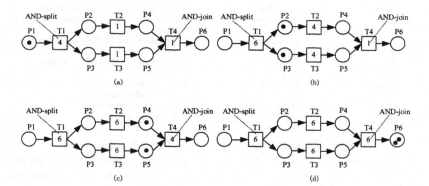

Fig. 4. Parallel pattern

（3） Selection pattern. For the selection pattern in workflow model, the associated rules to control workflow execution are that when some tokens as precondition in the place with OR-split are met for the firing condition of one or more than one of following transitions, they are fired. After they are executed, all of the tokens in places with OR-split are removed and places with OR-join are added the tokens whose number is equal to the number of token removed. The associated state modification and the rules of token operation are shown in Figure 5.

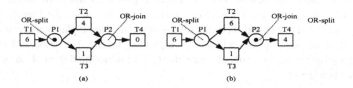

Fig. 5. Selection pattern

（4） Repetition pattern. For the repetition pattern in workflow model, its associated rules have the characteristics of both sequence pattern and selection pattern. The associated state modification and the rules of token operation are shown in Figure 6.

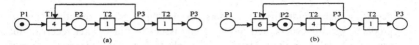

(a)   (b)

Fig. 6. Repetition pattern

3.2.3 Firing Mechanisms of Transition

The firing of transitions in the workflow model follows the behavior of the real life. In the model, a transition is enabled if all of its input places are valid. If a transition is enabled then it has qualification to fire. If an event occurs in the real life then the transition referring to this event must be fired in the model. Here we descript four different mechanisms about the firing of transition.

（1）Automation transitions. The firing of automation transition can occur instantaneously and automatically if all of its preconditions are fulfilled. The mark shown in Figure 7.a denotes the automation transitions.

（2）Operator intervention transitions. The firing of operator intervention transition is caused by operator interventions. Otherwise, the firing of transition can not occur without operator interventions while all of its preconditions are fulfilled. The mark shown in Figure 7.b denotes the operator intervention transitions.

（3）Message transitions. The firing of message transitions can not occur until it receives the desirable message. The mark shown in Figure 7.c denotes the message transitions.

（4）Non-primitive transitions. The firing of transition is associated with time. When the predefined time is over, the firing of transition can occur automatically. The mark shown in Figure 7.d denotes the non-primitive transitions.

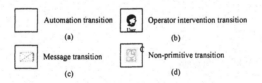

Fig. 7. Firing forms of transition

4 Case Study

In this section, we focus our works on three main parts. Firstly, process scenario as a WSCM system application is presented. Secondly, we translate it into a purchase workflow diagram. Finally, the conceptual framework is developed and the WSCM prototype is implemented for the typical business purchase processes.

4.1 Business Purchase Process Scenario

Business purchase is a typical case of supply chain management [5-8]. SCM project is a complementary skills working as a team for cost reductions and business process improvements. All participants contribute their expertise in different domains at various stages to reduce purchase cycle times. Purchasing activities include identifying vendors, evaluating vendors, selecting specific products, placing orders, and resolving any issues that arise after receiving the ordered goods or services. These issues might include late deliveries, incorrect quantities, incorrect items, and defective items. Therefore, by monitoring all relevant elements of purchase transactions, WSCM system can play an important role in maintaining and improving product quality, reducing cost, and optimizing performance of supply chain management.

4.2   Purchase Workflow Diagram

When a typical business purchase process is defined, we can translate it into a purchase workflow diagram, as shown in Figure 8.

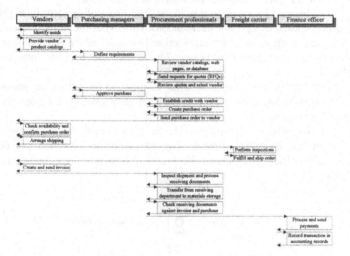

Fig. 8. Purchase workflow diagram

The diagram shows the detailed purchase workflow tasks and their corresponding team numbers. The purchase team consists of vendors, purchasing managers, procurement professionals, freight carriers, and finance officer. Based on the diagram, the workflow designer can establish a workflow template, as shown in Figure 9.

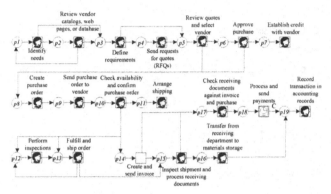

Fig. 9. Purchase workflow template

4.3 WSCM Framework and Implementation

Following the workflow approach, a prototype WSCM for supply chain management has been developed. Figure 10 shows the conceptual model of WSCM system. The three-tier architecture is implemented. The system includes user layer, workflow engine layer, and database layer.

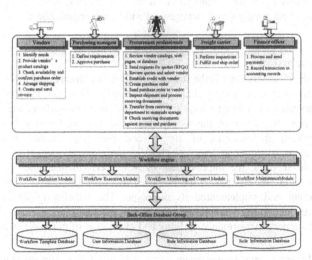

Fig. 10. WSCM Framework

Workflow designer corresponds with the process definition tool in general workflow product. In our prototype, the process definition interface is shown in Figure 11. It provides a graphic user interface by which workflow designer can model the control flow specification of workflows. Moreover, workflow designer can also assign all corresponding team members to specific tasks dynamically by dragging the elements from member's name list located at the right of the interface to workflow modeling panel.

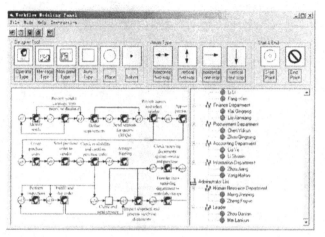

Fig. 11. Workflow Modeling Environment

After getting these information, WSCM will instantiate the workflow specification, create a workflow instance and handle its execution.

The implementation of the prototype presented in this paper is based on the four basic workflow patterns and firing mechanisms of transition. Our system mainly focuses on the implementation of the control flow perspective of workflow about supply chain management within one organization.

5   Conclusion

Supply chain management is the strategic, tactical, and operational level decision making that optimizes supply chain performance [5]. However, the dynamics of the organization and some exceptions can cause derivations from the business process plan. In particular, the supply chain management function is a critical link between the sources of supply and the organization. With most organizations spending at least one-third of their overall budget to purchase goods and services, the improvement of SCM performance holds significant business value. In this paper, we proposed the workflow-based supply chain management and implemented its prototype. The benefits of implementing WSCM are summarized as follows.

• It supports performance auditing and evaluation of purchase team in real time;

• Managers can optimize performance of business processes management of supply chain dynamically and flexibly;

• It supports the dynamic reengineering when business needs change;

• It provides the graphic panel with workflow designers to create and restructure workflow template.

However, our system has certain limitation. Our prototype WSCM supports supply chain management very well only within one organization. The implementation of the cross-organizational workflow product will be the focus of future research.

References

1. Workflow Management Coalition, Workflow Management Coalition Terminology & Glossary, Document Number WFMC-TC-1011 Document Status-Issue 3.0, 8-13(1999).
2. K.M. Hangos, *Intelligent control systems*, Kluwer Academic Publishers, 153-155 (2001).
3. C.J. Huang, J.C. Trappey and Y.H. Yao, "Developing an Agent-based Workflow Management System for Collaborative Product Design", *Industrial Management & Data Systems*, 106 (5), 680-699(2006).
4. H.B. Luo, Y.S. Fan, "CIMFlow: A Workflow Management System Based on Integration Platform Environment", *7th IEEE International Conference on Emerging Technologies and Factory Automation*, 233-241(1999).
5. L. S. Margaret, *Global Integrated Supply Chain Systems*, Hershey, PA, USA: Idea Group Publishing(2005).
6. V. N. Jeffrey, "Logical Channels: Using Web Services for Cross-organizational Workflow", *Business Process Management Journal*,11 (3), 224-236(2005).
7. U. Mihaela, W. B. Robert and S. W. Scott, "The Holonic Enterprise: AModel for Internet-enabled Global Manufacturing Supply Chain and Workflow Management", *Integrated Manufacturing systems*, 538-550(2002).
8. P. S. Gary, "Electronic Commerce, Seventh Annual Edition", *Thomson Learning*, 217-239 (2006).

Research on Evaluation Architecture of Marketing Performance for E-Commerce Websites

Yan Yang [1], Guangtian Zhou[2], Feng Yang [2]

1 School of Information Management, Heilongjiang University, Harbin
150080, yangyan9070@163.com
2 School of Computer Science Technology, Heilongjiang University,
Harbin 150080

Abstract. With the development of e-commerce websites, more and more firms use websites to advertise their products and brands and statues. How to evaluate marketing performance of firms on web-based e-commerce becomes more important problem. This paper analyses influencing factors of marketing performance under e-commerce websites. And it suggests an evaluation model based on combination of fuzzy logic and hierarchy methods. The model uses fuzzy set and average weights way to quantify the factors and thus, it can supplies a way to help firms to improve evaluating tools and modify their marketing strategies.

1 Introduction

E-commerce website is a very important tool that can help firms to implement marketing functions such as brands, products and services, information advertising, customer services and relationships, surveys, integrated resources and the Internet marketing. Under the condition of customers-centered websites, e-commerce framework integrates 4P(produce, price, place, promotion) strategies. Firms are focused on influencing factors, evaluation and assessment, measurement problems of web-based marketing performance. To research and solve these problems can effectively promote the levels of the Internet marketing and improve optimized design on websites. Therefore, the websites can obtain maximum visits and firms can obtain maximum profits by web-based e-commerce.

In general, the research on websites evaluation and influencing factors is divided into the following types: (1) from firms marketing management; (2) from online survey. A famous company, ForresterResearch uses online customers survey,

Please use the following format when citing this chapter:

Yang, Y., Zhou, G., Yang, F., 2007, in IFIP International Federation for Information Processing, Volume 251, Integration and Innovation Orient to E-Society Volume1, Wang, W. (Eds), (Boston: Springer), pp. 544-550.

statistical data from websites and expertise's analysis with "punchy evaluation method" to analyse a website; (3) websites evaluation and indexes based on customer demands and satisfactions[1]; (4) comparing e-commerce websites with not e-commerce websites to analyze index system of marketing profits and services effects[2]; (5) professional evaluation and analysis report on websites[3].

All above the kinds of research, to some degree, can supply influencing factors and methods on websites evaluation. Based on some results from local and other countries research, and also based on professinal evaluation and analysis report on websites , this paper surveys influencing factors on websites marketing performance in three catalogues of 15 subtypes with 45 items according to websites functions, website contents and customer actions, along with websites owners, builders, potential users and customers. At the same time, it suggests some detailed factors and constructs a model of index system architecture of e-commerce websites. [See Fig.1.]. It includes: (1) Interesting contents with specialty, fresh, updating, trust, practices; (2) Disturbing noises of browsers with unkind behaviors such as advertisements, components and reserved actions etc; (3) Security of information with no-cheating, no-healthy, misguides; quick-access with download speeds and shortest paths; (4) Function services with common and perfect.

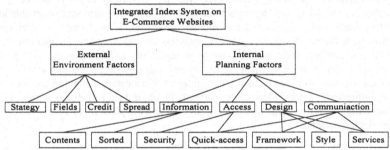

Fig 1. Evaluation architecture of integrated index system for e-commerce websites

E-commerce websites can supply business activities for enterprises on the Internet. The enterprises use the websites to advertise and communicate their information such as enterprises status, products, services and developing schedules etc by texts and images. Therefore, effective information is related to websites and enterprises operations. Websites internal planning factors depend on effective information, security, standerdized structure and style. So under the condition of fixed external environment, the effective analysis of internal information can improve the level of marketing on websites and realize maximal access and profits through optimized design. This gives firms a chance to use index system to evaluate and modify their websites.

The index sytsem can effectively avoid uncertainty on websites evaluation and unreality on seeking number of access websites. It can help websites owners to maintain information on the websites and get some formal e-commerce websites. In Fig 1.,external factors are common, but internal factors include effective information and sorted information such as fresh information, special information, real information and trusted information etc. Through these information, the goal of e-commerce websites is to absorb and hold customers, and also hope to make potential

customers to be permanent ones.One thing is to keep the websites fresh and
interesting; and special information shows some products and services of their
enterprises, it can be special point to absorb browsers'eyes; and also about real and
credited information can satify basic requirements which are those real materials of
products and services; The sorted information shows information sturcture on
websites. Effective access includes safe access and response quickly. Safe access
provides safe, realibility, stablity operation and contents. This asks the websites to
tolerate and against disturbance from other websites. And safe contents should be
healthful, legal and useful information. As usual, the websites can reply on any
quiries through reducing capacity of network and simplify access layers. The
different informations from websites become very important factors to build
websites.

Most firms use electronic commerce websites as the Internet marketing ways
which totally depend on quality of websites. They present quality by access of
customers from external environment leading into websites, and security of internal
planning and basic training of customers. Therefore, the quality of websites is from
the above three perceptions. In Fig.1., it shows an integrated index system
architecture of evaluating e-commerce websites in validity of some degree. The
index system architecture presents some kinds of factors and also impacts evaluation
of marketing performance under e-commerce websites. These factors are interacted
with each other. Through the factors analysis, the index system architecture is a
complex problem with multi-hierarchy, multi-factors and uncertainty. The paper
studies current existing influencing factors and suggests the evaluation model based
on e-commerce websites by using fuzzy integrated evaluation method to add weights
on influencing factors. Meanwhile, particularly single factor of different sub-index
hierarchies can also guide optimized design of website planning to satisfy maximal
marketing demands.

2 Fuzzy integrated evaluation model analysis

We can use fuzzy logic process to build fuzzy integrated evaluating model for the
above factors in Fig.1. The following part shows process steps.

First step, setting a total goal set of factors $U=\{u_1, u_2, u_3\}$,and a set of sub-
goal factors $u_1=\{u_{11}, u_{12}, u_{13}, u_{14}\}, u_2=\{u_{21}, u_{22}, ..., u_{27}\}$; and a set of
evaluation $V=\{v_1, v_2, ..., v_5\}$ separately equal to very good, good, common,
bad, very bad.

The second step, setting a fuzzy set $A=\{a_1, a_2, a_3\}$, a_i is weight of u_i.

The third step, setting R is fuzzy mapping function from U to V. $R(u_i)=(r_{i1}, r_{i2}, ..., r_{ij})$ is a member of R, it's subset of V, when the condition $0 \le r_{ij} \le 1$, it
describes that u_i is a membership of v_j.

In a finally, it is so called integrated evaluation exchanged matrix as a single
factor evaluated matrix $R=(r_{ij})$, which combines all of vector quantities from fuzzy
mapping function R. So it gets first fuzzy integrated evaluation model using fuzzy
matrix mixed operations[4].

$$B=A \cdot R=(b_1, \ b_2, \ ...,b_j)$$

$$b_j = \sum_{i=1}^{5} a_j r_{ij}, \ j=1,2,3,4,5; \quad b_j \text{ is a function of } r_{ij}.$$

It will be expended to form a multi-hierarchy fuzzy integrated evaluation model. This means that it makes initial model to apply multi-factors, the bottom layer's result becomes closed to above layer's input until the first layer.

About to obtain fuzzy evaluation matrix, first step is to select website owner and customers expression and some experts as an evaluation team, and then to evaluate single factor according to the second layer from the index system. It can use questionnaire tables to get single factor fuzzy evaluation matrix by surveying and analysis and statistic these tables.

$$R = \begin{bmatrix} r_{i11} & r_{i12} & \cdots & r_{i1n} \\ r_{i21} & r_{i22} & \cdots & r_{i2n} \\ \vdots & \vdots & \cdots & \vdots \\ r_{im1} & r_{im2} & \cdots & r_{imn} \end{bmatrix}, \quad (i=1, \ 2)$$

m is element number of the set of evaluation u_i

n is element number of the set evaluation V.

The integrated evaluation process is as following:

$$B_i = A_i \circ R_i = (b_{i1}, \ b_{i2}, \ b_{i3}, \ b_{i4}, \ b_{i5}), \quad R = \begin{bmatrix} B_1 \\ B_2 \end{bmatrix}$$

$$B = A \circ R = A \circ \begin{bmatrix} B_1 \\ B_2 \end{bmatrix} = A \begin{bmatrix} A_1 \circ R_1 \\ A_2 \circ R_2 \end{bmatrix} = (b_1, \ b_2, \ b_3, \ b_4, \ b_5)$$

3 The evaluating process of marketing performance

3.1 Calculating weights by hierarchy analysis methodology

During the process of fuzzy integrated evaluation, weights significantly affect the final results. Different weights sometimes achieve different results. We compute eigenvetor to get factors' weights from comparing evaluating matrix built by experts evaluation method and hierarchy analysis method. These methodologies can effectively correct the wrong real decisions and prevent from subjective minds. And also it can use weights to deal with filtering and restoration of evaluating matrix.

In Fig.1, there are four layers including: the final evaluating layer, factors evaluating layer, evaluating index layer and evaluating index sub-layer. Due to evaluating index sub-layer almost similar to evaluating index layer, the sub-layer only affects the four index layers. Therefore, about considering integrated evaluation, the evaluating index sub-layer belongs to evaluating index layer.

Setting the finial evaluating goal is A, factors evaluating layer has two elements: external environment and internal planning marked as A_1, A_2;

evaluating index layer belongs to A_1, A_2, marked as C_{11}, C_{12}, C_{13}, C_{14}; C_{21}, C_{22}, ..., C_{27} without crossing situation. The method's goal is to assign weights by relative their importance under the elements A_k (k=1,2).

(1) Ascertain weights from the factors in the first layer

Using average weight to calculate A_1, A_2 with final evaluating goal A given by experts team (including researchers, customers, field managers and other persons in this fields) A=(0.35, 0.65) (data from some relative questionaries).

(2)Calculating weights of A_1, A_2 in the factors layer

As we know, according to 1-9 marking methods, it can compare some degree importance of the indexes of A_1, A_2 each other. And then it builds weight table from consulting table by experts team.

$(C_{1j})_{4 \times 4}$ and $(C_{2m})_{7 \times 7}$ form decision matrix (j=1,2,3,4 ; m=1,2,3,4,5,6,7). For instance:

$$A_1 = (C_{1j})_{4 \times 4} = \begin{bmatrix} 1 & 1 & 1/5 & 1/7 \\ 1 & 1 & 1/3 & 1/7 \\ 5 & 3 & 1 & 1/3 \\ 7 & 7 & 3 & 1 \end{bmatrix}, \quad A_2 = (C_{2m})_{7 \times 7}$$

By calculating maximum features roots of deciding matrix and eigenvector, it sets that maximum eigenvector is λ_{max}, the standard eigenvector of λ_{max} is $W = (W_1, W_2, ..., W_n)^T$, then W_1, W_2, ..., W_n mapping index C_{11}, C_{12}, C_{13}, C_{14} and index C_{21}, C_{22}, ..., C_{27} as weights of importance degree to A_1, A_2.

And then inspecting consistence:

$$CI = \frac{\lambda_{max} - n}{n - 1}, \quad CR = CI / RI < 0.01$$

It can satisfy consistence between the two matrices.

At last, the model gives the weights result as following:

A_1=(0.15, 0.15, 0.2, 0.5), A_2=(0.2, 0.15, 0.10, 0.15, 0.15, 0.10, 0.15)

(3)Calculating weights from index layer

Setting current layer elements C_1, C_2, ..., C_m by above layer A_1, A_2 to weights vector $W_i = (W_{i1}, W_{i2}, ..., W_{in})^T$, i=1, 2, ..., m. And the elements C_1, C_2, ..., C_m related to weights a_1, a_2, ..., a_m, so the current elements A_1, A_2, ..., A_n integrated weights are the following:

$$\sum_{i=1}^{m} a_i W_{i1}, \quad \sum_{i=1}^{m} a_i W_{i2}, \quad ..., \quad \sum_{i=1}^{m} a_i W_{in}$$

3.2 Construct fuzzy evaluation matrix

Through the survey of affecting degree for some e-commerce websites, it shows the evaluating results seeing statistic table 1.

Table 1. The survey table of single factor evaluation

evaluation index	very good	good	common	bad	very bad
strategy					
standard					
credit rules					
path					
interesting					
sorted-information					
security					
quick-access					
framework					
styles					
function services					

Notes: R_1 is a matrix of 5 Rows 4 Columns, R_2 is a matrix of 5 Rows 7 Columns.

Through $A_1 = (0.15, 0.15, 0.2, 0.5)$ to obtain evaluating vector from external environment elements: $B_1 = A_1 \circ R_1$

Through $A_2 = (0.2, 0.15, 0.10, 0.15, 0.15, 0.10, 0.15)$ to obtain evaluating vector from internal planning elements: $B_2 = A_2 \circ R_2$

In general, the model can be operated to evaluate and check real websites. The article gives some useful factors and analysis process based on the model.

4 Conclusions

It is an important way that firms use some evaluating factors of marketing performance under web-based e-commerce to improve some marketing strategies. And it can use the evaluation process and results to analyse firms' competition abilities. They use the evaluation results to plan their websites and consider advanced minds by comparing with other firms' websites. However, because web-based e-commerce is a complex system of multi-attributes and the system is affected by customers' psychology, only one evaluating value can not express practical firm's good or bad totally and precisely. As we know, the index system has some degree fuzzification. Therefore, the fuzzy evaluating method combined with hierarchy analytic method is very useful to help firms from the quantities and quality analysis to evaluate marketing performance on e-commerce websites scientifically and systematically.

Acknowledgement

83.   This work is supported by the project of science and technology brainstorm of Heilongjiang Province: "Research on establishing modern logistic distribution center of characteristic products in Heilongjiang Province". (GB05D202-3)

References

1. W.J .Wang, Analysis and Comment on Study and Application of EC Websites
Evaluation, Information Science, 2003 (6), 639~642
2. S.W Zhou. X.J. Guo, A.P Sun., H.H Tang, Primary Discussion of Classification
and Evaluation of EC Web Station, *Chinese Journal of Management Science*,
VoL8. Special Issue, November. 2000 (11), 748~754
3. DR. Y.N. Feng, A new competition-professional evaluation and analysis report
on websites, http://www.jingzhengli.cn/pingjia.htm
4. S.L. Chen, J.G. Li, etc..*The Theory and Application of Fuzzy Assessment*,
Science publishing company, 2005.November, 235~241

The Simulation and Analysis of e-Business Model
A Case Study of Witkey

Yang-feng Ou, Hongdan Zhao, Guanglu Zheng,and Lan Wang
School of Business,Shantou University
NO.243, Daxue Road ,Shantou,Guangdong, China
{yangfeng , hdzhao1, g_glzheng, lwang4} @stu.edu.cn

Abstract. Based on the value-oriented ontology approach, we present a simulation analysis with the e^3-value software, and study the Witkey business model with structural analysis modeling method. The feasibility analysis on Witkey business model has been proved theoretically through the adjustment and estimate of parameters. Finally, the paper concludes with practical recommendations for business model innovation.

1   Introduction

The business model is one of the important factors to influence firm performance. It explains the business logic and the way of earning, as well as how to maintain the enterprise's competitive advantage. So far, we still hardly attain the conclusive definition in the business model literature. Eisenmann (2002) thought the concept of business model is widespread used but short defined [1]. Timmers (2000) deemed the scholar usually not be able to give any definition for the management mode [2]. But existing research about innovative motive and formed mechanism of the enterprise business model also are difficult to form a systemic, universal suitable theoretical analyze frame, for example, Weng Junyi (2004) defined business model as a value analysis system in three-dimensional space through the segment of the inside and outside of the enterprise operation environment. Value proposition, value support and value maintenance as three components of the value analysis system have provided the ideological method for business model design and analysis [3]. Luo Min (2005) explained the driving force for enterprise innovation from the economic perspective with the method of rent of enterprise [4]. Gao Chuang (2006) carried on a systemic and clear explanation from the view of value chain innovative theory to the realizable way of enterprise business model's innovation [5].

Please use the following format when citing this chapter:

Ou, Y., Zhao, H., Zheng, G., Wang, L., 2007, in IFIP International Federation for Information Processing, Volume 251, Integration and Innovation Orient to E-Society Volume1, Wang, W. (Eds), (Boston: Springer), pp. 551-559.

The study above mentioned mostly can be regarded as a theoretically analysis tool for business model innovation with the qualitative methods. We here think that it is necessary to do simulation analysis with the help of relevant simulation software to concisely illustrate the business model innovation and evolution. We can further explore the guideline for business model implementation and innovation. Simulation modeling based on the e^3-value ontology, can demonstrate the essence of e-business, value creation on the one hand, and give the concise description to business model on the other hand. So we can reason about that creative ideas for the study of e-business model can be derived from the application of the e^3-vallue simulation modeling.

2 The modeling analysis for e-business model

2.1 The e^3-value ontology for e-business

An e-business model gives a precise representation, which can be used to reach agreement among the stakeholders and can be used during the building of a commerce system as a specification. The key essence of e-business model is about who offer what to whom, and the expectative benefit. So, value, the core concept in e-business, plays the role of the linkage among various elements [6]. And value is also the key element of the e^3-value ontology, which aims at identifying exchanges of value objects between the actors in a business case. It also supports profitability analysis of business cases [7]. The ontology was designed to contain a minimal set of concepts and relations to make it easy to grasp for the intended users. In the case of e^3-value models without actor compositions a value exchange is a pair of value ports of opposite directions belonging to different actors. It represents one or more potential trades of value objects between these value ports. A value activity is an operation that can be carried out in an economically profitable way for at least one actor [7, 8, 13, and 14].

Therefore, we can deconstruct the value elements to study the innovation of an existing business value model [15]. And e^3-value ontology takes the value elements as the negative factors to the original value model, mainly including the following three components: (1) Value activity deconstruction: Find 'smaller' value activities, which can be assigned to different actors; (2) Value port deconstruction: Find ports with 'smaller' value objects; (3) Value interface deconstruction: Split up interfaces with ports > 2 into interfaces with fewer ports.

2.2 Theoretical feasibility analysis on e-business model

The e^3-value ontology not only provides the framework for e-business value model analysis and innovation, but also sets the foundation for us to simulation modeling. Then, before the application, we need to analyze the feasibility of a specific e-business model from the e^3-value ontology point of view. Then the following two questions need to be considered [6]:

Firstly, whether the value proposition of one business model is feasible. This refers to the existing meaning of an e-business model. Those practicable value propositions must be able to explicitly display the way of value creation and value exploitation, and has the ability to offer value for different stakeholders, such as customers, partners or employees. If this value proposition is accepted by the relevant actors, it in a sense shows its value for this e-business model. As far as the Witkey business model is concerned, the value proposition is to enhance the value of the knowledge. This value proposition is put forward on the condition of the improving environment for Witkey business model, the need for knowledge communication, as well as the situation of specific vertical website and comprehensive website co-existing, which could provide the feasibility theoretically [9].

Secondly, whether the process for implementation of this value proposition is consistent with business logic. That is, when we have solved the first question, the following question is about its feasibility in the existing business environment. For this question, we should consider about the value support and value maintenance in this business model. Value proposition, value support and value maintenance are interrelated with each other, value support has the role of promoting and keeping the value proposition in order. Value maintenance is contributed to the achievement of the formers. Many e-business application results have indicated that not all the advanced business model innovation is valuable in practice. An advanced and effective value proposition, if without proper value support and value maintenance, will not be implemented successfully. Even though the value proposition of Witkey is feasible theoretically, but if no suitable technologies support the relevant systems for offer, searching, knowledge database reserving, order-processing and trading, and on other business, such as the visiting volume, advertising, communication as well as the value-added activities, its value proposition of knowledge appreciation will not be achieved.

After the analysis of the theoretical feasibility, we can rely on the framework based on the e^3-value ontology to make structural analysis, integrate the relevant elements in the model, and collect the data needed to make simulation analysis.

3   The simulation analysis of Witkey e-business model

3.1   Brief introduction of Witkey business model

Witkey refers to those people who sell their intangible assets (intellectual goods) or make knowledge-related business on the internet. Witkey business model uses the wisdom of human to seek the solution for newly emergent events, which imply that knowledge makes money, which incorporate the value proposition of the Witkey business model [10].

Witkey websites coordinate multiply application systems, such as the inquiry and quoted price, search, knowledge database, order and the transaction system to achieve their value proposition. The tenders submit questions through inquiry and quoted price system, seek for the answer in knowledge database through search system. If no proper knowledge is available, relevant experts would offer the answers through the order system, and the website will add the new knowledge into the database to avoid the repetition of knowledge creation. The transaction system will finish the knowledge acquisition. The knowledge database system consists of variety of sub-knowledge database and is managed by different expert groups and Internet service providers. Internet service providers can benefit from every business trade, and also through advertisement, communication and other value-added business to support the model operation [9]. At present, Witkey website model can mainly be classified as two types: member score and cash transaction model. For reason of their similarity in the essence and mechanism, we mainly study the second model to carry out the simulation analysis.

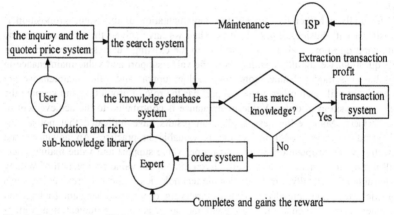

Fig. 1. Cash transaction Witkey website business model

According to the value activities of the Witkey business model, we can establish the Witkey business model with the e³-value software which is designed by Gordijn, as shown in figure 2.

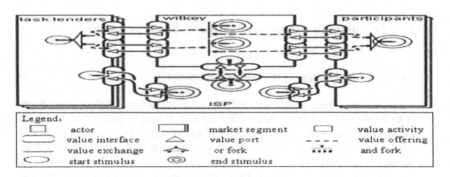

Fig. 2. The e^3-value model of Witkey business model

At present, Witkey business model emerge in our country in short time, they are still in the period of market entrance stage. The five key modules, the quoted price system, the search system, the knowledge database system, the order system and the transaction system, are not mature. The further cultivation is required, so we did not display the value activities detail in our model.

3.2   Value calculation

We choose an existing Witkey website, and give the presumption, say 1000 tenders pay 1000 RMB per person and 1000 task actors are involved. Every person average publishes and engages activities 5 times every year, and tenders get the satisfying answer with the likelihood of 4/5. The Witkey website will benefit 20% discount (no matter whether he or she can get the right works or not). Besides, the three parties all need pay for internet access service: the single user should pay 1000 RMB per year, and witkey website should pay 15000 RMB per year. We assume that the witkey website need 100000 RMB as the primary investment, other management and maintenance fee is 10000 RMB per year.

In order to take the non-monetary value in business environment and Witkey business model into consideration, we need further investigation for the real situation. We assume that tenders get more value from the right answer than the monetary value they have to pay. Participants get more than what they have to spend. The amount of the money, which witkey website and users pay the ISP, is less than the value they will get from the internet service. We assume that task tenders get the non-monetary value equal to 1500 RMB per task, the non-monetary value from the internet service equal 1300 RMB. Task participants spend the non-monetary cost to finish the task equal 100 RMB every time. The non-monetary value from the internet service equal 1200 RMB; Witkey websites gain the non-monetary value from ISP equal 20000 RMB per year. We input the parameters into the model; calculate the profitability sheet for witkey website, task tenders and participants as shown in table 1, 2, 3.

The profit sheets below have indicated that the amount of profit of Witkey website, task tenders, and participants is 895000 RMB, 2100 RMB, and 2900 RMB respectively. All of them gain the positive revenue, which show that Witkey business model has its feasibility in some sense.

Table 1. The profit table of Witkey website

Interface	Port	Transfer	Occurrences	Valuation	Value	Total
MONEY , ISP service			1		5000	
	out: MONEY	MONEY	1	15000	-15000	
	in: ISP service	(all transfers)	1	20000	20000	
MONEY, satisfaction			4000		-3200000	
	out: MONEY	MONEY	4000	800	-3200000	
	in: satisfaction	(all transfers)	4000	0	0	
satisfaction, MONEY			4000		4000000	
	out: satisfaction	(all transfers)	4000	0	0	
	in: MONEY	MONEY	4000	1000	4000000	
MONEY, dissatisfaction			1000		0	
	out: MONEY	MONEY	1000	0	0	
	in: dissatisfaction	(all transfers)	1000	0	0	
dissatisfaction, MONEY			1000		200000	
	out: dissatisfaction	(all transfers)	1000	0	0	
	in: MONEY	MONEY	1000	200	200000	
INVESTMENT					100000	
EXPENSES					10000	
total for actor						895000

Table 2. The profit table of task tenders

Interface	Port	Transfer	Occurrences	Valuation	Value	Total
MONEY , ISP service			1		300	
	out: MONEY	MONEY	1	1000	-1000	
	in: ISP service	(all transfers)	1	1300	1300	
MONEY, satisfaction			4		2000	
	out: MONEY	MONEY	4	1500	6000	
	in: satisfaction	(all transfers)	4	1000	-4000	
MONEY, dissatisfaction			1		-200	
	out: MONEY	MONEY	1	200	-200	
	in: dissatisfaction	(all transfers)	1	0	0	
COUNT	1000					
total for actor						2100

Table 3. The profit table of task participants

Interface	Port	Transfer	Occurrences	Valuation	Value	Total
MONEY , ISP service			1		200	
	out: MONEY	MONEY	1	1000	-1000	
	in: ISP service	(all transfers)	1	1200	1200	
satisfaction , MONEY			4		2800	
	out: satisfaction	(all transfers)	4	0	0	
	out: satisfaction	EXPENSE S	4	100	-400	
	in: MONEY	MONEY	4	800	3200	
dissatisfaction , MONEY			1		-100	
	out: dissatisfactio n	(all transfers)	1	0	0	
	out: dissatisfactio n	EXPENSE S	1	100	-100	
	in: MONEY	MONEY	1	0	0	
COUNT	1000					
total for actor						2900

3.3   Value analysis and the relevant countermeasures

We should pay emphasize to the logic behind the website well-running, not just give the simple evaluation to a website, so as to learn the effective way for e-business model practice and innovation [11]. We here don't mean the real estimate for the profitability with the profit sheet. The meanings of these data here lie in seeking for business opportunity and the condition for the opportunity [6]. So we can further reveal the real practicing process and the mechanism of the e-business model, and meanwhile contribute to our evaluation as well as seeking for the more effective innovative measure based on the e^3-value elements deconstruction. As the result of the estimation for the profitability of the e-business model above, we can recognize the existing problems and the relevant countermeasures:

First, the existing Witkey models are lack of the brand and the social influence, the quantity of Witkey participant are not enough, and cannot achieve the economies of scale. Some phenomena, such as knowledge-lacking about the witkey website, the low degree of the trust, and also the fraudulent events, have driven some brilliant witkey away [12]. In our opinion, witkey website should undertake the deconstruction in value activities and value ports, through some value behaviors activities, such as technologies-updating, management improving, content expanding. We could distribute some small value activities to participants for their value-adding profit. Through the deconstruction of the value ports, such as mass media propagandizing and the cooperation with other large website, they could seek for new ports with relevant value objects. We assume that the witkey website cost 100000 RMB per year for the content expanding and advertisement; consequently it attracts 500 new tenders and 500 participants. Then the website could gain 1295000 RMB.

Second, some problems, such as, low level of property management and running regulation, choke point of trust and intellectual property protection, are still existing. At present, network intellectual property and income tax which is brought by Witkey website still have no conclusion. Further more, the special transaction model of Witkey website made the intelligence achievement, which is provided by Witkey is extremely easy to be embezzled and imitated. How to coordinate trade operation of Witkey website have become the urgent issues that need to be solved [12]. It needs the Witkey website start with the deconstruction of value interface: through value interface deconstruction (improve its value activities of search system and knowledge database system) to split up interfaces into small interfaces with fewer ports. In other words, it may be attribute to avoid the repeated creation of knowledge with the help of searching system and knowledge database system, further save the trading expense, which not only increase utility of participants, but also can cause the decrease of website's management expense and increase the number of participants. We assume the expense that the Witkey website spend to enhance value activities quality of searching system and knowledge database system is 100000 RMB per year, which cause the participant's cost reduced 20 RMB for every time. Meanwhile, relevant expense reduction in management for 5000 RMB per year, and the increase of 500 tenders and 500 participants, then the website could benefit 1400000 RMB and participants' profit increases to 3000 RMB.

References

1. T. R. Eisenmann, *Internet Business Models: Text and Case* , McGraw-Hill Press, New York(2002).
2. P. Timmers , "Electronic Commerce: Strategies and Models for Business-to-Business Trading", *John Wiley & Sons*, Ltd Press, England(2000).
3. J. Y. Weng, Business Models Innovation , *Economy & Management Publishing House Press*, Beijing (2004).
4. M. Luo, T. Zeng and S. W. Zhou, "Business Model Innovation: Based on the Explanation for Rents", *China Industrial Economy* , No.7,73-81(2005).
5. C. Gao , X. Guan, "Achievement Ways and Evolutional Institution of Business Model Innovation—a Theoretical Explanation Based on the Innovation of Value Chain", *China Industrial Economy,* No.11, 83-90(2006)
6. R. Fu, "Based on Value to Express and Analyze the e-business mode-Case on the Knowledge resources website", *Science and Technology Management Research* No.8, 204 – 206(2006).
7. Z.Baida, J.Gordijn , A. Z. Morch ,H. Sale and H. Akkermans, "Ontology—based analysis of e-service bundles for networked enterprises", In the Proceedings of the 17th Bled eCommerce Conference. Bled, Slovenia (2004).
8. J.Gordijn and H. Akkermans, "Ontology-Based Operators for e-Business Model De-and Re-construction", In the Proceedings of the First International Conference on Knowledge Capture, Canada, October 21-23, 60–67 (2001).
9. X. He, "The New Topic of Saidi Consultant—Let the Knowledge Revalue", *E-business*, No.8, 36 (2006).

10. P. Zhao, "Try to Analyze the Present Situation and Development of Witkey Mode", Journal of Party School of CPC Zhengzhou Municipal Committee No.6, 123-125 (2006).

11. A. Afuah, C. L.Tucci, *Internet Business Models and Strategies: Text and Cases* ,Tsinghua University Press, Beijing (2002).

12. L. Li , " IT: The Witkey Walks to Us Quickly", *Business Culture*, No.1, 72-74 (2007).

13. J. Gordijn and H. Akkermans, "Value based requirements engineering: Exploring innovative E-business idea", *Requirements Engineering Journal* , No.2, 114-134(2003).

14. J.Gordijn, A.Osterwalder and Y.Pigneur, Comparing two Business Model Ontologies for Designing e-Business Models and Value Constellations, Proceedings of the 18th BLED conference (e-Integration in Action), D. R. Vogel, P. Walden, J. Gricar, G. Lenart (eds.),University of Maribor, CDrom (2005).

15. J.Gordijn and H. Akkermans, "e^3-value: Design and Evaluation of e-Business Models", *IEEE Intelligent Systems*, Special Issue on e-Business No.4, 11-17(2001).

Payment Scheme for Multi-Party Cascading P2P Exchange

Yichun Liu and Zemao Zhao
Hangzhou Dianzi University
Hangzhou 310018, China
liuyichun@126.com

Abstract. As a decentralized technology, P2P architecture arises as a new model for distributed computing and transaction in the last few years, consequently there is a need for a scheme to incorporate payment services to enable electronic commerce transaction via P2P systems. In this paper, the cascading sale model is described for multi-party P2P transaction, an efficient pricing and routing scheme is proposed for multi-party P2P transaction, and a new onion payment scheme is proposed, which can ensure that each middleman and digital content owner can obtain the payments due to them.

1 Introduction

P2P systems are network where peer nodes communicate and transport information directly each other. Unlike the conventional client-server model, a peer node of P2P network may act as both a client and a server simultaneously to share files or computing powers. It can request, serve, or relay services as needed. A major differentiating factor of P2P from traditional models is the lack of central management and control. This very important characteristic offers the ability to create efficient, scalable, and persistent services by taking advantage of the fully distributed nature of the systems.

In traditional electronic commerce transaction, some parties serve as vendors, who only sell goods, and the others act as buyers, who only purchase goods. However, in P2P transaction environment, peers serve as both vendors and buyers. A peer who has bought digital content might sell it to other for earning middleman commission.

Please use the following format when citing this chapter:

Liu, Y., Zhao, Z., 2007, in IFIP International Federation for Information Processing, Volume 251, Integration and Innovation Orient to E-Society Volume1, Wang, W. (Eds), (Boston: Springer), pp. 560-567.

Most of the current e-commerce researches are based on simple electronic transaction model. This is quite a distance away from what an electronic marketplace is envisioned to be. Nowadays, most of them are limited to simple exchange of funds and merchandise, and not sufficient for the complex transaction scenarios. Electronic commercial exchanges may be stymied because of a lack of a proper transaction model or protocol.

In this paper, we aim to propose a cascading transaction model for electronic commerce, in which multiple brokers relay the goods and payment between the goods owner and consumer according to the chained path. The related works are introduced in the next section; the cascading transaction model is described in section 3; the policy for transaction chain and price negotiation is discussed in section 4; the cascading payment model is proposed in section 5.

2 Related Work

A number of research projects have engaged in P2P computing and most have been focused on efficient resource location and load balancing; very few have addressed the need of payments in P2P environment.

An early P2P payment scheme is provided in [1], which relies on a fully trusted on-line escrow server. In this scheme, an escrow server is used as trusted thirty parties, which deal with the protocol commitment, transmission of decryption key and payment. The escrow server bearing too much burden will be inefficient and it might become the bottleneck of payment system, so the scheme has poor scalability.

Another P2P payment system is provided in [2], where a stamped digital note is introduced as token of transaction. The digital note is produced by the specific vendor and is stamped by the broker, and it can only be received and cashed by its issuer, so the scheme has still poor scalability.

The P2P payment scheme provided in [3] inherits the idea of the stamped digital note and delegates the vendor role to the agent during the payment phase, where the buyer peer does not need special digital notes for each vendor peer. Instead, he can buy digital goods from several vendor peers by interacting with only one agent who represents these vendor peers. In the scheme, the stamped digital note can only be used by a few vendors and an on-line third party is introduced, who is a heavy server in fact.

In the P2P payment protocol provided in [4], the buyer obtains the broker coin from the broker, and the vendor coin is produced by the vendor. The buyer and the vendor exchange their digital coins, and then buyer pays vendor coins to buy the goods from the vendor. The protocol is anonymous and secure, but it is neither practical nor convenient that the buyer must obtain special coin from different vendor before per transaction.

Ppay is a micropayment scheme for P2P environment [5], which presents the concept of floating and self-managed currency to greatly reduce broker involvement. The currency is allowed to float from one node to another without involving a centralized broker, and all security related to a coin, except for when the coin is first created or cashed. This currency is practical and efficient, but the related payment protocol is not presented.

Some complex transaction models are provided in [6], where the multi-party cascading transaction model is described as a transaction tree. The paper proposed some important requirement for complex transaction model, but the payment scheme has not been presented.

3 Cascading Transaction

With the globalization of economy, the commodity manufacturers wish selling their products over the world. It is necessary that goods producers sell their goods with the help of the middlemen. Usually, the hierarchical sale system includes the following levels: the manufacturer, the general agents, the district agents, the wholesalers, and the retailers. In the traditional chained model, the broker nodes are distributed in term of directed tree structure, and each node has only parent node. The traditional hierarchical sale model is described as Figure1.

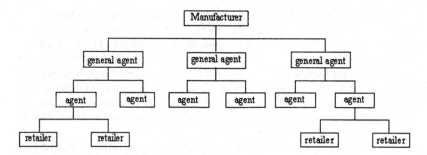

Fig. 1. Traditional Model for Multi-Party Cascading Sale

In the P2P cascading model, the broker nodes are peer-to-peer, and distributed in term of mesh structure, in which there are multiple path between any two nodes. In this model, theoretically unlimited parties can participate in the whole transaction. Among these parties, there should be a customer who is an end buyer and a supplier who is an end seller. The other parties are brokers who buy and resell the products.

The P2P model for multi-party cascading transaction is described as Figure2.

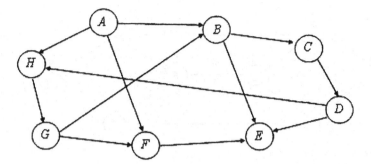

Fig. 2. Traditional Model for Multi-Party Cascading Sale

In the transaction shown as Figure2, the goods owner A might sell its goods along the path $A \rightarrow B \rightarrow C \rightarrow D \rightarrow E$, and it might also sell the goods along the path $A \rightarrow H \rightarrow G \rightarrow F \rightarrow E$, the path $A \rightarrow B \rightarrow E$, or the path $A \rightarrow F \rightarrow E$. The node B might obtain goods from A and might obtain other goods from G. The P2P members choose the path for obtaining suitable goods by considering the goods price and the trust of other peers, instead of regular hierarchical relation in traditional model.

In traditional commerce model, the customers only contact with the retailers, instead of contacting with the original goods owner. Usually, the items of P2P exchange are digital contents, which are easy to be duplicated and counterfeited. The P2P members are dynamical and changeable, so the payments should be distributed among both middle agent and goods owner, and it should be avoided that one party take the payment illegally which belongs to the others. In a P2P transaction, it should be guaranteed that the goods owner can obtain the royalties and the middleman brokers should get the commissions.

4 Exchange Chain And Price Negotiation

In multi-party cascading transaction, the goods price depends on the exchange chain that the goods and payment is transferred. Optimal exchange chain should be determined before the scheme is designed for P2P multi-party cascading transaction, so that the customers pay out at the lowest price.

When a P2P member wants to buy goods, it will send the purchase request to its neighbour node for searching the vendors. Each node which has received the request will relay the purchase message to their neighbour, until the goods owner receives the request. A larger P2P system has a mesh-like topological structure, in which there are many chain from a customer node to a merchant node, and it is possible that several merchant node have the requested goods.

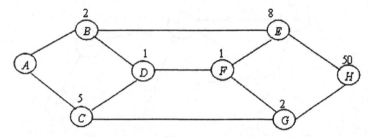

Fig. 3. Node Path of P2P Exchange

An example of multi-party P2P transaction is shown as Figure3. The nodes A, B, C, D, E, F, G and H denote the P2P members. A is an end buyer and H is the owner of the goods in the example. The weight on the node H denotes the royalty of the owner, and the weight on other nodes denotes the commissions of middleman agents. A's exchange cost can be expressed the sum of the weight on nodes along a path from A to H. There are different paths from A to H as follows: the sum of weight is 60 on the path $A{\rightarrow}B{\rightarrow}E{\rightarrow}H$; the sum of weight is 57 on the path $A{\rightarrow}C{\rightarrow}G{\rightarrow}H$; the sum of weight on the path $A{\rightarrow}B{\rightarrow}D{\rightarrow}F{\rightarrow}E{\rightarrow}H$ is 62; the sum of weight on the path $A{\rightarrow}C{\rightarrow}D{\rightarrow}F{\rightarrow}G{\rightarrow}H$ is 59; the sum of weight on the path $A{\rightarrow}B{\rightarrow}D{\rightarrow}F{\rightarrow}G{\rightarrow}H$ is 56; the sum of weight on the path $A{\rightarrow}C{\rightarrow}D{\rightarrow}F{\rightarrow}E{\rightarrow}H$ is 65. The path is shortest and A pay at lowest cost when the route $A{\rightarrow}B{\rightarrow}D{\rightarrow}F{\rightarrow}G{\rightarrow}H$ is selected. Selecting the shortest exchange path means selecting the lowest price. A famous method is Dijkstra algorithm for computing the shortest path.

In the P2P multi-party transaction, the disclosure of exchange information might lead to the broker's loss. The middle brokers don't wish that their exchange information and its neighbour nodes are not known by other parties in the same chain. It would be possible in Figure 3 that B contacts with F directly instead of node D for obtaining more commissions if B learns that D would get the goods from F.

This problem can be resolved efficiently by the aid of public key cryptography. A customer C selects a public/private key pairs, and then multicasts the purchase request and digital certificate to its neighbor nodes. The request receivers will relay the received messages on and on, until the original goods owner O receives the purchase request and digital certificate.

There are multiple routes from the customer C to the goods owner O. If a route is $C{\rightarrow}A_m{\rightarrow}A_{m-1}{\rightarrow}... \rightarrow A_1{\rightarrow}O$, here A_i is the i-th middle broker between O and C, O sends its royalty to the adjacent broker node A_1.

$O{\rightarrow}A_1 : PK_C(O, [royalty]_O)$

A_1 send its commission information $commission_1$ and the message from O to A_1.

$A_1{\rightarrow}A_2 : PK_C(A_1, [commission_1]_{A_1}, PK_C(O, [royalty]_O))$

Similarly, each A_i sends the message from A_{i-1} and A_i's commission information $commission_i$ to A_{i+1}.

$A_i \rightarrow A_{i+1}$: $PK_C(A_i, [commission_i]_{A_i}, PK_C(A_{i-1}, [commission_{i-1}]_{A_{i-1}}, ... PK_C(O,$
$[royalty]_O)...))$, $i=1 \sim m-1$

At last, the vendor A_m sends the price list *price_list* to the buyer C.

$A_m \rightarrow C$: $price\_list = PK_C(A_m, [commission_m]_{A_m}, PK_C(A_{m-1},[commission_{m-1}]_{A_{m-1}},$
$..., PK_C(O, [royalty]_O)...))$

The item $PK_X (message)$ denotes the encryption of the message *message* with X's public key. $[message]_X$ includes two parts, the message *message* and the digital signature on it with X's private key.

The customer C decrypts the price list with its private key and obtains the nodes information on each path $\{A_m, A_{m-1}, ..., A_1, O\}$, the commission information $\{commission_m, commission_{m-1}, ..., commission_1\}$ for every brokers, and the royalty information *royalty*. C can calculates the shortest path from C to O and obtain the optimal scheme for selecting the exchange path and pricing the exchange.

In the above negotiation process, RSA algorithm is recommended for the encryption and signature algorithm. DSA is an alternative algorithm for message signature. When the secure algorithms such as RSA or DSA are adopted, the malicious could not decode encrypted message or counterfeit valid signature.

5 Cascading Payment Model

A typical multi-party cascading payment system includes multiple parties: a customer C, a goods owner O, multiple intermediary peers $A_1, A_2, A_3, ...A_{m-1}$, A_m. The intermediaries buy the goods and sell it for obtaining the commissions.

The payments shall be distributed among peers (on a royalty-commission basis), where the content owner receives a fixed amount of the payment value. To ensure only the owner can claim payment for royalty, the payment for royalty shall be encapsulated for the owner at the payment origin. Content needs to be tagged with the owner's identity to enable this. Also, only payment meant for a peer may be redeemed by that peer, this requires the use of encryption techniques being applied. This enables the payments meant for content owners to be stored on other peers without them being wrongly redeemed.

We propose a new onion payment scheme to ensure that a goods owner can receive the royalty and all intermediaries can receive the commissions. In this scheme, the buyer peer encapsulates the payments for royalty and commissions into an onion payment package, and then transfers it to goods owner along the selected exchange path. Each intermediary peers on the exchange path strips the skin of onion payment package and gets its commission, until the owner obtain its royalty. The onion payment can be taken as a kind of onion route with payment information.

Let A_0 denotes the owner O, and *payment_i* denotes the payment for the commission of each intermediary peer A_i for $i=1 \sim m$. When the payment is transferred along the path $C \rightarrow A_m \rightarrow A_{m-1} \rightarrow ... \rightarrow A_1 \rightarrow O$, the onion payment package is as following:

$Onion\_Payment_0 = PK_{A_0} (payment_0)$

$Onion\_Payment_i = PK_{A_i}(payment_i, A_{i-1}, Onion\_Payment_{i-1}), i=1,2, ..., m$

The customer C encapsulate the onion payment package $Onion\_Payment_m$ and sends it to vendor A_m.

$C \rightarrow A_m$: $Onion\_Payment_m = PK_{Ai}(payment_m, A_{m-1}, Onion\_Payment_{m-1})$

A_m strip the exterior layer of onion payment package and get the payment for its commission $payment_i$ and the identifier of next broker A_{m-1}. Similarly, each A_i gets its payment $payment_i$ and then sends the onion payment message $Onion\_Payment_{i-1}$ to A_{i-1}.

$A_i \rightarrow A_{i-1}$: $Onion\_Payment_{i-1} = PK_{Ai-1}(payment_{i-1}, A_{i-2}, Onion\_Payment_{i-2})$
$$i = m \sim 2$$

At last, A_1 send the payment $payment_0$ for royalty to the owner O.

$A_1 \rightarrow O$: $PK_{A0}\ (payment_0)$

By using onion payment package with public key cryptography system, each exchange party can obtain its due, and no one can intercept the payment for other party.

The onion payment technology can guarantee the anonymity of payment information. By using onion payment technology for exchange payment, each broker can only get and learn its own payment information but it can't obtain the other's payment information by unpacking the payment package. The onion payment is efficient for multi-party cascading payment in complex exchange environment.

6 Conclusion

Nowadays most of researches on electronic commerce are focused on the simple exchange mode. Multi-party cascading exchange is a typical model of electronic commerce transaction. In this paper, the cascading exchange mode is described for multi-party P2P transaction, a new optimum strategy is presented for pricing and routing in multi-party P2P transaction, and the onion payment scheme is proposed so that the goods owner can obtain its royalty and each middleman broker can obtain its due commission in the complex multi-party transaction. By introducing public key cryptography system, our scheme is secure, and no one can illegally decode and counterfeit the confidential information or intercept the payment due to other peers.

Acknowledgments

This research was supported by the the Scientific Research Fund of Zhejiang Provincial Education Department under Grant No. 20060239.

References

1. B. Horne, Escrow Services and Incentives in Peer-to-peer Networks, Proceedings of the 3rd ACM conference on Electronic Commerce, 85-94 (2001).

2. L. Anantharaman, *An Efficient and Practical Peer-to-peer E-payment System*, Manuscript(2002).

3. J. A. Onieva, *Practical Service Charge for Peer-to-peer Content Distribution*, Springer-Verlag ,112-123 (2003).

4. P. Daras, A Novel Peer-to-peer Payment Protocol, *Proceedings of the EUROCON '2003,* 2-6 (2003).

5. B.Yang, Ppay: micropayments for peer-to-peer systems, *Proceedings of the 10th ACM conference on Computer and communication security,* 300 – 310 (2003).

6. G. Wang, Models and protocol structures for software agent based complex e-commerce transactions, *Springer-Verlag* , 121–131(2001).

A Research of Value-Net Based Business Model and Operating of M-Commerce

Yingliang Wu*, Chin E. Lin, Haosu Wu

School of e-Business, South China University of Technology, Guangzhou
510006, China
*e-mail: bmylwu@scut.edu.cn

Abstract. Recent advances in Internet and e-commerce have led industry to reengineer their organizational structures and value chains. One of the most prominent trends in this change is to conduct work and operation in the distributed or virtual environments. A new kind of business model, termed as value-net, is emerging. In this paper, the business and system mode from the value-net system is studied and proposed. The feature of this business model suitable for Mobile Commerce (M-Commerce) is analyzed on the basis of value-net. The ecosystems (ecology system) model based on value-net is presented for the M-Commerce with systematic structure, collaborate mode and working mechanism. A modified value-net based ecosystem for M-Commerce operators is proposed in this paper with practical case analysis.
Keywords: Collaborate Commerce (C-Commerce), Mobile Commerce (M-Commerce), Mobile Business Operator (MBP), Value-Net, Business Model, Ecosystems (Ecology System)

1   Introduction

The rapid development of information modernization and e-commerce (or e-business, EB) has caused the significant and deep changes [1-2] of management concept, method, system and business model. It also has caused the production and development of the new type business model and operating mechanism, challenging traditional supply chain management and value chain model [2]. As impacts to a lot of industries or enterprises, the management idea, management orientation, strategy implementation and technology strategy have made great changes to meet the new environment. People in the advancing front have already realized that traditional supply chain management (SCM), commercial mode and value creation mechanism of the value chain can't meet the needs of development. So contracture and operation

Please use the following format when citing this chapter:

Wu, Y., Lin, C. E., Wu, H., 2007, in IFIP International Federation for Information Processing, Volume 251, Integration and Innovation Orient to E-Society Volume1, Wang, W. (Eds), (Boston: Springer), pp. 568-577.

mechanisms in industrial ecosystems need a reengineering or optimizing work. This change is challenging people's traditional concept in information modernization and e-commerce application. This has already permeated through technology and equipment into e-commerce to confront with personnel and organization refreshing strategy and management with new concept and new culture for information modernization. We must expand the vision, resurvey and explore industrial development.

Then we can set up value system and ecosystems of M-Commerce step by step in the industry, field and society, which is steady, harmonious, sustainable development and rich in competitiveness and vitality. The technology and business model of E-Commerce could be used to provide the enable technical basis and management system to build and operate value-net [3] of M-Commerce.

For example, telecommunication industry is in the advancing front of competitive, reforming. From the "Report on International Competitiveness of China's Telecommunication Industry in 2003" [4], China is worthy of the name "Telecommunication Power". The order of the international competitiveness of China's Telecommunication Industry is No. 2 in 31 countries. However, the order in "System Competitiveness" and "Corporation Competitiveness" are 27th and the last, correspondingly. This is because system construction of China telecommunication operators does not keep up with the national demand. The operation mechanism of corporation is not strong enough and the development of telecommunication market is not perfect or well organized. Viewing from the potential development in China, telecommunication corporations are world class, but their profitability, operation capacity, innovation ability and management ability of corporation are significant gaps below comparing to the advanced corporations. When the competitiveness of value system in China telecommunication industry is compared to the developed countries, there are many gaps in market environment, in industry competitiveness, and especially in operation capacity of telecommunication corporations. Therefore, we must innovate business model, integrate industry chain, and improve competitiveness in order to transform from "Telecommunication Power" to "Telecommunication Great Power".

This paper has three objectives:

(1) to analysis and discuss systematic perspective and methodology of value-net, to explain the mechanism characteristic and operating model of the new type business;

(2) to study and describe the mechanism and system of value creation in mobile commerce in the age of e-commerce (or e-business), to show the construction and model of Ecosystems of value-net;

(3) to identify the necessity and feasibility on building, developing and optimizing the value-net based ecosystems of M-Commerce by the real world case studies.

2   The System Model of Value-Net

2.1 The definition of value-net

As a new business model, the value-net was brought forward as a new management theory and method by Mercer Management Consulting Company in year 2000 [3]. By means of advanced electronic business technology, the value-net is a value-create system whose core is customers through integrating industry chains, and is evolution of value chain and supply chain management (SCM) which can satisfy customers' increasing diversified, individual and smart serve requirements.   Being different from the traditional manage-object value chain and the linear chain model supply chain, the value-net is an interactive networked relation.   The logic value-net model is shown in Figure 1.

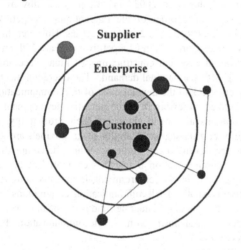

. **Fig. 1.** The Value-Net Model

The origin of the value-net is customer, that customers' requirement is the trigger of activating the whole network.   They can choose and integrate the most valuable product and value.   Surrounding the customer, there are the core company and business partners that control the marketing relationship with customers to collect customers' information, maintain relationship, serve customers and so on.   The outside suppliers constitute a strategic alliance with the inside core company, cooperate with development, carry a part function of research and development, and carry out material procurement, manufacture assembly and product shipment.   It is worthy to distinguish that "customers" here is different from "consumers".   The generalized customer may include individual consumers and consumer groups as well as companies.

2.2 Main characteristics of the value-net

To adopt the value-net, the characteristics can be compared with traditional business model based on an idea of supply chain as shown in Table 1.

(1) Customer-Focused. Customer's personalized requirements solicit activities of purchase, product and delivery on network in physical world or information world and marketplace. Different customer groups can get different customized service solution and customer command value-net. They are not passive accepter of supply chain product or service.

(2) Systematization and collaboration. On value-net, core companies apply themselves to constitute a bouncy electronic value-net combining supplier, customer and other business cooperative partner. On this network, each activity is accredited to the most effective cooperative partner. A great many of parts in operation are accredited to the professional suppliers. Because of cooperation of wide communication and information management, the whole network can deliver product and service perfectly and incarnate the value and life force of Collaborate Commerce (C-Commerce) [2, 5].

Table 1. Operating mode comparison.

Business Mode Characteristics	Supply Chain	Value-Net
Operating Concept	the Same Specification	Accordance to Customer
Competition Manner	Opposition for long time and Order	Cooperation and Systematic
Performance	Rigidity and Unchanged	Flexibility and Agility
Customer Reaction	Slowness and Stillness	Quick Reaction
Business Process	Analog	Digital
System Structure	Linear Chain	Distributed Network

(3) Agility and flexibility. By agile production, distribution and information flow design, the whole value-net's response is intelligent and agile to requirement change, new product coming into the market, speedy development or supplier network reconstitution. Furthermore value-net can reduce or eliminate the strictness of entity-limits and arise in flexibility.

(4) Fast response. On value-net, the cycle speeds from order to delivery. In the process of production and delivery, the company's entire multi-value relation network can assist customer design product or may deal with transferring real-time business information among suppliers. All these activities are carried out through distributed network. Additionally, high effective productivity and distribution system make the value-net to establish very low cycle time.

(5) Digitization and networking [4]. E-commerce is an important business method. Besides Internet, the information process design and intelligent application is the core of value-net. The new Internet based digital information channel connects and cooperates to all activities in the chain of companies, customers and suppliers. Based on business rules, the event-driven tools may substitute many management

decisions, the business intelligence (BI) can be used to provide the feasible solution quickly.

3   A Value-Net Based Ecosystem

With rapid development of technologies and applications of mobile communication, the progress of development from traditional voice services to added-value services for data, such as SMS (Small Message Service), MMS (Multimedia Message Service), social networking, and etc., has bring in a significant effect and strong impact on our daily life today.   It impacts consumer, entertainment and work profoundly and widely.   At the same time, as the mainstay, the industry on mobile communication services is transferred rapidly.   The market subjects and business principles are being changed deeply and evidently within days.   In essence, the aim of this change is to break the traditional industrial chain, and reform or optimize the mechanism and pattern of creating value and operating business [2].   The emerging trend of this change is to construct a new, cooperating, open and multi-win ecosystems based on value-net facing the network age.

3.1 Limitations of the traditional supply chain based business model

Though mobile communication, market has undergone a transferal course from monopolization and close to competition and open, because of limitations of technology, business circumstance and innovation being changed. The business models and operational principles of industry are based mainly on the traditional supply chain, that is to say the linear construction of supply chain management (SCM). It has been proven by practices and theories that the traditional industry construction has been not fitted to the social developments and customer's demands with the progress of technologies. Changes of customer's demands have confronted more and more competition, and also resulted in the expectation of Business Process Reengineering (BPR) by implementing M-Commerce. Some shortcomings of industry structure based on traditional supply chain and operating mode are described as follows.

(1) Monopolization and close. Market's subjects included by industry chain are so few and lack middle process. It is the same in mobile communication industry that new subjects are difficult squeeze into this market. This industry chain is monopolization and close comparatively.

(2) Single linear mode. Links among nodes of industry chain are not only simple. The relations among nodes are single linear and upright from up to down.

(3) Technology oriented. At this stage, the value of industry chain is mainly dependent on technology, so the power of technology is more important than power of market in the development of M-Commerce. Only technologies keep running ahead, the supplies for mobile service providers (MSP) by manufacturers of telecom facilities may upgrade to certain satisfaction level to meet customer demands.

With the developments and general applications of information modernization and e-commerce (or e-business), more professions and colligations of mobile communication join into operations day by day, bring in the emerging technologies of ISP (Internet Content Provider), IPP (Internet Platform Provider), ASP (Application Service Provider), and ISV (Independent Software Vendor). At the same time, the competition among mobile business operators is more and more intensive because of the open of mobile business market and the transfer from sell-side market to buy-side market. Facing to more and more mellow customers, mobile business operators have a few dependence on ICP, ASP and telecom equipment provider, to satisfy the cheap, abundant, and personal demands of customers. Therefore, mobile business operators are still the key position of industry chain by depending on predominance of network resources and customer aggregation, but it shall be fit to the change and adjust its' competition strategy. What's more, it shall integrate the different parts of industry chain to satisfy the demands of customers and gain the advantage of market competition.

3.2 The value-net based ecosystem architecture and operating mechanism

The changes and developments of new technology, market and social environment requires the existing industry-chain to dynamically evolve to new industry architecture with more vitality, stability and sustainability [5]. In the process, the mechanism of competition, value creation, and representation changes profoundly demand the mobile business operator (or provider) to utilize its advantages in resource and strength in status. By taking duty and responsibility of a certain degree in market supervision, the new industry may construct new rules and regulations, and integrate the industry chain on the basis of cooperation. A new win-win mode can be constructed an open, cooperative and integrative ecosystems with the customers, business partners and suppliers. This is because the customer-focused market competition is no longer the competition between business entities or traditional supply chains, but evolves to the comprehensive competition between the ecosystems of the industry and the other ecosystems.

3.2.1 The value-net based ecosystem architecture

The concept and principle of value-net was proposed by Mercer Consulting in year 2000 [3]. Because the e-commerce technologies and methods provides us with the technological and operational basis and means, so we can to construct and run a value-net based business model for M-Commerce effectively. We can present a value-net mode of mobile business by integrating technologies and e-commerce into the industry chain for mobile telecommunication service. Based on the development and mergence between the telecommunication industry and Internet business, we present a modified value-net based ecosystems model of M-Commerce using the e-commerce value integrating mechanism [2, 6].

The model architecture is shown in Figure 2 with definitions of elements of ecosystems of M-Commerce as follows.

(1) TDP: Terminal Device Provider;

(2) MBP: Mobile Business Operator, it includes the Internet Platform Provider (IPP) of software system platform;

(3) NDP: Network Device Provider, it includes the Internet Platform Provider (IPP) of hardware system platform;

(4) ISV: Independent Software Vendor;

(5) ICP: Internet Concept Provider;

(6) ASP: Application Service Provider.

At the same time, the collaborated business relation between these entities is very important. Besides the meaning of arrows or lines marked in Figure 2, the marked numbers are used to describe following business activities:

mark ①: to provide the network platform to ASP, ICP by MBP;

mark ②: concept services;

mark ③: application services;

mark ④: to provide content services;

mark ⑤: to provide application services.

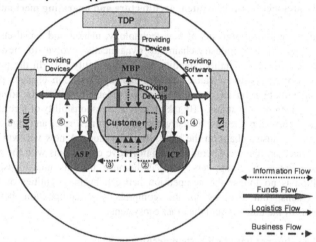

. **Fig.2.**The modified value-net based ecosystems mode of M-Commerce.

3.2.2 The operating mechanism of value-net based ecosystem of e-commerce

The operating system of the ecosystems model can be descried as following:

(1) Managing concept. It is a kind of customer-focused value creating system. The sustaining competitiveness and vitality of the value system requires constant improvement of both customer satisfaction and customer loyalty.

(2) System of value creating and distribution: The network operator still plays the role of value distributor. In realization of customer value, the funds flow uniformly goes from customers to the network operator. But in order to construct a vigorous ecosystem and to enhance the overall competitiveness, the network operators must share both profit and risk among suppliers and business partners of different value orientation in a cooperative, win-win, reasonable and effective way. Suppliers should be effectively motivated to cooperate and intensify R&D and innovation in addition to the payment of their products and services. The business

partners should be extensively invited on the basis of reasonable business regulations and win-win profit sharing systems. Competition should be encouraged with supervision reinforcement.

(3) Customer information flow. It does not simply flow to the operator but to related service providers according to the services they provide. Only under such mode can the operators, ASP and ICP run their corresponding SCM and CRM according to the services they each provide. Consequently, they can analyze the demand features to change the trends of their customers in order to develop new and better services. Furthermore, these activities will meet or even create the needs of their customers.

(4) Collaboration commerce. High level and extensive collaboration operating is one of the main features of this mode and system, which emphasizes the integration and collaboration of logistics flow, funds flow, information flow, knowledge flow, work flow, business flow and value flow. This is the crucial element of the core competitiveness of the value-net ecosystems.

(5) Information processing structure and technology frame [2, 5, 6]. The networked computing platform for the collaboration of the operators, business partners and customers is Intranet/Extranet/Internet, the integrated and distributed services provided by the ecosystems has excellent standardization, openness and integrity.

4   Case Analysis

China Mobile Limited (http: //www.chinamobileltd.com) is the top 1 of mobile service providers (MSP) in China. It has about 320 millions subscribers. Among them, China Mobile Limited provides E-mail and Internet accessing service for its mobile telephone users by Monternet.com. In the field of M-Commerce, China Mobile Limited creates a new service model by Monternet.com in China, which is a successful creation by composition of technology and marketing. As an example, China Mobile Limited establishes a perfect value-net integrated basic telecom managing and added-value telecom managing together.

In fact, we can use the above ecosystems model of M-Commerce which we proposed to delineate the business model of China Mobile Limited. This ecosystem is successfully constructed in the industry, with successful experiences accumulated in the practical operations. We do research on the key factor of China Mobile Limited 's success, abstract and generalize the following effective operating strategy of the ecosystems based on value-net.

(1) Constructing a multi-win business model. The mobile business Operator (MSP) should treat the symbiosis as strategic assets, and as a result, builds a integrated and effective industrial alliance. Such as cooperates and communication equipment providers, the multi-win business model in the industrial chain will be created by reasonable profit sharing plan and strategic relationship constructed by integrating capital and technology together.

(2) Networked and dynamic application integration. The MSP should establish an advanced E-Business system for virtual operation based on business rules, and integrates business partners and providers together in the system. As a result, the

customer requirement will be efficiently satisfied and the flexible alliance will be dynamically constructe

(3) Availability inspiration and monitor to value segment, Service Provider for example. The MSP should keep its outstanding achievement, brand, reputation, and quality of service to customers' expectation by maintaining the quality of the partners through some kinds of supports such as constituting technical standard, establishing a industry of business standard to assess and evaluate the SPs, setting up a well competitive mechanism, supplying fund and personnel to SPs.

(4) Building customer-focused brand and upgrading core competition. The core ability of MSP is about the operation capability on value-net and capability on CRM. In the communication age of ecological competition, an effective business model is the core competition, and it is the most important to build customer-focused brand.

5 Conclusion

The discussion of business model of M-Commerce based on value-net in China in this paper is a collaborative and multi-win model which can effectively cope with the complex variety and the intense competition in the market. And so as to offer a kind of new systemic view and methodology, and then effectively improve the competitiveness of the whole industry, the model constructs an ecosystems basing value-net in the industry and a vicious-cycle industrial ecosphere. But it must be mentioned that we shouldn't neglect the important factors such as technology, economy and society etc when we study and use the critical success factors of the system in the industry or field.

Acknowledgments

This research was supported by the key project of the National Natural Science Foundation of China under Grant 79931000, and the National Natural Science Foundation of China under Grant 70272047.

References

1. N. Adam, Y. Yesha, Electronic Commerce: *Current Research Issues and Applications*, New York: Springer Publisher, 1996.
2. Y. L. Wu, "Research on the Metasynthesis and Solution of e-Business Applications for Process System", the Research Report of the *Key Project of National Natural Science Foundation*, China (No. 79931000), March 2003 (in Chinese), pp. 1-9.
3. D. Bovet, J. Martha, R. Kirk Kramer, *Value-nets*, John Wiley & Sons, Inc., New York, 2000.
4. W. Cascio, "Managing a Virtual Workplace", Academy of Management Executive, Vol. 14, No.3, 2000, pp. 81-90.

5. B. M. Wiesenfeld, S. Raghuram, R. Garud, "Communications Patters as Determinants of Organizational Identification in a Virtual Organizations", *Organization Science*, Vol.10, No.6, 1999, pp. 777-790.

6. M. P. Koza, A. Y. Lewin, "The Co-Evolution of Network Alliances: A Longitudinal Analysis of an International Professional Service Network", *Organization Science*, No.50, 1999, pp. 1477-1490.

7. Definition of Social Bookmarking, en.wikipedia.org/wiki/Social_bookmarking. [2006-12-12]

8. P. Maes and R. Kozierok, , "Learning interface agents". *Proceedings of AAAI*, 459-465(1993).

On Developing China's Third Party Payment

Yong Jin, Wei Song, Jingyi Zhang

School of Management, Hubei University of Technology, P.R.China,

430068

jy6509@163.com, jy6509@21cn.com

Abstract: The development of the third party payment, which enhances electronic commerce's development greatly, provides a secure, efficient, convenient and low-cost way to transfer funds between the seller and the buyer. With fast development of electronic commerce and fierce competition in the third party payment market, the central bank of China sets about granting profession licenses to related companies. This paper theoretically analyses the third party payment's development situation, operation mode and operation feature, and then offers strategies to develop China's third party payment.

As a separate operating agency, the third party payment platform, acting as intermediation in the process of dealing under the supervision of banks and business management departments, provides secure guarantee and technological support to the two trading parties. The platform, also acting as witness and channel of the network transaction, offers abundant payment means and reliable service to customers decreases the possibility of fraudulent trade and relieves public worries on the security of network transaction.

The platform of third party payment was investment hotspot of the year 2005, which is called "on-line payment year". Due to relaxed qualification cognizance, small payment companies sprang up and the scale of platform increased by 100 percent a year. According to IReserach's investigation, the third party payment in 2004 is 2.3 billion RMB, while the number was more than 30 billion RMB in 2006 and with an expectation of 280 billion RMB in 2010.

It is said that the People's Bank of China sets about granting license to the third party payment companies which means 80 percent small ones will be eliminated, thus perfecting operation mode becomes the most important issue for this industry.

Please use the following format when citing this chapter:

Jin, Y., Song, W., Zhang, J., 2007, in IFIP International Federation for Information Processing, Volume 251, Integration and Innovation Orient to E-Society Volume1, Wang, W. (Eds), (Boston: Springer), pp. 578-585.

1. Development situation of China third party payment

The 21st century is an era of information with thorough development of computer and network technology, and EC stride ahead in this era. Meanwhile multitudinous information technology enterprises, venture investment companies, and production circulation enterprises involve in the field of EC. Realized high growth of 73.7% in 2004, the EC market paced into its steady growth stage since 2005, with a transaction sum 680 billion (increased by 41.7%) and 1020 billion in 2006(increased by 50%).

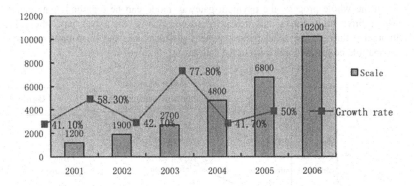

Fig. 1. Recent Development Tendency of China EC

Nowadays, two methods are widely used in the EC payment, one is electronic bank service and the other is the third party electronic payment service. According to the report of Ireserach, in China, 97% electronic payment is on-line payment, while only 3 percent is paid in form of mobile or telephone payment. All these prove that, in spite of the existence of immaturity and relaxed cooperation in this industrial chain, great achievement has been gained and on-line payment has been playing the most important role in the field of electronic payment. As to present case, on-line banks mainly deal with payments among enterprise (B2B), especially large and medium sized enterprises, whose sums of transacted money are large and their business partners are relatively stable, thus their interior ERP systems or self-constructed platforms are able to deal with the payments.

As for the domain of small–sum payments, such as B2C and C2C, services provided by single on-line bank could not satisfy the changing and flexible demands of small-sized customers. Similarly advanced technologies and costly maintenance expenses are beyond small-scaled network and business's management. Under such situation, the third party payment platform, a non-bank investment institution that is independent from both the payer and the payee, becomes a hot spot in the market of on-line payment. From 2001 to 2004, its annual compound growth rate is by 44.2 percent. By 2004, China's third party payment increased to 2.3 million RMB.

2. The Third Party's Payment Modes

The third party's payment mode can roughly divided into two kinds: One acts as bank gateway proxy which provides many bank connections to the users; the other acts as transaction intermediary (whose main function is to bridge the buyer and the sell, and also connect the EC platform and the bank) to realize on-line fund transaction.

2.1 The Mode of Payment Gateway

From the whole process, the payment gateway mode can be regarded as a channel which links multi-banks and treaty-signed merchants, the buyer pays the seller indirectly through the third party payment platform and the third party provides compatible connection platform to the sellers.

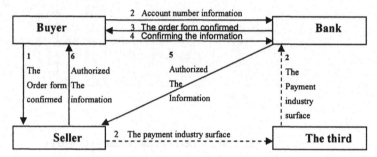

Fig. 2. Illustration of Payment Gateway Mode

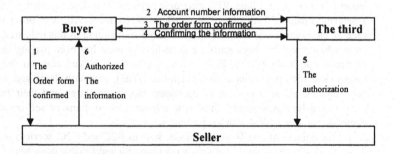

Fig. 3. Illustration of Credit Intermediary Mode

2. 2 The Mode of Credit Intermediary

In order to increase two sides' credit, ensure well circulation to fund and cargo, the third party payment service, acting as the credit intermediary, arises at the historic moment, implements "receiving and paying on other's behalf " and "the credit guarantees". Once transaction intention arrived, the buyer will firstly deposited his money into the third party's, after receiving and checking his ordered good, the buyer informs the third party, then the third party will transfer the fund deposited in its payment platform to the seller account. In this mode, the third party actually acts as credit intermediary; deposits funds for two sides before the buyer claim their wanted good. So in certain degree, the credit intermediary mode is a byproduct of on-line transaction's "Credit vacancy".

3. Operation Mode Analysis of the Third Party Payment

At present, the third party payment companies, banks, merchants, exterior competitors have already constitutes a complex chain in the electronic payment industry. The relationship between the third party payment and bank's large-scale electronic interactive platform is extremely subtle because they mutually and closely dependent on each other. Analysis each part's relationship among such chain and its dependence degree to others, we may classify this operation mode, adopted by the third party payment operation, into two kinds:

3.1 The Third Party's Gateway Operation Mode

This mode refers to the value-added service operation platform provided by third party to signed customers and it is independent from electronic payment industry chain. Such operation businessman only provides operation platform for product payment and payment system, its front end provides kinds of payments for on-line merchants and on-line consumers, which correspondingly relates to the bank's electronic connection in rear end. While the third party payment operation businessman is responsible for transferring accounts among banks, and providing value-added services, such as order management and account inquiry. In China, both Payeasy and Pay100 adopt this pattern.

This unique and flexible payment operation platform mainly faces B2B, B2C and G2C market, or provides payment settlement for small/medium-sized merchants and government-owned/private enterprises that are in need of payment. It's not consumers but banks and merchants (who are closely related to the third party operation business) who are users of the third party's gateway operation mode. This mode income mainly comes from bonus from banks' benefits, customers' annual expense and handling charge of transaction.

3.2 The Third Party Payment Operation Mode Widened by EC Businessman

3.2.1 Operation Mode Guaranteeing Payment Credit

This mode is independently exploited by the large-scaled electronic transaction platform or cooperatively exploited with other investors. Relying on its financial strength and good public praise, operation businessman cooperates with banks, offers middle guarantee for the trading parties by the third party payment operation mode. Through electronic transaction platform and payment platform, the third party, acting as credit intermediary, does business with customers and guarantees transaction operation being carried out smoothly.

Owning integrate electronic transaction platform and abundant network customer resources, such kind payment operation businessman, facing to C2C, B2C market, provides payment services to individuals and small/middle-sized business, plays the intermediary guarantee function, and establishes relatively reliable credit appraisal system for both sides according to the platform transaction recording. Its operating expense and benefit basically comes from network platform shop fee, commodity's landing fee, transaction service fee and so on. Nowadays popular domestic payments, such as Alipay, Paypal, Ebay and Tenpay, are using this operation mode.

3. 2 .2 Perfecting Payment Operation Mode Operated by EC Website

This operation mode, refers to payment gateway established by EC website (platform) who deals with special product (hypothesized product or entity product). This mode, originated from existed payment and management platform serving for EC operation businessman's commodity delivery and payment, owns solid background, abundant capital and ready-made stable net-work user and the cloud-net pays @ net. It's a typical representative of such mode.

This type operation business originates from mature EC enterprise, so they are familiar with customers' payment demands and they target on B2C market and provide on-line payment service to middle/small-scaled EC website then obtain annual service charge as well as transaction handling charge as operation income.

4. Prospective Analysis on the Third Party Payment

For the lack of systemic supervision and management, disorderly competition exists in the field of third party payment business. Meanwhile, the banks (who the third party payment relies on), together with reduced foreign/domestic investment and negative effects produced by well-known EC websites, cause the third party payment enterprise's survival surrounding becoming worse and worse.

Under such background, the central bank of China sets about granting license to the third payment business in order to regularize this field. Regardless of whether it's easy or hard to gain this license, turbulence will arise in this profession and reform is unavoidable. After these, surviving enterprises are bound to partition the market, which leads to competition pattern, and then it's vital for the third party payment enterprise to prospect its development strategy. Several aspects should be taken into strategy design:

4. 1 Strengthening Theoretical Research, Enriching Operation Mode and
Seeking Profit--making Points

The third party does not involve in particular transaction, which guarantees information security, but its individual credit safeguard system can be popularized in B2B and C2C transaction. On the other hand, B2B is rich in professions and each profession is characteristic and complicated, then sole and simple transaction or payment mode hinders B2B on-line payment's development. Consequently, while developing B2B on-line payment, the third party payment business must take profession difference into consideration, and intended acquaint it with particular profession demands. It should be aware of the key role of innovation, try hard to explore "value-added business". It's important for the third party to make good use of own resources superiority, localize its position accurately, divide market appropriately, and avoid homogeneity competition and unwise price war. It's equaled important to seek innovation spots from respects of business mode and product function, prominent good quality and well service of product, maintain and expands own superiority customer resources, and realize long-term stable development.

4. 2 Strengthening Governmental Supervision, Perfecting Monitoring System

At present, China lacks of correlation law or policy to regularize network market, which leads to the third party payment profession is too relaxed and beyond any supervision. The third party payment platform appearing in the form of profit-earned but not public welfare organization is facing with possible risk in its operating process. Furthermore, because its service involves fund circulation, which possible leads to serious exterior negative effect. All those call for reasonable supervision and management to the third party payment.
The third party payment business acts intermediary just as what banks do in the international trade. But banks, as an important part of social economy body, own strong ability to resist risk and mature management laws and regulations and good credit. In order to develop itself appropriately, the third party payment profession has to win trust from the public and exploit its service smoothly, as well as avoid risk timely. All this prompts us that while resetting our confidence in the third party payment profession market, we should reelect our credits.
Although our country has enacted "Electronic Signature Law " and " the Electronic Payment Direction (First) ", but for its particular features, the third party payment service has not included in these laws. The administrative departments should try to fulfill the third party business development requirements, instruct and supervise its business. Supervising and managing organization department should be established to provide unitive services to the third party, evaluate its business, collect profession cases, balance the relationship among government administrative department, the profession terminal organization as well as customers, and enhance the third party's development. Only these can form a harmonious market, which is advantageous to the third party payment business development.

4.3 Consummating Credit Safeguard System of On-line Payment System, Seeing Secure Payment

For the existence of low threshold and supervising and managing system flaw, certain payment company has to take over some illegal transactions to make a living, this kind of case jeopardizes on-line payment's public image, produces negative effects on its long-term development and harm network payment security.
Driven by malignant competition and surviving pressure, most payment companies, so long as having trade (which are so limited) to do, concern themselves with

transaction results, regardless of trade validity even though they are aware that many transactions are illegal money washing. Such continuous malignant competition withers the market and harms its harmonious development. It's well known that certain payment company provides a service (its maximum dealing amount is only several hundred Yuan.) which is nothing but providing operation convenience to wash illegal fund.

The existing weaknesses of the third party payment are partly due to the lack of network technology laws. The solutions to those problems lie in our whole society's efforts and the promotion of our overall qualities. Basing on service flow of the third party payment, administrative machinery and profession association should established fair and just evaluating system, regulate both sides' transaction behavior, establish credit appraisal organization for the third party, strengthen supervision and management to the transaction process. What's more, the EC profession itself should take care of these problems and promote the business's development by enhancing its immunity.

4.4 Locating Market Position, Perfecting Payment Service

On-line payment is an extension of finance industry network market, which should abide by corresponding national finance policy and rule. The third party payment industry should deepen its understanding to finance industry and EC, strengthen its service consciousness, cooperate with banks and obtain their financial guarantee, offer multiple terminal products and services to the users. All these contribute healthy development to the third party payment business.

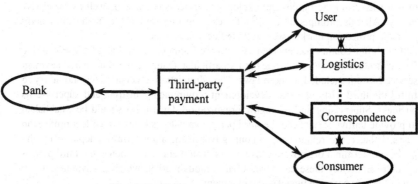

Fig. 4. The Third-party Payment Industry Chain Model

To enhance its profession competition ability, the third party payment enterprise should build and perfect its industrial chain, which is compatible with Internet and fulfilling electronic payment demand as to explore its value-added services. Based on development mode and capital background, the third party business must locate precisely its market position, identify its serving target, search for ways to stimulate its own development and satisfy customer various needs. At the same time, the third party business must build different managing pattern, enrich business concepts, perfect management structure and increase its payment pattern, carry out the plan of "vertical and horizontal alliance" in the field, rearrange professional resources, and enhance profession exterior competitive ability.

4.5 Constructing Urban New Payment Network

It's needed to construct the third party payment platform on the basis of urban synthetic safeguard system. This platform's front-end charge takes urban citizen (users of China telecom) as service terminal, its back-end charge takes urban non-profit organizations as service terminal, which include local public utility payment (the charge of water, electricity, gas, cable TV), cultural and educational business payment (such as network education, test training, school jot charge) and civilization payment (including traveling admission ticket, net-line expense, traveling special product, hotel reservation, electronic airplane ticket, electronic theater-including on-line and electronic bill)

This concept is far from maturity, but it offers development direction for the third party payment. With the help of today's highly developed information technology, we are confident to change this imagination into reality.

5. Summary

In brief, the third party payment platform, compared with other existent of on-line payment, is superior in secure payment and reliable trading credit, especially in B2C and C2C. What's more, its jot payment solves effectively the "payment bottleneck" problem, which puzzles EC transaction for years. Today, the third party payment profession has already been attracting attentions from government, banks, payment companies as well as risk investor. There's not doubt that the third party payment service will continue to play important role in future EC activity. Along with the emergence of related rules, the third party payment profession tends to be more mature and more perfect.

References

1. H. Chen, Evaluating development of the third party payment platform [J] South China finance computer, 2007 (1)
2. J.Y. Zheng, Present situation, question and supervising and managing suggestion of the Third party on-line payment market [J]. Financial accountant, 2006 (7)
3. Y. Zhao, The third party payment pattern analysis and question exploration [D] Beijing: Capital normal university, 2006
4. E.L. Li, Analyzing research on the third party payment [D] Chengdu: Southwest Finance and Economics University, 2006
5. http:// www.iResearch.com

On Chinese tourism e-business development on current stage

Yong Jin 1, 2, Xu song Xu 1

1 School of Economic and Management, Wuhan University, P.R.China,
430070
2 School of Management, Hubei University of Technology, P.R.China,
430068
jy6509@163.com, jy6509@21cn.com

Abstract. By analyzing the economy and technology background of appearance of tourism e-business, the paper describe the concept of tourism e-business and it's operation mode in order to master this modern alternative deeply and all-round. The author emphasizes on the discussion of the inter-promotion and inter-development relationship between e-business and tourism economy, meanwhile forecasts the future of Chinese tourism e-business based on the analysis of difficult position we are facing now in tourism e-business. Combining with successful cases, suggestions on the development of tourism e-business are put forward.

1 Introduction

Global economy is entering into the information time, digital economy, cyber-economy and information economy is gradually becoming the main trend of economy development. As the main economy and trade method in 21st century, e-business will bring great innovation to all countries' economy and become the growth motivation of economy and a new growth point.

2 Concept of tourism e-business

The so-called tourism enterprises are new business activities linked through computer calculation technology, electronic communication technology and enterprise buying and selling network system which based on internet technology provided by Internet. [1] They include on-line message sending and receiving; on-

---

Please use the following format when citing this chapter:

Jin, Y., Xu, X., 2007, in IFIP International Federation for Information Processing, Volume 251, Integration and Innovation Orient to E-Society Volume1, Wang, W. (Eds), (Boston: Springer), pp. 586-592.

line order, payment, customer service and other on-line selling, on-line before-selling recommendation and after-sale service; and various business activities like market investigation and analysis, financial accounting and manufacture arrangement which made use of Internet. It is a combination mode of information flow that based on information network poly-technology and business operation procedure. Functions of tourism e-business can be summed up to: tourism enterprises marketing information proclaim; EDI (Electronic Date Interchange), on-line order, e-account and on-line payment; service delivery, opinion seeking and consulting, trading management and so on. With the high speed development of information technology, as a new trading method and business mode, e-business is entering into every region of traditional business which involves tourism industry at an unprecedented rate.

3 Necessity of the development of tourism e-business

3.1 From market competition's standpoint

From external factors, after we entered WTO, with mature e-Business experience, abundant fund and first-class service, foreign tourism companies will be tremendous impact to Chinese tourism market. While from internal factors, tourism industry is the universal "sun-rise business" which has a good long term potential. Foreign investors want to occupy this market, however the original market occupants want to consolidate and expand their territory. It is an austere challenge for tourism enterprises to gain an advantage in competitions. Confronting with fierce market competition, it is necessary for tourism industry to take some measure to enlarge their scope, in order to realize the scale economy, reduce the margin cost and improve the efficiency. However expand in traditional way might leads to inflated departments and over-sized employees, which will lead to the inefficiency of management and costly payment. However tourism e-business can provide tourism enterprises with e-Business application operation platform, on which tourism product designation and suppliers purchasing can be easily completed, meanwhile, external advertisement and promotion, on-line selling enrollment, internal activity cooperation and communication can also be done there. All those can maintain the high efficiency and smooth for tourism operation. By using this, enterprises can improve their efficiency, reduce employees, lower cost and strengthen the enterprises' competition ability.

3.2 From tourism enterprises' standpoint

Since tourism industry belongs to service industry, its development depends on the level of customers' satisfaction on service they provided. It asks tourism enterprises to provide customers with abundant tourism attraction information timely, exactly and elaborately. At the same time, tourism enterprises should be aware of domestic and international customer market information, requirement of customer and provide various relevant services according to customers' requirement. Break up the region limitation, integrate all kinds of tourism resource to the maximum extend and pump new power into tourism enterprises to a large extent.

3.3 From customers' standpoint

With the improvement of people's material life, customers' psychological demand entered into a higher level, target of tourism increased to a high level of life experience, self-perfecting and self-value realization. People's tourism requirement is improving everyday, they would like to have an overall knowledge of all related information they need before they go out, and expect to enjoy all convenient and quick service. The appearance of tourism e-business meets the customers' requirement. Travelers can have a look of the brief introduction of the tourism company and pictures of the tourism spot, be aware of the journey, price quotation, accommodation and other information, meanwhile they can order service and tourism items through Internet.

4 Main problems that existed in Chinese tourism e-business

Problems that restrict the development of our tourism network are not only technology issues, but also operation environment existed in traditional tourism business and the whole development level of society economy. Main problems we are confronting of the development of our tourism internet are:

4.1 Imperfect information search

When searching tourism information on line, a big problem customers are facing is that how can they find the exact information through various websites, and obtain it at the lowest price. The search engine looks quite easy: user entered a key inquire word and the search engine will seek in the data base according to the key word and return with the most appropriate WEB page link. However according to the latest research result, currently at least 10 trillion web pages needs to build up a search engines on the internet, while existing search engines can only work 5 trillion web pages. There are still half of them can not use search engine. [2] This is not mainly because of the technology reason; on-line sellers want to protect the privacy of their product price. So when users browse information on-line, they have to search website by website, until they find a satisfied one.

4.2 Lower security of trading

Security of trading is still a main factor that influent the development of tourism e-business. Owing to the quick prevailing of Internet, tourism e-business causes widely attention and be considered to be the most potential new growth point of future IT industry. While when deal on the open network, how to make sure the security of data transfer is one of the most important factors that decide whether tourism e-business can be popularized. Investigation companies had ever taken the on-line survey about the application anticipation of tourism e-business. When asked why unwilling to shop on line, most of the worries are about the lost of credit card information in case of attacking by Hacker. So part of the people are not willing to use tourism e-business for worrying about the security issue. Security becomes the biggest obstacle of tourism e-business.

4.3 Lack of credit guarantee

Another obstacle of building up tourism e-business is the lack of credit. How is the trade credit of tourism enterprises? Are products we ordered in screen consistent with the real tourism? How about the quality? Due to the existing problems of the reliability of TV-ads, fears of on-line shopping will get more.

4.4 Similar operation mode

Main e-business business of tourism websites includes air-ticket; hotel and tourism group booking and every tourism website have them. When websites regard themselves as travel agencies, they found that there is nearly no predominance of their service comparing with traditional travel agencies, hotel booking center and air-ticket selling company. Therefore, to make profit, travel websites must provide better service, better products, or seeking new foothold and development opportunities, or quickly scale up their sales column. Otherwise, websites will get lost before nail down better development mode.

4.5 Guarantee of off-line service

Usually Internet companies lay particular stress on information flow and capital flow. Tourism websites should combine some good traditional marketing mode when they employ Internet to maximum advantages, only in this way can they provide users with integrated service. In fact, most network companies' off-line service can not get guarantee.

4.6 Disadvantage of payment method and consumption habit

In foreign countries, there is a close relationship between popularization of credit card, use of internet and good development of e-Business. In china, credit cards are not widely used and this way of payment is not be accepted by the society; meanwhile, not many Chinese get used to on-line consumption. Consumers' personal and companies' credit standing have not yet been set up on line and this must bring great obstacle to the development of tourism e-business.

4.7 lack of sustain of main tourism industry

Multitudinous tourism websites are lack of thorough and deep understanding of tourism industry when they layout, they cannot correctly find the breaking through point and therefore hardly to form their own characteristic and selling point. Usually they copy from foreign websites' existing mode and become the Chinese edition of developed countries' websites, for example American and Canada.

5 Countermeasures of development of Chinese tourism e-business

5.1 Characteristic orientation

Tourism industry is a typical service industry and tourism e-business is service oriented. According to CNNIC's report, among main factors that user select ISP, connecting speed takes the first place with 43%, service takes the second place with 24%; while among main factors of successful websites, service with plenty of information, in-time update and attractiveness takes the first place with 63.35%.[3] therefore, tourism website want to have higher visiting column and large quantity of trade, should have on-line trading platform which can provide special, multi-angle, multi-profile, diversified and good quality service to attract various kind of consumer. From case analysis below, we will have more direct understanding.

Ctrip.com holds items like routing, room-booking, ticket-booking and community, and the room-booking center whose scale is among the first three, its market orientation focus on self-tourism and business-tourism. Sales volume reached at 10 million RMB this May and hopefully accumulated to 1 trillion at the end of this year. Ctrip.com is built up from gateway model, depended on profit from room-booking; it aims at tourism Service Corporation. Before Ctrip.com, main business of tourism websites in China are information providing, for the first time tourism websites oriented at the service agency of tourism industry cause of the entrance of Ctrip.com. Revelation Ctrip.com brings to us is not only the technology promotion from Internet, but more important the re-definition of tourism service it digs out. [4]
Xoyo.com oriented at on-line hotel booking. Among various tourism resources, hotel industry is the easiest one of networking; moreover hotel booking is the most profitable part among e-Business. Investment always asks for return and blows off cyber-economy foam, Xoyo.com selected the most realistic method. Not pursuing high, great and integration, Xoyo.com established itself in brand-building and service-pursuing.

Sotrip.com locates its market breaking through point at culture tourism, which has profound inside culture information. The website oriented at "network edition of China national geography magazine", which currently has title of columns like tourism culture, tourism literature, community, professional homepage, theme tourism and so on. Concept of Sotrio.com is to grasp the great requirement of individuation that new age tourism asks for, then initiate "traveling all around, getting to know things and understanding diversified survival state; exploring deep and serene, meeting humanities and seeking trace of the ancients; visiting hardship and dangers, realizing spirit and feeling the free artistic conception of oneness of man and nature". Sotrip.com even did not plan to take business of on-line tourism group, ticket-booking, room-booking and so on, as for the way of making profit they have their own idea: consumer is the leader of digital economy, enterprises in the future need to take real time analysis and forecast consumer information, according to which provide customer-made product and service, in this way can they have necessary customer information. High visiting column plus customer loyalty plus sufficient and efficient customer data equals to the websites' future profit space, unlimited potential hided behind their new version.

5.2 Capital, resource, technology and market

Rushing forward is a rule in network industry. Winner is the one that keep merging the competitors after life and death struggles. Economy discipline from "all flowers bloom together" to "several branches outshine others" will finally complete the re-organization of capital, resource, technology and market. On the other facet, integration and strategy alliance between tourism websites and traditional tourism corporations is the main trend.

Tourism e-business breaks up the traditional mode and method and builds up modern tourism management information system, which avoids drawbacks of large organization and inefficient management from traditional scale expanding and form new structure of tourism development which is scaled, industry rationalized and standardized. At the same time, backed against traditional tourism industry and first-hand tourism material in detail provided by traditional corporations, tourism websites' content can get clear-cut and unique feature and service style. Tourism websites can also charge fees from services to Tourism Corporation to maintain its normal running and make profits. Tactic and strategy of Tourism Corporation and websites is a win-win measure. [5] Alliance method between Tourism Corporation and websites can be diversified and marketalized. Alliance can be done through capital way to take strategy re-organization, to form large-sized corporation group, it can also be done through tourism websites' netting of traditional tourism corporation. Tourism corporations and tourism websites can optimize their resources by forming corporation group and operation of capital, this makes management and operation easier and at the same time occupies double-themes of both sun-rise industry and network & high-tech, which makes financing from listing easier and promotes its core competition advantages. It is a good way for small and medium sized enterprises to consign tourism websites to finish their network building.

5.3 Operation method and scope

Among more than 3000 tourism agencies in china, 90% of them are small and medium sized, which continue traditional manual operation, operations with only a telephone plus a fax machine is not rare.[6] Those diversified, small and weak enterprise need network to reach low cost and efficiency, change the disorder situation of customer resource management by systematization. Large tourism service corporations emphasis good connection between subsidiaries and users through companies' network.

To develop tourism e-business, we also need to widen our field of observation, provide services with multi-language and different level of requirement according to our customer resource, like English edition, Japanese edition, and French edition and so on. For example, Sotrip.com has special English edition, compare with it, foreign websites can not deeply grasp Chinese culture's quintessence; while most of the

English edition of national websites are only translation of Chinese edition without taking into account the requirement difference between foreign and national customer. With the quick increase of Chinese entry tourism, this huge potential market is our important target in developing our tourism industry. At the time that foreign websites is coming, it seems to be more precious for our national websites to have the lofty sentiments to go out.

6 Conclusion

Tourism e-business is of special significance in reconstructing traditional inefficient business operation method and pushing up the promotion of market economy quality. However, problems still exist in the real development of tourism e-business, for example, unprofitable issue, payment issue, information problem and security problems and so on. Those problems are great obstacles for the development of tourism e-business. Our overall e-business is still on the stage of beginning, measurements of on-line security guarantee, identification of responsibility are universally be lacked of, big environments of e-Business still need to be improved. As the government and enterprises, we should regard "high starting point and internationalization" as the principle to support and push the development of tourism e-business, compromise tradition and modern, then tourism industry in information age will develop continuous and healthy.

Reference

1. L.D. Zhao, E-Business Theory and Practice, Beijing: People's Post and Telecommunication Press, 2001.
2. J.X. Zhang, (2001), "Opportunity and Challenge Tourism Industry's Information Management confronts under Network Environment", Science & Technology Progress and Policy, 2001, (6):131-132.
3. X.L Xu, C.F. Jiang, (2001), "Development of Travel Agency in Network Time", Tourism Science, 2001, (2):29-32.
4. M.X.Guo, (1999), "The fittest can survive; Development Tactic of Tourism Industry under the Impact of International Internet", Guilin Institution of Tourism Journal, 1999,(3):23-28.
5. L.Y. Zhang, Current Situation and Development Trend of our Tourism Internet, Beijing: China Travel and Tourism Press, 2000.
6. X.A. Wei, S.M. Zhang, Framing Conception of Chinese Tourism Industry E-Business Development, Beijing: China Travel and Tourism Press, 2000.
7. China Tourism News, [N].20050101-20051228.

The Information Characteristics and Controls in E-Commerce

Yong Liu1, Junping Qiu2

1 Information Science Department, Zhengzhou Institute of Aeronautical
Industry Management, Zhengzhou, P. R. China,
y_liu@zzia.edu.cn
2 Research Center for Chinese Science Evaluation, Wuhan University,
Wuhan, P.R.China

Abstract. The paper points out the significance of information control at first
and then arises some Characters of information in e-commerce. Further more,
the author analyzes the concept and ways of information integration and
information flow control.

1   The Inevitability of Information Control

All commercial activities take information as intermediary; the e-commerce
superiority lies in the full use of the commercial function of information network,
further strengthened the information intermediary function. Depends upon this
function, we may promote enterprise's management level and reduce the running
expenses greatly, orient the goal market quickly, more strive for and maintain the
customer relations, achieve the goal of improving efficiency of the commercial
activity. The success rate of the business activity is directly correlated with symmetry
of information exchange.

The information exchange of the traditional commercial activity takes hard
carrier of information as the core, such as paper carriers, magnetism carriers, optics
carriers, practicality carriers, communication establishment, terminal unit and vehicle,
etc. These carriers have a lot of limitation in information exchange, such as time,
space, region, specialty and personnel. But e-commerce is different, information
carrier which appears with high-efficient information transport apparatus with the
information network for main fact, not only has avoided all sorts of restrictions of
information exchange but also opened up the information exchange channel greatly.
In e-commerce era, information value among commercial activity is more prominent
than any time [1, 2]. Meanwhile, because of the e-commerce information characteristic
itself, its management problem will be more complicated. It is essential and urgent to

Please use the following format when citing this chapter:

Liu, Y., Qiu, J., 2007, in IFIP International Federation for Information Processing, Volume 251, Integration and
Innovation Orient to E-Society Volume1, Wang, W. (Eds), (Boston: Springer), pp. 593-600.

study information integration and information flow control on the basis of e-commerce.

2   The Inevitability of Information Control

Transmitting and processing commercial information by using the Web technology is an important technical feature of e-commerce, but information in e-commerce has own Characteristics.

From the angle of commodity exchange, e-commerce is not the operation transaction activity which completes by the physical exchange or the direct physical contact, but the operation transaction activity between transaction parts by the digital way, which indicated that information in the e-commerce has the digital feature.

From the angle of financial process, e-commerce is the commercial activity that transaction parts take the internet as platform to realize business contact, the data transmission, the commodity exchange, the bank credit payment and the settlement, which indicated that information in the e-commerce, has the integrated feature and collaboration or coordination feature.

From the angle of the operation pattern, e-commerce is the commercial activity that using modern information technology to change the traditional commerce pattern, which implied information in the e-commerce, has the control feature.

From the angle of technical application, e-commerce is the process that includes internet, digital information and commerce activity. In brief, e-commerce is informanization of commerce. In other words, the essence of e-commerce is the trade without paper, which means that there is massive information flow to process in the e-commerce activity, but logistics, the fund flow and other commercial factors must also process and transform as the form of information flow. One of e-commerce goals is the realization of complete alternation of entire commerce information, in order to gain more attachments value and the profit. This indicated that information in the e-commerce has the economical increment characteristics.

The development of network technology impelled the appearance and the development of e-commerce, and e-commerce through the information interaction affects information technology and value orientation of the social consumption behavior, which indicates information in the e-commerce has guiding feature.

Through the analysis above, information Characteristics in the e-commerce are extremely obvious, namely the information in the e-commerce has digital feature, the integration, the coordination, the controllability, the increment and the guidance feature and so on. In addition, the information in e-commerce also has the specialization, pertinence, large in quantity, the globality, the direct link, effectiveness, independence, openness, the interaction, sharing, inexpensive, authenticity, normative feature.[5,6,7] and so on.

3   Information Integration Control

3.1   Conception of information integration

As a technical methodology, Information Integration puts the information resources of e-commerce related application systems into the uniform information system architecture, thus realizes the division of work, cooperation, united management and effective utilization of information according to predetermined target. Information Integration does not mean simply gathering the information of related application systems, but mean integration based on technology, including the integration of application system interfaces, integration of information resource controlling agents, integration of organization and management model, integration of information users and services[3], etc. The core of Information integration is to merge information resources using modern information technology, and to realize the organic combination of information, technology, and intelligence, so that information resources can be well shared and effectively utilized.

The information integration of Enterprise Resource Planning and e-commerce technology is an effectual way for e-commerce information integration control, so it is focused and discussed in detail subsequently.

3.2   Information integration control

Two information chains exist in an enterprise: supply information chain, and market information chain. Thus, there are two separate application systems, namely Supply Chain Management system and Customer Relation Management system. ERP works as whole to link these two chains. The information exchanging relationship of them is displayed below as figure 1.

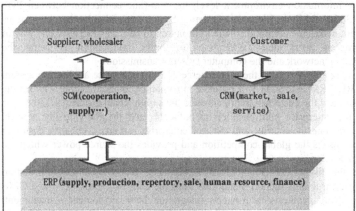

• **Fig. 1.** An AND/OR-network N on the left and a realization of N on the right side. AND-nodes are drawn as circles and OR-nodes as shaded squares

A unified information platform is essential for information integration control, which integrating independent application systems through network and e-commerce, and covering all the flows from suppliers to customers, to establish a unified e-commerce information integrating architecture. It's displayed as chart 2.

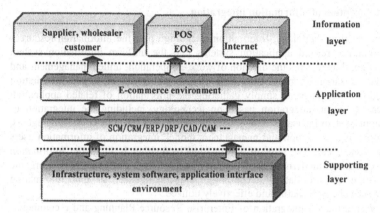

• **Fig. 2.** E-Commerce Information Integration Architecture.

The environmental structure of e-commerce information integration control is divided into three layers: supporting layer, application layer, and information layer. The e-commerce environment has integrated Web, EDI(Electronic Data Interchange), CA(Certificate authority) technology, etc., and provides interface for SCM(Supply Chain Management), CRM(Customer Relationship Management), ERP(Enterprise Resource Planning), DRP(Distribution Resource Planning), CAD(Computer Aided Design), CAM(Computer Aided Manufacturing) applications, so it plays a key part to build a information exchange channel.

In the information environment level, the real-time connection between POS (Point Of Sells) and EOS (Electronic Ordering System) provided by the e-commerce environment makes the commodity sale information to be read straightly. The way of online ordering work and exchanging the order information is using the communication network and the computer system transmission.

The integration between the e-commerce and the enterprise application system such as ERP, CRM and SCM will promote information communication between the supply chain and the customer chain, enhance the supply chain efficiency, satisfy the needs of the enterprise multiplication manufacture and the individuality service, effectively operate the interior and exterior enterprise resources, enhance customer satisfaction, meets the global competition and provides the source power which the enterprises develop.

With the further development of e-commerce technology, the information integration control construction transforms from the core with ERP, SCM and CRM to the core with synthesis information integration between content management, knowledge management and data warehouse, which will realize the more widespread information integration control.

Information integration control based on e-commerce will be the important way of future commerce development, which can avoid the unidirectional of the supply chain and customer chain information transmission in the traditional commerce pattern, effectively carry on the information track, the information record, the information storage, the information transmission, the information analysis and the policy-making consultation using the commercial network. Which will improve business management pattern, reduce the enterprise operation cost and the merchandise stock cost, fully use all kinds of resources, multi-way develop personalized products and open the customization service. It is important for enhancing the enterprise goodwill, improving the customer relations, enhancing enterprise's core competitive ability or executable ability, and finally obtaining sustainable development ability.

4 Information Flow Control in e-Commerce

The e-commerce information flow control is the establishment carries on in the information integration control foundation, if the information integration control provides is static integration frame, the information flow control then provides the dynamic information management method, belongs to the information collaboration or coordination control category.

4.1 Information flow in e-commerce

The traditional commercial activity has the concepts of the fund flows and the material flows, to the information flow had not taken the coordinate concept raises in, the main reason is the commercial information production and its transmission are most contains in the material flows, like the letter wraps mailing, facsimile receiving and dispatching, market information exchanging, transportation commodity information transmission and so on. In these ways, the information flow might be called the real scene information flow, also might become on the spot information flow. In this kind of situation, the obtaining, the processing, the transmitting and the exchanging of commercial information need to consume a mass of material flow.

The establishment in information superhighway foundation, e-commerce causes the information flow to separate itself from the material flow and the commercial flow, so that the information flow had the feature of non-real scene or not on the spot. The people use each kind of communication equipment and the information network carry on the information interactive, thus enable the information flow to have own cost and relatively independently comes out from each kind of commercial essential factor. Information flow independence, not only reduced the cost greatly which the material flows, moreover may provides the increment service for the material flow, the commercial flow, the fund flow and the economical management, this is significant difference between the e-commerce and the traditional commerce.

Is precisely because the Characteristics of independence and openness of information flow in e-commerce, in addition as mentioned earlier the Characteristics of digit, integration, the collaboration or coordination, the controllability, the increment and influence function of information and so on, the forming, obtaining, processing, the transmitting and the utilizing of e-commerce information then has many new problems, such as false information and information security questions[4]. Therefore, it is necessary to arise the information flow control concept and reasonable method through the effective way, by guaranteed the e-commerce activity with security and reliability while carries on the e-commerce construction.

4.2   E-Commerce information flow control method

The information flow control method is the core of information flow control. In the e-commerce system, the information has its own operators, such as producer, disseminators, consumers, managers and so on; therefore the information flow control also divides into subject oriented control method and the object oriented control method.

The information flow subject oriented control divides into five kinds of types as below: the producer control, the issue control, the disseminator controls, the consumer control and the manager control. The object attributes and the control method have the difference respectively, but have many same places included the information flow object oriented control. Summarizes, has the following several controls method:

4.2.1 E-Commerce information flow control method

The technical control is essential method for the e-commerce information flow control, which mainly solves the questions of order and security nature for the e-commerce information flow. At present, the e-commerce information technical control research are quite many, mainly includes the technical standard and the standard control, the control system and the management system control, the gateway website control, the firewall technical control, the data encryption technical control, the digital signature technical control, the digital time stamp technical control, the digital certificate control, the identification authentication and the access control, the information divulges protection technology, the e-commerce certification authorization organization transaction authentication control (CA, Certificate Authority), Internet's security agreement control etc.

The e-commerce information flow technical control belonging to the microscopic control is not the only useful means of information flow control, and could not solve all the problems. Therefore, we have to consider other complementary methods.

4.2.2 Policy method

The country and the government affairs have the macroeconomic regulation and control function to the e-commerce, through the management information, the economic information and the commercial information standard, overcomes the limitation of technical control, and solves the problems which the microscopic information control is not easy to solve.

Generally speaking, the country and the government have two ways to strengthen the macroeconomic regulation and control for e-commerce.

One is from the technology standard control, formulates and promulgates the e-commerce service standard, the data format standard as well as the relevant policies, like the digital signature implementation policy, the intellectual property rights protection policy, the electronic payment policy and so on, to play role of information standard and the policy guidance.

Two is macroeconomic regulation and control, like to promulgate the e-commerce tax policy, the financial policy, the credit policy, the service of material flows policy, the trade policy and the human resources policy and so on, in order to establish the e-commerce information safeguard system and information flow arrangement function.

4.2.3 Legal method

The perfect legal laws and regulations system is the guarantee to develop e-commerce, also is the important condition to control the information flow in the whole. The legal method may to supervise the e-commerce participant's information behavior and to restrict information source and transmission flow. Is same with the traditional commercial activity, the legal laws and regulations can maintain the e-commerce activity in the course of nature normally and protect legitimate benefit among all participates in the e-commerce.

4.2.4 Humanities method

Moral method, public opinion method and education method, all above methods belong to humanities method which may adjust human's information behavior, makes up flaw of the economical and technical management in the way of e-commerce, so to achieve the purpose that to strengthens the information flow reasonable use and the efficient management.

4.3   E-Commerce information synergetic control

The information synergetic control is the synthesis utilizes each information control method, forms the coupling the control system, and builds the harmonious e-commerce information environment. The way of information synergetic control may have the three ways as below:

4.3.1 Organization synergetic control

The function is to harmonize as well as adjust the business relations among each kind of organization or to establish unified e-commerce management organizations and agencies, like the establishment e-commerce information association and so on. We can then entrust them with the certain information control jurisdiction, in order to form the perfect organization and manage system which can synthesize utilizes each information control approaches to strengthen concentrated surveillance and control relate to the information flow.

4.3.2 Service synergetic control

The establishment of integrated e-commerce information service network will turn commercial information supply to integrated information supply. Meanwhile, through standardized the information integration service system, we can meet commerce information requirement for customers.

4.3.3 Operation synergetic control

All information flow control means and the methods must be performed through practical work by the operation layer. The synergetic of operation layer can influence the overall effect result from synthesis application of information control method directly. The operation synergetic involves several aspects like the e-commerce onstage website information management, backstage material flow information management and the intermediary information system. The information synergetic control plan in each aspect may be alone designed.

Acknowledgments

This article is supported by National Natural Science Foundation of China (Item No.70673071).

References

1.   F. Kleist, "An Approach to Evaluating E-Commerce Information Systems Projects". *Information Systems Frontiers,* Vol.5, No.3, 249-263(2003).
2.   I. Lewis and A. Talayevsky,"Improving the interorganizational supply chain through optimization of information flows". *Journal of Enterprise Information Management,* Vol. 8, 229-237(2004).
3.   P. Finnegal, "Systems Planning in Business-to-Business e-commerce Environments". *Information Technology and Management* , Vol.4, 183-198(2003).
4.   S. Rohrig, "Security Analysis of Electronic Business Processes", *e-commerce Research,* Vol.4, 59–81(2004).
5.   Y. Mao, "Information Flow in e-commerce", *Information Science,* Vol.6, 626-629(2002).
6.   Y. Liu and W. Z. Yang, "The Developing of Cyberspace and Controlling of Information Flow", *Archival Management,* Vol.3, 4-5 (2003).
7.   X. C. Lou and A. Z. Zhang, "Information integrated analysis process", *Information Theory and Application,* Vol.2, 101-104(2002).

An adaptive agent architecture for automated negotiation

Yong Yuan , Yong-quan Liang

College of Information Science and Engineering, Shandong University of
Science and Technology, Qingdao, 266510, China
elisen66@yahoo.com.cn

Abstract. Adaptability is regarded as an essential capability for negotiating
agent to deal with dynamic environments. In current literatures, however, little
attention has been paid on improving this capability. This paper presents a
new agent architecture to support adaptive negotiation, and discusses the
mechanisms of protocol parsing and strategy generation in detail. An
experiment is carried out on JADE platform to test the feasibility of this
architecture, and the results validate that agents can adaptively understand
protocols and respond with optimal strategies.

1 Introduction

With the amount of online commercial transactions increasing at a spectacular rate,
automated negotiation has become a key technique in developing intelligent and
flexible agent-mediated e-commerce (AMEC) systems [1]. Broadly speaking, current
research concentrates mainly on the autonomy and intelligence of negotiating agents,
aiming at empowering agents with capability of solving particular negotiating
scenarios with predefined protocols and specifically tailored strategies. In such open
and dynamic environments as Internet, however, adaptability is also essential. An
adaptive agent should have such capacities as (1) dealing with the interoperability
problem caused by heterogeneous knowledge sources; (2) understanding various
user-defined protocols and adapting to their dynamic changes; (3) generating optimal
strategies for arbitrary protocols without human intervention. Currently, the first
capacity can be obtained from the mapping of domain ontologies [2]. However, little
attention has so far been paid on the latter two problems.

The absence of adaptability hampers the real application of AMEC paradigm to
a large extent. This can be embodied from two facts: Firstly, negotiation protocols
are usually hard-coded implicitly in agents' code. As a result, agents can understand

Please use the following format when citing this chapter:

Yuan, Y., Liang, Y., 2007, in IFIP International Federation for Information Processing, Volume 251, Integration and
Innovation Orient to E-Society Volume1, Wang, W. (Eds), (Boston: Springer), pp. 601-609.

only predefined protocols and any modification to the protocol implies that agents must be taken offline to be reprogrammed. Secondly, it is hard for agents to respond an arbitrary protocol with optimal strategies. Two strategy-reasoning approaches are currently in use. One is deliberative agents' complex reasoning based on the logical argumentation and the other is reactive agents' direct response according to the past experience or predefined heuristic functions. Each has its drawbacks. The former is difficult to be realized for its high complexity while the latter usually generates sub-optimal strategies. Therefore, in order to improve adaptability, these two problems must be solved.

In this paper, an adaptive architecture of negotiating agents is put forward and tested on JADE platform. Our solution borrows some ideas from semantic web and co-evolutionary computation. In this architecture, negotiation protocol is annotated with semantic in terms of an explicit and shared protocol ontology so that it can be understandable to negotiating agent and separated from the agent kernel; Meanwhile, co-evolution is used to help the agent to generate optimal strategies adaptively.

The remainder of this paper is organized as follows: Section 2 introduces briefly the protocol ontology and co-evolution; Section 3 describes the agent architecture. Section 4 and 5 discuss the working principles of the protocol parser and the strategy generator respectively. A preliminary experiment is presented in section 6 based on JADE platform. Finally, section 7 concludes.

2   Theoretical Underpinnings

2.1   Protocol Ontology

Negotiation protocol is a set of rules that govern the interaction. To ensure an adaptive negotiation, a protocol should be: (1) Public. Unlike strategies are usually private, protocol must be public and explicit; (2) Sharable. Protocol should provide a common understanding to all agents; (3) Flexible. Protocol should be capable of being defined and modified dynamically without agents' code reprogrammed.

The emergence of ontology technique provides a perfect solution to satisfy above requirements. Ontology is a hot topic in semantic web and can be defined as a formal and explicit specification of a shared conceptualization [3]. In fact, each negotiating agent has its private ontology of negotiation protocol [4]. Thus their understandings of a same protocol may differ due to the structural or semantic heterogeneities between these ontologies. In this case, a common ontology is necessary, to which a mapping should be established to the private ontologies to ensure a common understanding. In dynamic scenarios, various concrete protocols can be instantiated and modified in terms of the common ontology. In this way, a negotiation protocol can be considered as a plug-in and consequently separated from the agent kernel.

2.2   Co-evolution

Co-evolution is a class of multi-population evolutionary algorithms dedicated to solve the dynamic self-adaptability problems in complex systems. According to the interspecies relationship, it can be classified into cooperative and competitive ones, which respectively imitate symbiosis and parasitism [5]. Currently, competitive co-evolution is often used to search for the optimal agent behaviors in strategic contexts. Its basic idea is to encode the strategy spaces as co-evolving strategy populations one for each competing agent. The co-evolution process starts with randomly generated populations and updates these strategies in successive iterations. Genetic operations are limited within the respective populations while the fitness evaluation lies on the direct interactions among strategies of different populations. Thus, these populations compete with and adapt to each other to form an evolutionary "arm race", and converge respectively. The optimal or approximate optimal strategy profiles are combinations of the best strategy individuals in the last generation.

3   Negotiating Agent Architecture

Technically speaking, a behavior-driven architecture is used in our design of the agent kernel. As is shown in figure 1, a negotiation task will be encapsulated into a composite behavior based on a finite state machine (FSM). A FSM behavior consists of a finite number of states and transition rules, and each state recursively contains a sub-behavior. Other functional components (represented by rectangular blocks) of the agent kernel coordinate to facilitate the generating, updating and scheduling of this FSM behavior.

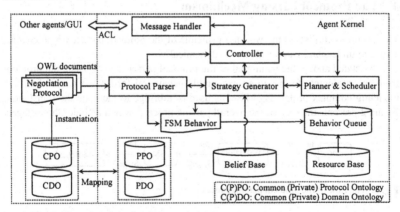

Fig.1. The architecture of an adaptive negotiating agent

As the functionalities of the above components are explicit, we hereby focus our emphasis on their coordination, which will be illustrated with a bilateral negotiation scenario. Typically, the negotiation process is as follows:

Step 1. As is shown in the left of figure 1, the initiating agent publishes the URLs of the CPO and CDO, defines a concrete negotiation protocol through instantiation from the CPO, and starts up a negotiation thread waiting for responders.

Step 2. Responding agent activates its controller and joins the negotiation thread. Based on lexical and semantic similarities, it establishes a mapping from its private ontologies to the common ones. Then negotiation protocol is sent to protocol parser.

Step 3. In terms of the CPO, the protocol parser parses the input protocol as a FSM behavior in which the sub-behavior of each state is empty. The strategy space of each agent is also generated and sent to the strategy generator.

Step 4. Strategy generator encodes the input strategy spaces as some co-evolving populations, and extracts current belief (especially of opponents) from the belief base as parameters of the co-evolution. Each population searches for one agent's strategy space and converges to its optimal strategies. Using a particular criterion, the planner will select one strategy for execution from these generated strategies. This strategy is used to fill or update the sub-behavior in each state of the FSM behavior. A belief revision operation will be performed to update the belief base if necessary.

Step 5. The FSM behavior is appended to the behavior queue, which is managed by the scheduler with a particular behavior-scheduling algorithm. Once the FSM behavior is executed, negotiation process begins.

Step 6. During negotiation, step 4 and step 5 are performed repeatedly until a final state of the FSM behavior is reached. In case the negotiation protocol changes, the protocol parser will be invoked once again to generate a new FSM behavior and provide the strategy generator with new strategy spaces.

4   The Protocol Parsing Mechanism

This section will discuss the working principle of the protocol parser, which enables agents to understand various protocols dynamically.

As stated above, the main goal of the protocol parser is to translate the protocol from an ontological format to an executable behavioral format. As a useful tool in modeling complex protocols, a FSM is used as a bridge to facilitate the translation. Figure 2 presents the flow of the overall parsing process, which includes three stages.

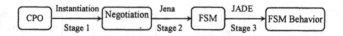

Fig. 2. The flow of the protocol parsing process

The first stage is the instantiation of the negotiation protocol from CPO. This is a precondition of the parsing process, and can be regarded as the semantic annotation of the protocol. In this stage, CPO plays an importance role. As a shared view of the commonalities across different protocols, CPO must capture the common concepts and their relationships. The instantiated protocol can be built from the instances of these concepts, and will be stored in OWL documents.

In the second stage, the OWL protocol will be parsed into a FSM. This can be done with the help of Jena. Jena is a Java framework for building semantic web applications and provides a java API for OWL manipulation [6]. Using Jena model interface, the protocol parser can explore the document structure of the OWL protocol, and extract instances of the CPO classes. In this way, the instances in the input OWL document can be considered as building blocks, from which a FSM can be assembled. In addition, the strategy space of each agent will also be generated in this stage simply by aggregating all possible actions in each move.

The last stage is to encode the FSM to an executable behavior. Fortunately, this can be done by the agent platform itself. The advantages of FSM lie not only in its rich expressive power, but also in the efficient supports from a variety of agent platforms. For instance, JADE [7], an open-source and fully FIPA compliant agent platform, provides a useful class jade.core.behaviours.FSMBehaviour which can translate from FSM to the corresponding FSM behavior conveniently. It is worth noting that in each state of the resulting FSM behavior, sub-behavior will be empty since only possible actions are specified in FSM. Which action is actually performed will be determined by the strategy generator.

5 The Strategy Generation Mechanism

This section presents the rationale of the co-evolutionary algorithm (CEA) used by strategy generator, which enables agents to generate optimal strategies adaptively.

As stated above, the strategy generator aims at specifying a determinate action for each move of an agent to maximize its payoff. This can be achieved using CEA. Essentially speaking, the co-evolution can be considered as an iterative searching and learning process in strategy spaces. The strategy generator will maintain several populations co-evolving with coupled fitness. In each generation, new strategies arise to defeat old ones, and this creates new challenges for the opponent populations. Consequently, fitter strategies must be found in the opponent populations to adapt to the challenges. This process will lead to an evolutionary "arm race" and eventually converge to the optimal strategies.

```
Input: An agentID id; Strategy spaces of N agents; Current belief; Instruction from the Planner;
Output: An optimal strategy of agent_id.
Begin
    Use the current belief to initialize the parameters of the co-evolution and set generation = 0;
    For i = 1 to N do Begin // Step 1: strategy encoding
        Encode agent_i's strategy space into a population P_i containing p_i random strategies;
    End;
    While (generation <= maximum generation) do // Iterative co-evolution
        For i =1 to N do Begin // Step 2: fitness evaluation
            For j =1 to p_i do Begin
                Select the j'th strategy s_j from P_i; //Host strategy
                Repeat //Negotiate with all parasite strategies
                    Select an untested strategy from each opponent population; //Parasite strategies
                    Calculate the payoff of s_j after negotiating with these strategies;
                Until (all opponent strategies are tested).
                Fitness of s_j = the average payoff obtained against all the opponent strategies;
            End;
        End;
        For i=1 to N do Begin // Step 3: genetic operation
            Perform the selection operation on P_i based on the fitness;
            For j=1 to p_i do Perform the crossover and mutation operation on strategy s_j.
        End;
        Set generation = generation+1;
    End;
    Select an optimal strategy from the individuals in P_id under the Planner's instruction and output it.
end
```

Fig. 3. Pseudo code of the co-evolutionary algorithm

The pseudo code of the detailed CEA is shown in figure 3. It consists of three main steps: strategy encoding, fitness evaluation and genetic operation. Specially, we will clarify the realization of the former two steps.

Strategy encoding is a mapping process from agent's strategy space to CEA's code space. Generally speaking, each input strategy space from the protocol parser will be encoded as a strategy population, in which a strategy individual is encoded as a chromosome. An action in each move of this strategy will be encoded as a gene on the chromosome, and all possible actions on one move constitute alleles.

Fitness evaluation of CEA differs from that of canonical evolutionary algorithm. Similarly as in [8], we use term "host" to refer to the population where the currently evaluated strategy is resided, and "parasites" to opponent populations. Each strategy of the host population competes against all the parasite strategies and its fitness will be the average payoff obtained against these parasite strategies. In this way, each population takes turns to be host and all strategies can be evaluated.

6   Experiment and Results

We implemented this adaptive agent architecture by integrating a protocol parser and a strategy generator with a JADE agent. In this section, we will carry out an experiment to validate that it can understand a simple protocol to which it has no prior knowledge, and respond with an optimal strategy.

6.1 Experiment Scenario

The experiment scenario involves two agents negotiating over a single issue. As is shown in figure 4(a), we initialized JADE with three containers: A main container serves as the E-market and two attached containers as the buyer host and seller host. The buyer and seller agents, denoted as ag_B and ag_S respectively, reside on their own host container initially and will migrate to the E-market later on. For simplicity, assume they are homogeneous and each has complete information about its opponent. In this case, ontology mapping and belief revision will not be taken into account.

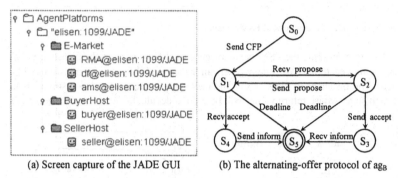

(a) Screen capture of the JADE GUI   (b) The alternating-offer protocol of ag_B

Fig. 4. The JADE set-up and the negotiation protocol

A finite-horizon version of the alternating-offer protocol depicted in [9] is used in our experiment. It has a unique sub-game perfect equilibrium (SPE), which can be used to check the optimality of strategies. In this protocol, agents offer alternately in discrete rounds $t = 1, 2, ..., T$ until reaching the deadline or agreement. Agents' time preferences are expressed by discount factors, denoted as δ_B and δ_S respectively. Without loss of generality, assume ag_B makes the first offer with a CFP message. The states and transitions of ag_B are depicted in figure 4(b), and those of ag_S can be obtained simply by exchanging the Send and Recv (abbr. of Receive) predicates.

6.2 Experiment Results

Let us first present the FSM behavior generated by the protocol parser. As stated above, this protocol must be semantically annotated based on CPO to be understood by agents. Due to space constraints, the class hierarchy of CPO will be omitted here. However, we think the concepts and instances below are sufficient to characterize this simple protocol: 1) six instances of class state from S0 to S5; 2) nine instances of class transition, each corresponding to an arrow in figure 4(b); 3) nine instances of class action, and each action triggers a transition; 4) seven instances of class message, each attached to a Send or Recv predicate.

```
registerFirstState(new S0Behavior(), S0); registerDefaultTransition(S0,S1);
registerState(new S1Behavior(), S1); registerTransition(S1,S2,1); registerTransition(S1,S4,2);
                              registerTransition(S1,S5,3); // 1,2,3 are return values of S1Behavior();
registerState(new S2Behavior(), S2); registerTransition(S2,S1,1); registerTransition(S2,S3,2);
                              registerTransition(S2,S5,3); // 1 2,3 are return values of S2Behavior();
registerState(new S3Behavior(), S3); registerDefaultTransition(S3,S5);
registerState(new S4Behavior(), S4); registerDefaultTransition(S4,S5);
registerLastState(new S5Behavior(), S5);
```

Fig. 5. The code of the generated FSM behavior

Figure 5 presents the FSM behavior generated from parsing these instances. We can see that each piece of code registers an instance of class state or transition within agent. The instances of class action and message are encapsulated in a sub-behavior of each state, whose return values will be used to decide the next state of a transition

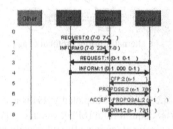

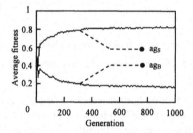

(a) Screen capture of the sniffer agent populations

(b) Average fitness of strategy

Fig. 6. Negotiation results

Next we will check the optimality of strategies resulting from the co-evolution in the strategy generator. Figure 6 shows the negotiation results in case the deadline $T = 3$ and discount factors $\delta_B = \delta_S = 0.8$. Similarly as in [9], if we assume the total negotiation surplus is equal to unity, the SPE in this case will be "Negotiation ends in the first round, and ag_S gets payoff 0.84 while ag_B gets the rest 0.16".

Figure 6(a) depicts the messages on the E-market container captured by a JADE sniffer agent. Obviously, negotiation will begin with the fifth CFP message. ag_B accepts the first offer of ag_S, and negotiation ends immediately. Figure 6(b) shows the average fitness of each agent's strategy population during the co-evolution. Here average fitness can be used to predict and interpret agent's payoff, and they converge stably to 0.84 and 0.16 respectively. These results are consistent with the SPE, which validates that optimal strategies have been obtained from the co-evolution.

7 Conclusions

This paper presents a new agent architecture capable of negotiating adaptively. Such techniques as ontology and co-evolution are employed to empower agents with capabilities of understanding ever-changing protocols and responding with optimal strategies adaptively. An experiment carried out on JADE platform indicates that this architecture is feasible and efficient. In the future work, we plan to experiment with more complex protocols and develop a practical AMEC prototype system.

8 References

1. N. R. Jennings, P. Faratin, A. R. Lomuscio, S. Parsons, C. Sierra and M. Wooldridge, "Automated Negotiation: Prospects, Methods and Challenges", *International Journal of Group Decision and Negotiation*, 10(2), 199-215, 2001.

2. N. Silva, P. Maio and J. Rocha, "An Approach to Ontology Mapping Negotiation", In: Proceedings of the Third International Conference on Knowledge Capture Workshop on Integrating Ontologies, Banff, Canada, 2005.

3. G. Antoniou and F. van Harmelen, *A Semantic Web Primer*, MIT Press, 2004.

4. V. Tamma, M. Wooldridge and I. Dickinson, "An Ontology for Automated Negotiation", In: Proceedings of the Workshop on Ontologies in Agent Systems, Bologna, Italy, 2002.

5. J. Paredis, "Co-evolutionary Computation", *Artificial Life*, 2(4), 355-375, 1995.

6. Jena-A Semantic Web Framework for Java. URL: http://jena.sourceforge.net/.

7. JADE-Java Agent Development Framework. URL: http://jade.tilab.com.

8. C. D. Rosin and R. K. Belew, "New Methods for Competitive Co-evolution", *Evolutionary Computation*, 5(1), 1-29, 1997.

9. A. Rubinstein, "Perfect Equilibrium in a Bargaining Model", *Econometrica*, 50(1), 97-110, 1982.

Technological Framework and Application of Exhibition Electronic Business

A Case Study of China Import & Export Fair

Yong-jun Chen[1], Shi Tan[2], Hai-jun Zhao[1], Cheng Hua[1], Ju Xiang[1]

1 Guangdong Electronic Business Market Application Key Laboratory,
Guangdong University of Business Studies. #21, Chisha Road, Haizhu
District, Guangzhou, Guangdong Province. 510320, P.R.C.
mikechen@gdcc.edu.cn
WWW home page: http://www.gdec.org.cn
2 Electronic Business Section of China Imports and Exports Commodity
Trade Fair

Abstract. The combination of the electronic business and the exhibition industry has become an inevitable trend of the development of the exhibition industry. Through the efforts of many years, China Import & Export Fair has built a solid basic hardware platform for electronic business, hence made the exhibition management and electronic service e-enabled and web-enabled, then established the outward communication service systems, and built up an OA platform for foreign trade center. This paper provides a demonstration research analysis, and proposes a general model for the framework of electronic business in the exhibition industry.

1 Introduction

Electronic business is an important means to enhance comprehensive national power and to make great strides in social productivity. The electronic business development is an inevitable trend of boosting the national economy and social information development. A report named" Electronic business is becoming a necessary means to increase city competitive competency" was recently issued by Ccidnet Consultant Company (www.ccidnet.com), an authorized IT consultation organization.

Exhibition industry is a new prosperous industry in china with wide potential market and promising future. It can directly promote economic development and boost trade communication in an effective way. With rapid development, it has become an important composition of the third industry in China. Exhibition industry is an integrated services trade industry tightly related to communication, traffic

Please use the following format when citing this chapter:

Chen, Y., Tan, S., Zhao, H., Hua, C., Xiang, J., 2007, in IFIP International Federation for Information Processing, Volume 251, Integration and Innovation Orient to E-Society Volume1, Wang, W. (Eds), (Boston: Springer), pp. 610-619.

transportation, city construction, tour and leisure, hotel and restaurant, advertisement and printing and others. It has been seeking to utilize information technology to improve operational efficiency and to increase the whole operating level. It has been an inevitable trend for the exhibition industry to take advantage of the electronic business to improve the exhibition industry in recent years. A system combined exhibition electronic business and information service with proper design, perfect function and friendly interface has been the infrastructure of the modern exhibition industry [1, 2, and 4].

2 The Construction of China Import & Export Fair Electronic Business System

Exhibition industry is playing an important role in Guangzhou. national economy[3]. As the biggest exhibition in China, the electronic business system of the China Import & Export Fair has an effect of demonstration and standardization, hence has significant reference to the construction of electronic business system in exhibition industry in China.

The electronic business system of China Import & Export Fair consists of five subsystems:

1) Business management service system.
2) Trade fair website,
3) Spot service system.
4) Foreign trade electronic administrative system.
5) Online hardware support platform.

2.1 The Business Management Service System

The business management service system can be divided into two parts: one is the business management service system facing exhibitors; the other is the service system facing the merchant customers. The former is based on the exhibitor database and the later is based on the merchant customer database. The information flow in the whole process of the exhibition business operation hence can be handled.

(1) The Management Service System Facing Exhibitors

The Management Service System Facing Exhibitors consists of subsystems such as online record management system, online card management system, transaction statistic system, online one-stop shop management system and others. It is a business management system that using modern electronic business technologies to establish the business between exhibitor enterprises and all levels of management departments in China Import & Export Fair. It aims at leveling up the exhibition and management of China Import & Export Fair by means of network, and increasing the visibility, fairness and transparency of the stall and card distribution in China Import & Export Fair. At present, it has helped China Import & Export Fair to implement the information management of some operations such as stall distribution, card management, and exhibition preparation.

1) Online Records Management System

The first stage of the record management system development was finished by the 90th session of China Import & Export Fair. It has become a mature system tool after several sessions perfecting. The exhibition preparation and exhibition electronic management level of China Import & Export Fair thus reached a new stage and the online administration of traditional operation thus became more convenient, more efficient, more visible and more transparent.

The functions of the system cover all traditional business related to China Import & Export Fair stall distribution such as the application submitting from the enterprises, the qualification check and approving of exhibition applications of the enterprises by the commercial association/trade group, the stall distribution inquiry/statistics. It made the process of charge for trade fair group stall information-enabled. In details,, the pre-charge notice and charge notice to each trade fair group are produced according to the situation of the stall distribution for the trade fair group; and then the exhibition refund form for each trade fair group is automatically built according to the exhibition map record, so that the checking and accounting of China Import & Export Fair stall management is web-enabled.

2) Management System of China Import & Export Fair Merchant Card

In the 91st session of China Import & Export Fair in Guangzhou the "Exhibitor Online Card Handling System" was issued, and merchant card dealing on online was then promoted in four exhibition groups. The range of the 92nd session experimental unit has extended to six chamber of commerce and 10 trade groups based on the success of the former two sessions.

A uniform China Import & Export Fair management platform was developed in the 93rd session of China Import & Export Fair with the range of card handling expended to all trade groups, chambers of commercial and exhibitors. All kinds of cards included in China Import & Export Fair such as exhibitor card, work card, temporary card, arrangement and withdrawal card, conference card, vehicle card, foreign representative card, accompanying card, interpreter card, and so on, were included and handled online, while the gests card was exclusive. Business functions such as information submission, card dealing, card changing, business statistics, card index checking, card handling fee, payment and settlement and so on, were provided online. With all cards handled online, the hidden trouble on safety of the traditional card dealing can be avoided; the card handling procedure can be simplified; and the pressure on the spot exhibition can be reduced.

3) Transaction Statistics System

Transaction Statistics System is mainly used in the statistic of exported transaction daily concluding to offer timely and precise data to support various departments to make decisions. According to the requirement and the instruction of the former ministry of foreign economy and trade, export transaction statistic method of China Import & Export Fair was regulated. As a result, the transaction statistic form delivery became timelier; the commodity classification became closer to custom statistic; and the classification details were specific to each transaction country. The statistic classification can really meet different needs of sponsors, chambers of commerce, and trade fair groups.

4) One-Stop Shop Service System

Traditional handwork operation mode was replaced by spot computer charge mode. Thus the efficiency of application procedure for dealing various service items of the exhibitors was increased. The One-Stop Shop Service System has become the core operational system during China Import & Export Fair arrangement period. At present, it has helped to implement the exhibition stall configuration confirmation from stall map, exhibition configuration prefabrication and repair, exhibitor spot services, background service and the whole processing electronic operation and data synchronization. Hence the precision and efficiency of the spot exhibition operation were greatly increased.

(2) Service System Facing Merchants

The Service System Facing Merchants includes subsystems such as the merchant invitation system, the merchant registration system, the electronic invitation and online card handling system, the VIP merchant management system and so on The operation of invitations and registering customers now can be managed electronically; the data support merchants to make decisions can be tracked and analyzed; the traditional business is extended successfully to the Internet; the procedures for merchants to deal with long-distance business become more convenient, and communication costs are saved.

1) Merchant Invitation System

The Merchant Invitation System is an operation system for merchants to communicate with China Import & Export Fair. Functions of system include invitation issue, investigation, analyses, and so on.

2) Merchant Registration System

The Merchant Registration System is and operation system handling card to merchants. Its main functions are register, card handling, statistic, analyses, and enquiry. It can offer complete and precise basic data to merchants and has gradually formed the core database of customers.

3) Electronic Invitation and Online Card Processing System

The Electronic Invitation and Online Card Processing System has functions such as electronic invitation, electronic invitation issue, electronic liaison, online investigation, PVC card preprocessing, pre-registration, and so on. All buyers are managed based on the membership system. Information can be self-maintained and transactions can be self-operated by buyers through Internet. Advanced online development technologies are adopted to extend clients invitation, card handling and liaison to Internet areas. Thus the capability of response to customers is greatly enhanced; the contact channel between the merchants is developed; and contact cost is reduced.

4) VIP Merchant Management System

VIP Merchant Management System is employed to systemically manage merchant invitation and liaison. It is executed to realize functions as: recording and inquiring basic information of the important customers, recording and checking visiting business and liaison process of important customers. Through related data collection, sorting, contrast and analysis, it offers scientific decisions and practical tools for the work of invitation.

2.2 Spot Information Service System

During the China Import & Export Fair, services of high quality including information field service, information tool service, and information services are offered to exhibitors through spot multi-form information service products such as scan enquiry, compact disc, broad band and electronic business center.

(1) SCAN Inquiry System

This system is based on the database of the exhibitors at China Import & Export Fair. It is an important information inquiry system to offer participants information, exhibition information, demand and supply information, as well as exhibition service information to the exhibitors during the trade fair. The classification of enterprise characteristics and products are more detailed, and is successfully integrated with the records system.

Information of more than 8000 exhibitor enterprises in each session of China Import & Export Fair has been collected, sorted and checked. There are 36 SCAN desks with consultants in the exhibition hall during the exhibition event to offer comprehensive, precise, and integrated information consulting services.

(2) Compact Disc (CD)

China Import & Export Fair information CD is a kind of information product to publicize trade fair and China Import & Export Fair exhibitor enterprises. It is issued twice annually by China Import & Export Fair which is held two sessions annually. It contains up to date data from the latest session of China Import and Export Fair, the 8000 participant enterprises, and 100000 exhibition products. The CD can be directly distributed free to more than 100000 merchants. it is a major reference tool for foreign merchants to contact exhibitor enterprises.

(3) Electronic Business Service Center

There are twelve electronic business service centers set in the exhibition hall in each session to offer exhibition participants various services such as email receiving and sending, selling card printing, online fax, information communication, online marketing, trade cooperation, member logging-on, and so on. In addition, various information products of China Import & Export Fair are actively publicized.

(4) Offering Broad Band and Rental Computers Service

High wire speed online communication service is offered to exhibitor enterprises; wireless Broad Brand service is offered to mobile users including foreign merchants and reporters; meanwhile, computer lease and hardware support services are offered.

2.3   The Official Website of China Import & Export Fair

The proposition of the Official Website of China Import & Export Fair is professional exhibition website for international trade. Found in autumn 1999, the website is completely updated in October 2001 and comprehensively offers lots of information and partially realizes some traditional online transaction. It has become the important window of China Import & Export Fair for invitation business and exhibition service. With the continual increasing in specialization and internationalization, the website construction of China Import & Export Fair is striding toward electronic business. The website of China Import & Export Fair features following functions:

(1) Publicity and business invitation

The website provides different language versions such as simplified Chinese, complicated Chinese, English, Japanese, German, French, Russian, Spanish, Arabic, and so on. Information is distinguishingly offered in different versions according to the targeted visitors on the website. Through merchant exhibition guides, exhibitor notice, news center and other columns, latest authority information of China Import & Export Fair can be timely issued. It is an important window of the business invitation by offering comprehensive and precise information on China Import & Export Fair to all exhibitors and merchants.

(2) Online Transactions of Traditional Business

1) Electronic Invitation and Online Card Processing System

The functions of this system are the same as the functions of the electronic invitation and online card processing system in service system facing merchants.

2) Easy-Connection between Exhibitors

"Easy-Connection between Exhibitors" online exhibition service center has been established for exhibitors; services to participant enterprises are gradually integrated; spot service, online reservation and information inquiry service are provided. In current phase, several contents such as exhibition information, transaction forms, and important notice are integrated by the platform; and some functions such as the declaration form enquiry, withdrawing stall configuration, examining chart result and other function are promoted; and services like broad band and information equipments reservation are offered online thus a new online approach for exhibitors to applying for services in advance is available.

3) Exhibitor Information Maintenance Online

At the beginning autumn of 2002, the transmission modes of SCAN information from exhibitor enterprises are partially changed from by mail of fax to by submitting directly online after logging on China Import & Export Fair website. Compared to the traditional mailing method, the way exhibitors submitting and maintaining information through web can ensure the accuracy and integrality of data. It is more convenient, faster, and more economic. Meanwhile, it can relieve typists from heavy workload.

4) "Authorized Purchase" Online Reservation

In order to cooperate with the event of "online purchasing" held in the 93rd session of China Import & Export Fair, an "online purchasing column" was issued on the website. Company information and purchasing lists from four purchasing companies including America Home Depot, were issued, and online reservations were offered on the website. Exhibitor enterprises can check event contents on the column, and can register their companies and main products according to the requirements. Buyer enterprises then can make appointments to carry on negotiation with exhibitor enterprises at China Import & Export Fair.

(3) Electronic Business Functions

Through columns like exhibitor enterprise, product inquiry, supply and demand information issuance, business affair section, and online business negotiation platform, the website offers international trade intermediaries service to national and international buyer companies. With multimedia means and multiple manners, the brand characteristics of China enterprises and culture are fully displayed, and China foreign trade export is boosted.

Online Trade Fair is improved version amended and perfected from the original online negotiation section. It has some new characteristics as following:

1) Better Customized Services

Business assistant offers multiple customized functions setting according to the requirements of users, and thus provides various customized services including "my negotiation", "my search", "my collection" and "customized services", "my statistics" and so on.

2) Offering multi-level information safety guarantee

Sensitive information is classified and set according to the safety level to guarantee the safety of key data from enterprises; the management mode of the authorized browsing products makes enterprises checking individually, through which the spying from competitors in the same industry is avoid; the detailed information resource instruction guarantees the legal use of enterprise information.

3) Multiple Technologies Supported Trade Negotiation

Two negotiation modes—one is based on online video and the other is based on trade forms, are offered. Enterprises can select either mode according to their actual requirements. The detailed and practical online training using streaming-media offers enterprises guidance and help on electronic business application.

4) Comprehensive statistics analysis function

Relevant data for the electronic business are offered to enterprises; business event situation on the China Import & Export Fair website is comprehensively analyzed; degrees of attentions on companies and products are reflect; data to support online marketing decision-making are offered.

2.4 Construction of Foreign Trade Center Electronic Administration

The objective of foreign trade electronic administration construction is to offer decision-makers assistant decision supports, and to help functional departments to make office work, decision-making and transactions e-enabled through constructing and employing OAS system. Thus foreign trade center affairs processed without paper, administration information e-enabled, and transactions processed simultaneously can be gradually realized. Efficiency and quality of transactions then can be enhanced.

Foreign trade center has constructed and promoted OA information management system in batches and in phases. At present, foreign trade personnel management, capital management, financial management, party affairs management, enterprise affairs management, daily exhibition management, and other administrative subsystems have been launched to use. The center electronic administrative network includes 15 subsidiary platforms, which is playing an important role to support the center business management, daily administration, and internal communication.

2.5 Network Hardware Support Platform

At present, China Import & Export Fair has high speed network system all over the China Import & Export Fair lobby, through which the network connection between two exhibition halls of Guangzhou is implemented, and kilo-mega trunk and hundred-mega port are basically made realized. There are 2500 hundred-mega-ports in the exhibition hall located in Liuhua Road and over 10000 hundred-mega-ports in the Pazhou exhibition hall. Thus the needs of the exhibition enterprises to use the network with high speed and with multimedia demonstration can be satisfied sufficiently. The core network safety project implemented centralized controlling of network anti-virus and supervision of malfunction retrievals; core data service server double-machine warm back-up project is finished; a batch of high performance service equipments are possessed of. Safe and reliable hardware support and network operation environment are offered to the electronic business of the China Import & Export Fair.

(1) Hardware Infrastructure

Some high performance computer equipments has been purchased for China Import & Export Fair. During the trade fair, the maximal number of running computers in the center (group) computer network reached 2500; various running servers are 46; and there are some printing equipments in different classes.

(2) Network System

The high speed network system all over at the trade fair is based on trunk- kilo mega, port hundred mega. There are 2500 of 10 mega information connecting point, through 200M bandwidth international internet connecting, which can fully meet the demand of the exhibitor enterprises to use the network with high speed and multimedia demonstration. In No. 1, No.2, No.3, No.5 hall, No.9 conference room, and in some public rest-rooms, there are wireless transmitting and receiving equipments that can meet the needs of wireless network communication service for mobile users; there are 3000 network access ports in transactions areas of the trade fair hall, which can meet the requirements of the foreign trade administration and transactions management system.

(3) Network Security

The implementation of core network safety project has realized the centralized controlling of network anti-virus and supervision of malfunction retrievals; the implementation of core data service server double-machine hot back-up project and the server optimizing project have provide reliable hardware support and network operation environment for the China Import & Export Fair electronic business.

3 Analysis of General framework of exhibition industry electronic business technology Architecture

Presently, there is no literature review on exhibition industry electronic business integrated framework. Through analyzing Guangzhou Import & Export Fair electronic business system, we proposed a general framework of exhibition electronic business technologies as following:

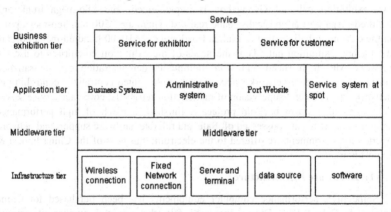

Fig 1 Exhibition electronic business framework model

The general framework of exhibition electronic business can be displayed as four tiers, which are 1) Infrastructure tier 2) middleware tier, 3) application tier, and 4) business display tier.

Infrastructure tier mainly offers basic software and hardware facilities. It consists of the network system, the system of servers and various terminals, the basic data source, and basic software. Network system includes wireless network ((GPRS/3G/WLAN/WIMAX/WIFI and etc) connecting, network connecting and exhibition intranet. The middleware tier mainly offers date integration of ground level data source, communication, encryption, and other services. It is mainly composed of various middleware. Application tier is made up of four parts which are the business system, the administration system, the portal website system, and the spot service system. The business exhibition tier mainly offers various services to participants. It mainly includes services facing exhibitors and services facing merchants.

The model of exhibition industry electronic business framework is a general mode which is abstracted from real exhibition electronic business framework. It is expected to offer beneficial guidance for the combination and development of China exhibition industry and electronic business.

4 Conclusion

The exhibition management and service system shall be e-enabled and web-enabled with the development of the exhibition industry; the outward communication service system and OA system shall be built up with core of professional exhibition website. Going on this premise, various advanced facilities and communication systems such as digital information transmission networks and satellite communication systems shall be built up, and the combination and development of exhibition industry and electronic business shall be achieved. Undoubtedly, it has important meanings of demonstration and reference to the construction of exhibition industry electronic business in China, if we generalize the course of China Import & Export Fair electronic business system, and abstract the framework model of exhibition industry electronic business in exhibition industry electronic business.

References:

1. X.J Yan, and W. Liu, *Some Problems for the Internet using for MICE*, Theory and Practice, 2004(1),pp54-85.
2. Bei Jin, "The Application of Electronic Commerce in the MICE of Modern City", *Journal of Beijing City College*, 71(3), pp.84-88(2005).
3. S. Tan, Electronic Business Promoting the Development of Gaungzhou Trade Fair. The Proceedings of Electronic Business and Guangzhou *Exhibition Development Salon*, Guangzhou, China. November, 2006(unpublished), pp1-6.
4. X.J Cao, The Prospect of MICE Electronic Business Development, The Proceedings of Electronic Business and Guangzhou *Exhibition Development Salon*, Guangzhou, China. November, 2006(unpublished), pp21-24.

A Digital Signature Scheme in Web-based Negotiation Support System

Yuxuan Meng[1] and Bo Meng[2]

1 Department of Computer Science, University of Saskatchewan, Saskatoon, Saskatchewan, S7N 5C9, Canada yxmeng68@yahoo.ca

2 School of Computer, Wuhan University, Wuhan, P. R. China, 430072 bmengwhu@sina.com

Abstract. With the rapid development of electronic commerce, digital signature is very important in preventing from forging, tampering, and disavowing electronic contract in web-based negotiation support system (WNSS). Based on the requirements of electronic contract in WNSS and several techniques widely used in digital signatures, a digital signature scheme for electronic contracts is presented in the paper. Public key algorithm, hash function and interceders are used in the scheme. The feasibility and implementation of the scheme in WNSS are discussed.

1 Introduction

The web-based negotiation support system (WNSS) has been developed and applied in electronic commerce, which could be used to support the negotiators to negotiate through Internet [1, 2]. WNSS can provide real-time remote supports and services in every phases of negotiation. Negotiators can use WNSS to deal with business negotiations and bargaining at any place of the world conveniently.

In the traditional business negotiations, two parties of the negotiation usually sign or stamp on the paper contract, if the negotiation is successful, namely 'black and white'. In this way we can identify trade associates, confirm the reliability of contract and prevent from disavowing. However, when the negotiators agree with a protocol or electronic contract in WNSS, we also need credible identification and implement digital signature to prevent from disavowing. Furthermore, the electronic contract without signatures is easily modified. And the integrity and authenticity of the contract can't be assured.

Based on the requirements of electronic contract in WNSS and several techniques widely used in digital signatures [3-8], this paper presented a digital

Please use the following format when citing this chapter:

Meng, Y., Meng, B., 2007, in IFIP International Federation for Information Processing, Volume 251, Integration and Innovation Orient to E-Society Volume1, Wang, W. (Eds), (Boston: Springer), pp. 620-626.

signature scheme for electronic contracts in WNSS, which use public key algorithm, hash function and interceders. The digital signature scheme can assure the reliability of electronic contracts and prevent from disavowing effectively. The feasibility and implementation of the digital signature scheme in WNSS are discussed.

2 Digital Signature and Digital Certificates

2.1 Digital Signature

The real purpose of a signature is for an individual/entity to provide a stamp of approval of the data or document under review. In today's world, almost every legal financial transaction is formalized on paper. A signature or multiple signatures on the paper guarantee its authenticity. The signature is typically used for the purposes of user authentication and document authentication. Signatures on the paper have two functions. One is preventing from disavowing, so that we can confirm that the file has been subscribed. Another is preventing from copying, so that we can confirm the reality of the file.

Digital signatures have the same functions of paper-based signatures. However, the digital signatures are more different from paper-based signatures. Because the digital signatures are so dependent on the actual data content, they are very suitable for digital data, which can be tampered with quite easily. The digital signatures have especial problems to be solved. Firstly, the digital file is easily to be copy, even the digital signature is difficult to forge, but cutting and plastering valid signature is so easy. Secondly, the digital file is easily to modify after the digital signature, and the modified file won't leave any trace. Thus simple graphic tag that simulates manual signature can't be used for digital signature.

Digital signature should have some characteristics as follows.

(1) Digital signature should use the information that can only identify signatory.

(2) The content of the message that would be signed can be authentication before signature.

(3) Digital signature could be validated by the third party in order to resolve dispute.

Obviously digital signature not only has the function of identification, but also authentication. Digital signature can be used to preventing from forging signature, tampering information, sending message in the name of other people and denying the information that has been sent/received.

2.2 Digital Signature Algorithms

2.2.1 Symmetric algorithms with interceder

The precondition of this algorithm is that sender and receiver fully trust interceder. Let S, T, R denote sender, interceder and receiver respectively. Then the algorithm is described as follows [3, 4].

(1) S and T share key K_A, R and T share key K_B.

(2) S encrypt file M with K_A to generates $K_A (M)$. Then S sends $K_A (M)$ to T.

(3) Because only S and T share K_A, if T can decrypt $K_A (M)$ with K_A, T can confirm the message coming from S. Then T write a declaration D to prove that he have received the M from S. At last T use K_B to encrypt M and D: $K_B (M, D)$.

(4) T sends $K_B (M, D)$ to S.

(5) S use K_B to decrypt $K_B (M, D)$, then gets M and D. From D, S could assure the M comes from S.

2.2.2 Public key algorithms

Public key algorithms are asymmetric algorithms, which are very suitable for digital signature, because they have public key and private key. It is very important to choose the private key for using Public key algorithms to encrypt file. The keys must meet three conditions: ① $SK(PK(M))=M$, $PK(SK(M))=M$. ② To calculate SK from PK is very difficult. ③ It is impossible to determine the M from part of plaintext. The algorithm is described as follows [3, 4].

(1) S encrypts plaintext M with his own private key SK to generate SK (M).

(2) S sends SK (M) to R.

(3) R decrypts with S's public key PK to get M.

If R could carry out step (3), the digital signature of S is valid.

2.2.3 Public key algorithm with hash function

The efficiency of using public key algorithm to encrypt long file is very low. Therefore hash function is always used with public key algorithm at the same time, in order to improve efficiency. In this way, sender needn't encrypt the whole file, he only to encrypt the hash value of the file. The sender and receiver should negotiate and determine the hash function and digital signature algorithm in advance. The algorithm is described as follows [3, 4].

(1) S uses a hash function to generate hash result H (M) of the file M.

(2) S encrypts H(M) with his own private key SK to get SK(H(M)), namely digital signature.

(3) S sends M and SK (H (M)) to R.

(4) R also uses the same hash function with S to generate H'(M) of the M, and decrypts SK(H(M)) with S's public key PK to get H(M). If H'(M)=H(M), then the digital signature is valid.

2.3 Digital Certificates

If digital signature is based on public key algorithms, there are two problems obviously. At first, how to ensure the owners of the public keys are authentic. Secondly, how to deal with the production, distribution and management of the public keys. Certification Authority (CA) can resolve above problems. The authenticity of public keys may be established by a trusted third party. A guarantee of the identity of the owner of a public key is called *certification* of the public key. A person or organization that certifies public keys is known as a Certification Authority (CA). The digital certificate is the evidence as identity of the person or organization on Internet. It includes the owner's name, public key, CA's digital signature, the period of validity of the digital certificate, etc. Digital certificate can provide identity and authenticity, so it is widely used in electronic commerce.

3 A Digital Signature Scheme in WNSS

3.1 Requirements of Digital Signature in WNSS

It is very important for both negotiators to sign the contract by the end of the negotiation, because the signed contract is the voucher of the business trade. To insure the validity, fairness of the signature and prevent from disavowing, the digital signature in WNSS should satisfy the following requirements.

(1) The digital signature of both negotiators of the negotiation is authentic. Any negotiator can confirm the signature he received comes from the other party of the negotiation, but not from someone else.

(2) The digital signatures of the negotiators can't be forged. Only negotiators can sign the contract, anyone else can't forge their signatures.

(3) The digital signatures of the negotiators can't be used repeatedly by other people. The signature is a part of the contract. Anyone else can't transfer the signature to other files.

(4) The context of the contract that both negotiators should sign must be same. In the process of transfer, the context of the contract can't be tampered.

(5) The digital signature of both negotiators is of non-repudiation. After both negotiators have signed the contract, they can't deny their signatures.

(6) The digital signature of both negotiators is fair. At the end of the process of signature, the result is both negotiators having received the other party's signature or both negotiators having not received the other party's signature.

(7) If the context of the contract was very confidential, it could be seen by both negotiators only.

3.2 The Digital Signature Scheme in WNSS

Taking into account of the requirements of digital signature in WNSS and several algorithms widely used in digital signatures, we designs a new digital signature scheme for electronic contracts in WNSS, which uses public key algorithm, hash function and interceders.

Let A and B be two negotiators of the negotiation respectively. Let PK_A, PK_B, PK_C be the public keys of the negotiator A, B and interceder respectively. Let SK_A, SK_B be private keys of the negotiator A, B respectively. Let H be hash function. Let M be the plaintext of the electronic contracts. The digital signature scheme is described as follows.

① A encrypts M with B's public key PK_B to generate $PK_B(M)$. A use hash function to generate hash result H(M). Then, A encrypts H(M) with his private key SK_A to sign the M. And $SK_A(H(M))$ is called the digital signature. Furthermore, A encrypts H(M) and SK_A(H(M)) with C's public key PK_C to generate a information packet ATC: PK_C(H(M), SK_A(H(M))), which would be transferred to C by B.

② A sends PK_B(M), H(M) and ATC to B.

③ B will decrypt PK_B(M) with his own private key SK_B to get M. Then B uses the same hash function as A to generate his own hash result H'(M). If H(M)= H'(M), then B can be sure M has not been changed during transference. Then B encrypts H'(M) with his own private key SK_B to sign the M. And SK_B(H'(M)) is B's digital signature.

④ B sends H'(M), SK_B(H'(M)) and ATC to C.

⑤ C decrypts ATC with SK_C to get H(M) and SK_A(H(M)). Then C will compare H(M) with H'(M). If it is different, then M is changed during transference. Hence the digital signatures of both negotiators are invalid. If it is same, then the M that B signed is the same as that A signed. Then C will decrypt SK_A(H(M)) and SK_B(H'(M)) with PK_A and PK_B respectively. If H(M)≠H'(M), the digital signatures by both negotiators are incorrect, then the signatures are invalid. If H(M)=H'(M), then C can ensure the signatures by both negotiators are valid.

⑥ If the digital signatures by A and B is valid, then SK_B(H'(M)) is time-stamped and sent to A by C, and SK_A(H(M)) is also time-stamped and sent to B by C.

3.3 The Feasibility Analysis of the Scheme

The feasibility of the scheme is analyzed as follows.

(1) The digital signatures are authentic. Because C is a trusted interceder by both negotiators, the digital signatures that received by each negotiator are verified and confirmed by C.

(2) The digital signatures are not forged. Because only negotiators have their own private keys, if interceder can decrypt signatures with negotiators' public keys respectively, he will know the signatures are not forged.

(3) The digital signatures can't be used repeatedly. Because that the negotiators signed is the hash result of contract, the signatures can't be copied to another contracts.

(4) The digital signature scheme can satisfy the integrity requirement of the contract. In the step ⑤ of the scheme, if the context of H'(M) and H(M) is different, we can discover the context of contract that each negotiator signed is different and the contract is changed by someone else in the transfer process.

(5) The digital signature scheme can satisfy the requirement of non-repudiation. Because both negotiators receive signed contract that is time-stamped and sent by interceder, they can't deny their signatures. The interceder can verify and prove the signatures of the both negotiators.

(6) The digital signature scheme can satisfy the fairness requirement. After the interceder has verified that the signatures are valid, both negotiators can receive the other negotiator's signature of the contract. Otherwise, both negotiators can't receive the other negotiator's signature of the contract. Both negotiators are in the strong fairness situation. And the interceder couldn't see the context of the contract.

(7) The execution efficiency of the scheme is very high, because negotiators only encrypt the hash result and the interceder needn't to transfer the contract. The interceder only do a few public key operations and signature verifications, then sent verified signatures to negotiators.

(8) In the digital signature scheme, the transferred contract can also be encrypted with keys that are different from signature keys in order to improve the security of the scheme further.

3.4 Implementation of the Digital Signature Scheme in WNSS

Generally a trusted third party is needed to provide service and intercede negotiation through WNSS. The third party can aid the negotiators in the process of the negotiation. Therefore, the trusted third party in WNSS can act as the interceder of the digital signature scheme. Because we use public key algorithm to encrypt contract, we need a CA to provide certificate service. In a similar way, the trusted third party can act as CA.

As we all know, MS NT 4.0 is widely used in Intranet and Internet. And in the Option Pack the software named Certificate Server1.0 can be used to construct our own CA conveniently and to realize the authorization and certification to the web server and client. The both negotiators can adopt X.509 certificate. The digital certificate can not only implement the bi-directional authentication in SSL connection, but also implement digital signatures with the keys in the certificate.

RSA is one of public key algorithm that is well known with its high security. It is especially suitable for using in digital signature. The algorithm of RSA is as follows.

Public key: $n = p \, q$. (p and q are two large prime numbers and are secret.)

Private key: $d = e^{-1} \bmod ((p-1)(q-1))$. (e is relatively prime to $(p-1)(q-1)$. e and n are public.)

Signature procedure: $S = M^d \bmod n$

Validation procedure: $V(M, S) = \text{TRUE} \Leftrightarrow M = S^e \bmod n$

Up to now many hashing algorithms have been designed, such as Rabin hash algorithm, N-hash algorithm, MD2, MD4, MD5, SHA and so on. MD5 produces a 128-bit (16-byte) hash result. The security of MD5 algorithm is higher and its operation speed is very fast, so that it is widely used. In WNSS we use RSA and MD5 to implement digital signatures for electronic contract.

As a network programming language, JAVA is rapidly developed and widely used in Internet. JAVA integrates a number of security tools. It can be used to develop multifunctional application programs that include identity certification, digital signature, encryption, decryption, etc. JAVA is also used to implement web-based negotiation support system. Therefore we use JAVA to develop and implement our digital signature application programs in WNSS.

4 Conclusions

Based on the requirements of electronic contract in WNSS and several techniques widely used in digital signatures, a new digital signature scheme for electronic contracts is presented in the paper. Public key algorithm, hash function and interceders are used in the scheme. The feasibility of the scheme is analyzed. It has been implemented in our web-based negotiation support system.

Digital signatures could be used to prevent from forging, tampering and disavowing, so it is one of the important techniques in electronic commerce. With the development of electronic commerce, the techniques in network security that include digital signature will be more and more important in our lives.

Acknowledgment

This research was supported by China Scholarship Council and the Natural Science Foundation of Hubei province of China (Project No. 2001ABB058).

References

1. B. Meng and W. Fu, An Overview of Theories and Models in Group Decision Making and Negotiation Support Systems, *Proceedings of '99 International Conference on Management Science and Engineering*, 1999.
2. W. Gao and B. Meng, Research and Development of Web-based Negotiation Support System, *Computer Engineering*, 29（19）, 63-65(2003) (in Chinese).
84. 3. Mohan Atreya, et al., *Digital Signatures* (McGraw-Hill, Berkeley, Calif., 2002).
85.   4. J. C. A. van der Lubbe, *Basic Methods of Cryptography* (Cambridge University Press, New York, 1998).
86.   5. Timothy P. Layton, *Information Security: Design, Implementation, Measurement, and Compliance* (Auerbach Publications, Boca Raton, 2007).
6. Elena Ferrari and Bhavani Thuraisingham, *Web and Information Security* (IRM Press, Hershey, Pa., 2006).
7. Aashish Srivastava, Electronic Signatures: A Brief Review of the Literature, Proceedings of the 8th International Conference on Electronic Commerce: The new e-commerce: Innovations for Conquering Current Barriers, Obstacles and Limitations to Conducting Successful Business on the Internet ICEC '06, August 2006.
8. Mark Stamp, *Information Security: Principles and Practice* (Wiley-Inter Science, Hoboken, N.J., 2006).

Analysis of E-Commerce Model in Transaction Cost Economics Framework

Zhao Duan

Information Management Department, HuaZhong Normal University
152 Luoyu Road.wuhan.hubei.P.R.China, 430079
victorduan@hotmail.com

Abstract. This paper introduces the theory and method of Transaction Cost Economics to identify the essence of e-commerce model by explicating its core objective and function. From the correspondence of transactions and governance structures, the author also discusses the design principle of an e-commerce model. The analysis shows that so-called e-commerce model in commercial practice could be identified as non-market governance structure in TCE framework. Also, under the high uncertainty of Internet, to minimize transaction costs, various e-commerce transaction distinguished by different assets specificity and transaction frequency should mutually correspond with governance structures having different expense and function. The analysis attempts to unify the existing definitions and classifications about e-commerce model in a multi-discipline framework, and bring people some new clues for the innovation in e-commerce application. At the same time, this heuristic perspective waits for the comprehensive examinations by further empirical researches.

1 Introduction

The Transaction Cost Economics developed by O. Williamson [1-13] on the base of R. Coase's [14-15] research, emphasizes transaction's attributes and the correspondences with governance structure. Nowadays, transaction cost economics has been the core theory of organization economics.

There are three key concepts involved in Transaction Cost Economics: assets specificity in the technical issues, bounded rationality hypothesis about the human nature, and opportunism on the behavior aspect. Williamson argued "a transaction occurs when a goods or service is transferred between technologically separable stages" [16]. The attributes of transaction can be identified from three lengths: assets specificity, uncertainty and transaction frequency. Under the bounded rationality

Please use the following format when citing this chapter:

Duan, Z., 2007, in IFIP International Federation for Information Processing, Volume 251, Integration and Innovation Orient to E-Society Volume 1, Wang, W. (Eds), (Boston: Springer), pp. 627-634.

hypothesis, it takes people high transaction cost to estimate the time and styles of opportunism's occurring and to make precautions. To ensure the proceeding of the transaction and save transaction costs, it is necessary to construct matches between transactions with different attributes and governance structures with different costs and efficiencies. Distinguishing from incentive intensity, administrative control and the contract law regime, the alternative modes of governance structure include market, hybrid and hierarchy. In this framework, transaction could be considered as the most basic and general form of human economic relationship. No matter what simple or complicated e-commerce activities, transaction could be taken into account as a basic analyzing unit.

Compared with traditional spot market, Internet involves higher uncertainty and more opportunism. Under this circumstance, the neoclassic contracts is hard to be applied to govern all e-commerce transaction relationships, only three choices can be made: aborting the transaction; integrating into organization internal transaction; or depending on certain hybrid governance structure that can not only ensure the relevant modifications of the contract ex ante with the continuing and the extending of the transactions, but also be able to defend opportunism and to save transaction cost. Hence, whether an e-commerce activity can realize and bring value for transactors depends on whether a kind of effective governance structure can be built to coordinate the mutual economic relationships between transactors. Actually so-called e-commerce model could be considered as a kind of exterior exhibition of governance structure in commercial practice. In this way, some new approaches might be offered for e-commerce practitioners by using the theory and methods of transaction cost economics to study the attributes of various e-commerce transactions, attributes of e-commerce transactions' governance structure, and researching their mutual correspondence.

Issues of two aspects will be discussed in this paper: part one will identify the essence and connotation of e-commerce model from the Transaction Cost Economics paradigm; part two will analyze the design principle of e-commerce models to correspond the attributes of e-commerce transaction.

2   Identification of E-Commerce Model from Transaction Cost Economics Paradigm

At present, there is no unified cognition for the definition and classification of e-commerce model yet. Except B2B, B2C and C2C models, many scholars such as Paul Timmers [17], Paul Bambury [18], Allan Afuah & Christopher Tucci [19], Magali Dubosson-Torbay [20], Peter Weil [21] and B. Mahadevan [22] etc. came up with nearly 20 kinds of various definitions and classifications. However, none of them is evaluated as perfectly complete and systematic.

Generally speaking, e-commerce model refers to the manners and approaches used to carry out business online. From the transaction cost economics paradigm, it could be considered as the governance structure constructed by a serial of contractual relationship among e-commerce transactors in order to ensure the value brought for the transactors. Specifically, two aspects' connotations are involved: one part is the incomplete contracts established ex ante by transactors, namely only a restrictive contractual framework is made to explain the business principle, performance program, mechanism of solving conflicts, and rights' attribution of the transactors etc; while the other part is the contract performance mechanism established to ensure the transaction take place, continue and produce value.

E-commerce transactions carry through partially or entirely online. Three reasons cause a complete contracts not able to be established by the transactors: (1) Because of the bounded rationality and asymmetric information, transactors are hard to estimate exactly plenty of occasional and random unborn events; (2) Even if those haphazards are exactly estimated and could be put into the contract clauses with no controversial wordings, the separation of the e-commerce transactors by Internet would make the bargaining costs pretty high; (3) After the establishment of the contract, there are still various difficulties to examine the execution of the contract clauses, even a third-party is involved, the cost of testifying who breaks the contracts and measure the loss would be very high. Hence, even an incomplete contracts exists lot of trouble of ex post adjustments, transactors establish an incomplete contract is still accord with a rational expectation. However, another problem is, incomplete contract would have to face with sorts of "post-contractual opportunistic behavior's hold-ups" [23]. For the transactor who involved transaction-specific assets, there exists risk that another side may depredate "the appropriable specialized quasi-rents " [23] from specific assets by using dishonest and deceitful means. So the side involving assets specificity must require for certain mechanism to minimize the risk of the hold-ups and to ensure the continuity of the transaction.

In the applications of e-commerce, various combinations of incomplete contracts and performance ensure mechanisms emerged through the bargaining between transactors or under unilateral authority, among the mutual competition, bring out some transplantable and imitable models, contribute the functions of crafting order, mitigating conflict and realizing mutual gains.

The Usual governance structures in the e-commerce include bilateral governance structure, trilateral governance structure, hierarchy and "contract enforcement mechanism" [24]. A governance structure may present as a formal and legally executable contractual form, or as a private arrangement outside law.

The contributions of identifying e-commerce model from transaction cost economics paradigm lies in the following three aspects: (1) In the research, transaction is regarded as the basic analysis unit, which can decrease the analysis complexity of e-commerce activities involved participants' roles, alternate relationships, product characteristic, behaviors and benefit sources etc; (2) E-commerce activities value source is attributed to the saving of the transaction cost and the continuity of the transaction, which clears an important direction of the innovation of e-commerce application; (3) E-commerce model is considered as a kind of governance structure, which can transfer the question of seeking an appropriate model into a question of seeking the effective correspondence among various attributes of e-commerce transaction and various governance structure, which can offer some new ideas for the innovation and optimization of e-commerce models.

3   The Correspondence of E-Commerce Transaction and Non-Market Governance Structure

Among the three identification lengths of transaction attributes, Williamson suggested that assets specificity is the most important factor [25]. Assets specificity refers to the attribute that the assets can not be reused for other purpose when it is involved in a specific transaction. For example, when some durable investment is used to support certain transaction, the assets formed during this period has this specificity. If the relative contractual relationship is terminated before the accomplishment of this transaction, the assets would be difficult for other utilities, and a part of sunk cost is involved. Therefore, the more assets specificity is involved in a transaction, the more continuity and harmony of the transaction would be cared about, and the more requirements to establish certain performance ensure mechanism would be brought out.

If no specific asset is involved in e-commerce, both sides of transactors can find other trade partners easily. They don't depend to each other, and none of them cares about the continuity of the transaction. Both sides always rules the transaction by the contracts they established ex ante and use court ordering to solve the conflicts ex post. Once the specific assets invested by one side arrives a critical level (use A' to express), the transaction cost of the e-commerce organized and managed by the traditional spot market governance structure will rise significantly, and it becomes necessary to introduce the hybrid governance structure or integration to replace spot market.

In e-commerce activities, the specific assets (use letter A to express) involved in a certain transaction can be scaled in the following formula: $A=(F/q)+S$. "F" represents the specific assets such as human resources, material resources and reputation which a transactor invest in the e-commerce platform serving for all e-commerce transactions; "q" represents the total amount of prospective congener e-commerce transaction; and "S" represents the specific assets correlating with the transaction itself, such as the resources invested for information screening, payment or logistics etc. Different from the traditional spot market, the necessary supportive facilities and the spatial and temporal elements in the e-commerce have decided that at least one side of the transactors can not keep away from some specific assets investment. In addition, the higher uncertainty and asymmetric information will increase transactors' sensitivity about contractual haphazards and cast enough influence on their decision-making and adjusting, which will put ulteriorly lower the lever of A'. Therefore, owing to the general existence of certain unevadable specific assets over A', nearly all of e-commerce transactions should be corresponding with non-market governance structures. It can partly explain why people feel the business way in the Internet market is different from that in the spot market.

4 The Correspondences of the E-Commerce Models with Various Attributes of E-Commerce Transaction

Uncertainty and transaction frequency are two others lengths to identify transaction attribute. Uncertainty comes from the asymmetric information between transactors, the impossibility to forecast all haphazard at ex ante, and the obstacle of high costs of forecasting or making precaution measure in contract. The meaning of uncertainty is to make people's choice become necessary, when a transaction is influenced by high uncertainty, people have to make choices between different governance structures under the principle of minimum transactions costs. The virtuality of transactor's identity, complexity during the course of transaction and the asymmetric information in the e-commerce activities make both transactors have to face a higher challenge of uncertainty from the environment and transaction itself, which increase their requirements about the flexibility of governance structure.

Transaction frequency refers to the rate of occurrence of repetitive transactions. It has direct impact on the relative value of transaction cost instead of absolute value. Though transaction cost decrease with the ascending of frequency, the cost can not reduce infinitely and approach to zero. The establishment and operation of a governance structure exists expense. To what extent can this expense be covered depends on the occurrence frequency of the transaction under such governance structure. More frequently transactions happen; easier expense of governance structure can be covered. Therefore, for an e-commerce transaction involving assets specificity and high uncertainty, frequency has direct impact on the mode of governance structure.

In the following analysis, uncertainty in e-commerce will be entirely supposed high enough and as a fixed factor, the attributes of e-commerce transaction will be partitioned as three main circumstances basis on the intensity and extension of assets specificity. In each circumstance, design principles of e-commerce model will be differentiated by the transaction frequency.

4.1 Both sides involving highly assets specificity (A1>>A1'∩ A2>>A2')

In such circumstances, once the transaction is interrupted the establishment of a new transaction relation will cost much. Both sides of transactors press for the stability of relation and continuance of transaction.

If the transaction frequency is very high, the expense of establishing a special organization to manage repetitive transactions can be covered easily, building of integration governance structure (hierarchy) would become cost-efficient, such as intranet e-commerce model.

If the frequency is low, the expense of integration are hard to be covered, the ex ante incomplete contract will need to be re-negotiated and re-adjusted frequently, and the post-contractual haphazard may cause endless bargaining and loss of time and money, even high risks of conflict. If transactors haven't mutual dependence relation in resource control, both sides would be unwilling to make specific asset investment ex ante, so transaction will be hard to realize, and the lack of investment will cause efficiency loss; but if one side has power of resource control, he could constitute "in-or-out" or "all-or-none" clauses in incomplete contract ex ante to increase the possibilities of transaction.

4.2   One side involving assets specificity, another not. （A1>A1' ∩ A2<A2'）

In such circumstances, both sides have different attitudes towards the continuance and harmony of transaction. The side involving assets specificity will press for certain "weapon" to defend potential hold-ups of appropriable specialized quasi-rents from the other side. Therefore, the core of designing e-commerce model is to set up possible contract self-enforcement mechanism to defend opportunism.

One adoptable way is to add personal penalty clauses on the observable business partner who has the tendency of breach of faith. Penalty clauses usually include two aspects: one is the threat of compensation in case of the transaction being interrupted by opportunism. If the quasi-rent coming from prospective opportunistic behaviors is less than the amount of compensation according to the clauses, hold-ups could be defended and the contract would be performed implicitly; the other is the devalue of reputation, which can bring the opportunist higher transaction costs in future business, so that reduces tendency of cheating.

Presently, the difficulties of transactor's identity investigation in e-commerce and lack of relevant legal regulation may cause the opportunist to escape from the penalty, so some other measures usually need to be combined for improving executing effect. If the transaction frequency is high, the side not involving assets specificity might temporarily abandon the option of hold-ups for a long-term interest, and once he can estimate exactly the amount of unborn transactions, opportunistic behaviors may take place in the ultimate transaction. In this case, for the side involving assets specificity, one alternative way is to combine personal penalty clauses with emotional attachment by the power of social routines, morality and spirit to defend opportunism; and another way is to use strategy of multi-part pricing according to the transaction accumulative times, which could induce the other side keep increasing the estimated amount of the future transaction and delaying opportunistic actions.

If the transaction frequency is low, penalty clauses should be combined with certain necessary legally retroactive measures, such as registration and authentication of verifiable information and setting reputation classification as entry barrier, etc.

4.3   Both sides involving certain assets specificity （A1>A1' ∩ A2>A2'）

In such circumstances, both sides will focus on the continuance of transaction and wish to establish some kind of ensure mechanism to reduce the uncertainty in transaction. It is the dominant circumstances in present e-commerce activities.

If the transaction frequency is low, the expense of establishing a special organization is hard to be covered; introducing third parties into a transaction is appropriate. This model is very popular in current e-commerce, for example, many e-commerce activities carry out through e-market platform provider, e-broker website, e-agency and online auction, or by using third-party security authentication, third-party payment system and logistics, etc.

If the transaction frequency is high, a bilateral governance structure will become more cost-efficient. The fashions of bilateral governance structure generally include establishing long-term contract, reciprocity, pledge and placing specific assets mutually. Under this model, both sides could not only keep independent relatively, but also balance transaction risks, make transaction relationship highly stable and sustainable, and increase mutual interests. In current e-commerce, B2B basis on supply-chain is a representative exhibition of this situation.

5 Conclusion

The rapid development of e-commerce owes to the saving of transaction cost coming from innovations and applications of computer science and information technology. Meanwhile, the higher uncertainty and opportunism in the Internet increase ex ante and ex post transaction costs from contract process on the other hand. The key of the substitution of e-commerce for traditional spot market, rely on whether we can establish certain corresponding governance structure to effectively organize and manage contractual relationship in e-commerce activities, and to minimize this transaction costs from contract process. Otherwise, the contribution of science and technology would regrettably be partially counteracted by the deficiency of institution.

But in practice, the diversiform and complex appearances of e-commerce model maybe make us be blind to its core objective and function, make us attend to trifles but neglect the essentials. Therefore, identifying e-commerce model as non-market governance structure and emphasizing the correspondence with transaction attributes in TCE framework will probably not be totally accepted by everyone, but if those multi-discipline perspectives could bring some new clues to the e-commerce scholars and practicers, the author's intention has achieved.

Reference

1. O. Williamson, *Markets and Hierarchies: analysis of antitrust implications* (Free Press, New York, 1975).
2. O. Williamson, *The Economic of Institute of Capitalism* (Free Press, New York, 1975).
3. O. Williamson, Comparative Economic Organization: The Analysis of Discrete Structural Alternatives, *Administrative Science Quarterly*; Vol. 36 Issue 2 (Jun 1991), pp. 269-296.
4. O. Williamson, Transaction Cost Economics and Organization Theory, *Industrial & Corporate Change*, Vol. 2 Issue 2 (1993), pp. 107-156.
5. O. Williamson, *The Mechanism of Governance* (Oxford Univ. Press, New York, 1996).
6. O. Williamson, Transaction cost economics: How it works; Where it is headed, *De Economist* (0013-063X); Vol. 146 Issue 1 (Apr 1998), pp. 23-59.
7. O. Williamson, The Institutions of Governance, *American Economic Review*, Vol. 88 Issue 2 (May 1998), pp. 75-79.
8. O. Williamson, Strategy Research: Governance and Competence Perspectives, *Strategic Management Journal*, Vol. 20 Issue 12 (Dec 1999), pp. 1087-1108.

9. O. Williamson, The New Institutional Economics: Taking Stock, Looking Ahead, *Journal of Economic Literature*, Vol. 38 Issue 3 (Sep 2000) p. 599.

10. O. Williamson, The Theory of the Firm as Governance Structure: From Choice to Contract, *Journal of Economic Perspectives*, Vol. 16 Issue 3 (Summer 2002), pp. 171-195.

11. O. Williamson, Examining Economic Organization through the Lens of Contract, *Industrial & Corporate Change*, Vol. 12 Issue 4 (Aug 2003), pp. 917-942.

12. O. Williamson, Transaction cost Economics and Business administration, *Scandinavian Journal of Management*, Vol. 21 Issue 1 (Mar2005), pp. 19-40.

13. Oliver. Williamson, The Economics of Governance, *American Economic Review*, Vol. 95 Issue 2 (May 2005), pp. 1-18.

14. Ronald. Coase, The Nature of the Firm, *Economics*, Vol. 4 (1937), pp. 386-405.

15. Ronald. Coase, The Problem of Social Cost, *Journal of law and Economics*, Vol. 3 (1960), pp. 1-44.

16. Oliver. Williamson, Strategy Research Governance and Competence Perspectives, *Book chapter of Competence, Governance & Entrepreneurship* (2000), p26.

17. Paul. Timmers, Business Models for Electronic Markets, *Journal on Electronic Markets*, Vol. 8 Issue 2 (1998), pp. 3-8.

18. Paul. Bambury, A taxonomy of Internet Commerce, *First Monday*, Vol. 10 Issue 3 (1998).

19. Allan. Afuah and Christopher. Tucci, *Internet Business Models and strategies, text and case* (McGraw Hill, Boston, 2001).

20. Magali Dubosson-Torbay, E-Business Model Design, Classification and Measurements, *Thunderbird International Business Review*, Vol. 4 (2001).

21. Peter Weil, *Place to space: Migrating to E-Business Models* (Harvard Business School Press, Boston, 2001).

22. B. Mahadevan, Business Models for Internet Based E-Commerce an anatomy, *California Management Review*, Vol. 42 Issue 4 (2000).

23. B. Klein, R. Crawford and A. Alchian, Vertical Integration, Appropriable Rents and Competitive Contracting Process, *Journal of Law and Economics*, Vol. 21 (1978), pp. 297-326.

24. B. Klein and K. Murphy, Vertical Restraints as Contract Enforcement Mechanisms, *Journal of Law and Economics*, Vol. 31 (1988), pp. 265-297.

25. O. Williamson, Asset Specificity and Economic Organization, *International Journal of Industrial Organization*, Vol. 3 Issue 4 (Dec 1985), pp. 365-379

A FOAF-based Framework for E-Commerce Recommender Service System

Yang Zhao

Wuhan University, Center for Studies of Information Resources
430072, Wuhan, P. R.China , zyaxjlgg_0813@hotmail.com
WWW home page: http://www.csir.whu.edu.cn/

Abstract. Recommender service systems have been widely and successfully applied in e-commerce to provide personalized recommendations to customers nowadays. The tremendous growth in the amount of available information and the number of visitors to websites poses some challenges for recommender service systems such as poor prediction accuracy, scalability, and dynamic changes of users. To address these issues and increase the performance of the systems, an e-commerce recommender service system framework based on FOAF (Friend of A Friend) is proposed in this paper. FOAF provides a RDF/XML vocabulary to describe individual users and their relationships with other users. A FOAF profile could allow a system to better understand users' personalized needs. Once the system extracts each user's preferences that are represented by FOAF document format, it can classify users with respect to their own preferences on real time, and also, it can recommend items in which some users are interested to a target user who has the highest similarity with them in the same group. Experimental results show that the proposed framework helps to reduce the recommendation time, while improving accuracy.

1 Introduction

With the fast development of internet infrastructure, recommender service systems have been successfully applied to improve the quality of service for users. A recommender service system on e-commerce has brought reduction of cost for searching by extracting information in which users are interested and listing the results that are likely to fit them. In order to provide more accurate recommendation results within an acceptable response time, a recommender service system is required to have the capacity to handle a large amount of information on real time.

Please use the following format when citing this chapter:

Yang, Z., 2007, in IFIP International Federation for Information Processing, Volume 251, Integration and Innovation Orient to E-Society Volume1, Wang, W. (Eds), (Boston: Springer), pp. 635-642.

Recommender service system framework generally applies the information filtering technique called collaborative filtering (CF)[1]to solve the problems in information processing. The typical CF approach employs statistical techniques to find a set of customers who have a history of agreeing with the target user. It has been widely used in a number of different applications, and overcomes lots of shortcomings of content-based recommender service systems. But with the rapid growth in the amount of users' information and products data, the calculation of the recommender algorithm becomes more and more complex, which leads to the scalability issue of CF. At the same time, the issue of dynamic changes of users' interests was not considered in CF, either. Recommender service systems are operated in the dynamic web environment in which at anytime a user may change his/her interests and decide to purchase some products. So the system should understand and handle users' interesting changes as quickly as it can. To solve these problems and increase the performance of e-commerce recommender service systems, a more effective system framework is needed.

In this paper, we proposed a Peer-to-Peer recommender service system framework based on FOAF (Friend of A of Friend) to improve the system scalability. FOAF[2]is a kind of semantic web technology that provides a RDF/XML vocabulary to describe a user's information, including name, mailbox, homepage URL, interests, friends, and so on. With the application of FOAF, it is easier to share and use information about users and their activities, to transfer information between web sites, and to automatically extend and re-use it on line[3]. User preference is asserted as a property of the FOAF document format by learning user's behaviors. Once the system learns user preference, it can classify users with respect to their preferences on real time, and also, it can recommend items in which users are interested to a target user who has the highest similarity with them in the same group on P2P network. Due to the reduced quantity of information processing, the system scalability will be greatly improved. At the same time, system can dynamically update and maintain the user profiles on real time by FOAF.

The paper is organized as follows: Section 2 introduces the approach for describing a user's information by FOAF profile. Section 3 presents the FOAF-based framework for implementing an e-commerce recommender service system and analyses the specific process of recommendation. Experiments with performance evaluation are given in Section 4. Section 5 concludes the paper.

2 Using FOAF Profiles for User Identification

We use the FOAF profile to identify a user. This type of profile contains information about social relations of the user next to traditional information that identifies the user. The profile could either be generated by hand, or more often, by copy, paste and edit of other people's FOAF, or by semi-automated tools such as FOAF-a-matic[4]. Part of an example profile is shown in Fig.1. This example illustrates several important things about FOAF. The *foaf:knows* property points to other people known by this person. Other FOAF profiles are linked through *rdfs:seeAlso*, allowing Semantic Web bots to crawl through FOAF space. At the same time, in this example we use the items that have been evaluated by this person to specify the interests of him/her. The $foaf:interest$ property can be used to represent the web pages about these items, including the items name, user rating results and other information[5]. But the item in which a user is interested may not be his/her preference, because the user may rate a low score on this item. The RDF syntax of FOAF allows a system to better understand users' needs. When a user publishes a FOAF profile (just like the example below) on the e-commerce websites, the system is able to make use of that information, and then extract this user's preferences.

```
<rdf:RDF xmlns:foaf="http://xmlns.com/foaf/0.1/" ... > ......
<foaf:Person>
<foaf:name>Zhao Yang</foaf:name>
<foaf:mbox rdf:resource="mailto:zymnesl@hotmail.com" />
<foaf:homepage rdf:resource="http://www.whu.edu.cn/zymnes" />
... ...
<foaf:interest dc:title="Gladiator"
rdf:resource="http://movielens.umn.edu/movieDetail?movieId=3578"/>
<foaf:interest dc:title="Harry Potter "
rdf:resource="http://movielens.umn.edu/movieDetail?movieId=40815"/>
<foaf:interest dc:title="Lord of the Rings"
......
</foaf:interest>
<foaf:knows><foaf:Person>
<foaf:name>Daisy Green</foaf:name>
<rdfs:seeAlso rdf:resource="http://martinmay.net/foaf.rdf"/>
</foaf:Person></foaf:knows>
... ...
</foaf:Person> </rdf:RDF>
```

Fig.1. Example of a user's FOAF profile

3   The Proposed FOAF-based Recommender Service System Framework

Fig.2. illustrates the overall framework which consists of three major components: FOAF profiles, recommender component and user interface. The FOAF profiles of different users are generated automatically by semi-automated tools in this system. Users' information comes from user database of this e-commerce website. A user database stores and mangers all kinds of users' information, such as registration information, past buying and rating behaviors, page view logs, and etc. Users can also maintain and update their own FOAF profiles dynamically. By the FOAF profiles, system can find in which items different users are interested. The recommender component is used to generate recommendations for users based on FOAF profiles. It is composed of user grouping, similarity calculation and recommendation generating modules. The output of an e-commerce recommendation system is a list of the top-N recommender items, and the goal of the user interface is to display these recommendation results in the manner such that the recommendation service user can absorb them easily and effectively. In this framework, in addition to FOAF method, some other recommendation algorithms have also been applied, such as collaborative filtering, associate rule based filtering, and etc. The specific process of the recommendation based on this FOAF framework will be analyzed below.

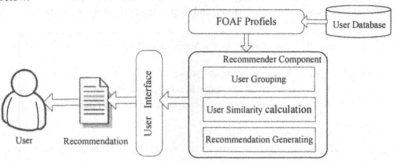

Fig. 2. The Proposed FOAF-based Recommender Service System Framework

3.1 Grouping Users According to Their Preferences

Grouping users makes it easy for the system to compute the similarity between users in the same group. Due to the extensibility of the FOAF-based distributed environment, it is possible to aggregate information from other users who have the same preference. The recommender service system extracts each user's preferences that are represented in FOAF profile. By the preferences of each user, recommender service system groups users. And then, when a user evaluates an item m_i, the system determines whether m_i is good enough to recommend to other users in the same group or not. In this paper, we take an online movie site as an example. We have distinguished movie genres into 15 categories [6]. Usually a user can have more than one preference about movie genre. Once a movie is rated by a user, the related page link of this movie will be added into the user's FOAF profile, and represented by the $foaf:interest$ property. The page includes some basic information of this movie, such as movie name, movie genre, actors, user ratings, and etc.

In order to extract accurate preferences from each user, we employed a probabilistic method as shown in equation (1). Assume there are the set of users $U=\{u_1,u_2,...,u_i\}$, the set of movies that is rated by a user u_i is $M=\{m_1,m_2,...,m_j\}$ and the set of genre is $G=\{g_1,g_2,...,g_k\}$. The function $f(P_{ik})$ extracts i-th user's preference about a genre g_k.

$$f(P_{ik}) = \sum_{j=1}^{n} \frac{g_k(m_j)}{\mu} R_{ij} \qquad \mu = \sum_{m=1}^{n} C_m(u_i,m_j) \qquad (1)$$

Where C_m is a set of genres included in movie m_j, and R_{ij} means a rating value of i-th user about movie m_j. Also μ means total count of genres that included in movies that are rated by user u_i. By comparing the value of $f(P_{ik})$, the system can classify users to different groups. Users in the same group have the same preference about movie genre. Sometimes, a user may have more than one preference, so he/she may be assigned to different groups at the same time.

3.2 Users Similarity Calculation

To an active visitor, users in the same group have different similarity. In order to improve the recommender accuracy for a particular user (active user), we should find which ones have the highest similarity with this user. There are a number of different ways to compute the similarity between users. The most widely and successfully way is neighborhood-based collaborative filtering [7]. But the traditional neighborhood-based collaborative filtering suffers from the poor scalability problem, i.e., the time used to search for a group of neighbors is proportional to the number of all users in the system. In the FOAF-base framework proposed in this paper, we have already grouped users according to their preferences, it is not necessary for all users in the database to be weighted according to their similarity with the active user. So the neighbor searching time is reduced. On the basis of user grouping, we use person correlation coefficient algorithm[8]that is a major approach of collaborative filtering to compute the similarity between active a and another user i, as equation (2).

$$sim(a,i) = \frac{\sum_{j \in I_{a,j}}^{n} (v_{a,j} - \bar{v}_a)(v_{i,j} - \bar{v}_i)}{\sqrt{\sum_{j \in I_{a,j}}^{n} (v_{a,j} - \bar{v}_a)^2} \sqrt{\sum_{i=1}^{n} (v_{i,j} - \bar{v}_i)^2}} \qquad (2)$$

Where $I_{a,i}$ denotes the set of items rated by both of user a and user i. $v_{a,j}$ denotes a rating value of active user a about item j. $v_{i,j}$ denotes a rating value of user i about item j. $\bar{v}_a$ and $\bar{v}_i$ indicate the average rating of active user a and user i on items. As shown in equation (2), it can be seen that the value of $sim(a,i)$ is proportional to the similarity of user a and i's rating results. And our main goal is to find a number of k-nearest neighbors who have the highest similarity and this process is based on their preferences and some partial information of the active user.

3.3 Generation of Recommendation

Recommendation is a list of TOP-N items that the active user will like most. It is derived from the k-nearest neighbors of the active user. These items are recommended to the user in the form of "customers who liked/rented this movie also rented...".

When the user is an old one, the system has kept track of use's history data, such as his click-streams, his transaction history data, ratings, and etc. Using these data, system can group users and find neighbors for an active user. As neighbors and active user have the highest similarity weights, we can predict the active user's rating value about an item according to his neighbors' rating value about it [9]. The TOP-N highest prediction items will be added to the list and recommended to active user. The prediction of the active user a on the items k that he doesn't purchase could be calculated as equation (3).

$$P_{a,k} = \overline{R_a} + \frac{\sum_{u \in N} sim(a,u)(R_{u,k} - \overline{R_u})}{\sum_{u \in N} |sim(a,u)|} \qquad (3)$$

$sim(a,u)$ denotes the similarity between user a and user u, $R_{u,k}$ denotes a rating value of user u about the item k, $\overline{R_a}$ and $\overline{R_u}$ denote the average rating made by users a and k respectively. N is a set of nearest neighbor of active user a.

4 Experimental Evaluation

We carried out several experiments to evaluate the performance of the proposed FOAF-based framework, and to compare it with some related work.

4.1 Data Set

We used experimental data from an open dataset of MovieLens which contains 100,000 ratings of 3,900 movies from $6,040$ users. Ratings are discrete values from 1 to 5 (1,2,3,4,5)[10]. We randomly selected 1,000 users who have rated 30 or more movies from the database. We divided the data into a training set (80%) and a test set (20%). We use data from the training set to compute predictions. Data from the test set is then used to evaluate efficiency and accuracy.

4.2 Evaluation Metric

Recommender service systems research has used several types of measures for evaluating the quality of a recommender service system. They can be mainly categorized into two classes: statistical accuracy metrics and decision support accuracy metrics [11]. Statistical accuracy metrics evaluate the accuracy of a system by comparing the numerical recommendation scores against the actual user ratings for the user-product pairs in the test dataset. Mean Absolute Error (MAE) between ratings and predictions is a widely used metric [12]. MAE is a measure of the deviation of recommendations from their true user-specified values. We choose MAE as our evaluation metric to report prediction experiments because it is most commonly used and easiest to interpret directly. MAE is defined as equation (4).

$$MAE = \frac{\sum_{i=1}^{N} |P_i - R_i|}{N} \qquad (4)$$

P_i denotes the predicted rating of product i, R_i denotes the true rating of product i and N denotes the number of items in the test set. Formally, the lower the MAE, the more accurately the recommendation engine predicts user ratings.

4.3 Experimental Results

After system made FOAF profiles of users, 1,000 users were divided into 15 groups according to their preferences. Therefore it was not necessary for all users in the database to be weighted according to their similarity with the active user. To confirm the effectiveness of the proposed improved recommendation method based on FOAF, we compare the traditional CF algorithm with the new recommendation algorithm. We carried out the experiment while changing the number of neighborhoods from 10 to 50, interval is 5.

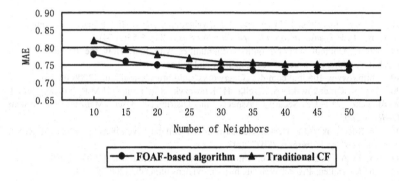

Fig. 3. Comparison of prediction quality of FOAF-based algorithms and traditional CF

In Fig.3, we could find that no matter how many neighbors we choose, the line of the traditional CF is higher than the line of our proposed one, which indicates that the FOAF-based algorithm can provide predictions of better quality than the traditional CF algorithm. Furthermore, the FOAF-based algorithm reduces the time used to search neighbors and generates the recommendations more quickly and effectively than traditional method.

5 Conclusions

Recommender service systems are a powerful new technology for extracting additional value for e-commerce websites from its users. These systems benefit users by enabling them to find items they like. Conversely, they help the e-commerce by generating more sales. Typical recommender service systems suffer from poor scalability and the lack of ability to handle dynamic changes of users' interests. In this paper, a new P2P recommender service system framework was proposed to address these issues. This framework is based on the FOAF. Since the recommendation system applies FOAF profiles for user describing and grouping, it reduces the averaged recommendation time and increases the recommending accuracy for users. The effectiveness comparison results also indicate that the proposed FOAF-based recommendation method performs better than the traditional CF algorithm in this recommender service system. The next research step is to validate and improve algorithm robustness of the proposed method.

Acknowledgment

The research reported in this paper is supported by the project Research on Digital Information Services in Network Environment under No. 06JJD870006, sponsored by Key Project of Key Institution in Humane and Social Science Research, Education of Ministry of P.R.China.

References

87.   1. A.K. Joseph, G.T. Loren and John, valuating Collaborative Filtering Recommender Systems, *ACM Transactions on Information Systems*, 22(1), 5-53(2004).

88.   2. E. Dumbill, Support online communities with foaf: How the friend-of-a-friend vocabulary addresses issues of accountability and privacy,

89.   http://www-106.ibm.com/developerworks/xml/library/x-foaf.htm. [2006-08-13].

90.   3. S. Grzonkowski, A. Gzella, H. Krawczyk, S.R. Kruk, F.J.M.R. Moyano and T. Woroniecki, D-FOAF-Security Aspects in Distributed User Management System, *TEHOSS'2005*.

91.   4. S.R. Kruk and S. Decker, Semantic Social Collaborative Filtering with FOAF Realm, *Semantic Desktop Workshop, ISWC* 2005.

92.   5. FOAF Vocabulary Specification. http://xmlns.com/foaf/0.1/. [2007-01-20].

93.   6. MovieLens Project Web site.http://movielens.umn.edu. [2007-01-20].

94.   7. S.J. Ko, Prediction of Preferences through Optimizing Users and Reducing Dimension in Collaborative Filtering System, *IEA/AIE* 2004, 1259-1268(2004).

95.   8. C. Zeng, C.X. Xing and L.Z. Zhou, Similarity Measure and Instance Selection for Collaborative Filtering, In *12th international conference on World Wide Web*, Budapest, Hungary, 2003.

96.   9. J. Herlocker, J. Konstan, A. Borchers and J. Riedl,, An Algorithmic Framework for Performing Collaborative Filtering, In *Proceedings of ACM SIGIR'99*.ACM press.

97.   10. B. Sarwar, G. Karypis, J. Konstan and J. Riedl, Analysis of recommendation algorithms for E-commerce, In *Proc. of ACM'00 Conf. on Electronic Commerce*, 158–167 (2000).

98.   11. Y.H. Guo and G.S. Deng, An improved Collaborative Filtering based E-Commerce Recommendation System with Case-based Reasoning, In *International Conference on Serveice System and Service Management*, 780-784(2004).

99.   12. W. Nejdl, M. Wolpers, W. Siberski, C. Schmitz, M. Schlosser, I. Brunkhorst and A. Loser, Super-Peer-Based Routing and Clustering Strategies for RDF-Based Peer-To-Peer Networks, In *Proc. of the Twelfth International World Wide Web Conference*,2003.

Experience-Based Trust in E-Commerce

Zhaohao Sun[1], Sukui Lu[2], Jun Han[3], Gavin Finnie[4]

1 Dept. of Computer Science, College of Mathematics and Information
Science, Hebei Normal University, Shijiazhuang, China, 050016,
zhsun@ieee.org

2 College of Mathematics and Computer, Hebei University, Baoding,
China, 071002, lsk@mail.hbu.edu.cn

3 School of Computer Science, Beihang University, Beijing 100083, China,
jun_han@buaa.edu.cn

4 School of Information Technology, Bond University, Gold Coast Qld
4229 Australia
gfinnie@staff.bond.edu.au

Abstract. Trust is significant for e-commerce and has received increasing attention in e-commerce, multiagent systems, and artificial intelligence (AI). However, little attention has been given to the theoretical foundation and intelligent techniques for trust in e-commerce from either a logical or intelligent systems viewpoint. This paper will fill this gap by examining knowledge-based trust, inference-based trust, case-based trust and experience-based trust in e-commerce and their interrelationships from an intelligent systems viewpoint. The proposed approach will facilitate research and development of trust, multiagent systems, e-commerce and e-services.

1 Introduction

Trust is significant for healthy development of e-commerce. Castelfranchi and Tan [2] assert that e-commerce can be successful only if the general public trusts in the virtual environment, because lack of trust in security is one of the main reasons for e-consumers and companies not to engage in e-commerce. Therefore, trust has received increasing attention in e-commerce and information technology (IT). For example, Salam et al [10] examine trust in e-commerce and note that "many customers may still not trust vendors when shopping online". Pavlou [9] integrates

Please use the following format when citing this chapter:

Sun, Z., Lu, S., Han, J., Finnie, G., 2007, in IFIP International Federation for Information Processing, Volume 251, Integration and Innovation Orient to E-Society Volume1, Wang, W. (Eds), (Boston: Springer), pp. 643-651.

trust with the technology acceptance model to explore the customer acceptance of e-commerce. Xiu and Liu [22] propose a formal definition of trust and discuss the properties of trust relation. Wingreen and Baglione [21] study the customer's trust in vendors (knowledge-based trust) from a business viewpoint. Olsson [8] examines trust in e-commerce and asserts that "if experience-based trust (EBT) can be evaluated automatically, then it would provide a foundation for decision support tool for e-commerce customers". Xiong and Liu [23] propose a formal reputation-based trust model by combining amount of satisfaction, number of interaction and balance factor of trust in a peer-to-peer e-communities. However, the majority of works is on trust in online purchase settings, while there is relatively less research on theoretical foundations of trust in e-commerce.

Multiagent systems (MAS) has been successfully applied in many fields such as e-commerce [14]. On the other hand, trust has also drawn some intention in MAS. Tweedale and Cutler discuss trust in MAS by proposing a trust negotiation and communication model for MAS architecture [18]. Chen et al [3] propose a fuzzy trust model for MAS taking into account direct trust, recommendation trust and self-recommendation trust. Schmidt et al [11] apply a fuzzy trust model to an e-commerce platform. This paper will examine trust in multiagent e-commerce systems (MECS) by examining experience-based trust and case-based trust in e-commerce and their interrelationships from an intelligent systems viewpoint. It also proposes knowledge-based and inference-based trust in e-commerce.

The rest of this paper is organized as follows: Section 2 examines trust in e-commerce from two different perspectives. Section 3 proposes an intelligent model of trust in e-commerce. Section 4 examines experience-based trust. Section 5 introduces a measure model for trust in e-commerce. Section 6 proposes a case-based model for trust in e-commerce and Section 7 concludes the paper with some concluding remarks and future work.

2 Two Perspectives to Trust in E-Commerce

Trust is an important ingredient in e-commerce, because the Internet is a source of trust and mistrust [19]. Therefore trust is essential for the success of e-commerce.

There are three main parties involved in e-transactions in e-commerce: the buyer, seller and intermediary [20]. In this study, buyers are either e-buyers or online customers or intelligent buyer agents [14]. Sellers are either Web merchants or Internet stores [12] or intelligent seller agents [14] or Web vendors [5], or online shops websites. Intermediaries are either e-agents or e-facilitators [20] or e-brokers or intelligent agents for any intermediary [15]. This consideration motivates the model of trust in e-commerce from a people-centered viewpoint as shown in Fig. 1.

The interrelationships between buyer trust, intermediary trust and seller trust have received substantial attention in e-commerce. For example, Verhagen, Meets & Tan [20] explore intermediary trust and seller trust. Intermediary trust refers to "the trustworthiness of the intermediary operating the system. It reflects perceptions of security during transaction to the presence of guarantees, regulations, safety nets or other structures that are introduced by these institutions" [20]. Intermediary trust is related to buyer trust and seller trust.

Seller trust refers to the "perceptions of trust in the counterpart of transaction" [20]. More specifically, it refers to the subjective belief with which consumers assess that sellers will perform potential transactions according to their confident expectations, irrespective of their ability to fully monitor them [20]. In e-commerce, the object of seller trust is the party selling the products. Trust in e-sellers is important in consumer-oriented e-commerce adoption decisions [12].

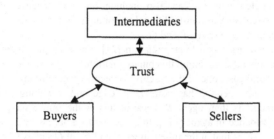

Fig. 1 A people-based model for trust in e-commerce [15]

In this model, buyer *B*, seller *S* and intermediary *I* are working together in e-commerce in order to complete an e-business transaction. However, all of them face trust issue in either e-commerce or MECS. Sometimes, they trust each other, sometimes they distrust one another. If they trust each other, it is easy for them to complete the e-business transaction satisfactorily. If they distrust each other, one of them might obtain the interest or benefit from the e-business transaction at one time.

From a system viewpoint, trust exists in the Web client, data transport, Web server, and operating system respectively. At the same time, trust constitutes a chain, which can be called a trust chain. The trust chain links Web client trust, data transport trust, Web server trust, and operating system trust as shown in Fig.2.

Trust can be propagated along the trust chain from Web client trust through data transport trust and Web server trust to operating system trust [16]. This trust propagation affects the trust of customer in the Web client, data transport, Web server, and operating system sequentially in general, in e-commerce in particular. At the same time, this trust propagation also promotes the improvement of the Web browser, data transport, Web server, and operating system. Therefore, the propagation of trust plays a vital role in e-commerce not only from the seller and buyer viewpoint, but also from a viewpoint of researcher or technology of e-commerce.

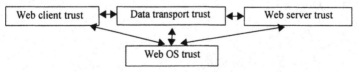

Fig. 2. A trust chain in e-commerce [15]

3 An Intelligent Model of Trust in E-Commerce

We assume that P is an agent and Q is another agent. P has a knowledge set K_P, which can be considered as the knowledge base in a knowledge based agent, reasoning methods set R_P, which can be considered the problem-solving methods. Q has knowledge base K_Q and reasoning set R_Q. Therefore, from a knowledge based systems viewpoint, the behavior of P and Q will be decided by (K_P, R_P) and (K_Q, R_Q) under the same environment.

It should be noted that K_P can also include one's experience, data, and information. R_P also consists of non-traditional reasoning methods.

Now we consider trust between P and Q.

As is well known, trust is a binary relation [22]. For example, agent P trusts agent Q. However, few have gone into this binary relation.

In the most general case, one of the essentially necessary conditions for "agent P trusts agent Q" is that agent Q has more knowledge and reasoning methods or problem solving methods than agent P, because this is the important premise of agent P placing confidence in agent Q [1]. In other words, a necessary condition for "agent P trusts agent Q" is that at the time t, agent P and agent Q satisfy:

$$K_P \subseteq K_Q \quad \text{and} \quad R_P \subseteq R_Q \quad \dotfill (1)$$

Based on (1), we can see that trust as a binary relation satisfying:

1. Reflectivity. Agent P trusts agent P itself.
2. Anti-symmetry. If agent P trusts agent Q, and agent Q trusts agent P, then $P=Q$. This is usually inconsistent with reality, because in e-commerce, agent P and agent Q can trust each other for an e-transaction. However, there are really many cases in e-commerce, in which, agent P trusts agent Q whereas agent Q might not trust agent P [1]. This model (1) is more suitable for the latter case. This is the limitation of this model. However, if one agrees that trust is temporary, whereas distrust or mistrust is ubiquitous, then this model is still of practical significance.
3. Transitivity. If agent P trust agent Q, and agent Q trust agent R, then agent P trust agent R. For example, it is very common in e-commerce if customer A trusts his friend B, and B trusts eBay.com, then A trusts eBay.com. This is a kind of transitive trust or trust propagation in customer-to-business e-commerce. However, trust is not transitive in some cases. For instance, customer A trusts his friend B, and B trusts an e-commerce website, however, A does not trust this website.

Therefore, a trust relation is conditionally symmetric and transitive [22].

In reality, the condition (1) can be weakened to three different possibilities that lead to "agent P trusts agent Q."

1. $K_P \subseteq K_Q$

2. $R_P \subseteq R_Q$

3. $K_P \subseteq K_Q$ and $R_P \subseteq R_Q$

The first possibility is that "agent P trusts agent Q" because agent Q has more knowledge and experience than agent P. For example, in a primary school, a student trusts his teacher, because the latter has more knowledge and experience than he. Therefore, the trust resulting from this possibility is called *knowledge-based trust*. In other words, knowledge-based trust is based on one's knowledge and experience about competencies, motives, and goals of the agent [1, 16].

The second possibility is that "agent P trusts agent Q" because agent Q has more reasoning methods or problem solving methods than agent P. For example, in a system development team, a young team member trusts his team leader, because the latter has more problem solving methods than the former in systems analysis. Therefore, the trust resulting from the second possibility is called *reasoning-based trust*. This implies that this trust is based on one's reasoning and problem solving abilities [1, 22]

The third possibility is that "agent P trusts agent Q" because agent Q has more knowledge, experience and more reasoning methods or problem solving methods than agent P. For example, a patient trusts an experienced doctor working in a clinic, because the doctor has more knowledge, experience and more methods in diagnosis and treatment. Therefore, the trust resulting from the third possibility is called *hybrid trust*. In other words, hybrid trust is a combination of knowledge-based trust and reasoning-based trust [16].

It is very common for agents P and Q in e-commerce or MECS to have a hybrid trust relationship, because the knowledge and reasoning methods of an agent are usually considered as his ability or reputation in particular in the case of trust as discussed in others' work such as Xiu and Liu [22]. Based on this idea, this investigation is more fundamental than reputation-based trust [6] and ability-based trust (see later).

4 Experience-Based Trust in E-Commerce

Experience-based trust has also been drawn attention in e-commerce [8]. Experience-based trust is to use past experiences to help build the trust in the potential buyers or sellers in e-commerce. The feedback from other peers to the potential buyers or sellers also plays an important role in building of trust which is the basis for recommendation and judgement on the potential buyers or sellers [23]. This section extends *reasoning-based* trust and hybrid trust to experience-based trust in e-commerce.

From a logic viewpoint, there are eight basic inference rules for performing EBR [15], which are summarized in Table 1, and constitute the fundamentals for all EBR paradigms [13]. The eight inference rules are listed in the first row, and their corresponding general forms are shown in the second row respectively. The eight inference rules are *modus ponens* (MP), *modus tollens* (MT), abduction, *modus ponens* with trick (MPT), *modus tollens* with trick (MTT), abduction with trick (AT), inverse *modus ponens* (IMP), inverse *modus ponens* with trick (IMPT). For simplicity, we denote them as $R = \{R_1, R_2, R_3, R_4, R_5, R_6, R_7, R_8\}$. The first four of them have been used in computer science, mathematics, mathematical logic, and other sciences [13, 14]. The rest were proposed in the past few years [13, 15], to our knowledge. However, they are all the abstraction and summary of EBR in real world problems.

Table 1. Experience-based reasoning: Eight inference rules

MP	MT	abdu-ction	MTT	AT	MPT	IMP	IMPT
P	$\neg Q$	Q	$\neg Q$	Q	P	$\neg P$	$\neg P$
$P \rightarrow Q$	$P \rightarrow Q$	$P \rightarrow Q$	$P \rightarrow Q$	$P \rightarrow Q$	$P \rightarrow Q$	$P \rightarrow Q$	$P \rightarrow Q$
$\therefore Q$	$\therefore \neg P$	$\therefore P$	$\therefore P$	$\therefore \neg P$	$\therefore \neg Q$	$\therefore \neg Q$	$\therefore Q$

It should be noted that "with trick" is only an explanation for such models. One can give other semantic explanations for them. For example, one can use exception or deception to explain them in the context of the stock market or systems diagnosis [13].

In the rest of this section, we will discuss reasoning-based trust in the context of EBR.

As is well known, one reasoning or problem solving consists of a chain of inference rules. In other words, one agent P's reasoning method consists of a few fundamental inference rules. Therefore, we can use inference rules (how many times has an inference rule been used? how many inference rules an agent has used for a problem solving?) to measure the reasoning methods or problem solving methods. Based on this discussion, let $R = \{R_1, R_2, R_3, R_4, R_5, R_6, R_7, R_8\}$, $R_P \subseteq R$ and $R_Q \subseteq R$, then agent P trusts agent Q with respect to EBR *iff* $R_P \subseteq R_Q$. This implies that "agent P trusts agent Q" because in the problem solving agent Q has used more inference rules in particular, more problem solving methods in general of EBR than agent P. For example, in a transaction of e-commerce, agent P trusts agent Q with respect to EBR, because agent Q uses *modus ponens* (MP), *modus tollens* (MT), abduction, inverse *modus ponens* (IMP) on some e-commerce occasions; that is, $R_Q = \{R_1, R_2, R_3, R_7\}$ and agent P only uses inference rules, $R_P = \{R_1, R_2, R_3\}$. In particular, in e-commerce negotiation, a seller agent might use any possible inference rules of the EBR to make an e-customer agent trust him [14]. Normally, an e-customer uses less inference rules of EBR in e-commerce negotiation.

6 Measure and Evaluation of Trust

Tweedale and Cutler examine trust in multiagent systems and note the measure of trust [18]. However, they have not gone into it. In what follows, we will introduce a unified measure of trust based on the discussion of the previous section.

Generally, let the cardinality (size) of knowledge set K and reasoning methods set R be $|K|$ and $|R|$ respectively. Then the trust degree of agent P in agent Q can be denoted as

$$T(P,Q) = \alpha\left(\frac{1-|K_P|}{|K_Q|}\right) + (1-\alpha)\left(\frac{1-|R_P|}{|R_Q|}\right) \quad \cdots\cdots\cdots\cdots\cdots\cdots \quad (2)$$

where when $\alpha = 1$, $T(P, Q)$ is the knowledge-based trust degree of agent P in agent Q. When $\alpha = 0$, $T(P, Q)$ is the reasoning-based trust degree of agent P in agent Q. When $0 < \alpha < 1$, $T(P, Q)$ is the hybrid trust degree of agent P in agent Q. For example, if knowledge-based trust degree of agent P in agent Q is 0.8, the reasoning-based trust degree of agent P in agent Q is 0.4, and $\alpha = 0.7$, then hybrid trust degree of agent P in agent Q is $T(P,Q) = 0.7 \times 0.8 + 0.3 \times 0.4 = 0.68$.

Further, $(1-|K_P|)/K_Q$ implies that agent P's trust degree is greater whenever the size of knowledge set of the agent Q is greater than that of agent P taking into account (1). Similarly, $(1-|R_P|)/R_Q$ implies that agent P's trust degree is greater whenever the size of reasoning methods of the agent Q is greater than that of agent P. The key idea behind it is that agent P easily trust agent Q if the latter has more knowledge and experience or problem solving ability than agent P taking into account (1). This case usually happens when a student trusts his teacher. With the age increasing the trust between any two persons will be decreasing. In other words, it is more difficult for one to trust others in the adult world. Therefore, $(1-|K_P|)/K_Q$ or $(1-|R_P|)/R_Q$ will be decreasing when the size of knowledge set of the agent P approaches to that of agent Q or the size of reasoning methods of the agent P approaches to that of agent Q. For simplicity, we use $T(P, Q)$ to denote either knowledge based trust degree or reasoning trust degree or hybrid trust degree and do not differ one from another without specification.

7 A Case-Based Model for Ability Based Trust

The intelligent model for trust introduced in Section 3 is not valid for dealing with the ability-based trust. This section will focus on this kind of trust.

Ability-based trust is related to the trustee's knowledge, skills or competency to perform as expected [22]. This kind of trust is related to one agent P and other agents or in particular agent team $Q = \{Q_1, Q_2, ..., Q_n\}$ with respect to task t. Assume that for the agent P, the satisfaction value that agent Q_i, $i \in \{1,2,...,n\}$ receives for completing task t is $s(P,Q_i,t)$, where $s(\quad, \quad, \quad) \in [0,1]$, then the trust degree of agent P in agent Q_i can be considered as $s(P,Q_i,t)$ [23] (more generally, agent P should be replaced by a special standard for completing a task.); that is,

$$T(P,Q_i,t) = s(P,Q_i,t) \qquad (3)$$

Therefore, the most trustworthy agent of agent P with respect to task t should be agent Q_k with a trust degree $T(P,Q_k,t)$ and $k \in \{1,2,...,n\}$ such that for any $i \in \{1,2,...,n\}$, $T(P,Q_k,t) \geq T(P,Q_i,t)$. We can briefly denote this as

$$T(P,Q,t)_{max} = T(P,Q_k,t) \qquad (4)$$

Now there is a new task t_0 to be done by one of the agents in Q. t_0 is similar to task t. The question is who should be most trustworthy agent for agent P to complete this task. In what follows we answer this question.

Let t be similar to t_0, then $T(P,Q_i,t) \approx T(P,Q_i,t_0)$, $\approx$ is a similarity metric [14], then the most trustworthy agent of agent P with respect to task t, agent Q_k with a trust degree $T(P,Q_k,t)$ that satisfies (4) will be recommended based on case-based reasoning [14] to complete the new task t_0, which is a kind of experience-based recommendation.

8 Concluding Remarks

This paper examined experience-based trust, knowledge-based trust, inference-based trust and case-based trust in e-commerce and their interrelationships from an intelligent systems viewpoint. The proposed approach will improve a formal understanding of trust and facilitate research and development of trust, multiagent systems, e-commerce and e-services.

In future work, we will develop a system prototype for the multiagent case based trust management system, which can be used for business recommendation and negotiation. We will also examine scalable trust in e-commerce and e-services.

References

M. Branchaud and S. Flinn , 2004, xTrust: A scalable trust management infrastructure, In *Proc 2nd Annual Conf on Privacy, Security and Trust*, Fredericton, New Brunswick, Canada, 14-15 October, pp. 207-218.

C. Castelfranchi, and Y.H. Tan (eds), 2001, *Trust and Deception in Virtual Societies*, Kluwer Academic Publishers, Norwell MA, USA.

G. Chen, Z. Li, Z. Cheng, Z. Zhao, and H. Yan, 2005, *A fuzzy trust model for multiagent systems*, LNCS 3612, Springer, Berlin, pp. 444-448.

G Finnie, Sun Z, and Barker J, 2005, Trust and deception in multi-agent trading systems: A logical viewpoint, In: Proc. 11th Americas Information Systems (AMCIS2005), The Association for Information Systems, Aug 11-14, 2005 Omaha, NE, USA, pp. 1020-1026.

D. H. McKnight, V. Choudhury, and C. Kacmar, 2002, The impact of initial customer trust on intentions to transact with a website: A trust building model, J of Strategic Information Systems, 11, 297-323.

M. Nielsen and K. Krukow, 2004, On the formal modelling of trust in reputation-based systems, LNCS 3113, Berlin Heidelberg Springer-Verlag, pp. 192-204.

N.J. Nilsson, 1998, Artificial Intelligence: A New Synthesis. San Francisco: Morgan Kaufmann Publishers.

O. Olsson, 2002, Trust in eCommerce - the ontological status of trust, Proc ECOM-02 - Electronic Commerce - Theory and Applications, B. Wiszniewski (ed), Gdansk, pp. 89-96.

P. A. Pavlou, 2003, Customer acceptance of electronic commerce: Integrating trust and risk with the technology acceptance model, Intl J of Electronic Commerce 7(3), 135-161.

Salam AF, Iyer L, Palvia P, and Singh R, 2005, Trust in e-commerce, Comm of The ACM, 48(2), 73-77.

S. Schmidt, R. Steele, T. Dillion and E. Chang, 2005, Applying a fuzzy trust model to e-commerce systems, LNAI 3809, Springer,pp 318-329.

C.V. Slyke, F. Belanger, and C.L. Comunale, 2004, Factors influencing the adoption of web-based shopping: The impact of trust, The Data Base for Advances in Information Systems, vol. 35, no. 2.

Z. Sun and G. Finnie, 2004a, Experience based reasoning for recognizing fraud and deception. In: Proc. Intl Conf on Hybrid Intelligent Systems (HIS 2004), December 6-8, Kitakyushu, Japan, IEEE Press, pp. 80-85.

Z. Sun and G. Finnie, 2004, Intelligent Techniques in E-Commerce: A Case-based Reasoning Perspective. Berlin Heidelberg: Springer-Verlag.

Z. Sun and G. Finnie, 2007, A fuzzy logic approach to experience based reasoning, Intl J Intell Syst. 22(8) 867-889.

Z. Sun, Y. Li, and S. Zhao, 2007, Trust, deception and security in e-commerce. In Columbus F (ed) E-Commerce Research and Trends, NY: Nova Science Publishers. In press.

Y.H. Tan and W. Thoen, 2001, Toward a generic model of trust for electronic commerce. Intl J of Electronic Commerce 5(2), 61-74.

J.Tweedale and P. Cutler, 2006, Trust in multiagent systems, LNCS 4252, Berlin Heidelberg Springer-Verlag, pp. 479-485.

Uslaner EM, 2004, Trust online, trust offline, Comm of The ACM, 47(4), 28-29.

T. Verhagen, S. Meents, and Y. H. Tan, 2006, Perceived risk and trust associated with purchasing at electronic marketplaces, European J of Information Systems, 15, 542-555.

S. C. Wingreen, S.L. Baglione, 2005, Untangling the antecedents and covariates of e-commerce trust: institutional trust vs. knowledge-based trust, Electronic Markets, 15 (3), 246 - 260.

D. Xiu, and Z. Liu, 2005, A formal definition for trust in distributed systems, LNCS 3650, Springer Verlag, Berlin Heidelberg, pp. 482-489.

L. Xiong and L. Liu, 2002, Building trust in decentralized peer-to-peer electronic communities, In Proc Intl Conf on Electronic Commerce Research (ICECR-5), Montreal, Canada, October, 2002.

Research on Design of Analysis-based CRMSystem for Mobile Communications Industry and its Application

Zheng-qing Luo [1], Shi-an Wang [1], Xu-fang Chen [2]

1 School of Management, Hefei University of Technology, Anhui,
230009, zqluojzz@mail.hf.ah.cn
2 Mail Box 218, Hefei University of Technology, Anhui, 230009
fangfang52065@sohu.com

Abstract: With the constant development of customer relationship management (CRM) theory and the maturity of business intelligence technology, the analysis-based CRM has become a hot topic in the academic field. Some enterprises have begun to put the analysis-based CRM to practice; however, there have been few successful applications because of the inadequate mastery of business intelligence technology and the insufficient understanding of business environment to apply the system. Through combining the characteristics of the mobile communications industry with those of mobile customer's consumption, this paper designs an analysis-based CRM system suitable for the mobile communications industry in China, which can provide useful references to the CRM of the mobile communications industry.

1 Introduction

We know that the domestic mobile communications industry has entered the steady development stage after its high speed development and that the market competition for the mobile communications industry has become more intense. The mobile communications industry is a typical industry needing huge fixed investment in its earlier stage, mainly including the construction of base-station and switch. The fixed expenditure in network and the equipment maintenance are relatively high, but the labor cost and other expenses are relatively small. The most remarkable characteristic of this industry is that the infrastructure investment has no direct relation with the quantity of its customer. That is to say, in a certain scope, there is no huge difference between having 10,000 customers and having only one customer

Please use the following format when citing this chapter:

Luo, Z., Wang, S., Chen, X., 2007, in IFIP International Federation for Information Processing, Volume 251, Integration and Innovation Orient to E-Society Volume1, Wang, W. (Eds), (Boston: Springer), pp. 652-662.

in the infrastructure investment. In other words, the marginal cost of winning a customer is low. Therefore, the market competition of the mobile communications industry, in essence, is to compete for more customer resources. The core competence of mobile communications industry is to attract new customers, to retain the old customers and to implement effective CRM.

2   Application and existing problems with t he CRM system of the domestic mobile communications industry

2.1   Current application of CRM system for the mobile communications industry in China and existing problems

At present, the domestic mobile communications industry has already established the mature service system, such as China Mobile's Business Operation Support System (BOSS), the former China Telecom's "97 projects" (like the networks administration system and the cost-calculating system) and China Unicom's synthetic account system. These systems have enabled the domestic mobile communications industry to operate automatically and they are similar to the analysis-based CRM system in certain aspects. However, each system does business in its own way and the data is dispersible among these systems. Therefore, it is difficult to integrate the customer's information, to say nothing of analyzing the data and mining valuable information. In this sense, the difficulty in the CRM implementation lies in how to establish a mature analysis-based CRM system by unifying the former operation system. In recent years, the overseas CRM suppliers have also developed the analysis-based CRM system in the mobile communications industry. There are few successful applications because the overseas suppliers have limited understanding of the commercial competition environment in China, and their models need perfecting.

2.2 Existing problems in the practice of CRM

(1) The incomplete and un-centralized customer information

The customer information that the mobile communications corporation has acquired is all dispersed in different departments. Usually, the market department acquires information through the name cards and the records of feedback table from the marketing campaign. In the sales department, the effective and dynamic information of important mobile customers is also fragmented and not comprehensive. The service sector only has the recorded information about customer's complaints and business applications.

(2) The more obvious limitation of customer value evaluation index

At present, the mobile communications corporation makes a rough judgment about customer value according to customer Average Revenue per User (ARPU). The ARPU value is unable to evaluate the customer value in the entire life cycle because it neglects the cost element and merely considers the customer current value instead of customer's latent value.

(3) The high percentage of customer loss and failure to analyze it comprehensively

At present, there is a high percentage of customer loss in the domestic mobile communications industry. According to the statistics of the China mobile, the customer loss in the four years spanning from 1999 to 2002 reaches as high as 11%, 9.5%, 16.3% and 20.8% respectively. The loss trend is on the obvious rise [1]. Despite the fact that the operation businessmen know the customer loss, they fail to take effective measures to control and manage the drained customers. They don't know why they drain away and the structure of the drained customers.

3 Structure of analysis-based CRM system and key technology

3.1 Structure of CRM system

Typical analysis-based CRM system consists of the interaction level, the operation level and the analysis level, which will be further explained in this paper.

3.2 Commercial intelligence, key technology of CRM system

In 1989, Commercial intelligence initially proposed by Howard Dresner in Gartner Group which is a consultant firm in the US. Commercial intelligence assists the business decision through the application of support system [2]. The commercial intelligence is generally composed of the data warehouse, on-line analytical processing (OLAP), data mining and analysis tool. The data warehouse is the integrated, non-updated data group, used to support policy-making process [3]. Data warehouse should be integrated with the operational data. OLAP is mainly used to analyze data. The data mining technology, also called knowledge discovering, is mainly used to acquire useful information and knowledge from massive incomplete data. The analysis tool presents the analysis result for the end-users. Integration of these four parts can be used to make a comprehensive and in-depth analysis of enterprise's administration.

4 Design of analysis-based CRM system for the mobile communications industry

4.1 Structure of analysis-based CRM system

According to the general structure of analysis-based CRM and mobile communications industry service pattern [4-6], the authors have designed an analysis-based CRM system for the mobile communications industry. This system mainly consists of the customer interaction level, the operation level and the analysis level, as is shown in figure 1.

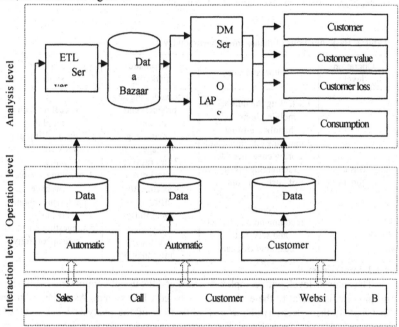

Figure 1 Analysis-based CRM system structure for mobile communications industry

4.2 Main functions of analysis-based CRM system for the mobile communications industry

4.2.1 Customer interaction level

The customer interaction level, the forepart of the analysis-based CRM system, is a direct contacting channel between the operation business and customers. The customer interaction level may achieve the following functions, as Table 1 shows.

Table 1 Contact points and basic functions of customer interaction level

Contact points	Self-support service hall, Call center, Important client manager, Client delegate, Agent service point, E-mail, Message, Website, Bill, Advertisement, etc.
Basic functions	Providing customers with uniform products and services effectively Responding to customer's personalized requests flexibly and quickly Collecting customer's information Finding out customer's demand Retaining customers

4.2.2 Management operation level

The management operation level includes the automatic sale, automatic marketing and the customer service support system. Basic functions of the management operation level are indicated in table 2.

Table 2. Basic functions of management operation level

Operation level	Automatic sale	Automatic marketing	Customer Service support
Basic functions	1.selecting the number of mobile phone and handling e-order 2.inputting ,changing and storing customer data 3.managing history of customer contact 4.checking customer credit 5.recommending product and service to customer delegate	1.popularizing new products and training 2.marketing management 3.interactive marketing 4.before and aftersales consultation 5.changing customer information	1. dealing with complaints 2. controlling and checking service quality 3. checking trouble in website 4.automatic phonic response 5.suggesting potential sale opportunity

4.2.3 Analysis level

The analysis level, with complex structure and the use of commercial intelligence technology, is crucial to the entire analysis-based CRM system. As is demonstrated in Chart 1, the system structure and work flow of the analysis level is clearly explained. The analysis level, first, constructs many data warehouses of the marketing sector and the service sector by extracting, transforming and loading data from the automatic sale, automatic marketing and customer service systems databases. Then, analysts from the above sectors can visit the DM server and the OLAP server through the customer end program, the browser and the report system tool, so that the customer analysis function can be achieved. The analysis content includes: the segmentation of customers, the analysis of customer behavior, the analysis of customer value, the analysis of cross sales, the analysis of customer loss and the analysis of customer loyalties.

5 Research on customer value of analysis-based CRM system in the mobile communications industry

This part researches on the analysis of the customer value because of the complex structure of the analysis-based CRM system and the limited pages .

5.1 Design of customer value evaluation index system

Based on the mobile communications customer value evaluation index system [7] designed by domestic scholar Qi Jia-yin in 2004, and resorting to China Mobile Business Analysis System Operation Criterion (the V1.0 version) [8] and China Unicom Business Analysis System Technology Criterion (the revised edition in 2004) [9], this paper has designed the following index system, as is shown in figure 2.

The system structure is divided into three levels. The first level mainly evaluates the customer value from the aspect of customer's current value and potential value. In the second level, income index and cost index can be used to evaluate the customer current value; the loyalty index and credit index can be used to show customer's latent value--the customer's stability and possibility of creating profits for the enterprise in the future. The third level is about the more concrete indexes.

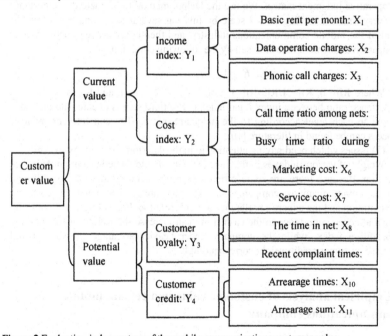

Figure 2 Evaluation index system of the mobile communications customer value

5.2 Computation model of Mobile customer value

(1) Customer value formula

Firstly, pre-establish the value extent for every index in the evaluation system, and ascertain customer value in every index through the mapping method. Then, put different weights to different indexes. At last, obtain the customer value through adding all products from each index multiplying with its weight. The formula is expressed below:

$$CV = \sum_{i=1}^{n} X_i \cdot R_i$$

Where CV stands for the customer value, Xi denotes the value of index i; Ri refers to the weight of index i; N is the number of index.

(2) The method of ascertaining index weights in the formula

In this customer value model, the index system is divided into three hierarchies. Therefore, it is suitable to determine the index weights by resorting to the analytic hierarchy process (AHP). The three concrete steps are as follows. The first step is to construct the hierarchy model. This paper thinks of the customer value as the target level, the customer current value and the latent value as the criterion level, then each detailed index as the lower project level. The second step is to construct mutual comparative judgment matrix. We use the Delphi method to evaluate the importance of every index according to 1-9 scale by inviting several marketing experts in the field of the mobile communications industry, and then construct reasonable mutual comparative judgment matrix to satisfy the following condition.

$$A = (R_{ij})_{m \times n}$$

Where Rij> 0, Rij= 1/Rji, Rii=1, also i, j= (1, 2......, n), and Rij is the relative importance ratio between index i and index j. The third step is to calculate the index weight in each level according to the judgment matrix. The concrete computation process can be found in literature [10].

(3) Issues which need paying attention to in the determining of index weight

Weight of various indexes in this index system should be dependent on the actual situation. Because there are some differences in the achievement goal of different mobile communications companies in different areas. The level of customer consumption and the expert's preference are different too. For example, the company which attaches importance to the cash flows can increase the weight of the monthly expenditure index, while the company under heavier arrearage pressure should increase customer credit weight correspondingly.

6 Empirical analysis of customer value in a certain mobile communications company

We investigated one of China Unicom companies in Anhui province during our research. This company is mainly engaged in comprehensive telecommunications service, such as GSM130, CDMA133 mobile phone, 193, the IP long-distance telephone, 165-net and so on. At present, the company possesses 12 business halls by itself, 89 associated business halls, 344 charge points, 1,400-kilometer cable, and the capacity of mobile exchanges for 485,000. The number of staff in the company is 345 and it has two subsidiaries.

6.1 Basic status of customers in this company

We referred to the basic information about GSM users and the CDMA users from the company's costs system and the account system in March, 2005. Through data handling, we obtained the value of user's ARPU and the distribution of total call charges, as is shown in table 4. Besides, we extracted call charges details of 1,000 customers from March to May in 2006 at random. Among them, details of a certain customer whose mobile phone number is 1308300**** are shown in table 3.

Table 3 A certain customer's detailed call charges list

Index\Time	Basic rent per month	Call charges	Value added charges	Arrear-age in the past	Advance payment	Overd-ue fees	Total call time (minutes)	Call time among nets (minutes)	Busy time call (minutes)
03/05	￥20.0	￥53.9	￥12.23	￥0.00	￥50.00	￥0.00	303.24	162.56	82.45
04/05	￥20.0	￥65.5	￥9.45	￥0.00	￥80.00	￥0.00	383.54	87.25	92.34
05/05	￥20.0	￥52.8	￥13.46	￥0.00	￥50.00	￥0.00	252.65	125.76	102.32

Table 4 GSM and CDMA customer's ARPU distribution

ARPU (Yuan)	Custo-mer amount	Ratio	Cumu-lative ratio	Call charges	Ratio	Cumul-Ative ratio	Aver-age ARPU
0-30	32653	0.094997	1.0000	869875.92	0.029150	1.00000	26.64
30-50	94273	0.274269	0.9050	4098808.91	0.137356	0.96703	43.48
50-100	162937	0.474033	0.6307	11641848.6	0.390134	0.82968	71.45
100-200	35556	0.103443	0.1567	6194566.32	0.207588	0.43954	174.22
200-300	9552	0.027790	0.0532	2414287.93	0.080906	0.23195	252.75
300-500	6702	0.019498	0.0254	2877436.68	0.096426	0.15105	429.34
500-800	1588	0.004620	0.0059	1145472.04	0.038386	0.05462	721.33
800-1000	331	0.000963	0.00135	315552.23	0.0105746	0.016239	953.33
>1000	133	0.000387	0.0003	282758.21	0.009475	0.00566	2126.0

According to table 4, we conclude that the customer data of this China Unicom company are approximately subject to the normal distribution through the statistical analysis and computation. We can obtain ARPU=86.81. Among them, 43.95% call charges is paid by 15.67% customers. The computation model is as follows.

6.2 Empirical analysis of customer value computation model

(1) Giving piecewise value to each index in the evaluation system

We first pre-establish the value extent for index X_1 to index X_{11}, and give corresponding value (20, 40, 60, 80, 100) to each different value extent by using centesimal mode. Considering there is little difference between each mobile customer's marketing cost index and service cost index and because it's difficult to obtain data of this subsidiary's marketing cost and service cost, indexes X_6 and X_7 are omitted. Piecewise value of other indexes is shown in table 5.

Table 5 Piecewise value of index

Index value	20	40	60	80	100
X_1: Basic rent per month	10	15	20	30	50
X_2:Data value-added operation charges	0-50	50-200	200-500	500-800	≥800
X_3 :Call charges	0-50	50-200	200-500	500-800	≥800
X_4:Call time ratio among nets	1-0.8	0.8-0.6	0.6-0.4	0.4-0.2	0.2-0
X_5 :Busy time ratio during call	1-0.8	0.8-0.6	0.6-0.4	0.4-0.2	0.2-0
X_8 :The time in net(year)	0-1	1-2	2-3	3-4	>4
X_9 :Recent times of complaint	>3	3	2	1	0
X_{10} :Times of arrearage	>8	8	4	2	0
X_{11} :Sum of arrearage	>200	200-100	100-50	50-20	20-0

We can obtain corresponding index value $X_1 = 60$, $X_2 = 20$, $X_3 = 40$, $X_4 = 80$, $X_5 = 80$, $X_8 = 40$,$X_9 = 100$, $X_{10} = 100$, $X_{11} = 100$ through computation by taking the customer whose mobile number is 1308300**** shown in table 4 for example.

(2) Selecting each index's weight

In order to clarify the importance of every correlated factor in the index system, we communicated sufficiently with related staff in the market administration department during our investigation. For the sake of computing simplicity, we apply the AHP method to ascertain weight for the income index level. For other levels, we use the direct evaluation method to ascertain weight. The judgment matrix of income index level is as follows:

$$Y_1 = \begin{bmatrix} 1 & 1/5 & 1/3 \\ 5 & 1 & 3 \\ 3 & 1/3 & 1 \end{bmatrix}$$

Where W=(0.105,0.637,0.258)',λmax=3.038,CI=0.019,RI=0.58,CR=0.033
According to the customer value computation model, we can obtain:
CV=0.6(0.8Y_1+0.2Y_2) +0.4(0.5Y_3+0.5Y_4)
WhereY_1=0.105X_1+0.637X_2+0.258X_3
Y_2=0.6X_4+0.4X_5,Y_3=0.3X_8+0.7X_9,Y_4=0.5X_{10}+0.5X_{11}
(3) Calculating customer's customer value (CV) in the sample

Substituting the customer data shown in Table 3 into the former CV formula, we can obtain customer value CV=98.1of No.1308300****, and other customers' CV can be computed by using the same principle.

In order to calculate the sample customer CV, we have established a programming using FOXPRO. Substitute the sample data into the programming to obtain the distribution of the 1,000 customers' CV. The statistics indicates the sample customer's CV is approximately subject to the normal distribution. Thus, we tested the reasonableness of this customer value computation model.

From the statistics, we may find two kinds of customers. One kind of customer's CV is high, but their ARPU value is low. This explains that this kind of customer's monthly consumption is low, but maybe their call time ratio among nets is smaller, the time they attend the net is longer, and their loyalty is higher. Therefore, it is unreasonable to evaluate this kind of customer by using the ARPU value merely. The other kind of customer's CV is lower, but their ARPU value is higher. This shows that this kind of customer's monthly consumption is high. However, their call ratio between nets is high, arrearage frequently occurs, their credit is low, and they are easy to drain away. For this kind of customers, if their customer value is evaluated by merely using the ARPU value, it is likely that the virtual height of the ARPU value will occur, which does harm to the marketing decision. Therefore, adequate importance should be attached to these two situations.

7 Conclusion:

This paper mainly analyzes problems existing in the CRM practice of domestic mobile communications industry. In order to solve these problems, we design the analysis-based CRM system for the mobile communications industry. The system structure has three levels, including the customer interaction level, the operation level and the analysis level. The functions for each part are designed and expatiated amply in the paper. According to the characteristics of domestic mobile communications industry and the characteristics of customer's consumption, we focus our research on the customer value. Moreover, we design a reasonable and comprehensive customer value evaluation index system. And we innovatively construct new model for the customer value computation. Finally, the paper tests the practicability and rationality of the analysis-based CRM system and the customer value computation model by giving an example. In a word, the paper has two scientific contributions. One is designing the structure and function of analysis-based CRM system for the mobile communications industry. The other is constructing a more scientific and new model for the customer value computation.

References:

1. D. Qi Jia-yin, Empirical research on customer entire life cycle management and mobile operation industry, Beijing University of Posts and Telecommunications, 2004
2. D. Peng Ying, Constructing analysis-based CRM by using commercial intelligence, University of International Business and Economics, 2003

3. M Inmon, W.H.Building, *Data Warehouse*, QED Technical Publishing Group, 1999:12-13

4. Tromp, S.; Versendaal, J.; Batenburg, R.; Van Duinkerken, W.; Business/IT-Alignment for Customer Relationship Management in the Telecommunication Industry: Framework and Case Study, *Information and Communication Technologies, 2006. ICTTA '06. 2nd.* Volume 1, 24-28 April 2006 Page(s):262 – 267

5. Camponovo, G.; Pigneur, Y.; Rangone, A.; Renga, F.; Mobile customer relationship management: an explorative investigation of the Italian consumer market, *Mobile Business, 2005. ICMB 2005,* International Conference on 11-13 July 2005 Page(s):42 – 48

6. Anderson, W.O., Jr, Customer relationship management in an e-business environment, Change Management and the New Industrial Revolution, 2001, *IEMC '01 Proceedings,* 7-9 Oct. 2001 Page(s):311 - 316

7. J. Qi Jia-yin, Designing customer value evaluation index system for mobile communications industry, *Chinese science and technology paper on-line,* 2004, 5

8. *China Mobile Business Analysis System Operation Criterion,* V1.0 version, China mobile communications company

9. China Unicom Business Analysis System Technology Criterion, in 2004, revised edition, The department of cost calculating, settlement, and information system from China Unicom Business headquarters

10. M. Du Dong, Pang Qing-hua, *Selection of modern comprehensive evaluation method and cases*, Qinghua University Press, 2005

Information Retrieval in Web2.0

Ziran Zhang , Jianyu Tang
Information Managment Department, Central China Normal University,
Wuhan, 430079 China.imdec2003@163.com

Abstract. The development of Web2.0 not only update the network industry, but also vastly impact on the traditional retrieval methods of networked information and put forward more new demands. The paper analyses the development of Web2.0 and the new demand of networked information retrieval, describes and evaluates the current mode of networked information retrieval. At last, the author put forwards a new conceptual mode which based on JXTA and P2P of networked information retrieval.

1 Introduction

With the development of the web2.0 and its typical application such as Blog, wiki, RSS, Tag, SNS and so on since 2004, users have become the center of information production and usage and they have more point to point channels of information transmission. This development and change not only update the network industry, but also vastly impact on the traditional retrieval methods of networked information and put forward more new demands. Researching these demands and new retrieval progress would be helpful in providing better retrieval service for information users. This paper is intended to analyze these new requirements under the circumstance of Web2.0, discuss and evaluate new retrieval mode of networked information.

2 Development and Networked Information Retrieval Requirements of Web2.0

2.1 Traditional Retrieval of Networked Information

Traditional retrieval of networked information is mainly depended on such following methods: key words-based retrieval which is represented by search engine; subject

Please use the following format when citing this chapter:

Zhang, Z., Tang, J., 2007, in IFIP International Federation for Information Processing, Volume 251, Integration and Innovation Orient to E-Society Volume1, Wang, W. (Eds), (Boston: Springer), pp. 663-670.

catalogue-based retrieval which is represented by Yahoo's classification system; metadata-based retrieval which is represented by subject gateway, such as AHDS, EELS, MathGuide, etc [1]; database and relative data pattern and retrieval language based deep web retrieval; professional portal retrieval and so forth. However, most of them use professional data that are selected by website editors or created beforehand as the main data, so massive knowledge produced by public can't be processed; the retrieval results to different users' search are the same, so individualized service can't be realized; as lacking of semantic relation among information, so the search engine which is the most common ways of network search can get good retrieval results only to the objective and fact-based information, thereby the subjective and personal opinion-based retrieval can't be well done that high quality retrieval results couldn't be got or even there isn't any results [2], Such retrieval methods can't be satisfied obviously.

2.2   New Requirements of Networked Information Retrieval

In the environment of Web2.0, information takes on characteristics that differ from Web1.0 and consequently brings forward new requirements to information retrieval, providing possibility for the coming of new retrieval ways.

(1)The popularization and massive of information production

In the times of Web1.0, the production of networked information is centered on relative minority professional companies and website editors, whereas, a large number of users offer massive information content for network in the environment of Web2.0.However, as the constantly growing of Web2.0 users, the original networked information has assumed a tendency of blowout, which would undoubtedly take tremendous difficulties to users who want to get essential and valuable information from innumerable information.

(2)The microcontent and semantics of information structure

Microcontent comes from various data created by users, such as a network log, review, image, collected bookmark, preferable music list, things that want to do, places wishing to go, new friends and so forth. Web2.0 creates massive microcotent and consume as much microcontent everyday, therefore, how to help users manage, maintain, store, share, transfer microcontent become the key point that users whether could exploit information effectively or not [3]. Although there is lots of microcontent in Web1.0, such as album online, speak and response of forum and so on, which are relatively closed to outside that can not be organized and exploited again fundamentally, the applications in Web2.0 could reused these microcontent, which makes it's possible to use these microcontent freely in any place, so these microcontent could be aggregated, managed, shared and transferred, and be remixed to individualized and abound applications further [4]. Moreover, traditional web data in HTML has no semantic label and the transmitted semantics is identified by human, which may be greatly differs from the original meaning of information provider, this is also the fundamental reason that traditional methods of information retrieval usually can only use the simple retrieval ways of key words or Boolean among key words and combination of the two, so that the agreed point can not be gotten between information provider and information users. In the environment of Web2.0, Tag is a kind of semantic mark and there are other semantic labels, such as label of resource relationship, label that is endowed automatically by computers according to the usage condition of resources and so on. Although these semantic labels couldn't fully identified automatically by computers at present, semantic matching and clustering could be done as least [5], even users' retrieval habits and retrieval characters could be recorded on the basis of semantic labels provided and concerned by users.

(3)The good and bad information quality is more intermingled

The massive and dispersive information results in lacking of necessary control on information releasing, so the quality of information is more intermingled. For users of mastering different knowledge structure, how to discriminate, filter and utilize information becomes a big difficulty, and also increase the difficulty of identifying tools of information retrieval. In the meantime, the information semantic is more complicated because of the using of Tag: it's a unavoidable problem for retrieval application of the environment of Web2.0 that the degree of authenticity and accuracy of semantic labels supplied by information provider or information consumer whether could directly become the important evidence of information acquisition or not.

(4) The bidirectional of information spreading

As Web2.0 network being readable and writable, users' information feedback may be done at any time and information source can update information at any times, which is a real communication pattern of twin-channel and information transmission might be well discriminated namely the spread of multipoint to multipoint. Therefore, the traditional situation that users are passive to receive information and different users' requirements receive the same information retrieval results can be changed, and it's possible to further perfect the technology of push and pull.

In view of the above characteristics of information, networked retrieval in the environment of Web2.0 should be popular, social and individual: in the first place, there is enough information retrieval scope so that the retrieval to multiple information sources can be provided to meet the increasing of popular and substantial information in the environment of Web2.0; secondly, one-stop retrieval resembling the function of integrated search engine ought to be offered, so that users don't need to log on multiply websites to obtain similar information ,in the same time, the reuse and store of microcontent should be supported to make use of the technology advantage of Web2.0; thirdly, semantic relationship among information can be analyzed and offer certain service of information evaluation, filter and convergence for consumers according to the relationship, so that the difficulty of information judgment and selection faced by users can be reduced to a certain degree; fourthly, users are able to quickly acquire their interested information in time through search activities and drive their knowledge to update, the retrieval tools can record and evaluate users' search activities to keep accuracy of knowledge update and individual of retrieval results; fifthly, community is created for users' identify marks according to their search activities, high quality information source is pushed to users actively based on their interests. By using such retrieval, users could quickly find their preferable information, finishing their work or tasks or goals in life, sharing knowledge with friends or meet new friends by sharing, and enrich global information and knowledge bank by making use of "root wisdom"[2].

3   New Information Retrieval Patterns in the Environment of Web2.0

3.1   Extended Service of Search Engine

According to the above analysis, the future search should be social and the search engine ought to be more concerned with knowledge content produced by users, so that users' demands are met in the environment of Web2.0. Presently, lots of search engine extends the functions of Web2.0, such as forum search of Google, Blog search, knowing and space of Baidu, My Web2.0 of English Yahoo and so on. My Web2.0 is to create a "social" search engine, which searches the often used and trustful website content of professional group, so the weakness of massive search can be made up. When doing individual search, not only the special index of setting by yourself can be searched, the index set by your friends and workmates can also be searched. For example, a group of physicists may share individual set mutually, hence, when one searches, he could make sure the results he obtains come from the essential index set that's set and selected by others[6]; Zhongsou' s forum search, post bar and so on. Even the search engine Wikiseek which specially searches wiki comes forth [7]; there are still some companies, for instance, Qihoo directly positions its search developing direction in Web2.0 search. Although functions provided by search engine could in some extent help people get information in Web2.0, several problems still exit in it: (1) the search scope is relative narrow. The search extent limits to internal network, for example, forum in Google only search the forum information registered in Google; Baidu's knowing, the Knowledge Hall of Yahoo, Prefer to Ask Intellectual of Sina all only retrieve the knowledge content exchanged by net friends from individual database; (2) the retrieval channels are finite. Only a few attributes are offered to retrieve, for instance, Qiku's Blog retrieval provides only two accesses by Blog article and writer, lacking of the limitations from Blog website, comment on article and property category; (3) the retrieval results are short of semantic analysis. The retrieval results are still the same with traditional web search that lacks of semantic analysis so that users only get the sorting results by matching key words not the results according to different demands; (4) the retrieved information is short of essential filtration, which resulting in the unsatisfied retrieval results, even some garbage information is received.

3.2   Vertical Search Engine

Just as its name implies, vertical search engine is to search the information sources of one industry or a kind, simply speaking, it is to break up the big and comprehensive search engine to professional search engines. It's exactly because these applications of Web2.0 combining with the abundant, fast update and timely characteristics of information, causes the traditional search engine to be in difficulty, so it becomes reasonable to develop the vertical search engine [8]. At present, some comprehensive search engines such as Google, Baidu, Yahoo and so on, also enter into the area of vertical search engine, but there are more professional vertical search engines. The common are map search, music search, video search, news search, pal search, region search, science search, job search, classification information search, shopping information search, etc. In essence, many vertical search engines don't' belong to the category of Web2.0 search, as they are devoid of the core idea of Web2.0 which is users creating content. However, the vertical search engine brings lots of convenience to users' information searching undoubtedly, users use the vertical search engine to gain information closely linked with life and the channels of information spreading and communication are increased consequently. In the meantime, there are also some vertical search engines trying to combine with Web2.0 successfully, for instance, the Jobui[9] (http://www.jobui.com) utilizes the vertical search engine to settle information collection, each job hunter is helped to hunt for a suitable job by using Blog to introduce himself. Job hunters release their Blogs to be acquainted by recruit enterprises fully by network, which changes the previous situation that resumes are monotonous and dull, and so employment opportunities are increased; furthermore, the Blog conduct system is also opened, so job hunters can import the previous Blog in other website.

The biggest problem faced by the vertical search engine is how to deeply mining the professional information, analyze and record users' activities, and offer deep and professional information to appropriate users through the technology platform of Web2.0.

3.3   Networked Favorite

Networked favorite is a kind of free service of social bookmark, which is also called Cyber Digest such as del.icio.us and Yahoo collection+. Besides, there are still baidusoucang, drawer, collection bar, Shouker, Haowangjiao and so on offering networked favorite. The favorite have strong and also weak points, but following problems exist in them: (1) users' credit is lacked. Web2.0 stresses that users produce knowledge content which is the starting point of networked favorite, so that links, evaluation, abstract are all produced and shared by users. However, how to assess users with credit and so to confirm and recommend users by sort isn't considered by above tools. (2) The rationality of folksonomy can't be judged. Most of favorites create classification system according to tags given by users, which is regarded as the main channel of searching Shoucang of users, these classification systems are not to be compared with classification systems created by experts. (3)The retrieval functions are finite. Most of them only offer the search function through key words resulting from defining tag, retrieval functions according to attributes such as user, date, and region are not offered. (4)The functions of creating user community are limited. Although users of collecting the same material can be found, most of favorites don't offer service of building user community, which greatly reduces communication chances between users.

3.4   Personal Portal

With the constantly developing of Web2.0, the portal concept is mixed with search engine gradually, resulting in birth of personal portal tools, such as IG. IG (Internet/Information Gateway) is a kind of internet personal portal whose access is based on desktop, centers on personal user which is put forward by China search, realizing individual service which internet information is got, transferred and reactive timely. IG integrates multiple network service items, such as IE browse, QQ, MSN, search engine, information customization, individual information portal, website navigation, facilitating citizens service, BBS, entertainment service, etc. In IG, users may choose the search engine which is used for searching forum, Blog, MP3, etc, and subscribe their interested news, information, Blog and so on. In addition, MSN Live of Microsoft, Google pack of Google and space of Baidu belong to the software of desktop search. These search software offers much convenience to users' search and store information in the environment of Web2.0, but the problems mentioned above are not solved primarily, such as the problems of controlling of information quality, judgment of user rank, etc. Moreover, in IG's latest edition 2.1, the functions of search and subscription through key words only offer methods of post bar, news and forum, service of searching and subscribing Blog, wiki and other website's post bar, wiki isn't offered, so the service items are very finite. As a result, IG is just regarded as the traditional search engine of integrating Web2.0 and desktop tools.

4   The Conceptual Model of Networked Information Retrieval Based on JXTA and P2P

There are many retrieval patterns of Web2.0 at present, the key problem that users exploit information of Web2.0 has not been settled yet, such as user credit, information quality, extent of information sharing and so on. Hence, a conceptual model of networked information retrieval based on JXTA and P2P is put forward here.

4.1   P2P and JXTA

Traditional application patterns of network adopt the method of server to end computer, so users are passive to receive information from servers, but the new modes of P2P desalinate the boundary between service provider and user, so as to make each participant user become a supplier. P2P has the power of timely communication in network which is independent on device, and can look for and connect with the needed person as real time. Hence, from the aspect of human, the development point is not just referring to how to construct P2P network, but connecting people in network by P2P, so people could solve the exchange problems in the convenient network medium, this is what information exchange and exploit of Web2.0 need [10].

JXTA is a plan that Sun aims at constructing the general technology foundation of P2P, which defines a group of protocols, such as Peer Discovery Protocol, Peer Revolver Protocol, Peer Information Protocol, Peer Membership Protocol, Pipe Binding Protocol and Peer Endpoint Protocol. The system of JXTA is showed as Fig.1 [11].

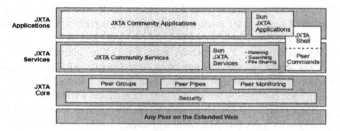

Fig. 1. P2P Software Architecture

4.3   The Conceptual Model of Networked Information Retrieval

The conceptual model of networked information retrieval based on JXTA is showed as Fig.2[12]. The JXTA Core and JXTA Services of the model can be fully referred to

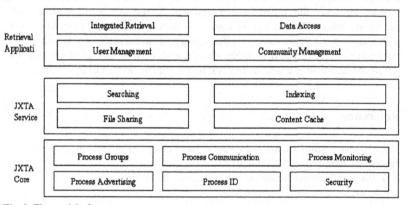

Fig. 2. The model of system structure

Retrieval Application mainly offers four kinds of functions such as integrated retrieval, data access, user management and community management. The integrated retrieval mainly provides retrieval request access, information filter, information retrieval and information sort. When a user or an information consumer submits a retrieval request, the request is submitted to system community and the set web search engine, such as Google, at the same time, the system searches corresponding results from process of community users or information providers who are related with the request, web search engine also returns retrieval results, and then the system integrates the results and feed back information consumers so that they can select the result that meet their needs. The selected files belong to the web or other users of the community who are information providers, the information consumer tags the files or directly chooses the tagged files and store then in his or her sharing process, so in the next retrieval process, information consumers are also information providers. Data access completes all the local data process and maintains a local cache space for community users' retrieval results. When there is same retrieval request, the local cache is searched firstly. User management is used for registration, login, allocating community, credit evaluation of users, so users can freely join in a community or are automatically classified to a community after the system analyzes their retrieval requests. Users' credit is evaluated according to the amount of files, the quality of tags and retrieval activity, the credit value is an important factor of sorting results when feeding back community retrieval results. Community management is used for managing sharing information of community in the system, such as users' past retrieval, community users and their credit and so on.

5 Conclusions

The paper analyzes these new demands in the environment of Web2.0, and evaluates and analyzes the tools and patterns of network information retrieval, and then a conceptual model of networked information retrieval based on JXTA and P2P is put forward. However, this is just the initial stage of the research, as the model is just a conceptual model. There is a lot of work to be done, such as how to extend scope of search, how to aggregate feedback information of different search circle, how to sort information effectively and so forth, which are all need to take great and continue efforts. At later time, we will do our best on the implementation of this model.

Reference

1. X. L. Zhang , "Semantics web and semantics-based networked information retrieval", *Journal of information*, 21(4),413-420 (2002).
2. Q. Zhang , "The search in times of web2.0"(January 10,2007). http://ysearchblog.cn/2006/12/web20.html.
3. "Microcontent in Web2.0" ,(November 18,2006). http://www.klogs.org/archives/2005/07/nieweb_20.html.
4. Incompleted, "Features of Web2.0"(November 18,2006). http://in.comengo.net/archives/feature-of-web2/.
5.W. Liu and. Q. Y. Ge , "From Web 2.0 to library2.0:service changed with users", *Modern information technology*, 9,8-12 (2006).
6. "Yahoo China lends Web2.0 activate to search mode"(December 1,2006). http://www.360doc.com/showWeb/0/0/159828.aspx.
7. "The catalog of search engine"(February 10, 2007). http://sskb.cn/sort/.
8. L. Liu , "Web2.0 of search engine. Journal of China Internet", 12, 32(2005).
9. Y. Liu., "Jobui: The new search of 'vertical search and Web2.0' ."(December 28,2006). http://net.chinabyte.com/chwssh/338/2232338.shtml.
10. W. T. Balke, "Supporting Information Retrieval in Peer-to-Peer Systems". *Springer-Verlag*, Berlin, Germany(2005).
11. G. Li., Project JXTA: A Technology Overview, 3(2002).
12.,M. Gnasa and Koblenz, "Congenial Web Search Conceptual Framework for Personalized", *Collaborative,Social Peer-to-Peer Retrieval*, MA, USA (2006).

Abnormal Data Detection for an E-Business using Object-Oriented Approach

Zongxiao Yang[1], Yanyi Zheng[1], Yanping Gao[1], Chuanye Cheng[1],
Sheng Xu[2] and Hiroyuki Yamaguchi[2]

1   Institute of Systems Science and Engineering,
HeNan University of Science and Technology, Luoyang 471003, China
zxyang@mail.haust.edu.cn,
WWW home page: http://www.haust.edu.cn/
2   Research Center,
Venture Link Communications Co. Ltd, Tokyo 107-6017, Japan

Abstract. An application service provider solution, named LINKCAFE
for the food industry, offers customers a new means to leverage the
internet to support line-of-business applications while reducing total cost
of ownership. It is necessary for managers to maintain data accuracy and
ensure data coherence in the online system. In this paper, abnormal data
detection applications (ADDA) based on object oriented approach was
developed by using unified modeling language models such as use-case
diagrams and sequence diagrams. The programming has been
accomplished for system managers for online service. Through
verification and validation of the application in functionality to practical
service for some years, the results have already proved that actual
application of ADDA has not only enhanced the accuracy of data
detection but also reduced data checking time to original 1/20 for system
managers.

1   Introduction

Partners in technology have been continuously searching for new technologies
that will enhance their client business. To most small- and medium-sized
enterprises, they cannot usually afford to buy expensive applications essential
for their development. In the late 1990s, a new kind of e-business called
applications service provider (ASP) appeared and developed rapidly and
vigorously these years. It offers the clients a new means of leveraging the
Internet to support line-of-business applications while reducing total cost of
ownership. [1-5]

An ASP solution named LINKCAFE has been put into practice successfully
in the food industry for many years. Customers and client managers can more
conveniently manipulate their service activities such as daily business
management, marketing prospect prediction and technical supports by lease of
the LINKCAFE system. They can experience immediate benefits through this
online e-business without the need to purchase, install, upgrade and maintain
costly servers, applications, databases and thus avoid hiring additional technical
support for upgrade and maintenance. But it is of vital importance for system

Please use the following format when citing this chapter:

Yang, Z., Zheng, Y., Gao, Y., Cheng, C., Xu, S., Yamaguchi, H., 2007, in IFIP International Federation for Information
Processing, Volume 251, Integration and Innovation Orient to E-Society Volume1, Wang, W. (Eds), (Boston: Springer),
pp. 671-678.

managers to ensure data coherency because large amounts of online business data are processed everyday.

OOA-based abnormal data detection applications (ADDA) for LINKCAFE system will be developed in this research. UML (Unified Modeling Language) models are applied to identify the functional structures for requirement analysis and construct the entity relation models for the architectural design of ADDA. The applications are implemented by 4GL (fourth-generation language) such as PL/SQL, HTML and JavaScript. The effectiveness and timesaving performance of ADDA will be verified through online verification and validation of the system managers.

2   LINKCAFE-An ASP Solution

LINKCAFE system, based on Website and RDBMS, consists of three functional parts shown in Fig.1, which include: (1) data maintenance and management of online business by inserting and updating real-time data, maintaining client commercial information, and saving & modifying business data in the system etc. (2) data analysis of sales, orders and costs to clients such as league users, owner users, leader users and supervisor users for their prediction estimation, business administration etc. (3) IT-based automatic franchise enterprise support by POS system, electronic order system and work procedure management system.

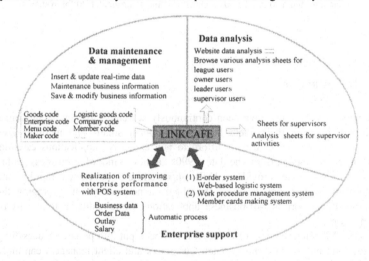

Fig.1. Outline of LINKCAFE system

The architecture of LINKCAFE shown in Fig.2 is mainly composed of data registries, basic sheets and TM (Technical Manual) sheets. In the data registry sub-system, twelve business data registry programs, such as enterprise calendar registry program, cashbook management program, can be provided for franchisor customers. For the basic sheets sub-system, three format categories including more than forty business report packages are developed for online business supports and enterprise activities to various franchise customers. Concerning TM sheets sub-system, nine profit-and-loss analysis packages are provided with many online supports such as prediction estimations, target analysis and administration. All of the functions make franchise clients manage their business more conveniently and economically.

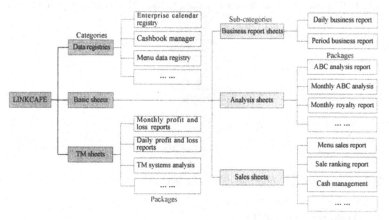

Fig.2. Architecture of LINKCAFE system (Partial)

To ensure accuracy and coherence of all the business data is necessary for system managers of this large-scale online system LINKCAFE everyday. The existence of abnormal data may affect the normal operation of the e-business and lower reputation of the franchise clients or even cause the ASP solution to face survival crisis. Therefore, it is necessary for the data managers to develop abnormal data detection package of the online system in order to improve labor efficiency and save working time.

3 OOA-based Construction of ADDA

3.1 Fault Tree Analysis for Abnormal Data

Abnormal data in LINKCAFE must be clarified in order to make development of ADDA more convenient. They are defined as 12 types which are stated as: (1) adjustment of department sales, (2) adjustment of sale data, (3) adjustment of goods sales, (4) adjustment of sum, (5) adjustment of owners and members, (6) adjustment of customer number, (7) adjustment of sale sum 35, (8) adjustment of sale sum 36, (9) overlap of sale data, (10) double business day, (11) presence of supplementary sales, and (12) adjustment of tax included in a discount.

Fault tree analysis (FTA)[6] is adopted to describe contribution of each abnormal data, and evaluates the reliability of a large-scale system qualitatively or quantitatively. The abnormal data are embodied through a fault tree in Fig.3. Every abnormal data is replaced with a capital Latin letter in order of alphabet. For instance, Type A represents the abnormal data of adjustment of department sales. Each abnormal data itself will alone lead to the occurrence of abnormal data, thus the twelve types are connected with an "OR" gate. By means of set theory, the cause-effect relationship can be expressed by the following equation:

$$D(A) = \bigcup_{i=1}^{12} Type(i) \qquad (1)$$

Where, D(A) represents the top event "abnormal data" while Type(i) denotes the abnormal data types. The employment of FTA can help system analysts find out abnormal data and perfect LINKCAFE system in a more high-efficient way.

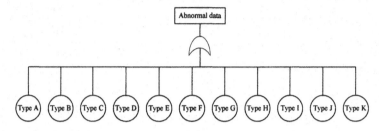

Fig.3. A fault tree for abnormal data in LINKCAFE

3.2 Architecture of ADDA

A functional flow chart of ADDA is constructed on the basis of requirement analysis for LINKCAFE system shown in Fig.4.

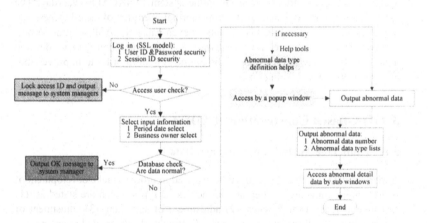

Fig.4. Functional flow chart of ADDA

In ADDA, we design the *Login* platform based on SSL (Security Socket Layer) model background with user ID, password security and session ID checking for system managers and database users. Certain access user would be locked if the access is not permitted and the application can output the access information to system managers for system security and safety; otherwise, the login user can select the input information including the period date and business owner code from the menu options, and then search the real time data from the online system. If the online data is identified on normal status, *OK* message will be output to the system managers; otherwise the abnormal data information including abnormal data number and abnormal data type list will be output. A popup window can be opened for abnormal data type definition help whenever necessary. The user can open sub-windows while he wants to check more abnormal detail data.

3.3 OOA-base Modeling

UML, which has become a standard modeling language for object oriented modeling [7-8], was applied to construct models of ADDA. The system requirements are discovered by means of discussion with various users or questionnaires etc., and are finally illustrated through use case diagrams. A high-level use case diagram shown in Fig.5 gives the general functions of the applications, which corresponds with the functional flow chart in Fig.4. As can be seen, the actor Users can inspect abnormal data by logging into the system, querying data and finally acquiring data.

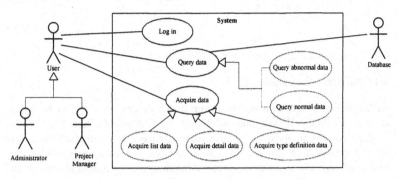

Fig.5. A use case diagram for the system general function

On the base of use case diagrams, classes can be identified. A class is a set of objects that share a common structure and common behavior called attributes and operations respectively. In ADDA, there are total ten kinds of classes named as *ProcShowList*, *ProcTop*, *ProcTopLeft* etc. For class *ProcTop*, its operations consist of *DataCheck*, *ListData*. Likewise, other classed contains a set of their own attributes and operations.

A sequence diagram shown in Fig.6 describes information exchange among all classes and models the behavior of objects during the process of abnormal data detection. Every object is an instance of a class in the class diagram, interacting with each other through messages in order of time. For example, to realize the function of data query, the object "User" sends message *ListData* to the object *ProcTop* first, and then the object *ProcTop* calls its method *FuncGetData* itself so as to search the abnormal data in the database of LINKCAFE system, finally the abnormal data can be detected. Entity-relationship diagrams about ADDA were easily constructed based on UML models but omitted here. They enabled us to develop ADDA by computer languages conveniently.

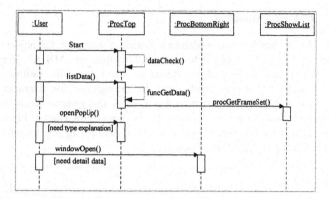

Fig.6. A sequence diagram for the abnormal data detection

3.4   Software Development

ADDA are easily implemented by means of 4th generation computer languages such as PL/SQL, HTML and JavaScript by OOA-based modeling [9]. The package body is composed of a main control procedure, seven platform control sub-procedures, five data control sub-procedures, one data catch sub-function and some common super-procedures for the diagnosis of twelve abnormal data types (symbolized by: A, B, C, D, ...) as well as some abnormal detail data. As an example, partial source codes of the method *FuncGetData* written with PL/SQL are given in Fig.7. And development of the ADDA was completed successfully in the same way for system managers in consideration of software performance tuning in programming [10].

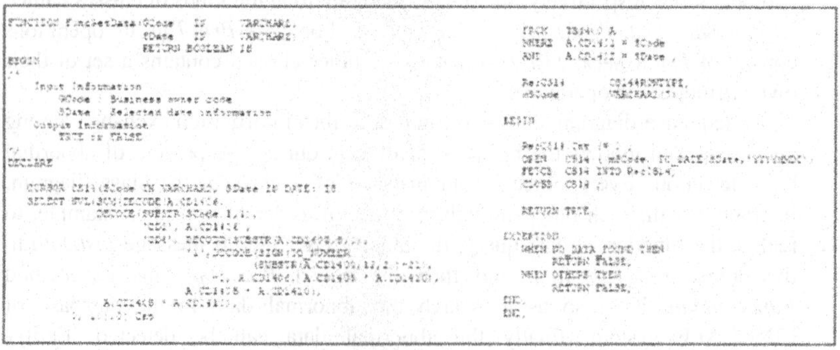

Fig.7. Sources of the Method *FuncGetData* (Partial)

4   Verification and Validation

The developed ADDA for LINKCAFE system have been put in practice for online verification and validation of the effectiveness, speediness and timesaving performance for some years.

When LINKCAFE system operates normally, a large quantity of online business data are inserted and updated automatically into the system everyday. The occurrence of abnormal data is unavoidable at any time. For instance, what if the salesperson in one of the shops received money but input wrong data into the POS system? This will cause inconsistency between the bill and actual total sum of money. Checking accuracy, coherence and trustiness of business data was a time-consuming task for data managers before ADDA was installed. Actually, to find out all the abnormal data will cost data managers too much of time that may even be counted by hours! But by employment of the diagnostic package, the abnormal data could be searched rapidly and the detection result was obtained within several minutes at most! It is given in the form of an abnormal data diagnostic list, which is illustrated by a screenshot shown in Fig.8.

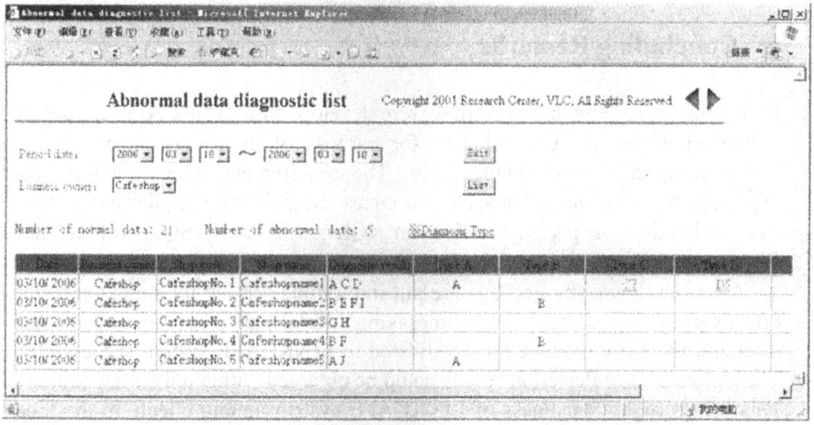

Fig.8. An abnormal data diagnostic list of ADDA

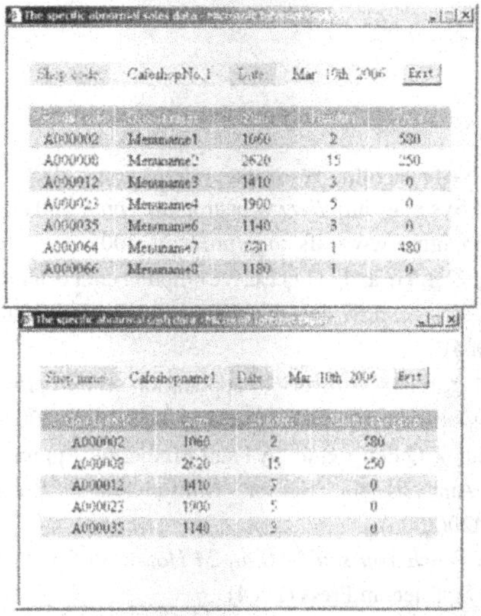

(a) An abnormal detail data for Type C   (b) An abnormal detail data for Type D

Fig.9. Diagnostic results for the detailed abnormal data

As is shown in Fig.8, the detection result is obtained when clicking the button *List* after *period date* and the *business owner code* are selected. Such symbols as A, B, C represent the types of abnormal data. Some sub-windows could be linked for more abnormal detail data information, for example C7 means that abnormal data type C has seven abnormal detail data records shown in Fig.9 (a). Another detailed detection result for D5 is illustrated in Fig.9 (b). The online verification and validation results have proved the applications improved the accuracy and coherence of data detection, increased the nonstop run trustiness of LINKCAFE system, saved data maintenance time of administrative staffs to original 1/20. Good reputation of LIKKCAFE system was established among the customers in food industry.

5 Concluding Remarks

In this research, OOA-based ADDA were developed for LINKCAFE system, an online e-business of ASP solution, for purpose of improving abnormal data detection accuracy and saving labor. The requirements were obtained and expressed by UML modeling such as use-case diagrams and sequence diagrams. The realization of package relied on 4GL such as PL/SQL, HTML and JavaScript.

After the diagnostic package are put into online service for some years, the effectiveness, speediness and timesaving performance of abnormal data detection have been verified and validated to LINKCAFE system successfully. The abnormal data detection results could be obtained within only a few minutes. This brings highly trustiness of LIKKCAFE system among clients in the food industry. Also the development of applications provides a methodology of online system management for abnormal data detection to system managers.

References

1. Universal Solution Systems, http://www.u-s-systems.com/, 2005.
2. Hitachi Information Systems, http://www.bistromate.com/, 2004.
3. Alphax Food System, http://www.afs.co.jp/product/, 2005.
4. S.Y.Jing, Z.Wang, S.H.Yu and C.D.Lu, "Computer-aided industrial design system based on application service provide", *Computer Integrated Manufacturing Systems*, 10(10), 1184-1190 (2004).
5. M.A.Smith and R.L.Kumar, "A theory of application service provider (ASP) use from a client perspective", *Information and Management*, 41(8) , 977-1002 (2004).
6. Z.X.Yang, X.B.Yuan, Z.Q.Feng, etal: "A Fault Prediction Approach for Process Plants using Fault Tree Analysis in Sensor Malfunction", *Proceedings of IEEE ICMA2006*,.3 ,2415-2420(2006).
7. J.Schmuller, *Sams Teach Yourself UML in 24 Hours*. In: Li H., Zhao L.G.: tran. 3rd Edition. Beijing: Posts & Telecom Press (2004).
8. I.Sommerville, *Software Engineering*, 7th Edition. New York: Pearson Education Limited (2004).
9. S.Urman,Oracle9i PL/SQL Programming. Tokyo: McGraw-Hill (2001).
10. M.Gurry and P.Corrigan, Oracle Performance Tuning. 2nd Edition. Paris: O'Reilly (1998).